Foundation

CAMBRIDGE
UNIVERSITY PRESS

University Printing House, Cambridge CB2 8BS, United Kingdom

Cambridge University Press is part of the University of Cambridge.

It furthers the University's mission by disseminating knowledge in the pursuit of education, learning and research at the highest international levels of excellence.

www.cambridge.org

Information on this title:
www.cambridge.org/9781107448094 (Paperback)
www.cambridge.org/9781107449909 (1 Year Online Subscription)
www.cambridge.org/9781107449855 (2 Year Online Subscription)
www.cambridge.org/9781107447998 (Paperback + Online Subscription)

© Cambridge University Press 2015

This publication is in copyright. Subject to statutory exception
and to the provisions of relevant collective licensing agreements,
no reproduction of any part may take place without the written
permission of Cambridge University Press.

First published 2015

Printed in Dubai by Oriental Press

A catalogue record for this publication is available from the British Library

ISBN 978-1-107-44809-4 Paperback
ISBN 978-1-107-44990-9 1 Year Online Subscription
ISBN 978-1-107-44985-5 2 Year Online Subscription
ISBN 978-1-107-44799-8 Paperback + Online Subscription

Additional resources for this publication at www.cambridge.org/ukschools

Cambridge University Press has no responsibility for the persistence or accuracy of URLs for external or third-party internet websites referred to in this publication, and does not guarantee that any content on such websites is, or will remain, accurate or appropriate.

....

NOTICE TO TEACHERS IN THE UK
It is illegal to reproduce any part of this work in material form (including photocopying and electronic storage) except under the following circumstances:
(i) where you are abiding by a licence granted to your school or institution by the Copyright Licensing Agency;
(ii) where no such licence exists, or where you wish to exceed the terms of a licence, and you have gained the written permission of Cambridge University Press;
(iii) where you are allowed to reproduce without permission under the provisions of Chapter 3 of the Copyright, Designs and Patents Act 1988, which covers, for example, the reproduction of short passages within certain types of educational anthology and reproduction for the purposes of setting examination questions.

....

This resource is endorsed by OCR for use with specification J560 GCSE Mathematics.

In order to gain OCR endorsement this resource has undergone an independent quality check. OCR has not paid for the production of this resource, nor does OCR receive any royalties from its sale. For more information about the endorsement process please visit the OCR website **www.ocr.org.uk**

Contents

INTRODUCTION	**vi**
1 Basic calculation skills	**1**
Section 1: Basic calculations	3
Section 2: Order of operations	8
Section 3: Inverse operations	10
2 Whole number theory	**13**
Section 1: Review of number properties	15
Section 2: Prime numbers and prime factors	17
Section 3: Multiples and factors	19
3 Algebraic expressions	**24**
Section 1: Algebraic notation	26
Section 2: Simplifying expressions	28
Section 3: Multiplying out brackets	30
Section 4: Factorising expressions	33
Section 5: Using algebra to solve problems	34
4 Functions and sequences	**37**
Section 1: Sequences and patterns	39
Section 2: Finding the nth term	41
Section 3: Functions	44
Section 4: Special sequences	46
5 Properties of shapes and solids	**51**
Section 1: Types of shapes	53
Section 2: Symmetry	57
Section 3: Triangles	60
Section 4: Quadrilaterals	63
Section 5: Properties of 3D objects	66
6 Construction and loci	**72**
Section 1: Geometrical instruments	74
Section 2: Bisectors and perpendiculars	78
Section 3: Loci	81
Section 4: More complex problems	84
7 Further algebraic expressions	**88**
Section 1: Multiplying two binomials	89
Section 2: Factorising quadratic expressions	94
Section 3: Apply your skills	99
8 Equations	**103**
Section 1: Linear equations	105
Section 2: Quadratic equations	111
Section 3: Simultaneous equations	115
Section 4: Using graphs to solve equations	121
Section 5: Using equations and their graphs	125
9 Angles	**130**
Section 1: Angle facts	132
Section 2: Parallel lines and angles	135
Section 3: Angles in triangles	138
Section 4: Angles in polygons	141
10 Fractions	**147**
Section 1: Equivalent fractions	149
Section 2: Operations with fractions	151
Section 3: Fractions of quantities	155
11 Decimals	**159**
Section 1: Revision of decimals and fractions	160
Section 2: Calculating with decimals	163
12 Units and measurement	**171**
Section 1: Standard units of measurement	173
Section 2: Compound units of measurement	180
Section 3: Maps, scale drawings and bearings	185
13 Percentages	**193**
Section 1: Review of percentages	195
Section 2: Percentage calculations	198
Section 3: Percentage change	202
14 Algebraic formulae	**207**
Section 1: Writing formulae	209
Section 2: Substituting values into formulae	211
Section 3: Changing the subject of a formula	213
Section 4: Working with formulae	215
15 Perimeter	**222**
Section 1: Perimeter of simple and composite shapes	224
Section 2: Circumference of a circle	230
Section 3: Problems involving perimeter and circumference	236

Find answers at: cambridge.org/ukschools/gcsemaths-studentbookanswers

16 Area — 242
- Section 1: Area of polygons — 244
- Section 2: Area of circles and sectors — 251
- Section 3: Area of composite shapes — 253

17 Approximation and estimation — 262
- Section 1: Rounding — 264
- Section 2: Approximation and estimation — 271
- Section 3: Limits of accuracy — 273

18 Straight-line graphs — 277
- Section 1: Plotting graphs — 279
- Section 2: Using the features of straight-line graphs — 280
- Section 3: Parallel lines — 289
- Section 4: Working with straight-line graphs — 292

19 Graphs of equations and functions — 297
- Section 1: Review of linear graphs — 299
- Section 2: Graphs of quadratic functions — 302
- Section 3: Other polynomials and reciprocals — 307
- Section 4: Plotting, sketching and recognising graphs — 311

20 Three-dimensional shapes — 315
- Section 1: Review of 3D solids — 317
- Section 2: Drawing 3D objects — 320
- Section 3: Plan and elevation views — 326

21 Volume and surface area — 333
- Section 1: Prisms and cylinders — 334
- Section 2: Cones and spheres — 341
- Section 3: Pyramids — 345

22 Calculations with ratio — 349
- Section 1: Introducing ratios — 351
- Section 2: Sharing in a given ratio — 353
- Section 3: Comparing ratios — 355

23 Basic probability and experiments — 361
- Section 1: The probability scale — 363
- Section 2: Calculating probability — 365
- Section 3: Experimental probability — 368
- Section 4: Mixed probability problems — 373

24 Combined events and probability diagrams — 380
- Section 1: Representing combined events — 383
- Section 2: Theoretical probability of combined events — 390

25 Powers and roots — 400
- Section 1: Index notation — 402
- Section 2: The laws of indices — 405
- Section 3: Working with powers and roots — 407

26 Standard form — 412
- Section 1: Expressing numbers in standard form — 414
- Section 2: Calculators and standard form — 417
- Section 3: Working in standard form — 419

27 Plane vector geometry — 424
- Section 1: Vector notation and representation — 426
- Section 2: Vector arithmetic — 428
- Section 3: Mixed practice — 430

28 Plane isometric transformations — 432
- Section 1: Reflections — 434
- Section 2: Translations — 439
- Section 3: Rotations — 443

29 Congruent triangles — 450
- Section 1: Congruent triangles — 452
- Section 2: Applying congruency — 456

30 Similarity — 461
- Section 1: Similar triangles — 463
- Section 2: Enlargements — 467
- Section 3: Similar shapes — 476

31 Pythagoras' theorem — 480
- Section 1: Finding the length of the hypotenuse — 482
- Section 2: Finding the length of any side — 484
- Section 3: Proving that a triangle is right-angled — 487
- Section 4: Using Pythagoras' theorem to solve problems — 489

32 Trigonometry — 495
- Section 1: Trigonometry in right-angled triangles — 497
- Section 2: Exact values of trigonometric ratios — 505
- Section 3: Solving problems using trigonometry — 507

33 Discrete growth and decay — 513
- Section 1: Simple and compound growth — 514
- Section 2: Simple and compound decay — 518

34 Direct and inverse proportion — 522
- Section 1: Direct proportion — 524
- Section 2: Algebraic and graphical representations — 527
- Section 3: Inverse proportion — 532

35 Collecting and displaying data — 536
- Section 1: Populations and samples — 538
- Section 2: Tables and graphs — 541
- Section 3: Pie charts — 549
- Section 4: Line graphs for time series data — 551

36 Analysing data — 558
- Section 1: Summary statistics — 560
- Section 2: Misleading graphs — 567
- Section 3: Scatter diagrams — 571

37 Interpreting graphs — 578
- Section 1: Graphs of real-world contexts — 580
- Section 2: Gradients — 583

38 Algebraic inequalities — 587
- Section 1: Expressing inequalities — 589
- Section 2: Number lines — 590
- Section 3: Solving inequalities — 591
- Section 4: Working with inequalities — 592

GLOSSARY — 596

INDEX — 599

Note
The colour of each chapter corresponds to the area of maths that it covers:

- Number
- Algebra
- Ratio, proportion and rates of change
- Geometry and measures
- Probability
- Statistics

Find answers at: cambridge.org/ukschools/gcsemaths-studentbookanswers

GCSE Mathematics for OCR (Foundation)

Introduction

This book has been written by experienced teachers to help build your understanding and enjoyment of the maths you will meet at GCSE.

Each chapter opens with a list of skills that are covered in the chapter. The **real-life applications** section describes an example of how the maths is used in real life.

All chapters build on knowledge that you will have learned in previous years. You might need to revise some topics before starting a chapter. To check your knowledge, answer the questions in the **Before you start...** table. You can check your answers using the free answer booklet available at www.cambridge.org/ukschools/gcsemaths-studentbookanswers. If you answer any questions incorrectly, you might need to revise the topic from your work in earlier years.

The chapters are divided into sections, each covering a single topic. Some chapters may cover topics that you already know and understand. You can use the **Launchpad** to identify the best section for you to start with. Answer the questions in each step. If you find a question difficult to answer correctly, the step suggests the section that you should look at.

Throughout the book, there are features to help you build knowledge and improve your skills:

- This means you might need a calculator to work through a question.
- This means you should work through a question without using a calculator. If this is not present, you can use a calculator if you need to.
- This shows the question is from a past exam paper.

Tip

Tip boxes provide helpful hints.

Calculator tip

Calculator tips help you to use your calculator.

Learn this formula

Learn this formula boxes contain formulae that you need to know.

Key vocabulary

Important maths terms are written in **green**. You can find what they mean in **Key vocabulary** boxes and also in the **Glossary** at the back of the book.

Did you know?

Did you know? boxes contain interesting maths facts.

WORK IT OUT

Work it out boxes contain a question with several worked solutions. Some of the solutions contain common mistakes. Try to spot the correct solution and check the free answer booklet available at www.cambridge.org/ukschools/gcsemaths-studentbookanswers to see if you're right.

WORKED EXAMPLE

Worked examples guide you through model answers to help you understand methods of answering questions.

Some chapters contain a **Problem-solving framework**, which sets a problem and then shows how you can go about answering it.

Checklist of learning and understanding

At the end of a chapter, use the **Checklist of learning and understanding** to check whether you have covered everything you need to know.

Chapter review

You can check whether you have understood the topics using the **Chapter review**, which contains questions from the whole chapter.

A booklet containing answers to all exercises is free to download at www.cambridge.org/ukschools/gcsemaths-studentbookanswers.

You can find more resources, including interactive widgets, games and quizzes on **GCSE Mathematics Online**.

Acknowledgements

Questions from OCR past question papers © OCR.

These questions are indicated by .

Questions from Cambridge IGCSE® Mathematics reproduced with permission of Karen Morrison and Nick Hamshaw.

The authors would like to thank Fran Wilson for her work on GCSE Mathematics Online.

Cover © 2013 Fabian Oefner www.fabianoefner.com; p1 (top) Henry Gan/Photodisc/Thinkstock; p1 Denis Kuvaev/Shutterstock; p5 StockLite/Shutterstock; p13 (top) Yuriy S/iStock/Thinkstock; p13 Tyler Olson/Shutterstock; p21 Elnur/Shutterstock; p24 (top) agsandrew/iStock/Thinkstock; p24 wavebreakmedia/Shutterstock; p35 Andresr/Shutterstock; p37 (top) © PhotoAlto/Alamy; p37 © Monty Rakusen/Cultura/Corbis; p40 © Roger Bamber/Alamy; p47 murengstockphoto/Thinkstock; p48 Shaiith/Thinkstock; p51 (top) Monarx3d/iStock/Thinkstock; p62 kilukilu/Shutterstock; p63L Marafona/Shutterstock; p63R Huang Zheng/Shutterstock; p67 © Owen Franken/Corbis; p69 Alex Tarrasov/Shutterstock; p72 (top) Huskyomega/iStock/Thinkstock; p72 Franz Pfluegl/Shutterstock; p72,74,75 Yulia Glam/Shutterstock; p83L UMB-O/Shutterstock; p83R Vector House/Shutterstock; p86 Gemenacom/Shutterstock; p88 (top) Leigh Prather/iStock/Thinkstock; p88 Dariush M/Shutterstock; p103 (top) Alison Bradford Photography/iStock/Thinkstock; p103 Andrey Popov/Shutterstock; p111 Raulin/Shutterstock; p124 © Manuel Sulzer/cultura/Corbis; p130 (top) Mark Stillwagon/iStock/Thinkstock; p130 Mikio Oba/Shutterstock; p134 Dmitry Kalinovsky/Shutterstock; p141 Ryan Lewandowski/Shutterstock; p147 (top) SDivin09/iStock/Thinkstock; p147 Chameleons Eye/Shutterstock; p154 Jon Milnes/Shutterstock; p159 (top) Andrey Popov/iStock/Thinkstock; p159 Leah-AnneThompson/Shutterstock; p161 William West/Staff/Getty Images; p163 © JUMANAELHELOUEH/Reuters/Corbis; p171 (top) Mike Watson Images/moodboard/Thinkstock; p178 Taiga/Shutterstock; p180 Brenda Carson/Shutterstock; p193 (top) shutter_m/iStock/Thinkstock; p199 tr3gin/Shutterstock; p207 (top) deyan georgiev/iStock/Thinkstock; p207 Leah-Anne Thompson/Shutterstock; p215 © PCN Photography/Alamy; p219 Suppakij1017/Shutterstock; p222 (top) David Chapman/Designpics/Valueline/Thinkstock; p222 itman__47/Shutterstock; p223 dkART/Shutterstock; p231 Karl Weatherly/Thinkstock; p233 iceink/Shutterstock; p242 (top) imagean/iStock/Thinkstock; p242 Federico Rostagno/Shutterstock; p249 stefanospezi/Shutterstock; p262 (top) Joe McDaniel/iStock/Thinkstock; p262 Dmitry Kalinovsky/Shutterstock; p266 ILYAAKINSHIN/Shutterstock; p271 Pixsooz/Shutterstock; p277 (top) Kerem Yucel/iStock/Thinkstock; p277 Dan Breckwoldt/Shutterstock; p297 (top) shaunnessey/iStock/Thinkstock; p297 © Jenny E. Ross/Corbis; p302 herreid/Thinkstock; p315 (top) alfimimnill/iStock/Thinkstock; p319L Thomas Demarczyk/Thinkstock; p319R Vitaly Edush/Thinkstock; p320L AnthonyBaggett/Thinkstock; p320R merial/Thinkstock; p333 (top) Phil Ashley/Photodisc/Thinkstock; p333 govicinity/Shutterstock; p334 lsantilli/Shutterstock; p338 Dmitry Kalinovsky/Shutterstock; p340 Sergio Bertino/Shutterstock; p342 © Daniel Mogan/Alamy; p344L Courtesy of Newcastle International Airport; p344R © 2ebill/Alamy; p346L kravka/Shutterstock; p346R Chameleons Eye/Shutterstock; p348 cpphotoimages/Shutterstock; p349 (top) Eugen Weide/Hemera/Thinkstock; p349 T.Fabian/Shutterstock; p351 Anteromite/Shutterstock; p353 zentilia/Shutterstock; p354 Adam Gilchrist/Shutterstock; p357 Valentyn Volkov/Shutterstock; p361 (top) Chemik11/iStock/Thinktstock; p363 levradin/Shutterstock; p368 Tamara Kulikova/Shutterstock; p380 (top) maury75/iStock/Thinkstock; p380 angellodeco/Shutterstock; p400 (top) Jeffrey Collingwood/Hemera/Thinkstock; p400 Candy Box Images/Shutterstock; p412 (top) agsandrew/iStock/Thinkstock; p412 Sergey Kamshylin/Shutterstock; p422 Iakov Kalinin/Shutterstock; p424 (top) sutichak/iStock/Thinkstock; p424 © Michael Winston Rosa/Shutterstock; p430 Herbert Kratky/Shutterstock; p432 (top) ninjacpb/iStock/Thinkstock; p434 Pal Teravagimov/Shutterstock; p450 (top) Pietro Ballardini/iStockEditorial/Thinkstock; p450 Ross Strachan/Shutterstock; p461 (top) Comstock/Stockbyte/Thinkstock; p461 Kletr/Shutterstock; p474 Lucy Clark/Shutterstock; p480 (top) © Emma Smales/VIEW/Corbis; p480 © Paul Doyle/Alamy; p487 racorn/Shutterstock; p494 © Rob Wilkinson/Alamy; p495 (top) Digital Vision/Photodisc/Thinkstock; p495 GECOUK/Science Photo Library; p498 © Andrew Ammendolia/Alamy; p512 Svetlana Jafarova/Shutterstock; p513 (top) shutter_m/iStock/Thinkstock; p513 Pressmaster/Shutterstock; p517 vetroff/Shutterstock; p522 (top) Karol Kozlowski/iStock/Thinkstock; p522 Michael Jung/Shutterstock; p523T larik_malasha/Shutterstock; p523B terekhovigor/Shutterstock; p527 Christian Delbert/Shutterstock; p536 (top) cherezoff/iStock/Thinkstock; p536 Chad McDermott/Shutterstock; p539 © Detail Nottingham/Alamy; p558 (top) marekuliasz/iStock/Thinkstock; p558 Brian A. Jackson/Shutterstock; p561 Peter G./Shutterstock; p578 (top) zentilia/iStock/Thinkstock; p578 Zryzner/Shutterstock; p585 pfshots/Shutterstock; p587 (top) © Tabor Gus/Corbis; p587 © Olaf Doering/Alamy; p593 Jamie Duplass/Shutterstock.

Find answers at: cambridge.org/ukschools/gcsemaths-studentbookanswers

1 Basic calculation skills

In this chapter you will learn how to …

- use non-calculator methods to calculate with positive and negative integers.
- perform operations in the correct order based on mathematical conventions.
- recognise inverse operations and use them to simplify and check calculations.

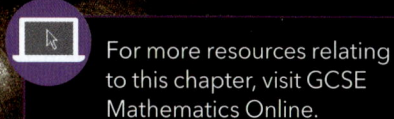

For more resources relating to this chapter, visit GCSE Mathematics Online.

Using mathematics: real-life applications

Everyone uses numbers on a daily basis often without really thinking about them. Shopping, cooking, working out bills, paying for transport and measuring all rely on a good understanding of numbers and calculation skills.

Tip

You probably already know most of the concepts in this chapter. They have been included so that you can revise concepts if you need to and check that you know them well.

"Number puzzles and games are very popular and there are mobile apps and games available for all age groups. Our website offers free games where you have to identify the correct order of operations to use to solve different number puzzles."

(Website designer)

Before you start …

KS3	You should be able to add, subtract, multiply and divide positive and negative numbers.	**1** Copy and complete each statement to make it true. Use only <, = or >. **a** $2 + 3 \;\square\; 4 - 7$ **b** $^-3 + 6 \;\square\; 4 - 7$ **c** $^-1 - 4 \;\square\; 20 \div {}^-4$ **d** $^-6 \times 2 \;\square\; {}^-7 - ({}^-5)$
KS3	You should know the rules for working when more than one operation is involved in a calculation (BIDMAS).	**2** Spot the mistake in each calculation and correct the answers. **a** $3 + 8 + 3 \times 4 = 56$ **b** $3 + 8 \times 3 + 4 = 37$ **c** $3 \times (8 + 3) \times 4 = 130$

KS3	You should understand that addition and subtraction, and multiplication and division are inverse operations.	**3** Identify the inverse operation by choosing the correct option.
		a $14 \times 4 = 56$
		    A $56 \times 4 = 14$ B $14 \div 4 = 56$ C $56 \div 4 = 14$
		b $200 \div 10 = 20$
		    A $200 \div 20 = 10$ B $200 = 10 \times 20$ C $10 \times 200 = 2000$
		c $27 + 53 = 80$
		    A $80 = 4 \times 20$ B $80 - 27 = 53$ C $80 + 27 = 107$

Find answers at: cambridge.org/ukschools/gcsemaths-studentbookanswers

GCSE Mathematics for OCR (Foundation)

Assess your starting point using the Launchpad

STEP 1

1 Calculate without using a calculator and show your working.
  a 647 + 786
  b 1406 − 289
  c 45 × 19
  d 414 ÷ 23

GO TO Section 1: Basic calculations

STEP 2

2 Choose the correct answer.
  a 9 ÷ (2 + 1) − 2
     A 9   B $3\frac{1}{2}$ C 1   D 0
  b (3 × 8) ÷ 4 + 8
     A 2   B 30   C 16   D 14
  c 12 − 6 × 2 + 11
     A 78   B 23   C 1   D 11
  d [5 × (9 + 1)] − 3
     A 53   B 47   C 40   D 43
  e (6 + 5) × 2 + (15 − 2 × 3) − 6
     A 40   B 20   C 32   D 25

GO TO Section 2: Order of operations

STEP 3

3 The perimeter of a square is equal to four times the length of a side. If the perimeter is 128 cm, what is the length of a side?

4 What should you add to 342 to get 550?

5 If a number divided by 45 is 30, what is the number?

GO TO Section 3: Inverse operations

GO TO Chapter review

Section 1: Basic calculations

You will not always have a calculator so it is useful to know how to do calculations using mental and written strategies.

It is best to use a method that you are confident with and always **show your working**.

Remember that when a question asks you to find the:
- **sum** you need to add.
- **difference** you need to subtract one number from another.
- **product** you need to multiply.
- **quotient** you need to divide.

> **Tip**
> These are the kind of skills that are tested in the non-calculator examination papers.

WORK IT OUT 1.1

Look at these calculations carefully.

Discuss with a partner what methods these students have used to find the answer.

Which method would you use to do each of these calculations? Why?

① 489 + 274
$$400 + 200 \rightarrow 600$$
$$80 + 70 \rightarrow 150$$
$$9 + 4 \rightarrow 13$$
$$763$$

② 284 − 176
$$2\overset{7}{\cancel{8}}\overset{1}{4}$$
$$-176$$
$$108$$

③ 29 × 17
$$\rightarrow 30 \times 17 - 17$$
$$\rightarrow 3 \times 170 - 17$$
$$\rightarrow 510 - 17$$
$$\rightarrow 493$$

④ 15 × 62
$$= 30 \times 31 \quad 310$$
$$= 930 \quad\quad 310$$
$$\quad\quad 310$$
$$\quad\quad 930$$

⑤ 207 × 47

×	200	0	7
40	8000	0	280
7	1400	0	49

$$9400 + 0 + 329$$
$$= 9729$$

⑥ 2394 ÷ 42
$$2394$$
$$-1680 \quad \text{(40)}$$
$$714$$
$$-420 \quad \text{(10)}$$
$$294$$
$$-210 \quad \text{(5)}$$
$$84$$
$$-84 \quad \text{(2)} = 57$$
$$0$$

$42 \times 10 = 420$
$42 \times 20 = 840$
$42 \times 40 = 1680$
$42 \times 5 = 210$
$42 \times 2 = 84$

Find answers at: cambridge.org/ukschools/gcsemaths-studentbookanswers

Problem-solving strategies

Many of the written calculations that you have to do will be to solve word problems.

Everyone has their own method of solving problems but there are some useful strategies and techniques that you can use for problem solving.

The problem-solving framework below outlines the steps that you can take to break down most problems to help you solve them more easily.

If you follow these steps each time you are faced with a problem you will become more skilled at problem solving and more able to self-check.

These are important skills both for your GCSE courses and for everyday life.

Problem-solving framework

Sally buys, repairs and sells used furniture at a market.

Last week she bought a table for £32 and a bench for £18.

She spent £12 on wood, nails, varnish and glue to fix them up.

She then sold the two items on her stall for £69.

How much profit did she make on the two items?

Steps for approaching a problem-solving question	What you would do for this example
Step 1: Work out what you have to do. Start by reading the question carefully.	Find the profit on the two items.
Step 2: What information do you need? Have you got it all?	Cost of items = £32 + £18 Cost of repairs = £12 Selling price = £69
Step 3: Is there any information that you don't need?	In this problem you don't need to know what she spent money on for repairs. You just need to know how much she spent. Many problems contain extra information that you don't need to test your understanding.
Step 4: Decide what maths you can do.	Profit = selling price − cost You can add the costs and subtract them from the selling price.
Step 5: Set out your solution clearly. Check your working and make sure your answer is reasonable.	Cost = £32 + £18 + £12 = £62 Profit = £69 − £62 = £7 Sally made £7 profit.
Step 6: Check that you have answered the question.	Yes. You needed to find the profit and you have found it.

EXERCISE 1A

Solve these problems using written methods.
Set out your solutions clearly to show the methods you chose.

> **Tip**
>
> You don't always need to write anything for the first few steps in the problem-solving framework, but you should try to mentally answer the questions as you read problems to decide what to do. You should always show how you worked to solve the problem.

1 After checking the prices at three different supermarkets, Nola found out that the cheapest pack of pens was £3.90 for three. She bought fifteen pens.

How much did she pay in total and what does this work out to per pen?

   a How many packs of pens did she buy? Why do you need to know this?

   b What is the total cost of the fifteen pens?

   c What is the cost of each pen?

2 Sandra bought a pair of jeans for £34, a scarf for £9.50 and a top for £20.

If she had saved £100 to buy these items, how much money would she have left?

3 How many 16-page brochures can you make from 1030 pages?

4 Jason can type 48 words per minute.

   a How many words can he type in an hour and a half?

   b Approximately how long would it take him to type an article of 2000 words?

5 At the start of a year the population of Greenside Village was 56 309.

During the year 617 people died, 1835 babies were born, 4087 people left the village and 3099 people moved into the village.

What was the population at the end of the year?

6 The Amazon River is 6448 km long, the Nile River is 6670 km and the Severn is 354 km long.

   a How much longer is the Nile than the Amazon?

   b How much shorter is the Severn than the Amazon?

7 What is the combined sum of 132 plus 99 and the product of 36 and 127?

8 What is the result when the difference between 8765 and 3087 is added to the result of 1206 divided by 18?

> **Did you know?**
>
> The Severn is the longest river in the UK.

GCSE Mathematics for OCR (Foundation)

Key vocabulary

integers: whole numbers belonging to the set {... ⁻3, ⁻2, ⁻1, 0, 1, 2, 3, ...}; they are sometimes called directed numbers because they have a negative or positive sign.

Tip

You will be expected to work with negative and positive values in algebra, so it is important to make sure you can do this early on in your GCSE course.

Working with negative and positive integers

When doing calculations involving positive and negative **integers**, you need to remember to apply the following rules:

- Adding a negative number is the same as subtracting the number:
  4 + ⁻3 = 1.

- Subtracting a negative number is the same as adding a positive number:
  5 − ⁻3 = 8.

- Multiplying or dividing the same signs gives a positive answer:
  ⁻4 × ⁻2 = 8 and $\frac{-4}{-2}$ = 2.

- Multiplying or dividing different signs gives a negative answer:
  4 × ⁻2 = ⁻8 and $\frac{-4}{2}$ = −2.

EXERCISE 1B

1 Calculate.

a	12 − 5 + 8	b	⁻3 − 4 − 8	c	3 + 5 − 6
d	⁻2 − 8 + 5	e	14 − 3 − 9	f	9 − 3 − 4
g	⁻34 + 18 − 12	h	25 − 19 − 42	i	⁻9 − (⁻7)
j	⁻3 − (⁻10)	k	⁻4 − (⁻12)	l	8 − (⁻9)
m	9 − (⁻8)	n	⁻14 − (⁻14)	o	⁻3 − 8 − (⁻9)

2 Calculate.

a	⁻2 × ⁻4 × ⁻4	b	⁻4 × 3 × ⁻6	c	⁻3 × ⁻4 × 3
d	⁻4 × ⁻8 × 3	e	3 × 6 × ⁻4	f	12 × 2 × ⁻3
g	1 × ⁻1 × 10	h	⁻3 × ⁻8 × 9	i	24 ÷ 3
j	⁻24 ÷ 3	k	⁻28 ÷ 2	l	⁻48 ÷ ⁻6
m	⁻300 ÷ ⁻10	n	400 ÷ ⁻40	o	42 ÷ ⁻7
p	⁻22 ÷ ⁻22	q	⁻33 ÷ 11	r	⁻27 ÷ ⁻3
s	45 ÷ ⁻9	t	⁻64 ÷ ⁻8	u	⁻81 ÷ 3

3 Calculate.

a $\frac{-40}{5}$ b $\frac{-28}{-4}$ c $\frac{30}{-5}$

d $\frac{12}{-2}$ e $\frac{65}{-5}$ f $\frac{-48}{-6}$

g $\frac{-330}{-10}$ h $\frac{-400}{40}$ i $\frac{-63}{7}$

j $\frac{-60}{-20}$ k $\frac{60}{-6}$ l $\frac{-36}{6}$

4 Apply the operations in the first row to the given number to complete each table.

a

	−10	× −2	+ 4	÷ −2	− 8	+ 1
−5						

b

	× −4	÷ −5	+ 8	− 3	× 2	− 9
10						

c

	− 10	× −2	+ 4	÷ −2	− 8	+ 1
0						

5 Here are some bank transactions.

Calculate the new balance in each case.

a Balance of £230, withdraw £100.

b Balance of £250.50, withdraw £300.

c Balance of −£450, deposit £900 then withdraw £300.

d Balance of −£100, deposit £2000 then withdraw £550.

6 The opening of an oil well 5000 feet below sea level, caused a massive oil spill in the Gulf of Mexico in 2010.

The oil well itself extended to a depth of 13 000 feet.

Express the answers to these questions as directed numbers.

a How deep was the deepest part of the oil well below the sea bed?

b How far did oil travel from the bottom of the well to reach the surface of the water?

c The oil company involved estimated that they were losing money at the rate of $15 000 000 per day. Use an integer to express the money lost after:

i one week.   ii thirteen weeks.

> **Tip**
>
> Feet is a standard unit of imperial measurement for length; the metric measurement for length is metres. You will learn more about metric measurements in Chapter 12.

7 Here is a set of integers.

{−8, −6, −3, 1, 3, 7}

a Find two numbers with a difference of 9.

b Find three numbers with a sum of 1.

c Find two numbers whose product is −3.

d Find two numbers which, when divided, will give an answer of −6.

8 One more than −6 is added to the product of 7 and six less than 3.

What is the result?

9 The temperature in Inverness is 4 °C at 7 pm at night.

By 1 am the same night, it has dropped by 12 degrees.

a What is the temperature at 1 am?

b What is the average hourly change in the temperature?

c By noon the next day, the temperature is 7 °C.
How many degrees warmer is this than it was at 1 am?

Find answers at: cambridge.org/ukschools/gcsemaths-studentbookanswers

GCSE Mathematics for OCR (Foundation)

Section 2: Order of operations

Jose posted this calculation on his wall on social media.

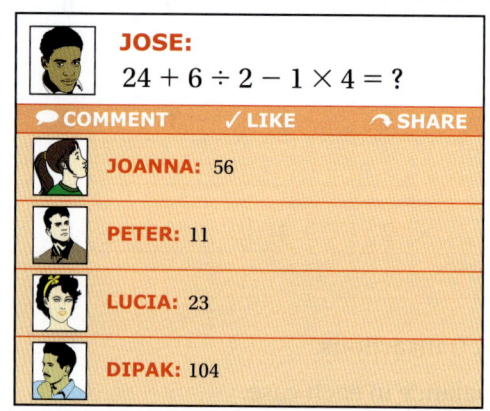

> **JOSE:**
> $24 + 6 \div 2 - 1 \times 4 = ?$
>
> 💬 COMMENT   ✓ LIKE   ↗ SHARE
>
> **JOANNA:** 56
>
> **PETER:** 11
>
> **LUCIA:** 23
>
> **DIPAK:** 104

Within minutes, his friends had posted four different answers.

Which one (if any) do you think is correct? Why?

There is a set of rules that tell you the order in which you need to work when there is more than one operation.

The order of operations is:
1 Do any operations in brackets first.
2 If there are any indices (powers or exponents) in the calculation, do them next.
3 Do division and multiplication next, working from left to right.
4 Do addition and subtraction last, working from left to right.

Tip

Many people remember these rules using the letters BIDMAS (or sometimes BODMAS).
Brackets
Indices (or **O**rders)
Divide and/or **M**ultiply
Add and/or **S**ubtract

Brackets and symbols

Brackets are used to group operations. For example:

$(3 + 7) \times (30 \div 2)$

When there is more than one set of brackets, it is best to work from the **innermost set** to the **outermost set**.

WORKED EXAMPLE 1

Solve $2((4 + 2) \times 2 - 3(1 - 3) - 10)$

$2((4 + 2) \times 2 - 3(1 - 3) - 10)$ Highlight the different pairs of brackets to help if you need to.

$2((4 + 2) \times 2 - 3(1 - 3) - 10)$
$= 2(6 \times 2 - 3(^-2) - 10)$
$= 2(6 \times 2 - 3 \times {}^-2 - 10)$

The red brackets are the innermost, so do the calculations inside these ones first. There are two lots of red brackets, so work from left to right. **Note** that you can leave $^-2$ inside brackets if you prefer because $3(^-2)$ is the same as $3 \times {}^-2$.

$2(6 \times 2 - 3 \times {}^-2 - 10)$
$= 2(12 - {}^-6 - 10)$
$= 2(8)$
$= 2 \times 8$
$= 16$

Black brackets are next. Do the multiplications first from left to right, then the subtractions from left to right.

Often a different style of bracket will be used to make it easier to identify each pair. For example, the following different types of brackets have been used below: ( ), [ ], { }.

$\{2 - [4(2 - 7) - 4(3 + 8)] - 2\} \times 8$

Other symbols can also be used to group operations. For example:

Fraction bars: $\dfrac{5 - 12}{3 - 8}$

Roots: $\sqrt{16 + 9}$

These symbols are treated like brackets when you do a calculation.

WORK IT OUT 1.2

Which of the solutions is correct in each case?

Find the mistakes in the incorrect option.

	Option A	Option B
1	$7 \times 3 + 4$ $= 21 + 4$ $= 25$	$7 \times 3 + 4$ $= 7 \times 7$ $= 49$
2	$(10 - 4) \times (4 + 9)^2$ $= 6 \times 16 + 81$ $= 96 + 81$ $= 177$	$(10 - 4) \times (4 + 9)^2$ $= 6 \times (13)^2$ $= 6 \times 169$ $= 1014$
3	$45 - [20 \times (4 - 3)]$ $= 45 - [20 \times 1]$ $= 45 - 21$ $= 24$	$45 - [20 \times (4 - 3)]$ $= 45 - 20 \times 1$ $= 45 - 20$ $= 25$
4	$30 - 4 \div 2 + 2$ $= 26 \div 2 + 2$ $= 13 + 2$ $= 15$	$30 - 4 \div 2 + 2$ $= 30 - 2 + 2$ $= 30$
5	$\dfrac{18 - 4}{4 - 2}$ $= \dfrac{18}{2}$ $= 9$	$\dfrac{18 - 4}{4 - 2}$ $= \dfrac{14}{2}$ $= 7$
6	$\sqrt{36} \div 4 + 40 \div 4 + 1$ $= \sqrt{9} + 10 + 1$ $= 3 + 11$ $= 14$	$\sqrt{36} \div 4 + 40 \div 4 + 1$ $= \sqrt{9} + 40 \div 5$ $= 3 + 8$ $= 11$

Calculator tip

Most modern calculators are programmed to use the correct order of operations. Check your calculator by entering $2 + 3 \times 4$. You should get 14.

If the calculation has brackets, you need to enter the brackets into the calculator to make sure it does these first.

Find answers at: cambridge.org/ukschools/gcsemaths-studentbookanswers

EXERCISE 1C

1 Calculate.
Show the steps in your working.

a $5 \times 10 + 3$
b $5 \times (10 + 3)$
c $2 + 10 \times 3$
d $(2 + 10) \times 3$
e $23 + 7 \times 2$
f $6 \times 2 \div (3 + 3)$
g $10 - 4 \times 5$
h $12 + 6 \div 2 - 4$
i $3 + 4 \times 5 - 10$
j $18 \div 3 \times 5 - 3 + 2$
k $5 - 3 \times 8 - 6 \div 2$
l $7 + 8 \div 4 - 1$
m $\dfrac{15 - 5}{2 \times 5}$
n $(17 + 1) \div 9 + 2$
o $\dfrac{16 - 4}{4 - 1}$
p $17 + 3 \times 21$
q $48 - (2 + 3) \times 2$
r $12 \times 4 - 4 \times 8$
s $15 + 30 \div 3 + 6$
t $20 - 6 \div 3 + 3$
u $10 - 4 \times 2 \div 2$

2 Check whether these answers are correct.
If the answer is wrong, work out the correct answer.

a $12 \times 4 + 76 = 124$
b $8 + 75 \times 8 = 698$
c $12 \times 18 - 4 \times 23 = 124$
d $(16 \div 4) \times (7 + 3 \times 4) = 76$
e $(82 - 36) \times (2 + 6) = 16$
f $(3 \times 7 - 4) - (4 + 6 \div 2) = 12$

3 Use the numbers listed to make each number sentence true.

a ☐ − ☐ ÷ ☐ = ☐   0, 2, 5, 10
b ☐ − ☐ ÷ ☐ = ☐   9, 11, 13, 18
c ☐ ÷ (☐ − ☐) − ☐ = ☐   1, 3, 8, 14, 16
d (☐ + ☐) − (☐ − ☐) = ☐   4, 5, 6, 9, 12

Section 3: Inverse operations

Operations are inverses of each other if one undoes (cancels out) the effect of the other.

- Adding is the inverse of subtracting, for example +5 is undone by −5.
- Multiplying is the inverse of dividing, for example ×2 is undone by ÷2.
- Taking a square root is the inverse of squaring a number, for example 4^2 is undone by $\sqrt{16}$.
- Taking the cube root is the inverse of cubing a number, for example 2^3 is undone by $\sqrt[3]{2}$.

When you add a number to its inverse the answer is always 0.

For example, $1 + {}^-1 = 0$, ${}^-1$ is known as the **additive inverse** of 1.

When you multiply a number by its inverse, the answer is always 1.

For example, $2 \times \dfrac{1}{2} = 1$

$\dfrac{1}{2}$ is known as the **multiplicative inverse** of 2.

The multiplicative inverse of a number is also called its **reciprocal**.

For example, $\dfrac{1}{3}$ is the reciprocal of 3.

Inverse operations are useful for checking the results of your calculations because carrying out the inverse operation gets you back to the number you started with.

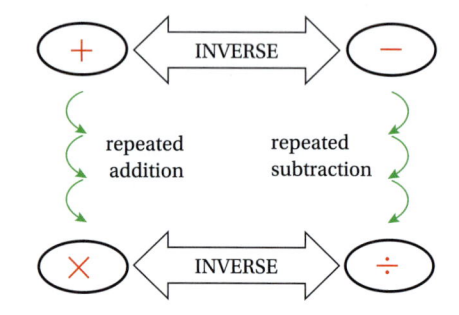

For example, is 4320 − 500 = 3820 correct?

Check by adding 500 back to the result (i.e. doing the inverse operation) to see if you get 4320.

3820 + 500 = 4320 so the original calculation is correct.

EXERCISE 1D

1 Find the additive inverse of each of these numbers.
   a 5   **b** 2   **c** 100   **d** −3   **e** −16   **f** −12

2 By what number would you multiply each of these to get an answer of 1?
   a 5   **b** 10   **c** −3   **d** $\frac{1}{3}$ **e** 9   **f** $\frac{1}{9}$

3 Use inverse operations to check each calculation.
Correct those that are wrong. (You can correct the question or the answer.)
   a 6172 − 3415 = 2757
   b 488 − 156 = 322
   c 219 − 361 = −142
   d 264 + 469 = 723
   e 4019 + 217 = 4235
   f 617 + 728 = 1345
   g 512 ÷ 4 = 43
   h 672 ÷ 12 = 56
   i 1274 ÷ 15 = 85
   j 3840 ÷ 30 = 128
   k 30 × 125 = 3770
   l 214 × 8 = 1732
   m $\sqrt{900} = 30$
   n $\sqrt{15\,625} = 120$
   o $400^2 = 16\,000$
   p $2500 = 50^2$

4 Use inverse operations to find the missing values in each of these calculations.
   a ☐ + 217 = 529
   b ☐ + 388 = 490
   c ☐ − 218 = 182
   d 121 × ☐ = −605
   e −6 × ☐ = 870
   f ☐ ÷ 40 = 5400

> **Tip**
> You will use inverse operations to solve equations and when you deal with functions, so it is important that you understand how they work.

Checklist of learning and understanding

Basic calculations
- Written methods are important for when you do not have a calculator.
- You can use any method as long as you show your working.
- Negative and positive numbers can be added, subtracted, multiplied and divided as long as you apply the rules to get the correct sign in the answer.

Order of operations
- In maths there is a standard order for working when there is more than one operation.
- Always work out brackets (or other grouping symbols) first, then powers. Multiply and/or divide next, then add and/or subtract.

Inverse operations
- An inverse operation undoes the previous operation.
- Addition is the inverse of subtraction.
- Multiplication is the inverse of division.
- Squaring is the inverse of taking the square root.
- Cubing is the inverse of taking the cube root; this is the same for any power and root.

Find answers at: cambridge.org/ukschools/gcsemaths-studentbookanswers

Chapter review

For additional questions on the topics in this chapter, visit GCSE Mathematics Online.

1 The cross-number puzzle on the left contains the solutions.

The clues are all calculations that involve using the correct order of operations.

Write a set of clues that would give these results.

2 Use integers and operations to write ten different questions that give an answer of ⁻17.

3 **a** Work out these calculations.

   i $4 + 3 \times (1 + 2)$ (1 mark)

   ii $\dfrac{4}{2} + 1 \times 3$ (1 mark)

   iii $\dfrac{4 \times 3}{2 + 1}$ (1 mark)

   b Fern is finding calculations that follow these rules
   - You must use **all** the digits 1, 2, 3 and 4, but they can be used only once
   - You can add, subtract, multiply or divide as many times as you like
   - You can use brackets.

   For example when Fern was looking for a calculation with an **answer of 9**, she wrote down

   $(4 + 3 + 2) \times 1$

   Find a calculation, using her rules, which has an answer of

   i 8 (1 mark)

   ii 15 (1 mark)

   © OCR 2012

4 On a page of a magazine there are three columns of text.

   Each column contains 42 rows.

   If there is an average of 32 letters per row, approximately how many letters are there on a page?

5 A stadium has seats for 32 000 people.

   How many rows of 125 is this?

6 Two numbers have a sum of ⁻15 and a product of ⁻100.

   What are the numbers?

7 The sum of two numbers is 1, but their product is ⁻20.

   What are the numbers?

8 Josie's bank account was overdrawn.

   She deposited £1000 and this brought her balance to £432.

   By how much was her account overdrawn to start with?

2 Whole number theory

In this chapter you will learn how to …
- identify the properties of different sets of numbers and use the correct words to talk about them.
- identify prime numbers and express any whole number as a product of its prime factors.
- find the HCF and LCM of two numbers by listing and by prime factorisation.

For more resources relating to this chapter, visit GCSE Mathematics Online.

Using mathematics: real-life applications

Numbers and basic calculations are used by people on a daily basis. A market stall holder has to quickly calculate the cost of a customer's order; a logistics manager has to order stock and divide the supplies so that they are never over or under stocked. There are many applications of basic calculation.

> **Tip**
> You probably already know most of the concepts in this chapter. It is included so you can revise the concepts if you need to and check that you know them well.

"Counting in multiples saves quite a bit of time. If I know that each shelf has 15 boxes and each box contains 5 reams of paper, then I know straightaway that you have 75 reams on each shelf without having to count each ream." *(Logistics manager)*

Before you start …

KS3	You should be able to recognise and find the factors of a number and to list multiples of a number.	**1** If these are the factors, what is the number? **a** 1, 5, 25 **b** 1, 2, 3, 6 **c** 1, 11 **2** If these are all multiples of a number, what is the number? **a** 8, 10, 12, 14 **b** 18, 21, 27, 33 **c** 5, 20, 35, 60	
KS3	You should know the first few prime numbers, square numbers and cube numbers.	**3** Which of the numbers below are: **a** prime numbers? **b** square numbers? **c** cube numbers? 0, 1, 2, 3, 4, 5, 6, 7, 8, 9, 10, 11, 12, 13, 14, 15, 16, 17, 18, 19, 20	
KS3	You will need to be able to express a number as a product of its prime factors.	**4** Match each number to the product of its prime factors. **a** 450 **b** 180 **c** 120 **d** 72 A $2 \times 2 \times 2 \times 3 \times 3$ B $2 \times 2 \times 3 \times 3 \times 5$ C $2 \times 2 \times 2 \times 3 \times 5$ D $2 \times 3 \times 3 \times 5 \times 5$	

Find answers at: cambridge.org/ukschools/gcsemaths-studentbookanswers

Assess your starting point using the Launchpad

STEP 1

1 Say whether each statement is true or false.
   a 1 is the smallest prime number.
   b If you square 7 you get 14.
   c 8 is the cube of 2.
   d Any whole number that ends in 1 is an odd number.
   e 33, 43 and 53 are prime numbers.
   f 7, 14 and 21 are factors of 7.

2 There is one incorrect number in each of these sets.
Work out what the number property of the set is and find the incorrect number.
   a 20, 22, 24, 26, 28, 29, 30
   b 11, 22, 33, 44, 56, 66
   c 1, 2, 3, 4, 8, 12
   d 27, 30, 33, 36, 39, 41
   e 1, 2, 3, 4, 6, 9, 12, 18, 24, 36
   f 12, 24, 48, 60, 72, 86
   g 2, 3, 5, 7, 9, 11, 13, 17, 19
   h 1, 4, 9, 16, 20, 25

GO TO
Section 1:
Review of number properties

STEP 2

3 Choose the correct product of prime factors for each number.
   a 48
       A $2 \times 2 \times 2 \times 3 \times 3$ B $2 \times 2 \times 2 \times 2 \times 3$
   b 100
       A $2 \times 2 \times 5 \times 5$ B $2 \times 5 \times 5$

GO TO
Section 2:
Prime numbers and prime factors

STEP 3

4 Given that $72 = 2 \times 2 \times 2 \times 3 \times 3$ and $120 = 2 \times 2 \times 2 \times 3 \times 5$, choose the correct answers.
   a The HCF of 72 and 120 is:
       A 360   B 12   C 24   D 5
   b The LCM of 72 and 120 is:
       A 30   B 2   C 120   D 360

GO TO
Section 3:
Factors and multiples

GO TO
Chapter review

Section 1: Review of number properties

Mathematical terms and their meanings

Make sure you remember the correct mathematical terms for the different types of numbers shown in the table.

Mathematical term	Definition	Example
Odd number	A whole number that cannot be divided exactly by 2; it has a remainder of 1.	1, 3, 5, 7, …
Even number	A whole number that can be divided exactly by 2.	0, 2, 4, 6, 8, …
Prime number	A whole number greater than 1 that can only be divided exactly by itself and by 1. (It only has two factors.)	2, 3, 5, 7, 11, 13, 17, 19, …
Square number	The product when an integer is multiplied by itself. For example $2 \times 2 = 4$, so 4 is a square number.	1, 4, 9, 16, … 3×3 can be written as using powers as 3^2.
Cube number	The product when an integer is multiplied by itself twice. For example $2 \times 2 \times 2 = 8$, so 8 is a cube number.	1, 8, 27, 64, … $5 \times 5 \times 5$ can be written as using powers as 5^3.
Root ($\sqrt{}$)	The number that produces a square number when it is multiplied by itself is a square root. The number that produces a cube number when it is multiplied by itself and then by itself again is a cube root.	The square root of 25 is 5. $\sqrt{25} = 5 \ (5 \times 5 = 25)$ The cube root of 8 is 2. $\sqrt[3]{8} = 2 \ (2 \times 2 \times 2 = 8)$
Factor (also called divisor)	A number that divides exactly into another number.	Factors of 6 are 1, 2, 3 and 6. Factors of 7 are 1 and 7. Factors of 25 are 1, 5 and 25.
Multiple	A multiple of a number is found when you multiply that number by a whole number. Your times tables are really just lists of multiples.	Multiples of 3 are 3, 6, 9, 12, … Multiples of 7 are 7, 14, 21, …
Common factor (divisor)	A common factor is a factor shared by two or more numbers. 1 is a common factor of all numbers.	Factors of 6 are 1, 2, 3, and 6. Factors of 12 are 1, 2, 3, 4, 6 and 12. 1, 2, 3 and 6 are common factors of 6 and 12.
Common multiple	A common multiple is a multiple shared by two or more numbers.	Multiples of 2 are 2, 4, 6, 8, 10, 12, … Multiples of 3 are 3, 6, 9, 12, … 6 and 12 are common multiples of 2 and 3.

You might also find it helpful to know the following:

Integers are positive and negative whole numbers.

Rational numbers can be expressed as a fraction where both the numerator and the denominator are integers. Decimal numbers that terminate (e.g. 1.5) or are recurring (e.g. 1.666666666…) are rational numbers.

Irrational numbers are decimals that do not terminate nor are recurring and so cannot be expressed as rational numbers. Examples include π, $\sqrt{2}$ and $\sqrt{3}$.

> **Tip**
>
> You will learn more about these types of number in Chapter 10.

Find answers at: cambridge.org/ukschools/gcsemaths-studentbookanswers

EXERCISE 2A

1 Here is a list of numbers.

1 2 3 4 5 6 7 8 9 10 11 12 13 14 15
16 17 18 19 20 21 22 23 24 25 26 27 28 29 30

Choose and list the numbers in the box that are:

- **a** odd
- **b** even
- **c** prime
- **d** square
- **e** cube
- **f** factors of 24
- **g** multiples of 3
- **h** common factors of 8 and 12
- **i** common multiples of 3 and 4

2 Write down:

- **a** the next four odd numbers after 207.
- **b** four **consecutive** even numbers between 500 and 540.
- **c** the square numbers between 20 and 70.
- **d** the factors of 23.
- **e** four prime numbers greater than 15.
- **f** the first ten cube numbers.
- **g** the first five multiples of 8.
- **h** the factors of 36.

3 Say whether the results will be odd or even.

- **a** The sum of two odd numbers.
- **b** The sum of two even numbers.
- **c** The difference between two even numbers.
- **d** The square of an odd number.
- **e** The product of an odd and an even number.
- **f** The cube of an odd number.

> **Key vocabulary**
>
> **consecutive**: following each other in order. For example 1, 2, 3 or 35, 36, 37.

Place value

Consider the number 22<u>2</u> 222.

Each of the 2s in the number has a different place value.

The place value tells you the value of the digit; the underlined 2 in the number above has a value of 2 thousands or 2000.

Hundred thousands 100 000	Ten thousands 10 000	Thousands 1000	Hundreds 100	Tens 10	Ones/units 1
2	2	2	2	2	2

Each column in the place value table is ten times the value of the place to the right of it.

2 Whole number theory

EXERCISE 2B

1 Write each set of numbers in order from smallest to biggest.
  a 432   456   348   843   654
  b 606   660   607   670   706
  c 123   1231   312   1321   231
  d 12 700 71 200 21 700 21 007

2 What is the value of the 5 in each of these numbers?
  a 35   b 534   c 256   d 25 876
  e 50 346 987 f 1 532 980   g 5 678 432   h 356 432

3 What is the biggest and smallest number you can make with each set of digits?
  Use each digit only once in each number. (Do not begin a number with 0.)
  a 4, 0 and 6   b 5, 7, 3 and 1   c 1, 0, 3, 4, 6 and 2

Section 2: Prime numbers and prime factors

Prime numbers have only two factors: 1 and the number itself.

The number 1 is not a prime number because it only has one factor.

2 is the only even prime number.

The prime numbers less than 20 are:

2, 3, 5, 7, 11, 13, 17, 19.

> **Tip**
> You need to know all the prime numbers less than 20, but it will help you work faster if you can recognise them all up to 100.

Prime factors

If a factor of a number is a prime number it is called a **prime factor**.

Every integer greater than 1 can be written as a product of its prime factors.

Finding the prime numbers that multiply together to make a given number is known as **prime factorisation**.

You can find the prime factors of a number by **repeatedly dividing by prime numbers**, or by using **factor trees**.

> **Key vocabulary**
> **prime factor**: a factor that is also a prime number.

WORKED EXAMPLE 1

Express 48 as a product of its prime factors:
a by division.   **b** using a factor tree.

a
```
2 | 48
2 | 24
2 | 12
2 |  6
3 |  3
```
2 × 2 × 2 × 2 × 3

Divide by prime numbers; you should always divide to get integers. Start with the lowest divisor that is prime; always try 2 first. Divide by 2 repeatedly until you can't any more and then try the next prime number, 3, and so on.

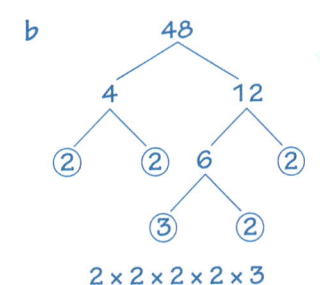

b
```
        48
       /  \
      4    12
     / \   / \
    2   2 6   2
         / \
        3   2
```
2 × 2 × 2 × 2 × 3

Write the number as a product of any two of its factors. Keep doing this for the factors until you cannot divide a factor any more (i.e. until you get to a prime factor); the numbers should all be integers.

Find answers at: cambridge.org/ukschools/gcsemaths-studentbookanswers

> **Tip**
>
> The **unique factorisation theorem** in mathematics says that each number can be written as a product of prime factors in one way only.
>
> It means that different numbers cannot have the same product of prime factors.

You get the same result with both methods. An integer can only be expressed in terms of its prime factors one way.

Even if you do the division in a different order and split the factors differently in the factor tree, you will always get the same result for a given number.

Here are four ways of finding the prime factors of 280.

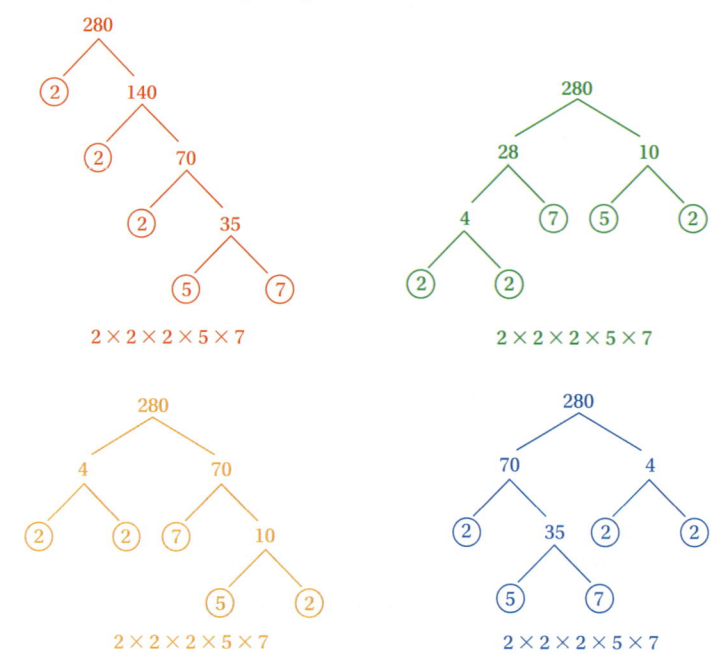

$2 \times 2 \times 2 \times 5 \times 7$

$2 \times 2 \times 2 \times 5 \times 7$

$2 \times 2 \times 2 \times 5 \times 7$

$2 \times 2 \times 2 \times 5 \times 7$

You can use powers to write the product of factors of a number in a shorter, more efficient way.

$$\underbrace{2 \times 2 \times 2 \times 5 \times 7}_{\text{expanded form}} = \underbrace{2^3 \times 5 \times 7}_{\text{power notation}}$$

Using power notation, $2 \times 2 \times 2$ is simplified to 2^3.

EXERCISE 2C

1 Identify the prime numbers in each set.

   a 1, 2, 3, 4, 5, 6, 7, 8, 9, 10

   b 50, 51, 52, 53, 54, 55, 56, 57, 58, 59, 60

   c 95, 96, 97, 98, 99, 100, 101, 102, 103, 104, 105

2 Express each of the following numbers as a product of their prime factors. Use the method you prefer. Write your final answers using power notation.

   a 36   **b** 65   **c** 64   **d** 84

   e 80   **f** 1000   **g** 1270   **h** 1963

3 A number is expressed as $2^3 \times 3^3 \times 5$.

   a What is the number?

   b Could it be any other number? Explain why.

Section 3: Multiples and factors

The lowest common multiple

The lowest common multiple (LCM) of two or more numbers is the smallest number that is a multiple of all the given numbers.

To find the LCM, list the multiples of the given numbers until you find the first multiple that appears in all the lists.

> **WORKED EXAMPLE 2**
>
> Find the LCM of 4 and 7.
>
> 4, 8, 12, 16, 20, 24, 28, 32, …   List the multiples of 4.
>
> 7, 14, 21, 28, …   List the multiples of 7.
>
> LCM of 4 and 7 = 28   Stop listing at 28 as it appears in the both lists.

The highest common factor

The highest common factor (HCF) of two or more numbers is the largest number that is a factor of all the given numbers. To find the HCF, list all the factors in each number, and pick the highest number that appears in all the lists.

> **WORKED EXAMPLE 3**
>
> Find the HCF of 8 and 24.
>
> 8: <u>1</u>, <u>2</u>, <u>4</u>, <u>8</u>
>
> 24: <u>1</u>, <u>2</u>, 3, <u>4</u>, 6, <u>8</u>, 12, 24   Underline the common factors.
>
> HCF of 8 and 24 = 8   The highest underlined number is the HCF.

> **Tip**
>
> The LCM is used to find the lowest common denominator when you add or subtract fractions.
> The HCF is useful for cancelling fractions. You will also use them in Chapter 10 on fractions, as well as in Chapter 3 to factorise algebraic expressions.

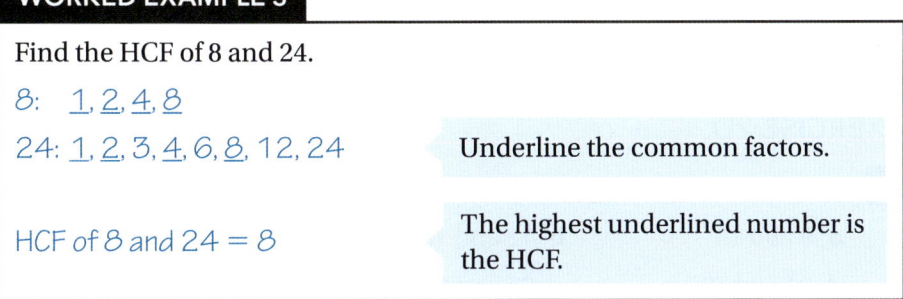

With word problems you need to work out whether to use the LCM or HCF to find the answers.

- Problems involving the LCM usually include repeating events. You might be asked how many items you need to 'have enough' or when something will happen again at the same time.
- Problems involving the HCF usually involve splitting things into smaller pieces or arranging things in equal groups or rows.

Finding the HCF and LCM using prime factors

When you work with larger numbers you can find the HCF and LCM by writing the numbers as products of prime factors (i.e. by prime factorisation).

Once you've done that you can use the factors to quickly find the HCF and LCM.

Find answers at: cambridge.org/ukschools/gcsemaths-studentbookanswers

WORKED EXAMPLE 4

a Find the HCF of 72 and 120.   b Find the LCM of 72 and 120.

a $72 = \underline{2} \times \underline{2} \times \underline{2} \times \underline{3} \times 3$
   $120 = \underline{2} \times \underline{2} \times \underline{2} \times \underline{3} \times 5$

> First express each number as a product of prime factors.
>
> Underline the common factors. Here the common factors are three '2's and one '3'. 72 has an extra '3' not shared with 120, and 120 has a '5' not shared with 72.

$2 \times 2 \times 2 \times 3 = 24$.
HCF of 72 and 120 = 24

> Write down the common factors and multiply them out.

b $72 = \underline{2} \times \underline{2} \times \underline{2} \times \underline{3} \times \underline{3}$.
   $120 = 2 \times 2 \times 2 \times 3 \times \underline{5}$

> First express each number as a product of prime factors.
>
> Underline the largest set of multiples of each factor across **both** lists. Here, there are three '2's in each list so underline one set; '3' appears twice in one list and once in the other, so underline the set of two '3's. The one '5' in the bottom set is the largest set of '5's so underline that one.

$2 \times 2 \times 2 \times 3 \times 3 \times 5 = 360$.
LCM of 72 and 120 is 360

> Write down each set of multiples and multiply them out.

Tip

Use the letters to help you remember what to do. LCM requires the **L**argest set of **M**ultiples

EXERCISE 2D

1 Find the LCM of the given numbers.

   a 9 and 18   b 12 and 18   c 15 and 18
   d 24 and 12   e 36 and 9   f 4, 12 and 8
   g 3, 9 and 24   h 12, 16 and 32

2 Find the HCF of the given numbers.

   a 12 and 18   b 18 and 36   c 27 and 90
   d 12 and 15   e 20 and 30   f 19 and 45
   g 60 and 72   h 250 and 900

3 Find the LCM and the HCF of the following numbers by using prime factors.

   a 27 and 14   b 85 and 15   c 96 and 27
   d 24 and 60   e 450 and 105   f 234 and 66
   g 550 and 128   h 315 and 275

2 Whole number theory

4 Sian has two rolls of cotton fabric.

One roll has 72 metres on it, the other has 90 metres on it.

She wants to cut the fabric to make pieces of equal length without wasting any of it.

  a What is the longest possible length the pieces can be?

  b How many pieces can be cut from each roll for that length?

5 In a shopping centre promotion every 30th shopper gets a £10 voucher and every 120th shopper gets a free meal.

How many shoppers must enter the mall before one receives both a voucher and a free meal?

6 Amanda has 40 pieces of fruit and 100 sweets to share among the students in her class.

She is able to give each student an equal number of pieces of fruit and an equal number of sweets.

What is the largest possible number of students in her class?

7 Samir and Li start to walk in opposite directions around a walking track.

They start at the same point at the same time.

It takes Samir 5 minutes to walk round the track and it takes Li 4 minutes.

If they walk at this pace, how long will it be before they meet again at the starting point?

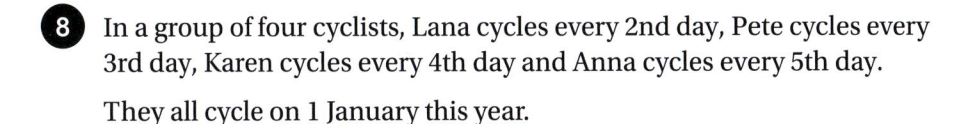

8 In a group of four cyclists, Lana cycles every 2nd day, Pete cycles every 3rd day, Karen cycles every 4th day and Anna cycles every 5th day.

They all cycle on 1 January this year.

  a How many days will pass before they all cycle on the same day again?

  b How many times a year will they all cycle on the same day?

9 Mr Abbot has three pieces of ribbon with lengths 2.4 m, 3.18 m and 4.26 m.

He wants to cut the ribbons into pieces that are all the same length.

He doesn't want any of the ribbon left over.

What is the greatest possible length for the pieces?

10 Two warning lights in a tunnel flash every 20 seconds and 30 seconds, respectively.

They flashed together at 4.30 pm.

When will they next flash at the same time?

Find answers at: cambridge.org/ukschools/gcsemaths-studentbookanswers

Checklist of learning and understanding

Properties of numbers
- Even numbers are multiples of 2, odd numbers are not.
- Factors are numbers that divide exactly into a number.
- Prime numbers have only two factors, 1 and the number itself.
- Square numbers are the product of a number and itself ($n \times n$).
- Cube numbers are the product of a number multiplied by itself twice ($n \times n \times n$).
- The value of a digit depends on its place in the number.

Prime numbers
- The prime numbers less than 20 are: 2, 3, 5, 7, 11, 13, 17 and 19.
- If a factor is a prime number it is called a prime factor.
- Integers can be written as the product of their prime factors.
  You find the prime factors by:
    - repeated division by prime numbers (starting from 2 and working upwards).
    - using a factor tree and breaking down factors until they are prime factors.

Factors and multiples
- The lowest common multiple (LCM) of two numbers can be found by:
    - listing the multiples of both numbers and choosing the lowest multiple that appears in both lists.
    - finding the largest set of multiples of each of the prime factors and multiplying them together.
- The highest common factor (HCF) of two numbers can be found by:
    - listing the factors of both numbers and choosing the highest factor that appears in both lists.
    - finding the common prime factors and multiplying them together.

For additional questions on the topics in this chapter, visit GCSE Mathematics Online.

Chapter review

1. Complete the crossword puzzle on the handout provided by your teacher.

Clues

Across
1. The times tables are examples of these.
2. Whole numbers divisible by 2.
3. Another word used for factor.
4. Numbers in the sequence 1, 4, 9, 16, …
5. An even prime number.
6. The result of a multiplication.

Down
a. $n \times n \times n$ is the __ of n.
b. Numbers with only two factors.
c. Whole numbers that are not exactly divisible by 2.
d. Number that divides into another with no remainder.
e. HCF of 12 and 18.

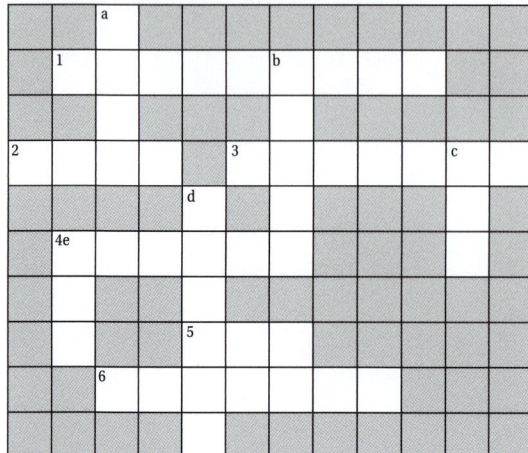

2 Is 149 a prime number? Show how you decided.

3 34   6   16   17   48   20   21

Choose from this list of numbers

a a multiple of 5 *(1 mark)*

b a factor of 24 *(1 mark)*

c a prime number *(1 mark)*

d two numbers that add up to 50 *(1 mark)*

e a square number *(1 mark)*

© OCR 2011

4 Find the HCF and the LCM of 20 and 35 by listing the factors and multiples.

5 Express 800 as a product of prime factors, giving your final answer using powers.

6 Determine the HCF and LCM of the following by prime factorisation.

a 72 and 108   b 84 and 60

7 Jo, Mo and Jenny were jumping up a flight of stairs.

Jo jumped 2 steps at a time, Mo jumped 3 steps at time while Jenny managed 4 steps at a time.

They started together on the bottom step. What is the first step they will all jump on?

Find answers at: cambridge.org/ukschools/gcsemaths-studentbookanswers

3 Algebraic expressions

In this chapter you will learn how to …
- use algebraic notation and write algebraic expressions.
- simplify and manipulate algebraic expressions.
- use common factors to factorise expressions.
- use algebra to solve problems in different contexts.

For more resources relating to this chapter, visit GCSE Mathematics Online.

Using mathematics: real-life applications

Algebra lets you describe and represent patterns using short mathematical language. This is useful in many different careers including accounting, navigation, building, plumbing, health, medicine, science and computing.

"You are unlikely to think about algebra when you watch cartoons or play video games, but animators use complex algebra to program the characters and make objects move." (Games designer)

Before you start …

KS3	You need to understand the basic conventions of algebra.	**1**	Choose the correct way to write each of these.
			a $n \times n$
			   A $2n$ B n^2 C 2^n D $2(n)$
			b c multiplied by 3 and then added to 5
			   A $3c + 5$ B $3(c + 5)$ C $c + 15$
			c n squared and then multiplied by 2
			   A $2n^2$ B $(2n)^2$ C $4n^2$

KS3	You should be able to substitute numbers for letters and evaluate expressions.	**2**	**a** Evaluate the following expressions for $n = 5$ and $n = {-}5$. **i** $3n + 4$ **ii** $3(n + 4)$ **b** What is the value of $\dfrac{(2 + 4)^2}{6}$?
Ch 2	You should be able to find the highest common factor in a group of terms.	**3**	Write down the HCF of: **a** $12xy$ and $18y^2$. **b** $45x$, $50xy$ and $15x$.

Assess your starting point using the Launchpad

STEP 1

1 Write each statement as an algebraic expression.
   a Multiply n by 3 and add 4 to the result.
   b Subtract 4 from n and multiply the result by 3.
   c Multiply n squared by 4, add 3 and divide the result by 2.

GO TO Section 1: Algebraic notation

STEP 2

2 Simplify these expressions by collecting like terms.
   a $3a + 2b + 2a - b$
   b $4x + 7 + 3x - 3 - x$
   c $4a^2 + 8ab - 10a^2 - 5ab$

GO TO Section 2: Simplifying expressions

STEP 2

3 Multiply out the brackets and simplify.
   a $m(n - p)$ b $3(x + 5) + 4(x + 2)$ c $2z(z + 4) - z(z + 5)$

GO TO Section 3: Multiplying out brackets

STEP 3

4 Complete the following.
   a $3x + 12 = \Box(x + 4)$ b $5x + 10y = \Box(x + 2y)$
   c $x^2 - 3x = \Box(x - 3)$ d $ab - ac = a(\Box - \Box)$
   e $^-x + 7x^2 = {}^-x(\Box \Box \Box)$

5 Factorise each expression and write it as a product of its factors.
   a $2x + 4y$ b $^-3x - 9$ c $5x + 5y$

GO TO Section 4: Factorising expressions

GO TO Section 5: Using algebra to solve problems

Find answers at: cambridge.org/ukschools/gcsemaths-studentbookanswers

Section 1: Algebraic notation

In algebra letters are used to represent unknown numbers.

For example $x + y = 20$.

This tells you that two numbers add up to 20.

The letters can represent many different numbers so they are called **variables**.

Letters and numbers can be combined and linked together with operation signs to form **expressions** such as $5a^3 - 2xy + 3$. This expression has three **terms**.

Terms are separated by + or − signs and the sign belongs with the term that follows it. Terms should always be written in the shortest, simplest way:

$2 \times h$ is written as $2h$ and $x \times x \times y$ is written as x^2y.

$4x \div 3$ is written as $\frac{4x}{3}$ and $(x + 4) \div 2$ is written as $\frac{x + 4}{2}$.

The rules for the four operations are the same for letters as they are for numbers.

For example, to find a **product**, you multiply together the factors:

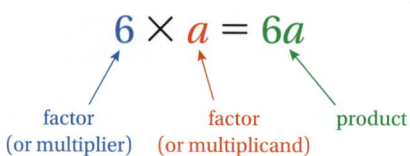

$6 \times a = 6a$

factor (or multiplier)   factor (or multiplicand)   product

In algebraic notation, multiplication is shown by writing the factors next to each other. You write $a \times b$ as ab and $5 \times z$ as $5z$.

Equations and identities

An equation is a mathematical statement that includes an equals sign, for example $a + 3 = 27$. An identity is an equation that includes the symbol '≡', which means 'exactly the same as' or 'identical to'. This means that the left-hand side is a different way of representing the right-hand side. For example, the following are all identities:

$a \times b \equiv ab$ $5 \times z \equiv 5z$ $a \div b \equiv \frac{a}{b}$ $5 \div z \equiv \frac{5}{z}$

Identities are true for all values of the variables.

An identity is not the same as two equivalent terms. For example, you can say $2n = n + 2$ but you cannot say $2n \equiv n + 2$.

$2n = n + 2$ is an equation and has one unique answer, $n = 2$ but $2n$ and $n + 2$ are **not** identical terms. When $n \neq 2$, then $2n \neq 2$ so it is **not** true for all values of n, and is not an identity.

> **Key vocabulary**
>
> **variable**: a letter representing an unknown number.
> **expression**: a group of numbers and letters linked by operation signs.
> **term**: a combination of letters and/or numbers. Each number in a sequence is called a term.
> **product**: the result of multiplying numbers and/or terms together.

> **Tip**
>
> When you have numbers and letters in a term, the number is written first and letters are usually written in alphabetical order.
> So, you write $5x$ not $x5$ and $3xy$ not $3yx$.

> **Tip**
>
> It is fine to use an = sign instead of an ≡ for example, $2 + 3 = 5$ and $2 + 3 \equiv 5$ are both accurate. But it is **not** okay to use a ≡ sign for anything other than an identity.

WORK IT OUT 3.1

Johan was asked to write three identities and to justify his choices.

Is each choice correct or incorrect? Why?

Option A	Option B	Option C
$3(x - 5) \equiv 15 - 3x$ $3x - 15 \equiv 15 - 3x$ LHS is the same as the RHS, true for all values of x.	$(2x)^2 + 1 \equiv 4x^2 + 1$ LHS $= 2x \times 2x + 1$ $= 4x^2 + 1$ $=$ RHS ∴ this is an identity, true for all values of x.	$\frac{2y + 2}{3} \equiv \frac{3}{2(y + 1)}$ $2y + 2 = 2(y + 1)$ $2y + 2 = 2y + 2$ LHS is divided by 3 and on RHS 3 is divided by the expression. ∴ this is an identity, true for all values of x.

EXERCISE 3A

1 a Are these true or false?
    i $2n \equiv n + 2$ **ii** $2n \equiv n + n$ **iii** $2n \equiv n^2$ **iv** $2n^2 \equiv (2n)^2$
b Is there a value of n so that $2n = n^2$?

2 Write the algebraic expression for:
  a x multiplied by 3 and added to y multiplied by 7.
  b 4 subtracted from x squared and the result multiplied by 5.
  c x cubed added to y squared and the result divided by 4.
  d 6 added to x, the result multiplied by 4 and then y subtracted.
  e x multiplied by itself and then divided by 2.

3 Match each statement to the correct algebraic expression.

a	Take a number and multiply it by 3 then add 2 to it.	i	$\dfrac{6 + x}{2}$
b	Take a number and add 3 to it, then double it.	ii	$3x + 2$
c	Take a number, multiply it by itself then add 3 to it.	iii	$5(x - 4)$
d	Add 6 to a number then divide it by 2.	iv	$9x^2$
e	Subtract 4 from a number and multiply the result by 5.	v	$x^2 + 3$
f	Square a number then multiply it by 9.	vi	$2x^2 - 3x^3$
g	Square a number and multiply it by 2, then subtract the same number cubed and multiplied by 3.	vii	$2(x + 3)$

4 Use algebra to write these in as short a form as possible.
  a $2 \times 3a$ **b** $4b \times 5$ **c** $d \times (^-9)$ **d** $4a \times 3b$ **e** $5c \times 2d$
  f $^-3m \times 4n$ **g** $^-2p \times (^-3q)$ **h** $a \times a$ **i** $m \times m$ **j** $2a \times 4a$
  k $^-3a \times 5a$ **l** $^-2m \times (^-4m)$ **m** $7a \times 8ab$ **n** $^-6cd \times (^-2de)$ **o** $2a \times 2a \times 2a$

5 Rewrite each division using algebraic conventions. Simplify them if possible.
  a $15x \div 5$ **b** $27y \div 3$ **c** $24a^2 \div 8$ **d** $7 \times 15p \div 21$ **e** $24x \div (8 \times 3)$
  f $18y \div (6 \times 2)$ **g** $^-18x^2 \div 9$ **h** $^-16a^2 \div (^-4)$ **i** $15 \div (3 \times n \times n)$

6 Write each of the following without multiplication or division signs.
  a $2 \times 5n$ **b** $p \times q$ **c** $a \times (b + c)$ **d** $(x + y) \div z$ **e** $n^2 \times n^3$ **f** $p^3 \times p$

7 Write expressions to represent the perimeter and area of each shape:

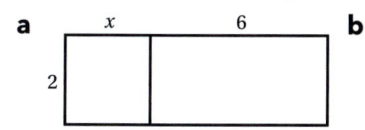

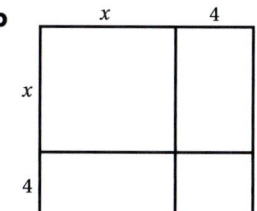

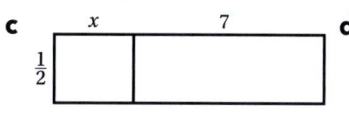

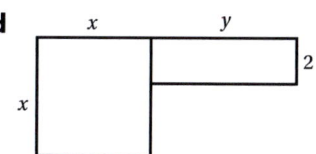

a rectangle with sides x, 6, and 2
b square-like shape with sides x, 4, x, 4
c rectangle with sides x, 7, and $\frac{1}{2}$
d L-shape with sides x, y, 2, x

8 A man is x years old.
  a How old will he be ten years from now?
  b How old was he ten years ago?
  c His daughter is a third of his age. How old is his daughter?

Find answers at: cambridge.org/ukschools/gcsemaths-studentbookanswers

GCSE Mathematics for OCR (Foundation)

Key vocabulary

evaluate: to find the value of, to solve.

substitute: to replace letters in an expression, equation or formula with numbers.

Tip

When you substitute values into a term such as 2y you need to remember that 2y means $2 \times y$. So, if $y = 6$, you need to write 2y as 2×6 and not as 26.

Tip

Substitution is an important skill. You will need to substitute values for letters when you work with formulae for perimeter, area and volume of shapes and when you solve problems involving Pythagoras' theorem.

Substitution

You can **evaluate** expressions if the letters are given values. This is known as **substitution**.

For example, if $x = {}^-2$, you can work out that $2x + 1 = 2 \times {}^-2 + 1 = {}^-4 + 1 = {}^-3$.

WORKED EXAMPLE 1

Given that $a = {}^-2$ and $b = 8$, evaluate:

a ab **b** $3b - 2a$ **c** $2a^3$ **d** $2(a + b)$

a $ab = a \times b$
$= {}^-2 \times 8$
$= {}^-16$

b $3b - 2a = 3 \times b - 2 \times a$
$= 3 \times 8 - 2 \times {}^-2$
$= 24 - ({}^-4)$
$= 28$

c $2a^3 = 2 \times a^3$
$= 2 \times ({}^-2)^3$
$= 2 \times {}^-8$
$= {}^-16$

d $2(a + b) = 2 \times (a + b)$
$= 2 \times ({}^-2 + 8)$
$= 2 \times 6$
$= 12$

Remember to do the calculation in brackets first.

EXERCISE 3B

1 Given that $x = 3$ and $y = 6$, evaluate these expressions.

a $2x + 3y$ **b** $3x + 2y$ **c** $10y - 2x$ **d** $x + 2y$

e $6x + y$ **f** $5x - 5y$ **g** $2xy$ **h** $\frac{1}{2}xy$

i $3x^2 + 7y$ **j** ${}^-x - y$ **k** $\sqrt{x + y}$ **l** $\sqrt{x^2}$

2 Find the value of each expression when $a = {}^-2$ and $b = 5$.

a ${}^-5ab + 10$ **b** ${}^-3ab - 6$ **c** $\frac{10}{b}$ **d** $\frac{400}{a}$

e $\frac{6}{a} - \frac{15}{b}$ **f** $\frac{15}{b} - \frac{24}{2a}$ **g** $8 - 2a + 2b$ **h** $7a - 4 + 2b$

i $\left(\sqrt{{}^-10ab}\right)$ **j** $\frac{2a}{3y}$ **k** $4a - 7b + 35$ **l** $11a - b - 4b$

Section 2: Simplifying expressions

When you are asked to simplify an expression, you need to use the rules of arithmetic and algebra to write an expression as simply as possible.

Adding and subtracting like terms

Like terms have exactly the same letters or combination of letters and powers.

You can simplify expressions by adding or subtracting like terms.

$3a$ and $4a$ are **like** terms. $7xy$ and $2xy$ are **like** terms. $5x^2$ and $3x^2$ are **like** terms.

$3a + 4a = 7a$ $7xy - 2xy = 5xy$ $5x^2 - 3x^2 = 2x^2$

$5ab^2$ and $2a^2b$ are **not like** terms so $5ab^2 - 2a^2b$ cannot be simplified further.

WORK IT OUT 3.2

Here are two terms: $3x^2y$ and $2xy^2$.

Student A said that these two terms are like terms and can be added together to be written as: $5x^2y^2$

Student B said that these two terms are not like terms and can only be written added together as: $3x^2y + 2xy^2$

Which student is correct? Why?

When an expression contains many different terms you might be able to simplify it by collecting and combining like terms.

WORKED EXAMPLE 2

Simplify $2x - 4y + 3x + y$

$= 2x + 3x - 4y + y$ Rearrange the terms so like terms are together. Keep the signs with the terms they belong to.

$= 5x - 3y$ Combine the like terms. Remember $y = 1y$.

Multiplication and division

In Section 1 you saw how to simplify expressions by writing them without multiplication or division signs.

When you divide, you can simplify fractions by cancelling them down to lowest terms.

WORKED EXAMPLE 3

Simplify.

a $\;5 \times 4a$ b $\;2x \times 6y$ c $\;2a^2 \times 7ab$ d $\;12a \div {}^-4$

e $\;\dfrac{6x^2}{2}$ f $\;\dfrac{{}^-8xy}{{}^-16}$ g $\;\dfrac{12ab^2}{36ab}$

a $\;5 \times 4a = 20a$

b $\;2x \times 6y = 12xy$ Multiply numbers by numbers and write letters in alphabetical order.

c $\;2a^2 \times 7ab = 14a^3b$ $a^2 = a \times a$, so $a^2 \times a = a \times a \times a = a^3$

d $\;12a \div {}^-4 = \dfrac{12a}{{}^-4} = {}^-3a$ Write the division as a fraction and reduce it to its lowest terms by cancelling.

e $\;\dfrac{6x^2}{2} = 3x^2$

f $\;\dfrac{{}^-8xy}{{}^-16} = \dfrac{xy}{2}$

g $\;\dfrac{12ab^2}{36ab} = \dfrac{b}{3}$ Write the numerator as b not $1b$ by convention.

Tip

Remember that $\dfrac{12a}{{}^-4} = \dfrac{12}{{}^-4} \times \dfrac{a}{1}$.

You will revise using the four operations on fractions in Chapter 10.

Find answers at: cambridge.org/ukschools/gcsemaths-studentbookanswers

EXERCISE 3C

1 Say whether each of these are like or unlike terms.
- **a** $4a$ and $3b$
- **b** $5b$ and ^-3b
- **c** $3b$ and $9b$
- **d** $4p$ and $6p$
- **e** $8p$ and ^-4q
- **f** $5a$ and $6b$
- **g** $7mn$ and $3mn$
- **h** $4ab$ and ^-2ab
- **i** ^-6xy and ^-7x
- **j** $9ab$ and $3a$
- **k** $9x^2$ and $6x^2$
- **l** $6a^2$ and $^-7a^2$

2 Simplify.
- **a** $9x + 4y - 4y - 3x + 5y$
- **b** $3c + 6d - 6c - 4d$
- **c** $2xy + 3y^2 - 5xy - 4y^2$
- **d** $2a^2 - ab^2 + 3ab^2 + 2ab$
- **e** $5f - 7g - 6f + 9g$
- **f** $7a^2b + 3a^2b - 4a^2b$
- **g** $6mn^3 - 2mn^3 + 8mn^3$
- **h** $3st^2 - 4s^2t + 5s^2t + 6st^2$

3 Copy and complete.
- **a** $2a + \square = 7a$
- **b** $5b - \square = 2b$
- **c** $8mn + \square = 12mn$
- **d** $11pq - \square = 6pq$
- **e** $4x^2 + \square = 7x^2$
- **f** $6m^2 - \square = m^2$
- **g** $8ab - \square = {^-2ab}$
- **h** $^-3st + \square = 5st$

4 Copy and complete.
- **a** $8a \times \square = 16a$
- **b** $9b \times \square = 18b$
- **c** $8a \times \square = 16ab$
- **d** $5m \times \square = 15mn$
- **e** $3a \times \square = 12a^2$
- **f** $6p \times \square = 30p^2$
- **g** $^-5b \times \square = 10b^2$
- **h** $4m \times \square = 12m^2n$

5 Rewrite each expression in the simplest possible form.
- **a** $7 \times 2x \times {^-2}$
- **b** $4x \times 2y \times 2z$
- **c** $2a \times 5 \times a$
- **d** $ab \times bc \times cd$
- **e** $^-4x \times 2x \times {^-3y}$
- **f** $\frac{1}{4x} \times 4y \times {^-y}$
- **g** $^-9x \div 3$
- **h** $^-24y \div 2x$
- **i** $18x^2 \div 6$

6 Simplify.
- **a** $\frac{4x}{6}$
- **b** $\frac{3a}{9}$
- **c** $\frac{^-12m}{18}$
- **d** $\frac{14p}{21}$
- **e** $\frac{22x^2}{33}$
- **f** $\frac{15xy}{20}$
- **g** $\frac{12ab}{a}$
- **h** $\frac{2xy}{6xy}$

> **Key vocabulary**
>
> **expanding**: multiplying out an expression to get rid of the brackets.

> **Tip**
>
> Remember that $2(a + b)$ means $2 \times (a + b)$. But in algebraic notation you don't write the multiplication sign.
> Pay careful attention to the rules for multiplying negative and positive numbers when you multiply out.

Section 3: Multiplying out brackets

Removing brackets is called **expanding** the expression.

To expand an expression such as $2(a + b)$ you multiply each term inside the bracket by the value outside the bracket.

$$2(a + b) = 2 \times a + 2 \times b$$
$$= 2a + 2b$$

$$^-2(a + b) = {^-2} \times a + ({^-2} \times b)$$
$$= {^-2a} - 2b$$

WORKED EXAMPLE 4

Expand.
a $3x(y + 2z)$ b $-2x(4 + y)$ c $-(3x - 2)$

a $3x(y + 2z) = 3x \times y + 3x \times 2z$
$= 3xy + 6xz$

b $-2x(4 + y) = -2x \times 4 + (-2x \times y)$
$= -8x - 2xy$

c $-(3x - 2) = -1 \times 3x + (-1 \times -2)$
$= -3x + 2$

Multiply each term inside the brackets by the term outside the brackets; write out each term and then simplify.

When there is just a negative sign outside the brackets like here, it is the same as multiplying by -1.

You are able to expand brackets this way because multiplication is distributive over addition and subtraction. The distributive law says that

$a(b + c) \equiv ab + ac$

Both sides of these expressions are identical so we can use the $\equiv$ symbol.

If two algebraic expressions are identical, the values calculated will be equal for any numbers that are substituted for the variables.

We call identical expressions identities.

You can prove this rule works by substituting in values.

WORKED EXAMPLE 5

Show that $3(2x - 4) \equiv 6x - 12$.

LHS $= 3(2x - 4)$ Begin with the left-hand side.

$= 3 \times 2x + 3 \times (-4)$ Expand the bracket (multiply each term inside the bracket by 3).

$= 6x - 12 =$ RHS Simplify. This is exactly the same expression as on the right-hand side!

WORKED EXAMPLE 6

Use substitution to determine whether $(a + b)^2 \equiv a^2 + b^2$.

Let $a = 1$ and $b = 2$ Choose small values to make your calculations as simple as possible.

$(a + b)^2 = (1 + 2)^2 = (3)^2 = 9$
$a^2 + b^2 = 1^2 + 2^2 = 1 + 4 = 5$
$9 \neq 5$ So the expressions are not identical.

Find answers at: cambridge.org/ukschools/gcsemaths-studentbookanswers

GCSE Mathematics for OCR (Foundation)

When you have expanded an expression it might contain like terms.
Add or subtract like terms to simplify the expression further.

> **WORKED EXAMPLE 7**
>
> Expand and simplify. **a** $6x - 3(2x + 1)$ **b** $2x(x + y) - x(3x - 4y)$
>
> **a** $6x - 3(2x + 1)$
> $= 6x - 6x - 3$
> $= -3$
>
> **b** $2x(x + y) - x(3x - 4y)$
> $= 2x^2 + 2xy - 3x^2 + 4xy$
> $= -x^2 + 6xy$

EXERCISE 3D

1 Some of these expansions are incorrect.

Check each one and correct those that are wrong.

a $4(a + b) = 4a + b$
b $5(a + 1) = 5a + 6$
c $8(p - 7) = 8p - 56$
d $-3(p - 5) = -3p - 15$
e $a(a + b) = 2a + ab$
f $2m(3m + 5) = 6m^2 + 10m$
g $-6(x - 5) = 6x + 30$
h $3a(4a - 7) = 12a^2 - 7$
i $4a(3a + 5) = 12a^2 + 20a$
j $3x(2x - 7y) = 6x^2 - 21y$

2 Expand and simplify.

a $2(c + 7) - 9$
b $(a + 2) + 7$
c $5(b + 3) + 10$
d $2(e - 5) + 15$
e $3(f - 4) - 6$
f $2a(4a + 3) + 7a$
g $5b(2b - 3) + 6b$
h $2a(4a + 3) + 7a^2$
i $3b(3b - 5) - 7b^2$

3 Expand and simplify.

a $2(y + 1) + 3(y + 4)$
b $2(3b - 2) + 5(2b - 1)$
c $3(a + 5) - 2(a + 7)$
d $5(b - 2) - 4(b + 3)$
e $x(x - 2) + 3(x - 2)$
f $2p(p + 1) - 5(p + 1)$
g $3z(z + 4) - z(3z + 2)$
h $3y(y - 4) + y(y - 4)$

4 The expression in each box is found by adding the expressions in the two boxes directly below it.

```
              | 9x + 14y |
         | 5x + 5y | 4x + 9y |
    | 2x + y | 3x + 4y | x + 5y |
```

Complete these two pyramids.

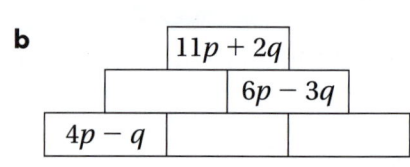

a
```
    |      |      |      |
    |      |      |      |
| 2x − 3y | 4x + y | 5x − 2y |
```

b
```
    |      |      | 11p + 2q |
    |      | 6p − 3q |
| 4p − q |      |      |
```

5 Use substitution to show that the following expressions are **not** identities.

a $a + a$ and a^2
b $3x + 4 - x + 2$ and $2x + 2$
c $(m + 2)^2$ and $m^2 + 4$
d $\dfrac{x + 3}{3}$ and $x + 1$

Section 4: Factorising expressions

Factorising is the opposite of expanding.

When you factorise an expression you use brackets to write it as a product of its factors.

If you expand $5(x + 7)$ you get $5x + 35$.

To factorise $5x + 35$ you find the highest common factor of the terms.

5 is the HCF of $5x$ and 35, so 5 is written outside the bracket and the remaining factors are written in brackets.

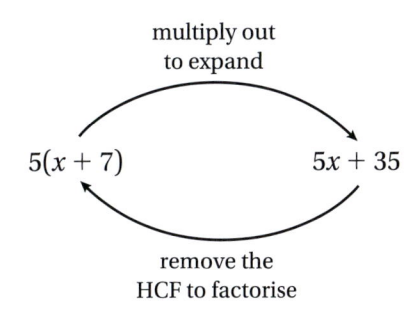

$5(x + 7)$ ⟷ $5x + 35$

multiply out to expand

remove the HCF to factorise

Key vocabulary

factorising: writing a number or expression as a product of its factors.

Tip

The highest common factor can be a number or a variable. It can also be a negative quantity.

WORKED EXAMPLE 8

Factorise each expression.   a $10a + 15b$ b $^-2x - 8$ c $3x^2 - 6xy$ d $3(m + 2) - n(m + 2)$

a $10a + 15b$
   $10a + 15b = 5(2a + 3b)$

HCF of 10 and 15 is 5. There are no common variables.

b $^-2x - 8$
   $^-2x - 8 = ^-2(x + 4)$

HCF of $^-2$ and $^-8$ is $^-2$.

c $3x^2 - 6xy$
   $3x^2 - 6xy = 3x(x - 2y)$

HCF is $3x$.

d $3(m + 2) - n(m + 2)$
   $3(m + 2) - n(m + 2) = (m + 2)(3 - n)$

This looks like an expansion, but you are asked to factorise! $(m + 2)$ is common to both terms, so it is the HCF.

EXERCISE 3E

1 Factorise each expression and write it as the product of its factors.

a $2x + 4$ b $12m - 18n$ c $3a - 3b - 6$ d $xy - xz$
e $5xy - 15xyz$ f $14ab - 21bc$ g $pq - pr$ h $x^2 - x$
i $18abc - 12ac$ j $2x^2 - 4xy$ k $2x^2y - 4xy^2$ l $^-6a - 12$
m $^-3a - 9$ n $^-xy - 5x$ o $^-x^2 + 6x$ p $4x^2 - 8xy + 16x^2y$

2 Factorise.

a $7x - xy + x^2$ b $2xy + 4xz + 10x$
c $10x - 5y + 15z$ d $x(x - 2) + 5(x - 2)$
e $a(a - 7) - (a - 7)$ f $(x - 3) - 3(x - 3)$

Tip

You will learn other methods of factorising expressions in Chapter 7.

Find answers at: cambridge.org/ukschools/gcsemaths-studentbookanswers

Section 5: Using algebra to solve problems

Algebra lets you describe and make sense of patterns.

This is very useful for solving problems, particularly if they involve unknown amounts. Working with expressions you can work out and prove rules.

WORKED EXAMPLE 9

Prove that $3n + 3 =$ the sum of three consecutive numbers.

n
$n + 1$
$n + 2$

Let the first number be n. If the numbers are consecutive, you know that each number is 1 more than the previous number.
The next number must be 1 more than n, so let it be $n + 1$.
The third number is 1 more than $n + 1$, so let it be $n + 1 + 1 = n + 2$.
The three consecutive numbers are n, $n + 1$ and $n + 2$

$n + n + 1 + n + 2 = 3n + 3$.

The sum of the three numbers when the first number, n, is known is $3n + 3$.

Sum the numbers to write a general rule.

$n = 205$
$3 \times 205 + 3 = 615 + 3 = 618$
Check: $205 + 206 + 207 = 618$

Test your rule using a set of consecutive numbers, for example 205, 206, 207.
Substitute 205 for n in $3n + 3$.

General expressions like that in Worked example 9 are very useful for programmed operations and repeated calculations involving different starting numbers.

EXERCISE 3F

1 Are the following statements true or false?

  a The expression $3z^2 + 5yx - z^2 - 6yx$ simplifies to $2z^2 - 11xy$.

  b If you expand the brackets $2p(3p + q)$ you get the expression $6p^2 + 2pq$.

  c This is a correct use of the identity symbol: $4(a + 1) \equiv 4a + 4$.

  d $\frac{4}{x}$ always has the same value as $\frac{x}{4}$.

  e x squared and added to 7 with the result divided by 3 is $\frac{x^2 + 7}{3}$.

2 In a magic square the sum of each row, column and diagonal is the same. Is the square on the left a magic square?

$m - p$	$m + p - q$	$m + q$
$m + p + q$	m	$m - p - q$
$m - q$	$m - p + q$	$m + p$

3 **a** Write an expression for each missing length in this rectangle.

  b Write an expression for P, the perimeter of the rectangle.

  c Given that $a = 2.1$ and $b = 4.5$, calculate the area of the rectangle.
(Area = length × width)

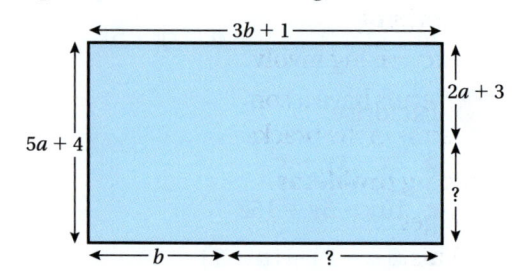

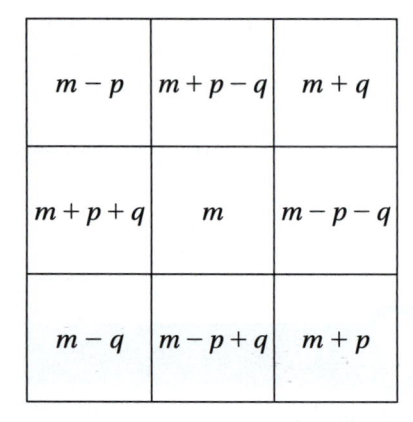

Rectangle with top side $3b + 1$, right side $2a + 3$, bottom left portion b, bottom right portion $?$, left side $5a + 4$, and right bottom $?$.

4 a The area of a rectangle is $2x^2 + 4x$. Suggest possible lengths for its sides.
 b If the perimeter of a rectangle is $2x^2 + 4$, what could the lengths of the sides be?

5 Draw two diagrams representing areas to prove that $(3x)^2$ and $3x^2$ are different.

6 The number in each cell is made by adding the numbers in the two cells beneath it.
Fill in the missing expressions for each cell. Write each expression as simply as possible.
(The first entry in diagram **a** has been completed in red.)

a

	$2a + 4b$	
$2a$	$4b$	$5a$

b

	$48a^2b$	
	$24a$	
		$2b$

c

	$96m^2n^2q$	
	$16mn^2$	
	$2m$	

7 a Paul plays a 'think of a number game' with his friends and predicts what their answer will be.

These are the steps he tells his friends to follow:
- Think of a number. Double it.
- Add 6. Halve it.
- Take away the number you first thought of.

Paul then guesses that the answer is 3.

Use algebra to show why Paul will guess correctly, no matter what number his friends choose as a starting number.

b Make up a 'think of a number' problem.
Use algebra to check it works and to see which number you end up with.
Try it on a classmate to check that it works.

Checklist of learning and understanding

Algebraic notation
- You can use letters (called variables) in place of unknown quantities.
- An expression is a collection of numbers, operation signs and at least one variable.
- Each part of an expression is called a term.
- To evaluate an expression you substitute numbers in place of the variables.

Simplifying expressions
- Like terms have exactly the same variables.
- Expressions can be simplified by adding or subtracting like terms.

Multiplying out brackets
- You can multiply and divide unlike terms.
- If an expression contains brackets you multiply them out and then add or subtract like terms to simplify it further.

Factorising
- Factorising involves putting brackets back into an expression.
- If terms have a common factor, write it in front of the bracket and write the remaining terms in the bracket as a factor. (You can check by multiplying out.)

Solving problems
- Algebra allows you to make general rules that apply to any number.
This is useful in problem solving.

Find answers at: cambridge.org/ukschools/gcsemaths-studentbookanswers

Chapter review

1 Simplify if possible.

  a $12x - 7x$ **b** $4a - 12b - 3a + 4b$ **c** $5xy \times z \times 2 + 8xyz$

2 $7(x + 4) - 3(x - 2)$ simplifies to $a(2x + b)$. Calculate a and b.

3 Check whether each expression has been fully simplified. If not, simplify it further.

a	$5(g + 2) + 8g$	$5g + 10 + 8g$
b	$4z(4z - 2) - z(z + 2)$	$15z^2 - 10z$
c	$^-5ab \times (^-3bc)$	$15ab^2c$
d	$\dfrac{18x^3}{3x}$	$\dfrac{6x^3}{x}$

4 a Work out the value of $x^2 - 3x$ when

  i $x = 5$ *(1 mark)*

  ii $x = ^-4$ *(2 marks)*

  b Multiply out.

  $y(y + 5)$ *(1 mark)*

  c Factorise fully.

  $4p^2 - 8p$ *(2 marks)*

  © OCR 2013

5 The nth even number is $2n$. The next even number after $2n$ is $2n + 2$.

  a Explain why.

  b Write an expression, in terms of n, for the next even number after $2n + 2$.

  c Show algebraically that the sum of any three consecutive even numbers is always a multiple of 6.

6 Determine by substitution whether the following pairs of expressions are identities or not. For those that you think are identities, show that the left hand side is identical to the right hand side.

  a $5(x + 3)$ and $5x + 3$

  b $^-3(m - 2)$ and $^-3m - 6$

  c $4(y - 3) + 2(y + 4)$ and $6y - 4$

4 Functions and sequences

In this chapter you will learn how to ...
- generate sequences and find unknown terms in a sequence.
- interpret expressions as functions with inputs and outputs.
- write rules or functions to find any term in a sequence.
- recognise and use a variety of special sequences.

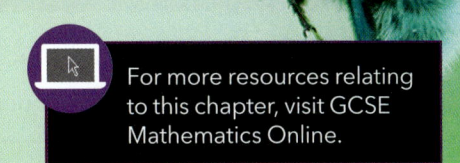

For more resources relating to this chapter, visit GCSE Mathematics Online.

Using mathematics: real-life applications

Finding a pattern and working out how the parts of the pattern fit together is important in scientific discovery. Scientists use sequences to model and solve real-life problems, such as estimating how quickly diseases spread.

Tip

When you work with sequences you can draw diagrams, flow charts or tables to organise the patterns and make sense of them.

"When a new outbreak of a disease occurs I need to work out how quickly it is spreading. To do this I look at the sequence in which the numbers of victims are increasing. I use the sequence to predict how many people will become infected in a certain length of time." *(Medical researcher)*

Before you start ...

KS3 Ch 2	You need to know your multiplication tables and recognise multiples of numbers.	**1** a What are the first five multiples of 7? b Which of these are multiples of 6? 56, 66, 86, 18, 54, 36
KS3 Ch 2	You need to be able to recognise square numbers and cube numbers.	**2** a Which of these are square numbers? 1, 16, 66, 50, 25, 4, 6, 9, 49 b Which of these are **not** cube numbers? 9, 15, 27, 64, 1, 8, 125
KS3	You need to be able to spot and describe patterns.	**3** a Describe this pattern in words. Shape 1 Shape 2 Shape 3 b How many matchsticks would you need to build the sixth shape in the pattern?

Find answers at: cambridge.org/ukschools/gcsemaths-studentbookanswers

GCSE Mathematics for OCR (Foundation)

Assess your starting point using the Launchpad

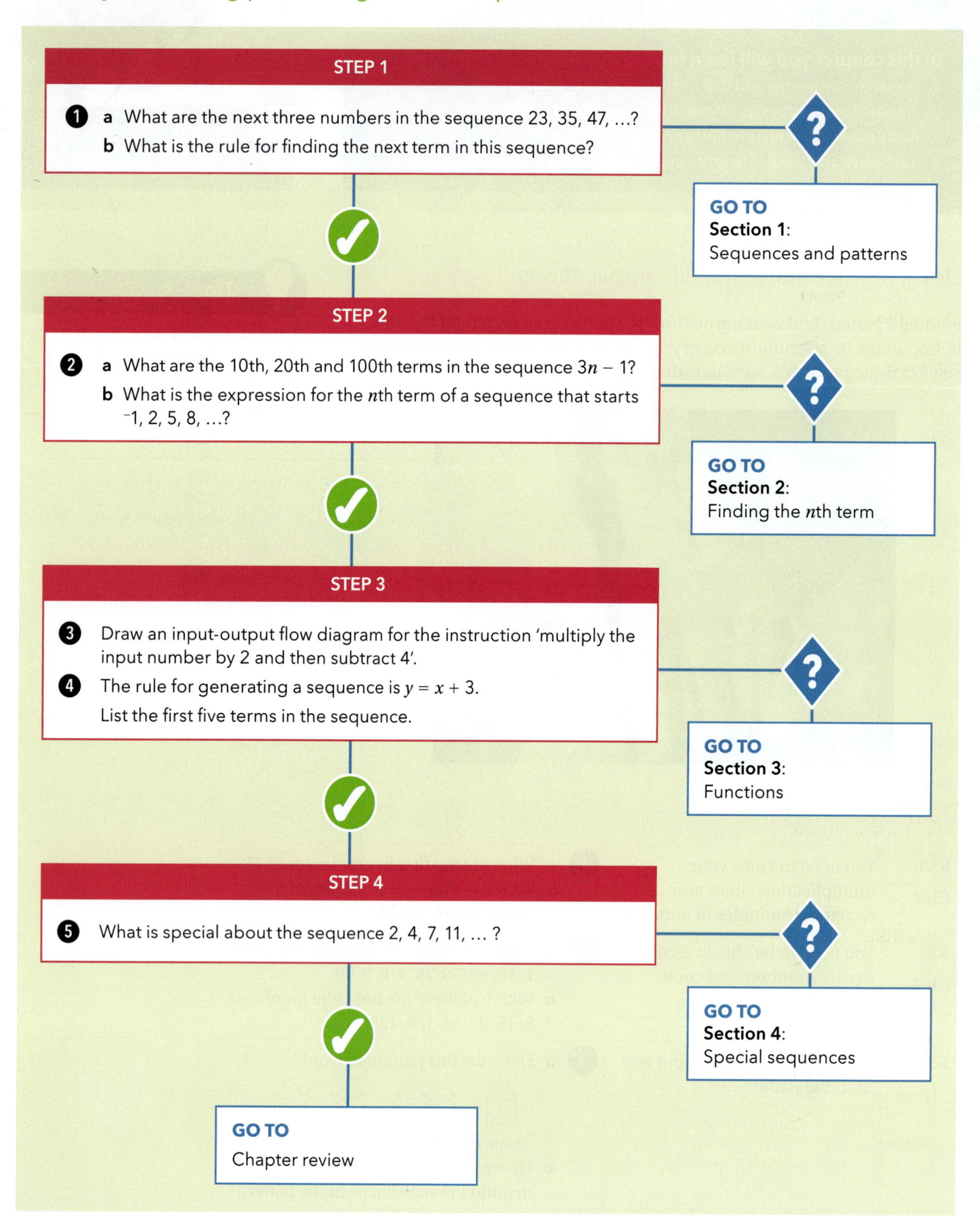

STEP 1

1 a What are the next three numbers in the sequence 23, 35, 47, …?
    b What is the rule for finding the next term in this sequence?

GO TO
Section 1: Sequences and patterns

STEP 2

2 a What are the 10th, 20th and 100th terms in the sequence $3n - 1$?
    b What is the expression for the nth term of a sequence that starts −1, 2, 5, 8, …?

GO TO
Section 2: Finding the nth term

STEP 3

3 Draw an input-output flow diagram for the instruction 'multiply the input number by 2 and then subtract 4'.

4 The rule for generating a sequence is $y = x + 3$.
    List the first five terms in the sequence.

GO TO
Section 3: Functions

STEP 4

5 What is special about the sequence 2, 4, 7, 11, … ?

GO TO
Section 4: Special sequences

GO TO
Chapter review

Section 1: Sequences and patterns

The term-to-term rule

A **sequence** is an ordered list or pattern.

Terms that follow each other in a sequence are called **consecutive terms**.

The first term in a sequence is called T(1), the second T(2) and so on.

You can find the next term in the sequence by working out what the difference is between each term. This is called the **first difference**.

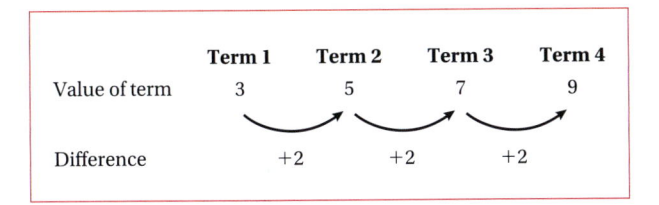

	Term 1	Term 2	Term 3	Term 4
Value of term	3	5	7	9
Difference	+2	+2	+2	

The **term-to-term rule** for this sequence is 'add two'.
9 + 2 = 11 so the next term in the sequence is 11.

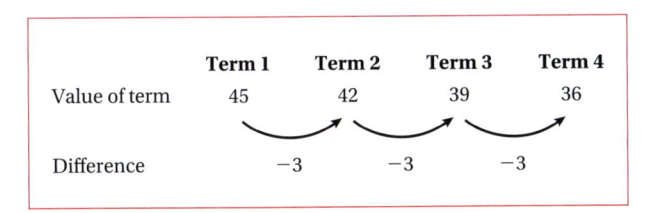

	Term 1	Term 2	Term 3	Term 4
Value of term	45	42	39	36
Difference	−3	−3	−3	

The term-to-term rule for this sequence is 'subtract three'.

3, 5, 7, 9, ... and 45, 42, 39, 36, ... are both **arithmetic sequences**.
In an arithmetic sequence the terms are generated by adding or subtracting a constant difference.

In a **geometric sequence**, the terms are generated by multiplying or dividing by a constant factor.
3, 6, 12, 24, ... and 1000, 500, 250, 125, ... (below) are both geometric sequences.

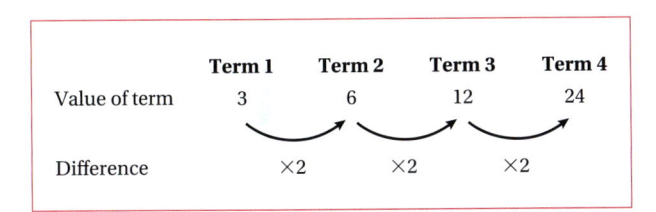

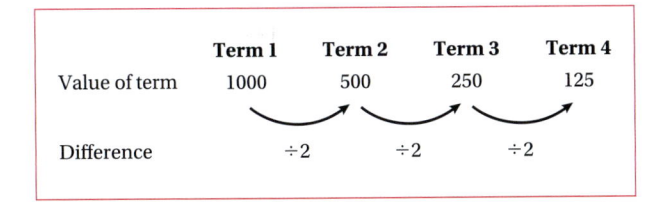

	Term 1	Term 2	Term 3	Term 4
Value of term	3	6	12	24
Difference	×2	×2	×2	

	Term 1	Term 2	Term 3	Term 4
Value of term	1000	500	250	125
Difference	÷2	÷2	÷2	

Key vocabulary

sequence: a number pattern or list of numbers following a particular order.

consecutive terms: terms that follow each other in a sequence.

first difference: the difference between one term and the next.

term-to-term rule: operations applied to any number in a sequence to generate the next number in the sequence.

Tip

Each number in a sequence is called a term.

Key vocabulary

arithmetic sequence: a sequence where the difference between each term is constant.

geometric sequence: a sequence where each term is found by multiplying the previous term by a constant factor.

Find answers at: cambridge.org/ukschools/gcsemaths-studentbookanswers

GCSE Mathematics for OCR (Foundation)

WORKED EXAMPLE 1

"I use term-to-term rules in my job. I know that each row of bricks will have three fewer bricks than the row below it, so I can work out how many bricks I need in each row."

(Bricklayer)

The first row of the wall has 57 bricks.

Use a term-to-term rule to find the number of bricks in the next three rows.

The term-to-term rule is 'subtract three'.

> The number of bricks decreases by 3 for each new row.

57 in the first row

57 − 3 = 54 in the second row

> Subtract 3 from 57 to get the next term.

54 − 3 = 51 in the third row
51 − 3 = 48 in the fourth row

> Continue to do this for the next two terms.

EXERCISE 4A

1 Find the next three terms in each of these sequences. Explain how you found them.

- **a** 4, 7, 10, 13, …
- **b** 38, 43, 48, 53, …
- **c** 27, 23, 19, …
- **d** 63, 57, 51, …
- **e** 1, 2, 4, 8, …
- **f** 64, 32, 16, …
- **g** 4, 12, 36, …
- **h** 729, 243, 81, …

2 Give the term-to-term rule for each of these sequences.

- **a** 7, 14, 21, 28, …
- **b** 19, 15, 11, 7, …
- **c** 2, 8, 32, 128, …
- **d** 84, 42, 21, …

Tip

It can help to write out the sequence and label the difference between each term.

3 Find the term-to-term rule for each of these sequences. Use it to generate the next three terms in each sequence.

- **a** 3.5, 5.5, 7.5, …
- **b** 1.2, 2.4, 4.8, …
- **c** $1\frac{1}{2}$, 3, $4\frac{1}{2}$, …
- **d** 8, 5, 2, …
- **e** 72, 36, 18, …
- **f** −10, −7, −4, …

4 When a ball is dropped it bounces back to half its original height.

With each new bounce it bounces back to half the height of the previous bounce.

   a If a ball is dropped from 96 cm, how high will it bounce on its 4th bounce?

   b How many times will it bounce before it bounces to below 1 cm?

> **Tip**
> Look for the term-to-term rule to answer this question.

5 T(1) of a sequence is 4 and the term-to-term rule for the sequence is 'add x'.

Find a value for x so that:

   a every second term is an integer.

   b every third term is a multiple of 4.

   c T(2) is smaller than T(1).

Section 2: Finding the nth term

The position-to-term rule

Term-to-term rules are useful for generating the first few terms of a sequence and for finding the next term in a given sequence. They are less useful when you want to find the 50th or 100th term.

A **position-to-term** rule allows you to work out the value of any term in a sequence if you know its position in the sequence.

The sequence 1, 3, 5, 7… can be generated using the position-to-term rule 'position number ×2, subtract 1' by substituting the position number into the rule.

> **Key vocabulary**
> **position-to-term rule**: operations applied to the position number of a term in a sequence in order to generate that term.

Position in sequence	Position-to-term rule 'position ×2, −1'	Term
1	(1 × 2) − 1	1
2	(2 × 2) − 1	3
3	(3 × 2) − 1	5
4	(4 × 2) − 1	7
5	(5 × 2) − 1	9
6	(6 × 2) − 1	11
7	(7 × 2) − 1	13
8	(8 × 2) − 1	15
9	(9 × 2) − 1	17
10	(10 × 2) − 1	19

The nth term

The notation T(n) refers to 'any term' in the sequence, where n is the position of the term. T(n) is known as the 'nth term'.

Sometimes you will be given a sequence and you will need to find a rule to find any term, T(n), in that sequence. You can usually find a rule for a sequence by looking at the difference between consecutive terms.

Find answers at: cambridge.org/ukschools/gcsemaths-studentbookanswers

Remember that this is called the **first difference**.

Once you have found the first difference you can compare it with number patterns you already know to find the rule for the sequence.

Problem-solving framework

Find an expression for the nth term of the sequence: 5, 8, 11, 14, 17 …

Steps for approaching a problem-solving question	What you would do for this example
Step 1: Identify what you have to do.	You are trying to find an expression to work out the value of any term in the sequence.
Step 2: If it is useful to have a table draw one.	Draw a table showing the position and the term: | n | 1 | 2 | 3 | 4 | 5 | |---|---|---|---|---|---| | $T(n)$ | 5 | 8 | 11 | 14 | 17 |
Step 3: Start working on the problem using what you know.	Label the table with the difference between each term: | n | 1 | 2 | 3 | 4 | 5 | |---|---|---|---|---|---| | $T(n)$ | 5 | 8 | 11 | 14 | 17 | +3 +3 +3 +3 The difference in this sequence is '+ 3'.
Step 4: Connect to other sequences and compare.	Another sequence that has the same term-to-term rule of 'add 3' is the multiples of 3. (If the difference was '+2' you would compare to $2n$; if it was '−4' you would compare it to $-4n$.) Add this sequence to your table: | n | 1 | 2 | 3 | 4 | 5 | |---|---|---|---|---|---| | $T(n)$ | 5 | 8 | 11 | 14 | 17 | | **Multiples of $3n$** | 3 | 6 | 9 | 12 | 15 | +2 Compare the multiples of 3 to the terms of the original sequence. Each term is the corresponding multiple of 3 with 2 added. So the expression for the nth term of this sequence could be $3n + 2$.
Step 5: Check your working and that your answer is reasonable.	Test for $n = 5$: $(3 \times 5) + 2 = 15 + 2$ $15 + 2 = 17$ The fifth term is 17 so the expression is correct.
Step 6: Have you answered the question?	Yes. The expression for the nth term is $3n + 2$.

> 💡 **Tip**
>
> The rule for an arithmetic sequence can also be calculated using the following formula: $(a + d(n - 1))$ where a = first term, and d = common difference. The **common difference** is the constant difference between terms. Try this for the example above.

WORK IT OUT 4.1

A sequence is defined by the rule T(n) = $3n - 2$.

What are the first 5 terms of the sequence?

Only one answer below is correct. Explain why the other two are wrong.

Option A	Option B	Option C
−2, 1, 4, 7, 10	1, 4, 7, 10, 13	−1, 1, 3, 5, 7

EXERCISE 4B

1 A sequence is created using the position-to-term rule 'position ×3 subtract 1'.
   a What are the first 6 terms of the sequence?
   b What is the 20th term of the sequence?
   c Would the 40th term of the sequence be double the value of the 20th term? Explain your answer.

2 Find the value of the following terms for each position-to-term rule.

   i 1st term ii 2nd term iii 3rd term iv 4th term
   v 10th term vi 20th term vii 100th term

   a $4n + 1$ b $4n - 5$ c $8n + 2$
   d $5n - \dfrac{1}{2}$ e $\dfrac{n}{2} + 1$ f $-2n + 1$

3 Find the expression for the nth term in the sequence that begins 5, 9, 13, 17…

4 Find the expressions for the nth term of the following sequences.
   a 3, 5, 7, 9, …   b 3, 7, 11, 15, …   c −1, 4, 9, 14, …
   d 7, 12, 17, 22, …   e −3, 0, 3, 6, …   f −1, 6, 13, 20, …

5 Majid conducts an experiment in science and gets the following pattern of results:

   67, 73, 79, 85

   Write an expression for the nth term of Majid's results.

6 Sam has planted a sunflower and notices that it measures 4.5 cm at the end of the first week, 6.7 cm at the end of the second week and 8.9 cm at the end of the third week.
   a Find an expression for the nth term of this sequence, assuming the sunflower continues to grow at the same rate.
   b How big will the sunflower be at the end of the 100th week?
   c Explain why this is unlikely to be true.

7 Tammy has £100.
   She saves £4 per week. At the end of the first week she has £104.
   a If she continues to save at this rate, how much will she have after 52 weeks?
   b How long will it take her to save £400?

Find answers at: cambridge.org/ukschools/gcsemaths-studentbookanswers

GCSE Mathematics for OCR (Foundation)

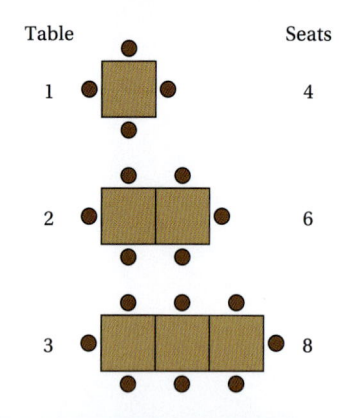

Table		Seats
1	▢	4
2	▢▢	6
3	▢▢▢	8

> 🔑 **Key vocabulary**
>
> **function**: an operation between values where each input value gives back only one output value. The square root of 4 can be $^+2$ or $^-2$ so it is not a function.

> 💡 **Tip**
>
> You can think of a function as 'the answer you will get' if you apply this rule to a number.

8 A restaurant uses square tables that can seat 4 people.

Tables can be pushed together to create different seating arrangements.

   a How many people can fit around 6 tables pushed together in this way?

   b How many people can fit around 10 tables pushed together this way?

   c Is it possible to seat 31 people around tables pushed together like this with no spaces?

Section 3: Functions

A **function** is a rule for changing one number into another.

'Multiply by two', 'add three' and 'divide by 2 and then add 1' are examples of functions.

You can use algebra to write functions, for example 'multiply by 2' can be written as the expression '$2n$'.

Functions can be expressed in different ways:

$y = x + 3$ $x \rightarrow x + 3$

These both mean the same thing: take any value of x and add 3 to it to get a result.

The steps you take to work out the value of a function can be shown as a simple flow diagram or function machine.

A function machine shows the input, operation and output for a given rule.

Input ⟶ | rule ⟩ ⟶ Output

In a function there is only **one** possible output for each input.

Generating a sequence using a function

You can generate a sequence using a function.

The table shows the outputs when you input the values 1 to 10 into the function $y = 2n + 4$

$n \rightarrow$ | ×2 ⟩ $\rightarrow$ | +4 ⟩ $\rightarrow 2n + 4$

Input	Function	Output
1	× 2 + 4	6
2	× 2 + 4	8
3	× 2 + 4	10
4	× 2 + 4	12
5	× 2 + 4	14
6	× 2 + 4	16
7	× 2 + 4	18
8	× 2 + 4	20
9	× 2 + 4	22
10	× 2 + 4	24

If you know the values of a sequence, you can find the function that generates the sequence by working out the position-to-term rule.

WORKED EXAMPLE 2

A sequence has the following terms: 3, 8, 13, 18, 23 ...
Write down the function machine that generates this sequence.

n	1	2	3	4	5
Tn	3	8	13	18	23

+5 +5 +5 +5

Draw a table showing the position and term.
Work out the difference between consecutive terms.
The terms increase by 5.

n	1	2	3	4	5
Tn	3	8	13	18	23
$5n$	5	10	15	20	25

Compare the sequence with the sequence for $5x$.
Each term in the sequence is 2 less than the term in the sequence $5x$.

$x \to \boxed{\times 5} \to \boxed{-2} \to 5x - 2$

The function could be 'multiply by 5, subtract 2'; test it using a term from the sequence.

$4 \to \times 5 \to 20 \to -2 \to 18$ ✓

EXERCISE 4C

1 The numbers 1 to 10 are the input for the function $x \to x + 3$.
What sequence does this create?

2 Input the numbers 1 to 10 into each function to generate a sequence.
  a $x \to x - 5$ **b** $x \to 3x$ **c** $n \to n + 7$ **d** $n \to \dfrac{n}{2}$

3 Input the numbers 21 to 30 into each function to generate a sequence.
  a $y = 2x$ **b** $y = x - 8$ **c** $y = \dfrac{x}{3}$ **d** $y = x + \dfrac{1}{2}$

4 Look at this pattern.

  a Write the number of coins used to build each shape as a sequence.

  b How many coins would you need to build the next shape in the pattern?

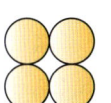

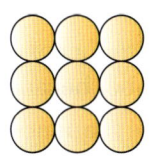

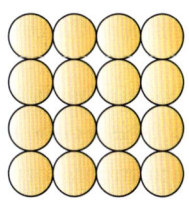

  c Complete this function machine for calculating the number of coins used to make any shape in the pattern:

  input $(n) \to \boxed{} \to$ output

  d Use your function to work out the number of coins you would need to build the 6th and 10th shapes in the pattern.

Find answers at: cambridge.org/ukschools/gcsemaths-studentbookanswers

5 Jess earns £6.25 per hour at her part-time job.
Write a function for calculating how much she will earn if she works n hours.

6 Zena is a salesperson.
She earns a basic salary of £500 plus £3 for every item she sells.

   a Write a function for calculating her salary if she sells p items.

   b Apply your function to work out her earnings if she sells 10, 20, 30 or 40 items.

Section 4: Special sequences

Some patterns and sequences of numbers are well known.
You need to be able to recognise and use the following patterns.

Special sequence	Description
Simple arithmetic progression (or linear sequences)	The **difference** between each term is constant, for example, 3, 5, 7, ... or 14, 11, 8, ...
Geometric sequences	The **ratio** between each term is constant, for example, 3, 6, 12, 24, ...
Triangular numbers	These are made by arranging dots to form equilateral triangles. 1 dots 3 dots 6 dots 10 dots 15 dots The sequence is 1, 3, 6, 10, 15 ...
Square numbers	A square number is the product of multiplying a whole number by itself. For example, $3^2 = 3 \times 3 = 9$ Square numbers form the sequence: 1, 4, 9, 16, 25, 36, ...
Quadratic sequences	These sequences are linked to square numbers. A quadratic sequence has a position-to-term rule that involves squaring one of the variables. For example, the sequence formed by the rule $n^2 + 3$ is: 4, 7, 12, 19, 28, ... The terms in a quadratic sequence do **not** increase or decrease by a constant amount. The first difference is **not** constant but the **second difference** is constant. The second difference is the difference between each term in the first difference.
Cube numbers	A cube number is the product of multiplying a whole number by itself and then by itself again. 64 is a cube number because $4^3 = (4 \times 4 \times 4) = 64$. Cube numbers form the sequence: 1, 8, 27, 64, 125, ...
Fibonacci sequences	Leonardo Fibonacci was an Italian mathematician who developed the number pattern 1, 1, 2, 3, 5, 8, 13, 21, ... while he was trying to work out how many offspring a pair of rabbits would produce over different generations. These numbers are now called Fibonacci numbers. If you start the sequence with the number 1, the term-to-term rule is 'add the previous two terms together'.

4 Functions and sequences

Did you know?

The Fibonacci pattern is found in many natural situations.

In the Fibonacci series, the sequence of numbers is created by adding the 1st and 2nd term together to make the 3rd term; adding the 2nd and 3rd terms together to make the 4th term and so on.

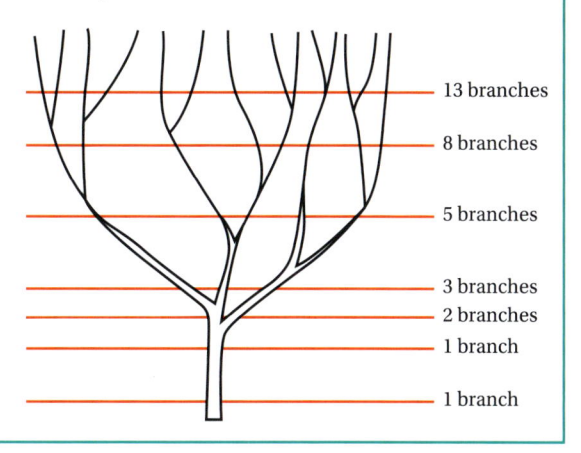

13 branches
8 branches
5 branches
3 branches
2 branches
1 branch
1 branch

EXERCISE 4D

1 a Write down the sequence of the first 10 square numbers.

   b How could you use this sequence to find the next 2 square numbers?

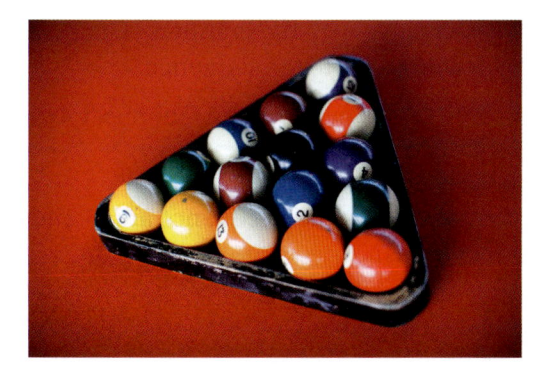

2 a What type of number is shown here? Explain how you know this.

   b The picture represents the fifth term in the sequence.
   Write down the first 10 numbers in the same sequence.

   c Find the first and second differences between the terms of the sequence.

   d What type of sequence is this?

3 Honeybees live in colonies known as hives.

   There is one queen bee, a female, who is the only one able to lay eggs.

   All other female bees are called workers, they are made when a male fertilises the queen's eggs. This means that worker bees have a mother and a father.

   The males are called drones, and are made when the queen's eggs hatch without being fertilised by a male. This means that a drone has a mother but not a father.

Find answers at: cambridge.org/ukschools/gcsemaths-studentbookanswers

This is a family tree of a drone; a family tree shows each generation of bee in terms of their parents.

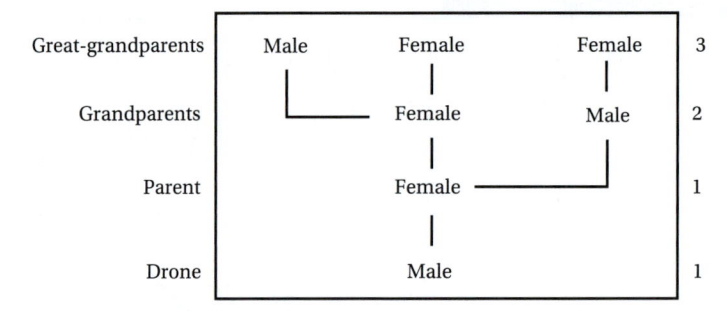

Generation		Count
Great-grandparents	Male — Female Female	3
Grandparents	Female Male	2
Parent	Female	1
Drone	Male	1

a How many great-great-grandparents does the male bee have?

b The family tree shows four generations of bee.

  i Copy and complete the tree so that it shows six generations.

  ii Use the family tree to write a sequence for the number of bees there are in each generation.

  iii Continue the sequence to find how many bees there are in the ninth generation.

  iv What is the relationship between the number of bees in each generation? Do you recognise the sequence?

4 a Find the first 10 terms of a Fibonacci sequence that starts with the numbers 3, 4, …

b Start a Fibonacci sequence with the numbers ⁻2 and 3. Write down the first 10 terms of the sequence.

c Compare your sequence in part **b** with a Fibonacci sequence starting with 2, ⁻3. What do you notice?

> **Tip**
> You know the term-to-term rule of the Fibonacci sequence. How can you use this to help you?

5 The 6th and 7th terms of a Fibonacci sequence are 31 and 50. What are the first two terms?

6 Copy and complete the table below.

Position-to-term rule	1st term	2nd term	3rd term	5th term	10th term	20th term	50th term
$n^2 + 5$							
$n^2 - 3$							
$2n^2 + 1$							
$2n^2 - 7$							

7 Write down the first six terms of the sequence formed by the rule $n^3 + 1$.

8 Write down the first 10 terms of the sequence formed by using the rule $n^2 + n$.

9 Compare your answer to Question **8** with your answer from Question **2**.

a What is the position-to-term rule for triangular numbers?

b Use your rule to find the 10th and 25th triangular numbers.

Checklist of learning and understanding

Sequences
- Sequences can be formed using a term-to-term rule. Each term is generated by applying the same rule to the previous term.
- The position-to-term rule is used to find the value of any term, known as the nth term in a sequence using its position in the sequence.

Functions
- A function is an expression or rule for changing one number (the input) into another number (the output).
- A sequence can be generated by inputting an ordered set of numbers into a function.

Special sequences
- It is important to be able to recognise familiar sequences such as square numbers, cube numbers, triangular numbers and Fibonacci numbers.
- In a quadratic sequence the first difference between the terms is not constant but the second difference is, and the pattern is linked to square numbers.

Chapter review

For additional questions on the topics in this chapter, visit GCSE Mathematics Online.

1 For each sequence:
   a find the missing terms.
   b write an expression in terms of n to find any term in the sequence.
   c use your expression to find the 25th term in each sequence.

   i 1.5, 2, ☐, 3, 3.5, ☐, ...
   ii ☐, -8, -4, ☐, 4, 8, ☐, ...
   iii $\frac{1}{2}, \frac{1}{4},$ ☐, $\frac{1}{16}, \frac{1}{32},$ ☐, ...
   iv 5, ☐, 17, 23, 29, ☐, ...

Tip

Look at the sequence of numbers in the denominators. Do you recognise it?

2 a Here are the first four terms of a sequence.

   8   11   14   17

   Write an expression for the nth term of this sequence. *(2 marks)*

   b The nth term of another sequence is given by $12 - 5n$.
   Write down the first three terms of this sequence. *(2 marks)*

   © OCR 2012

3 This array of numbers is called Pascal's triangle.

Each number is the sum of the two numbers above it, except for the edges which are all 1.

There are many different number patterns in the triangle.

```
            1
          1   1
        1   2   1
      1   3   3   1
    1   4   6   4   1
  1   5  10  10   5   1
```

Find answers at: cambridge.org/ukschools/gcsemaths-studentbookanswers

The first row (containing the number 1) is the 0th row.

a Copy and complete Pascal's triangle to the 10th row.

b Find the total for each row.

Describe the sequence that is created by these totals.

c What sequence is represented by the diagonal series of numbers that begins in the second row 1, 3, 6, 10, ...?

4 A virus is infecting the population of a village.

The table shows how the number of infections increased over four days.

Day	1	2	3	4
Number of infections	8	13	18	23

a If the virus continues to infect people at the same rate, how many people will be infected on day 5?

b Assume the infection rate is constant.

Find an expression to calculate how many people will be affected on any day.

c There are 126 people in the village.

How long will it be before everyone is infected?

5 Look at this pattern.

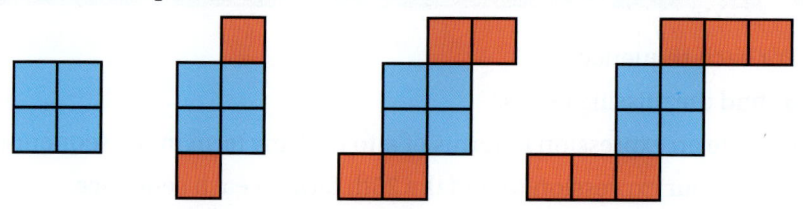

a Write the number of tiles used to build each shape as a sequence.

b How many tiles would you need to build the fifth shape in the pattern?

c Complete this function machine for calculating the number of tiles used to make any shape in the pattern:

input (n) → ☐ → ☐ → output

d Use your function to work out the number of tiles you would need to build the 20th, 25th and nth patterns.

6 Tamsyn is an ecologist.

She gets 28 days holiday every year plus $\frac{1}{2}$ a day holiday for each overnight bat survey she completes.

a Write a function for calculating how much holiday she will get if she does b bat surveys in a year.

b Tamsyn expects to do 16 bat surveys this year.
How much holiday will she get?

5 Properties of shapes and solids

In this chapter you will learn how to ...
- use the correct geometrical terms to talk about lines, angles and shapes.
- recognise and name common 2D shapes and 3D objects.
- describe the symmetrical properties of various polygons.
- classify triangles and quadrilaterals and use their properties to identify them.

For more resources relating to this chapter, visit GCSE Mathematics Online.

Using mathematics: real-life applications

Many people use geometry in their jobs and daily lives. Artists, craftspeople, builders, designers, architects and engineers use shape and space in their jobs, but almost everyone uses lines, angles, patterns and shapes in different ways every day.

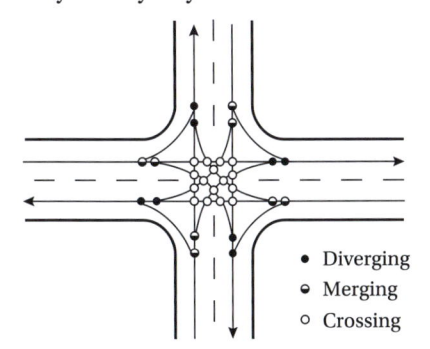

- Diverging
- Merging
- Crossing

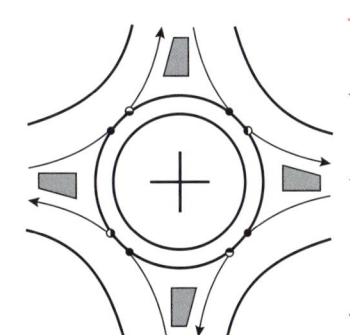

"I use a CAD package to plot lines and angles and show the direction of traffic flow when I design new road junctions."

(Civil engineer)

Before you start ...

KS3	You should be able to use geometrical terms correctly.	1	Choose the correct labels for each letter on the diagram.
			base vertex acute angle point
			edge right angle height face
KS3	You need to be able to recognise and name different types of shapes.	2	**a** Identify three different shapes in this diagram and use letters to name them correctly.
			b ABCE is one face of a solid with 6 faces. What type of solid could it be?

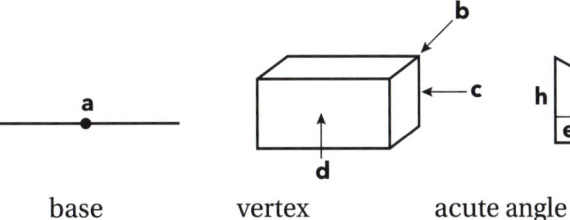

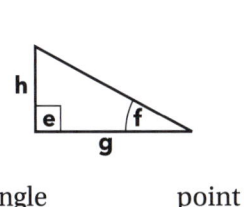

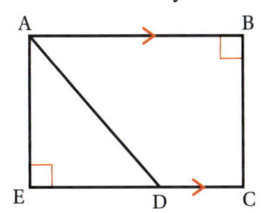

Find answers at: cambridge.org/ukschools/gcsemaths-studentbookanswers

GCSE Mathematics for OCR (Foundation)

Assess your starting point using the Launchpad

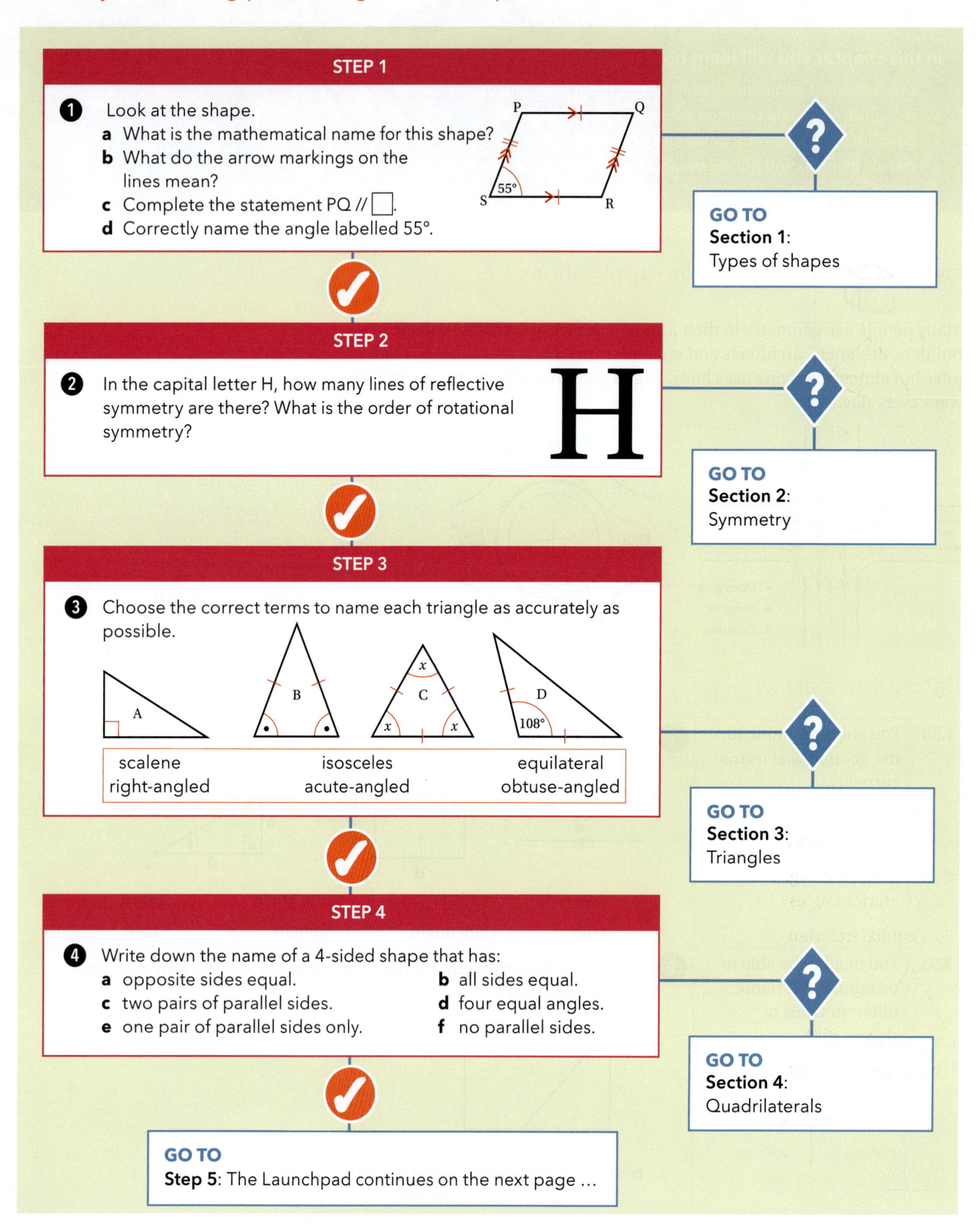

STEP 1

1 Look at the shape.
 a What is the mathematical name for this shape?
 b What do the arrow markings on the lines mean?
 c Complete the statement PQ // ☐.
 d Correctly name the angle labelled 55°.

GO TO Section 1: Types of shapes

STEP 2

2 In the capital letter H, how many lines of reflective symmetry are there? What is the order of rotational symmetry?

GO TO Section 2: Symmetry

STEP 3

3 Choose the correct terms to name each triangle as accurately as possible.

| scalene | isosceles | equilateral |
| right-angled | acute-angled | obtuse-angled |

GO TO Section 3: Triangles

STEP 4

4 Write down the name of a 4-sided shape that has:
 a opposite sides equal.
 b all sides equal.
 c two pairs of parallel sides.
 d four equal angles.
 e one pair of parallel sides only.
 f no parallel sides.

GO TO Section 4: Quadrilaterals

GO TO Step 5: The Launchpad continues on the next page …

5 Properties of shapes and solids

Launchpad continued ...

STEP 5

5 Copy and complete this table.

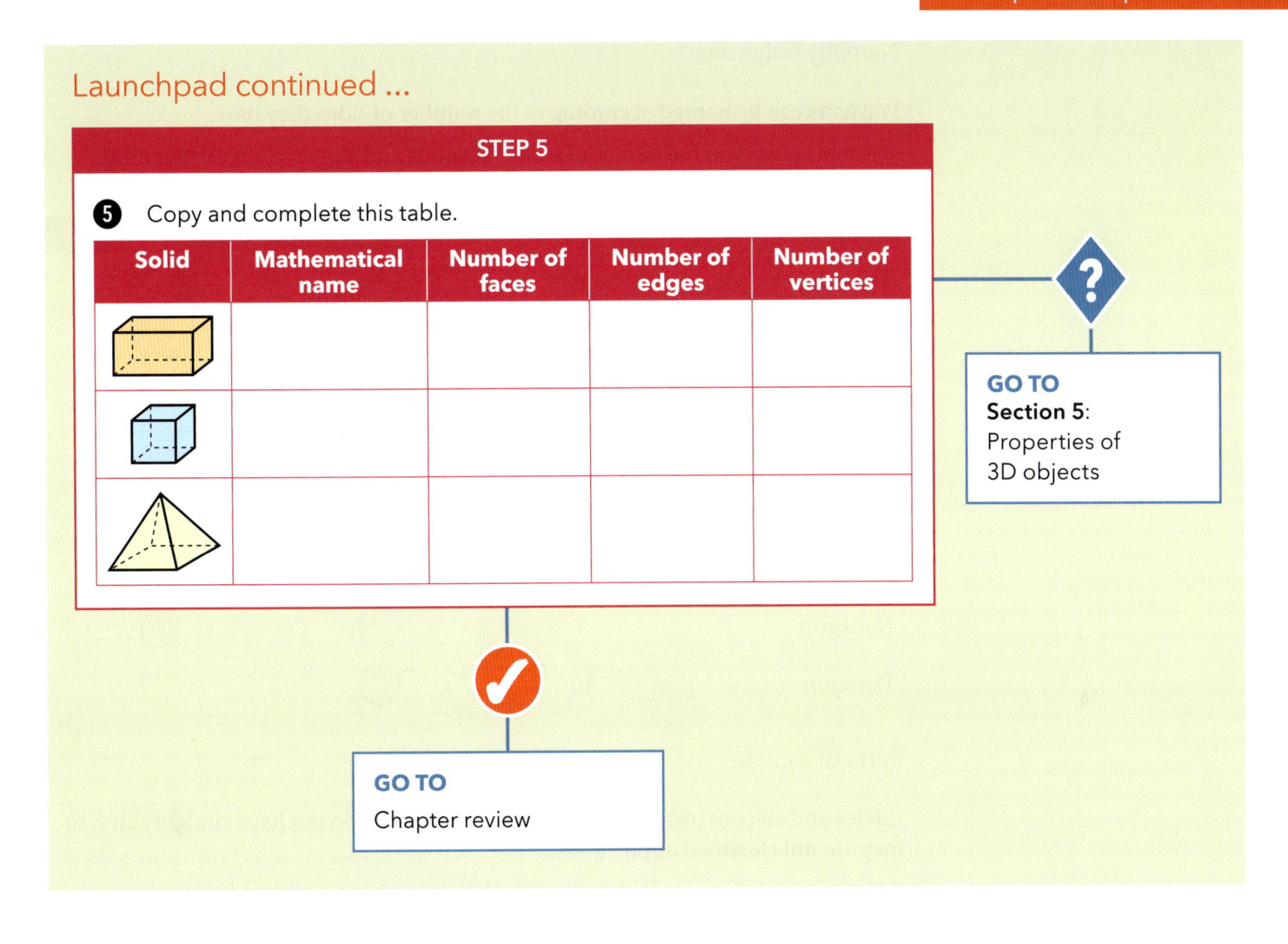

Solid	Mathematical name	Number of faces	Number of edges	Number of vertices

GO TO
Section 5: Properties of 3D objects

GO TO
Chapter review

Section 1: Types of shapes

Flat shapes are called **plane shapes** or two-dimensional (2D) shapes.

A **polygon** is a closed plane shape with three or more straight sides.

If the sides of a polygon are all the same length and the angles between the sides (interior angles) are equal, then the polygon is a **regular polygon**.

This equilateral triangle is a regular polygon.

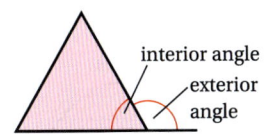

If a polygon is regular, the angles formed by extending the sides (exterior angles) are also equal.

If a polygon does not have equal sides and equal angles it is called an **irregular polygon**.

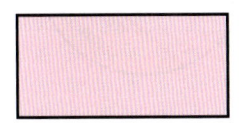

This rectangle is an irregular polygon because its sides are not all equal in length.

The fact that the angles are all equal to 90° does not make it a regular polygon.

Key vocabulary

plane shape: a flat, two-dimensional shape.

polygon: a closed plane shape with three or more straight sides.

regular polygon: a polygon with equal sides and equal angles.

irregular polygon: a polygon that does not have equal sides and equal angles.

Find answers at: cambridge.org/ukschools/gcsemaths-studentbookanswers

53

Naming polygons

Polygons can be named according to the number of sides they have.

The table gives you the names of some polygons and shows you a regular and irregular example of each one.

Name of polygon	Number of sides	Regular polygon	Irregular polygon
Triangle	3		
Quadrilateral	4		
Pentagon	5		
Hexagon	6		
Heptagon	7		
Octagon	8		
Nonagon	9		
Decagon	10		

Parts of a circle

Circles and ellipses (ovals) are plane shapes, but they do not have straight sides, so they are **not** classified as polygons.

A circle is a set of points that are an equal distance from a central point.

The main parts of a circle are shown below; make sure you are familiar with them.

Key vocabulary

circumference: the distance round the outside of a circle.
diameter: a straight line from one point on the circumference to another, that passes through the centre of the circle; it is twice the length of the radius.
radius: the distance of any point on the circumference from the centre of the circle.
arc of a circle: a section of circumference between two points; a minor arc is the shorter distance between the two points, the major arc is the larger distance.
sector: part or slice of a circle that is enclosed by two radii and an arc; the minor sector is the smaller of the two sectors created, the major sector is the larger.
semicircle: exactly half of a circle; the diameter splits a circle into two semicircles.
chord: a straight line from one point on the circumference to another. The diameter is a chord that goes through the centre of the circle.
segment: a chord splits a circle into two segments; the smaller segment is known as the minor segment and the larger is the major segment.
tangent: a straight line that touches the circumference of a circle at only one point.

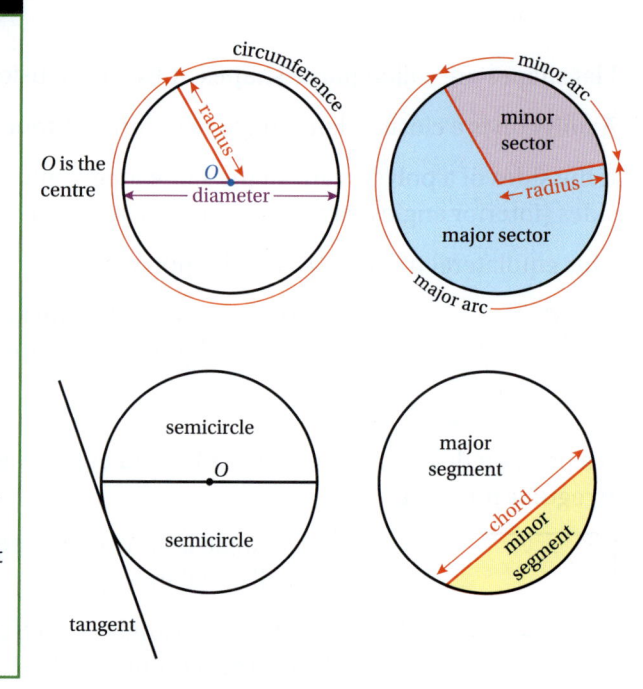

Solids

Solids are three-dimensional (3D) objects.

The parts of a solid are given specific names.

Flat surfaces of a solid are called faces. Two faces meet at the edge of a solid.

Three or more faces meet at a point called a vertex. (The plural of vertex is vertices.)

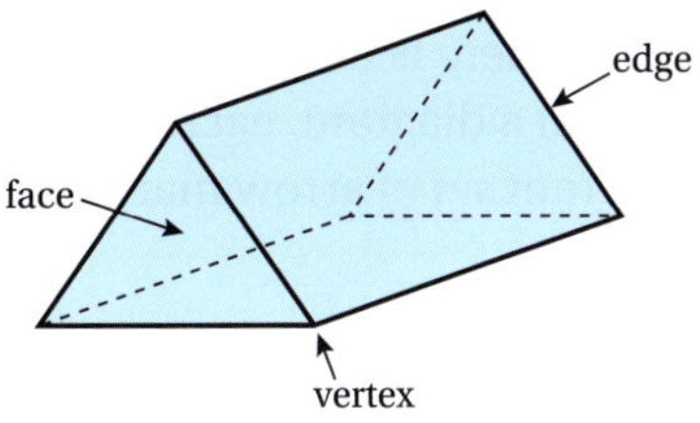

A solid with flat faces and straight edges and elevations is a **polyhedron**. (The plural of polyhedron is polyhedra.)

Polyhedra are solid objects with flat faces that are polygons.

Cylinders, spheres and cones are not polyhedra. They are solids with a curved surface.

> **Tip**
>
> 3D means an object has three dimensions or measurements: length, depth and height.

> **Key vocabulary**
>
> **polyhedron**: a solid object with flat faces that are polygons.

EXERCISE 5A

1 What is the correct mathematical name for each of the following shapes?

   a A plane shape with three equal sides.

   b A polygon with five equal sides.

   c A polygon with six vertices and six equal angles.

   d A plane shape with eight equal sides and eight equal internal angles.

2 Where might you find the following in real life?

   a A regular octagon.   **b** A cube.

   c A regular quadrilateral.   **d** An irregular pentagon.

Perpendicular and parallel lines

Perpendicular lines meet at right angles.

The symbol ⊥ means 'perpendicular to'.

In the diagram AB ⊥ CD.

The shortest distance from a point to a line is the perpendicular distance between them.

The sides of shapes are perpendicular if they form a 90° angle.

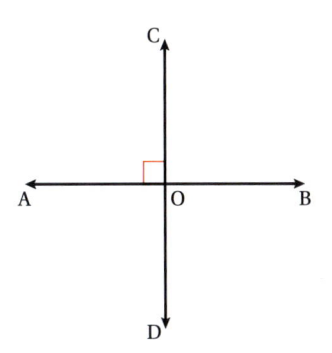

Lines are parallel if they are the same perpendicular distance apart at any point along their length.

We can say that parallel lines are **equidistant** along their length.

The symbol // means 'parallel to'. In the diagram AB // CD and MN // PQ.

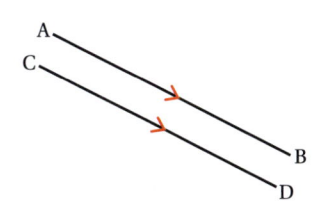

> **Key vocabulary**
>
> **equidistant**: means 'the same distance from'; if all points are equidistant they are the same distant apart.

Find answers at: cambridge.org/ukschools/gcsemaths-studentbookanswers

Small arrow symbols are drawn on lines to indicate that they are parallel to each other. When there is more than one pair of parallel lines in a diagram, each pair is usually given a different set of arrow markings.

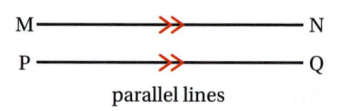

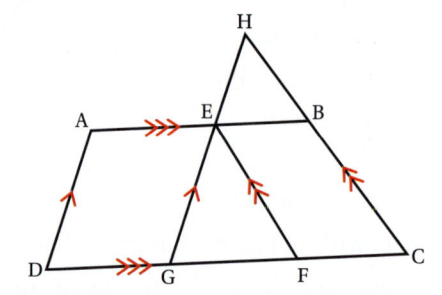

parallel lines

In this diagram AB // DC, AD // EG and EF // HC.

Drawing and labelling diagrams

Mathematical diagrams are drawn and labelled in particular ways so that their meaning is clear to anyone who uses them.

Shapes are labelled using capital letters on each vertex.

The letters are usually written in alphabetical order as you move round the shape.

This triangle has three vertices labelled A, B and C.

The shape would be called △ABC.

Each side of this triangle can be named using the capital letters on the vertices: AB, BC and CA.

The angles can be named in different ways. The angle at vertex A can be named A, BAC or CAB. Symbols can be used to label angles. For example ∠BAC or BÂC

Sometimes single letters are used to name the sides.

In this example, side BC can also be called side a because it is opposite angle A.

This convention is often used when you work with Pythagoras' theorem and in trigonometry.

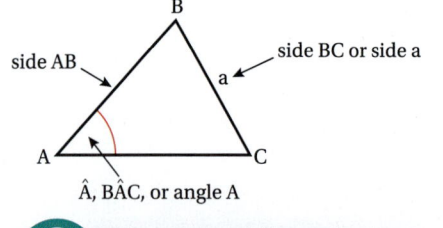

> **Tip**
>
> Greek letters are sometimes used to label angles. Don't be surprised to see α (alpha), β (beta), γ (gamma), δ (delta), and θ (theta) used to label angles, particularly in trigonometry.

Marking equal sides and angles

Small lines can be drawn on the sides of a shape to show whether the sides are equal or not. Sides that have the same markings are equal in length.

Curved lines and symbols such as dots or letters can be used to show whether angles are equal or not. Angles that are equal have the same marking, symbol or letter.

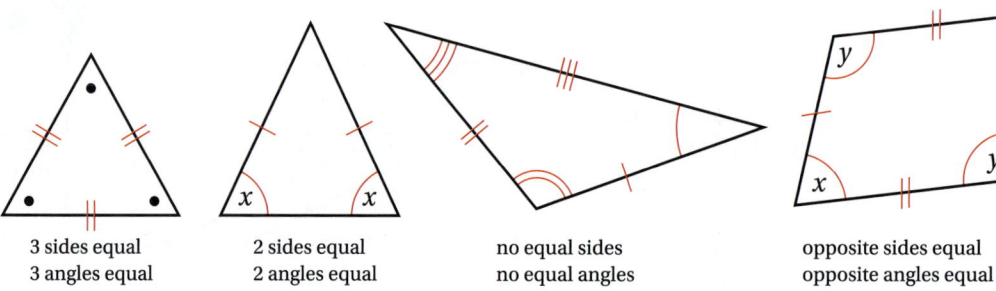

3 sides equal
3 angles equal

2 sides equal
2 angles equal

no equal sides
no equal angles

opposite sides equal
opposite angles equal

EXERCISE 5B

1 Match each description to its term.

a	A shape that has two fewer sides than an octagon.	i	Decagon
b	A shape that has two sides more than a triangle.	ii	Hexagon
c	A shape with four sides.	iii	Equilateral triangle
d	A stop sign is an example of this shape.	iv	Two-dimensional
e	A figure that has length and height.	v	Pentagon
f	A closed plane shape with all sides x cm long and all angles the same size.	vi	Quadrilateral
g	A ten-sided figure	vii	Square
h	Another name for a regular 4-sided polygon.	viii	Regular polygon
i	The more common name for a regular 3-sided polygon.	ix	Octagon

2 Look at the diagram.

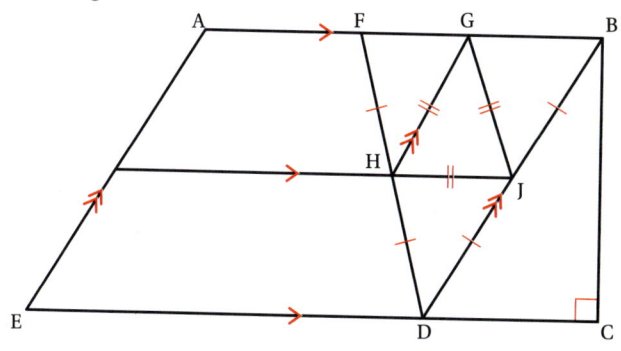

Say whether the following statements are true or false.

a AF // EC.
b △BFD is isosceles.
c CE ⊥ BC.
d AE // BD.
e ABCE is a regular polygon.
f GB // BC.
g In △DHJ, angle H = angle J = angle D.
h △GHJ is a regular polygon.

3 Draw and correctly label a sketch of each of the following shapes.

a A triangle, ABC with angle B = angle C and side AB ⊥ AC.
b A regular four-sided polygon DEFG.
c Quadrilateral PQRS such that PQ // SR but PQ ≠ SR and ∠PSR = ∠QRS

Section 2: Symmetry

Symmetry is an important property of shapes. You can use it to identify shapes, find missing lengths and angles, and solve problems.

You need to recognise two types of symmetry in plane shapes: line symmetry and rotational symmetry.

Find answers at: cambridge.org/ukschools/gcsemaths-studentbookanswers

Line symmetry

> **Key vocabulary**
>
> **reflection**: an exact image of a shape about a line of symmetry.
>
> **line (axis) of symmetry**: a line that divides a plane shape into two identical halves, each the reflection of the other.

If you can fold a shape in half to create a mirror image (**reflection**) on either side of the fold the shape has line symmetry.

The fold is known as the **line of symmetry**.

Each half of the shape is a reflection of the other half so this type of symmetry is also called reflection symmetry.

Triangle A has line symmetry. The dotted line is the line of symmetry.

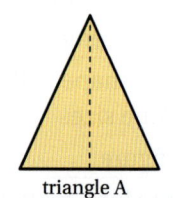

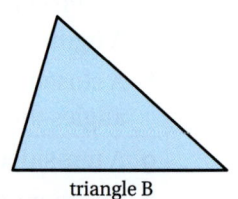

triangle A   triangle B

If you fold the shape along the line of symmetry the two parts will fit onto each other exactly.

Triangle B is not symmetrical. You cannot draw a line to divide it into two identical parts.

A shape can have more than one line of symmetry.

For example, a regular pentagon has five lines of symmetry.

Lines of symmetry can be horizontal, vertical or diagonal.

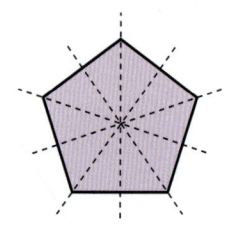

> **Tip**
>
> The line of symmetry is sometimes called the mirror line. If you place a small mirror on the line of symmetry you will see the whole shape reflected in the mirror.

Rotational symmetry

A rotation is a complete turn (a movement of 360°).

A shape has **rotational symmetry** if you rotate it around a fixed point and it looks identical in different positions.

To look identical, the shape has to fit onto itself.

The **order of rotational symmetry** tells you how many times the shape will look identical before it returns to the starting point.

If you have to rotate the shape a full 360° before it appears identical again then it does **not** have rotational symmetry.

The order of rotational symmetry of a regular polygon depends on the number of sides it has.

A square has an order of rotational symmetry of 4 around its centre.

You can see this in the diagram.

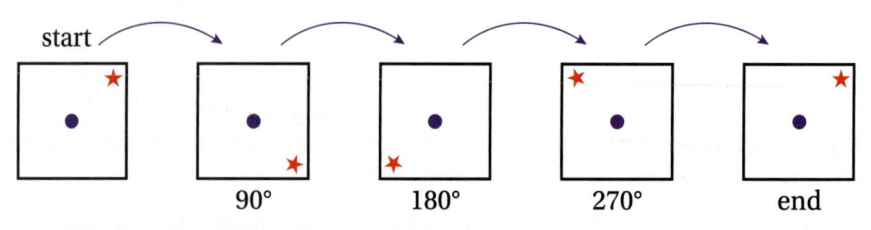

start   90°   180°   270°   end

The star shows the position of one vertex of the square as it rotates.

> **Key vocabulary**
>
> **rotational symmetry**: symmetry by turning a shape around a fixed point so that it looks the same from different positions.
>
> **order of rotational symmetry**: how many times a shape will fit exactly onto itself when you rotate it through 360°.

> **Tip**
>
> You will deal with reflections in mirror lines and rotations about a fixed point again in Chapter 28 when you deal with transformations.

This symbol is the national symbol for the Isle of Man.

It has an order of rotational symmetry of 3 about its centre.

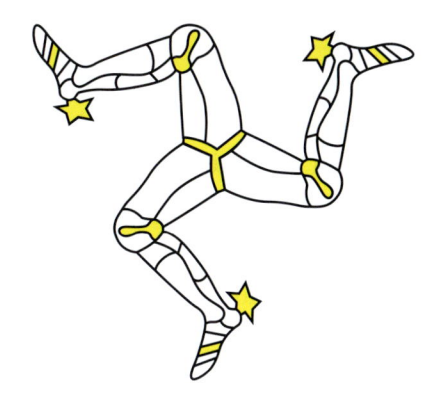

EXERCISE 5C

1 Which of the dotted lines in each figure are lines of symmetry?

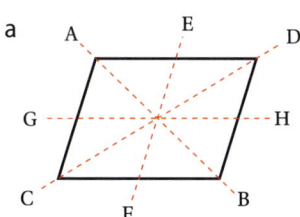

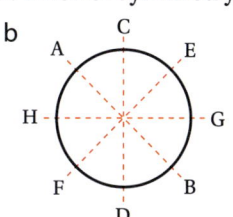

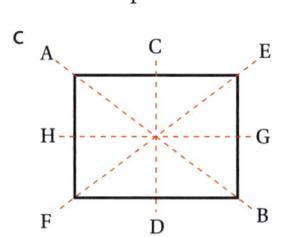

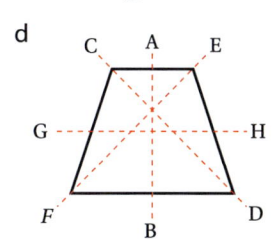

a (parallelogram with dotted lines A–B, C–D, E–F, G–H)

b (circle with dotted lines A–B, C–D, E–F, G–H)

c (rectangle with dotted lines A–B, C–D, E–F, G–H)

d (trapezium with dotted lines A–B, C–D, E–F, G–H)

2 By sketching, work out the number of lines of symmetry and the order of rotational symmetry of each shape.

Copy and complete the table to show your results.

Shape	Number of lines of symmetry	Order of rotational symmetry
Square		
Rectangle		
Isosceles triangle		
Equilateral triangle		
Parallelogram		
Regular hexagon		
Regular octagon		

3 Give an example of a shape which has rotational symmetry of order 3 but which is not a triangle?

4 Which of the following letters have rotational symmetry?

C H A R

Find answers at: cambridge.org/ukschools/gcsemaths-studentbookanswers

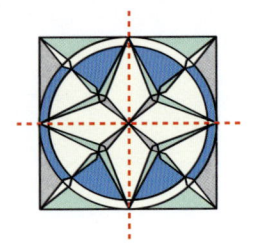

5 Look at the design on the left. Describe its symmetrical features in as much detail as possible.
Use sketches if you need to.

6 Metal alloy rims for tyres are very popular on modern cars.
Find and draw five alloy rim designs that you like.
For each one, state its order of rotational symmetry.

7 Sketch five different symmetrical designs or logos that you can find in your environment.
Label your sketches to indicate how the design is symmetrical.

Section 3: Triangles

Triangles are three-sided polygons that are given special names according to their properties.

Type of triangle	Properties
Scalene	• No equal sides. • No equal angles. • No line of symmetry. • No rotational symmetry.
Isosceles	• Two equal sides. • Angles at the base of the equal sides are equal. • One line of symmetry. • Line of symmetry is the perpendicular height. • No rotational symmetry.
Equilateral	• All sides equal. • Three equal angles, each is 60°. • Three lines of symmetry. • Rotational symmetry of order 3.
Acute-angled	• All angles are less than 90° (acute).
Right-angled	• One angle is a right angle (90°).
Obtuse-angled	• One angle is greater than 90° (obtuse).

Triangles can be a combination of types.

For example an isosceles triangle could be a right-angled isosceles triangle, an acute-angled isosceles triangle or an obtuse-angled isosceles triangle depending on the size of the angles.

Triangle MNO on the right is a right-angled isosceles triangle.

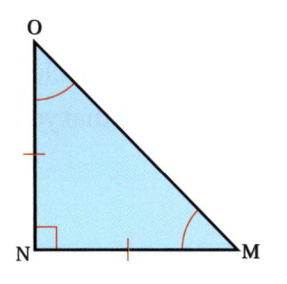

Angle properties of triangles

The angles inside a shape are called interior angles.

The three interior angles of any triangle always add up to 180°.

If you extend the length of one side of a triangle you form another angle outside the triangle. Angles formed outside the triangle in this way are called exterior angles.

If you tear off the angles of any triangle and place them against a straight edge (180°) you can see that the interior angles add up to 180°.

You can also see that the exterior angle is equal to the sum of the two interior angles that are opposite it.

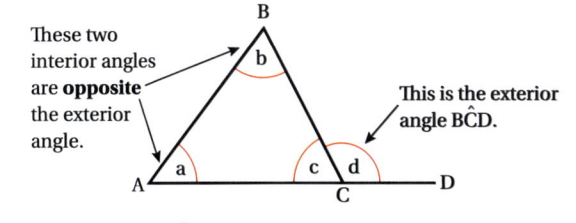

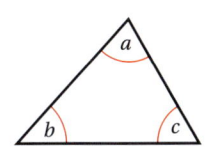

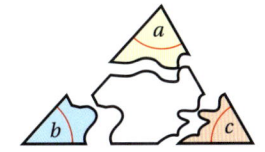

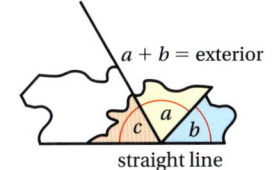

These two interior angles are **opposite** the exterior angle.

This is the exterior angle $B\hat{C}D$.

Tip

You will learn how to prove these properties using mathematical principles in Chapter 9.

Using the properties of triangles to solve problems

You can use the properties of triangles to solve problems involving unknown angles and lengths of sides.

Problem-solving framework

Triangle ABC is isosceles with perimeter 85 mm. AB = BC and AC = 25 mm. Angle ABC = 48°.

Calculate: **a** the length of each equal side. **b** the size of each equal angle.

Steps for approaching a problem-solving question	What you would do for this example
Step 1: Work out what you have to do. Start by reading the question carefully.	You need to use the properties of isosceles triangles and the given information to find the length of two sides and the size of two angles.
Step 2: What information do you need? Have you got it all?	Draw a labelled sketch to see whether you have the information you need. 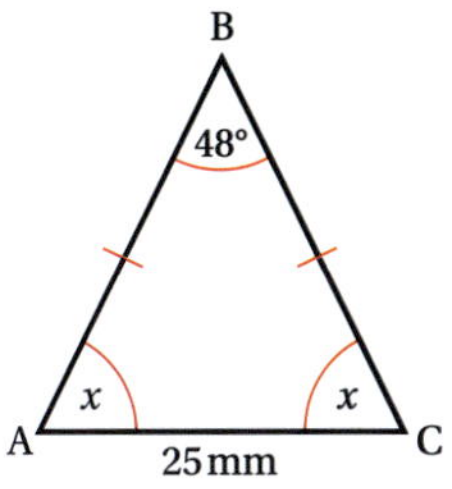
Step 3: Decide what maths you can do.	You can use the values you already have to make equations to find the missing values.

Continues on next page …

Find answers at: cambridge.org/ukschools/gcsemaths-studentbookanswers

61

Step 4: Set out your solution clearly. Check your working and that your answer is reasonable.	a Perimeter = AC + AB + BC = 85 mm So, 85 = 25 + AB + BC 85 − 25 = AB + BC 60 = AB + BC But AB = BC, so AB = BC = 30 mm Check: 30 + 30 + 25 = 85. b Let each equal angle be x. 48 + 2x = 180 (angle sum of triangle) 2x = 180 − 48 2x = 132 x = 66 Check: 66 + 66 + 48 = 180
Step 5: Check that you've answered the question.	Each equal side is 30 mm long. Each equal angle is 66°.

Tip

You will use properties of triangles often when you deal with trigonometry in Chapter 18.

In many problems you will have to find the size of unknown angles before you can move on and solve the problem.

EXERCISE 5D

1. What type of triangle is this? Explain how you decided without measuring.

2. What type of triangle is this? Choose the correct answer.
    A obtuse-angled scalene
    B right-angled isosceles
    C acute-angled isosceles
    D obtuse-angled isosceles

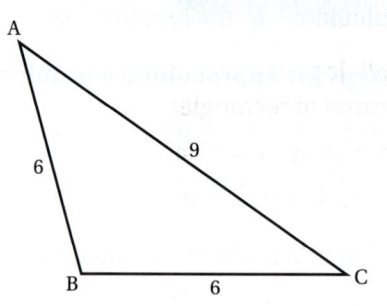

3. Which of the following triangles are not possible? Explain why.
    a An isosceles triangle with an obtuse angle.
    b A scalene triangle with two angles > 90°.
    c A scalene triangle with three angles 34°, 64° and 92°.
    d An obtuse-equilateral triangle.
    e An isosceles triangle with side lengths 6.5 cm, 7 cm and 7.5 cm.

4 Two angles in a triangle are 38° and 104°.

  a What is the size of the third angle?

  b What type of triangle is this?

5 Find the size of angles **a** to **e**.

Show your working and give mathematical reasons for any deductions you make.

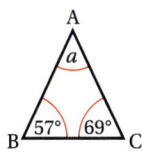

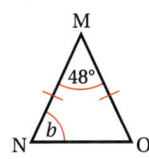

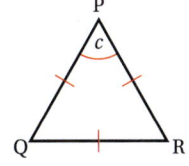

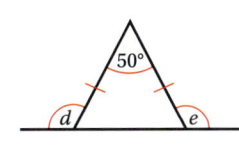

[Triangle ABC with angle a at A, 57° at B, 69° at C]
[Triangle MNO isosceles with 48° at M, angle b at N]
[Triangle PQR equilateral with angle c at P]
[Triangle isosceles with 50° at apex, angles d and e at base]

6 Isosceles triangle DEF with DE = EF has a perimeter of 50 mm. Find the length of EF if:

  a DF = 15 mm.

  b DF = $\sqrt{130}$.

Section 4: Quadrilaterals

A quadrilateral is a four-sided plane figure.

Quadrilaterals are probably the most common shape in your environment.

In the photographs here you can find rectangles, squares and trapezia.

Parallelograms and rhombuses are less common in everyday life, but the shadows of rectangles and squares often produce these shapes.

Quadrilaterals are classified and named according to their properties.

You can see from the definitions that some properties overlap.

For example, a rectangle is actually a special type of parallelogram.

The rectangle meets the definition of a parallelogram (in other words it has both pairs of opposite sides parallel), so all rectangles are parallelograms.

In this case the reverse of the statement (the converse) is not true. All parallelograms are not rectangles.

Did you know?

In mathematics we call a reverse statement the converse.

You need to know the names and basic properties of the quadrilaterals shown in the table.

Quadrilateral	Properties
Trapezium	• One pair of opposite sides are parallel.
Kite	• Two pairs of **adjacent** sides are equal. • Diagonals are perpendicular. • One diagonal **bisects** the other. • One diagonal bisects the angles.
Parallelogram	• Both pairs of opposite sides are parallel. • Both pairs of opposite sides are equal. • Both pairs of opposite angles are equal. • Diagonals bisect each other.
Rhombus	A rhombus is a parallelogram with all sides equal. It has the same properties listed for parallelograms, but has the following special features: • All sides are equal. • Diagonals bisect at right angles. • Diagonals bisect the angles.
Rectangle	A rectangle is a parallelogram with angles of 90°. It has the same properties as listed for parallelograms, but with the following special features: • All angles are 90°. • Diagonals are equal in length.
Square	A square is a rectangle with all sides equal. It has the same properties as a rectangle, but also has these special features: • All sides are equal. • Diagonals bisect at right angles. • Diagonals bisect the angles.

> **Key vocabulary**
>
> **adjacent**: next to each other; in shapes, sides that intersect each other.
>
> **bisect**: to divide exactly into two halves.

Using the properties of quadrilaterals to solve problems

You can use the properties of a quadrilateral to identify and name it.

You should always say what properties you are using to justify your answer.

WORKED EXAMPLE 1

A plane shape has two diagonals. The diagonals are perpendicular.

a What shape(s) could this be?   **b** The diagonals are not the same length. Which shape(s) could it **not** be?

a Two diagonals means that the shape is a quadrilateral.

Only the square, rhombus and kite have diagonals that intersect at 90°.

The shape could be a square, rhombus or kite.

> Remember to include your reasoning as part of your answer.

b Of the three shapes, only the square has diagonals that are equal in length.

Therefore, it could not be a square.

The angle sum of quadrilaterals

All quadrilaterals have two (and only two) diagonals. If you draw in one diagonal you divide the quadrilateral into two triangles.

You already know that the interior angles of a triangle add up to 180°.

Therefore, the interior angles of a quadrilateral are equal to 2 × 180° = 360°.

This is an important property of all quadrilaterals.

You can use it together with the other properties of quadrilaterals to find the size of unknown angles.

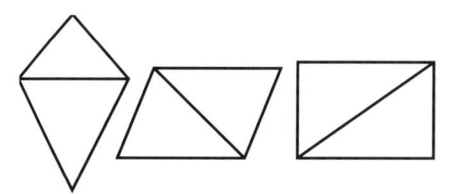

WORKED EXAMPLE 2

Find the size of the unknown angles.

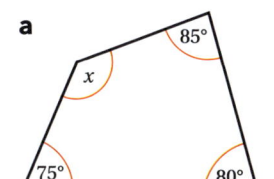

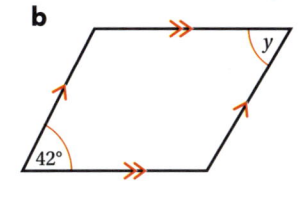

a $75° + 80° + 85° + x = 360°$

$240° + x = 360°$

$x = 360° - 240°$

$x = 120°$

> Shape is a quadrilateral, angles of a quadrilateral add up to 360°, so you can write an equation and solve for x.

b $y = 42°$

> Shape is a parallelogram, so the opposite angles are equal.

EXERCISE 5E

1 Identify the quadrilateral from the description.
There may be more than one correct answer.

    a All angles are equal.

    b Diagonals are equal in length.

    c Two pairs of sides are equal and parallel.

    d No sides are parallel.

    e The only regular quadrilateral.

    f Diagonals bisect each other.

Find answers at: cambridge.org/ukschools/gcsemaths-studentbookanswers

2. You can identify a quadrilateral by considering its diagonals. Copy and complete this table.

Shape	Diagonals are equal in length	Diagonals bisect each other	Diagonals are perpendicular
Rhombus			
Parallelogram			
Square			
Kite			
Rectangle			

3. What is the most obvious difference between a square and a rhombus?

4. Millie says that a quadrilateral has all four sides the same length.
Elizabeth says it must be a square.
Is Elizabeth correct? Give an explanation for your answer.

5. A kite has one angle of 47° and one of 133°.
What sizes are the other two angles?

6. State whether each statement is always true, sometimes true or never true. Give a reason for your answer.
   a A square is a rectangle.
   b A rectangle is a square.
   c A rectangle is a rhombus.
   d A rhombus is a parallelogram.
   e A parallelogram is a rhombus.

Tip

You need to know the properties of the basic polyhedra and other 3D solids.

You will use these properties to draw plans and elevations of solids in Chapter 20 and you will apply them when you solve problems relating to volume and surface area in Chapter 21.

Key vocabulary

congruent: identical in shape and size.

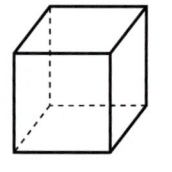

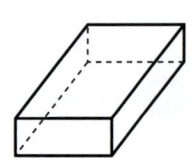

Section 5: Properties of 3D objects

In Section 1 you learned that solids are 3D objects that have length, depth and height, and that polyhedra are solids with polygon faces.

Cubes, cuboids, prisms and pyramids are all types of polyhedra.

Each type of polyhedron has some properties that are not shared by the others.

For example, a cuboid has six rectangular faces. A cube also has six faces, but to be classified as a cube, the faces must all be **congruent** squares.

Cubes and cuboids

Cubes and cuboids are box-shaped polyhedra.

They have six faces, twelve edges and eight vertices.

A cube has square faces.

A cuboid has rectangular faces.

All cubes are cuboids, but not all cuboids are cubes.

Prisms

A prism is a 3D object with two congruent, parallel faces.

If the prism is sliced parallel to one of these faces the cross-section will always be the same shape.

The diagram shows a prism with two triangular end faces.

You can see that slicing it anywhere along its length gives a triangular cross-section.

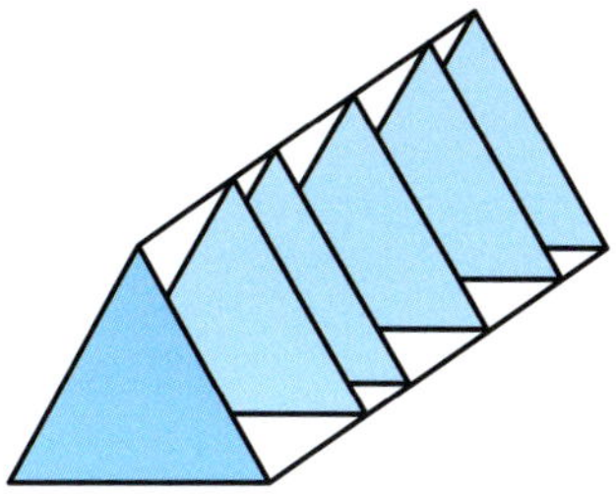

The parallel faces of a prism can be any shape.

If the prism is a polyhedron all of the other faces are rectangular.

Prisms are named according to the shape of their parallel faces.

pentagonal prism **hexagonal prism** **octagonal prism**

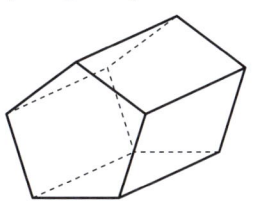

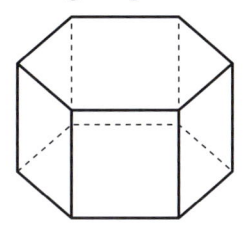

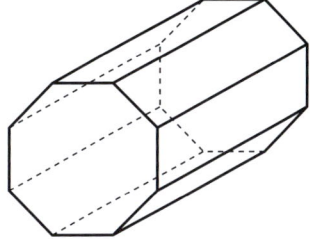

2 pentagonal faces   2 hexagonal faces   2 octagonal faces
5 rectangular faces   6 rectangular faces   8 rectangular faces

A cube is a square prism and a cuboid is a rectangular prism.

Pyramids

A pyramid is a polyhedron with a polygon base and triangular faces that meet at a vertex. (Sometimes called the apex of the pyramid.)

Pyramids are named according to the shape of their base.

triangular-based pyramid   **square-based pyramid** 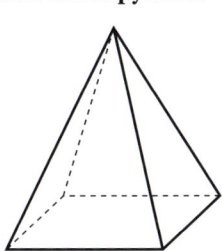   **pentagonal-based pyramid** 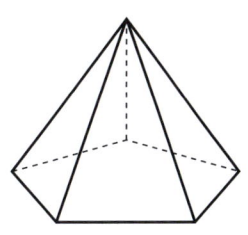   **hexagonal-based pyramid**

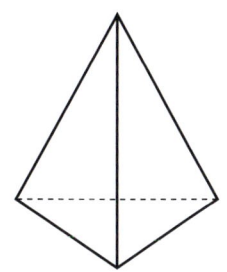

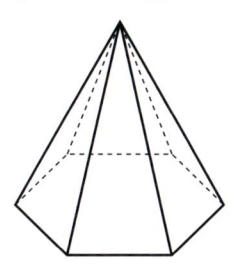

The number of sides of the base can be used to work out how many triangular faces the pyramid has.

A square has four sides, so a square-based pyramid has four triangular faces.

The Louvre Museum in Paris is famous for the massive glass square pyramid at its entrance.

There is another smaller, inverted square pyramid in the underground shopping mall behind the museum.

Find answers at: cambridge.org/ukschools/gcsemaths-studentbookanswers

A regular polyhedron is a solid whose faces are all congruent regular polygons.

There are only five regular polyhedra. These are shown in the table below.

Polyhedron	Vertices	Edges	Faces
Tetrahedron	4	6	4
Cube/hexahedron	8	12	6
Octahedron	6	12	8
Dodecahedron	20	30	12
Icosahedron	12	30	20

Other solids

Cylinders, cones and spheres are also 3D objects.

They do not have straight edges or flat faces that are polygons so they are not polyhedra.

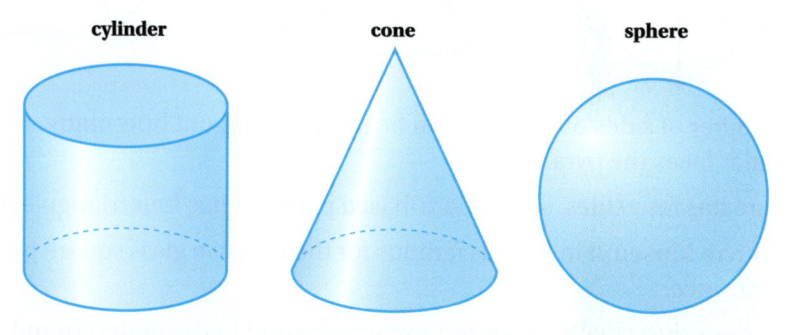

cylinder   cone   sphere

A cylinder has two circular end faces and a curved surface along its length.

A cone has a circular base and a curved surface that forms a point.

A sphere is shaped like a ball. It has only one continuous curved surface.

EXERCISE 5F

1 Sketch an example of each of the following solids.

   a A tall thin cylinder.

   b A cube.

   c A rectangular prism.

   d An octagonal pyramid.

   e A prism with a parallelogram-shaped cross-section.

2 What is the difference between a sphere and a circle?

3 Compare a cone and a cylinder. How are they similar? How are they different?

4 Name two solids that have six flat faces.

5 Copy and complete this table.

3D Shape	Faces	Vertices	Edges
Cube			
Cuboid			
Triangular pyramid			
Square pyramid			
Triangular prism			
Hexagonal prism			

6 In total how many faces, edges and vertices does the tower have?

Find answers at: cambridge.org/ukschools/gcsemaths-studentbookanswers

Checklist of learning and understanding

Types of shapes
- Polygons are closed plane shapes with straight sides.
- Triangles, quadrilaterals, pentagons and hexagons are all polygons.
- Circles and ovals are plane shapes, but they are not polygons.

Symmetry
- Shapes have line symmetry if they can be folded along a line of symmetry to produce two identical mirror images.
- Shapes have rotational symmetry if they fit onto themselves more than once during a 360° rotation.

Triangles
- Triangles are 3-sided polygons.
- Triangles can be classified and named using their side and angle properties.
- The sum of the interior angles of a triangle is 180°.

Quadrilaterals
- Quadrilaterals are 4-sided polygons.
- Quadrilaterals can be classified and named using their side, angle and diagonal properties.
- The sum of the interior angles of a quadrilateral is 360°.

Properties of 3D objects
- 3D objects are solids with length, depth and height.
- Polyhedra are solids with flat polygon faces and straight edges.
- Prisms and pyramids are polyhedra.
- Cylinders, cones and spheres are 3D objects but they are not polyhedra.

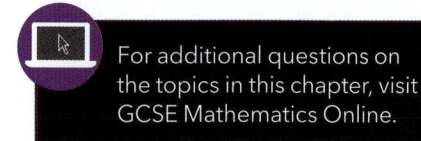

For additional questions on the topics in this chapter, visit GCSE Mathematics Online.

Chapter review

1 True or false?
  a A slice of pizza can be accurately described as a triangle.
  b A triangular pyramid has 4 vertices, 4 faces and 6 edges.
  c A pair of lines that are equidistant and never meet are described as being perpendicular.

2 Describe the symmetrical features of a regular hexagon as fully as possible.

3 Find the missing angles in this isosceles trapezium.

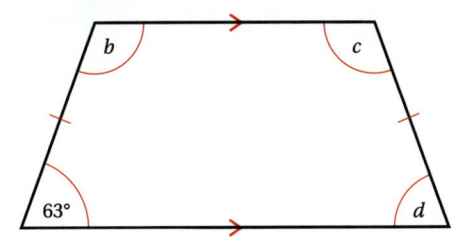

4 Is the missing angle a right angle? Explain.

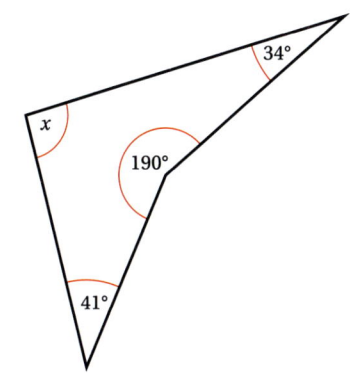

6 Construction and loci

In this chapter you will learn how to …
- use a ruler, protractor and pair of compasses effectively.
- use a ruler and a pair of compasses to bisect lines and angles and construct perpendiculars.
- use construction skills to construct geometrical figures.
- construct accurate diagrams to solve problems involving loci.

For more resources relating to this chapter, visit GCSE Mathematics Online.

Using mathematics: real-life applications

Draughtspeople and architects need to draw accurate scaled diagrams of the buildings and other structures they are working on. Although the drawings are complicated, they still use ordinary mathematical instruments like pencils, rulers and pairs of compasses to draw them.

"I prepare technical drawings and plans that are given to me by an architect. I use a CAD program, but I always start with a drawing board and plans that I draw using my ruler, set squares and pair of compasses." *(Draughtsperson)*

Before you start …

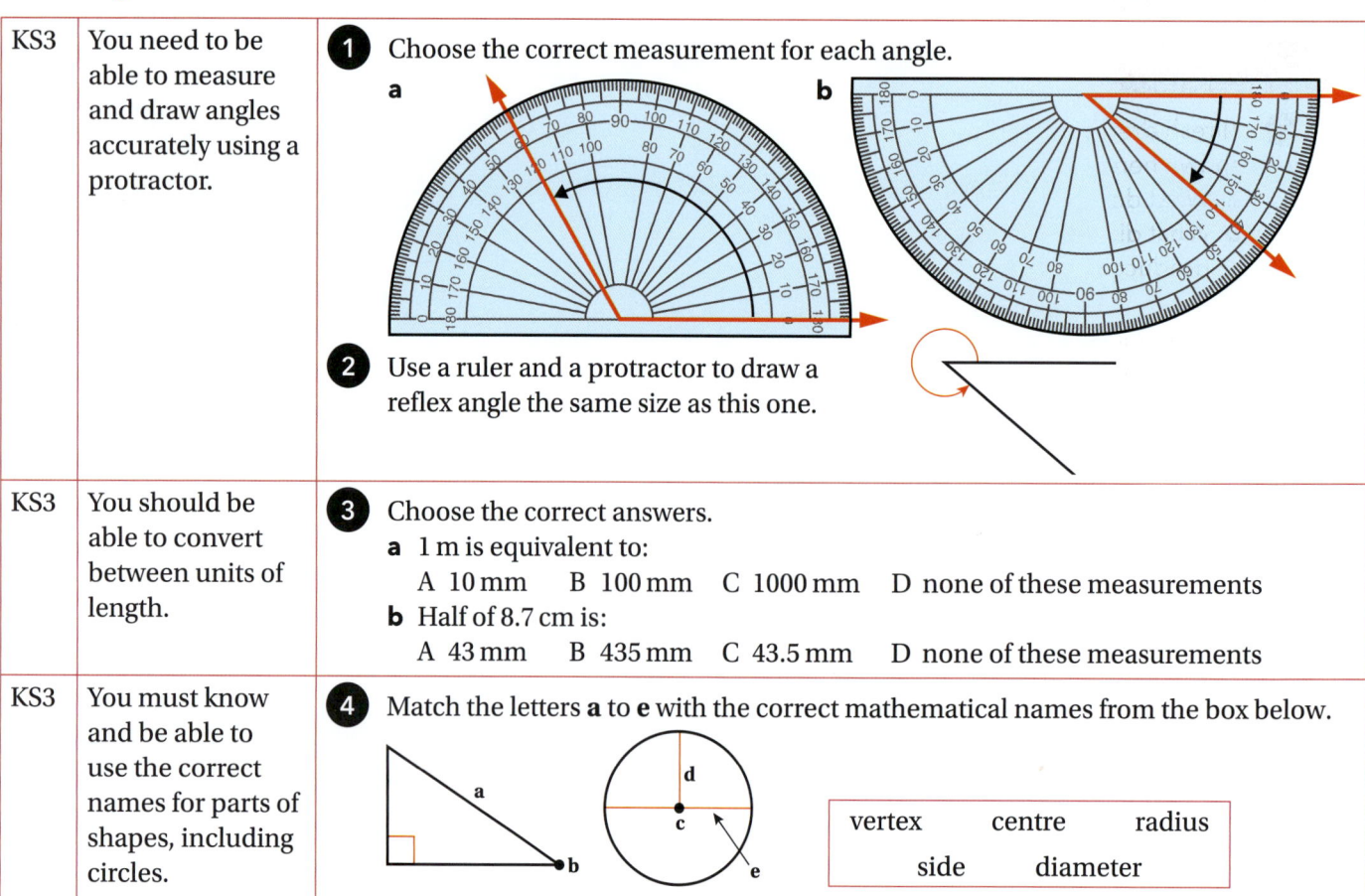

KS3	You need to be able to measure and draw angles accurately using a protractor.	**1** Choose the correct measurement for each angle. **a** **b**
		2 Use a ruler and a protractor to draw a reflex angle the same size as this one.
KS3	You should be able to convert between units of length.	**3** Choose the correct answers. **a** 1 m is equivalent to: A 10 mm B 100 mm C 1000 mm D none of these measurements **b** Half of 8.7 cm is: A 43 mm B 435 mm C 43.5 mm D none of these measurements
KS3	You must know and be able to use the correct names for parts of shapes, including circles.	**4** Match the letters **a** to **e** with the correct mathematical names from the box below. vertex centre radius side diameter

6 Construction and loci

Assess your starting point using the Launchpad

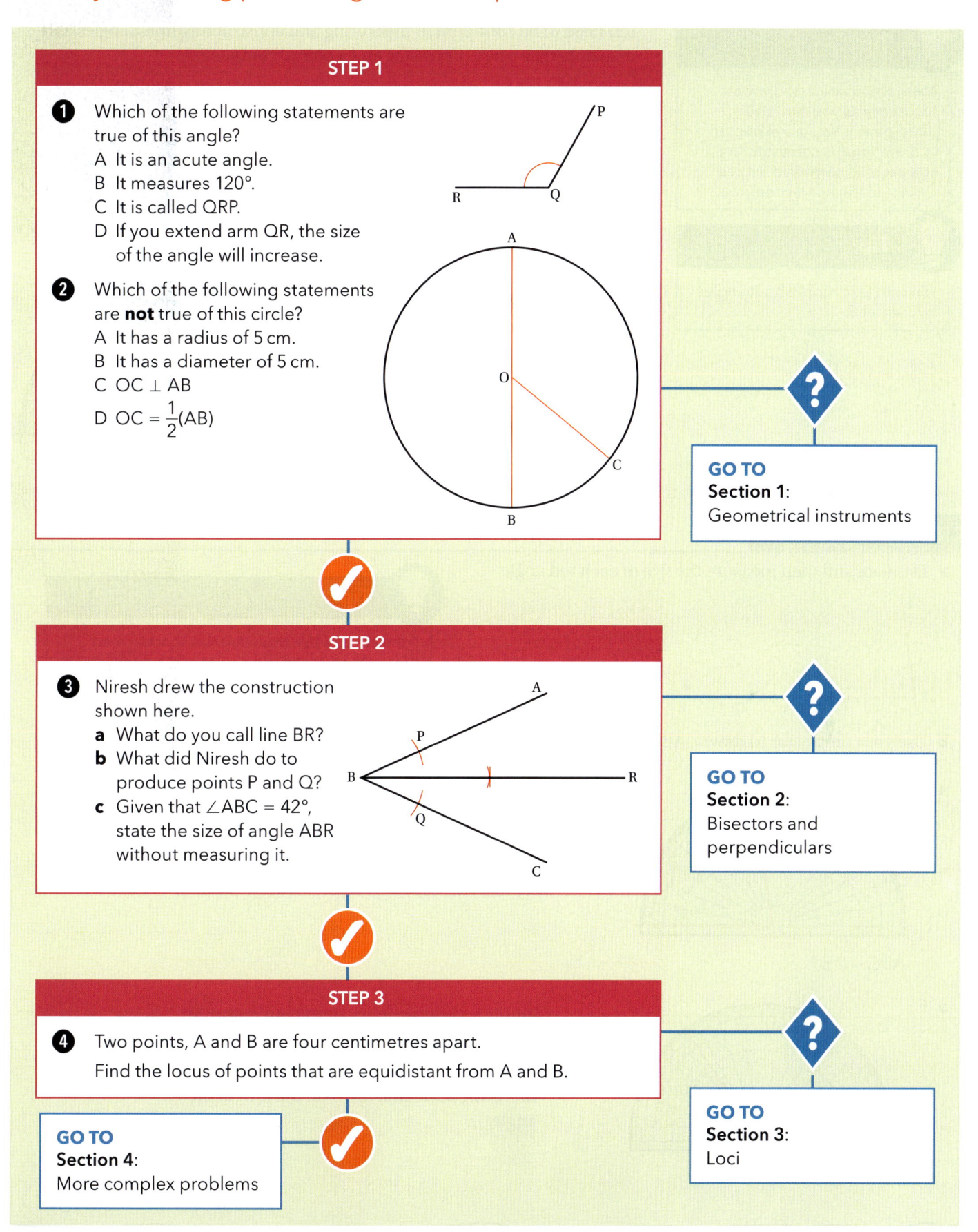

STEP 1

1 Which of the following statements are true of this angle?
  A It is an acute angle.
  B It measures 120°.
  C It is called QRP.
  D If you extend arm QR, the size of the angle will increase.

2 Which of the following statements are **not** true of this circle?
  A It has a radius of 5 cm.
  B It has a diameter of 5 cm.
  C OC ⊥ AB
  D OC = $\frac{1}{2}$(AB)

GO TO
Section 1: Geometrical instruments

STEP 2

3 Niresh drew the construction shown here.
  a What do you call line BR?
  b What did Niresh do to produce points P and Q?
  c Given that ∠ABC = 42°, state the size of angle ABR without measuring it.

GO TO
Section 2: Bisectors and perpendiculars

STEP 3

4 Two points, A and B are four centimetres apart.
Find the locus of points that are equidistant from A and B.

GO TO
Section 3: Loci

GO TO
Section 4: More complex problems

Find answers at: cambridge.org/ukschools/gcsemaths-studentbookanswers

GCSE Mathematics for OCR (Foundation)

Section 1: Geometrical instruments

You need to be confident in measuring and constructing lines, angles and shapes using a ruler, protractor and a pair of compasses.

Measuring and drawing angles

Angles are created when two line segments (or rays) meet at a point. The point is called the **vertex** of the angle, and the two line segments are called its sides (sometimes referred to as the 'arms' of the angle).

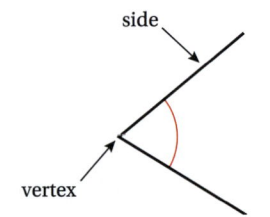

You use a protractor to measure and draw angles.

This protractor has two scales so that we can measure angles facing different directions.

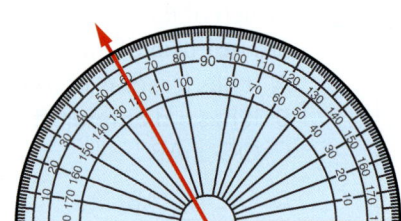

To avoid measuring on the wrong scale, estimate the size of the angle before you measure. Use your knowledge of acute, right and obtuse angles to estimate as accurately as possible.

> **Tip**
>
> Always measure and draw as accurately as you can. Use a sharp pencil. You are expected to draw lengths correct to the nearest millimetre and angles correct to the nearest degree.

> **Tip**
>
> You will learn more about angles in Chapter 9.

WORKED EXAMPLE 1

a Estimate and then measure the size of each red angle.

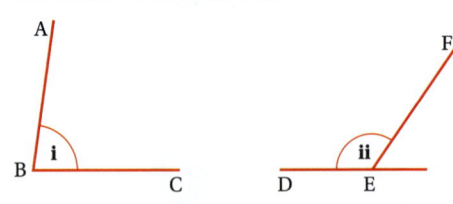

> **Tip**
>
> If the arms of the angle are too short to read the scale correctly use a ruler and a pencil to extend them. This doesn't change the size of the angle but it lets you read the measurement more accurately. If you cannot draw on the angle (because it is in a book) you can extend the arm with the straight edge of a sheet of paper.

b Use your protractor to draw ∠ABC = 76°.

a i

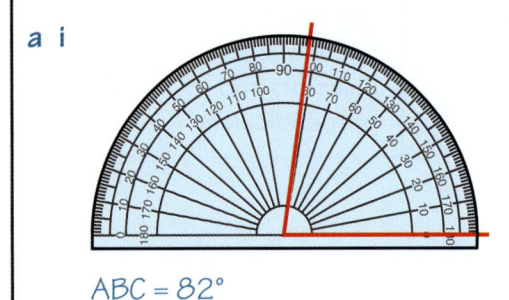

ABC = 82°

This is an acute angle but it is close to 90°.
Estimate about 80°.

Use the inner scale to measure, counting from 0.

a ii

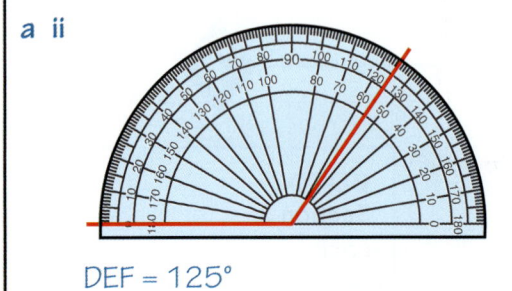

DEF = 125°

This is an obtuse angle. It is about one-third bigger than a right angle. Estimate about 130°.

Use the outer scale to measure because now this is the scale that has 0 on the arm of the angle.

Continues on next page …

74

6 Construction and loci

b
Draw a horizontal line using your ruler. Mark B, the vertex in ∠ABC.

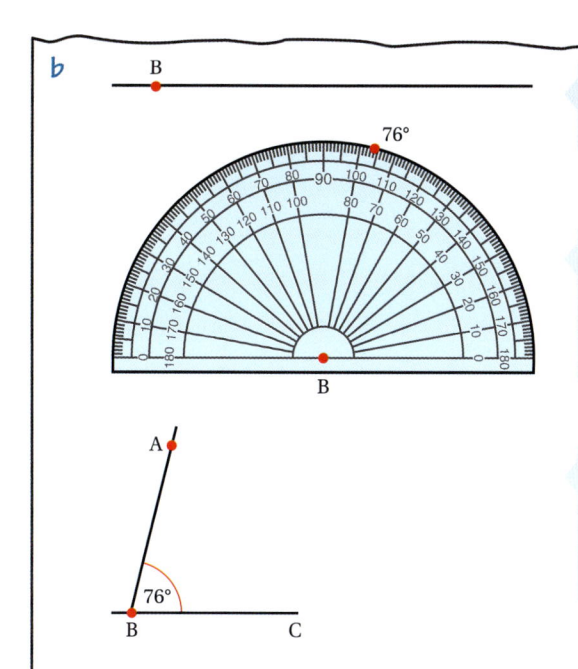

Place your protractor with its centre on B and baseline on the horizontal line.
Measure and mark 76°.

Remove the protractor. Draw a line from B through the 76° marking using a ruler. Label the angle correctly.

Using a pair of compasses

A pair of compasses (sometimes just called compasses or a compass) is very useful for drawing circles and angles, and marking accurate line lengths.

Using a pair of compasses effectively takes practice.

Make sure your pencil point is sharp and that the pair of compasses are not too loose.

WORKED EXAMPLE 2

a Draw a circle with a radius of 4.5 cm.

a 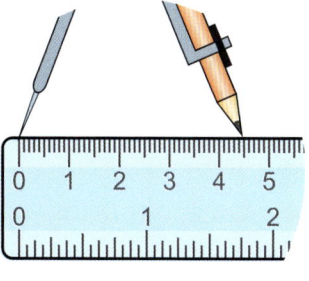
Place the pair of compasses alongside a ruler and open it to 4.5 cm.

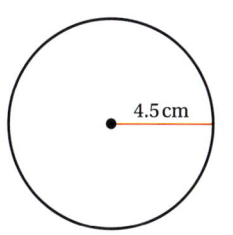

Draw a circle by pressing down on the point of the compasses, holding it at 0 (the centre of the circle) and sweeping the pencil round in a circle.

Continues on next page ...

Find answers at: cambridge.org/ukschools/gcsemaths-studentbookanswers

75

b Make an accurate copy of this figure.

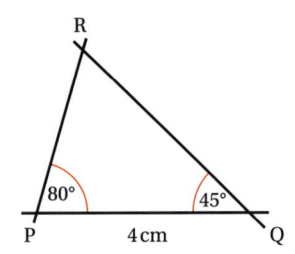

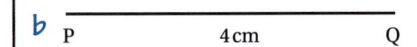

You have been given the length of one line and the size of two angles. First draw the base line of 4 cm using a ruler, and label this PQ.

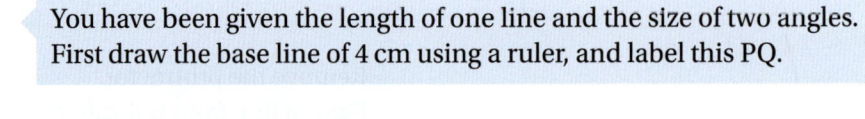

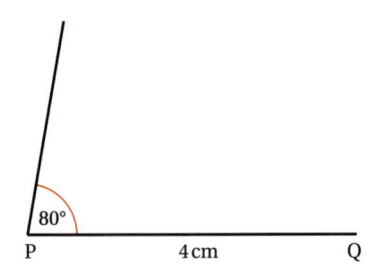

Use a protractor to measure and mark the angle 80° from point P, as per instructions in Worked example 1. Then draw a line from the mark to P.

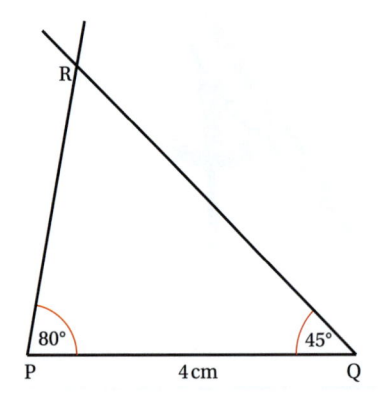

From point Q measure the angle 45° and draw a line from Q extending out so that it crosses the other line. Where the two lines cross is point R. This is the apex of the triangle.

c Construct an equilateral triangle with side lengths 6 cm.

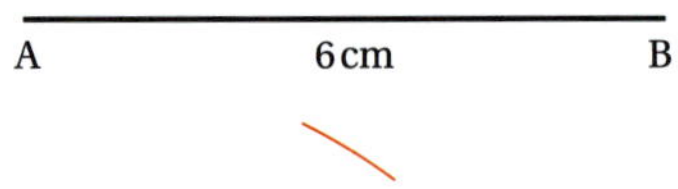

Here, you have not been given the size of any angles but you have been given the length of each side. First draw the base line of 6 cm with a ruler and label it AB.

Then set your pair of compasses to 6 cm with the point of your compasses on A. Draw an arc above the line AB, roughly where you would estimate C to be.

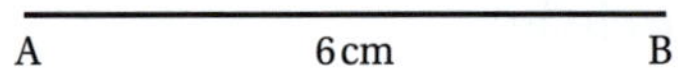

Continues on next page …

Repeat this from the other side at point B.

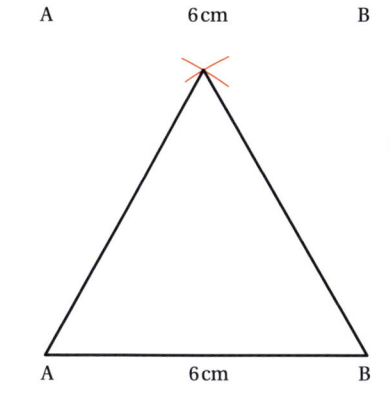

A — 6 cm — B

Where the two arcs cross is the apex of the triangle, that is, where the point C is. Use this point to complete the triangle. This method can be used for triangles with sides of different lengths by setting your pair of compasses to whatever the lengths of the sides are.

Tip

Leave the construction markings (arcs made using your pair of compasses) on your diagrams as this shows the method you used to construct them.

EXERCISE 6A

1 Use a ruler and protractor to draw and label the following angles.
   a ∠PQR = 25°   **b** ∠DEF = 149°   **c** ∠XYZ = 90°

2 How could you use a protractor marked from 0° to 180° to measure an angle of 238°?

3 **a** Draw line MN which is 8.4 cm long.
   At M, measure and draw ∠NMP = 45°.
   At N, measure and draw ∠RNM = 98°.
   b Explain why the lengths of MP and NR do not matter in this diagram.

4 Use a pair of compasses to construct:
   a a circle of radius 4 cm.   **b** a circle of diameter 12 cm.
   c a circle of diameter 2 cm which shares a centre, O, with another circle of radius 5 cm.

5 Draw a line AB which is 70 mm long.
Construct the circle for which this line is the diameter.

6 Draw a circle of radius 3.5 cm and centre O.
Use a ruler to draw any two radii of the circle. Label them OA and OB.
Join point A to point B to form triangle AOB.
Measure angles AOB, OBA and BAO. Write the measurements on your diagram.

Find answers at: cambridge.org/ukschools/gcsemaths-studentbookanswers

7 Accurately copy the following diagrams.

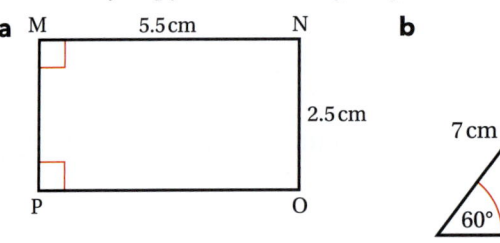

a Rectangle MNOP with MN = 5.5 cm and NO = 2.5 cm.

b Triangle ABC with angle A = 36°, angle B = 60°, angle C = 84°, and AB = 7 cm.

8 Write step-by-step instructions for using only a ruler and a pair of compasses to construct:

   a an equilateral triangle ABC with sides of 6.4 cm.

   b a semicircle with a radius of 30 mm.

Section 2: Bisectors and perpendiculars

Bisecting a line

You can use a ruler and a pair of compasses to **bisect** any line without measuring it.

Tip

Remember, bisect means divide exactly in two.

WORKED EXAMPLE 3

Bisect line AB by construction.

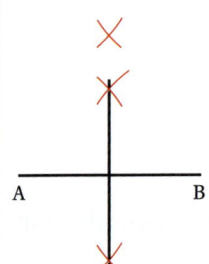

Place the point of a pair of compasses on A, then open them to any length that is **greater** than half way along the line AB. Draw arcs above and below the line. Keep the compasses open to the same width and place the point on B. Draw arcs above and below the line so that they cut the first set of arcs.

Use a ruler to join the points where the arcs intersect. This is the bisector of the line AB.

The point where the constructed line cuts AB is called the **midpoint** of AB.

The distance from A to this point is equal to the distance from B to this point.

The constructed line is perpendicular to AB, so it is called the **perpendicular bisector** of AB.

Key vocabulary

midpoint: the centre of a line; the point that divides the line into two equal halves.

perpendicular bisector: a line perpendicular to another that also cuts it in half.

Constructing perpendiculars

Tip

Remember perpendicular means 'at right angles to'.

You can use your pair of compasses to construct:
- a line perpendicular to any point on a given line.
- a perpendicular line from a point above or below a given line.

Construct a perpendicular at a given point on a line

WORKED EXAMPLE 4

Construct XY $\perp$ AB at point X.

Open your pair of compasses to a width of about 4 cm. Place the point of your compasses on X. Draw two arcs to cut AB on either side of X.

Construct the perpendicular bisector of the line segment between the arcs (as per Worked example 3). Draw a line through the intersecting arcs. Label one end of it Y to produce XY.

> **Tip**
>
> Remember the symbol $\perp$ means 'perpendicular to'; see Chapter 5 if you need to.

Construct a perpendicular from a point to a line

The shortest distance from any point to a line, is the perpendicular distance from the point to the line.

WORKED EXAMPLE 5

Construct PX perpendicular to line AB from point P.

Place the point of your pair of compasses on P. Draw an arc that cuts AB in two places. Label these places C and D.

Open the pair of compasses to a width more than half the distance between C and D. Place the point on C and draw an arc on the opposite side of the line to point P. Place the point on D and draw an arc which intersects the one you just drew. Draw a line from the intersecting arcs to P. Label PX and mark the perpendicular.

Find answers at: cambridge.org/ukschools/gcsemaths-studentbookanswers

Bisecting an angle

An angle bisector divides any angle into two equal halves.

WORKED EXAMPLE 6

Use a protractor to draw an angle PQR of 70°.

Construct the angle bisector of this angle without measuring.

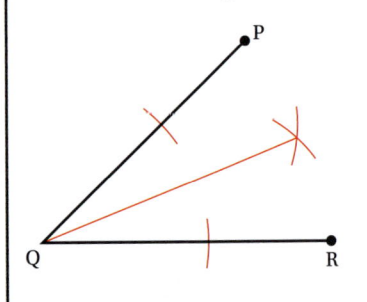

Place the pair of compasses on the vertex (Q) of the angle. Open your compasses a few centimetres and draw arcs that cut each arm of the angle.

Place the point of your compasses on each arc where it cuts the arm of the angle, and keeping the width the same, draw arcs between the arms of the angle.

Draw a line from the vertex of the angle through the intersection of the arcs.

This is the angle bisector.

EXERCISE 6B

1. Measure and draw the following line segments.
   Find the midpoint of each by construction.

   a AB = 9 cm   **b** MN = 48 mm   **c** PQ = 6.5 cm

2. **a** Draw any three acute angles. Bisect each angle without measuring.

   b How could you check the accuracy of your constructions?

3. Draw the angles shown and then, using only a ruler and pair of compasses, bisect each angle.

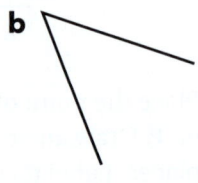

4. Draw any triangle ABC.

   a Construct the perpendicular bisector of each side of the triangle.

   b Use the point where the perpendicular bisectors meet as the centre, and vertex A as a radius, and draw a circle.

   c What do you notice about this circle?

5. Construct equilateral triangle DEF with sides of 7 cm.

   a Bisect each angle of the triangle by construction. Label the point where the angle bisectors meet as O.

   b Measure DO, EO and FO. What do you notice?

6. Draw MN = 80 mm. Insert any point A above MN.

   a Construct AX ⊥ MN.   **b** Draw AB // MN.

Section 3: Loci

A **locus** is a set of points that follow a certain rule. You can think of a locus as the path that shows all the possible positions for a point.

The halfway line on a football pitch is the set of points that follow the rule: '*must be equidistant between both penalty spots*'.

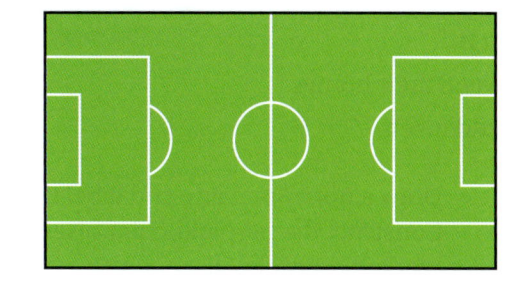

Some of the rules for loci produce shapes and lines (paths) that you are already familiar with from your work on constructions.

If you recognise the paths made by common loci you can apply what you know about those paths to solve problems.

For example, the locus of points at a given distance from a fixed point forms a circular path, that is, a circle. You can use what you know about drawing circles to use a pair of compasses to construct this locus.

> **Key vocabulary**
>
> **locus (plural loci):** a set of points that satisfy the same rule.

> **Tip**
>
> The locus of a point at distance (*r*) from a fixed point (O) is a circle with centre O and radius (*r*).

WORKED EXAMPLE 7

A tap is located at point X.

Draw the locus of points that are exactly 50 metres from the tap.

Your diagram does not need to be to scale.

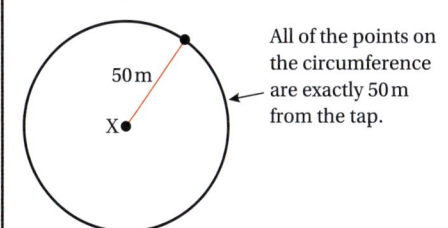

All of the points on the circumference are exactly 50 m from the tap.

Diagram is not to scale.

Use a pair of compasses to draw a circle (as per Worked example 2). Draw a point in the centre and label this 'X'. Draw in a line for the radius and label this '50 m'. Label the diagram to indicate it is not to scale. Any point on the circumference of this circle is 50 m from the tap.

In Worked example 7 the locus of points that are **less than** 50 m from the tap is the region **inside** the circle.

If you were asked to construct this locus, you would shade the interior of the circle to show that all the points inside the circumference meet the conditions of the locus.

You would also show the circumference as a **broken line** to indicate that it is **not** included in the locus.

> **Tip**
>
> If a line is included in the locus you draw it as a solid line. If the line is not included, but just shows the edge of the locus, you draw it as a broken, or dashed, line.

Find answers at: cambridge.org/ukschools/gcsemaths-studentbookanswers

The locus of points equidistant from two fixed points is the perpendicular bisector of the line joining the points.

WORKED EXAMPLE 8

Anna lives at point A. Josie lives at point B.

They want to meet exactly midway between their homes.

Draw a diagram to show where they could meet.

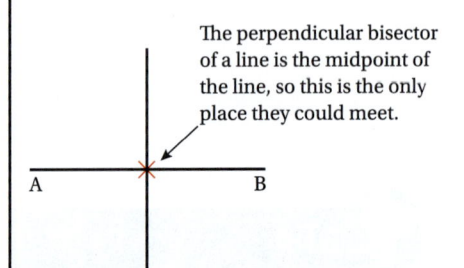

The perpendicular bisector of a line is the midpoint of the line, so this is the only place they could meet.

Draw a horizontal line and label the ends A, and B. Construct the perpendicular bisector of this line (as per Worked example 4).

The point where the lines cross is exactly midway between their homes.

In Worked example 8 you can take any point on the perpendicular bisector and it will be the same distance from A and B.

If Anna and Josie wanted to meet at a point that was the same distance from their homes, they could meet anywhere along the perpendicular bisector of the line AB.

However, the question asked you to find the point **exactly midway** between A and B, and the midpoint of line AB is the only point that meets that condition.

> **Tip**
>
> Remember a line continues to infinity in both directions, so it has no end points.

The locus of points equidistant from a line is a pair of parallel lines at the given distance. The locus lines will be on either side of the given line.

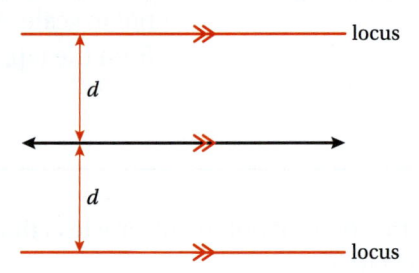

A line segment has a fixed length. The locus of points equidistant from a line segment has to be the same distance from the line and also the same distance from its end points.

> **Tip**
>
> The locus of points a fixed distance (d) from a line is the pair of parallel lines which are d cm away from the given line.
>
> The locus of points at a fixed distance (d) from a line segment is a pair of parallel lines d cm away from the line segment along with the semicircles of radius d cm at the ends of the line segment.

This produces an oval 'racing track' shape with all points the same distance (d) from the line segment.

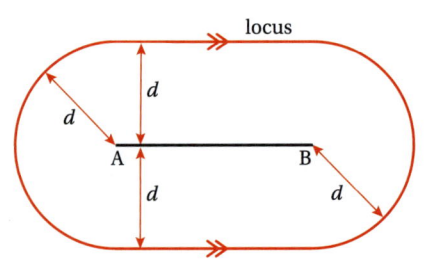

The locus of points that are equidistant from the arms of ∠ABC is shown.

If you take any point on the line BP, it will be the same distance from AB and BC.

You should recognise that BP is the angle bisector of ∠ABC.

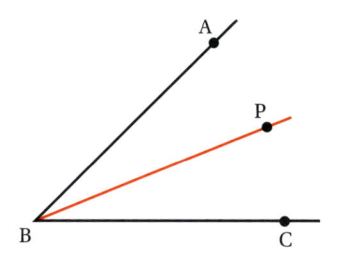

> **Tip**
>
> The locus of points an equal distance from two intersecting lines is their angle bisector.

EXERCISE 6C

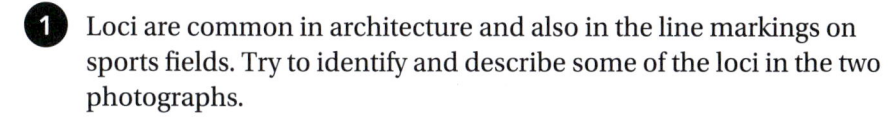

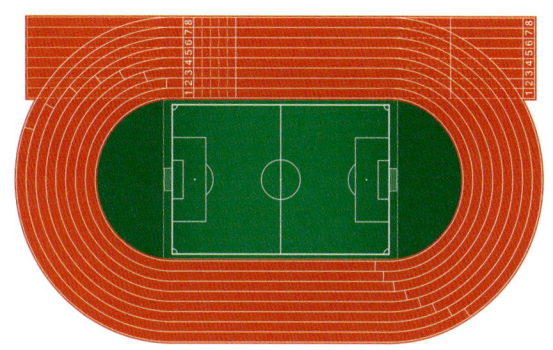

1 Loci are common in architecture and also in the line markings on sports fields. Try to identify and describe some of the loci in the two photographs.

2 Without drawing them, describe the point, path or area that each locus below will produce.

　a Points that are 200 km from a shop at point X.

　b Points that are more than 2 km but less than 3 km from a straight fence 1 km long.

　c Points that are equidistant from the two baselines of a tennis court.

　d Points that are equidistant from the four corners of a soccer field.

　e Points that are within 1 km of a railway line.

3 Accurately construct the locus of points 4 cm from a point O.

4 Draw ∠MNR = 50°.

Accurately construct the locus of points equidistant from MN and NR.

5 Draw PQ 4 cm long.

Construct the locus of points 1 cm from PQ.

6 PQ is a line segment of 5 cm.

X is a point exactly 4 cm from P and exactly 2.5 cm from Q.

Show by construction the possible locations of point X.

Find answers at: cambridge.org/ukschools/gcsemaths-studentbookanswers

GCSE Mathematics for OCR (Foundation)

7 Draw a rectangle ABCD with AB = 6 cm and BC = 4 cm.

   a Construct the locus of points that are equidistant from AB and BC.

   b Shade the locus of points that are less than 1 cm from the centre of the rectangle.

   c Construct the locus of points that are exactly 1 cm outside the perimeter of the rectangle.

Section 4: More complex problems

You need to be able to combine the construction techniques you have learned to construct accurate diagrams of shapes and to construct loci to show different situations.

In many cases you will need to decide which construction technique to use. For example, to construct a rectangle without measuring the right angles, you would need to construct the perpendiculars at two points on the base of the rectangle.

Many of the loci problems that you will have to solve could be presented in context. You might be asked to draw scaled diagrams to solve these problems. The scale might be given. For example, 1 cm : 10 km. If you are not given a scale, always state the scale that you have used.

Problem-solving framework

A, B and C represent three towns.

A mobile phone tower is to be erected in the area.

The tower is to be equidistant from towns A and B and within 30 km of town C.

Show by accurate construction on a scale diagram all possible sites for the tower.

Use a scale of 1 cm : 10 km.

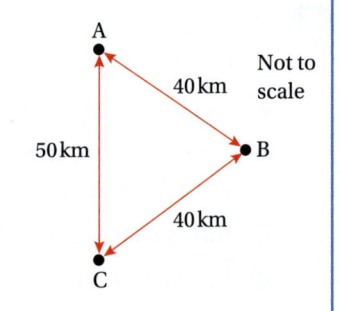

Steps for approaching a problem-solving question	What you would do for this example
Step 1: Work out what you have to do. Start by reading the question carefully.	Although it doesn't say so, this is a locus problem. You have to find the locus of points equidistant from A and B and the locus of points that are less than 30 km from C. The solution is where these loci overlap.
Step 2: What information do you need? Have you got it all?	You have to draw a scale diagram. The distances and the scale are given. The conditions for the loci are given.

Continues on next page ...

Step 3: Decide what maths you can do.	First work out the lengths you have to construct using the scale. The scale is 1 cm : 10 km. So: $\frac{40 \text{ km}}{10} = 4 \text{ cm}$ $\frac{50 \text{ km}}{10} = 5 \text{ cm}$. Next use these lengths to construct a triangle using your ruler and pair of compasses. Once you have the triangle you can find the loci by construction.
Step 4: Set out your solution clearly. Check your working and that your answer is reasonable.	The tower could be built at any position along the thick red line
Step 5: Check that you've answered the question.	You have shown the overlapping loci and written a statement to answer the question.

EXERCISE 6D

1. Draw line AB = 5.2 cm.

   Construct DE, the perpendicular bisector of AB.

   Draw DE so that it is 44 mm long.

   Mark point F on DE such that DF = FE = 22 mm.

   Construct MN //AB and passing through point F.

2. Construct a parallelogram with sides of 46 mm and 28 mm and a longest diagonal of length 60 mm. Measure and write in the length of the other diagonal.

3. Accurately construct a square of side 45 mm.

4. Construct quadrilateral ABCD such that ABC = 90°, AB = DC = 2.2 cm and AD = BC = 5 cm. What kind of quadrilateral is this?

5. On a treasure map, the position of buried treasure is known to be 10 metres from the castle at point Y and 12 metres from the cave at point Z.

   Y and Z are 15 metres apart.

   Draw a scale diagram and mark with an X all the places where the treasure might be buried.

   Use a scale of 1 cm to 2 m.

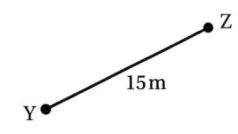

6 A monkey is in a rectangular enclosure which is 10 m by 17.5 m.
The monkey is able to stretch through the fence around its enclosure and reach a distance of 25 cm.

   a Draw a scale diagram to show the locus of points that the monkey can reach outside its enclosure.

   b Show on your diagram where you would place a safety barrier to make sure that people cannot touch the monkey.
   Give a reason for your choice.

Checklist of learning and understanding

Geometry constructions

- A protractor is used to measure and draw angles.
- You can use a ruler and pair of compasses to construct perpendicular lines and to bisect lines and angles.
- The perpendicular bisector of any line cuts the line at its midpoint.
- The shortest distance from a point to a line is always the perpendicular distance.

Loci

- A locus is a set of points that meet the same conditions.
- The locus of points can be a single point, a line, a curve or a shaded area.
- Loci can be used to solve problems involving equal distances and overlapping areas.

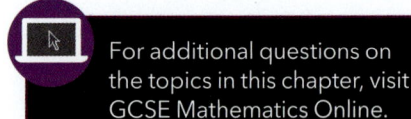

For additional questions on the topics in this chapter, visit GCSE Mathematics Online.

Chapter review

1 **a** Use a protractor to measure angles a and b on this clock face.
   b Draw two angles which are the same size as a and b.
   c Bisect the two angles you have drawn by construction.

2 Draw a line AB of length 6.5 cm and find its midpoint by construction.
Indicate the locus of points that are equidistant from A and B on your diagram.

3 Town X is due north of Town Y and they are 20 km apart.
Town Z is 25 km from Town X and 35 km from Town Y.

   a Draw a scale diagram to show the location of Town Z in relation to the other two towns.
   Use a scale of 1 cm : 5 km.

b A railway runs between towns X and Y such that it is equidistant from both towns. Show the position of the railway on your drawing.

c The electricity supply from town X is carried on a cable that is the same distance from XZ and XY along its length.
Show where this cable would be.

4 Here is a scale diagram of a field ABCD with a canal crossing it.

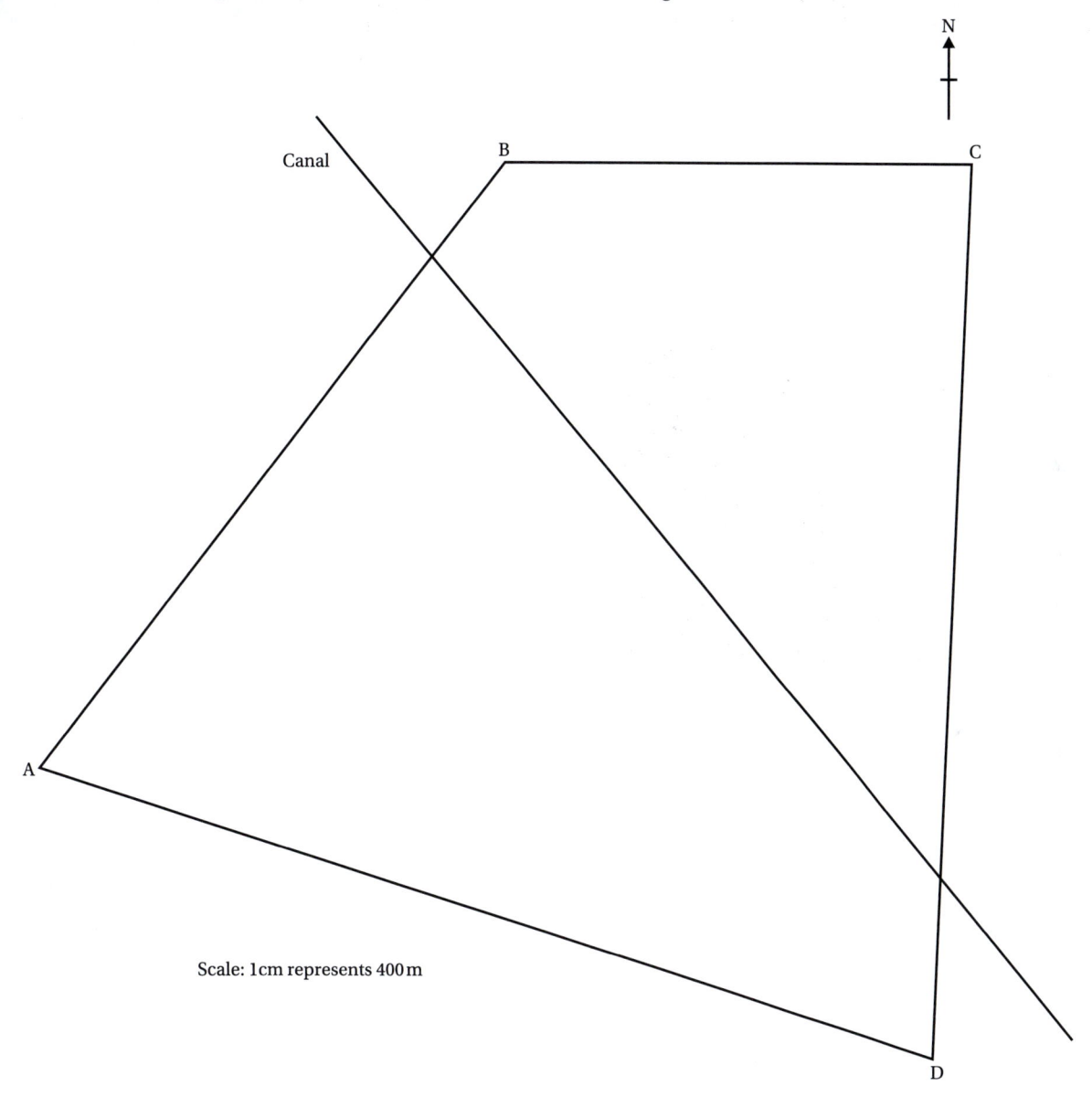

Scale: 1cm represents 400m

The council want to put a runway inside the field.
The whole runway has to be:
- Nearer to AB than to AD
- At least 800 m from the canal
- In an East-West direction
- 2000 m long.

Show that it is possible to put this runway inside the field.
You must leave in all your construction lines.

(4 marks)

© OCR 2012

Find answers at: cambridge.org/ukschools/gcsemaths-studentbookanswers

7 Further algebraic expressions

In this chapter you will learn how to …

- expand the product of two binomial expressions.
- factorise quadratic expressions of the form $x^2 + bx + c$.
- solve problems involving quadratic expressions.

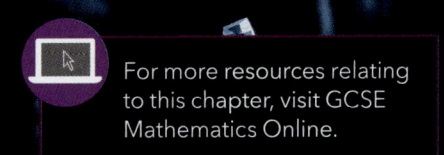

For more resources relating to this chapter, visit GCSE Mathematics Online.

Using mathematics: real-life applications

Quadratic expressions and formulae can be used to model motion, including acceleration, stopping distance, velocity and distance travelled (displacement).

"At the site of a crash, I measure the length of the tyre skid marks and apply an equation to work out the speed at which vehicles were moving before the accident." (Police road accident investigator)

Before you start …

Ch 3	Check you remember how to simplify expressions.	1	Simplify. $3x + 6y + 2xy + 2x$
Ch 3	Make sure you can multiply out brackets.	2	Expand. $2x(x - y)$
Ch 3	Make sure you can factorise simple expressions.	3	Factorise fully. $27xy - 9x$
Ch 3	You should be able to recognise an identity.	4	Is the identity symbol used correctly in each example? Explain why or why not. **a** $3(2a^2 - 4) \equiv 6a^2 - 12$ **b** $2x + 4 \equiv 7x - 8$
Ch 3	You should be able to express situations using algebra.	5	3 is added to a number and this new number is multiplied by 6 more than another number. Which expression represents this situation? **a** $6x(3 + y)$ **b** $(3 + y)(x + 6)$
Ch 1, 3	Make sure you remember the rules for multiplying negative and positive quantities.	6	Simplify. **a** $6 \times {}^-5$ **b** ${}^-3 \times {}^-7$ **c** ${}^-2a \times b$ **d** ${}^-y \times {}^-y$ **e** ${}^-2a \times {}^-5a$

88

7 Further algebraic expressions

Assess your starting point using the Launchpad

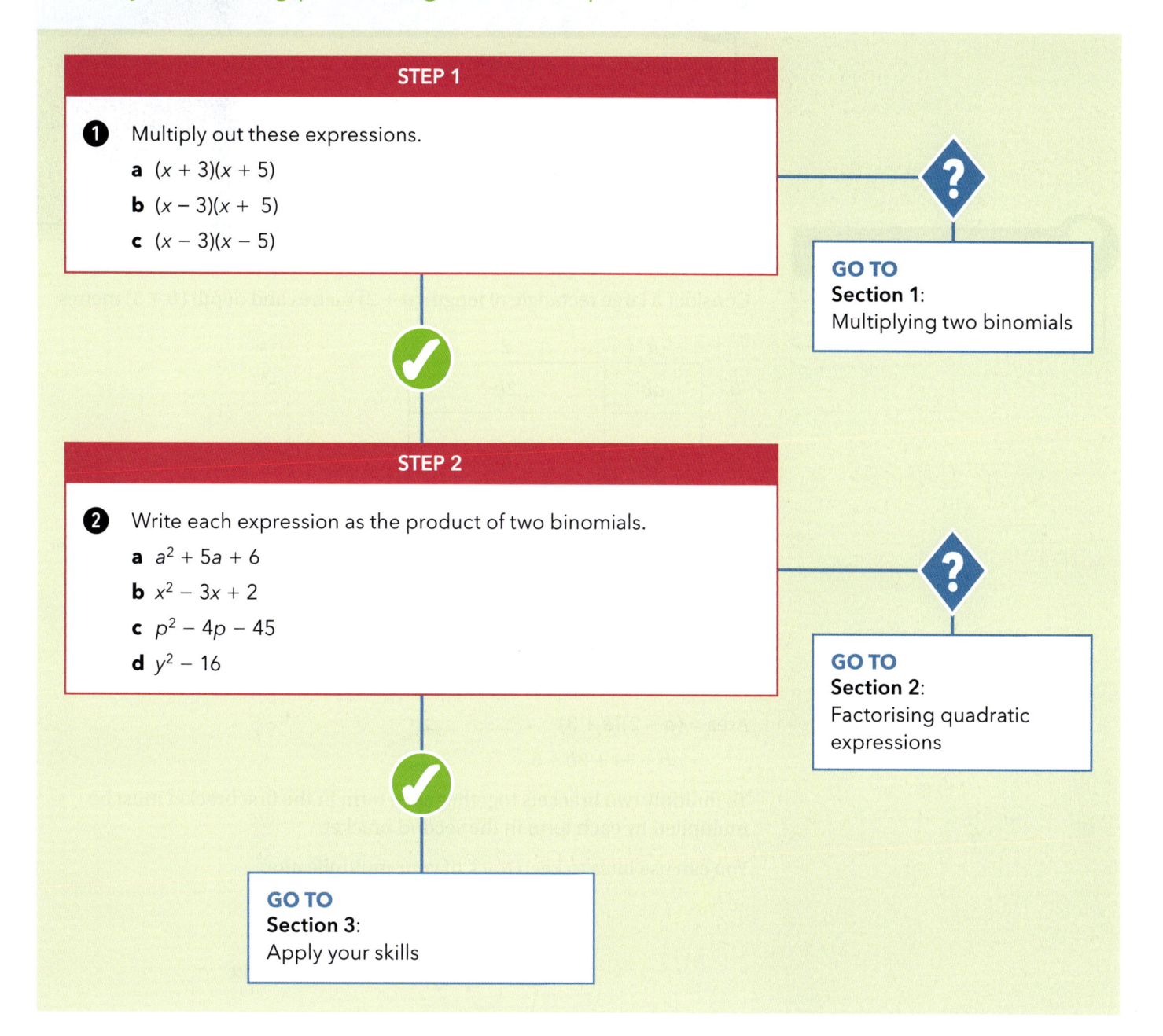

STEP 1

1. Multiply out these expressions.
   a $(x + 3)(x + 5)$
   b $(x − 3)(x + 5)$
   c $(x − 3)(x − 5)$

GO TO
Section 1: Multiplying two binomials

STEP 2

2. Write each expression as the product of two binomials.
   a $a^2 + 5a + 6$
   b $x^2 − 3x + 2$
   c $p^2 − 4p − 45$
   d $y^2 − 16$

GO TO
Section 2: Factorising quadratic expressions

GO TO
Section 3: Apply your skills

Section 1: Multiplying two binomials

A **binomial** is an expression that contains two terms.

For example:

$x + 2$ $x − 4$ $3x^2 + 4$ $2x^2 − 5y^3$

A **binomial product** is the product of two binomials.

Multiplying the first two binomials above gives the binomial product $(x + 2)(x − 4)$.

You expand the product of two binomials by multiplying out the brackets.

$(x + 2)(x − 4) = x^2 − 2x − 8$

Key vocabulary

binomial: an expression consisting of two terms.

binomial product: the product of two binomial expressions; for example, $(x + 2)(x + 3)$.

Find answers at: cambridge.org/ukschools/gcsemaths-studentbookanswers

89

> **Tip**
>
> Writing numbers in expanded notation to do long multiplication is similar to finding a binomial product.
>
> 14×27 can be written as
>
> $(10 + 4) \times (20 + 7) = 10 \times 20 + 10 \times 7 + 4 \times 20 + 4 \times 7$
> $= 200 + 70 + 80 + 28$
> $= 378$

The area of a rectangle is useful for showing how to multiply two binomials.

Consider a large rectangle of length $(a + 2)$ metres and depth $(b + 3)$ metres.

	a	2
b	ab	$2b$
3	$3a$	6

> **Tip**
>
> Breadth and depth mean the same as width.

The area of the whole rectangle must be equal to the sum of the four smaller rectangular areas shown on the diagram.

So, total area $= ab + 2b + 3a + 6$.

But the area (length × depth) of the whole rectangle is also the binomial product $(a + 2)(b + 3)$.

Area $= (a + 2)(b + 3)$
$= ab + 3a + 2b + 6$

To multiply two brackets together each term in the first bracket must be multiplied by each term in the second bracket.

You can use lines to keep track of your multiplication.

$(a + 2)(b + 3) = ab + 6 + 2b + 3a$

You can also use a grid to make sure you have multiplied all the terms.

×	a	2
b	ab	$2b$
3	$3a$	6

The product of two binomials gives you four terms.

In the example above there are no like terms so you cannot simplify the expression any further. When the product contains like terms you add these to simplify the expression.

> **Tip**
>
> Expanding a binomial product will not always give you four terms. Simplifying the expression might result in fewer terms.

7 Further algebraic expressions

> **WORKED EXAMPLE 1**
>
> Expand and simplify, if possible.
>
> $(x + 3)(x + 5)$.
>
> | × | x | 3 |
> |---|-----|---|
> | x | x^2 | $3x$ |
> | 5 | $5x$ | 15 |
>
> $(x + 3)(x + 5) = x^2 + 3x + 5x + 15$
> $\qquad\qquad\qquad = x^2 + 8x + 15$
>
> Use lines or draw a grid to help you find the four products.
> $x^2 + 3x + 5x + 15$
>
> $5x$ and $3x$ are like terms, so add them.

The expression $x^2 + 8x + 15$ is a **quadratic expression**, because the highest power of x in the expression is x squared (x^2).

The general form of a quadratic expression is $ax^2 + bx + c$.

You need to pay careful attention to the signs when you multiply binomials. Remember the rules of multiplication for positive and negative numbers:

- negative × positive = negative
- negative × negative = positive

🔑 **Key vocabulary**

quadratic expression: an expression that can be written in the form $ax^2 + bx + c$, where $a \neq 0$, there are no negative or fractional powers and the highest power is 2.

> **WORKED EXAMPLE 2**
>
> Expand and simplify, if possible.
>
> **a** $(x - 2)(x + 9)$ **b** $(x - 4)(x - 7)$
>
> **a** $(x - 2)(x + 9) = x^2 + 9x - 2x - 18$
> $\qquad\qquad\qquad\;\; = x^2 + 7x - 18$
>
> Notice that you get a positive and a negative like term here.
>
> **b** $(x - 4)(x - 7) = x^2 - 7x - 4x + 28$
> $\qquad\qquad\qquad\;\; = x^2 - 11x + 28$
>
> Notice that the like terms are both negative here.

> **WORK IT OUT 7.1**
>
> These are the results three students got when they were asked to expand $(x - 5)(x + 6)$.
>
> Student A: $x^2 + 11x + 30$ Student B: $2x - 30$ Student C: $x^2 + x - 11$
>
> What did each student do wrong?
> What is the correct answer?

Perfect squares

A perfect square is the resulting product when a number, variable or expression is multiplied by itself.

1, 4, 9, 16, 25 and 36 are perfect squares (square numbers).

a^2, x^2, $(xy)^2$ and $(2x)^2$ are all perfect squares.

A term such as $16x^2$ is a perfect square because it is equivalent to $(4x)^2$.

A term such as $5y^2$ is not a perfect square because only the y is a perfect square, the 5 is not.

Find answers at: cambridge.org/ukschools/gcsemaths-studentbookanswers

GCSE Mathematics for OCR (Foundation)

> **Key vocabulary**
>
> **perfect square**: a binomial product of the form $(a \pm b)^2$.

When a binomial is multiplied by itself the product is called a **perfect square**.

For example:

$$(x + 8)^2 = (x + 8)(x + 8)$$
$$= x^2 + 8x + 8x + 64$$
$$= x^2 + 16x + 64$$

Expanding a perfect square always produces the same pattern. This pattern can be used to expand them without doing any working.

$(a + b)^2 = a^2 + 2ab + b^2 \qquad (a - b)^2 = a^2 - 2ab + b^2$

↑ first term squared ↑ twice the product of the two terms ↑ second term squared ↑ first term squared ↑ twice the product of the two terms ↑ second term squared

Note that this is a helpful shortcut rather than a strict rule to be learnt.

EXERCISE 7A

1 Expand and simplify.
   - **a** $(x + 2)(x + 5)$
   - **b** $(x - 2)(x - 5)$
   - **c** $(x + 2)(x - 5)$
   - **d** $(x - 2)(x + 5)$
   - **e** $(x + 3)(x - 4)$
   - **f** $(x + y)(x + y)$

2 Find these products and simplify.
   - **a** $(x - 5)(x - 1)$
   - **b** $(a - 7)(a - 4)$
   - **c** $(m + 4)(m - 5)$
   - **d** $(p - 6)(p + 4)$
   - **e** $(x - 7)(x + 6)$
   - **f** $(x + 11)(x - 3)$
   - **g** $(x - 11)(x - 7)$
   - **h** $(x + 8)(x - 3)$
   - **i** $(x - 12)(x - 6)$

3 Expand and simplify.
   - **a** $(2x + 4)(3x + 3)$
   - **b** $(3x + 4)(5x + 2)$
   - **c** $(2x - 5)(3x + 1)$
   - **d** $(4y - 3)(5y + 1)$
   - **e** $(3a - 5)(2a - 1)$
   - **f** $(2b - 5)(b - 3)$
   - **g** $(2y - 3)(3y - 5)$
   - **h** $(2x + 4)(2x - 6)$
   - **i** $(5x - 3)(4x - 1)$

4 Expand these perfect squares.
   - **a** $(x + 5)^2$
   - **b** $(x - 5)^2$
   - **c** Write a sentence to explain in words how to multiply out a perfect square.

5 Expand each of these perfect squares.
   - **a** $(x + 2)^2$
   - **b** $(x + 7)^2$
   - **c** $(x - 3)^2$
   - **d** $(x - 9)^2$
   - **e** $(2x + 1)^2$
   - **f** $(1 - 3x)^2$

6 If $A = 3x + 2$ and $B = 2x - 1$ determine:
   - **a** AB
   - **b** $A^2 + B^2$
   - **c** $(A - B)(A + B)$

7 Find the area, in terms of x, of each of these squares.

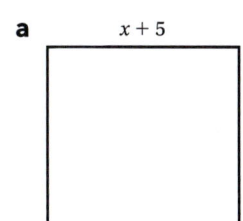

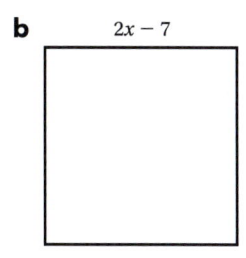

a $x + 5$

b $2x - 7$

c Calculate the area of each square when $x = 8$.

The difference of two squares identity

Work through the investigation in Exercise 7B to find a shortcut for expanding binomials in the form of $(a + b)(a - b)$.

EXERCISE 7B

1 Expand each of the following binomials.

a $(x + 1)(x - 1)$ b $(a + 2)(a - 2)$ c $(2x - 1)(2x + 1)$ d $(x - 2y)(x + 2y)$

2 How many terms are there in your answers? Can you explain why this happens?

3 What is special about each term in the binomials you expanded?

4 Write down a rule that you can use to quickly find the answer to any similar expansion.

5 Copy this expansion and fill in the gaps.
$(x + y)(x - y)$
$= x^2 + \Box - xy - \Box$
$= \Box - \Box$

6 The example in Question 5 shows that $(x + y)(x - y) \equiv x^2 - y^2$.

This is called **the difference of two squares identity**.

a Which are the two squares?

b How can you recognise when a binomial expansion is a difference of two squares?

c Is $(3y + 2x)(2x - 3y)$ a difference of two squares? Explain why or why not.

> **Tip**
>
> You learnt about identities in Chapter 3. Remember that the $\equiv$ means that both sides are equal for all values of the variable.

The diagram opposite illustrates the difference of two squares.

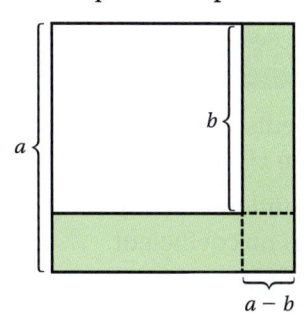

The biggest square has an area of a^2.
The smaller unshaded square has an area of b^2.

Find answers at: cambridge.org/ukschools/gcsemaths-studentbookanswers

The difference in area between these two squares is the shaded part of the diagram.

The total shaded area is formed of two rectangles and one square.

The area of the small shaded square is:

$(a - b)(a - b) = a^2 - ab - ab + b^2$ This is a perfect square.
$= a^2 - 2ab + b^2$ (collecting like terms)

The area of the two rectangles is:

$2 \times b(a - b) = 2ab - 2b^2$

The total area of the shaded part is:

$a^2 - 2ab + b^2 + 2ab - 2b^2 = a^2 - b^2$

The difference between two squares $a^2 - b^2 \equiv (a + b)(a - b)$.

Section 2: Factorising quadratic expressions

In Chapter 3 you learned that factorising an expression is the opposite of expanding it. For example, $2(x + 7)$ is the factorised form of $2x + 14$.

2 is a common factor of $2x$ and 14, and dividing each term by 2 leaves $(x + 7)$.

You now also know that expanding a binomial such as $(x + 3)(x + 4)$ gives you a quadratic expression.

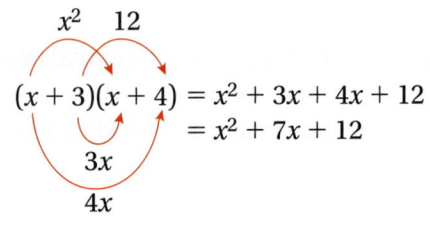

$$(x + 3)(x + 4) = x^2 + 3x + 4x + 12$$
$$= x^2 + 7x + 12$$

Factorising an expression involves writing it as the product of its factors. In other words, factorising means 'putting the brackets back into the expression'.

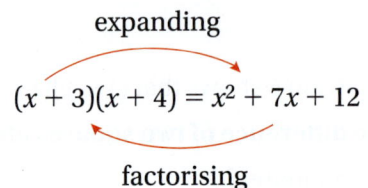

expanding
$$(x + 3)(x + 4) = x^2 + 7x + 12$$
factorising

In this section you will learn how to factorise quadratic expressions in the form of $x^2 + bx + c$. Note that **not all** quadratic expressions can be factorised.

In this expression x is the variable, b is the **coefficient** of x and c is a **constant**.

> **Tip**
>
> Do you remember how to factorise an expression by taking out a common factor?
> Revise that section in Chapter 3 if you are not sure.

> **Key vocabulary**
>
> **coefficient**: the number in front of a variable in a mathematical expression. In the term $5x^2$, 5 is the coefficient and x is the variable.
>
> **constant**: in algebra, a constant is a fixed number.

WORK IT OUT 7.2

Two students were asked to identify the coefficient of x^2 in the expression $x^2 + bx + c$

The first student said the coefficient was 1 and the second student said that x^2 has no coefficient.

Which student is correct?

How would you explain to the other student why their answer is wrong?

Factorising a quadratic is the inverse of finding the product of (multiplying) two binomials.

In general:

$(x + a)(x + b) = x^2 + (a + b)x + ab$.

So, the middle term is the sum of a and b in the original binomials or $(a + b)$.

The third term is the product of a and b or (ab).

This pattern can be used to develop a strategy for factorising quadratics.

Work through the examples to see how to do this systematically.

WORKED EXAMPLE 3

Factorise $x^2 + 7x + 12$.

$x^2 + 7x + 12$ — Write down the expression you have been asked to factorise.

$= (x + \Box)(x + \Box)$ — Start by writing brackets and insert an x in each. You can do this because to get x^2 you know you need to multiply x by x. (**Note** you do not have to include a '+' or '−' sign in the brackets at this stage, you can wait until you've identified the factors.)

Factor pairs for 12 are

1×12
2×6
3×4

Now look at the value of the constant; you know that the constants in each bracket are multiplied together to get the constant of the quadratic, and that the sum of the two constants becomes the coefficient of x in the quadratic. So, what factors of 12 will add up to give 7 and multiply to give 12? Write down some factor pairs for 12.

$3 + 4 = 7$
$3 \times 4 = 12$

Identify which factor pair meets the conditions and substitute one factor into each bracket.

So, $x^2 + 7x + 12 = (x + 3)(x + 4)$

$(x + 3)(x + 4) = x^2 + 3x + 4x + 12$
$= x^2 + 7x + 12$

Expand the brackets to check your answer. Yes, this is the expression you started with.

Quadratics that have negative terms need a bit more care.

Consider factorising $x^2 - 7x + 12$.

You can start by writing $x^2 - 7x + 12 = (x - \Box)(x - \Box)$ as before.

Put negative signs in both brackets because the constant is $+12$ but the coefficient of x this time is a negative number, $^-7$.

The product of two negative numbers is positive so the factor pairs must be negative:

$^-1 \times {}^-12$

$^-2 \times {}^-6$

$^-3 \times {}^-4$

$^-3 + (^-4) = {}^-7$, so this is the factor pair you need.

$x^2 - 7x + 12 = (x - 3)(x - 4)$

Find answers at: cambridge.org/ukschools/gcsemaths-studentbookanswers

The example below shows you how to work systematically to factorise a quadratic which has negative terms.

WORKED EXAMPLE 4

Factorise $x^2 - 4x - 12$.

$x^2 - 4x - 12$
$= (x + \square)(x - \square)$

Make two sets of brackets and write an x in each as before. The constant of the quadratic is negative. To get a negative product you have to multiply a negative number by a positive number, so one bracket will have a negative sign and the other will have a positive sign. (**Note** you do not have to include a '+' or '−' sign in the brackets at this stage, you can wait until you've identified the factors.)

Factor pairs are:
1×12
2×6
3×4

Now look at the constant. It is ⁻12. Which factor pair has a difference of 4? There is a difference of 4 between 2 and 6.

$-2 + 6 = 4$
$-6 + 2 = -4$

Which factor pair will give you ⁻4 if you add the numbers together and give you ⁻12 if you multiply them? So, the 6 goes in the bracket with the negative sign. The 2 goes in the bracket with the positive sign.

$x^2 - 4x - 12 = (x + 2)(x - 6)$

$(x + 2)(x - 6) = x^2 - 4x - 12$

Check your answer by expanding the binomial. Yes, this is the expression you started with.

Work out the signs before you factorise by looking at the signs in the quadratic.

If the **constant is positive**, the brackets will have the **same** sign.
- If the x term is positive, both brackets will have positive signs.
- If the x term is negative, both brackets will have negative signs.

If the **constant is negative**, the brackets will have **different** signs.
- The x term is the difference between the two factors.
- The largest number in the factor pair will have the same sign as the x term in the quadratic.

When you factorise any expression, the first step should be to check for, and remove, **common factors**.

Once you have done this, you factorise the brackets as before.

WORKED EXAMPLE 5

Factorise $4x^2 - 12x - 40$.

$= 4(x^2 - 3x - 10)$ Take out the common factor of 4.

$= 4(x - 5)(x + 2)$ Factorise the trinomial independently of the '4' outside the brackets, but remember to reinsert the '4' outside of the brackets when you have finished factorising.

7 Further algebraic expressions

EXERCISE 7C

1 Find two numbers that meet each set of conditions.

   a Have a sum of 5 and a product of 6.
   b Add to give 8 and multiply to give 7.
   c Have a product of ⁻8 and a sum of 2.
   d Multiply to give 24 and add to give ⁻10.
   e Produce ⁻24 when multiplied, and sum to 5.
   f Have a sum of 3 and a product of ⁻18.

2 Factorise each of the following.

   a $x^2 + 14x + 24$ **b** $x^2 + 3 + 2$ **c** $x^2 + 7 + 12$ **d** $x^2 + 12x + 35$
   e $x^2 + 12 + 27$ **f** $x^2 + 7 + 6$ **g** $x^2 + 11x + 30$ **h** $x^2 + 10x + 16$
   i $x^2 + 11x + 10$ **j** $x^2 + 8 + 7$ **k** $x^2 + 24x + 80$ **l** $x^2 + 13x + 42$

3 Factorise each of the following.

   a $x^2 - 8x + 12$ **b** $x^2 - 9x + 20$ **c** $x^2 - 7x + 12$ **d** $x^2 - 6x + 8$
   e $x^2 - 12x + 32$ **f** $x^2 - 14x + 49$ **g** $x^2 - 8x - 20$ **h** $x^2 - 7x - 18$
   i $x^2 - 4x - 32$ **j** $x^2 + x - 6$ **k** $x^2 + 8x - 33$ **l** $x^2 + 10x - 24$

4 Factorise fully.

   a $2x^2 + 6x + 4$ **b** $6x^2 - 24x + 18$ **c** $5x^2 - 5x - 10$
   d $2x^2 + 14x + 20$ **e** $2x^2 + 4x - 6$ **f** $3x^2 - 30x - 33$

The difference of two squares

Earlier you saw that multiplying out binomials in the form $(a + b)(a - b)$ gives a product that is the difference of two squares.

$$(a - b)(a + b) = a^2 + ab - ab - b^2$$
$$= a^2 - b^2 \text{ (simplifying)}$$

When you are asked to factorise a quadratic of the form $a^2 - b^2$, you can apply what you know about the difference of two squares to find the factors.

> **Tip**
>
> You can also think of factorising a difference of squares as taking the square root of each term and writing these in brackets, one with a negative sign and one with a positive sign. The order in which you write down the brackets doesn't matter.
> $(a - b)(a + b) = (a + b)(a - b)$

WORKED EXAMPLE 6

Factorise: **a** $x^2 - 4$ **b** $x^2 - 36$ **c** $4a^2 - 9$ **d** $100 - y^2$

a $x^2 - 4 = x^2 - (2)^2$ Express both terms as squares.

          $= (x + 2)(x - 2)$ Apply the identity: $a^2 - b^2 \equiv (a + b)(a - b)$.

b $x^2 - 36 = x^2 - (6)^2$
           $= (x + 6)(x - 6)$

c $4a^2 - 9 = (2a)^2 - (3)^2$
           $= (2a + 3)(2a - 3)$

d $100 - y^2 = (10)^2 - y^2$
           $= (10 + y)(10 - y)$

Find answers at: cambridge.org/ukschools/gcsemaths-studentbookanswers

Mathematically a difference of two squares such as $x^2 - 4$ is a special case of the quadratic expression $x^2 + bx + c$. Here, the coefficient of x is 0, so there is no x term ($x \times 0 = 0$) and the constant (c) is a negative number.

Using the difference of two squares in number problems

You can use the difference of two squares to subtract square numbers such as $86^2 - 14^2$ without working out the square values.

WORKED EXAMPLE 7

Solve $86^2 - 14^2$.

$86^2 - 14^2 = (86 + 14)(86 - 14)$ — Write the subtraction as the product of its factors.

$= 100 \times 72$ — Add and subtract the values in each bracket.

$= 7200$ — Find the product.

This method can also be used to find one of the shorter sides in a right-angled triangle.

Tip

You should remember Pythagoras' theorem from KS3.

The theorem says that for a right-angled triangle, the square of the length of the hypotenuse (longest side) is equal to the sum of the squares of the lengths of the other two sides.

So in the triangle below, $a^2 + b^2 = c^2$.

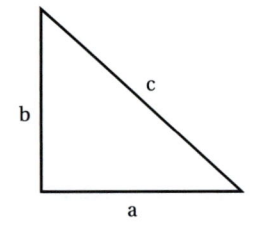

You will need to know the theorem from memory.

See Chapter 31 for more information and practice.

WORK IT OUT 7.3

In this right-angled triangle, the hypotenuse measures 13 cm and one of the shorter sides measures 5 cm.

Use the difference of squares and Pythagoras' theorem to calculate the size of the unknown length.

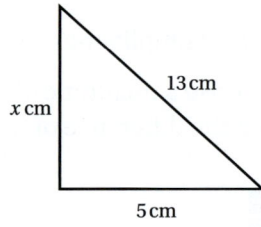

Which of these options is correct?

What mistakes are there in the other options?

Option A	Option B	Option C
$13^2 - x^2 = 5^2$	$x^2 = 13^2 - 5^2$	$x^2 = 13^2 - 5^2$
$(169 + x)(169 - x) = 25$	$x^2 = (13 + 5)(13 - 5)$	$x^2 = (13 - 5)(13 - 5)$
$169 - x^2 = 25$	$x^2 = 18 \times 8$	$x^2 = 8 \times 8$
$x^2 = 194$	$x^2 = 144$	$x^2 = 64$
$x = \sqrt{194}$	$x = \sqrt{144}$	$x^2 = \sqrt{64}$
$x = 13.9$ cm	$x = 12$ cm	$x = 8$ cm

EXERCISE 7D

1 Factorise each of the following.

  a $x^2 - 36$ **b** $p^2 - 81$ **c** $w^2 - 16$
  d $p^2 - 36q^2$ **e** $144s^2 - c^2$ **f** $64h^2 - 49g^2$

2 Using $(a - b)(a + b) = a^2 - b^2$, evaluate the following.

  a $100^2 - 97^2$ **b** $50^2 - 48^2$ **c** $639^2 - 629^2$
  d $98^2 - 45^2$ **e** $83^2 - 77^2$ **f** $1234^2 - 999^2$

3 Use the difference of two squares method to find the value of a in each triangle. Leave the answer in square root form.

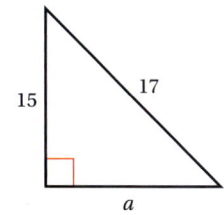

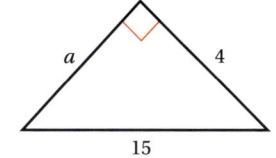

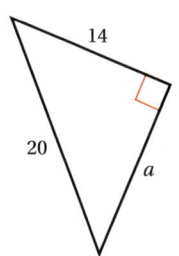

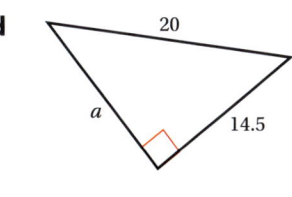

a (right triangle with sides 15, 17, and a)

b (right triangle with sides a, 4, and 15)

c (right triangle with sides 14, 20, and a)

d (right triangle with sides 20, 14.5, and a)

> **Tip**
>
> When you leave the answer in square root form you are giving the exact answer. If your answer is an irrational decimal, that is, one that does not terminate or recur, then the square root form is known as a surd. Examples of surds are $\sqrt{2}$ and $\sqrt{3}$.

Section 3: Apply your skills

For the rest of your GCSE course you will use what you have learned about expanding, simplifying and factorising algebraic expressions to work out the value of unknown quantities in different types of problems.

These skills also give you the tools to describe problems algebraically so that you can solve them efficiently.

EXERCISE 7E

Answer these questions to review what you have learned in this chapter.

1 Decide whether each statement is true or false.

  a $(x + 11)(x - 5) = x^2 + 6x - 55$

  b $x^2 + 2x + 4$ is a perfect square

  c $(a - 8)^2 = a^2 - 64$

  d $69^2 - 11^2$ can be solved by calculating $(69 + 11)(69 - 11)$

Tip

Remember:
Area of a square = side × side
Area of rectangle = length × width
Area of triangle
= $\frac{1}{2}$ × base × height

2 Write an expression for the area of each shape.

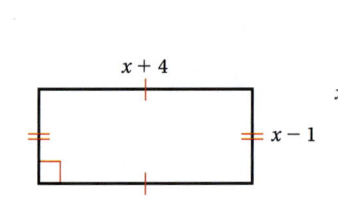

   a (square/rhombus with side $x + 3$)
   b (rectangle with length $x + 4$ and width $x - 1$)
   c (right-angled triangle with height $x - 2$ and base $2x + 6$)

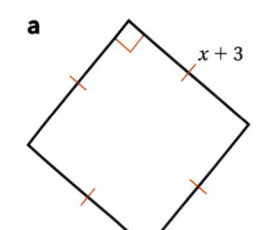

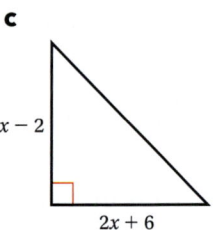

3 The cost of rubber matting for a children's play area is £19.50 per square metre.
   The rectangular play area is $(x + 4)$ metres wide and $(x + 7)$ metres long.
   a Write an expression for the area to be covered by rubber matting.
   b Write an expression for the cost of the rubber matting.
   c Given that $x = 12$, find the cost of the rubber matting.

4 A carpet fitter has a square piece of carpet with sides of x metres.
   He does the following sketches to work out how to carpet a rectangular area.

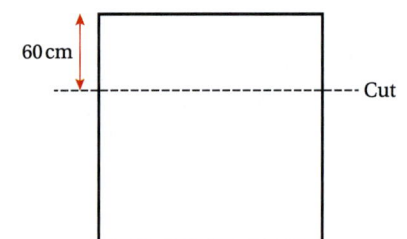

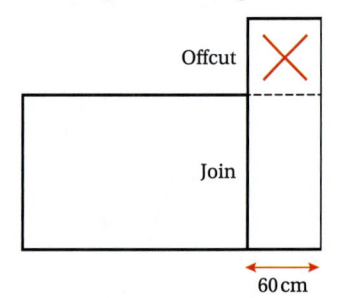

   (Diagram: square with 60 cm marked on left side with "Cut" line; rectangle with "Offcut" marked with X on top right, "Join" and 60 cm marked)

   He plans to cut a 60 cm wide strip off the square carpet and place it along the adjacent side of the square as shown in the diagram.
   The area marked with a cross will be cut off and discarded.
   a Express the length and width of the rectangular carpet in terms of x.
   b Write an expression for the area of the rectangular carpet.
   c What type of expression is this?
   d Form an expression and work out the difference in the areas of the original square carpet and the rectangular carpet.

5 The area of each rectangle and an expression for the length of one side are given.
   Find an expression for the length of each missing side.

   a Area = $8a + 12$
      (rectangle with $2a + 3$ on top, ? on left)

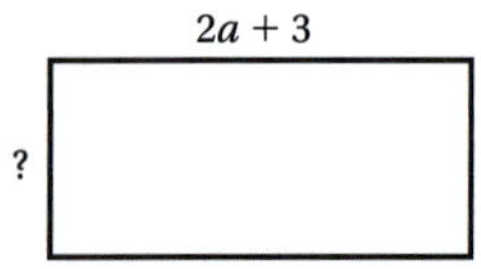

   b Area = $10mn + 15$
      (rectangle with $5n$ on top, ? on left)

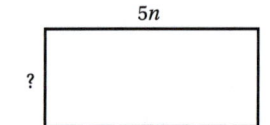

   c Area = $(2y)^2 - 49$
      (rectangle with $2y + 7$ on top, ? on left)

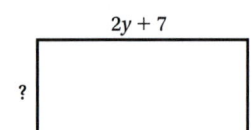

   d Area = $x^2 + x - 30$
      (rectangle with $x + 6$ on top, ? on left)

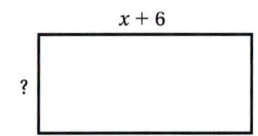

6 Fill in the blanks.

  a $(x + 5)(x + 7) = x^2 + \square x + \square$

  b $(x + \square)(x + 6) = x^2 + 9x + \square$

  c $(x + 4)(x - \square) = x^2 - 2x - \square$

  d $(2x + 3)(x + \square) = 2x^2 + 7x + \square$

  e $(\square x + \square)(2x + 5) = 4x^2 + 12x + \square$

7 Factorise these two quadratic expressions.

  a $x^2 - 11x + 24$ **b** $x^2 - 25x + 24$

  c Write another two quadratic expressions with a first term of x^2 and a constant term of 24.

8 Use $a^2 - b^2 = (a + b)(a - b)$ to evaluate $1999^2 - 1998^2$.

9 The area of a quadrilateral is expressed as $x^2 - 25$.

  a Explain why this quadrilateral cannot be a square.

  b Another quadrilateral has an area of $x^2 + 10x + 25$.
  Can it be a square? How do you know that?

Checklist of learning and understanding

Expanding two binomials

- A binomial expression is one that contains two terms.
- Expand means remove the brackets and multiply out the terms.
- A binomial product is the product of two binomial expressions, for example, $(x \times 2)(x \times 3)$.
- After you expand binomial products you simplify further by collecting any like terms.
- A binomial multiplied by itself is a perfect square.
    $(a + b)^2 \equiv a^2 + 2ab + b^2$
    $(a - b)^2 \equiv a^2 - 2ab + b^2$
- A binomial in the form of $(a - b)(a + b)$ gives a product that is a difference of two squares: $(a - b)(a + b) \equiv a^2 - b^2$.

Factorising

- Factorising is the inverse operation to expanding brackets.
- You can factorise by taking out a common factor: $6ab + 3ad \equiv 3a(2b + d)$
- You can factorise a quadratic by writing it as a product of its two binomial factors: $x^2 - x - 6 \equiv (x + 2)(x - 3)$
- The rules for multiplying positive and negative signs are important when you factorise quadratics.

Find answers at: cambridge.org/ukschools/gcsemaths-studentbookanswers

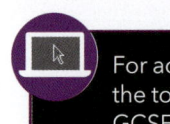

For additional questions on the topics in this chapter, visit GCSE Mathematics Online.

Chapter review

1 Expand and simplify by collecting like terms.

a $(x-2)^2 + (x-4)^2$

b $(x-2)^2 + (x+2)^2$

Tip

Expand and simplify each bracket first and then simplify by collecting like terms.

2 Fill in the blanks.

a $(x+3)(x-\square) = x^2 - 2x - \square$

b $(x+3)(x+\square) = x^2 + 10x + \square$

c $(x+2)(x-\square) = x^2 - x - \square$

d $(x+6)(\square + \square) = x^2 + 11x + 30$

e $(x+4)(\square + \square) = x^2 + 10x + 24$

3 a Factorise $6x + 8$. *(1 mark)*

b Work out the value of $x^2 - 9$ when

  i $x = 5$ *(1 mark)*

  ii $x = {}^-4$ *(1 mark)*

c Factorise $x^2 - 9$ *(1 mark)*

© OCR 2013

4 A rectangular field has an area of $x^2 - 4x - 5$ metres.

a Express the length and breadth of the field in terms of x.

b Write an expression in simplest terms for the perimeter of the field.

5 Use the difference between two squares to simplify the expression $(x+8)^2 - (x-8)^2$.

6 Write an expression in its simplest form for the area of the shaded part of this rectangle.

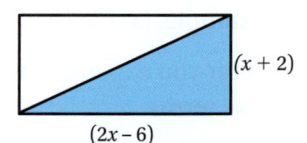

$(x+2)$, $(2x-6)$

7 The sides of a triangle are $(x+8)$ cm, $(x+6)$ cm and $(x-1)$ cm.

If the square of the longest side is equal to the sum of the squares of the other two sides, the triangle is right-angled.

a Which is the longest side in this triangle? How do you know that?

b What is the square of the longest side?

c Find the sum of the squares of the other two sides.

d $x = 9$.

Is this triangle right-angled?

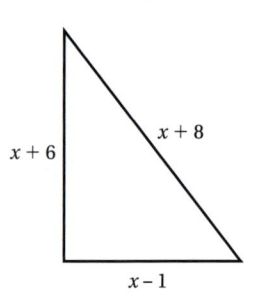

In this chapter you will learn how to …

- solve linear equations and apply them in context.
- solve quadratic equations.
- set up and solve simultaneous equations.
- use graphs to find approximate solutions to equations.

For more resources relating to this chapter, visit GCSE Mathematics Online.

Using mathematics: real-life applications

Accounting involves a great deal of mathematics. Accountants set up computer spreadsheets to calculate and analyse data. Programs such as Microsoft Excel® work by applying different equations to values in columns or cells, so you need to know what equations or formulae to use to get the results you need.

"Although the computer does the actual calculations, I have to insert different equations to tell it what operations to perform and in which order to perform them." *(Accountant)*

Before you start …

Ch 3	Check you can write an equation to represent a problem mathematically.	**1** Which of the equations below correctly represent this problem? "I think of a number, multiply it by 6 and add 1. The answer is 37. What is my number?" A $6x + 1 = 37$ B $y \times 6 = 37 + 1$ C $6a = 37$ D $6(x + 1) - 37 = 0$
Ch 1	You should be able to recognise and apply inverse operations.	**2** Complete the following statements. a $7 + \square = 0$ b $\square - 8 = 0$ c $^-4a + \square = 0$ d $5 \times \square = 1$ e $\frac{1}{6} \times \square = 1$ f $\square \times 12x = x$
Ch 7	You need to know how to factorise quadratic expressions.	**3** Match each expression to its factors. a $x^2 - 5x + 6$ b $x^2 + 3x$ c $x^2 - 25$ d $x^2 - 5$ A $x(x + 3)$ B $(x + 5)(x - 5)$ C $(x - 2)(x - 3)$ D $(x + \sqrt{5})(x - \sqrt{5})$

Find answers at: cambridge.org/ukschools/gcsemaths-studentbookanswers

103

GCSE Mathematics for OCR (Foundation)

Assess your starting point using the Launchpad

STEP 1

1 Match each equation to its solution.

Equations
a $x + 7 = 19$
b $x - 6 = 11$
c $2x + 5 = 7$
d $8x = {}^-24$
e $2 - 3x = 8$

Solutions
A $x = 1$ B $x = 17$ C $x = {}^-2$ D $x = 12$ E $x = {}^-3$

f How can you check whether a solution is correct?

2 Solve.
a $9a - 7 = 7a + 3$
b $3(x + 5) = 2(x + 6)$

3 When 16 is added to twice Jack's age, the answer is 44. Write an equation and solve it to find Jack's age.

GO TO
Section 1:
Linear equations

STEP 2

4 If $x^2 - 2x - 3 = 0$, which pair of values is the solution?
A $x = 3$ or $x = {}^-1$
B $x = {}^-3$ or $x = 1$.

5 What are the possible values of x given that $x^2 - 16 = 0$?

GO TO
Section 2:
Quadratic equations

STEP 3

6 a How many whole number solutions can you find for $x + y = 6$?
b Which of those solutions are correct if $x + y = 6$ and $x - y = 2$?

GO TO
Section 3:
Simultaneous equations

GO TO
Step 4:
The Launchpad continues on the next page …

Launchpad continued ...

STEP 4

7 A company hires out meeting rooms.

The total cost (*y*) can be worked out using the equation
$y = 15x + 40$, where *x* represents the number of hours the room is hired for. The graph of this equation is the straight line shown here.

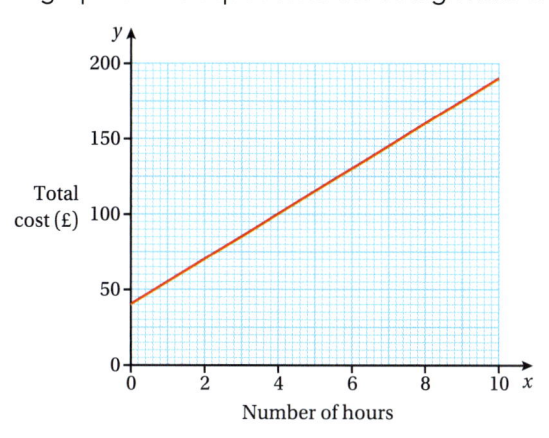

a Use the graph to find cost of hiring a meeting room for 4 hours.
b What is the value of *x* when *y* is 175?
c What is the value of *y* when *x* is 5?

GO TO
Section 4:
Using graphs to solve equations

GO TO
Section 5:
Using equations and their graphs

Section 1: Linear equations

An equation is a mathematical statement that contains an equal sign. For example:

$3 + 2 = 5$ $3 + x = 5$ $3 + 2 = x$ $2x + 3 = 6$

The unknown value is called a **variable** and can be represented by any letter but *x* and *y* are used most often.

The same letter can represent different values in different equations.

For example, in the equation $x + 1 = 4$, the value of *x* is 3, but in the equation $x + 2 = 3$, the value of *x* is 1.

If the highest power of the unknown is 1, and there are no negative or fractional powers, the equation is a **linear equation**.

Solving an equation means finding the value of the unknown letter.

In simple equations like $x + 3 = 7$ you can solve for *x* by inspection.

Key vocabulary

variable: a letter representing an unknown number.

linear equation: an equation where the highest power of the unknown is 1, for example $x + 3 = 7$.

In more complex equations you can find the solution by carrying out inverse operations on both sides of the equation.

Worked example 1 shows how an equation can be changed without altering the solution (the value of x) if you carry out the same operation on both sides.

> **WORKED EXAMPLE 1**
>
> Let $x = 3$. Write an equivalent equation.
>
> | Add 5 | $x + 5 = 3 + 5$ | To keep the equation balanced, do the operation on both sides. |
> |---|---|---|
> | Now | $x + 5 = 8$ | |
> | Subtract 1 | $x + 5 - 1 = 8 - 1$ | |
> | Now | $x + 4 = 7$ | |
> | Multiply by 2 | $2(x + 4) = 2(7)$ | |
> | Now | $2x + 8 = 14$ | |
>
> Is the solution to $2x + 8 = 14$ still $x = 3$?
>
> $2(3) + 8 = 6 + 8 = 14$
>
> The left-hand side (LHS) is equal to the right-hand side (RHS) so $x = 3$
>
> Check this by substituting $x = 3$ into the left-hand side of the equation.

Look at the next example to see how you can start with $2x + 8 = 14$ and perform inverse operations to get back to the solution $x = 3$.

> **WORKED EXAMPLE 2**
>
> Solve each equation for x.   **a** $2x + 8 = 14$ **b** $2(x + 1) = 10$
>
> **a** $2x + 8 = 14$
>
> $\therefore 2x + 8 - 8 = 14 - 8$ Subtract 8 from both sides.
>
> $\therefore 2x = 6$
>
> $\therefore \dfrac{2x}{2} = \dfrac{6}{2}$ $2x$ means $2 \times x$, so divide each side by 2 to find x.
>
> $\therefore x = 3$
>
> **b** $2(x + 1) = 10$
>
> $\dfrac{2(x + 1)}{2} = \dfrac{10}{2}$ Get rid of $\times 2$ by dividing both sides by 2.
>
> $\therefore x + 1 = 5$
>
> $\therefore x = 4$ Subtract 1 from both sides.

Tip

The symbol $\therefore$ is used a lot in mathematics to save time writing. It means 'therefore'.

Tip

The examples here show each step in detail to help you understand the process of solving an equation. In your own work you might find it more efficient to combine steps or leave out some of the working.

EXERCISE 8A

1 Work with another student.

Solve each equation by inspection.

Check your answers by substitution.

- **a** $x + 11 = 8$
- **b** $x - 6 = 11$
- **c** $^-2x = 16$
- **d** $x + 7 = 29\frac{1}{2}$
- **e** $3x = {}^-24$
- **f** $6x - 21 = 3$

2 Solve each equation by writing down at least two steps.
Check your answers.

- **a** $2a - 5 = 7$
- **b** $3b + 4 = 19$
- **c** $5d - 7 = 23$
- **d** $3e - 2 = 16$
- **e** $5h + 21 = 11$
- **f** $6a + 17 = {}^-1$
- **g** $3a - 16 = {}^-31$
- **h** $4b + 12 = {}^-16$
- **i** $2t - 8 = 5$

3 Solve each equation. Try to do this without expanding the brackets.

- **a** $2(x + 3) = 8$
- **b** $3(x - 2) = 15$
- **c** $4(b - 1) = 12$
- **d** $5(p + 1) = 10$
- **e** $3(x - 3) = 18$
- **f** $2(y + 4) = 14$
- **g** $2(3x + 4) = 0$
- **h** $2(y - 3) = {}^-8$

i Explain how not expanding the brackets in these equations means you can solve them in fewer steps.

4 Consider the equation $2(x + 1) - 3(x - 2) = 6$.

a Why does it make sense to expand the brackets before solving the equation in this example?

b Expand the brackets, collect like terms on the left of the equation and then solve for x.

> **Tip**
>
> When you are asked to **check by substitution** you are being asked to substitute your answer back into the original equation to check it works. You learnt how to substitute in Chapter 3.

> **Tip**
>
> You learnt about expanding brackets in Chapter 7.

> **Tip**
>
> When you are asked to solve an equation for x you cannot give an answer in the form of $^-x = 3$ or $^-x = {}^-4$ because the solution is in terms of x not negative x. If you end up with a negative unknown, divide both sides of the equation by negative 1 to get a positive value ($- \div - = +$). Don't confuse this with $x = {}^-3$; the value of the unknown can be negative, but the variable used to represent it in an equation, for example the letter 'x', cannot be negative.

Equations with the unknown on both sides

Some equations have the unknown in expressions on both sides of the equation. In these equations you take steps to get all the terms containing the unknown onto the same side of the equation.

The expressions may also contain brackets. If that is the case, you need to expand the brackets first.

Work through the examples to see how to deal with different types of equations.

Find answers at: cambridge.org/ukschools/gcsemaths-studentbookanswers

> **Tip**
>
> Remember you can combine steps in your own working. These examples show all the steps in detail.

WORKED EXAMPLE 3

Solve for x.

a $5x - 5 = 3x + 1$ **b** $2y + 17 = 5 - 6y$ **c** $2(3x - 1) = 2(x + 1)$

a $5x - 5 = 3x + 1$

$5x - 5 - 3x = 3x + 1 - 3x$	Subtract $3x$ from each side.
$2x - 5 = 1$	Add like terms.
$2x - 5 + 5 = 1 + 5$	Add 5 to each side.
$2x = 6$	Simplify.
$x = 3$	Divide both sides by 2.

b $2y + 17 = 5 - 6y$

$2y + 17 + 6y = 5 - 6y + 6y$	Add $6y$ to both sides (this helps you get rid of negative signs).
$8y + 17 = 5$	Add like terms.
$8y + 17 - 17 = 5 - 17$	Subtract 17 from each side.
$8y = {}^-12$	Simplify.
$\dfrac{8y}{8} = \dfrac{{}^-12}{8}$	Divide both sides by 8.
$y = \dfrac{{}^-3}{2}$	Reduce the fraction to its simplest terms.

c $2(3x - 1) = 2(x + 1)$

$6x - 2 = 2x + 2$	Expand the brackets paying attention to the signs.
$6x - 2 - 2x = 2x + 2 - 2x$	Subtract $2x$ from each side.
$4x - 2 = 2$	Add like terms.
$4x - 2 + 2 = 2 + 2$	Add 2 to each side.
$4x = 4$	
$x = 1$	Divide both sides by 4.

> **Tip**
>
> **Alternatively**, you could start by dividing both sides of the equation by 2, instead of expanding the brackets. This eliminates the '2' on both sides, leaving you with the equation $3x - 1 = x + 1$.

EXERCISE 8B

1 Solve the following equations. Check each answer by substitution.

a $13x + 1 = 11x + 9$ b $5t - 4 = 3t + 6$ c $4y + 3 = 2y + 8$
d $5y + 1 = 3y + 13$ e $3y + 10 = 5y + 3$ f $12x + 1 = 7x + 11$
g $5x - 2 = 3x + 6$ h $5x + 12 = 20 - 11x$ i $8 - 8a = 9 - 9a$
j $5x + 3 = 2(x + 2)$

2 Solve these equations by expanding the brackets first.

a $2(x + 1) + 4(x + 2) = 22$ b $3(x + 1) = 2(x + 2)$
c $5(t + 3) = 3(2t + 1)$ d $7(x + 2) = 4(x + 5)$
e $4(x - 2) + 2(x + 5) = 14$ f $3(x + 1) = 2(x + 1) + 2x$
g $-2(x + 2) = 4x + 9$ h $4 + 2(2 - x) = 3 - 2(5 - x)$

3 a Try to solve these two equations.
   i $2(x + 8) - 3x = x + 16$ ii $4(3 + x) + 4x = 4(2x + 3)$

   b If an equation is true for any value of x, it is an identity.
      Which of these two equations is an identity? How do you know this?

   c Do you think there is a solution for the other equation?
      Give a reason for your answer.

Forming and solving linear equations

You can use algebra to set up and then solve your own equations.

When you set up an equation you must say what the letters stand for.

WORKED EXAMPLE 4

Write an equation to represent the following problem:
The sum of two number is 54.
If one number is 14 more than the other number, find the two numbers.

Let one of the numbers be x.	Start by giving a letter to one of the unknown values.
So the other number is $(x + 14)$	
The numbers are x and $(x + 14)$	You are told that the other number is 14 more than this
The two numbers add up to 54.	
$x + (x + 14) = 54$	
$2x + 14 = 54$	Use this information to form an equation and then solve for x.
$2x = 54 - 14$	
$2x = 40$	
$x = 20$	
$x = 20$, $\therefore x + 14 = 34$	By solving the equation you have found one of the numbers (x). You still have to find the value of the other number.
The two numbers are 20 and 34.	
Check that his works $20 + 34 = 54$	
Yes, the solution is correct.	

Find answers at: cambridge.org/ukschools/gcsemaths-studentbookanswers

WORKED EXAMPLE 5

a In a triangle, the largest angle is four times the size of the smallest angle. The third angle is 24° bigger than the smallest angle.

Write an equation and solve it to find the size of each angle in this triangle.

What type of triangle is this?

b The length of a rectangle is three times its width.

If the perimeter is 24 centimetres, find the area of the rectangle.

a

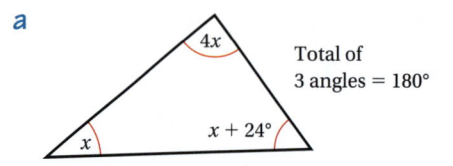

Total of 3 angles = 180° ◁ Draw a sketch and mark the angles using the information given.

Let the smallest angle be x.
The greatest angle is therefore $4x$.
The other angle is $(x + 24)$.

◁ Label the angle that the others are related to with a variable; you can then write an expression for each of the other angles.

So, $x + 4x + x + 24 = 180$
$6x = 180 - 24$
$6x = 156$
$x = 26$

◁ You know that the sum of angles in a triangle is 180°.

So $4x = 4 \times 26 = 104$.
And $x + 24 = 26 + 24 = 50$.

◁ Use the value of x to find the size of the other angles.

The angles are 26°, 50° and 104°.
The triangle is obtuse-angled.

b Let the width be x.
∴ the length is $3 \times x = 3x$.

◁ Write an expression for the length and the width.

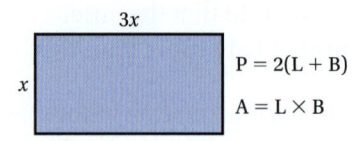

$P = 2(L + B)$
$A = L \times B$

◁ Draw a sketch and label it.

$2(x + 3x) = 24$
$x + 3x = 12$
$4x = 12$
$x = 3$

◁ You need to find the lengths of the sides so you can use them to work out the area.

The width is 3 cm, the length is $3 \times 3 = 9$ cm.
The area is $3 \times 9 = 27$ cm².

Tip

When the problem involves a shape it is useful to draw a sketch and label it to help you set up the equation.

Tip

Make sure you know what the unknown is and state what letter you are using to represent it. We tend to let x be the unknown, but you can choose any letter as long as you define it.

EXERCISE 8C

1 For each of the following, write an equation and solve it to find the unknown number.

  a Three times a certain number is 348, what is the number?
  b 7 less than a number is ⁻2, what is the number?
  c 6 greater than a number is ⁻4, what is the number?
  d Two less than four times a number is 66, what is the number?
  e Two consecutive numbers have a sum of 63, what are the numbers?
  f Three less than twice a number is ⁻2. What is the number?

2 Form an equation and solve it to answer each question.

  a When 16 is added to twice Lucy's age, the answer is 44. How old is Lucy?
  b Stephen buys 8 pens and receives 80p change from £20.00. How much does a pen cost, assuming each pen costs the same amount?
  c Multiplying a number by 2 and then adding 5 gives the same answer as subtracting the number from 23. What is the number?
  d Nick is twenty years older than his daughter. His daughter has worked out that in five years' time, she will be half her dad's age. How old is she now?

3 A square has sides of $3x$ cm.
A parallelogram has sides of $2x$ cm and $(x + 9)$ cm.

  a Write an expression for the perimeter of the square.
  b Write an expression for the perimeter of the parallelogram.
  c Given that the two quadrilaterals have the same perimeter, form an equation and solve it to find the length of one side of the square.

4 The area of this rectangle is 10 cm². Calculate the value of x and use it to find the length and width of the rectangle.

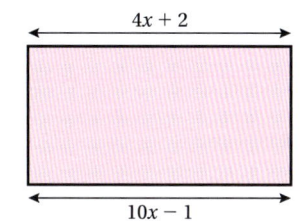

(Rectangle with width $4x + 2$ and length $10x - 1$)

Section 2: Quadratic equations

A quadratic equation has at least one term with a variable that is squared (x^2) and no variables with a power higher than 2.

Consider the simple quadratic equation $x^2 = 9$. You know that $3^2 = 9$ and that $(-3)^2 = 9$. This means that the equation $x^2 = 9$ has two possible roots (or solutions). Indeed, all square numbers can have a positive or negative root.

In a quadratic equation, because you are dealing with a squared variable, you might have two **roots**.

When you are asked to solve a quadratic equation you need to give a **solution** that contains **both** roots.

So, for the quadratic equation $x^2 = 9$:

$x = \pm\sqrt{9} = \pm 3$

So the two possible solutions to the quadratic equation are $x = 3$ or $x = -3$.

Key vocabulary

roots: of an equation are the value(s) that makes the equation true; the root of a function is the value that makes the function equal to zero.

solution: all possible roots of an equation

Tip

You learnt about functions in Chapter 4.

Find answers at: cambridge.org/ukschools/gcsemaths-studentbookanswers

You already know that the general form of a quadratic trinomial is $ax^2 + bx + c$.

The standard form of a quadratic expression with an x^2 term with a coefficient of 1 is $x^2 + bx + c$.

You can solve a quadratic equation in many ways. One way is to factorise the equation first.

Before you learn how to solve quadratic equations by factorising them, you need to consider what it means if the product of two factors is 0.

For example, if $7 \times a = 0$, then you know that $a = 0$.

Similarly, if $a \times b = 0$ then either $a = 0$ or $b = 0$ or both $a = 0$ and $b = 0$.

This means that if $(x - 1)(x - 2) = 0$ then either $(x - 1) = 0$ or $(x - 2) = 0$.

If $x - 1 = 0$, then $x = 1$.   If $x - 2 = 0$, then $x = 2$.

This zero factor principle lets you factorise the left-hand side of a quadratic equation and use the fact that one of the factors must be zero to solve it.

> **Tip**
>
> Make sure you remember these three methods of factorising quadratic expressions covered in Chapter 7:
> - taking out a common factor, e.g., $x^2 - 6x = x(x - 6)$
> - writing a trinomial as a product of binomials, e.g., $x^2 + 5x + 4 = (x + 1)(x + 4)$
> - applying the difference of two squares identity, e.g., $x^2 - 100 = (x + 10)(x - 10)$

WORKED EXAMPLE 6

Solve.

a $x^2 - 3x + 2 = 0$ **b** $x^2 - 4 = 0$ **c** $x^2 - 6x = 0$ **d** $x^2 - 8x = {-}12$

a $x^2 - 3x + 2 = 0$

$(x - 1)(x - 2) = 0$ — Factorise the left-hand side.

Either $(x - 1) = 0$ or $(x - 2) = 0$ — Apply the zero factor principle.

$x - 1 = 0$ — Solve both equations.
$\therefore x = 1$ — Add 1 to each side.

$x - 2 = 0$
$\therefore x = 2$ — Add 2 to each side.

So, $x = 1$ or $x = 2$ — State the solution.

b $x^2 - 4 = 0$

$(x + 2)(x - 2) = 0$ — Factorise using the difference of squares identity.

Either $(x + 2) = 0$ or $(x - 2) = 0$ — Apply the zero factor principle.

$x + 2 = 0$
$\therefore x = {-}2$ — Solve the equations.

$x - 2 = 0$
$\therefore x = 2$

So, $x = {-}2$ or $x = 2$ — State the solution.

Continues on next page …

c $x^2 - 6x = 0$

   $x(x - 6) = 0$ — Factorise by taking out a common factor of x.

   Either $x = 0$ or $(x - 6) = 0$ — Apply the zero factor principle.
   $x - 6 = 0$
   ∴ $x = 6$ — In this case you already have one value for x so you need only solve one equation.

   So, $x = 0$ or $x = 6$. — State the solution.

d $x^2 - 8x = -12$
   $x^2 - 8x + 12 = 0$ — Add 12 to each side to get the equation in the standard form of $x^2 + bx + c$.

   $(x - 2)(x - 6) = 0$ — Factorise the trinomial.
   $(x - 2) = 0$ or $(x - 6) = 0$ — Apply the zero factor principle.
   $x - 2 = 0$
   ∴ $x = 2$
   $x - 6 = 0$ — Solve the equations.
   ∴ $x = 6$
   So, $x = 2$ or $x = 6$. — State the solution.

After working through these examples you should be able to see a clear set of steps for solving a quadratic equation in the form of $x^2 + bx + c = 0$.

Step 1
If necessary, take all the terms to the left-hand side so the right-hand side = 0 to get the equation in the standard form, $x^2 + bx + c = 0$.

Step 2
Factorise the quadratic trinomial by either:
• checking for common factors; or
• checking for difference of squares; or
• writing trinomials as a binomial product.

Step 3
Write each factor equal to 0.
Solve the equations to find the roots.

EXERCISE 8D

1 Solve for x.
   a $x^2 - 5x = 0$
   b $x^2 - x = 0$
   c $4x^2 + 8x = 0$
   d $8x^2 - 2x = 0$
   e $5x^2 + 2x = 0$
   f $2x^2 + x = 0$

2 Solve for x.
   a $x^2 - 16 = 0$
   b $100 - x^2 = 0$
   c $x^2 - 1 = 0$
   d $9x^2 - 36 = 0$
   e $4x^2 - 1 = 0$
   f $9x^2 - 4 = 0$

3 Find the roots of each equation.
   a $x^2 + 9x + 18 = 0$
   b $x^2 - 10x + 9 = 0$
   c $x^2 + 2x - 8 = 0$
   d $x^2 - 9x + 20 = 0$
   e $x^2 - 4x - 12 = 0$
   f $x^2 + 4x - 21 = 0$

Find answers at: cambridge.org/ukschools/gcsemaths-studentbookanswers

GCSE Mathematics for OCR (Foundation)

4 Solve these equations.

a $x^2 - x = 12$
b $(x + 3)^2 = 25$
c $2x^2 + x = 0$
d $4x^2 = 3x$
e $x^2 + 4x = 5$
f $x^2 + 6x - 13 = 14$
g $3x - 18 = {}^-x^2$
h $3x^2 - 21x + 36 = 0$
i $x^2 + 8x = 20$

Forming and solving quadratic equations

As with linear equations, you can set up and solve quadratic equations.
Always define the letters you are using in your equation.

WORKED EXAMPLE 7

A number is added to its square and the result is 12.
What could the number be?

Let the number be x.   *Define the unknown values.*

$\therefore$ its square is x^2.

$x + x^2 = 12$ *Set up an equation using the information in the problem. Rearrange the equation so that it is in standard form and equal to zero.*

$\therefore x^2 + x - 12 = 0$

$\therefore (x + 4)(x - 3) = 0$ *Factorise the quadratic trinomial.*

Either $x + 4 = 0$ or $x - 3 = 0$ *Solve the equations.*

$x + 4 = 0$

$\therefore x = {}^-4$

$x - 3 = 0$

$\therefore x = 3$

The number could be 3 or $^-4$.   *State the solution **in the context of the problem**.*

Tip

If the problem involves square units then you can probably use a quadratic equation to solve it.

When you use quadratic equations to model real-life situations you might find that one of the solutions is not possible.

For example, if x is the length of the side of a box in metres, and you get the roots $x = 2.5$ or $x = {}^-1.75$ you can ignore the value of $^-1.75$ as this cannot be the length of an object. You use 2.5 as the length of the side.

WORKED EXAMPLE 8

A rectangle with an area of 28 cm² has one side 3 cm longer than the other.
How long are each of the shorter sides?

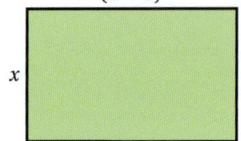

Draw a diagram and label the sides.

Let the shorter side be x.

$\therefore$ the longer side is $x + 3$.

Continues on next page …

$A = x(x + 3)$	Next form your equation. The area of a rectangle is length × breadth.
$28 = x(x + 3)$	But we are told the area is 28.
$x(x + 3) = 28$ $x^2 + 3x = 28$ $x^2 + 3x - 28 = 0$	Rearrange the equation to get a quadratic in standard form and equal to zero. Expand the brackets. Subtract 28 from each side.
$(x + 7)(x - 4) = 0$	Factorise.
Either $(x + 7) = 0$ or $(x - 4) = 0$	Apply the zero factor principle.
$x + 7 = 0$ $\therefore x = {}^-7$ $x - 4 = 0$ $\therefore x = 4$	Solve the equations.
The shorter sides are 4 cm long.	State the answer. In this problem you can ignore the $x = {}^-7$ solution because $^-7$ cm is not a possible length for the side of a rectangle.

EXERCISE 8E

1 Write an equation and solve it to find the unknown numbers.

   a The product of a certain whole number and four more than that number is 140. What could the number be?

   b The product of a certain whole number and three less than that number is 108. What could the number be?

   c When three times a number is subtracted from the square of the number the answer is $^-10$. What are possible values of the number?

   d The product of two consecutive positive even numbers is 48. What are the numbers?

2 The base of a triangle is 4 cm longer than twice its height. If the area of the triangle is 48 cm², calculate its height.

> **Tip**
>
> Remember the area of a triangle is half the length of the base × height.

3 A rectangular hall has a floor area of 210 m².

The length of the hall is 1 m more than its width.

Form an equation and solve to find the dimensions of the hall.

Section 3: Simultaneous equations

Some equations contain two unknowns. For example, $x + y = 4$.

You can suggest some values for x and y, for example, $1 + 3 = 4$ or $2 + 2 = 4$.

To find the correct solution to this equation, you need more information.

Find answers at: cambridge.org/ukschools/gcsemaths-studentbookanswers

GCSE Mathematics for OCR (Foundation)

> **Key vocabulary**
>
> **simultaneous equations**: a pair of equations with two unknowns that can be solved at the same time.

In reality, x and y could take many different values, including negative and fractional values.

If you are told that $x + y = 4$ and that $3x - y = 2$ you have a pair of equations in two unknowns that are true at the same time.

These are called **simultaneous equations**.

You can use the fact that both these equations are true to solve them at the same time (simultaneously).

Simultaneous equations are used to solve problems that involve two conditions that are met at the same time. The example below shows how this works.

WORKED EXAMPLE 9

There are 30 rose bushes in a nursery. Some are red and others are white.

There are twice as many red rose bushes as white.

How many rose bushes of each colour are there?

Let w = the number of white rose bushes,   To solve this you need to set up two equations.
r = the number of red rose bushes

$r + w = 30$ There are 30 rose bushes altogether.

$w = 2r$ The number of red bushes is twice the number of white bushes.

$r + w = 30$ You can draw up a table for each equation to show some values of r and w.

r	0	10	20	30
w	30	20	10	0

$w = 2r$

r	0	5	10	15
w	0	10	20	30

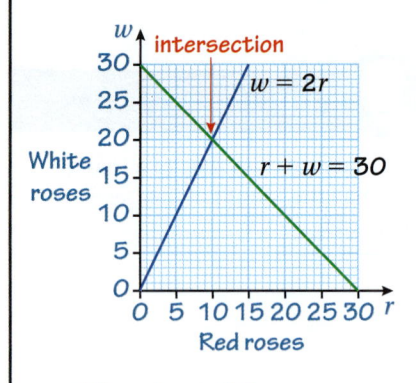

If you draw the graph of each set of values you get two lines that intersect in one place only. Where the graphs intersect, the values on the axes must be the same.

The coordinates (r, w) of the point of intersection are $(10, 20)$, so $r = 10$ and $w = 20$.

$r = 10$ and $w = 20$ This is the simultaneous solution of the two equations.

$r + w = 30$ Check by substitution in both equations.
$10 + 20 = 30$

$w = 2r$
$20 = 2(10) = 20$

You can draw graphs to solve simultaneous equations but this method takes a long time and it might not be very accurate, especially if the solution values are fractions.

There are two methods of solving simultaneous equations using algebra: substitution and elimination.

The method you choose depends on how the equations are written.

Solving simultaneous equations by substitution

In this method, you substitute the algebraic value of one of the unknowns into the other equation to solve for the other unknown. Then substitute the resulting value back into one of the equations to solve for the first unknown.

> **Tip**
>
> The substitution method is suitable when one of the equations already has x or y on its own on one side or when you can easily rearrange one of the equations to have x or y on its own.

WORKED EXAMPLE 10

Solve these simultaneous equations by substitution.

$x - 2y + 1 = 0$ and $y + 4 = 2x$

$x - 2y + 1 = 0$ (1) — Number the equations (1) and (2).
$y + 4 = 2x$ (2)

$y = 2x - 4$ (2) — Rearrange one equation so x or y is on its own; equation 2 seems simpler to rearrange.

$x - 2(2x - 4) + 1 = 0$ (3) — Substitute the value of y from equation 2 in place of y in equation (1). Label this equation (3).

$x - 2(2x - 4) + 1 = 0$ — Solve the equation 3, which now only has one unknown.
$x - 4x + 8 + 1 = 0$
$-3x + 9 = 0$
$-3x = -9$
$x = 3$

$y + 4 = 2 \times 3$ (2) — Substitute the solution into either of the original equations to find the other unknown. Substitute $x = 3$ into (2) and solve.
$y + 4 = 6$
$y = 6 - 4$
$y = 2$

So, $x = 3$ and $y = 2$ — Write out the full solution.

EXERCISE 8F

1 Solve the following pairs of simultaneous equations by substitution.

Check that your solutions are correct for **both** equations.

a $y = x - 2$
     $y = 3x + 4$

b $y = 2x + 6$
     $y = 4 - 2x$

c $y = x + 1$
     $x + y = 3$

d $y = x - 2$
     $3x + y = 14$

e $y = 2x + 1$
     $x + 2y = 12$

f $y = 1 - 2x$
     $x + y = 2$

Find answers at: cambridge.org/ukschools/gcsemaths-studentbookanswers

GCSE Mathematics for OCR (Foundation)

2 Solve these simultaneous equations.

a $x + 2y = 11$
   $2x + y = 10$

b $x - y = {}^-1$
   $2x + y = 4$

c $5x - 4y = {}^-1$
   $2x + y = 10$

d $3x - 2y = 29$
   $4x + y = 24$

e $3x + y = 6$
   $9x + 2y = 1$

f $3x - 2 = {}^-2y$
   $2x - y = {}^-8$

Solving simultaneous equations by elimination

In this method you add or subtract the equations eliminate (get rid of) one of the unknown variables.

You might need to multiply or divide one equation by a factor before you do this.

WORKED EXAMPLE 11

Solve the simultaneous equations $2x + y = 8$ and $x - y = 1$ by elimination.

$2x + y = 8$ (1)
$x - y = 1$ (2)

Number the equations (1) and (2).

(1) + (2)

$2x + y = 8$
$x - y = 1$
─────────
$3x = 9$ (3)

Decide whether you can add or subtract to eliminate a variable. (1) has a variable of y and (2) has a variable of ^-y. If you add the equations, these terms will cancel out. Label the new equation (3).

$3x = 9$
$x = 3$

Solve the combined equation (3), which now only has one unknown.

$3 - y = 1$ (2)
$^-y = 1 - 3$
$^-y = {}^-2$
$y = 2$

Substitute the solution into either of the original equations to find the other unknown. Substitute $x = 3$ into (2).

So, $x = 3$ and $y = 2$

Write out the full solution.

In some examples, you will need to subtract the equations.

Tip

Here, addition will not eliminate one of the variables, so you need to subtract.

Add if the signs are different and one variable can be eliminated.

Subtract when the signs are the same, including when they are both negative.

WORKED EXAMPLE 12

Solve the pair of simultaneous equations by elimination.

$x + 3y = 7$ (1)
$x + y = 5$ (2)

$(x + 3y) - (x + y) = 7 - 5$ Subtract (2) from (1).

$x + 3y - x - y = 2$ Remove the brackets.

$2y = 2$ Simplify.

$y = 1$ Solve for y.

$x + 1 = 5$ (2)   Substitute in equation (2).

$x = 4$ Solve.

The solutions are $x = 4$ and $y = 1$.

In the following example, x and y cannot be eliminated by either addition or subtraction. A new equation must be written. In order to use the elimination method, the coefficient of either x and y must be identical.

Sometimes two new equations are required to create a pair of x or y terms that will eliminate.

WORKED EXAMPLE 13

Solve the pair of simultaneous equations by elimination.

$2x + y = 3$ (1)
$5x - 2y = 12$ (2)
$4x + 2y = 6$ (3)   Multiply equation (1) by 2 to create equation (3).

$9x = 18$ Add (2) and (3) to eliminate y.

$x = 2$ Divide both sides by 9.

$4 + y = 3$ Substitute $x = 2$ in (1).

$y = -1$ Subtract 4 from both sides.

So $x = 2$ and $y = -1$ Check these solutions satisfy both equations (1) and (2).

Tip

In this example it is possible to solve by substitution by rewriting equation (1).
Unless a particular method is requested to solve a question, you can choose either method: substitution or elimination.

EXERCISE 8G

1 Solve the following pairs of simultaneous equations by elimination.
Check your solutions are correct for **both** equations.

- **a** $x - y = 2$
  $3x + y = 14$
- **b** $2x - 3y = 3$
  $x + 3y = 6$
- **c** $3x + y = 4$
  $2y - 3x = {}^-10$
- **d** $2x - y = 13$
  $5x + y = 13$
- **e** $x + 2y = 14$
  $4x - 2y = 14$
- **f** $^-x - y = 3$
  $x + 5y = {}^-11$
- **g** $x + y = 5$
  $3x + y = 9$
- **h** $3x + 4y = 15$
  $x + 4y = 13$
- **i** $2x - y = 7$
  $4x - y = 15$

2 Solve each pair of simultaneous equations.
Choose the most suitable method for doing this.

- **a** $2x + y = 7$
  $3x + 2y = 12$
- **b** $^-2x + 8y = 6$
  $2x = 3 - y$
- **c** $4x + 2y = 50$
  $x + 2y = 20$
- **d** $x + y = {}^-7$
  $x - y = {}^-3$
- **e** $y = 1 - 2x$
  $5x + 2y = 0$
- **f** $y = 2x - 5$
  $y = 3 - 2x$

Forming and solving simultaneous equations

Some problems can be described using a pair of simultaneous equations. Once you have defined the variables and set up the equations you can use algebra to solve them.

Tip

If a problem asks for two different pieces of information then it means there are two unknowns and you will need two equations to solve it.

Find answers at: cambridge.org/ukschools/gcsemaths-studentbookanswers

GCSE Mathematics for OCR (Foundation)

Problem-solving framework

A field contains a number of goats and chickens.
Altogether there are 60 heads and 200 legs.
How many are there of each type of animal?

Steps for approaching a problem-solving question	What you would do for this example
Step 1: Work out what you have to do. Start by reading the question carefully.	You have to find the number of goats (g) and the number of chickens (c).
Step 2: What information do you need? Have you got it all?	You need to know how many there are altogether. You're not told this, but you can work it out because each goat and each chicken must have one head. $g + c = 60$ Now you need another equation to link the goat and chickens. You've already used the number of heads, so it must be something to do with the legs. Goats have 4 legs each, so the number of goat legs is $4 \times g$. Chickens have 2 legs each, so the number of chicken legs is $2 \times c$. There are 200 legs in total so: $4g + 2c = 200$
Step 3: Decide what maths you can do.	There are two unknowns so you should use simultaneous equations.
Step 4: Set out your solution clearly. Check your working and that your answer is reasonable.	Let the number of goats = g and the number of chickens = c. $g + c = 60$ (1) $4g + 2c = 200$ (2) $g = 60 - c$ Make g the subject of equation (1). Substitute $(60 - c)$ for g in (2) and solve. $4(60 - c) + 2c = 200$ $240 - 4c + 2c = 200$ $240 - 2c = 200$ $240 - 200 = 2c$ $40 = 2c$ $20 = c$ Substitute $c = 20$ into equation (1) to find g. $g + 20 = 60$ so $g = 40$ Check your result by substituting c and g into original equation (2). $4(40) + 2(20) = 200$ $160 + 40 = 200$ Yes, this works.
Step 5: Check that you've answered the question.	There are 20 chickens and 40 goats.

EXERCISE 8H

1. The sum of two numbers, a and b, is 120.
   When b is subtracted from $3a$, the result is 160. Find the value of a and b.

2. Two numbers have a sum of 76 and a difference of 48. What are the numbers?

3. A taxi company charges a flat fee plus an amount per mile.
   A journey of 10 miles costs £7 and a journey of 15 miles costs £9.
   What would you pay for a journey of 8 miles?

4. Josh and Sanjita both spent £2.20 on sweets.
   Josh bought five fizzers and four toffees.
   Sanjita bought two fizzers and six toffees.
   Work out the cost of each type of sweet.

5. Sam got eighteen 5p and 10p coins totalling £1.65 as change when he went to the shop. How many of each coin did he get?

6. Two children have a total of 264 stickers between them.
   One child has 6 fewer stickers than 5 times the other child's stickers.
   How many do they each have?

Section 4: Using graphs to solve equations

If you have a graph you can use it to solve an equation or to answer questions based on the equations.

WORKED EXAMPLE 14

This is the graph of the linear equation $4x + y = 2$.

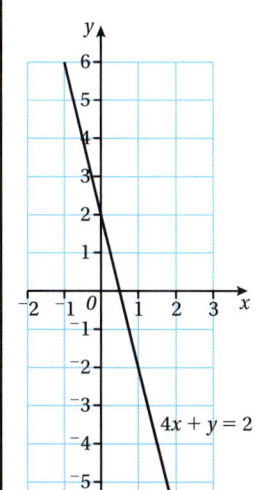

a Use the graph to estimate the value of y when:

   i $x = 0$.

   ii $x = 1$.

   iii $x = 2$.

b What is the value of x when $y = {}^-4$?

Continues on next page …

Find answers at: cambridge.org/ukschools/gcsemaths-studentbookanswers

GCSE Mathematics for OCR (Foundation)

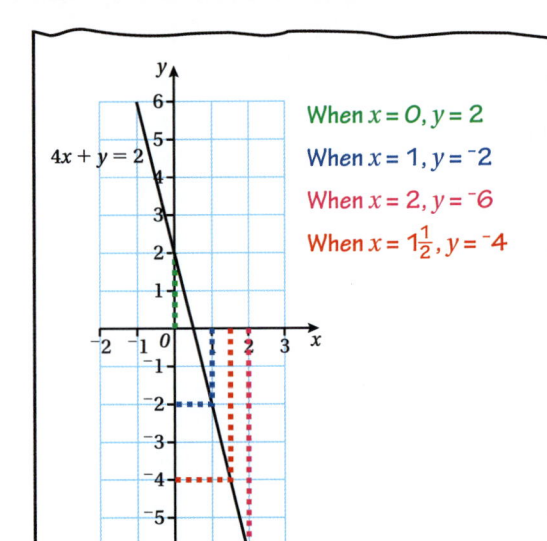

$4x + y = 2$

When $x = 0$, $y = 2$
When $x = 1$, $y = -2$
When $x = 2$, $y = -6$
When $x = 1\frac{1}{2}$, $y = -4$

Each point on the graph represents a value of x and y that work in this equation.

To find the solutions for different values of x or y, you need to use the value you have been given as one of the coordinates of a point. If you take a line from this point to the graph you can estimate the value of the other coordinate.

Key vocabulary

parabola: the symmetrical curve produced by the graph of a quadratic function.

If there are two equations, you need two graphs. In Section 3 you used a pair of graphs to find the solution to a pair of simultaneous equations. If the equation is a quadratic, the graph will be a curve called a **parabola**. You can use the graph to find the solution of the equation; it is where $y = 0$, that is, where the curve cuts the x-axis.

Tip

You will work with graphs and equations again in Chapters 18 and 19.

EXERCISE 8I

1. This graph represents the distance travelled by a cyclist over time.

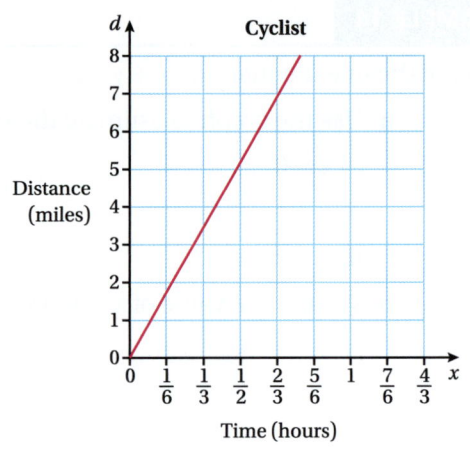

   a Use the graph to estimate how far the cyclist has travelled after 30 minutes.

   b How long did it take the cyclist to cover a distance of 8 miles?

   c The equation $s = \dfrac{d}{t}$ can be used to work out the speed (s) of the cyclist.

   Use values for d (distance) and t (time) from the graph to estimate the speed at which this cyclist was travelling.

2 This graph shows the distance covered over time by a motorist in a car.

  a Estimate how long it took the driver to travel 70 km.

  b How far did the driver travel in the first 20 minutes?

  c By using two points on the graph, estimate the speed at which the driver was travelling.

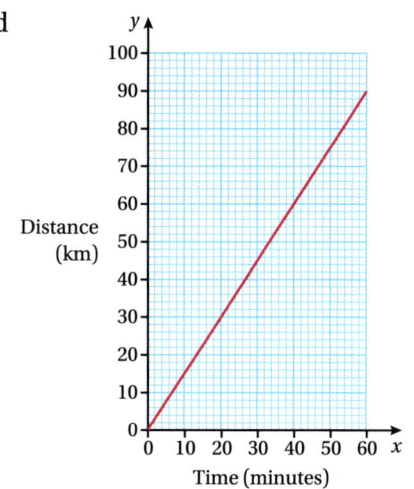

3 Use this graph of the equation $y = 3x - 2$ to estimate the value of y for the following values.

  a $x = 0$ **b** $x = 1$ **c** $x = 2$

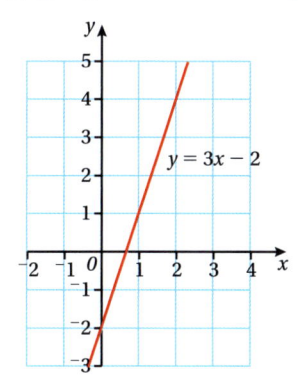

4 This graph shows how water drains from a tank at a constant rate.

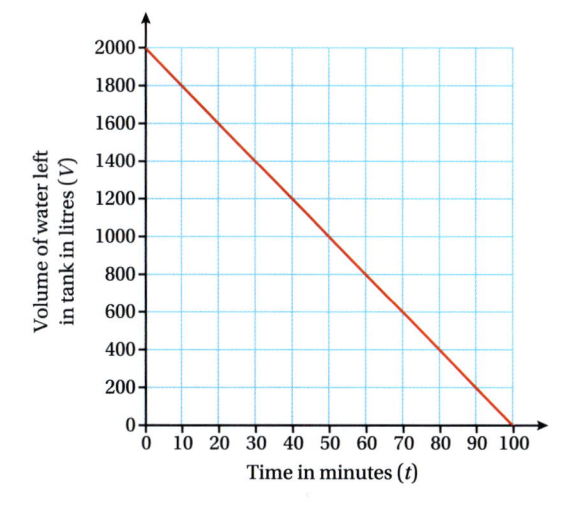

  a How much water was in the tank to start with?

  b How long did it take for the tank to empty?

  c Zena says the equation for this graph is $y = 2000 - 20x$ and Leane says it is $y + 20x = 2000$.

  Show using different points from the graph that they are both correct.

Find answers at: cambridge.org/ukschools/gcsemaths-studentbookanswers

123

5 This graph shows the cost of producing goods and how much money is earned from sales (revenue).

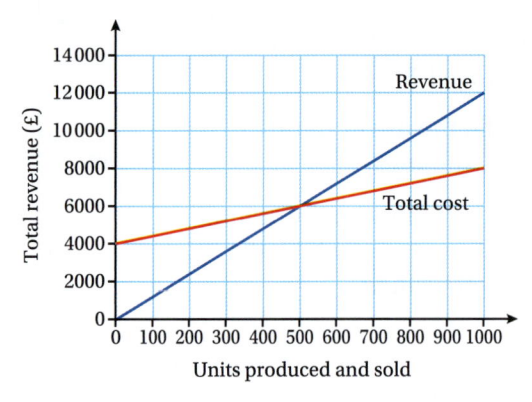

a Use the graph to estimate the point at which the costs and revenue are equal.

b The point at which costs and revenue are equal is called the break even point.

How does knowing this help a business owner?

6 This diagram show the graphs of two linear equations $y = 2x$ and $y = {}^-2x + 8$.

Use the graph to find the solution to the two equations.

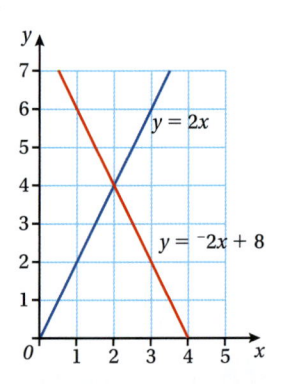

7 This graph of a quadratic equation models a stunt rider's path in the air as he does a jump.

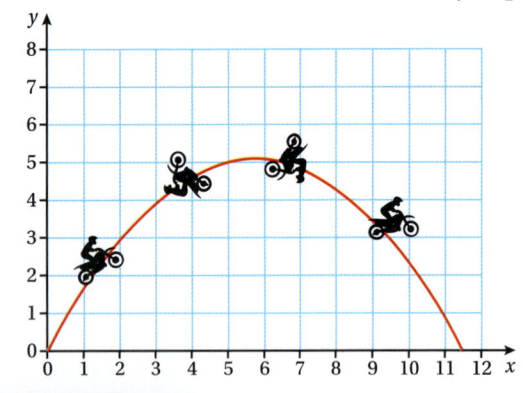

Tip

The solution of a quadratic function is the value of x when $y = 0$. On a graph, these values are found where the graph intersects the x-axis.

a What do you think the axes represent in this case?

b What values on the horizontal axis represent the rider taking off and landing again?

c Why are these two values useful in terms of the equation?

d Use the graph to estimate the coordinates of the maximum height reached during this jump.

8 The graphs of two quadratic equations are given here.

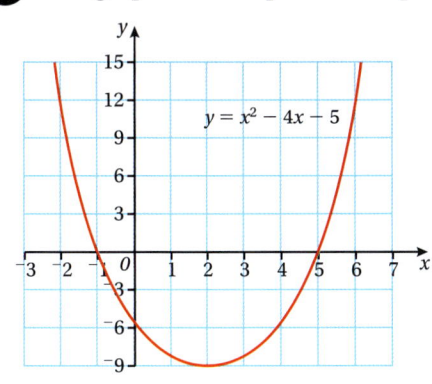

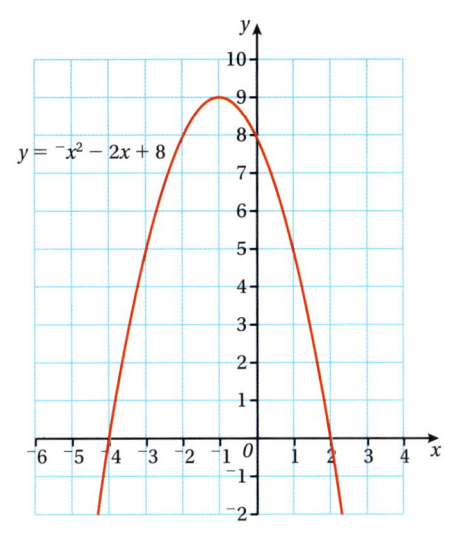

Use the graphs to estimate the roots of each equation.
Check your solutions by substitution.

9 This is the graph of a quadratic equation but the equation is not given.

Explain how you can use the graph to find the roots of the equation even though you don't know what the equation is.

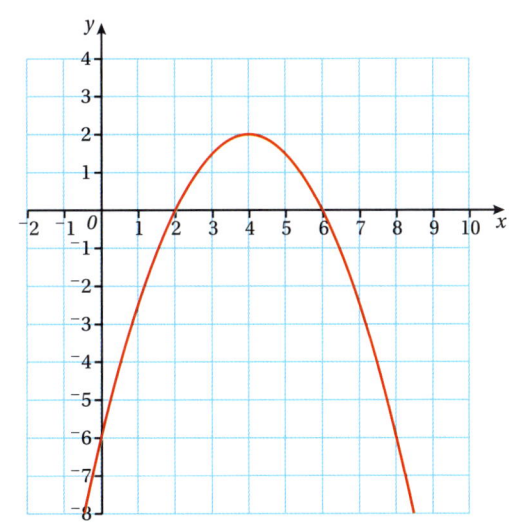

Section 5: Using equations and their graphs

In this chapter you have learnt how to solve linear, quadratic and simultaneous equations using algebraic and graphical methods.

You have also learnt how to form your own equations and use them to solve word problems in different contexts.

In this section you are going to work through a mixed exercise to practise and apply your skills.

EXERCISE 8J

1 Read each statement and decide whether it is true or false.
If it is false, explain why.

  a $5(x - 2) = 15$ so $x = 2$.

  b The statement 'four is subtracted from a number x which has been multiplied by 5 and this is equal to the number x subtracted from 14' can be represented as $5x - 4 = 14 - x$.

Find answers at: cambridge.org/ukschools/gcsemaths-studentbookanswers

c The two solutions to the quadratic equation $x^2 - 2x - 15 = 0$ are $x = 3$ and $x = {^-5}$.

d $x = 2$ and $y = 1$ are the simultaneous solutions to the pair of equations $y = x + 4$ and $y = 2x + 3$.

e This graph represents a quadratic equation whose roots are $x = 1$ and $x = {^-2}$.

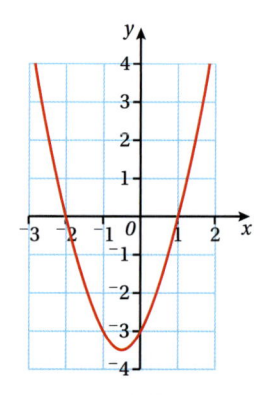

2 Solve.

a $4a = 36$

b $3x + 19 = 46$

c $4(2x - 3) = 84$

d $2x + 7 = x + 9$

3 A rectangular floor has a width 8 m shorter than its length and a perimeter of 80 m.

Find the length and width of the room by writing a linear equation and solving it.

4 Factorise and solve these quadratic equations.

a $x^2 - 7x + 12 = 0$

b $x^2 + 18x + 81 = 0$

c $x^2 - 64 = 0$

d $x^2 - 1 = 0$

e $x^2 + 7x = 0$

f $x^2 + 3x = 18$

5 Solve each pair of simultaneous equations by substitution.

a $y = 3x - 5$
$y = 6x - 11$

b $y = 2x - 3$
$y = 3x - 5$

c $x = 2y - 1$
$2x + y = 11$

6 Solve the following simultaneous equations by elimination.

a $x + y = 2$
$3x - y = 10$

b $2x + y = 5$
$x + y = 2$

c $2x - 3y = 1$
$3x + 3y = 9$

7 The difference between two numbers is 5.
The sum of three times one number and two times the other is 25.
Find the two numbers.

8 A line of best fit has been drawn through this data to create a linear graph that plots BMI (Body Mass Index) against mass in pounds (lb) for a specific group of people.

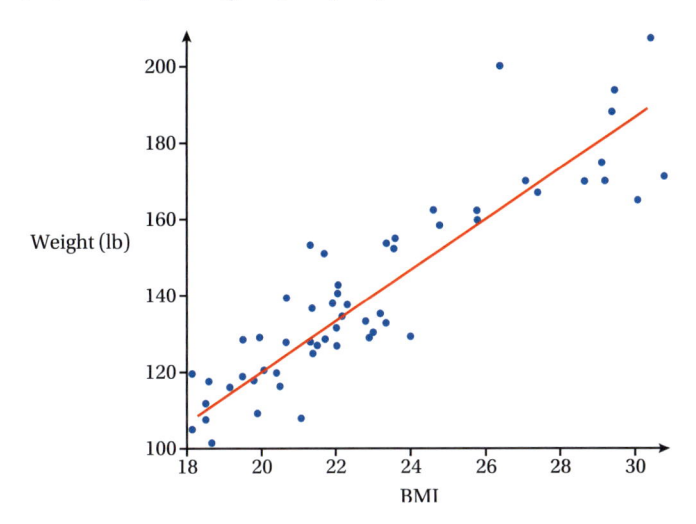

a Use the graph to estimate the mass of a person whose BMI is 24.5.

b Estimate the BMI of a person who weighs 165 lb.

c Given that 1 kilogram is equivalent to 2.2 pounds, find the BMI of a person with a mass of 55 kg.

9 Samuel is going to study in the USA and he needs to buy a data package for his mobile so he can text home.

This graph shows the costs of three different options.

The number of text messages is shown on the *x*-axis and the related costs are shown on the *y*-axis in dollars.

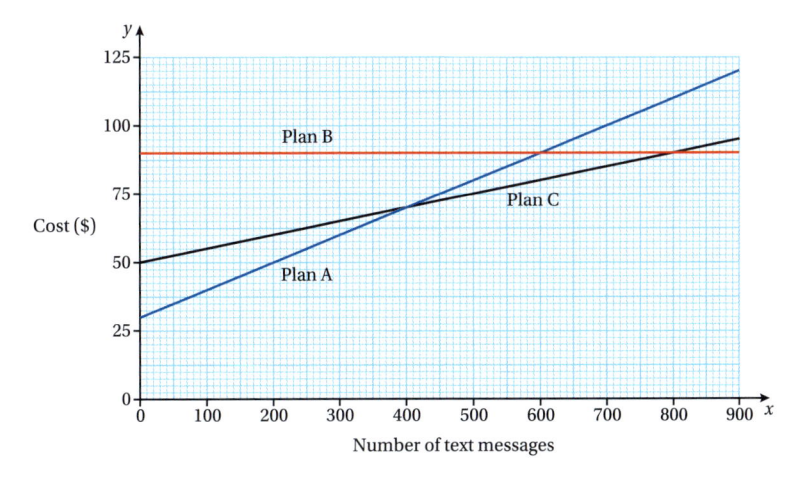

a Which plan represents a set monthly fee? How do you know?

b Use the graph to estimate the point at which Plan C and Plan A cost the same.

c What is the maximum number of texts you can send on Plan C before it begins to cost more than plan B?

d Which plan is best for Samuel if he sends more than 800 texts per month? Why?

Find answers at: cambridge.org/ukschools/gcsemaths-studentbookanswers

10 This diagram shows the graphs of two quadratic equations, $y = x^2 - 4x + 4$ and $y = {}^-x^2 - 3x - 3$.

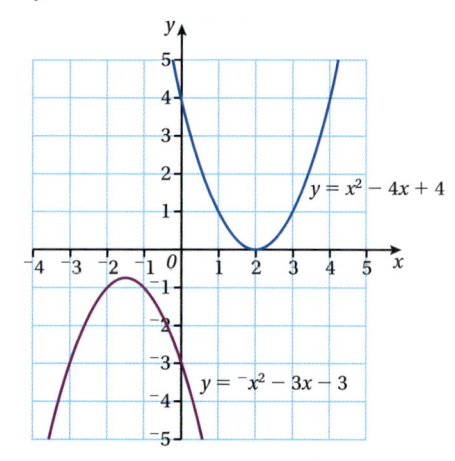

a What value does the graph give for the solution to $x^2 - 4x + 4 = 0$?

b Why is there only one root to this equation?

c Verify that there is only one root by factorising the equation $x^2 - 4x + 4 = 0$.

d Look at the graph of the equation $y = {}^-x^2 - 3x - 3$.

What do you think will happen if you try to find the roots of this equation? Why?

Checklist of learning and understanding

Linear and quadratic equations

- A linear equation has one unknown and will have one unique value as a solution.
- A quadratic equation has a square as the highest power for the variable.
- Quadratic equations in the form of $x^2 + bx + c = 0$ can be solved by factorising.
- Quadratic equations have a maximum of two roots. Sometimes there is only one because the values are the same and sometimes there is only one because one value doesn't work in a particular context.

Simultaneous equations

- Simultaneous equations are a pair of equations with two unknowns that have solutions that satisfy both equations.
- Simultaneous equations can be solved graphically using the point of intersection, or algebraically by substitution or by elimination.

Graphs and problems

- Equations are useful for setting up problems mathematically.
- You can find or estimate the solutions of equations using graphs.
- You need two graphs to solve simultaneous equations. The solution is the point of intersection of the graphs.
- The solution of a quadratic equation is where the curve cuts the x-axis, that is, where $y = 0$.

Chapter review

1 Solve for x.

a $8x + 5 = 3(2x - 11)$
b $x^2 = 8 - 2x$
c $4(x + 2) = 3(x + 1)$
d $-x^2 = 8x + 12$
e $(x + 2)^2 = 36$
f $(x + 4)(x + 3) = 6$

2 Study this graph.

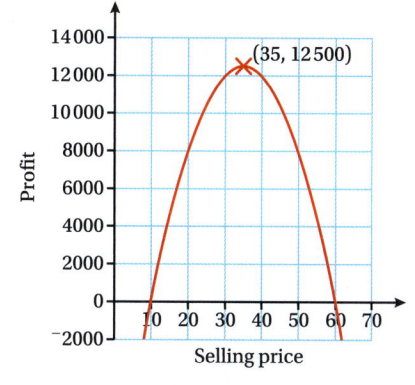

a What are the roots of the quadratic equation modelled by this graph?
b What does the graph tell you about the selling price?

3 Is $y = x + 2$ equivalent to $5y = 5x + 10$?

How can you tell this without solving the equations?

4 a What happens when you try to solve this pair of equations?

$x + y = 2$
$x + y = 4$

b What would their linear graphs show?

5 If you drew the graph of $y = x^2 + 2x - 15$ where would the curve cut the x-axis?

6 The sum of two numbers is 19 and their difference is 5.

a Write a set of equations in terms of x and y to show this.
b Solve the equations simultaneously to find the two numbers.

9 Angles

In this chapter you will learn how to ...
- apply basic angle facts to find unknown angles.
- use the angles associated with parallel lines to find unknown angles in a range of diagrams.
- prove that the sum of angles in a triangle is 180°.
- use known angle facts to find the sum of exterior and interior angles of polygons.
- use angle facts and properties of shapes to justify and prove results.

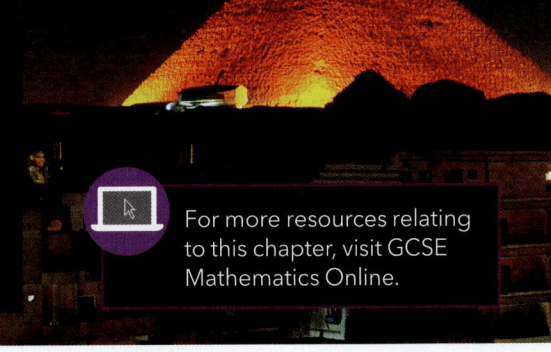

For more resources relating to this chapter, visit GCSE Mathematics Online.

Using mathematics: real-life applications

People who work in many different jobs rely on an understanding of angles and spatial relationships in their daily work. These include designers, architects, opticians and tree surgeons among others.

"I had to work quite carefully with the 360 degrees around the centre to place each of the 32 pods correctly on the London Eye." (Structural engineer)

Before you start ...

Ch 1	You should be able to use inverse operations to make 180 and 360.	① Copy and complete. a 180 − 96 = ☐ b 180 − ☐ = 116 c 173 + ☐ = 360 d 360 − 55 − 97 = ☐
Ch 5	You need to know and apply the basic properties of triangles and quadrilaterals.	② Use the marked properties to name each polygon as accurately as possible. a, b, c diagrams with 45° angles, rhombus, and quadrilateral with angles x and y. ③ What can you say about angles x and y in figure **c**? Why?
Ch 6	You need to know how to use a protractor to measure angles.	④ Measure the following angles. a, b

130

Assess your starting point using the Launchpad

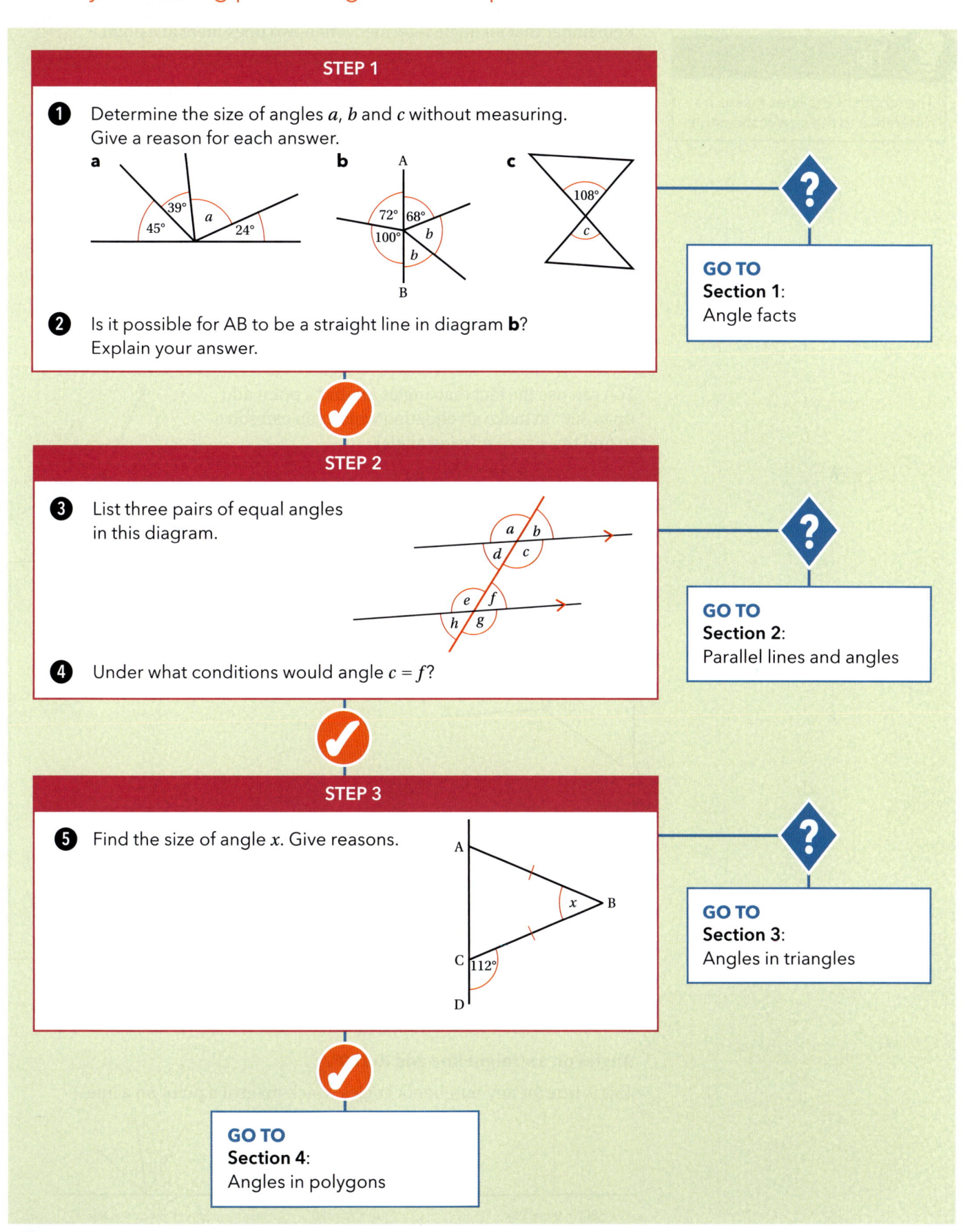

STEP 1

1 Determine the size of angles a, b and c without measuring. Give a reason for each answer.

a (angles 39°, 45°, a, 24° on a straight line)

b (angles around a point: 72°, 68°, b, 100°, b; points A at top, B at bottom)

c (108° and c in bowtie/vertical angles figure)

GO TO Section 1: Angle facts

2 Is it possible for AB to be a straight line in diagram **b**? Explain your answer.

STEP 2

3 List three pairs of equal angles in this diagram.

(Two parallel lines cut by a transversal, with angles a, b, d, c at upper intersection and e, f, h, g at lower intersection.)

GO TO Section 2: Parallel lines and angles

4 Under what conditions would angle $c = f$?

STEP 3

5 Find the size of angle x. Give reasons.

(Isosceles triangle with vertex at B, equal sides AB and CB, point D below C on line, angle at C (below, 112°) given, angle x at B.)

GO TO Section 3: Angles in triangles

GO TO Section 4: Angles in polygons

Find answers at: cambridge.org/ukschools/gcsemaths-studentbookanswers

GCSE Mathematics for OCR (Foundation)

Section 1: Angle facts

Remember that an angle is formed when two lines meet at a point.

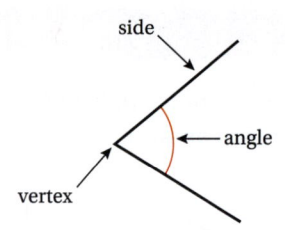

> **Tip**
> The length of the lines makes no difference to the size of the angle.

Angles around a point

The sum of angles around a point is 360°.

A 90° angle is one quarter turn, two 90° angles are half a turn and so on.

There are four quarter turns around a point: 4 × 90° = 360°.

You can use the fact that angles around a point add up to 360° to make an equation which you can solve to find the size of missing angles.

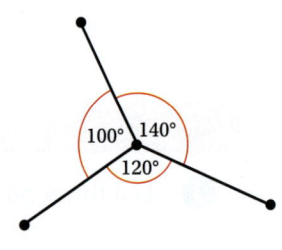

WORKED EXAMPLE 1

Find the size of x.

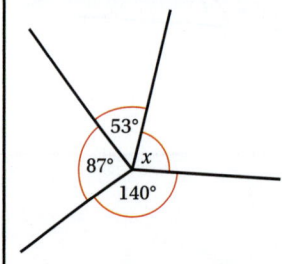

$87° + 53° + x + 140° = 360°$

$x = 360° - 140° - 53° - 87°$

(Angles round a point.)

$= 360° - 280°$

$= 80°$

When you use an angle rule to calculate a value, you **must** state the rule you have used alongside the equation in which you have used it.

Angles on a straight line

Angles on a straight line add to 180°.

This is true for any number of angles which meet at a point on a line.

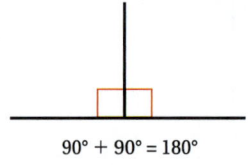

90° + 90° = 180° 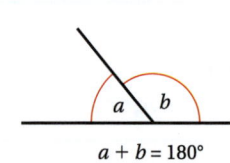 $a + b = 180°$ 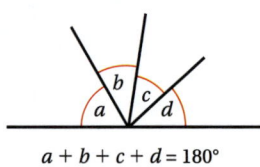 $a + b + c + d = 180°$

You can use the fact that the angles on a line add up to 180° to write and solve equations to find missing angles.

> **WORKED EXAMPLE 2**
>
> Determine the size of x. 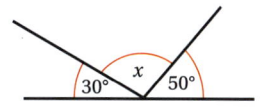
>
> $x = 180° - 30° - 50°$ (Angles on a line.)
>
> $\quad = 100°$

Vertically opposite angles

When two lines cross, or intersect, they form four angles.

The angles a and b are vertically opposite each other and the angles x and y are vertically opposite each other.

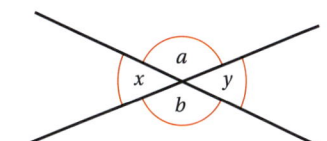

Vertically opposite angles are equal.

$a = b$

$x = y$

Key vocabulary

vertically opposite angles: angles that are opposite one another at an intersection of two lines. Vertical here means 'of the same vertex or point', not up and down.

You need to know these angle facts:

- Angles around a point add up to 360°.
- Angles on a straight line add up to 180°.
- Vertically opposite angles are equal.

EXERCISE 9A

1. Calculate the size of the missing angles.

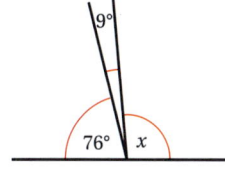

   a (42°, 130°, x)

   b (x, 40°, 33°, 87°)

   c (9°, 76°, x)

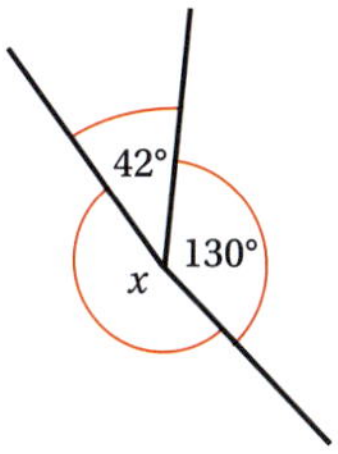

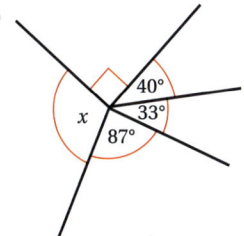

   d What type of angle is x in each case?

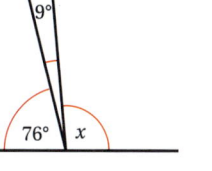

Tip

Angles can be acute (less than 90°), obtuse (between 90° and 180°) or reflex (between 180° and 360°). A right angle is exactly 90°. An angle of 180° is a straight line.

2. Find the marked angles in each diagram. Give reasons for any deductions you make.

   a Find x and y.

   (10°, 41°, x, y)

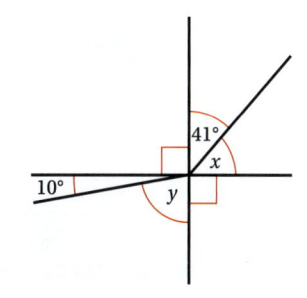

Find answers at: cambridge.org/ukschools/gcsemaths-studentbookanswers

b Find x.

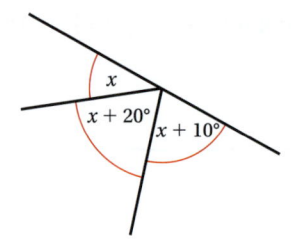

c Find p.

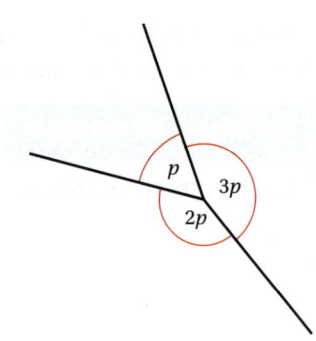

3 Explain why AE cannot be a straight line.

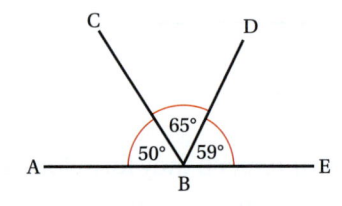

4 Calculate the size of the marked angles in each figure.

The lines are straight lines but the diagrams are not to scale.

Show your working and give reasons for any deductions you make.

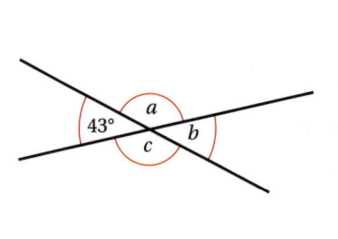

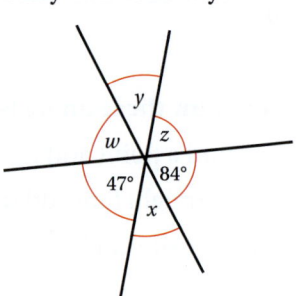

5 Given that $x = 50°$ find the size of angle z.

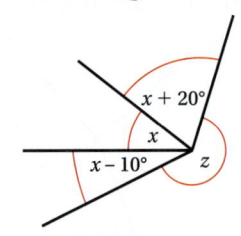

"When I'm designing and making clothes I need to be able to cut on the bias (at a given angle) and also bisect angles to add darts and fit sleeves." (Fashion designer)

Section 2: Parallel lines and angles

A line intersecting two or more parallel lines is called a **transversal**.

When a transversal intersects with parallel lines, it creates pairs of angles. These angle pairs have particular properties.

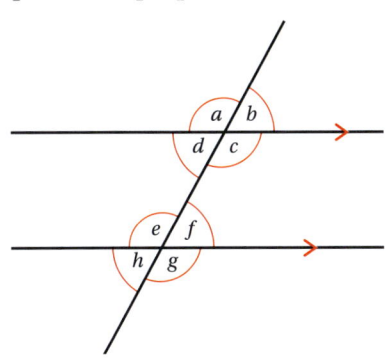

> **Key vocabulary**
>
> **transversal:** a straight line that crosses a pair of parallel lines.

Vertically opposite angles are equal, so

$a = c$ $\qquad$ $b = d$ $\qquad$ $e = g$ $\qquad$ $f = h$

Angles on a straight line add to 180° so

$a + d = 180°$ $\qquad$ $b + c = 180°$ $\qquad$ $a + b = 180°$ $\qquad$ $c + d = 180°$

Corresponding angles

Corresponding angles formed between a transversal and each parallel line are equal.

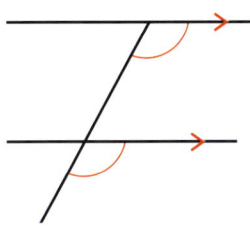

> **Key vocabulary**
>
> **corresponding angles:** angles that are created at the same point of the intersection when a transversal crosses a pair of parallel lines.

When a transversal crosses two parallel lines, there are four pairs of corresponding angles.

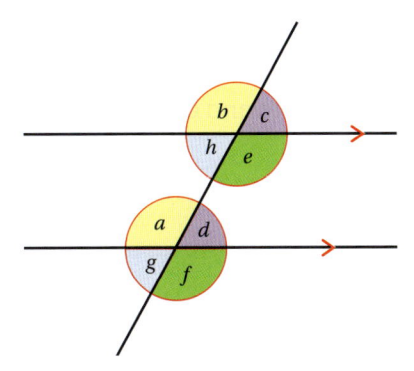

The corresponding angle pairs are:

$a = b$ $\qquad$ $c = d$ $\qquad$ $e = f$ $\qquad$ $g = h$

The pairs of corresponding angles form an F-shape because they are on the same side of the transversal and on the same side of the parallel lines (either both above, or both below).

> **Tip**
>
> The F-shape that you can see is what helps you identify the type of angle.
>
> F-shape = corresponding angles.
> The F can be facing back-to-front as well.

Find answers at: cambridge.org/ukschools/gcsemaths-studentbookanswers

Key vocabulary

alternate angles: the angles on parallel lines on opposite sides of a transversal.

Alternate angles

Alternate angles on opposite sides of the transversal on parallel lines are equal.

They can be seen as a Z-shape.

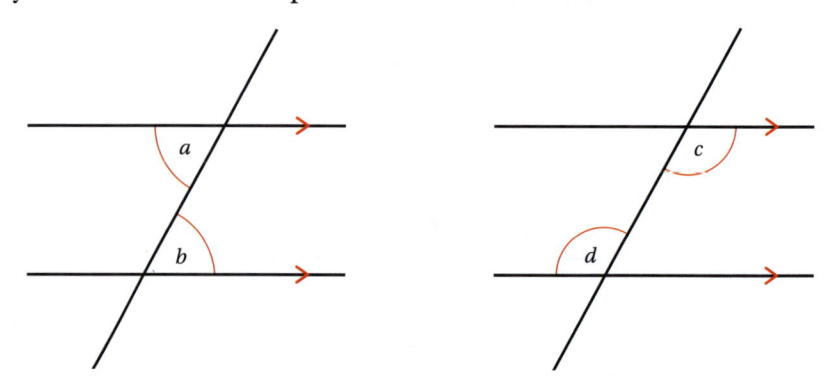

When a transversal crosses two parallel lines, four pairs of alternate angles are formed.

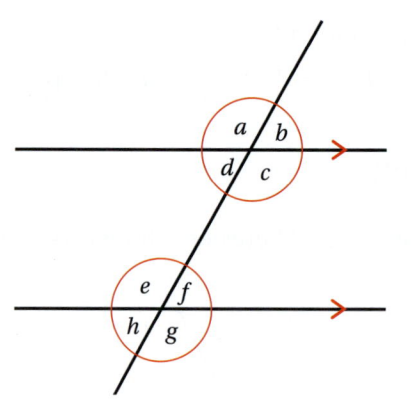

Tip

The Z-shape you can see helps you to identify the pairs of alternate angles.

Think **A** to **Z**: **A**lternate angles are **Z**-shaped.

The **Z** can be facing back-to-front as well.

The alternate angle pairs are:

$a = g$ $\qquad b = h \qquad c = e \qquad d = f$

Key vocabulary

co-interior angles: the angles within the parallel lines on the same side of the transversal.

Co-interior angles

The angles inside the parallel lines and on the same side of the transversal are called **co-interior angles**.

These angles are **supplementary**, which means that they add up to 180°.

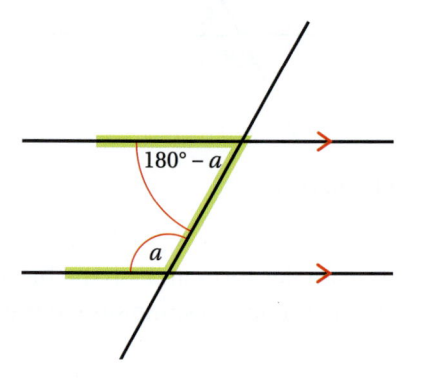

Summary of angle facts

This table summarises the facts you need to know about the angles associated with parallel lines.

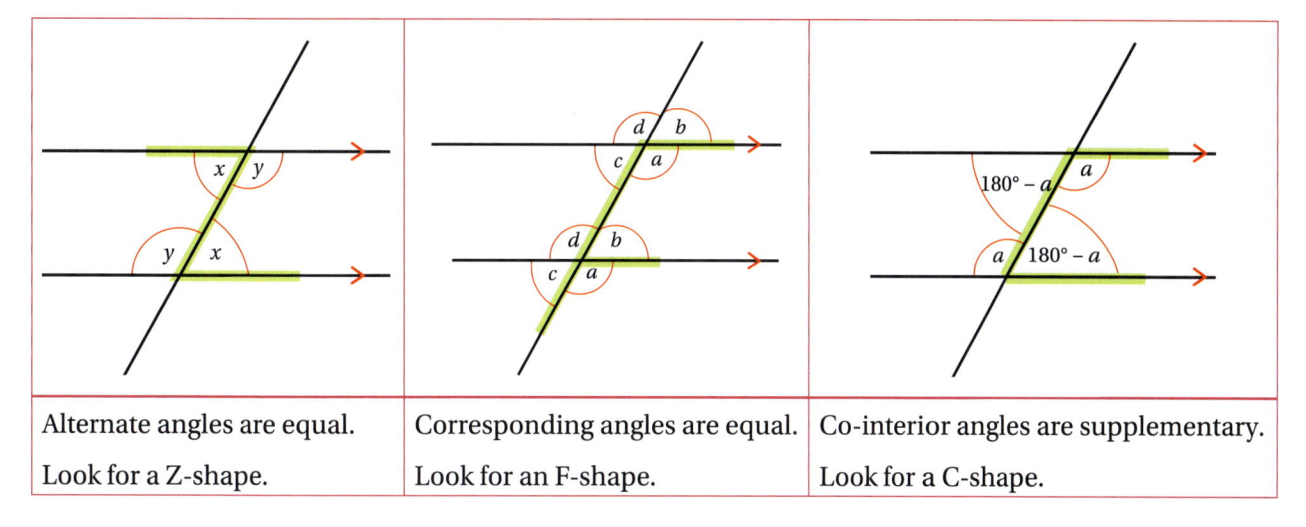

Alternate angles are equal. Look for a Z-shape.	Corresponding angles are equal. Look for an F-shape.	Co-interior angles are supplementary. Look for a C-shape.

EXERCISE 9B

1 Find the size of the missing angles a, b, c and d.

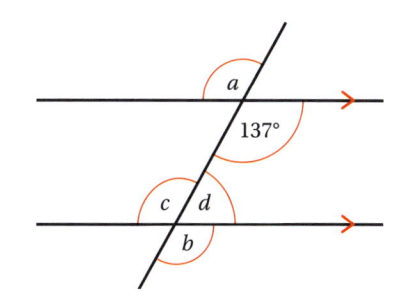

Tip

Remember, the Z, F and C shapes can be facing back-to-front as well.

2 Given that the two poles are parallel to each other, find the angle x that the second pole makes with the incline upwards.

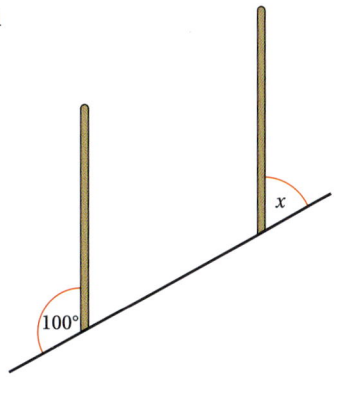

3 Find the size of the missing angles a, b and c.

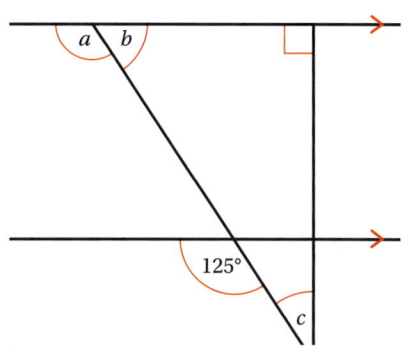

Find answers at: cambridge.org/ukschools/gcsemaths-studentbookanswers

4 Find the size of angles *x* and *y*.

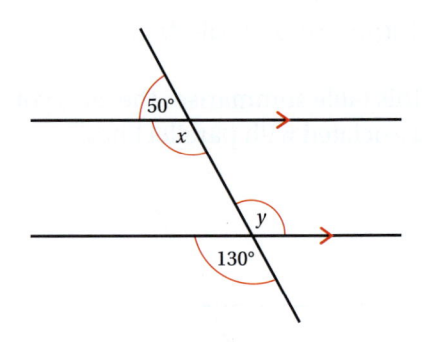

5 Find the size of the missing angles.

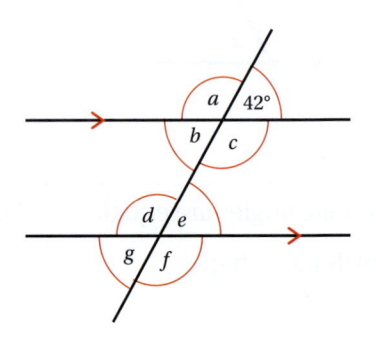

6 Find the size of ∠CEG.

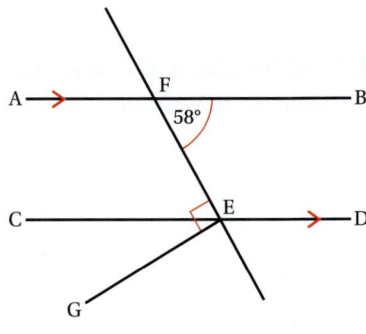

7 Find the size of ∠DCF.

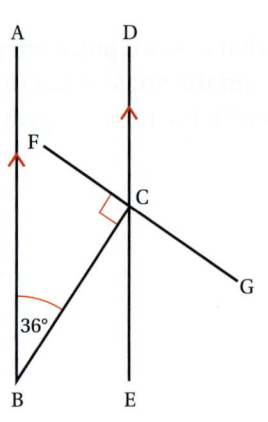

Tip

Make sure you know the differences between an equilateral triangle, a right-angled triangle, an isosceles triangle and a scalene triangle. Look back at Chapter 5 if you need to revise the properties of these triangles.

Section 3: Angles in triangles

In Chapter 5, you saw that when you tear off the interior angles of any triangle and place them on a straight edge, they will form an angle of 180°.

Tearing off the angles shows that the interior angles of a triangle add up to 180° but it is **not** a mathematical proof.

Angle sum of a triangle

To prove that the angles in a triangle add up to 180° you can construct a line parallel to one side of the triangle like this:

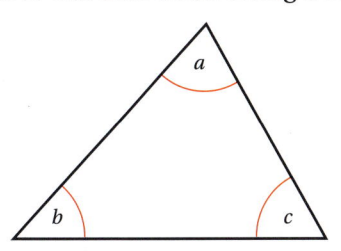

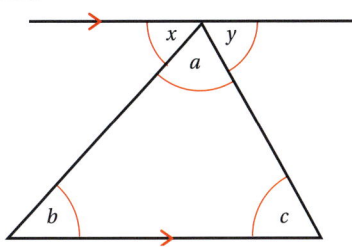

Once you have done that, you can prove that $a + b + c = 180°$ using mathematical principles.

$x + a + y = 180°$ (Angles on a line sum to 180°.)

But: $x = b$ and $y = c$ (Alternate angles are equal.)

Substitute b for x and c for y and you prove that $a + b + c = 180°$.

Therefore the three angles of a triangle always add up to 180°.

> **Tip**
>
> Some other important angle facts about triangles that you should learn are:
> - all angles in an equilateral triangle are 60° (all angles are equal and 180° ÷ 3 = 60°).
> - the base angles in an isosceles triangle are equal; this means if you know one of the base angles, or the third non-base angle, you can calculate the other angles inside the triangle.

The exterior angle is equal to the sum of the opposite interior angles

In Chapter 5 you also saw that the exterior angle of a triangle is equal to the sum of the two opposite interior angles.

There are different ways to prove this using mathematical principles.

Read through the example to see how you can prove it using angles on a line and the angle sum of triangles.

WORKED EXAMPLE 3

Show that $a + b = x$, and therefore prove that the exterior angle of any triangle is equal to the sum of the opposite interior angles.

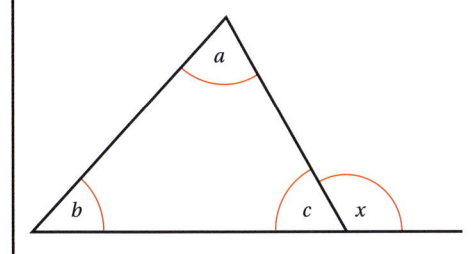

$c + x = 180°$ (Angles on a line sum to 180°.)
$\therefore c = 180° - x$
$a + b + c = 180°$ (Angle sum of a triangle.)
$\therefore c = 180° - (a + b)$
But, $c = (180° - x)$ (Proven above.)
So, $180° - (a + b) = 180° - x$
$\therefore a + b = x$

You can now combine basic angle facts, angle facts related to parallel lines and angle facts about triangles to find unknown angles in different figures.

Always give reasons for any statements you make based on known facts.

Find answers at: cambridge.org/ukschools/gcsemaths-studentbookanswers

EXERCISE 9C

1 Calculate the size of the missing angles.

a

b

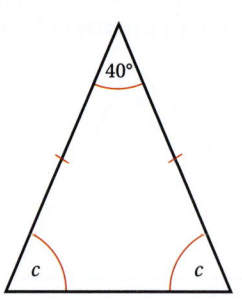

2 Find x and y.

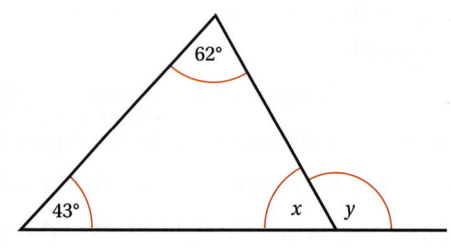

3 Find a and b.

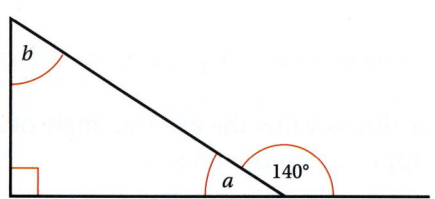

4 Find x, y and z.

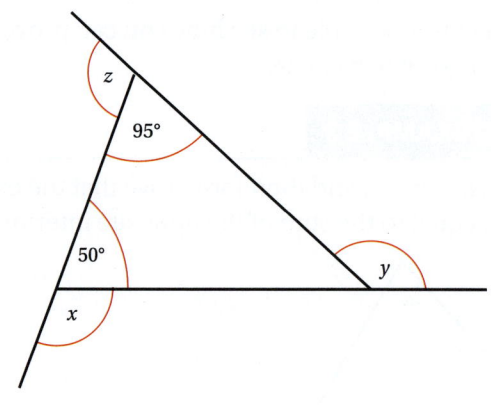

5 Work out the sizes of the angles marked a, b and c.
Give reasons to justify your answers.

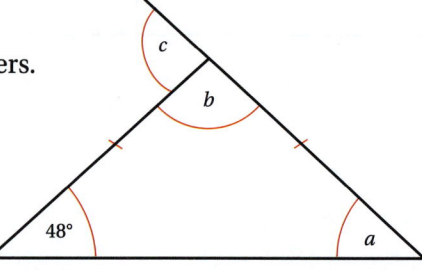

6 Calculate x.

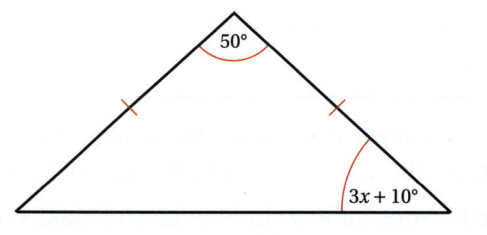

Section 4: Angles in polygons

You learnt about polygons in Chapter 5. Remember:
- A polygon is a plane shape with three or more straight sides.
- Polygons are regular if all their sides and angles are equal.
- Polygons are named according to how many sides they have: triangle (3), quadrilateral (4), pentagon (5), hexagon (6), heptagon (7) and octagon (8).

These basalt columns are formed naturally when lava cools.

The end faces are almost perfectly hexagonal.

The angle sum of a polygon

You can divide any polygon into triangles by drawing in the diagonals.

This allows you to use the angle sum of triangles to work out the sum of the interior angles in a polygon.

This is a regular hexagon.

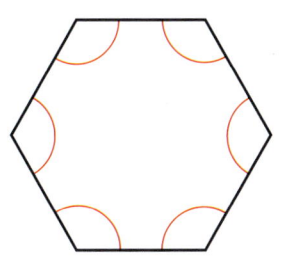

It has six **interior angles** which are all equal.

The diagonals divide the hexagon into four triangles.

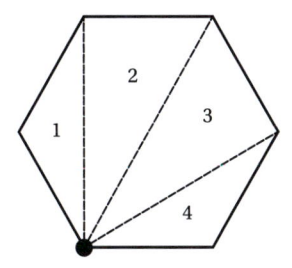

So the sum of the interior angles of a hexagon is 4 × 180° = 720°.

The hexagon is regular, so the six interior angles are equal in size.

720° ÷ 6 = 120°. So, each interior angle is 120°.

Work through the investigation in Exercise 9D to develop a rule for finding the angle sum of any polygon.

> **Key vocabulary**
>
> **interior angles**: angles inside a two-dimensional shape at the vertices or corners.

Find answers at: cambridge.org/ukschools/gcsemaths-studentbookanswers

141

GCSE Mathematics for OCR (Foundation)

WORK IT OUT 9.1

Three students attempted to calculate the size of interior angles in a regular pentagon.

Which is the correct solution?

What mistakes have been made by the other students?

Option A	Option B	Option C
There are three triangles within the pentagon. $3 \times 180° = 540°$ Five angles in a pentagon. $540° \div 5 = 108°$ Each interior angle = 108°.	There are five triangles in a pentagon. $5 \times 180° = 900°$ $900° \div 5 = 180°$ Interior angle = 180°.	There is a trapezium and a triangle inside the pentagon. $360° + 180° = 540°$ There are five angles inside the pentagon including the central 360° which gives a total of 900°. Interior angle = $900° \div 5 = 180°$.

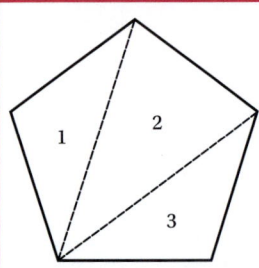

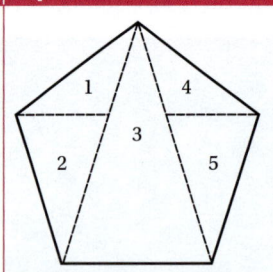

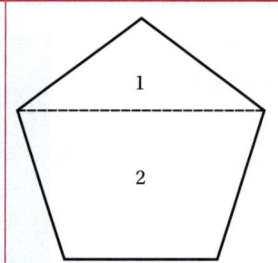

EXERCISE 9D

1. Draw the following polygons and divide them into triangles by drawing diagonals from one vertex as with the hexagon above.

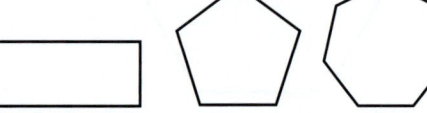

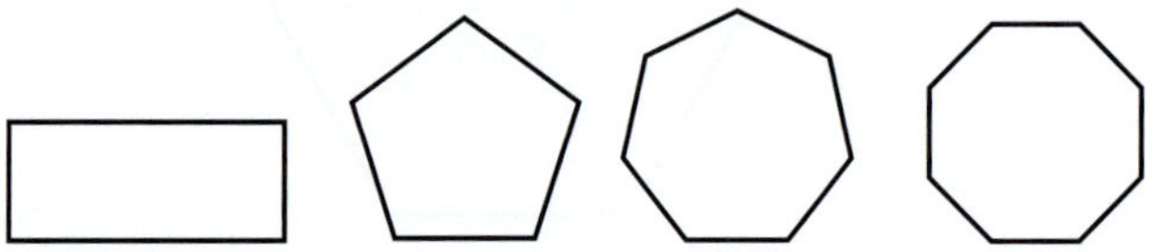

2. Predict how many triangles you could form if you did the same for a 10-sided and 20-sided polygon.

3. Copy and complete this table using your results from Questions **1** and **2**.

Number of sides in polygon	3	4	5	6	7	8	10	20
Number of triangles	1			4				
Angle sum of interior angles	180°			720°				

4. What is the relationship between the number of sides in a polygon and the number of triangles you can form in this way?

5. If a polygon has n sides, how many triangles can you form in this way?

6. Write a rule for finding the angle sum of a polygon:

    a in words. b in general algebraic terms for a polygon of n sides.

7 Use your rule to find the angle sum of a polygon with 12 sides.

8 How could you find the size of each angle of a regular 12-sided polygon?

The sum of exterior angles of a polygon

Look at the regular hexagon again.

You know that each interior angle is 120°.

By extending each side, we can form six **exterior angles**.

Like this:

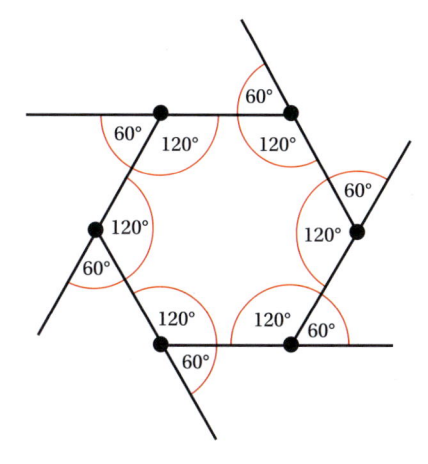

> **Key vocabulary**
>
> **exterior angles**: angles produced by extending the sides of a polygon.

There are six sides, so this produces six pairs of angles (one interior and one exterior per pair) on straight lines.

The sum of angles on a straight line is 180°.

So, the sum of these six angle pairs is 6 × 180° = 1080°.

But, you already know that the sum of interior angles is
180°(n – 2) = 180° × 4 = 720°.

The sum of the interior and exterior angles is 1080°.

The sum of the interior angles is 720°.

So, the sum of the exterior angles of the hexagon is 1080° – 720° = 360°.

Now consider any polygon with n sides.

The sum of interior plus exterior angles can be found using 180n, where n is the number of sides.

The sum of the interior angles can be found using 180(n – 2) where n is the number of sides.

So, for a pentagon, the sum of the exterior and interior angles would be
180° × 5 = 900° because there are five sides.

The sum of interior angles is 180(5 – 2) = 180° × 3 = 540°.

The sum of the exterior angles = the sum of the interior and exterior angles – the sum of the interior angles

= 900° – 540°

= 360°

> **Tip**
>
> Exterior angles of any polygon = 360° or one complete turn. For a regular polygon, the size of one exterior angle = $\frac{360}{n}$ where n is the number of sides.

You can use these rules to find the angle sum of any polygon.

If the polygon is regular, you can also work out the size of each interior and exterior angle.

> **WORKED EXAMPLE 4**
>
> For a regular 10-sided polygon, find:
>
> **a** the sum of the interior angles.
>
> Angle sum = $180(n - 2) = 180(8) = 1440°$ *In a 10-sided figure n = 10.*
>
> **b** the size of each interior angle.
>
> There are 10 interior angles, so one angle = $\frac{1440}{10} = 144°$
>
> **c** the size of each exterior angle.
>
> $180 - 144 = 36$

EXERCISE 9E

1 Copy and complete the following table.

Regular polygon	Sum of interior angles	Size of internal angle	Size of external angle
Triangle			120°
Quadrilateral		90°	
Pentagon			
		120°	60°
Heptagon			

2 Calculate the sum of interior angles of a polygon with:

    a 9 sides.   **b** 12 sides.   **c** 25 sides.

3 A regular polygon has 15 sides. Find:

    a the sum of the interior angles.   **b** the sum of the exterior angles.
    c the size of an interior angle.   **d** the size of an exterior angle.

4 A regular polygon has an interior angle that is three times the size of the exterior angle.

    a What is the size of each exterior angle?
    b What is the size of each interior angle?
    c What is the name of the regular polygon?

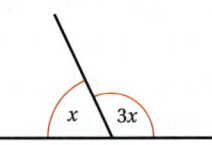

5 Find the size of x in each of the following polygons.

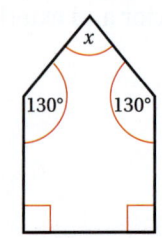

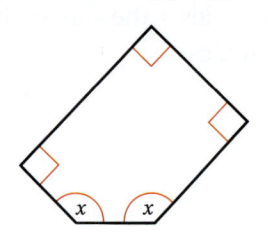

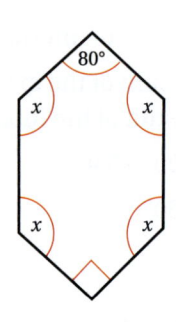

Checklist of learning and understanding

Basic angle facts
- Angles around a point add up to 360°.
- Angles on a straight line add up to 180°.
- Vertically opposite angles are equal.

Angles associated with parallel lines
- Corresponding angles are equal.
- Alternate angles are equal.
- Co-interior angles sum to 180°.

Geometric proofs
- Using properties of alternate and corresponding angles, you can prove that the three interior angles of any triangle add up to 180°.
- Using the angle sum of triangles and properties of angles at a line and at a point, you can find the interior and exterior angles of any polygon.

Chapter review

For additional questions on the topics in this chapter, visit GCSE Mathematics Online.

1 Select the correct size for the marked angle in each diagram.

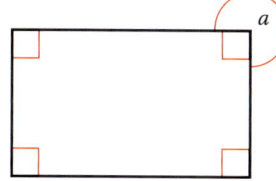

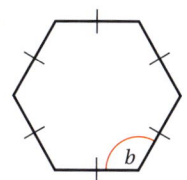

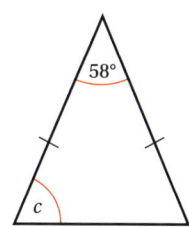

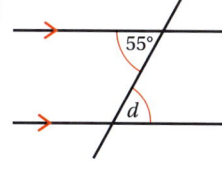

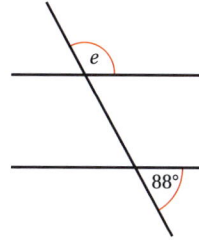

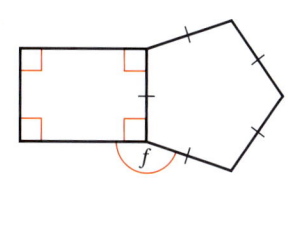

| 270° | 92° | 120° | 162° | 61° | 55° |

2 If the interior angle of a regular polygon is 108° what type of polygon is it?

3 Calculate $p + q + r + s + t$.

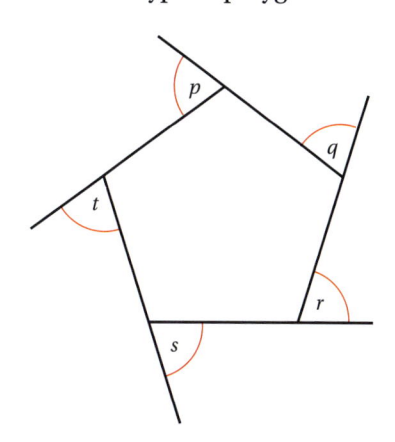

Find answers at: cambridge.org/ukschools/gcsemaths-studentbookanswers

4. In this irregular hexagon, calculate the value of z.

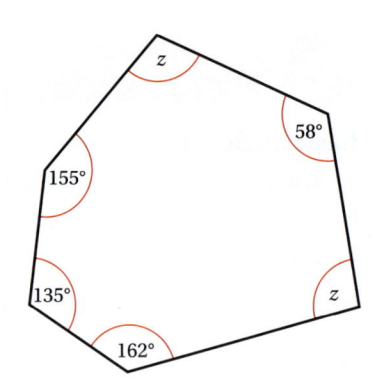

5. This diagram shows part of a regular polygon. The interior angle is 144°.

   Calculate the number of sides of the polygon.

   What is the name given to this polygon?

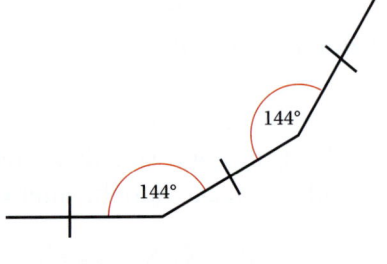

6. Calculate the exterior angle of a regular 10-sided polygon.

7. Show mathematically why the sum of the exterior angles of any polygon is 360°.

8. Find the value of x and y.

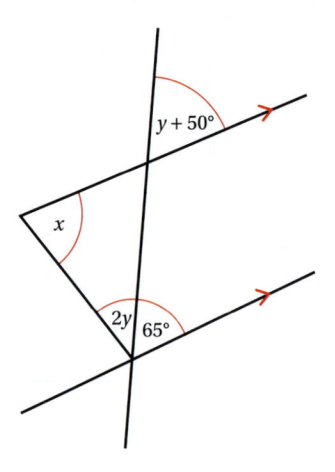

9. In the diagram ADE is a triangle.
   BC is parallel to DE and DBA is parallel to EF.

   Work out angle x.
   Give a reason for each step of your working.

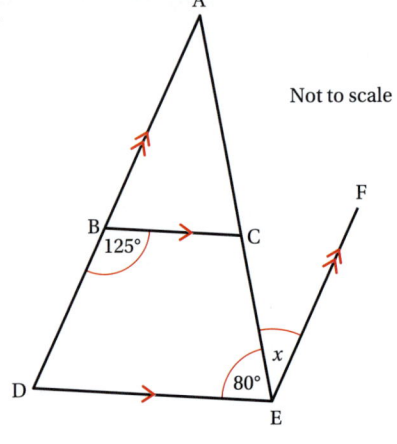

   Not to scale

   (5 marks)
   © OCR 2013

146

10 Fractions

In this chapter you will learn how to …

- recognise equivalence between fractions and mixed numbers.
- carry out the four basic operations on fractions and mixed numbers.
- work out fractions of an amount.

For more resources relating to this chapter, visit GCSE Mathematics Online.

Using mathematics: real-life applications

Nurses and other medical support staff work with fractions, decimals, percentages, rates and ratios every day. They calculate medicine doses, convert between different systems of measurement and set the patients' drips to supply the correct amount of fluid per hour.

"We have to record how much fluid patients drink when they are recovering from surgery. So for example, if we give the patient a 300 ml glass of orange juice and they only drink $\frac{2}{3}$ of it, we have to work out that they have taken in 200 ml of fluid." *(Nurse)*

Before you start …

Ch 2	Check that you can find common factors of sets of numbers.	① 18 24 27 28 30 32 36 From this set of numbers, choose numbers that have: **a** a common factor of 9. **b** common factors 2 and 3. **c** common factors 3, 4 and 12. **d** common factors of 3 and 6.
Ch 2	Find the lowest common multiple of sets of numbers.	② Choose the lowest common multiple of each set of numbers. **a** 5 and 10 A 15 B 50 C 10 D 20 **b** 8 and 12 A 12 B 96 C 36 D 24 **c** 2, 3 and 5 A 1 B 30 C 10 D 6
Ch 1	Know the correct order for performing operations. (BIDMAS)	③ Which calculation is correct in each pair? Why? |	Student A	Student B | |---|---|---| | a | $-3 - 2 \times -6 - 4 = 5$ | $-3 - 2 \times -6 - 4 = 50$ | | b | $-60 \div 5 + 3 \times -4 - 8 = 28$ | $-60 \div 5 + 3 \times -4 - 8 = -32$ | | c | $13 - 2 \times -6 - 5 \times 4 = 80$ | $13 - 2 \times -6 - 5 \times 4 = 5$ |

Find answers at: cambridge.org/ukschools/gcsemaths-studentbookanswers

GCSE Mathematics for OCR (Foundation)

Assess your starting point using the Launchpad

STEP 1

1 Which fraction does not belong in each set?

a $\dfrac{3}{15}, \dfrac{1}{5}, \dfrac{6}{30}, \dfrac{5}{35}, \dfrac{4}{20}$

b $\dfrac{4}{7}, \dfrac{8}{14}, \dfrac{12}{21}, \dfrac{9}{16}, \dfrac{52}{91}$

c $\dfrac{22}{10}, \dfrac{11}{4}, 2\dfrac{3}{4}, \dfrac{33}{12}, 2\dfrac{18}{24}$

GO TO
Section 1:
Equivalent fractions

STEP 2

2 Each calculation contains a mistake. Find the mistake and write the correct answer.

a $\dfrac{2}{3} + \dfrac{3}{4} = \dfrac{5}{7}$

b $\dfrac{4}{5} - \dfrac{9}{10} = \dfrac{1}{10}$

c $\dfrac{2}{7} \times \dfrac{4}{5} = \dfrac{6}{35}$

d $30 \div \dfrac{1}{2} = 15$

GO TO
Section 2:
Operations with fractions

STEP 3

3 Which is greater in each pair?

a $\dfrac{5}{8}$ of 40 or $\dfrac{3}{5}$ of 60

b $\dfrac{3}{4}$ of 240 or $\dfrac{7}{10}$ of 300

c $\dfrac{1}{4}$ of $\dfrac{1}{2}$ or $\dfrac{1}{2}$ of $\dfrac{3}{4}$

GO TO
Section 3:
Fractions of quantities

GO TO
Chapter review

Section 1: Equivalent fractions

Fractions tell you what share you have of a quantity.

Fractions that look different can be describing the same share.

For example, you could have $\frac{1}{4}$ of a pizza and a friend could have $\frac{2}{8}$ of a pizza.

The fractions look different but the share of the pizza is the same.

The fractions $\frac{1}{4}$ and $\frac{2}{8}$ are equivalent.

You can find equivalent fractions by multiplying the numerator and denominator by the same number ; the multiplier can be any number so long as the same is used for both the numerator and the denominator.

For example:

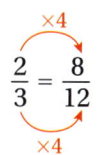

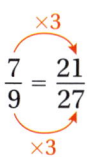

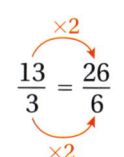

$$\frac{2}{3} = \frac{8}{12} \qquad \frac{7}{9} = \frac{21}{27} \qquad \frac{13}{3} = \frac{26}{6} \qquad 2\frac{1}{2} = \frac{5}{2} = \frac{10}{4}$$

(×4) (×3) (×2) (×2)

Convert to improper fraction before finding equivalent fraction.

You can also find equivalent fractions by dividing the numerator and denominator by the same number.

This is known as simplifying, cancelling or reducing the fraction to its lowest terms.

When you give an answer in the form of a fraction, you usually give it in its simplest form.

$\frac{6}{18} = \frac{1}{3} \qquad \frac{12}{27} = \frac{4}{9} \qquad 3\frac{5}{30} = 3\frac{1}{6}$

$$\frac{6}{18} = \frac{1}{3} \qquad \frac{12}{27} = \frac{4}{9} \qquad 3\frac{5}{30} = 3\frac{1}{6}$$

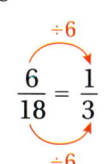

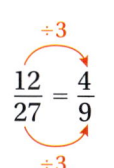

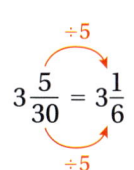

(÷6) (÷3) (÷5)

When you cancel out numbers in a fraction you are dividing the numerator and denominator by the same number.

For example, $\frac{6}{18} = \frac{1}{3}$. This is the same result as dividing both the numerator and denominator by six.

When you are asked to compare fractions that look different, you might need to write them both with the same denominator (a **common denominator**) so that you can tell whether they are equivalent, or one is larger than the other.

Find answers at: cambridge.org/ukschools/gcsemaths-studentbookanswers

---

Tip

Fractions:
- belong to the set of real numbers (numbers that can be found on a number line).
- are written in the form $\frac{a}{b}$ where b is not equal to zero.
- are rational numbers (they can be written as terminating or recurring decimals).
- a proper fraction is one where the numerator is smaller than the denominator.
- an improper fraction is one where the numerator is larger than the denominator; these can also be written as mixed numbers.
- a mixed number is written as an integer and a fraction, for example, $2\frac{1}{2}$ is a mixed number.

Tip

Remember, to convert a mixed number to an improper fraction, you multiply the integer part by the denominator and then add the numerator; the denominator stays the same. For example, in $2\frac{1}{2}$ the integer, 2, is equivalent to $\frac{1}{2} + \frac{1}{2} + \frac{1}{2} + \frac{1}{2}$, that is, $\frac{4}{2}$, so the numerator of the improper fraction will be $\frac{4}{2} + \frac{1}{2}$ which is $\frac{5}{2}$.

Key vocabulary

common denominator: a number into which all the denominators of a set of fractions divide exactly.

GCSE Mathematics for OCR (Foundation)

WORKED EXAMPLE 1

a Is $\frac{5}{6}$ equivalent to $\frac{7}{8}$?

$\frac{5}{6} = \frac{20}{24}$ and $\frac{7}{8} = \frac{21}{24}$ — Write both fractions with the same denominator.

$\frac{5}{6} \neq \frac{7}{8}$ — When the fractions have the same denominator it is easy to see whether they are equivalent or not. It is also easy to tell which one is bigger or smaller.

b Is $3\frac{3}{4}$ equivalent to $\frac{45}{12}$?

$3\frac{3}{4} = \frac{15}{4}$ — Write the mixed number as an improper fraction.

$\frac{15}{4} = \frac{45}{12}$ — Write $\frac{15}{4}$ with a denominator of 12, or write $\frac{45}{12}$ with a denominator of 4.

Tip

You can use the LCM of the denominators to find a common denominator, but any common denominator works (not just the lowest).

EXERCISE 10A

1 Complete each statement to make a pair of equivalent fractions.

a $\frac{3}{4} = \frac{\square}{44}$
b $\frac{1}{3} = \frac{1000}{\square}$
c $\frac{1}{2} = \frac{\square}{300}$
d $\frac{-2}{5} = \frac{-18}{\square}$

e $\frac{-6}{-10} = \frac{42}{\square}$
f $\frac{\square}{5} = \frac{36}{20}$
g $\frac{4}{3} = \frac{28}{\square}$
h $\frac{10}{14} = \frac{50}{\square}$

2 List five fractions that are equivalent to each of these fractions.

a $\frac{5}{7}$
b $\frac{4}{5}$
c $\frac{12}{8}$
d $\frac{-5}{-3}$

3 Write each mixed number as an improper fraction in its simplest form.

a $2\frac{1}{3}$
b $3\frac{1}{3}$
c $5\frac{4}{8}$
d $4\frac{6}{12}$

e $2\frac{14}{21}$
f $1\frac{12}{36}$
g $2\frac{30}{50}$
h $3\frac{35}{45}$

4 Rewrite each fraction as an equivalent mixed number.

a $\frac{12}{5}$
b $\frac{7}{3}$
c $\frac{8}{5}$
d $\frac{-11}{5}$

e $\frac{12}{11}$
f $\frac{13}{9}$
g $\frac{-9}{-4}$
h $\frac{21}{9}$

5 Determine whether the following pairs of fractions are equivalent (=) or not ($\neq$).

a $\frac{2}{5}$ and $\frac{3}{4}$
b $\frac{2}{3}$ and $\frac{3}{4}$
c $\frac{3}{8}$ and $\frac{5}{12}$
d $\frac{2}{11}$ and $\frac{1}{10}$

e $\frac{3}{5}$ and $\frac{9}{15}$
f $\frac{10}{25}$ and $\frac{4}{10}$
g $\frac{6}{24}$ and $\frac{5}{20}$
h $\frac{11}{9}$ and $\frac{121}{99}$

6 Reduce the following fractions to their simplest form.

a $\frac{3}{15}$
b $\frac{4}{6}$
c $\frac{25}{100}$
d $\frac{-5}{-10}$

e $\frac{4}{12}$
f $\frac{7}{21}$
g $\frac{36}{24}$
h $\frac{60}{100}$

i $\frac{-14}{21}$
j $\frac{18}{27}$
k $\frac{-15}{-21}$
l $\frac{18}{42}$

10 Fractions

Section 2: Operations with fractions

You have already learnt in earlier school years how to add, subtract, multiply and divide fractions and mixed numbers.

Read through the examples to remind you of the key rules for operations on fractions.

Multiplying fractions

This rectangle has been divided into 12 smaller squares, or twelfths.

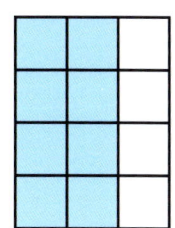

$\frac{2}{3}$ of this rectangle is blue

$\frac{3}{4}$ of the $\frac{2}{3}$ have been marked with a ★

From the diagram you can see that $\frac{3}{4}$ of $\frac{2}{3}$ is 6 of the original 12 parts.

$\frac{3}{4}$ of $\frac{2}{3} = \frac{3}{4} \times \frac{2}{3} = \frac{6}{12}$

The example above gives you a general rule for multiplying fractions.

To multiply fractions multiply the numerators and then multiply the denominators.

If possible, cancel before you multiply to make the calculations easier.

WORKED EXAMPLE 2

a $\frac{3}{4} \times \frac{2}{7} = \frac{3 \times 2}{4 \times 7}$

$= \frac{6}{28}$ — Multiply numerators by numerators and denominators by denominators.

$= \frac{3}{14}$ — Give the answer in its simplest form.

b $\frac{5}{7} \times 3 = \frac{5 \times 3}{7 \times 1}$ — Think of a whole number as a fraction with a denominator of 1.

$= \frac{15}{7}$ — $\frac{15}{7}$ cannot be simplified further but it can be written as a mixed number.

$= 2\frac{1}{7}$

c $\frac{3}{8} \times 4\frac{1}{2} = \frac{3}{8} \times \frac{9}{2}$ — Rewrite the mixed number as an improper fraction.

$= \frac{27}{16}$ — $\frac{27}{16}$ cannot be simplified but it can be written as a mixed number.

$= 1\frac{11}{16}$

> **Tip**
>
> Cancelling in the first step means you don't have to simplify the fraction to get an answer.
>
> $\frac{3 \times 2^1}{{}^2\cancel{4} \times 7}$
>
> $= 3 \times \frac{1}{2} \times \frac{1}{7} = \frac{3}{14}$

> **Tip**
>
> You can cancel before you multiply to make it easier to simplify the answers.

Find answers at: cambridge.org/ukschools/gcsemaths-studentbookanswers

Adding and subtracting fractions

To add or subtract fractions they must have the same denominators. Find a common denominator and then find the equivalent fractions with that common denominator before you add or subtract the numerators.

> **Tip**
> Think of $\frac{2}{4}$ as 2 lots of 4ths, and $\frac{1}{4}$ as 1 lot of 4ths. If you combine them, you have 3 lots of 4ths, or $\frac{3}{4}$. You never add the denominators.

WORKED EXAMPLE 3

a $\frac{1}{2} + \frac{1}{4}$ — Use 4 as a common denominator.

$= \frac{2}{4} + \frac{1}{4}$ — Write $\frac{1}{2}$ as its equivalent $\frac{2}{4}$.

$= \frac{3}{4}$ — Add the numerators.

b $2\frac{1}{2} + \frac{5}{6}$

$= \frac{5}{2} + \frac{5}{6}$ — Rewrite mixed numbers as improper fractions.

$= \frac{15}{6} + \frac{5}{6}$ — Find a common denominator.

$= \frac{20}{6}$ — Add the numerators.

$= \frac{10}{3}$ or $3\frac{1}{3}$ — Simplify the answer.

c $2\frac{3}{4} - 1\frac{5}{7}$ — Rewrite mixed numbers as improper fractions.

$= \frac{11}{4} - \frac{12}{7}$ — Find a common denominator.

$= \frac{77}{28} - \frac{48}{28}$ — Subtract the numerators.

$= \frac{29}{28}$ or $1\frac{1}{28}$ — Write the answer as a mixed number.

Dividing fractions

Dividing a fraction such as $\frac{9}{10}$ by another fraction, such as $\frac{1}{2}$, means finding out how many $\frac{1}{2}$s there are in $\frac{9}{10}$.

You are trying to find $\frac{9}{10} \div \frac{1}{2}$ which is the same as the fraction $\frac{\frac{9}{10}}{\frac{1}{2}}$.

If you multiply the numerator and the denominator by 2, you can get rid of the fractional denominator.

$$\frac{\frac{9}{10}}{\frac{1}{2}} = \frac{\frac{9}{10} \times \frac{2}{1}}{\frac{1}{2} \times \frac{2}{1}} = \frac{9}{10} \times \frac{2}{1} = \frac{18}{10} = \frac{9}{5}$$

You can do this calculation faster by just inverting (flipping over) the fraction you are dividing by.

This gives the general method for dividing by a fraction.

To divide one fraction by another fraction you multiply the first fraction by the **reciprocal** of the second fraction.

WORKED EXAMPLE 4

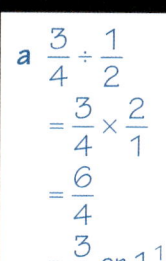

a $\dfrac{3}{4} \div \dfrac{1}{2}$

$= \dfrac{3}{4} \times \dfrac{2}{1}$ — Multiply by the reciprocal of $\dfrac{1}{2}$, that is, flip the fraction to get $\dfrac{2}{1}$.

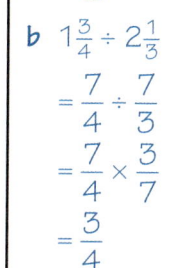

$= \dfrac{6}{4}$

$= \dfrac{3}{2}$ or $1\dfrac{1}{2}$

b $1\dfrac{3}{4} \div 2\dfrac{1}{3}$

$= \dfrac{7}{4} \div \dfrac{7}{3}$ — Convert mixed numbers to improper fractions.

$= \dfrac{7}{4} \times \dfrac{3}{7}$ — Multiply by the reciprocal of $\dfrac{7}{3}$. Cancel the 7s.

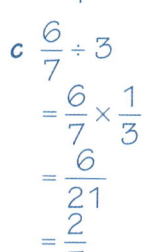

$= \dfrac{3}{4}$

c $\dfrac{6}{7} \div 3$

$= \dfrac{6}{7} \times \dfrac{1}{3}$ — Multiply by the reciprocal of 3.

$= \dfrac{6}{21}$

$= \dfrac{2}{7}$

> **Key vocabulary**
>
> **reciprocal:** the reciprocal of a number, x, is 1 divided by x, i.e. $\dfrac{1}{x}$. Any number multiplied by its reciprocal is 1. For the fraction $\dfrac{a}{b}$, the reciprocal is $\dfrac{b}{a}$.

> **Tip**
>
> Dividing by a number is the same as multiplying by its reciprocal, which in some calculations may be easier. To find the reciprocal of a fraction you invert it. So, the reciprocal of $\dfrac{3}{4}$ is $\dfrac{4}{3}$ and the reciprocal of $\dfrac{7}{4}$ is $\dfrac{4}{7}$. The reciprocal of a whole number is a unit fraction. For example, the reciprocal of 3 is $\dfrac{1}{3}$ and the reciprocal of 12 is $\dfrac{1}{12}$.

The rules for order of operations and negative and positive signs also apply to calculations with fractions.

EXERCISE 10B

1 Write each set of fractions in increasing order of size.

a $\dfrac{3}{5}, \dfrac{1}{4}, \dfrac{9}{4}, 1\dfrac{3}{4}, \dfrac{4}{7}$

b $\dfrac{5}{6}, \dfrac{3}{4}, \dfrac{11}{3}, \dfrac{19}{24}, 2\dfrac{2}{3}$

c $2\dfrac{3}{7}, \dfrac{1}{7}, \dfrac{7}{7}, \dfrac{8}{14}, \dfrac{10}{21}, \dfrac{13}{7}$

2 Calculate.

a $\dfrac{3}{4} \times \dfrac{2}{5}$

b $\dfrac{1}{5} \times \dfrac{1}{9}$

c $\dfrac{5}{7} \times \dfrac{1}{5}$

d $\dfrac{7}{10} \times \dfrac{2}{3}$

e $\dfrac{4}{7} \times \dfrac{3}{8}$

f $\dfrac{6}{11} \times \dfrac{-5}{6}$

g $\dfrac{3}{4} \times 24$

h $\dfrac{4}{9} \times \dfrac{8}{10}$

i $\dfrac{3}{8} \times \dfrac{4}{9}$

j $\dfrac{7}{25} \times \dfrac{3}{4}$

k $1\dfrac{1}{2} \times {}^-10$

l $1\dfrac{4}{5} \times {}^-6$

m $1\dfrac{2}{7} \times 3\dfrac{1}{2}$

n $4\dfrac{1}{11} \times {}^-3\dfrac{1}{8}$

o $\dfrac{7}{25} \times \dfrac{7}{9}$

p $3\dfrac{1}{3} \times 9\dfrac{2}{5}$

3 Simplify.

a $\dfrac{1}{5} \times \dfrac{3}{8} \times \dfrac{-5}{9}$

b $\dfrac{2}{3} \times \dfrac{3}{4} \times \dfrac{4}{5}$

c $\dfrac{1}{2} \times \dfrac{2}{3} \times \dfrac{4}{11}$

d $\dfrac{5}{8} \times \dfrac{3}{7} \times \dfrac{2}{3}$

e $\dfrac{4}{25} \times \dfrac{-3}{5} \times \dfrac{-7}{8}$

f $\dfrac{9}{20} \times \dfrac{10}{11} \times \dfrac{1}{12}$

> **Tip**
>
> When you are asked to order fractions, it will help to write all the fractions with the same denominator first so that you only need to compare the numerators to order them. Remember to return them to their original form when you write them in order in your answer.

Find answers at: cambridge.org/ukschools/gcsemaths-studentbookanswers

4 Simplify.

a $\frac{2}{7} + \frac{1}{2}$ b $\frac{1}{2} + \frac{1}{4}$ c $\frac{1}{4} + \frac{3}{8}$ d $\frac{5}{6} + \frac{6}{10}$

e $\frac{5}{8} - \frac{1}{4}$ f $\frac{7}{9} - \frac{1}{3}$ g $\frac{3}{4} + \frac{2}{5}$ h $\frac{3}{4} - \frac{1}{3}$

i $\frac{4}{5} - \frac{1}{3}$ j $\frac{4}{5} - \frac{3}{10}$ k $\frac{3}{4} + \frac{1}{6}$ l $\frac{4}{9} - \frac{1}{4}$

m $\frac{2}{3} - \frac{3}{10}$ n $\frac{7}{8} - \frac{3}{5}$ o $14 - \frac{1}{5}$ p $\frac{13}{2} - \frac{8}{5}$

5 Simplify.

a $2\frac{3}{4} + 2\frac{1}{2}$ b $1\frac{3}{4} - 1\frac{1}{3}$ c $2\frac{7}{8} + 1\frac{3}{5}$ d $3\frac{7}{10} + 2\frac{9}{11}$

e $4\frac{3}{4} + 1\frac{5}{6}$ f $8\frac{2}{5} - 3\frac{1}{2}$ g $7\frac{1}{4} - 2\frac{9}{10}$ h $9\frac{3}{7} - 2\frac{4}{5}$

i $6\frac{3}{5} - 1\frac{11}{13}$ j $2\frac{11}{20} - 1\frac{9}{10}$ k $8 - 2\frac{3}{4}$ l $9\frac{3}{5} - 7\frac{1}{2}$

6 Simplify.

a $\frac{1}{4} \div \frac{1}{4}$ b $\frac{1}{2} \div \frac{1}{4}$ c $\frac{1}{5} \div \frac{2}{7}$ d $\frac{-6}{7} \div \frac{2}{5}$

e $\frac{1}{8} \div \frac{7}{9}$ f $\frac{2}{11} \div \frac{-3}{5}$ g $\frac{5}{9} \div \frac{3}{7}$ h $\frac{-5}{12} \div \frac{-1}{2}$

i $\frac{3}{4} \div -2\frac{1}{2}$ j $2\frac{1}{2} \div \frac{2}{5}$ k $3\frac{1}{5} \div 2\frac{1}{2}$ l $1\frac{7}{8} \div 2\frac{3}{4}$

7 Calculate.

a $4 + \frac{2}{3} \times \frac{1}{3}$ b $2\frac{1}{8} - \left(2\frac{1}{5} - \frac{7}{8}\right)$ c $\frac{3}{7} \times \left(\frac{2}{3} + 6 \div \frac{2}{3}\right) + 5 \times \frac{2}{7}$

d $2\frac{7}{8} + \left(8\frac{1}{4} - 6\frac{3}{8}\right)$ e $\frac{5}{6} \times \frac{1}{4} + \frac{5}{8} \times \frac{1}{3}$ f $\left(5 \div \frac{3}{11} - \frac{5}{12}\right) \times \frac{1}{6}$

g $\left(\frac{5}{8} \div \frac{15}{4}\right) - \left(\frac{5}{6} \times \frac{1}{5}\right)$ h $\left(2\frac{2}{3} \div 4 - \frac{3}{10}\right) \times \frac{3}{17}$ i $\left(7 \div \frac{2}{9} - \frac{1}{3}\right) \times \frac{2}{3}$

8 Nicci buys a 4 kg packet of nuts and raisins. She notices that $\frac{3}{8}$ of the contents are raisins.
How many kilograms of nuts were there?

9 Josh eats 8 packets of crisps each week. Nick eats $1\frac{3}{4}$ times as many packets. How many packets do they eat altogether?

10 Kevin is a professional deep-sea diver.
He needs to keep track of how much time he spends underwater to make sure he has enough air left in his tank.
If he spends $9\frac{3}{4}$ minutes swimming to a wreck, $12\frac{5}{6}$ minutes exploring the wreck and $3\frac{5}{6}$ minutes examining corals, how much time has he spent in total?

11 $\frac{5}{12}$ of the people at a conference are from Britain, $\frac{3}{16}$ are from India, $\frac{7}{24}$ are from Brazil and the rest are from Malaysia.

a What fraction of the people at the conference are from Malaysia?

b Which country has most people at the conference?

c Which country has the fewest people at the conference?

d The Indian delegation left the conference a day before everyone else. What fraction of the original number of people is left?

12 In a café, $\frac{1}{4}$ of the customers order coffee and $\frac{2}{5}$ order tea. The rest of the customers order juice.
   a What fraction of the customers ordered hot drinks?
   b What fraction of the customers ordered juice?

13 A litre carton of milk is $\frac{3}{4}$ full. Sandra uses $\frac{1}{3}$ of a litre to make breakfast. What fraction of a litre is left after breakfast?

14 Mrs Smith spends $\frac{1}{4}$ of her wages on rent and $\frac{2}{5}$ on other expenses. What fraction does she have left?

15 There are $1\frac{3}{4}$ cakes left over after a party. These are shared out equally among 6 people.

What fraction does each person get?

16 If I have $5\frac{2}{3}$ litres of juice, how many cups containing $\frac{2}{15}$ of a litre can I pour?

17 Nico buys 6 trays of chicken pieces for his restaurant.

Each tray contains $2\frac{1}{2}$ kg of chicken. Each chicken meal served uses $\frac{3}{8}$ kg of chicken. How many chicken meals can he serve?

Section 3: Fractions of quantities

Read and think about these statements.

- I'll pay half of the £50 costs.
- $\frac{1}{3}$ of the 24 apples in this pack are bad.
- I save $\frac{1}{10}$ of my income of £1200 every month.
- I make about 220 calls a month and about $\frac{4}{5}$ of them are for business.

Some of the fractions in the statements are easy to work out.

- You know that half of 50 is 25.

    $\frac{1}{2} \times 50 = \frac{50}{2} = 25$

- $\frac{1}{3}$ of 24 is 8.

    $\frac{1}{3} \times 24 = \frac{24}{3} = 8$

- $\frac{1}{10}$ of 1200 = 120

    $\frac{1}{10} \times 1200 = \frac{1200}{10} = 120$

This shows that the word 'of' means 'multiply' ($\times$).

Look at the last statement. It isn't so easy to work out $\frac{4}{5}$ of 220 straight away.

Multiplying by $\frac{4}{5}$ gives you the answer.

$\frac{4}{5} \times \frac{220}{1} = \frac{880}{5} = 176$.

When you see the word 'of' in a fraction problem, replace it with $\times$ and do the multiplication as you normally would.

Find answers at: cambridge.org/ukschools/gcsemaths-studentbookanswers

GCSE Mathematics for OCR (Foundation)

Expressing one quantity as a fraction of another

It is easy to express one quantity as a fraction of another if you remember that the numerator in a fraction tells you how many parts of the whole quantity you are dealing with.

The denominator represents the whole quantity.

So, a fraction of $\frac{3}{5}$ means you are dealing with 3 of the 5 parts that make up the whole.

WORKED EXAMPLE 5

a What fraction is 20 minutes of 1 hour?
b Express 35 centimetres as a fraction of a metre.

a 20 minutes is part of 60 minutes.

$\frac{20}{60} = \frac{2}{6} = \frac{1}{3}$ of an hour.

> 20 minutes is the part of the whole, so it is the numerator.
> The hour is the whole, so it is the denominator.
> You cannot form a fraction using one unit for the numerator and another for the denominator, so you need to convert the hour to minutes.

b 35 cm is part of 100 cm.

$\frac{35}{100} = \frac{7}{20}$ of a metre.

> 35 cm is the part of the whole, so it is the numerator.
> The metre is the whole, so it is the denominator.
> Again, you cannot use centimetres and metres in the same fraction, so you convert 1 m to 100 cm.

To write a quantity as a fraction of another quantity make sure the two quantities are in the same units and then write them as a fraction and simplify.

EXERCISE 10C

1 Calculate.

a $\frac{3}{4}$ of 12
b $\frac{1}{3}$ of 45
c $\frac{2}{9}$ of 36
d $\frac{3}{8}$ of 144
e $\frac{4}{5}$ of 180
f $\frac{1}{3}$ of 96
g $\frac{1}{2}$ of $\frac{3}{4}$
h $\frac{1}{3}$ of $\frac{3}{10}$
i $\frac{4}{9}$ of $\frac{3}{14}$
j $\frac{1}{4}$ of $2\frac{1}{2}$
k $\frac{3}{4}$ of $2\frac{1}{3}$
l $\frac{5}{6}$ of $3\frac{1}{2}$

2 Calculate the following quantities.

a $\frac{3}{4}$ of £28
b $\frac{3}{5}$ of £210
c $\frac{2}{5}$ of £30
d $\frac{2}{3}$ of £18
e $\frac{1}{2}$ of 3 cups of sugar
f $\frac{1}{2}$ of 5 cups of flour
g $\frac{1}{2}$ of $1\frac{1}{2}$ cups of sugar
h $\frac{3}{4}$ of $2\frac{2}{3}$ cups of flour
i $\frac{2}{3}$ of $1\frac{1}{2}$ cups of sugar
j $\frac{2}{3}$ of 4 hours
k $\frac{1}{3}$ of $2\frac{1}{2}$ hours
l $\frac{3}{4}$ of 5 hours
m $\frac{1}{3}$ of $\frac{3}{4}$ of an hour
n $\frac{2}{3}$ of $3\frac{1}{2}$ minutes
o $\frac{3}{15}$ of a minute

3 Express the first quantity as a fraction of the second.

  a 12p of every £1
  b 35 cm of a 2 m length
  c 12 mm of 30 cm
  d 45 minutes per 8 hour shift
  e 5 minutes per hour
  f 150 m of a kilometre
  g 45 seconds of 30 minutes
  h 575 ml of 4 litres

4 Nick earns £18 000 per year. His friend Samir earns £24 000 per year.

What fraction of Samir's salary does Nick earn?

5 The floor area of a room is 12 m². Pete buys a rug that is 110 cm wide and 160 cm long.

What fraction of the floor area will be covered by this rug?

Checklist of learning and understanding

Equivalent fractions

- Fractions that represent the same amount are called equivalent fractions.
- You can change fractions to their equivalents by multiplying the numerator and denominator by the same value or by dividing the numerator and denominator by the same value (simplifying).

Operations on fractions

- To add or subtract fractions, find equivalent fractions with the same denominator, then add or subtract the numerators; the denominators do not get added or subtracted.
- To multiply fractions, multiply numerators by numerators and denominators by denominators.
- To divide fractions, multiply the fraction being divided by the reciprocal of the divisor.

Fractions of a quantity

- The word 'of' means multiply; so to find a fraction of an amount, you multiply that amount by the fraction.
- A quantity can be written as a fraction of another as long as they are in the same units. Write one quantity as the numerator and the other as the denominator and simplify.

Chapter review

1 Simplify.

  a $\dfrac{15}{90}$
  b $\dfrac{195}{230}$
  c $4\dfrac{18}{48}$

2 Write each set of fractions in increasing order of size.

  a $\dfrac{8}{9}, \dfrac{4}{5}, \dfrac{5}{6}, \dfrac{3}{7}$
  b $2\dfrac{2}{5}, \dfrac{23}{7}, 1\dfrac{3}{5}, \dfrac{16}{9}$

Find answers at: cambridge.org/ukschools/gcsemaths-studentbookanswers

For additional questions on the topics in this chapter, visit GCSE Mathematics Online.

3 Evaluate.

a $\frac{7}{5} + \frac{3}{8}$ b $\frac{7}{5} \times \frac{3}{8}$ c $\frac{7}{5} \div \frac{3}{8}$

d $3\frac{1}{7} + 2\frac{2}{5}$ e $3\frac{1}{15} - 1\frac{3}{5}$ f $\frac{1}{7}$ of $3\frac{3}{12}$

g $\frac{2}{7} \times \frac{8}{18} \div 3$ h $28 \div \frac{3}{4}$ i $\frac{2}{9}$ of $\frac{3}{4}$

4 Simplify.

a $\left(\frac{3}{8} \div \frac{13}{4}\right) + \left(\frac{5}{9} \times \frac{3}{5}\right)$ b $2\frac{2}{3} \times \left(8 \div \frac{4}{7} + \frac{7}{8}\right)$

5 a Write 425 g as a fraction of $2\frac{1}{2}$ kg.

b Write 12 000 g as a fraction of 40 kg.

6 Sandy has $12\frac{1}{2}$ litres of water.

How many bottles containing $\frac{3}{4}$ litre can she fill?

7 A surveyor has to divide a 15 km² area of land into equal plots each measuring $\frac{1}{2}$ km².

How many plots can she make?

11 Decimals

In this chapter you will learn how to …
- write decimals as fractions and fractions as decimals.
- convert decimals to fractions and fractions to decimals.
- order fractions and decimals.
- carry out the four basic operations on decimals without using a calculator.
- solve problems involving decimal quantities.

For more resources relating to this chapter, visit GCSE Mathematics Online.

Using mathematics: real-life applications

Food technologists analyse the contents of different raw and prepared foods to work out what they contain and how much there is of each ingredient. For example, how much water, protein and fat there is in a cut of meat. They use decimal fractions to give the quantities correct to tenths, hundredths or even smaller parts of a gram.

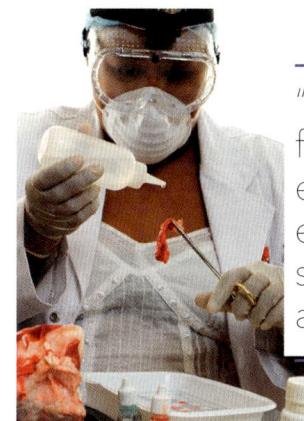

"The laws about labelling food are fairly strict. Manufacturers need to state exactly what is in their product and give exact amounts of different ingredients so I have to measure things very accurately." *(Food technologist)*

Before you start …

KS3	You need to be able to work confidently with place value.	1	31.098 0.0398 300.098 0.98308 19.308 Choose the number from the set that has a 3 in the: **a** hundreds position. **b** hundredths position. **c** tenths position. **d** thousandths position. **e** tens position.
KS3	Check that you can compare decimal fractions and order them by size.	2	Fill in <, = or > between each pair of decimal fractions. **a** 0.65 ☐ 0.7 **b** 0.08 ☐ 0.01 **c** 0.8 ☐ 0.85 **d** 2.87 ☐ 0.99 **e** 4.230 ☐ 4.23
KS3	You need to know the fractional equivalents of some common decimals.	3	Make equivalent pairs by matching the decimals in the left-hand box with the fractions in the right. **a** 0.25 $\frac{3}{4}$ **b** 0.375 $\frac{3}{8}$ **c** 0.4 $\frac{45}{90}$ **d** 0.75 $\frac{2}{5}$ **e** 0.5 $\frac{1}{40}$ **f** 0.025 $\frac{4}{16}$
KS3	You need to round numbers to estimate answers.	4	Find the approximate answer to each calculation. **a** 0.4×0.6 **b** $5.40 + 3.52 + 8.99$ **c** $99 \div 24$

Find answers at: cambridge.org/ukschools/gcsemaths-studentbookanswers

GCSE Mathematics for OCR (Foundation)

Assess your starting point using the Launchpad

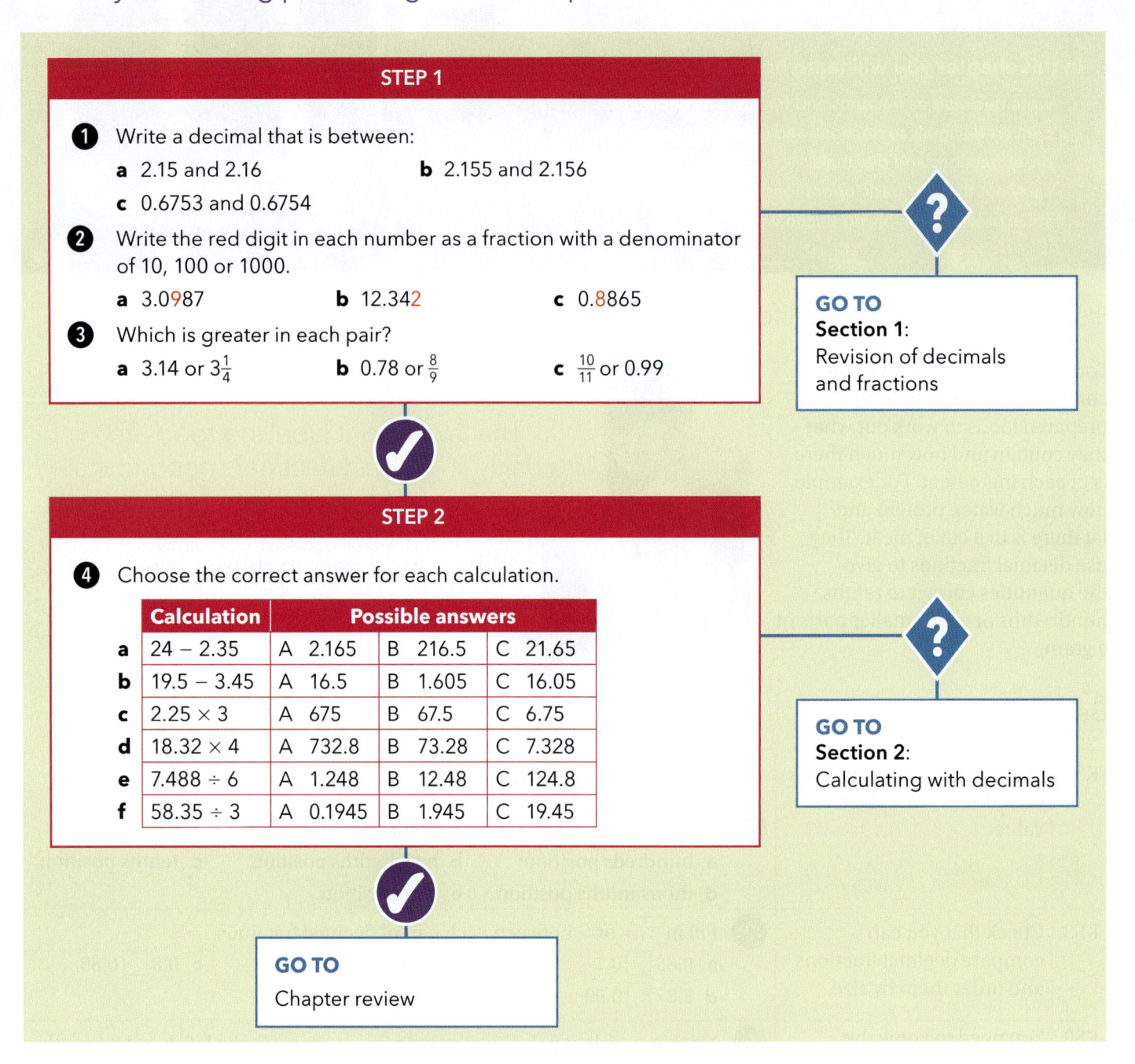

STEP 1

1. Write a decimal that is between:
   a 2.15 and 2.16
   b 2.155 and 2.156
   c 0.6753 and 0.6754

2. Write the red digit in each number as a fraction with a denominator of 10, 100 or 1000.
   a 3.0987
   b 12.342
   c 0.8865

3. Which is greater in each pair?
   a 3.14 or $3\frac{1}{4}$
   b 0.78 or $\frac{8}{9}$
   c $\frac{10}{11}$ or 0.99

GO TO Section 1: Revision of decimals and fractions

STEP 2

4. Choose the correct answer for each calculation.

	Calculation	Possible answers		
a	24 − 2.35	A 2.165	B 216.5	C 21.65
b	19.5 − 3.45	A 16.5	B 1.605	C 16.05
c	2.25 × 3	A 675	B 67.5	C 6.75
d	18.32 × 4	A 732.8	B 73.28	C 7.328
e	7.488 ÷ 6	A 1.248	B 12.48	C 124.8
f	58.35 ÷ 3	A 0.1945	B 1.945	C 19.45

GO TO Section 2: Calculating with decimals

GO TO Chapter review

Section 1: Revision of decimals and fractions

> **Tip**
> This section has been included so that you can revise concepts if you need to, and check that you know them well.

Comparing decimals

The table shows the results of the men's 4 × 100 m relay final at the 2010 Commonwealth Games in New Delhi.

Five teams completed the race.

Team	Time (seconds)
Australia	39.14
Bahamas	39.27
England	38.74
India	38.89
Jamaica	38.79

The winning times are given as decimals. The digits that follow the decimal point indicate parts of a second (decimal fractions). There are two digits after the decimal place so the times are given correct to a hundredth of a second.

To write the times in order from fastest to slowest, compare the whole number parts of each time first. If those are the same, compare the decimal parts.

You can see that England, India and Jamaica ran the relay in less time than Australia and the Bahamas just by looking at the whole number part.

To decide who came first, second and third between England, India and Jamaica, you need to look at the decimal parts.

Here are the times written in a place value table.

	Tens	Ones/units	.	Tenths	Hundredths
England	3	8	.	7	4
India	3	8	.	8	9
Jamaica	3	8	.	7	9

Tip

Remember you are comparing winning times, so you are looking for the smallest fraction of a second as this is the fastest time. The greater the fraction, the slower the team ran.

Start by looking at the tenths.

8 > 7 so India came third.

England and Jamaica both have 7 in the tenths place value so compare the hundredths.

4 < 9 so England was faster.

The places were: England (1st), Jamaica (2nd) and India (3rd), followed by Australia then the Bahamas.

Converting decimals to fractions

Decimals can be written as fractions using place value.

Look at the time England ran the relay.

Tens	Ones/units	.	Tenths	Hundredths
3	8	.	7	4

You can see that the team ran the relay in 38 seconds and $\frac{74}{100}$ of a second.

The fraction can be simplified further: $\frac{74}{100} = \frac{37}{50}$.

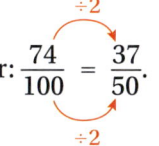

$\div 2$

$\div 2$

Find answers at: cambridge.org/ukschools/gcsemaths-studentbookanswers

Any decimal can be converted to a fraction in this way. For example:

$$0.6 = \frac{6}{10} = \frac{3}{5} \quad (\div 2)$$

$$0.25 = \frac{25}{100} = \frac{1}{4} \quad (\div 25)$$

$$0.375 = \frac{375}{1000} = \frac{3}{8} \quad (\div 125)$$

Converting fractions to decimals

Fractions can be converted to decimals. There are different methods of doing this and you should choose the method that is easiest for the fraction involved.

Method 1:	Method 2:	Method 3:
Equivalent fractions with denominators that are powers of 10, for example, 10, 100, 1000 and so on.	Pen and paper division. Using the 'traditional' written method of division.	Calculator division.
Example: express $\frac{61}{125}$ as a decimal. Multiply the numerator and the denominator by 2 repeatedly until you reach a denominator that is a power of 10. $\frac{61}{125} = \frac{122}{250} = \frac{244}{500} = \frac{488}{1000} = 0.488$ $\frac{61}{125} = 0.488$ This method works well if the denominator is a factor of 10, 100 or 1000.	Example: express $\frac{5}{8}$ as a decimal. Work out $5 \div 8$ using division. Set up a line with 5.0 below it, and write in digits of the answer above the line as you go. $\quad 0.625$ — insert decimal point so that it aligns with the decimal point in the number you are dividing $\overline{5.0}$ $\underline{4.8} \quad 0.6 \times 8$ 0.20 $\underline{0.16} \quad 0.02 \times 8$ 0.040 $\underline{0.040} \quad 0.005 \times 8$ 0.00 $\frac{5}{8} = 0.625$	Example: express $\frac{2}{3}$ as a decimal. Input $2 \div 3$ on your calculator. [2][÷][3][=] [0.666666666] The 6s continue forever (they recur). Show this by writing the answer as $0.\dot{6}$. **Tip** Remember you write a dot above the first and last digits of the recurring number if more than one digit recurs, so 5.134134134... would be written $5.\dot{1}3\dot{4}$.

EXERCISE 11A

Tip

When you have to compare and order ordinary fractions you can convert them all to decimals and compare them easily using place value. This is often quicker than changing them all into equivalent fractions with a common denominator.

1. Write each of the following decimals as a fraction in its simplest form.
   a 0.6 b 0.84 c 1.64 d 0.385 e 0.125
   f 1.08 g 0.875 h 0.008 i 3.064 j 0.333

2. Convert the following fractions to decimals without using a calculator.
   a $\frac{3}{5}$ b $\frac{3}{4}$ c $\frac{18}{25}$ d $\frac{19}{20}$ e $\frac{34}{50}$
   f $\frac{110}{250}$ g $\frac{89}{200}$ h $\frac{76}{500}$ i $\frac{185}{20}$ j $\frac{145}{50}$
   k $\frac{11}{6}$ l $\frac{3}{8}$ m $\frac{9}{4}$ n $\frac{8}{9}$ o $\frac{19}{8}$

3 Use a calculator to convert the fractions from $\frac{1}{9}$ to $\frac{8}{9}$ into decimals.
  a What pattern do you notice?
  b What do you call decimals of this nature?
  c Repeat this for the fractions from $\frac{1}{6}$ to $\frac{5}{6}$.
    Write each decimal correctly using the notation for recurring decimals as necessary.
  d Convert $\frac{1}{11}$ and $\frac{2}{11}$ to decimals.
    Write the decimals correctly using notation for recurring decimals.
  e Predict what $\frac{3}{11}$ and $\frac{4}{11}$ will be if you convert them to decimals.
    Check your prediction using a calculator.

4 Arrange the following in decreasing order of size.
  a 5.2, 5.29, 8.62, 4.92, 4.09
  b 7.42, 0.76, 0.742, 0.421, 3.219
  c 14.3, 14.72, 14.07, 14.89, 14.009
  d 0.23, 0.26, 0.273, 0.287, 0.206
  e 0.403, $\frac{1}{2}$, $\frac{2}{3}$, 0.68, 0.45, $\frac{5}{11}$
  f $\frac{7}{9}$, $\frac{3}{8}$, 0.625, 0.88, 0.718

5 Fill in the boxes using <, = or > to make each statement true.
  a 13.098 ☐ 13.099
  b 0.312 ☐ 0.322
  c $\frac{5}{6}$ ☐ 0.84
  d 0.375 ☐ $\frac{3}{8}$
  e 2.05 ☐ $\frac{205}{1000}$
  f $\frac{3}{5}$ ☐ 0.7
  g $\frac{2}{5}$ ☐ 0.35
  h $\frac{18}{25}$ ☐ 0.67
  i $\frac{1}{3}$ ☐ 0.37

6 Write a decimal fraction that is between each pair of decimals.
  a 3.135 and 3.136
  b 0.6645 and 06646
  c 4.998 and 4.999

7 The lengths of some of the world's longest roller coaster rides are given in the table.

Roller coaster	Country	Length of ride (km)
The Beast	USA	2.243
California Screaming	USA	1.851
Formula Rossa	United Arab Emirates	2.0
Fujiyama	Japan	2.045
Steel Dragon	Japan	2.479
The Ultimate	UK	2.268

  a Which is the longest roller coaster?
  b Which is the shortest?
  c Is the Steel Dragon longer or shorter than $2\frac{1}{2}$ km?
  d Which roller coasters are longer than $2\frac{1}{4}$ km?
  e Write the lengths in order from longest to shortest.

Section 2: Calculating with decimals

You need to be able to add, subtract, multiply and divide decimals without using a calculator.

Working through the following activities will help you revise this.

Find answers at: cambridge.org/ukschools/gcsemaths-studentbookanswers

Tip

You will learn more about approximation in Chapter 17.

Estimating

When you calculate with decimals it is useful to first estimate the answer.

An estimate helps you decide if your solution is reasonable and whether you have the decimal point in the correct place. There's a big difference between £10 and £0.10!

WORKED EXAMPLE 1

Lucy bought three items from a market stall.

One item cost £4.39, another cost 55p and the third cost £13.25.

The market stall holder asked for £72.64.

Lucy had estimated the expected price and knew this was far too much. She asked the market stall holder to check his calculations.

His calculator screen showed the following:

    4.39 + 55 + 13.25
                72.64

a What is a possible estimate for the cost of Lucy's items?

b What did the market stall holder do wrong?

a 4.39 + 0.55 + 13.25 — Round each answer to a 'reasonable' number. As these are money amounts, to the nearest pound or 50p is sensible.

4.50 + 0.50 + 13 — Add together the rounded amounts.

5 + 13 = 18 — It should have cost around £18.

Lucy's items should cost ≈ £18

b The market stall holder didn't enter 55p correctly as 0.55.

When doing calculations, it's important to make sure that all terms of the calculation are converted to the same units by multiplying or dividing by a power of 10. To convert from pence to pounds, divide by 100.

Tip

You will learn more about converting between units in Chapter 12.

EXERCISE 11B

For each of the following problems estimate the answer. Record what you did to estimate.

1 The masses of some coins are given below.

7.1g   6.6g   8.1g   9.5g

a What is the approximate difference in mass between the heaviest and lightest coins?

b Approximate the combined mass of the four coins.

   c What is the approximate total mass of a £1 coin and two 10p coins?

   d Nick has five £1 coins in his pocket. Approximately how much do they weigh altogether?

   e Xena has a packet of 50p coins that weighs 162 grams.
      Approximately how many coins are in the packet?

   f Will ten 10p coins weigh more or less than six £1 coins?

   g Ana has a pile of twenty 2p coins and Ben has a pile of twenty 10p coins. What is the approximate difference in the mass of the two piles?

2 A bottle of medicine contains 0.375 litres and costs £2.55.

   a Can you buy two bottles for £5?

   b About how many litres of medicine will you need to fill 5 bottles?

   c Estimate how many bottles you can fill with 1 litre of the medicine.

   d Tanja has to take 15 ml of the medicine twice a day. Approximately how long will the bottle last?

   e Nina buys two bottles of the medicine and pays with a £20 note. Estimate how much change she should get.

   f In one day, the pharmacy sold 23 bottles of this medicine. Is that more or less than 5 litres in total?

   g What is the approximate cost per 100 ml of this medicine?

3 Compare your work with a partner.

   a Explain how you estimated the answers.
      How did you use rounding and approximation?
      How did you decide what to do?

   b Look at your answers.
      Did you get the same estimates? If not, is one estimate closer than the other? Try to explain why.

Adding and subtracting decimals

Add or subtract decimals in columns by lining up the places and the decimal points.

WORKED EXAMPLE 2

Calculate.

a 12.7 + 18.34 + 3.087

```
   12.7
   18.34
+   3.087
_____
   34.127
```

b 399.65 − 245.175

```
   399.650
-  245.175
_____
   154.475
```

Write a 0 as a place holder here.

Find answers at: cambridge.org/ukschools/gcsemaths-studentbookanswers

Multiplying and dividing decimals

> **Tip**
>
> This is really a place value movement by the digits as you multiply or divide by a power of 10, but visually, it looks like the decimal point is moving.

To **multiply or divide by a power of 10** (10, 100, 1000, and so on):
- The digits move as many places to the left as the number of zeros when multiplying.
- The digits move as many places to the right as the number of zeros when dividing.

To **multiply decimals by decimals**:
- Ignore the decimal points and multiply the numbers.
- Place the decimal point in the answer so it has the same number of digits after the decimal point as there were altogether in the multiplication problem.

To **divide by a decimal**:
- Make the divisor a whole number by multiplying the divisor and the dividend by the same power of 10.
- Then divide as normal, keeping the decimal point in the answer directly above the decimal point in the number you are dividing; be careful to insert digits according to their correct place value.

To **divide a decimal by a whole number**:
- Use the 'traditional' written method of division but make sure you align the decimal point in the answer with the decimal point in the dividend, and keep the decimals aligned in all your working; be careful to insert digits according to their correct place value.

WORKED EXAMPLE 3

Calculate.

a $0.4 + 0.3$ **b** 5.408×3.2 **c** $1.144 \div 0.02$

a 0.4×0.3
$= \dfrac{4}{10} \times \dfrac{3}{10}$
$= \dfrac{12}{100}$
$= 0.12$

b 5.408×3.2
$5408 \times 32 = 173\,056$ *There are 3 dp and 1 dp in the calculation.*
$5.408 \times 3.2 = 17.3056$ *There are four decimal places.*

c $1.144 \div 0.02$
$= \dfrac{0.144}{0.02}$
$= 0.144 \times \dfrac{100}{0.02} \times 100$
$= \dfrac{14.4}{2}$
$= 7.2$

WORK IT OUT 11.1

Work with a partner.

Read through the notes about how to multiply and divide with decimals. Provide two numerical examples to show how to do each of the following.

a Multiply by a power of 10.

b Divide by a power of 10.

c Multiply a decimal fraction by a decimal fraction.

d Divide by a decimal.

e Divide a decimal by a whole number.

> **Tip**
>
> You might find it helpful to use a place value chart and estimate your answer first.

Reasoning

You use decimals when you deal with money, distances and other measurements.

When you solve problems involving decimals you need to make sure that your answer is both reasonable and sensible in the context.

For example, if you work out the price of an item and you get an answer of £15.987, it makes sense to round it to £15.99 because you don't have coins smaller than 1p (a hundredth of a pound).

Problem-solving framework

Salman saved £20 to go and see an exhibition at the Natural History Museum in London.

His train ticket cost £6.35. The ticket for the exhibition was £8.00. He bought an exhibition booklet for £2.50 and spent £1.55 on a snack at the museum café.

How much money did he have left?

Steps for approaching a problem-solving question	What you would do for this example
Step 1: Work out what you have to do. Start by reading the question carefully.	The words 'how much does he have left' tell you that you need to find the change. So you have to add up what he spent and then subtract it from the money he had.
Step 2: What information do you need? Have you got it all?	You need the starting amount and how much he spent. You have that information.
Step 3: Is there any information that you don't need?	You don't need to know where he went or what he spent the money on. That detail is unnecessary.
Step 4: Decide what maths you can do.	Money left = money saved − costs. You can add the costs and subtract them from the amount Salman had saved.

Continues on next page …

Find answers at: cambridge.org/ukschools/gcsemaths-studentbookanswers

Steps for approaching a problem-solving question	What you would do for this example
Step 5: Set out your solution clearly. Check your working and that your answer is reasonable.	6.35 8.00 2.50 + 1.55 ――― 18.40 20.00 − 18.40 ――― 1.60
Step 6: Check that you've answered the question.	Salman has £1.60 left over.

EXERCISE 11C

1 Estimate first then calculate.

   a 0.8 + 0.78   **b** 12.8 − 11.13   **c** 0.8 + 0.9

   d 15.31 − 1.96   **e** 2.77 × 8.2   **f** 9.81 × 3.5

2 Evaluate without a calculator.

   a 12.7 + 18.34 + 35.01   **b** 12.35 + 8.5 + 2.91   **c** 6.89 − 3.28

   d 34.45 − 12.02   **e** 345.297 − 12.39   **f** 56 + 8.345 − 34.65

   g 27.4 + 9.01 − 12.451   **h** 0.786 × 100   **i** 54.76 × 2000

   j 1.234 × 0.65   **k** 87.87 × 2.341   **l** 1.83 ÷ 61

   m 0.358 ÷ 4   **n** 5.053 ÷ 0.62   **o** 31.72 ÷ 0.04

3 The world record for the men's 4 × 100 m relay is 36.84 seconds (Jamaica, 2008) and the Commonwealth Games record is 38.20 seconds (England, 1998).

   a What is the time difference between the World Record and the Commonwealth Games Record?

   b In the 2010 Commonwealth Games, the English team ran the relay in 38.74 seconds.
      How much slower is this than their record in 1998?

   c Each of the four runners in a relay runs 100 m.
      Calculate the average time taken for 100 m during the World Record winning race.

   d Do you think each runner takes the same amount of time? Explain your reasoning.

4 Nadia wants to make a dish that requires 1.5 litres of cream.

   She has four 0.385 litre cartons of cream. Does she have enough?

5 Josh takes a multivitamin every morning.

He calculates that if he takes one tablet every day for a week he will take in 1166.69 g of vitamin C, 54.6 mg of boron and 257.95 mg of calcium.

Work out how much of each ingredient there is in a tablet.

6 The Chetty household uses about 25.75 kilowatt hours of electricity per day.

Calculate how much they will use in:

   a one week.
   b one (non-leap) year.

7 Sandra has £87.50 in her purse. She buys two sweaters that cost £32.99 each. How much money does she have left?

8 George travels from York to Oxford by car.

His odometer reads 123 456.8 km when he leaves York and 123 642.7 km when he arrives in Oxford.

How far did he travel?

9 If I have 5.67 litres of juice, how many cups containing $\frac{2}{15}$ of a litre can I pour?

10 Find 0.75 of 2400.

11 Sheldon placed fence posts 0.84 m apart all along his boundary fence.

If the total fence is 60 metres long, how many posts will there be?

12 June bought 6.65 litres of petrol at £1.29 per litre. How much did she pay?

13 Toni earns £28 650 per year.

   a How much is this per day?
   b How much is this per five-day week? Give your answer correct to two decimal places.
   c If Toni is paid the amount in part **b** every week for 52 weeks of a year, will she earn more or less than the original total? Why?

> **Tip**
>
> Remember there are 365.25 days in a year.

Checklist of learning and understanding

Decimals and fractions

- You can express decimals as fractions by writing them with a denominator that is a power of ten and then simplifying them. For example, $0.4 = \frac{4}{10} = \frac{2}{5}$.
- You can change fractions to decimals by dividing the numerator by the denominator. The bar in a fraction stands for division.
  For example, $\frac{3}{4} = 3 \div 4 = 0.75$.
- Changing ordinary fractions to decimals makes it easier to compare their sizes using place value.

Calculations with decimals

- Pen and paper methods are important in a non-calculator exam paper; you can use any method as long as you show your working.

Find answers at: cambridge.org/ukschools/gcsemaths-studentbookanswers

- Decimals can be added and subtracted by lining up the places and the decimal points.
- Decimals can be multiplied like whole numbers as long as you insert the decimal point so there are the same number of decimal places in the answer as there were altogether in the numbers being multiplied.
- Decimals can be divided by making the divisor a whole number (multiply both numbers by a power of ten to do this). Then divide normally and align the decimal point in the answer with the decimal point in the number being divided; be careful to insert digits according to their correct place value.
- When dividing a decimal by a whole number, use the 'traditional' written method of division but make sure you align the decimal point in the answer with the decimal point in the dividend, and keep the decimals aligned in all your working; be careful to insert digits according to their correct place value.

For additional questions on the topics in this chapter, visit GCSE Mathematics Online.

Chapter review

1. Arrange each set of numbers in increasing order of size.

   a 4.2, 4.8, 4.22, 4.97, 4.08
   b 2.96, 2.955, $2\frac{46}{50}$, $2\frac{9}{25}$, 2.12
   c $\frac{3}{4}$, 0.86, $\frac{4}{5}$, 0.78, $\frac{5}{6}$, 0.91

2. Convert to decimals and insert <, = or > to compare the fractions.

   a $\frac{3}{5}$ □ $\frac{12}{20}$
   b $\frac{5}{6}$ □ $\frac{7}{11}$
   c $\frac{2}{9}$ □ $\frac{1}{7}$

3. Write each as a fraction in its simplest terms.

   a 0.88
   b 2.75
   c 0.008

4. a Increase $\frac{2}{5}$ by 2.75
   b Reduce 91.07 by $\frac{1}{2}$ of 42.8
   c Divide 4 by 0.125
   d Multiply 0.4 by 0.8

5. a Add 4.726 and 3.09
   b Subtract 2.916 from 4.008
   c Multiply 8.76 by 100
   d Divide 18.07 by 1000
   e Multiply 4.12 by 0.7
   f Simplify $\frac{32.64}{2.4}$

6. Jarryd and Kate have £16 each. Jarryd spends 0.416 of his money and Kate spends $\frac{4}{15}$ of hers.

   Who has more money left? How much more?

12 Units and measurement

In this chapter you will learn how to …

- work with and convert standard units of measurement.
- use and convert compound units of measurement.
- work with map scales and bearings.
- construct and use scale diagrams to solve problems.

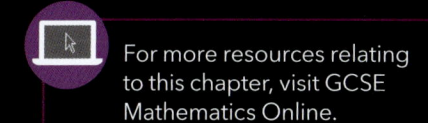

For more resources relating to this chapter, visit GCSE Mathematics Online.

Using mathematics: real-life applications

Measurement has practical applications in many different jobs, but it is also important in everyday activities. Being able to read and work with measurements is important when you make or alter clothes, work out what materials you need to build things, and weigh ingredients to make a recipe.

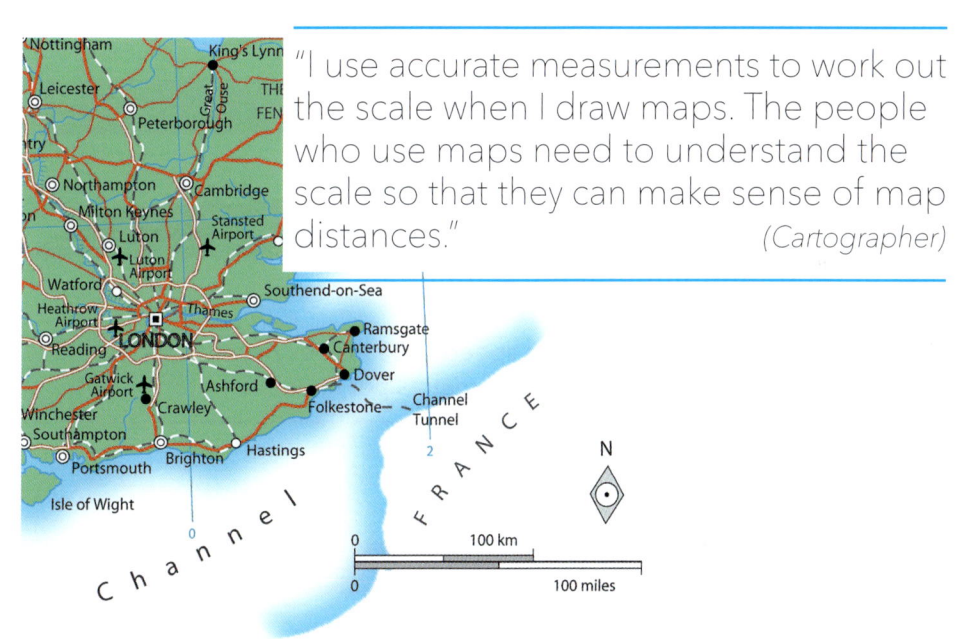

"I use accurate measurements to work out the scale when I draw maps. The people who use maps need to understand the scale so that they can make sense of map distances."
(Cartographer)

Before you start …

KS3	You must be able to multiply and divide using multiples of 10.	**1** Work out. **a** 1000×10 **b** $10 \div 1000$ **c** $100 \div 1000$
KS3 Ch 3	You should be able to substitute numbers into a simple formula.	**2** Use the formula to work out the pay of each person: pay = hours worked × rate of pay **a** Amelia: 20 hours worked at £7 per hour. **b** Billy: 15 hours worked at £6 per hour. **c** Catrin: 40 hours worked at £5.50 per hour.
KS3	You should be able to solve problems involving direct proportion.	**3** Six pencils cost 90p. Work out the cost of: **a** 12 pencils. **b** 1 pencil. **c** 4 pencils.

Find answers at: cambridge.org/ukschools/gcsemaths-studentbookanswers

GCSE Mathematics for OCR (Foundation)

Assess your starting point using the Launchpad

STEP 1

1 Convert.
  a 11 569 grams into kilograms
  b $4\frac{1}{2}$ hours into seconds
  c 123 456 pence into pounds (£)
  d 5 cm² into m²

GO TO
Section 1:
Standard units of measurement

STEP 2

2 A car travels 16 kilometres in 20 minutes.
  a What is the average speed of the car in kilometres per hour?
  b Express this speed in m/s.

3 An object is travelling at a speed of 25 metres per second. Express this as a speed in kilometres per hour.

GO TO
Section 2:
Compound units of measurement

STEP 3

4 A helicopter is drawn using a scale of 1 : 100. On the scale drawing the length of the helicopter blade is 8 cm. How long is the actual blade?

5 The helicopter takes off from a point X and flies due north for 30 km to reach point Y.

It then flies on a bearing of 150° for 15 km to reach point Z.
  a Use a scale of 1 cm to represent 10 km to make a scale drawing showing this journey.
  b Use your diagram to find the bearing from X to Z.
  c By measuring your diagram, find the actual distance directly between X and Z.

GO TO
Section 3:
Maps, scale drawings and bearings

GO TO
Chapter review

12 Units and measurements

Section 1: Standard units of measurement

We use standard metric units of measurement for recording length, area, volume, capacity, mass and money.

In the metric system, units of measurement are divided into sub-units with prefixes such as milli-, centi-, deci-, deca-, hecto- and kilo-.

The same prefixes are used for length, mass and capacity.

	×10	×10	×10	×10	×10	×10
length	millimetre	centimetre	decimetre	metre	decametre	hectometre	kilometre
mass	milligram	centigram	decigram	gram	decagram	hectogram	kilogram
capacity	millilitre	centilitre	decilitre	litre	decalitre	hectolitre	kilolitre
	÷10	÷10	÷10	÷10	÷10	÷10

> **Did you know?**
>
> The USA, Liberia and Myanmar are the only three countries in the world that do not officially use the metric system of measurement. All other countries have adopted the metric system.

Each sub-unit is 10 times bigger than the one before it.

Centimetres are 10 times bigger than millimetres, decimetres are 10 times bigger than centimetres and so on.

Converting between units

To convert between units in the metric system you need to multiply or divide by powers of 10.

This diagram shows how to convert between centimetres and metres.

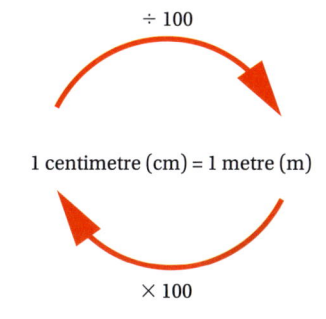

÷ 100

1 centimetre (cm) = 1 metre (m)

× 100

The **conversion factor** is 100 because you are changing across **two** sub-units.

Each sub-unit is 10 times greater or smaller than the one next to it, so here you have to multiply or divide by $10^2 = 100$.

You will use the following conversions often, so it will be useful to remember them.

1 centimetre (cm) = 10 millimetres (mm)
1 metre (m) = 100 centimetres (cm)
1 kilometre (km) = 1000 metres (m)
1 kilogram (kg) = 1000 grams (g)
1 tonne (t) = 1000 kilograms (kg)
1 litre (l) = 1000 millilitres (ml)
1 litre (l) = 1000 cubic centimetres (cm^3)
1 cubic centimetre (cm^3) = 1 millilitre (ml)

> **Tip**
>
> When you convert from a smaller to a larger unit there will be fewer of the larger units, so you **divide by a power of 10**.
>
> When you convert from a larger to a smaller unit there will be more of the smaller units, so you **multiply by a power of 10**.

> **Key vocabulary**
>
> **conversion factor**: the number that you multiply or divide by to convert one measure into another smaller or larger unit.

Find answers at: cambridge.org/ukschools/gcsemaths-studentbookanswers

173

GCSE Mathematics for OCR (Foundation)

WORK IT OUT 12.1

In a sponsored swim the total number of lengths swum is 94.

Each length is 25 metres.

How many kilometres were swum in total?

Which of the answers below is correct?

Option A	Option B	Option C
Total number of metres = 25 × 94 = 2350 metres	Total number of metres = 25 × 94 = 2350 metres	Total number of metres = 25 × 94 = 2350 metres
Conversion: 100 metres = 1 km	Conversion: 100 metres = 1 km	Conversion: 1000 metres = 1 km
2350 ÷ 100 = 23.5 km swum in total.	2350 × 100 = 235 000 km swum in total.	2350 ÷ 1000 = 2.35 km swum in total.

Converting areas and volume

Area is measured in square units such as mm² (square millimetres), cm², m² or km² so any conversion factor also has to be squared.

For example, to convert cm to mm you would multiply by 10, but to convert cm² to mm² you would need to multiply by 10² which is 100.

The two blue rectangles below have the same area.

The conversion factor from m² to cm², and vice versa, is 10 000.

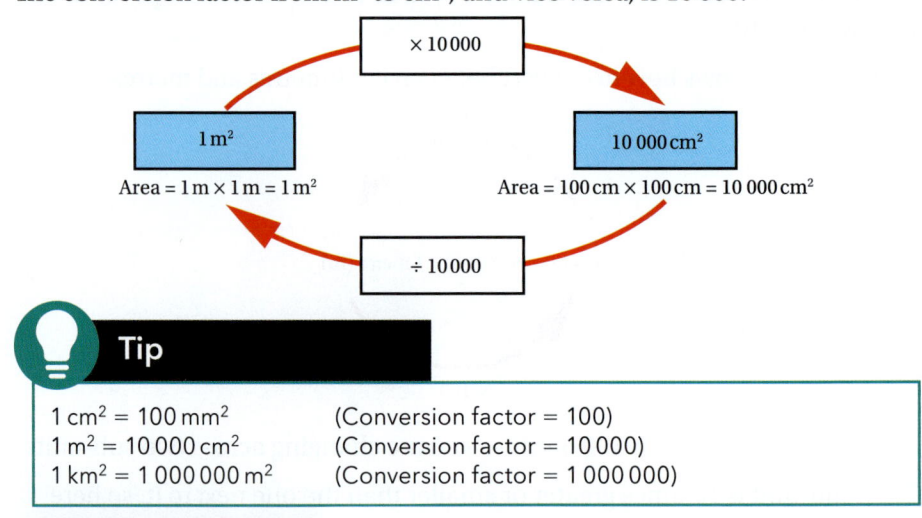

```
                    × 10 000
              ┌──────────────→
    ┌─────┐                    ┌──────────┐
    │ 1m² │                    │10 000 cm²│
    └─────┘                    └──────────┘
  Area = 1m × 1m = 1m²     Area = 100 cm × 100 cm = 10 000 cm²
              ←──────────────┐
                    ÷ 10 000
```

Tip

1 cm² = 100 mm²   (Conversion factor = 100)
1 m² = 10 000 cm²   (Conversion factor = 10 000)
1 km² = 1 000 000 m²   (Conversion factor = 1 000 000)

WORKED EXAMPLE 1

Convert each measure to the units given.

a 10 m² to cm²   b 8.6 km² to m²   c 3500 mm² to cm²

a 10 m² to cm²
   = 10 × 10 000 = 100 000 cm²   Conversion factor = 10 000

b 8.6 km² to m²
   = 8.6 × 1 000 000 = 8 600 000 m²   Conversion factor = 1 000 000

c 3500 mm² to cm²
   = 3500 ÷ 100 = 35 cm²   Conversion factor = 100

Volume is measured in cubic units such as mm³ (cubic millimetres), cm³ or m³ so any conversion factor also has to be cubed.

Again, to convert cm to mm you would multiply by 10, but to convert cm³ to mm³ you would need to multiply by 10^3 which is 1000.

The two cuboids below have the same volume.

The conversion factor from m³ to cm³, and vice versa, is 1 000 000.

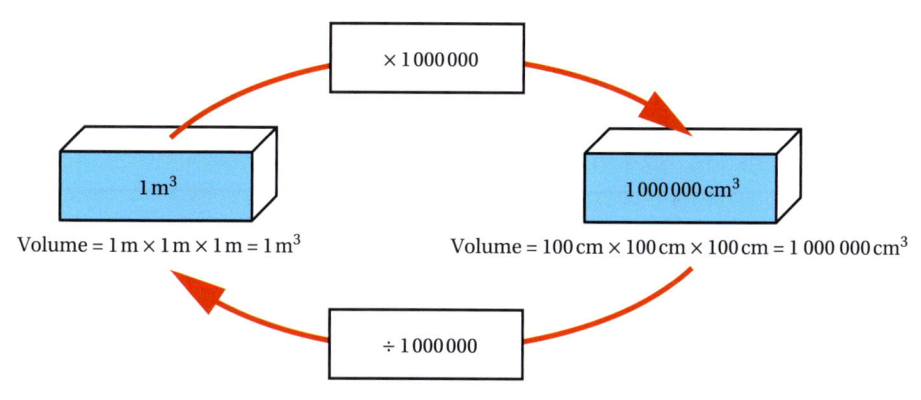

$1\,m^3$ ⇄ $1\,000\,000\,cm^3$

× 1 000 000

÷ 1 000 000

Volume = 1 m × 1 m × 1 m = 1 m³

Volume = 100 cm × 100 cm × 100 cm = 1 000 000 cm³

> **Tip**
>
> 1 cm³ = 1000 mm³ (Conversion factor = 1000)
> 1 m³ = 1 000 000 cm³ (Conversion factor = 1 000 000)
> 1 litre = 1000 cm³ (Conversion factor = 1000)

WORKED EXAMPLE 2

Convert each measurement to the unit given.

a 6.3 m³ to cm³ **b** 96 500 000 cm³ to m³ **c** 750 cm³ to mm³

a 6.3 m³ to cm³
  = 6.3 × 1 000 000 = 6 300 000 cm³   Conversion factor = 1 000 000

b 96 500 000 cm³ to m³
  = 96 500 000 ÷ 1 000 000 = 96.5 m³   Conversion factor = 1 000 000

c 750 cm³ to mm³
  = 750 × 1000 = 750 000 mm³   Conversion factor = 1000

Look at this plan of a room.

The real length of each section of wall is given but the units of measurement are different.

It is easy to make mistakes if you try to calculate with measurements in different units, so it makes sense to convert them all to the same unit before doing any calculations.

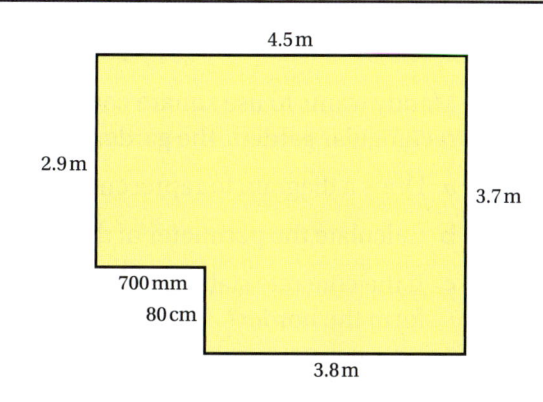

4.5 m
2.9 m
3.7 m
700 mm
80 cm
3.8 m

Find answers at: cambridge.org/ukschools/gcsemaths-studentbookanswers

WORKED EXAMPLE 3

A builder is to put masking tape all along the line where the walls meet the ceiling of the room drawn above. How many metres of masking tape does the builder need?

80 cm ÷ 100 = 0.8 m

700 mm ÷ 1000 = 0.7 m

Total distance around the room:
2.9 + 4.5 + 3.7 + 3.8 + 0.8 + 0.7 = 16.4 m

The builder needs 16.4 m of masking tape.

In this example, it makes sense to work in metres, as the answer needs to be given in metres.

Tip

You will use measurement conversions when you deal with scale drawings and maps in Section 3 and when you deal with perimeter, area and volume in Chapters 15, 16 and 21.

EXERCISE 12A

1 Match the measurement on the left to the equivalent measurement on the right.

10 000 mm	10 l
10 000 ml	10 g
10 kg	10 m
0.01 kg	1 mm
0.1 cm	10 000 g

2 Convert the following lengths and masses into the given units to complete the following.

a 2.5 km = ☐ m b 85 cm = ☐ mm c 34 m = ☐ mm

d 1.55 m = ☐ mm e 0.07 m = ☐ cm f 5.4 kg = ☐ g

g 0.9 kg = ☐ g h 102 g = ☐ kg i 14.5 g = ☐ kg

3 Add the following capacities. Give your answers in the units indicated in brackets.

a 3.5 l + 5 l (ml) b 2.3 l + 450 ml (l) c 20 l + 4.5 l + 652 ml (l)

4 Mandy wants to use square concrete slabs to form a border around a rectangular garden. The garden is 480 cm wide and 7.2 metres long.

a Draw a diagram to represent the garden.

b Calculate the perimeter of the garden in metres.

c If the concrete slabs are 120 cm long, how many will Mandy need to form the border?

d The slabs cost £4.55 each. Work out how much it will cost Mandy to buy the slabs she needs.

e What is the cost per metre for the concrete border?

5 Convert each of the following into the required units.

  a Total weight in kg of 3 bags of flour, each of mass 1200 g.

  b The length in cm of a 7.763 m long whale.

  c 3567 kg of lead into tonnes.   **d** Area of 5 m² into mm².

  e 96.35 m³ of sand into cm³.   **f** 345 cm³ of water into litres.

Time

The units of time we use on a daily basis are not decimal units.

To convert units of time you have to work out how many sub-units there are in the units you are working with.

For example, to convert from weeks to days, you would need to multiply by 7 as there are 7 days in a week.

To convert from seconds to hours, you would need to divide by 60 to get minutes and then by 60 again to get hours.

You can also do this in one step by dividing by 3600.

> **Tip**
>
> 1 year = 365 days
> (366 in a leap year)
> 1 day = 24 hours = 1440 minutes
> 1 hour = 60 minutes
> = 3600 seconds
> 1 minute = 60 seconds

Time is sometimes given in decimal form, for example 4.8 hours.

You can convert these times back to ordinary units in different ways.

There are 60 minutes in an hour, so

4.8×60 minutes = 288 minutes = 4 hours 48 minutes.

Or, you can think of this as 4 hours and 0.8 hours.

$0.8 \times 60 = 48$, so the time is 4 hours and 48 minutes.

In athletics and other timed sporting events the times are often given using decimal fractions of a second.

For example, in August 2009, Usain Bolt ran the 100 m in the World Record time of 9.580 seconds.

In the metric system, 1 second = 1000 milliseconds.

9.580 is time recorded exact to $\frac{1}{1000}$ of a second.

This is 9 seconds and 580 milliseconds. You cannot convert it in any other way.

> **Calculator tip**
>
> Modern scientific calculators have a mode that you can use to do hexadecimal calculation (hours, minutes and seconds). Different models work in different ways, so read the manual or check online to see how your calculator works.

12-hour and 24-hour times

The 12-hour time system uses **am** to show times from midnight to noon and **pm** for time from noon till midnight.

The 24-hour time system shows the times 00:00 to 23:59. Midnight is 00:00.

> **Tip**
>
> Add 12 to write a pm time using the 24-hour clock,
> for example 10.35 pm + 12 = 22:35.
> Subtract 12 to write a time between 13:00 and 23:59 using the 12-hour clock,
> for example 15:40 − 12 = 3.40 pm.

Find answers at: cambridge.org/ukschools/gcsemaths-studentbookanswers

Problem-solving framework

Mr Smith is in Moscow. He needs to return to London for a meeting in the morning.

The flight from Moscow to London takes 3.6 hours. The local time in Moscow is 3 hours ahead of the UK.

The flight is scheduled for take-off at 18:55 local time. On arrival it will take 45 minutes to pass through customs and exit the airport.

Mr Smith will stop to buy a coffee for the train.

Trains for central London leave at 5, 27 and 46 minutes past the hour, and the journey will take 29 minutes.

There is a 7 minute walk from the train station to his hotel.

What is the earliest time that Mr Smith can expect to arrive at his hotel?
Give your answer using the 12-hour system of time.

> **Tip**
>
> When you work with time, treat hours and minutes separately. If you carry over from hours to minutes, remember you are carrying 60 minutes.

Steps for approaching a problem-solving question	What you would do for this example
Step 1: What have you got to do?	Work out the time of arrival in London and then work out how long it takes from there to the hotel.
Step 2: What information do you need?	Flight departure times: 18:55 (local time) Time difference between London and Moscow: 3 hours Flight time: 3.6 hours Time to pass through customs: 45 minutes Train departure times: 5 past, 27 minutes past, 46 minutes past the hour Length of train journey: 29 minutes Walk time: 7 minutes
Step 3: What information don't you need?	Assume time to buy a coffee is too short to include.

Continues on next page …

12 Units and measurements

Step 4: What maths can you do?	18:55 minus 3 hours = 15:55 (London time)
	Convert 3.6 from a decimal to time in hours and minutes:
	3 hours and 0.6×60 = 3 hours 36 mins
	Arrival time in London: 15:55 + 3 hours 36 mins = 19:31
	Add on time in customs: 19:31 + 45 mins = 20:16
	Next possible train is 20:27
	Time at end of train journey: 20:27 + 29 mins = 20:56
	Arrival time at venue following walk: 20:56 + 7 mins = 21:03
	21:03 − 12 = 9.03 pm or three minutes past nine in the evening
Step 5: Have you used all the information? At this point you should check to make sure you have calculated what was asked of you.	Flight departure time ✓ Time difference ✓ Flight time ✓ Time through customs ✓ Train departure times ✓ Length of train journey ✓ Walk time ✓
Step 6: Is it correct?	Estimate to check
	$3\frac{1}{2}$ hours flying + 45 mins at airport + 10 mins wait + 30 mins train + 7 mins walk = about 5 hours
	Take off the time difference leaves 2 hours
	Leave 7 pm + 2 hours = 9 pm

Money

You already know how to convert between pence and pounds.

£1 = 100p   So, £x = 100x pence   and x pence = £$\frac{x}{100}$

The rate at which one currency is converted to another is called an **exchange rate**.

For example £1 = €1.26 and €1 = £0.794 or 79.4p (at 2014 rates).

When the exchange rate is given as 1 unit of A = x units of B, you can convert A to B by multiplying by x.

For example £1 = €1.26

So, £400 = 400 × 1.26 = €504

Currency B can be converted to currency A by dividing by x.

For example £1 = €1.26

So, €400 = $\frac{400}{1.26}$ = £317.46

> **Key vocabulary**
>
> **exchange rate:** the value of one currency used to convert that currency to an equivalent value in another currency.

Find answers at: cambridge.org/ukschools/gcsemaths-studentbookanswers

EXERCISE 12B

1. The starting pistol for a road race is fired at 12:15:30.
   The first runner crosses the finishing line at 14:07:22.
   What was the winning time for the race?

2. Sandra is exactly 16 years old. Calculate her age in:
   a weeks.   b days.   c hours.   d seconds.

3. A boat leaves port at 14:35 and arrives at its destination $6\frac{1}{2}$ hours later.
   At what time does the boat arrive?

4. An area of 250 000 cm² needs to be painted. A pot of paint can cover an area of 10 m².
   How many pots of paint are needed?

5. The table gives the value of the pound against four other currencies in mid-2014.

British pound (£)	Euro (€)	US dollar ($)	Australian dollar (AS$)	Indian rupee (INR)
1	1.26	1.70	1.80	102.28

   a Convert each of the currencies into pounds using the rates in the table.
   b Convert £125 to US dollars.
   c How many Indian rupees would you get if you converted £45 at this rate?
   d Dilshaad has 8000 Indian rupees. What is this worth in pounds at this rate?

Section 2: Compound units of measurement

Compound measures involve more than one unit of measurement.

For example:

- Rate of pay (such as pounds per hour) involves units of money and time.
- Unit pricing (such as pence per gram) involves units of money and mass (or capacity or volume).

Compound measures usually express how many of the first unit correspond with 1 of the second unit. For example, a rate of pay of £8.20/hour shows how many pounds you earn for 1 hour of work.

You can simplify compound measures by multiplying or dividing both units by the same factor.

Tip

A forward slash symbol / is often used instead of the word 'per'. So £8.20/hour means the same as £8.20 per hour.

WORKED EXAMPLE 4

40 litres of petrol cost £52.

a What is the cost in £/litre?

b Convert the cost in £/litre to pence per millilitre.

a £$\frac{52}{40}$ = £1.30 — The compound measure £/litre tells you that pounds are the first unit.

The cost is £1.30/litre

b £1.30 = 130p
1 l = 1000 ml

You want a compound measure comparing pence and millilitres. So, convert pounds to pence, and litres to millilitres.

130p per 1000 ml — Compare the two quantities.

130 ÷ 1000 = 0.13
1000 ÷ 1000 = 1

You want a rate per one millilitre, so divide both quantities by 1000.

So 130p per 1000 ml = 0.13p/ml

Speed

Speed compares the distance travelled to the time taken.

The units of speed depend on the situation.

A car or train's speed is often given in km/h or mph (kilometres or miles per hour).

An athlete's running speed may be given in m/s (metres per second).

You need to know the formula for calculating speed:

Learn this formula

Average speed = $\frac{\text{distance travelled}}{\text{time taken}}$

The speed is an average speed because a journey may involve faster and slower speeds over the given period. You can see the different speeds at different points in a car journey by looking at the speedometer. The speed shown on the speedometer is the speed at that particular time.

The triangle shows the relationship between speed, distance and time.

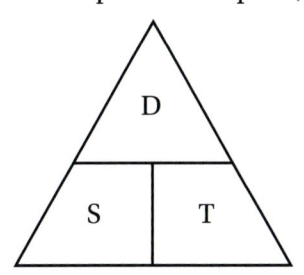

The units of speed given in a problem usually let you know what units to use.

For example, if the problem talks about km/h, then express distances in kilometres and time in hours to calculate the speed.

Find answers at: cambridge.org/ukschools/gcsemaths-studentbookanswers

Did you know?

Speed isn't just a measure of how fast something is travelling. Run rates per over in cricket and the number of words you can type per minute are both examples of speed.

Tip

Using the triangle:
- To find distance: cover D with your finger. The position of S next to T tells you to multiply speed by time.
  Distance = Speed × Time
- To find time: cover T with your finger. The position of D over S tells you to divide distance by speed.
  Time = Distance ÷ Speed
- To find speed: cover S with your finger. The position of D over T tells you to divide distance by time.
  Speed = Distance ÷ Time

WORK IT OUT 12.2

A car travels 330 miles in $5\frac{1}{2}$ hours.

What is the average speed of the car in miles per hour (mph)?
Which of the answers below is correct?

Option A	Option B	Option C
Speed = Distance ÷ Time	Speed = Distance × Time	Speed = Distance − Time
D = 330 miles	D = 330 miles	D = 330 miles
T = $5\frac{1}{2}$ hours = 5.5 hours	T = $5\frac{1}{2}$ hours = 5.5 hours	T = $5\frac{1}{2}$ hours = 5.5 hours
S = 330 ÷ 5.5 = 60 mph	S = 330 × 5.5 = 1815 mph	S = 330 − 5.5 = 324.5 mph

To convert speeds from one set of units to another, you need to work systematically and take care with the units.

WORKED EXAMPLE 5

An athlete runs at an average speed of 10.16 m/s. Is this faster or slower than an average speed of 40 km per hour?

10.16 × 60 = 609.6 m/min

609.6 × 60 = 36 576 m/hour

Convert 10.16 m/s so that both speeds are in km per hour.

Convert seconds to hours:
× 60 to get metres per minute
× 60 to get metres per hour

$\frac{36\,576}{1000}$ = 36.576 km/h

Convert metres to kilometres:
÷ 1000 to get kilometres per hour

So the athlete's speed is slower than 40 km per hour.

Tip

You will work with speed again in the context of kinematics when you deal with time-distance graphs and rates of change in Chapter 34.

EXERCISE 12C

1. Joe is 18 years old and works for a minimum wage of £5.03 per hour. If he works for 14 hours, how much will he earn?

2. Henry earns £8.75 per hour.
   One week he worked 36.5 hours.
   Sian earned £202.40 for working 22 hours.
   How much more than Henry does Sian earn per hour?

3. A bricklayer lays 680 bricks in 4 hours.
   How many does she lay per minute, to the nearest brick?

4. Bernie cycles 168 km in 8 hours. What is his average speed?

5. A car travels 528 km at an average speed of 88 km/h. Work out the time taken.

6. Usain Bolt set an Olympic Record over 100 m at the London Olympics in 2012 with a time of 9.63 seconds.
   a Express this speed in m/s.
   b How fast is this in kilometres per hour?

Density and pressure

Density is the ratio between the mass and the volume of an object.

You need to know the formula for calculating the density of an object.

The triangle below helps you see the relationship between density, mass and volume.

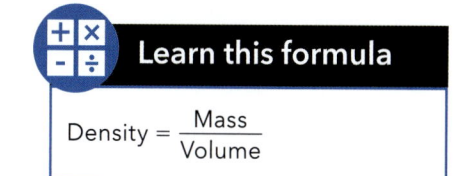

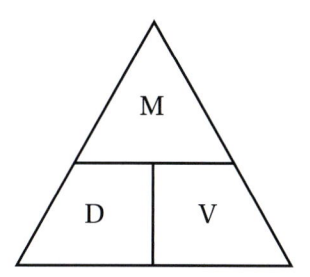

Learn this formula

$$\text{Density} = \frac{\text{Mass}}{\text{Volume}}$$

Mass = Density × Volume

$$\text{Volume} = \frac{\text{Mass}}{\text{Density}}$$

$$\text{Density} = \frac{\text{Mass}}{\text{Volume}}$$

The units of density are grams per cubic centimetre (g/cm³) or kilograms per cubic metre (kg/m³).

Express the mass and the volume in the units given when you solve problems involving density.

WORKED EXAMPLE 6

A gold bar has a volume of 725 cm³ and a mass of 14.5 kg.

What is the density of the gold bar in g/cm³?

M = 14.5 kg = 14.5 × 1000 = 14 500 g
V = 725 cm³
Density = 14 500 ÷ 725 = 20 g/cm³

Density = Mass ÷ Volume

(Units of density are g/cm³ so mass must be in g.)

Pressure is defined by the formula:

$$\text{Pressure} = \frac{\text{Force}}{\text{Area}}$$

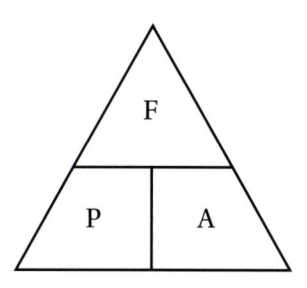

The units given for force and area give you compound units for the pressure.

For example, if force is measured in Newtons and area in mm², the compound unit of pressure would be N/mm² (newtons per mm²).

Find answers at: cambridge.org/ukschools/gcsemaths-studentbookanswers

WORKED EXAMPLE 7

A brick exerts a force of 5N.

Calculate the pressure exerted on the ground when the brick is in each of the following positions.

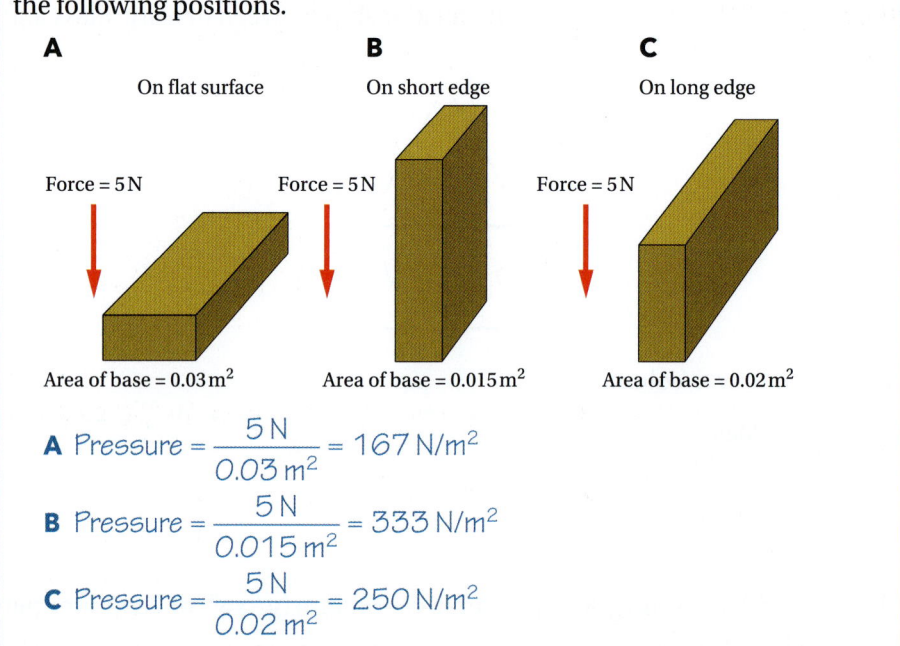

A On flat surface, Force = 5N, Area of base = 0.03 m²

B On short edge, Force = 5N, Area of base = 0.015 m²

C On long edge, Force = 5N, Area of base = 0.02 m²

A Pressure = $\dfrac{5\,N}{0.03\,m^2}$ = 167 N/m²

B Pressure = $\dfrac{5\,N}{0.015\,m^2}$ = 333 N/m²

C Pressure = $\dfrac{5\,N}{0.02\,m^2}$ = 250 N/m²

EXERCISE 12D

1 The mass of 1 cm³ of different substances is shown in the diagram.

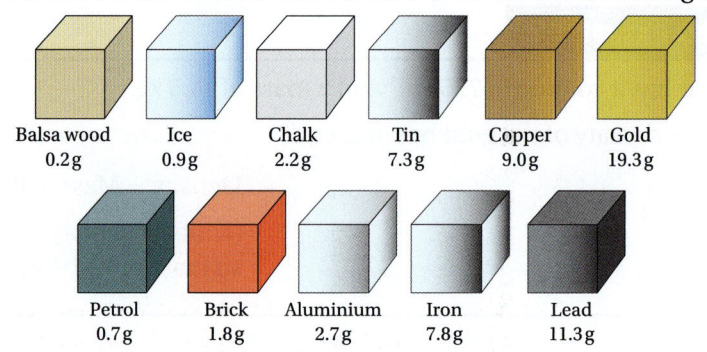

Balsa wood 0.2 g | Ice 0.9 g | Chalk 2.2 g | Tin 7.3 g | Copper 9.0 g | Gold 19.3 g

Petrol 0.7 g | Brick 1.8 g | Aluminium 2.7 g | Iron 7.8 g | Lead 11.3 g

   a Calculate the density of each substance in g/cm³.

   b Express each density in g/m³ and then convert each to kg/m³.

2 A cube of material with side length 30 mm has a mass of 0.0642 kg. Calculate the density of the material in g/cm³.

3 Calculate the volume of a piece of wood with a mass of 0.1 kg and a density of 0.8 g/cm³.

4 Two metal blocks both exert a force of 18 N.
Block A is a cube with sides 100 cm long. Block B is a cuboid with a base of area 6 m² in contact with the floor.
Calculate the pressure exerted by each block in N/m².

5 A car exerts a force of 6000 N on the road.
Each of the four wheels has an area of 0.025 m² in contact with the road.
What pressure does the car exert on the road?

Section 3: Maps, scale drawings and bearings

A **scale drawing** is a diagram in which measurements are either reduced or enlarged by a **scale factor**.

The scale tells you by how much the dimensions were reduced or enlarged.

Maps are scaled representations of areas of the real world.

The scale of a map describes the relationship between lengths in real life and lengths on the map.

The scale allows you to convert distances that you measure on the map to real-life distances.

Map scales are shown in different ways.

- **Bar or line scales.** The divided line or bar shows you distances on the map but the number on the bar tells you what the real distances are (usually in km).
- **Ratio scales.** You will often see scale given as a ratio, for example: 1 : 25 000. This means that one unit measured on the map is equivalent to 25 000 of the same units in real life. So, 1 cm on the map represents 25 000 cm = 0.25 km in real life.

> **Key vocabulary**
>
> **scale factor**: a number that scales a quantity up or down.

Using the map scale

Bar or line scales are useful for finding small distances. You measure the distance and then compare it with the line scale.

On the line scale below, each block is 1 cm long, so 1 cm on the map represents 1 km in real life.

To find a distance in real life:

- Measure the map distance using a piece of paper.
- Make pencil marks on the paper to record the distance.

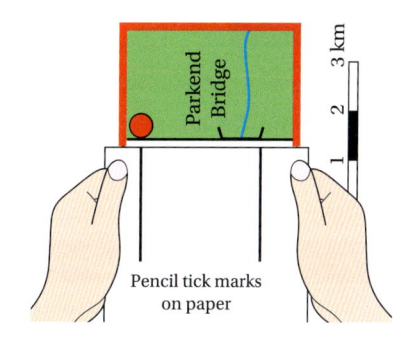

- Compare your marked distance with the line scale.
- Read off the real distance.

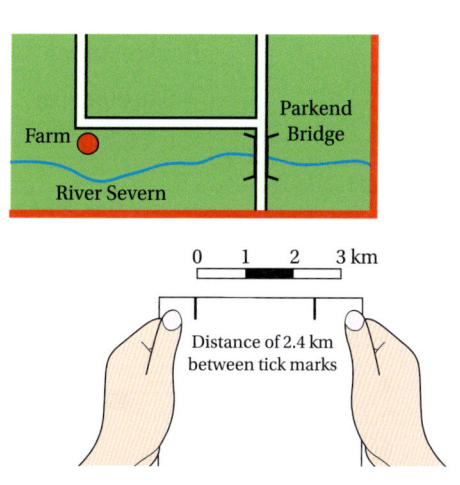

For bigger distances it is more efficient to use the ratio scale. You can convert any distance on a map to a real distance using the following formula.

Distance on the map × scale factor = distance on the ground

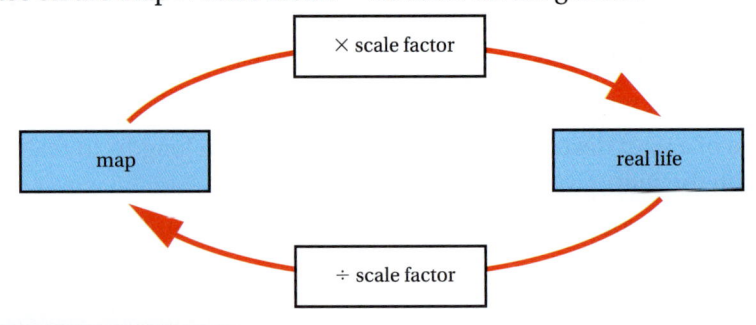

```
                    × scale factor
         ┌─────┐                    ┌──────────┐
         │ map │                    │ real life│
         └─────┘                    └──────────┘
                    ÷ scale factor
```

WORKED EXAMPLE 8

A scale drawing has a scale of 1 : 10.

a Calculate the real-life length when a length on the drawing is 5 cm.

  5 cm on the drawing = 5 × 10 = 50 cm in real life

b Calculate the length on the drawing when the real-life length is 30 cm.

  30 cm in real life = 30 ÷ 10 = 3 cm on the drawing.

Take care with the units.

When you multiply by the scale factor your answer will be in the same units that you used to measure on the map.

If the question asks for different units, you will need to convert the measurement to get the units you need.

WORK IT OUT 12.3

The distance between two towns on a 1 : 25 000 map is 3.4 cm.

How many kilometres apart are these towns in reality?

Which student has worked out the correct answer?
What have the other two done incorrectly?

Student A	Student B	Student C
$\dfrac{1}{25\,000} \times \dfrac{3.4}{1}$ = 0.000 136 cm = 1.36 km	Map distance = 34 mm Scale = 1 : 25 000 Real distance 34 × 25 000 = 850 000 mm = 8.5 km	3.4 × 25 000 = 85 000 The distance is 85 000 cm ÷ 100 = 850 m ÷ 1000 = 0.85 km

EXERCISE 12E

1 Here are three line scales. Work out what distance is represented by 1 cm in each case.

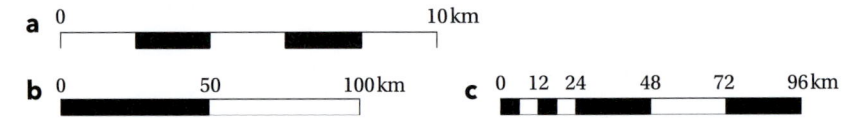

a 0 ———————————— 10 km

b 0 ——— 50 ——— 100 km

c 0 12 24   48   72   96 km

2 Work out the real distance (in kilometres) that a map distance of 45 mm would represent at each scale.

   a 1 : 120 **b** 1 : 1200 **c** 1 : 12 000 **d** 1 : 120 000
   e 1 : 1 200 000 **f** 1 : 12 000 000 **g** 1 : 120 000 000 **h** 1 : 1 200 000 000

3 Andrew says that a map drawn to a scale of 1 : 15 000 is a larger scale map than one drawn to 1 : 150 000.

Is he correct? How do you know?

4 The map opposite shows three towns.

The map has a scale of 1 : 75 000.

Work out the actual distance directly from Coltown to Bracwich.

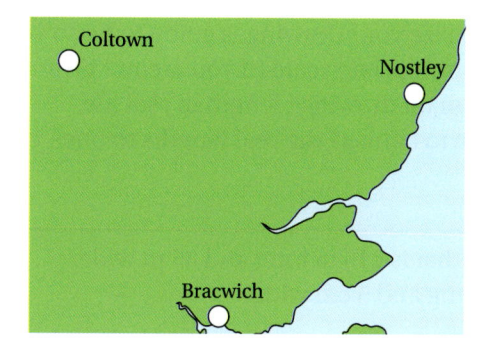

5 The red line on the map shows the flight path of a plane flying from Edinburgh to London. The flight took 55 minutes.

   a Calculate the distance flown in kilometres.
   b What was the plane's average speed on this flight?

1 : 10 000 000

6 A set of toy furniture is manufactured using a scale of 1 : 50.

Work out:

   a the height of a cupboard if the model is 5 cm high.
   b the width of the toy bed if the actual bed is 1.5 m wide.
   c the length of a table if the model is 2.7 cm long.

7 A model of an F15 fighter jet has a scale of 1 : 32.

The real aircraft is 12.5 m long.

What is the length of the model?

Find answers at: cambridge.org/ukschools/gcsemaths-studentbookanswers

GCSE Mathematics for OCR (Foundation)

Tip

You will use scale factors again in Chapter 30 when you deal with similar triangles and also in Chapter 28 when you deal with enlargements of shapes.

8 A map of Scotland on an A4 sheet of paper has a scale of 1 : 2 000 000.
   a The map distance from Inverness to Glasgow is 90 mm.
      What is the real distance between these places?
   b The actual distance by road from Aberdeen to Dundee is 96.5 km.
      How long would this road be on the map?

Constructing scale drawings

To make a scaled drawing or simple map you need to:
- Find out or measure the real lengths involved.
- Decide what size your drawing is going to be so you can work out a scale.
- Choose an appropriate scale (if you are not given one to use). Use ratio to work this out.
  Scale = length on drawing : length in real life.
- Use the scale to convert the real lengths to ones you need for the scaled drawing.

WORKED EXAMPLE 9

Draw a scale plan of a rectangular park that is 115 m long and 85 m wide.
Your plan must fit into a space 7.5 cm long and 5 cm wide.

Scale = length on drawing : length in real life

= 6 cm : 115 m

= 6 cm : 11 500 cm

= 1 : 1917

Scaled length = 115 m ÷ 2000 = 0.0575 m = 5.75 cm
Scaled width = 85 m ÷ 2000 = 0.0425 m = 4.25 cm

Step 1: The real measurements are 115 m and 85 m.

Step 2: A scale drawing 6 cm long will fit into the given space.

Convert the metres to centimetres.

Step 3: Work out the scale.
Divide both sides of the ratio by 6 to get 1 on the left.
1 : 1917 is a clumsy scale.
Most scales are rounded.
So try a scale of 1 : 2000.

Step 4: Use the scale to convert the real distances.

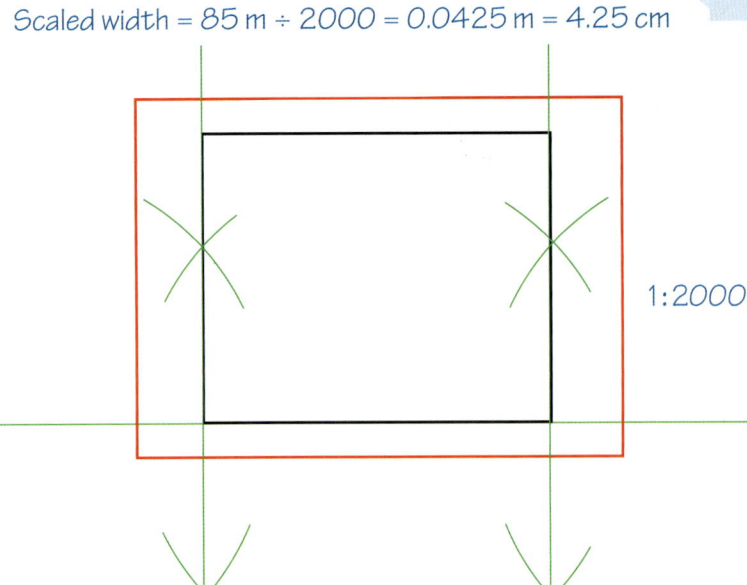

1 : 2000

Draw a 5 cm by 7.5 cm frame.
Use your construction skills to draw an accurate rectangle 4.25 cm by 5.75 cm.
Remember to write the scale you used on the diagram.

188

12 Units and measurements

EXERCISE 12F

1 The floor of a school hall is 40 m long and 20 m wide.
Draw scaled diagrams to show what it would look like at each of these scales.
   a 1 : 250   **b** 1 : 500   **c** 1 : 1000

2 Measure the dimensions of your desk in centimetres.
Work out a suitable scale and draw a scaled diagram of your desk, including anything on it.

3 Jules drew this rough plan of a classroom block at her school.
She wrote the actual measurements on the plan.
Use the dimensions on the plan to draw a scaled diagram of this classroom block that fits into the width of your exercise book.
Indicate windows and doors as shown on the plan.

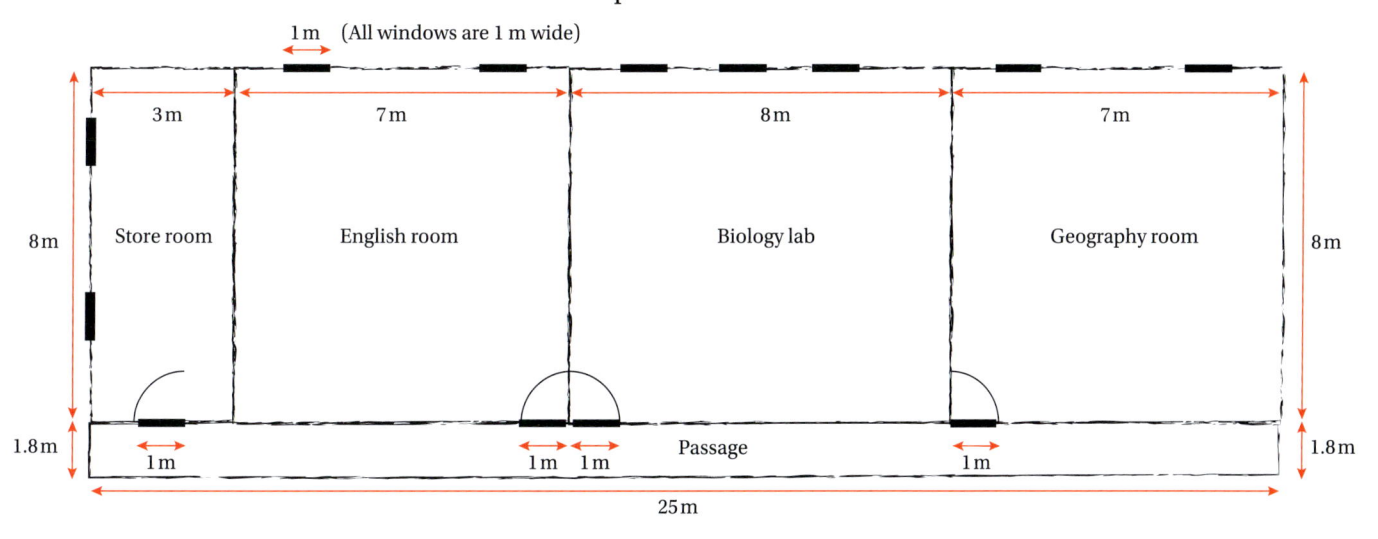

1 m (All windows are 1 m wide)

3 m	7 m	8 m	7 m
Store room	English room	Biology lab	Geography room

8 m

1.8 m 1 m   1 m 1 m Passage   1 m   1.8 m

25 m

4 A plan of a house is to be drawn at a scale of 1 : 80.
   a What should the scaled dimensions of the kitchen be if the real dimensions are 4900 mm by 3800 mm?
   b Calculate the scaled length of the sink unit if it is 1.2 metres long in reality.

Bearings

Compass directions can be given using cardinal points as shown on the compass rose.

More accurate directions can be given using degrees or bearings.

Bearings are measured in degrees from 0° (North) around in a clockwise direction to 360° (which is back at North).

To measure bearings, you must place the baseline of your protractor in line with the compass direction north. Then you measure the angle from there to the given point.

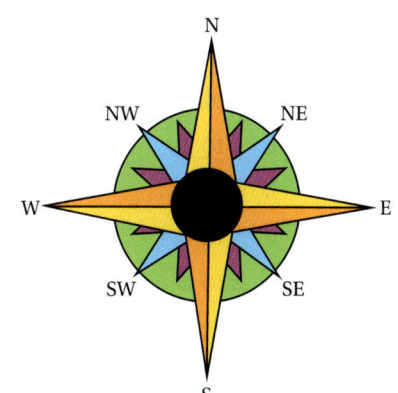

Tip

You might have to draw a perpendicular to a point to make your own north line if it is not on the diagram.

The bearing is normally written as a three-figure number, so a bearing of 90° would be written as 090° (this bearing corresponds with the direction East).

Find answers at: cambridge.org/ukschools/gcsemaths-studentbookanswers

GCSE Mathematics for OCR (Foundation)

WORKED EXAMPLE 10

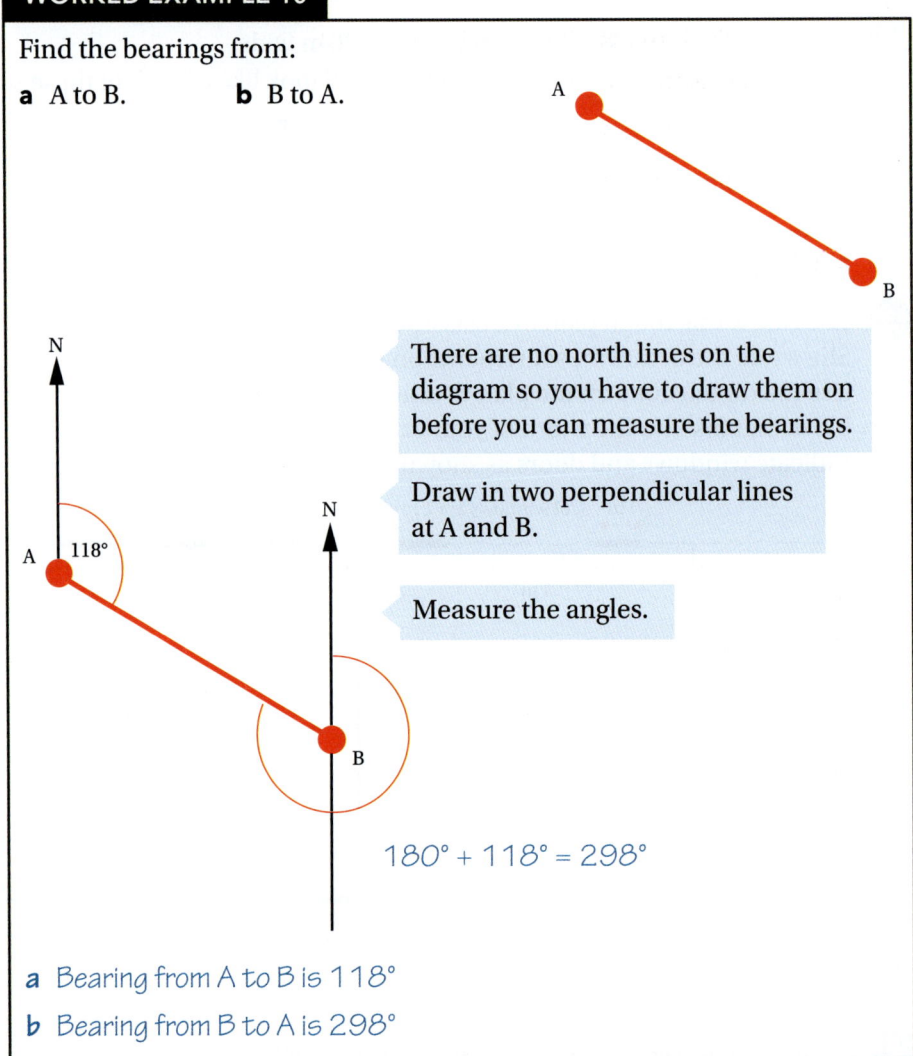

Find the bearings from:

a A to B.   b B to A.

There are no north lines on the diagram so you have to draw them on before you can measure the bearings.

Draw in two perpendicular lines at A and B.

Measure the angles.

180° + 118° = 298°

a Bearing from A to B is 118°
b Bearing from B to A is 298°

EXERCISE 12G

1 Write the three-figure bearing that corresponds with each direction.

  a Due south   b North-east   c West

2 Use a protractor to measure each of the following bearings on the diagram.

  a A to B
  b B to A
  c A to C
  d B to D
  e D to A
  f D to B

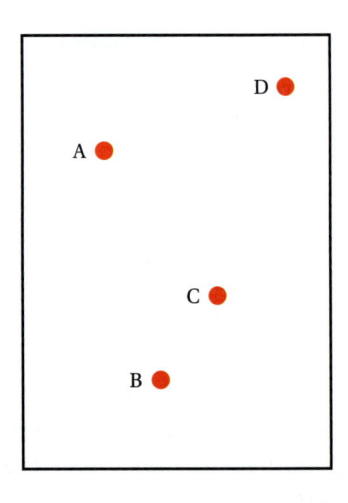

190

3 Beville is 140 km west and 45 km north of Lake Salina.

Draw a scale drawing with a scale of 1 cm to 20 km and use it to find:

a the bearing from Lake Salina to Beville.

b the bearing from Beville to Lake Salina.

c the shortest distance between the two places in kilometres.

Checklist of learning and understanding

Standard units of measurement

- You can convert between metric units of length, mass and capacity by multiplying or dividing by powers of ten.
- To convert squared units, you need to square the conversion factors.
- To convert cubed units, you need to cube the conversion factors.
- Units of time are not metric, so you need to use the number of parts in the sub-units when you convert units of time.

Compound units of measurement

- Compound units of measurement involve more than one unit.
- Rates such as £/hour or cost per kilogram are compound units.
- Speed = $\frac{\text{distance}}{\text{time}}$
- Density = $\frac{\text{mass}}{\text{volume}}$
- Pressure = $\frac{\text{force}}{\text{area}}$

Maps, scales and bearings

- The scale of a map or diagram describes how much smaller (or bigger) the lengths on the diagram are compared to the original lengths.
- Real length = map length × scale factor
- The scale can be written as length on diagram : real length
- Bearings are accurate directions given in degrees from 0° to 360°. 0° corresponds with north.
- Bearings are measured clockwise from 0° and written using three figures.

Chapter review

For additional questions on the topics in this chapter, visit GCSE Mathematics Online.

1 Match each statement to the correct number in the box below.

| 5 | 475 | 182.5 | 259 200 |

a The number of seconds in 3 days.

b The number of kilometres travelled in $2\frac{1}{2}$ hours by a car travelling at 73 km/h.

c The distance in km in real life of a length of 5 cm on a map with a scale of 1 : 1000.

d The number of litres in 475 000 millilitres.

Find answers at: cambridge.org/ukschools/gcsemaths-studentbookanswers

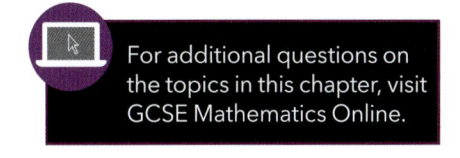

GCSE Mathematics for OCR (Foundation)

2 True or false?

  a Tony's fish tank contains 72 litres of water.
  He says this is 72 000 millilitres.

  b The school is 15 km from the bus stop. The bus travels at 40 km/h.
  Molly says it will take her half an hour to get to school.

  c The distance from Liverpool to Manchester is about 55 km.
  The scale of a map is 1 : 250 000.
  The distance on the map would be 5.2 cm.

3 Convert 60 000 cm^2 into m^2.

4 How many mm^2 are there in 2 m^2?

5 A car is travelling at an average speed of 80 km/h for one hour on a bearing of 120°.

  a Use a scale of 1 cm to 20 km to show this journey.

  b After 45 km, the driver stopped for petrol. Mark this spot on the diagram. If this was after 40 minutes, calculate his speed for that part of the journey.

6 The density of an object is 8 kg/m^3.

Work out the mass of 25 m^3 of the object.

7 A cyclist travels due east from point A for 10 km to reach point B.

She then travels 6 km on a bearing of 125° from B to reach point C.

  a Use a scale of 1 cm to 2 km to represent her journey on a scale diagram.

  b Find the bearing from C to A.

  c Find the direct distance from C to A in kilometres.

  d If it takes the cyclist $1\frac{1}{2}$ hours to cycle back using the direct route from C to A, find her average speed:

  i in km/h.   **ii** in m/s.

13 Percentages

In this chapter you will learn how to ...
- change between fractions, decimals and percentages.
- calculate a percentage of an amount.
- write a quantity as a percentage of another.
- increase and decrease amounts by a given percentage.
- solve problems involving percentage change.

For more resources relating to this chapter, visit GCSE Mathematics Online.

Using mathematics: real-life applications

Percentages are often used in daily life to express fractions. For example, you might see adverts claiming that 76% of pets prefer a particular brand of food or that 90% of dentists recommend a particular type of toothpaste. Sale price reductions, discounts and interest rates are usually given as percentages.

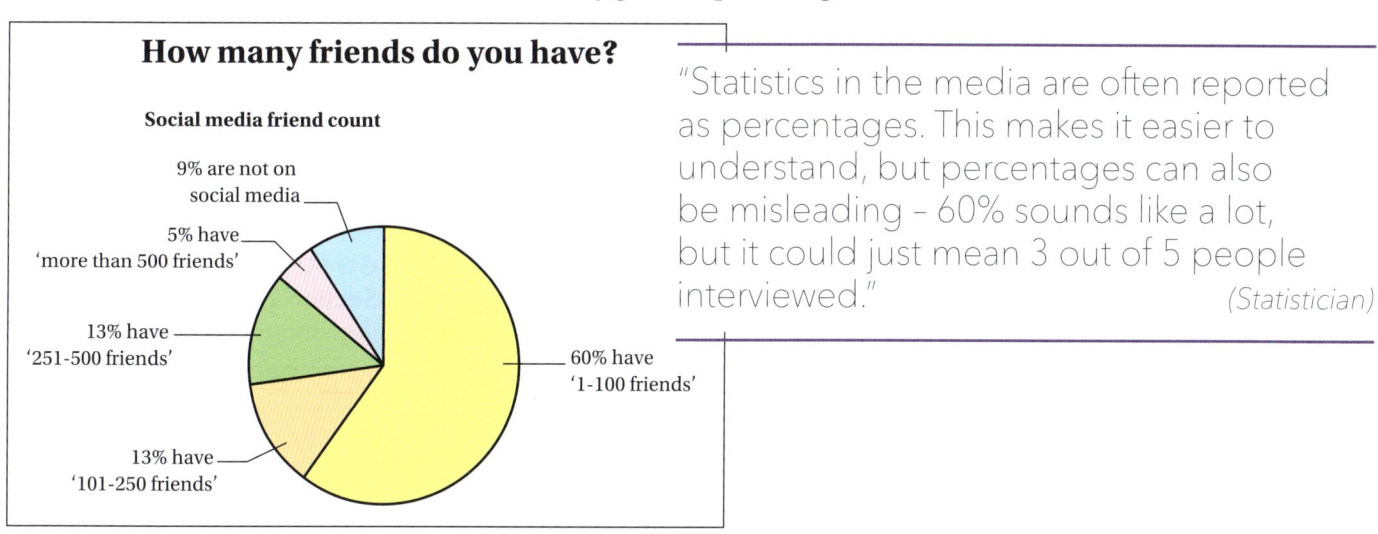

How many friends do you have?

Social media friend count
- 9% are not on social media
- 5% have 'more than 500 friends'
- 13% have '251-500 friends'
- 13% have '101-250 friends'
- 60% have '1-100 friends'

"Statistics in the media are often reported as percentages. This makes it easier to understand, but percentages can also be misleading – 60% sounds like a lot, but it could just mean 3 out of 5 people interviewed."
(Statistician)

Before you start ...

Ch 11	You need to be able to confidently multiply and divide by 100.	① Where should the decimal place go in each answer? **a** $210 \div 100 = 21$ **b** $21 \div 100 = 21$ **c** $0.24 \times 100 = 24$ **d** $0.024 \times 100 = 24$
Ch 10	You need to be able to express fractions in simplest terms by cancelling.	② Match the fractions in box A to their equivalent fraction in box B. Box A: $\frac{16}{36}$ $\frac{15}{35}$ $\frac{30}{36}$ $\frac{9}{36}$ $\frac{39}{52}$ $\frac{13}{39}$ Box B: $\frac{1}{4}$ $\frac{3}{4}$ $\frac{1}{3}$ $\frac{5}{6}$ $\frac{3}{7}$ $\frac{4}{9}$
Ch 11	You should be able to express any percentage as a decimal.	③ Are the following statements true or false? **a** $20\% = 0.02$ **b** $25\% = 1.4$ **c** $3\% = 0.3$ **d** $12.5\% = 0.125$ **e** $1.25\% = 0.125$

Find answers at: cambridge.org/ukschools/gcsemaths-studentbookanswers

GCSE Mathematics for OCR (Foundation)

Assess your starting point using the Launchpad

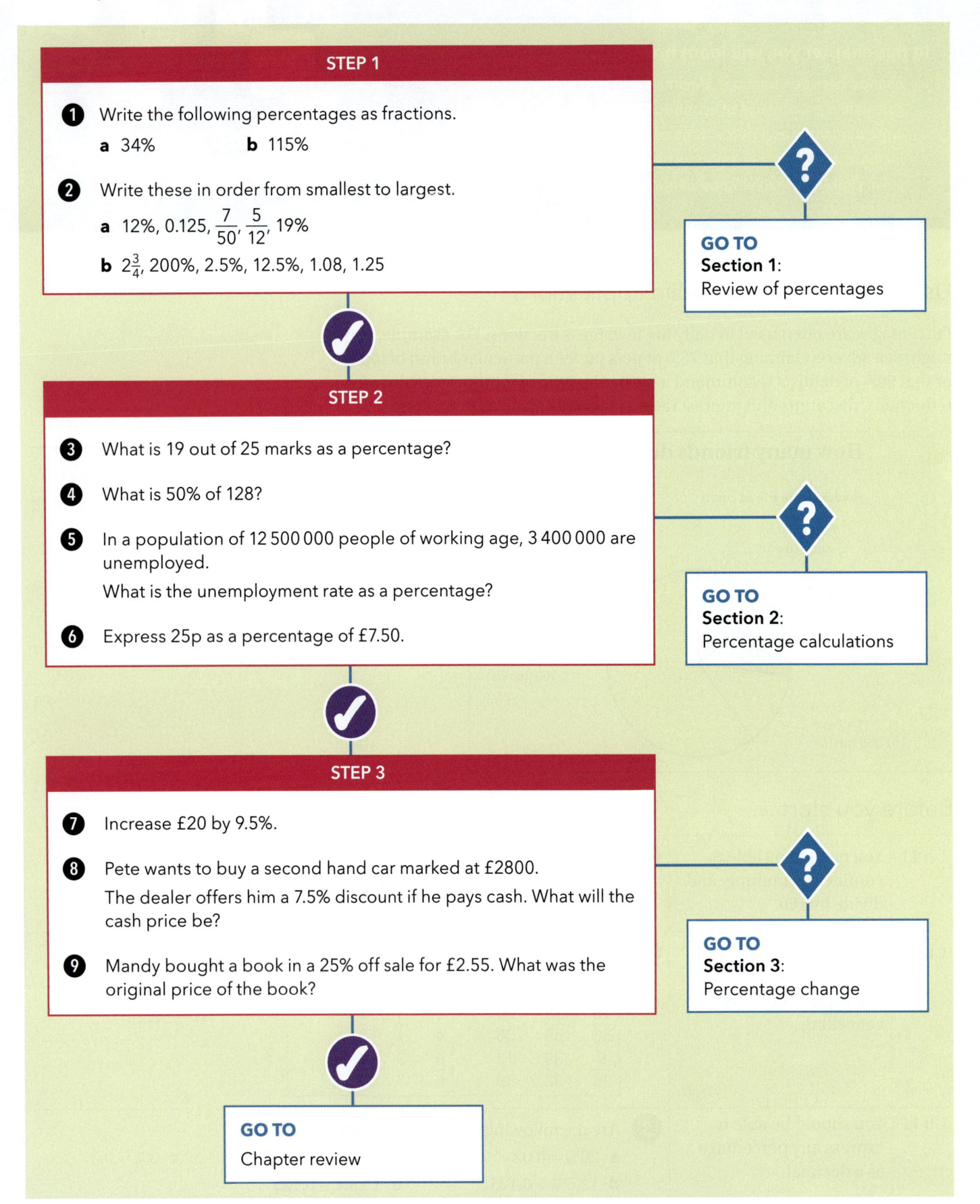

STEP 1

1. Write the following percentages as fractions.
   a 34%   b 115%

2. Write these in order from smallest to largest.
   a 12%, 0.125, $\frac{7}{50}$, $\frac{5}{12}$, 19%
   b $2\frac{3}{4}$, 200%, 2.5%, 12.5%, 1.08, 1.25

GO TO
Section 1:
Review of percentages

STEP 2

3. What is 19 out of 25 marks as a percentage?

4. What is 50% of 128?

5. In a population of 12 500 000 people of working age, 3 400 000 are unemployed.
   What is the unemployment rate as a percentage?

6. Express 25p as a percentage of £7.50.

GO TO
Section 2:
Percentage calculations

STEP 3

7. Increase £20 by 9.5%.

8. Pete wants to buy a second hand car marked at £2800.
   The dealer offers him a 7.5% discount if he pays cash. What will the cash price be?

9. Mandy bought a book in a 25% off sale for £2.55. What was the original price of the book?

GO TO
Section 3:
Percentage change

GO TO
Chapter review

Section 1: Review of percentages

A percentage shows the number of parts per hundred.

During 2014, the maker of a mobile phone case did a survey of 872 people.

The survey results showed that 92% of people said they would feel stressed if their phone battery ran out and 81% of people said that running out of power on their phones had led to them having a bad experience.

- 92% means 92 out of every 100.
- 81% means 81 out of every 100.

Percentages, fractions and decimals

Percentages, fractions and decimals are different ways of showing a part of a whole.

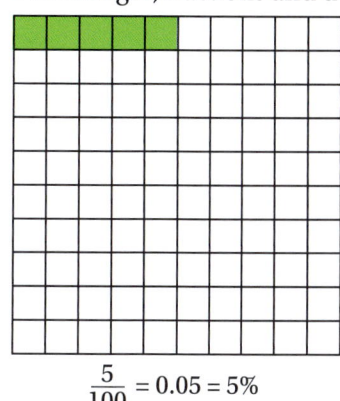

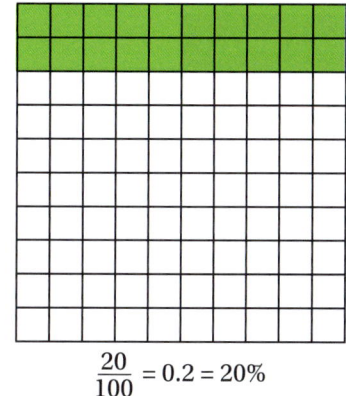

$\dfrac{5}{100} = 0.05 = 5\%$ $\dfrac{20}{100} = 0.2 = 20\%$

Percentages can be changed to fractions by writing the fraction with a denominator of 100 and simplifying.

$92\% = \dfrac{92}{100} = \dfrac{23}{25}$

$81\% = \dfrac{81}{100}$

> **Tip**
>
> Remember that a percentage shows the number of parts per hundred.

To change a percentage to a decimal, write it as fraction with a denominator of 100 and then convert it to a decimal.

$92\% = \dfrac{92}{100} = 0.92$

$81\% = \dfrac{81}{100} = 0.81$

To change a fraction to a percentage, you can write it as an equivalent fraction with a denominator of 100, then multiply by 100 and add the percentage symbol.

$\dfrac{1}{2} = \dfrac{50}{100} = 50\%$ Do **not** simplify, write the fraction of 100 as a percentage.

You can also use a calculator.

To convert $\dfrac{2}{3}$ to a percentage, enter [2] [÷] [3] [×] [1] [0] [0]

Your display will show 66.666666667.

This is the percentage. Write it as 66.67% (correct to two decimal places).

> **Tip**
>
> When you use a calculator to convert a fraction to a percentage you are actually first changing $\dfrac{2}{3}$ to a decimal (2 ÷ 3 = 0.6666666667) and then converting the decimal to a percentage. You do not enter the percentage sign in the calculation because the values you are entering are not percentages. The percentage is the answer you get.

Find answers at: cambridge.org/ukschools/gcsemaths-studentbookanswers

GCSE Mathematics for OCR (Foundation)

To change a decimal to a percentage write it as a fraction with a denominator of 100 and multiply it by 100, or use your calculator to multiply it by 100 directly, and write the percentage symbol.

$0.3 = \frac{3}{10} = \frac{30}{100} = 30\%$ $\qquad\qquad$ $0.3 \times 100 = 30\%$

$0.025 = \frac{0.25}{10} = \frac{2.5}{100} = 2.5\%$ $\qquad\qquad$ $0.025 \times 100 = 2.5\%$

$3.75 = \frac{37.5}{10} = \frac{375}{100} = 375\%$ $\qquad\qquad$ $3.75 \times 100 = 375\%$

Comparing percentages, fractions and decimals

When you have to compare a mixed set of percentages, fractions and decimals you can compare them by changing them all to percentages.

Tip

You can also change all the values to decimals or equivalent fractions to compare them if that is easier for you.

WORKED EXAMPLE 1

Write the following in ascending order. $35\%, \frac{1}{3}, 0.38, \frac{2}{5}, \frac{2}{7}$.

$\frac{1}{3} \times 100 = 33.33\%$

$0.38 \times 100 = 38\%$

$\frac{2}{5} \times 100 = 40\%$

$\frac{2}{7} \times 100 = 28.57\%$

$\frac{2}{7}, \frac{1}{3}, 35\%, 0.38, \frac{2}{5}$

Convert all the fractions and decimals to percentages.

Remember to use the original fractions or decimals when you write down your answer.

Tip

Ascending order means from smallest to largest; descending order means from largest to smallest.

Some common conversions that might be useful to learn:

Fraction	Decimal	Percentage
$\frac{1}{2}$	0.5	50%
$\frac{1}{4}$	0.25	25%
$\frac{3}{4}$	0.75	75%
$\frac{1}{3}$	$0.3\dot{3}$	$33\frac{1}{3}\%$
$\frac{2}{3}$	$0.6\dot{6}$	$66\frac{2}{3}\%$

EXERCISE 13A

1 Write the following as percentages.

Use fractional ($32\frac{1}{2}\%$) or decimal (2.5%) percentages where you need to.

a $\frac{5}{100}$ $\qquad$ b $\frac{27}{50}$ $\qquad$ c $\frac{11}{25}$ $\qquad$ d $\frac{17}{20}$

e $\frac{1}{2}$ $\qquad$ f $\frac{2}{3}$ $\qquad$ g $\frac{5}{8}$ $\qquad$ h $\frac{92}{50}$

i 0.3 $\qquad$ j 0.04 $\qquad$ k 0.47 $\qquad$ l 1.12

m 2.07 $\qquad$ n 2.25 $\qquad$ o 0.035 $\qquad$ p 0.007

13 Percentages

2 Write each of the following percentages as a fraction in its simplest terms.
   a 25%   b 80%   c 90%   d 12.5%
   e 50%   f 98%   g 60%   h 22%

3 Write the decimal equivalent of each percentage.
   a 82%   b 97%   c 45%   d 28%
   e 0.05%   f 0.08%   g 0.006%   h 0.0007%
   i 125%   j 300%   k 7.28%   l 9.007%

4 State whether the following are true or false.
   a $\frac{3}{5} > 70\%$ b $\frac{7}{9} < 83\%$ c $\frac{1}{3} = 30\%$
   d $67\% > 0.666$ e $\frac{3}{4} \neq 75\%$ f $0.55 \neq \frac{1}{2}$

5 a If 93.5% of the students in a school have wifi at home, what percentage do not?
   b If $\frac{2}{3}$ of all the sim cards sold in a mobile phone shop are pre-paid, what percentage are not pre-paid?
   c 0.325 of computer users back up their work every day. What percentage do not do this?

6 Zack spends 24.7% of a day playing computer games, 0.138 of the day doing homework and $\frac{3}{8}$ of the day playing sport.
   What percentage of the day is spent doing other things?

7 What percentage of each pie chart is shaded?

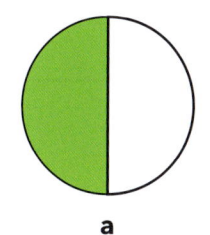

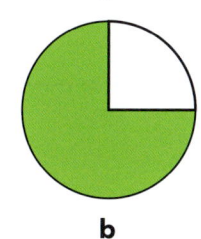

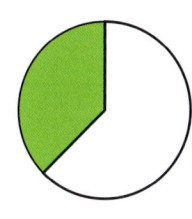

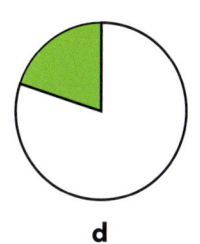

   a   b   c   d

8 Write the following in ascending order.
   a $\frac{1}{20}$, 30%, 0.1, $\frac{3}{5}$, 0.8%   b 0.75, 57%, 0.88, $\frac{1}{4}$, 0.15
   c $\frac{2}{3}$, 0.75, 60%, $\frac{9}{10}$, 0.25   d $\frac{3}{7}$, 0.43, 45%, 0.395, $\frac{4}{9}$
   e $\frac{5}{6}$, 80%, $\frac{19}{25}$, 55%, 49.3%

9 A media company states that 83.5% of its customers read the news online every day.
   What fraction of the customers is this?

10 Anna pays 0.06 of her salary into her credit card account.
   What percentage of her salary is this?

Find answers at: cambridge.org/ukschools/gcsemaths-studentbookanswers

GCSE Mathematics for OCR (Foundation)

Tip

Remember that
mean = $\frac{\text{sum of values}}{\text{number of values}}$.
You will cover statistics in more detail in Chapter 36.

11 During a work shift, Sandy spent $\frac{9}{20}$ of her time texting on her phone.

What percentage of the shift was she not texting?

12 Angie gets the following marks for three maths assignments:

$\frac{31}{40}, \frac{27}{30}$ and $\frac{13}{15}$.

a In which assignment did she get the best marks?

b What is her mean result for the three assignments as a percentage?

Section 2: Percentage calculations

The word 'of' means multiply.

To find a percentage of an amount you have to multiply the amount by the percentage.

You need to write the percentage as a fraction with a denominator of 100, or as a decimal, unless you are using a calculator.

WORK IT OUT 13.1

Which of the following methods was used to calculate that 9% of 400 is 36?
Explain why the other methods won't work.

Method A	Method B	Method C	Method D	Method E
$\frac{9}{100} \times 400$	$\frac{400}{9} \times 36$	0.009×400	9×400	$\frac{9}{400} \times 100$

WORKED EXAMPLE 2

What is 12% of 700?

Calculate the answer using:

a fractions. **b** decimals. **c** a calculator.

a $\frac{12}{100} \times 700 = 84$

Simplify by cancelling if you can, then do the calculation. Divide by 100 to simplify the calculation to 12×7.

b 0.12×700

$= 0.12 \times 100 \times 7$

$= 12 \times 7$

$= 84$

Write 12% as the decimal 0.12. Then use what you know about multiplying decimals to do the calculation.

Tip

You were reminded how to multiply decimals in Chapter 11.

c [1][2][%][×][7][0][0][=]
[84]

Enter the calculation on your calculator as shown. **Note** that the sequence of buttons might differ on different calculators so check your manual!

Calculator tip

Make sure you know how to use the % button on your calculator.

You might need to enter '12% × 700' or '700 × 12%' (some calculators will work both ways).

On some calculators you need to press the = .

Check how your calculator works by finding 12% of 350. The answer should be 42.

You **do** enter the percentage sign in these calculations because one of the values you are working with is a percentage.

EXERCISE 13B

1 Calculate.

- **a** 5% of 250
- **b** 9% of 400
- **c** 20% of 120
- **d** 65% of 4500
- **e** 12% of 75
- **f** 75% of 360
- **g** 32% of 50
- **h** 110% of 60
- **i** 150% of 90

2 Calculate, give answers as mixed numbers or decimals as necessary.

- **a** 19% of £50
- **b** 60% of 70 kg
- **c** 45% of 35 cm
- **d** 90% of 29 kg
- **e** $3\frac{1}{2}$% of £400
- **f** 2.6% of 80 minutes
- **g** 7.4% of £1000
- **h** 3.8% of 180 m
- **i** $9\frac{2}{3}$% of 600 litres

Tip

Remember your answer will have a unit not a percentage sign. You are not working out a percentage here, you are working out what a given percentage of a quantity is.

3 Annie got 85% for a test that was out of 80 marks.

What was her mark out of 80?

4 A salesperson at a mobile phone shop estimates that about 3% of phones come back for some sort of repair in the first week.

If the shop sells 180 phones, how many can they expect to come back for repairs in the first week?

5 46% of residents in an area throw out the local free newspaper without even looking at it, the rest read some or all of it.

If there are 2450 residents, how many people:

- **a** don't look at the paper?
- **b** read some or all of it?

6 Of 240 trains arriving at King's Cross, 2.5% arrived early and 13.8% arrived late.

How many trains were on time?

7 A tablet computer is advertised for £899 excluding VAT.

VAT is 20% of the sale price.

Nisha wanted to buy it when VAT was 17.5% of the sale price but she didn't get round to it.

How much would she have saved if she had bought it when VAT was 17.5%?

Find answers at: cambridge.org/ukschools/gcsemaths-studentbookanswers

8 7.5% of a 620 m² market garden is set aside for growing tulips and the rest is used to grow vegetables.

How many square metres of land is used to grow:

a tulips? b vegetables?

9 The population of a town in Cornwall increases by about 24.8% each summer.

If the population of the town is 12 760 before summer, approximately how many people are likely to move in during the summer?

10 Pure gold contains 24 parts (called carats) of gold to every 24 parts.

$\frac{24}{24}$ = 100% gold.

18 carat gold contains 18 parts pure gold per 24 parts and 9 carat gold contains 9 parts pure gold per 24 parts.

a Work out the percentage of pure gold in

  i 9 carat gold   ii 18 carat gold.

b If Naz buys an 18 carat gold ring that weighs 7.3 grams, how much pure gold does it contain?

c If Vishnu buys a 9 carat gold pendant that has a mass of 16.3 grams, how much pure gold does it contain?

d Do you think it is accurate to label 9 carat gold as gold? Explain your answer.

Expressing one quantity as a percentage of another

To write one quantity as a percentage of another, write the first quantity as a fraction of the second quantity and then multiply by 100 to get a percentage. The two quantities must be in the same units before you write them as a fraction.

> **Tip**
> You expressed one quantity as a fraction of another in Chapter 10. Read through that work again if you cannot remember how to do this.

> **Tip**
> When you convert quantities to get them to the same unit you can avoid decimal values by choosing the smaller units (for example, making both units metres in this example rather than making them both kilometres).

> **Tip**
> Remember the steps in the problem-solving framework.

WORK IT OUT 13.2

Brian has run 1500 m of a 5 km race when he gets a cramp in his foot.

What percentage of the race has he completed at this stage?

Which of these two students has got the correct answer? Why is the other one wrong?

Student A	Student B
$\frac{1500}{5} \times 100$	$\frac{1500}{5000} \times 100$
$= 300 \times 100$	$= \frac{3}{10} \times 100$
$= 300\%$	$= 30\%$

Sometimes you will need to find intermediate values before you can work out the percentage. Make sure you always read the question carefully so that you know what it is that you are trying to calculate.

WORKED EXAMPLE 3

Andrew has 1 kilogram of apples.

He gives 300 g to his neighbour, 400 g to his mother and keeps the rest.

What percentage of the apples does he keep for himself?

$300 + 400 = 700$

$1000 - 700 = 300$

> You need to calculate what mass of apples he kept before you can calculate the percentage.

$\dfrac{300}{1000} = 0.3 \times 100 = 30\%$

> Work out the number of grams he kept as a percentage of the total number of grams. (You could have converted the quantities to kilograms instead; it would make no difference to the final percentage.)

EXERCISE 13C

Try to answer some of the questions without using your calculator; use the non-calculator techniques you have learnt for decimals and fractions.

1 Write the first amount as a percentage of the second.

Give your answer correct to no more than two decimal places (if necessary).

- **a** 400 m of 5 km
- **b** 45 m of 3 km
- **c** 150 m of 1 km
- **d** 8 cm of 2 m
- **e** 14 mm of 4 cm
- **f** 19 cm of 3 m
- **g** 25p of £4
- **h** 66p of £3.50
- **i** 20 seconds of a minute
- **j** 25 seconds of 1.5 minutes
- **k** 750 g of 23 kg
- **l** 800 g of 1.5 kg
- **m** 4 days of a week
- **n** 3 days of 6 weeks
- **o** 800 kg of 3 tonnes
- **p** 8.4 tonnes of 50 000 kg
- **q** 500 mm of 2 m
- **r** 90 mm of 14 cm
- **s** 350 ml of 2 litres
- **t** 5 ml of 0.5 litres

2 Sandra got 19 out of 24 for an assignment and Nina got 23 out of 30.
Which girl got the higher percentage mark?

3 In a local election there were 5400 registered voters. Of these, 3240 voted.
What percentage of registered voters voted?

4 Mel improved his running time for the 400 m race by 3 seconds.
If his previous running time was 50 seconds, what is his percentage improvement?

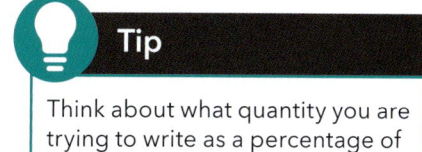

5 Kenny had a box of 40 chocolates. He ate 32 of them.
What percentage of the chocolates remain?

> **Tip**
> Think about what quantity you are trying to write as a percentage of another quantity.

6 Sylvia keeps a record of how many sets she wins when she plays tennis against her sister.
In the past month she won 19 out of 27 sets.
What percentage of the sets did she lose?

7 The longest kiss lasted 58 hours, 35 minutes and 58 seconds and was achieved by Ekkachai Tiranarat and Laksana Tiranarat at an event organised by 'Ripley's Believe It or Not! Pattaya', in Pattaya, Thailand, on 12–14 February 2013.
What percentage of the three-day event was this?

Find answers at: cambridge.org/ukschools/gcsemaths-studentbookanswers

Muesli	
Nutritional values	
(Per 30 g serving)	
Carbohydrates	19 g
(of which sugars)	6.2 g
Fat	3.8 g
Sodium	93 mg

8 Read the label and answer the questions.

  a Calculate the combined percentage of fat and sugar in a serving of muesli.

  b What percentage of a serving is sodium?

Section 3: Percentage change

You will often see increases or decreases in amounts written as percentages.

For example, you might read that the price of petrol is going to increase by 5.5%, or that the cost of mobile broadband has decreased by 15% over the past year.

> **Tip**
> You will learn more about percentage change in Chapter 33.

Increasing or decreasing an amount by a percentage

WORK IT OUT 13.3

Last September, the enrolment of students to Scaltback School was 650.

This September, the student enrolment increased by 12%.

At the same time, the registration fee of £120 decreased by 15%.

Work out:

a the new student enrolment.

b the new registration fee.

Students A and B solved this problem using different methods. **Both** methods are correct.

Their workings are shown below.

Which method do you prefer?

Could you use your calculator to do these calculations? How?

Student A	Student B
a 650 increased by 12% 12% of 650 = $\frac{12}{100} \times 650$ = 78 650 + 78 = 728 728 students enrolled this September.	a 650 increased by 12% Old population = 100% New population = old + increase = 100% + 12% = 112% 112% = $\frac{112}{100}$ = 1.12 650 × 1.12 = 728 728 students enrolled this September.
b 120 decreased by 15% 15% of 120 = $\frac{15}{100} \times 120$ = 18 £120 − £18 = £102 The new registration fee is £102.	b £120 decreased by 15% | % (of £120) | Amount (£) | |---|---| | 10 | 12 | | 5 | 6 | | 15 | 18 | £120 − £18 = £102 The new registration fee is £102.

> **Tip**
> Multiplying by 1.12 is the same as multiplying by $\frac{112}{100}$.

The new registration fee could also have been calculated as follows:

£120 decreased by 15%

Original value = 100%

New value = 100% − 15% = 85%

So the new value is 85% of the original value.

$\frac{85}{100} \times 120 = £102$

> **Tip**
>
> You can express any percentage increase or decrease as a decimal or fractional multiplier.
>
> To increase a number by x%, multiply the original value by $\left(1 + \frac{x}{100}\right)$.
>
> To increase by 30% multiply by 1.3. To increase by 3% multiply by 1.03.
>
> To decrease a number by x%, multiply the original value by $\left(1 - \frac{x}{100}\right)$.
>
> To decrease by 16% multiply by 0.84. To decrease by 6% multiply by 0.94.

EXERCISE 13D

1 Increase each amount by the given percentage.
   a £48 increased by 14%
   b £700 increased by 35%
   c £30 increased by 7.6%
   d £40 000 increased by 0.59%
   e £90 increased by 9.5%
   f £80 increased by 24.6%

2 Decrease each amount by the given percentage.
   a £68 decreased by 14%
   b £800 decreased by 35%
   c £90 decreased by 7.6%
   d £20 000 decreased by 0.59%
   e £85 decreased by 9.5%
   f £60 decreased by 24.6%

3 A building is worth £125 000.
   If its value increases by $3\frac{1}{2}$%, what will it be worth?

4 Josh currently earns £3125 per month.
   If he receives an increase of 3.8% per month, what will his new monthly earnings be, correct to the nearest pound?

5 Sally earns £25 per shift. Her boss says she can either have £7 more per shift or a 20% increase.
   Which is the better offer?

6 The membership of a sports club increased by 26% one year.
   If they had 284 members the previous year, how many do they have now?

7 Sammy bought £2500 worth of shares.
   At the end of the first month their value had decreased by 4.25%.
   At the end of the second month Sammy checked the value again and found it had gone up 1.5% from the previous month.
   Work out the value of the shares at the end of each month.

8 Amira earns £25 000 per year plus 12% commission on any sales she generates.
   Calculate her annual earnings if she sold £145 250 worth of goods.

Find answers at: cambridge.org/ukschools/gcsemaths-studentbookanswers

Finding original values

If you know the percentage by which an amount has increased or decreased, you can use it to find the original amount. Problems involving original values are often called reverse or inverse percentages. When you work with these problems you need to remember that you are dealing with percentages of the **original** values.

WORKED EXAMPLE 4

A shop is offering a 10% discount on all sale goods.

Jessie bought a bike in the sale and paid £108.

What was the original price of the bike?

Let x represent the original price of the bike.

90% of x = £108 — If the cost is reduced by 10% then you are actually paying 90% of x, the original price.

$\frac{90}{100}x = 108$ — You can write an equation and solve it to find the value of x.

$90x = 100 \times 108$

$90x = 10\,800$

$x = \frac{10\,800}{90}$

$x = 120$

The original price was £120. — Check this answer by decreasing £120 by 10%.

Tip

Undoing a 10% decrease is not the same as just increasing the sale price by 10%. If you add 10% to the sale price of £108, you will be adding 10% of £108 (to get £118.80), which is **NOT** the right answer.

WORKED EXAMPLE 5

Sameen sells some shares she has in a company for £3450. She makes a profit of 15%.

What did she pay for the shares originally?

Let the cost price be x. — Let x be the cost of the shares originally. Write an equation and solve for x.

$1.15x = 3450$ — Profit = selling price − cost price.

$x = \frac{3450}{1.15}$ — So here, '15% profit' means her profit is 15% of the amount she paid for the shares (the cost). So, 3450 is a 15% increase on the cost value.

$x = 3000$

She paid £3000 for the shares originally.

$3000 \times 1.15 = 3450$ ✓ — Check this by increasing 3000 by 15%

EXERCISE 13E

1 Find the original values if:

    a 25% is £30.

    b 8% is 120 grams.

    c 120% is 800 kg.

    d 115% is £2000.

2 VAT of 20% is added to most goods before they are sold.

Tourists to the UK can claim back the VAT when they leave the country.

Work out the price of each of these items without VAT to see what a tourist would pay for them.

The prices given here include VAT.
- **a** Necklace £1200
- **b** Camera £145.50
- **c** Painting £865
- **d** Boots £54.99

3 Misha paid £40 for a DVD box set in a 20% off sale.

What was the original price of the DVD set?

4 240 students are in Year 10. This is 20% of the school population.
- **a** How many students are there in total in the school?
- **b** How many students are in the other years at this school?

5 Susie was told that her pay had increased by 15%. Her new pay is £172.50.

What was her pay before the increase?

6 9 carat gold is 37.5% pure gold.

A piece of 9 carat gold jewellery contains 97.5 grams of pure gold.

What does the piece of jewellery weigh?

7 A maraton runner reduces her weight by 5% over a three-month period.

If she weighs 58 kg at the end of the period, what did she weigh at the start?

8 310 runners completed an ultramarathon within the cut-off time.

If this represents 62% of the runners, how many runners started the race?

Checklist of learning and understanding

Review of percentages
- Percentage means 'parts per hundred'. Remember that percentages, fractions and decimals are all expressions of part of a whole and you can convert between them all.
- To convert a percentage to a fraction write the percentage with a denominator of 100 and simplify.
- To convert percentages to decimals, write the percentage with a denominator of 100 then divide by 100 to convert it to a decimal.
- To change a fraction to a percentage, find the equivalent fraction with a denominator of 100, then multiply by 100 and add the percentage sign or use your calculator to divide the numerator by the denominator and multiply by 100.
- To change a decimal to a percentage write it as a fraction with a denominator of 100 and multiply it by 100, or use your calculator to multiply it by 100 directly, and write the percentage symbol.
- To order a mixture of fractions, decimals and percentages change them all to percentages or decimals first.

Find answers at: cambridge.org/ukschools/gcsemaths-studentbookanswers

Percentage calculations

- To find a percentage of an amount, express the percentage as a fraction over 100 and then multiply the amount by the fraction.
- To express one quantity (quantity A) as a percentage of another quantity (quantity B), make sure the units are the same and then calculate $\frac{\text{quantity A}}{\text{quantity B}} \times 100$.

Percentage change

- To increase or decrease an amount by a percentage,
  - find the percentage amount and add or subtract it from the original amount
  - or, use a fractional or decimal multiplier:
    - to increase an amount by $x\%$, the multiplier is $\left(1 + \frac{x}{100}\right)$;
    - to decrease an amount by $x\%$, the multiplier is $\left(1 - \frac{x}{100}\right)$.
- To find an original value when you know the percentage increase or decrease and the new amount, write an equation and use reverse percentages to solve for x.

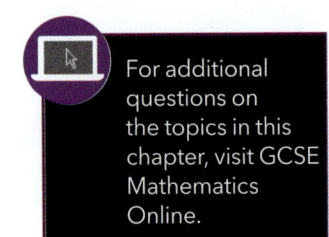

For additional questions on the topics in this chapter, visit GCSE Mathematics Online.

Chapter review

1 Write as fractions in their simplest form.
  a 25%   b 30%   c 3.5%

2 Write each of these as a percentage.
  a $\frac{1}{20}$ b $\frac{1}{8}$ c $\frac{8}{15}$ d 0.5   e 1.25   f 0.005

3 Put these values in ascending order.
  15.24, $15\frac{23}{86}$, (15×1.015), $15\frac{56}{45}$

4 The value of an investment increased from £120 000 to £124 800.
  What percentage increase is this?

5 The population of New Orleans was 484 674 before Hurricane Katrina.
  Afterwards, the population was found to have decreased by 53.9%.
  What was the population afterwards?

6 Mark has a voucher that gives him 22% off the prices at *Cordula's Hardware Store*.
  Estimate how much he will pay for an electric drill that normally costs £87.99.
  (3 marks)
  © OCR 2012

7 Shaz works 30 hours per week. She wants to increase this by 12%.
  How many hours will she then work per week?

8 Write: a 3 hours as a percentage of a day.
  b 750 metres as a percentage of 2 km.

9 The price of a plane ticket was reduced by 8% to £423.20.
  What was the original price of the ticket?

10 Nick sold his shares for £1147.50 and made a 35% profit.
  What did he pay for the shares?

14 Algebraic formulae

In this chapter you will learn how to ...
- use formulae to write and solve problems.
- change the subject of a formula.
- substitute numbers into formulae to find the value of the subject.
- understand and use a range of formulae, including kinematics formulae.

For more resources relating to this chapter, visit GCSE Mathematics Online.

Using mathematics: real-life applications

Formulae are used by engineers, scientists, pharmacists, vets and many other professionals. Vets use formulae to make sure they give animals the correct dosage of medicines for their age and weight. A poodle weighing 6 kg needs a far smaller dose of medicine than a 35 kg retriever.

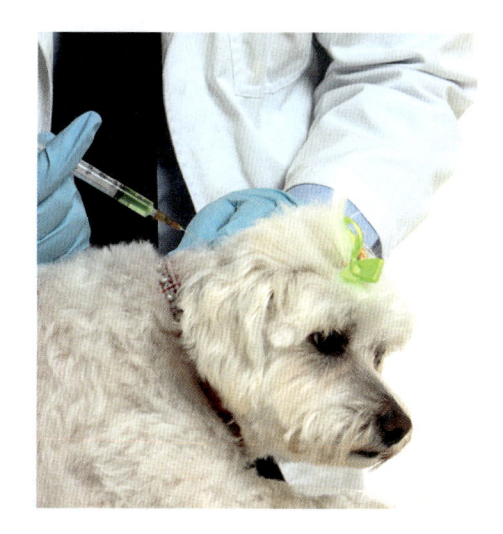

"I need to make sure I give the animals I treat the correct amount of medicine. I do this by using formulae that take into account their age, weight and the ratio between any other prescribed medicines." *(Vet)*

Before you start ...

Ch 1, 3	You need to be able to substitute values into expressions.	1 Evaluate $\dfrac{x + 2y}{z}$ when: **a** $x = 7, y = 4$ and $z = 2$　　**b** $x = 7, y = {}^-2$ and $z = 2$ **c** $x = {}^-7, y = 4$ and $z = 4$　　**d** $x = {}^-7, y = {}^-2$ and $z = {}^-2$
Ch 8	You should be able to solve simple equations.	2 Solve. **a** $6x = x + 35$　　**b** $5x = 64 - 3x$ **c** $2(2x + 3) = x + 7$　　**d** $5x - 8 = 3x + 12$
Ch 3, 5, 7, 8, 12	You should be familiar with some formulae already, and be able to identify the subject, variable(s) and any constants.	3 Look at these two formulae for finding the area of shapes. $A = \tfrac{1}{2}bh$　　$A = \pi r^2$ **a** What do the variables represent? **b** What is the constant in each formula? **c** What is the subject of each formula? **d** What tells you that the second formula applies to circles?

Find answers at: cambridge.org/ukschools/gcsemaths-studentbookanswers

207

GCSE Mathematics for OCR (Foundation)

Assess your starting point using the Launchpad

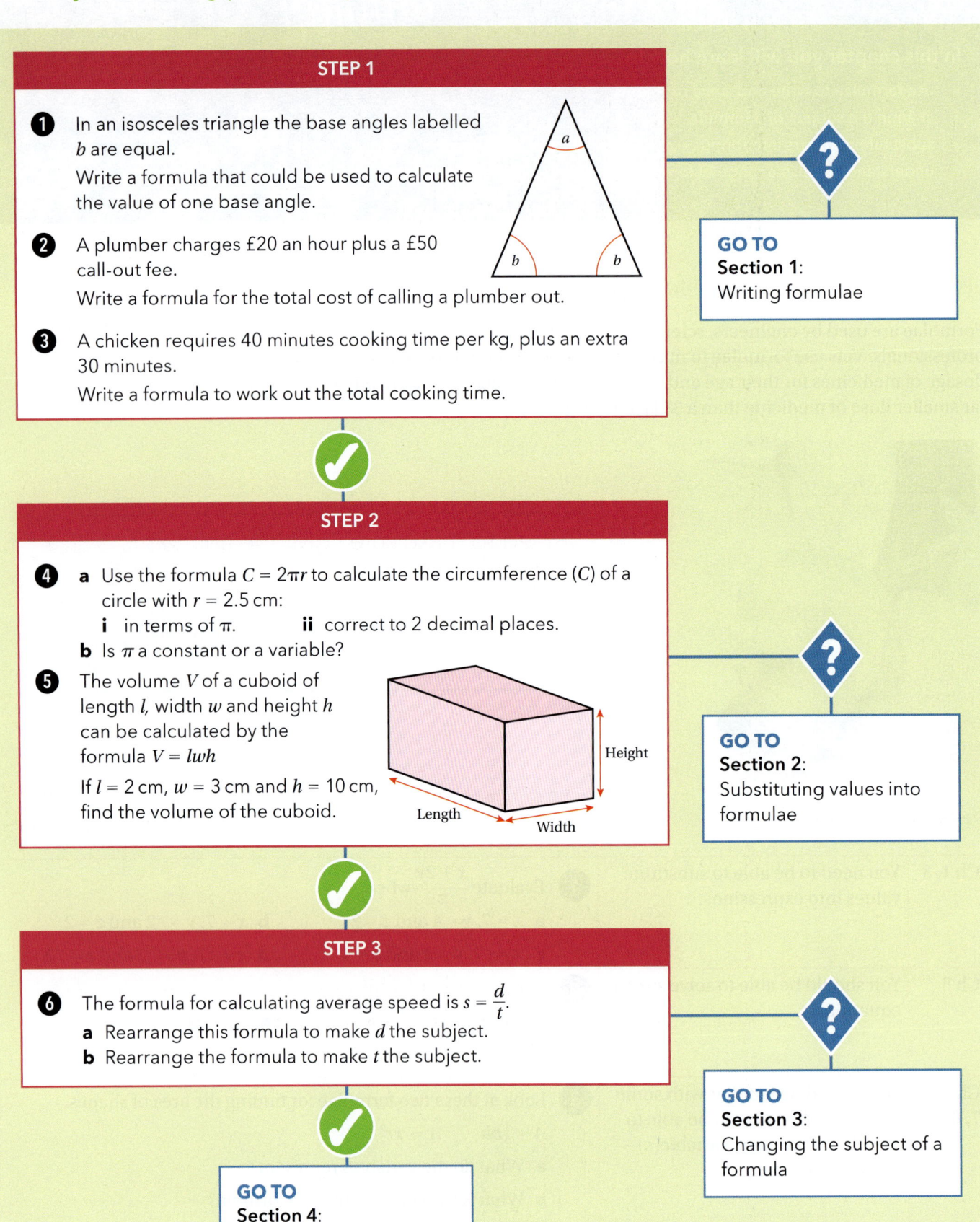

STEP 1

1 In an isosceles triangle the base angles labelled *b* are equal.
Write a formula that could be used to calculate the value of one base angle.

2 A plumber charges £20 an hour plus a £50 call-out fee.
Write a formula for the total cost of calling a plumber out.

3 A chicken requires 40 minutes cooking time per kg, plus an extra 30 minutes.
Write a formula to work out the total cooking time.

GO TO Section 1: Writing formulae

STEP 2

4 a Use the formula $C = 2\pi r$ to calculate the circumference (C) of a circle with $r = 2.5$ cm:
  i in terms of π. **ii** correct to 2 decimal places.
b Is π a constant or a variable?

5 The volume V of a cuboid of length l, width w and height h can be calculated by the formula $V = lwh$
If $l = 2$ cm, $w = 3$ cm and $h = 10$ cm, find the volume of the cuboid.

GO TO Section 2: Substituting values into formulae

STEP 3

6 The formula for calculating average speed is $s = \dfrac{d}{t}$.
a Rearrange this formula to make d the subject.
b Rearrange the formula to make t the subject.

GO TO Section 3: Changing the subject of a formula

GO TO Section 4: Working with formulae

14 Algebraic formulae

Section 1: Writing formulae

Formulae

A **formula** is a special type of equation that shows the relationship between two or more unknown quantities.

For example, the rule for working out cooking time for a roast chicken might be cook for 40 minutes per kilogram plus an extra 20 minutes.

To make sense of a formula you need to know what the variables represent. In the formula to calculate the area of a triangle, $A = \frac{1}{2}bh$:

- A is the area in square units.
- b is the length of the base of the triangle.
- h is the perpendicular height of the triangle.

A, b and h are variables. The letters can be replaced by many different values. $\frac{1}{2}$ is a constant. No matter what value you use for b or h, you have to multiply by $\frac{1}{2}$ in the formula to find the area of a triangle.

A single variable on one side of the formula is called the **subject** of the formula. It is the variable (or quantity) that is being **expressed in terms of** the other variables in the formula.

In $A = \frac{1}{2}bh$, A is the subject of the formula.

Writing formulae to represent real-life contexts

In Chapter 8 you wrote equations to represent information given in problems and then solved the equations to calculate the value of the unknowns. You use the same procedures to write formulae.

1. List the quantities involved. Work out whether they represent the subject, a variable, a constant or a coefficient.
2. Work out the relationship between each quantity. What is the subject being expressed in terms of?
3. Write the formula as simply as possible using algebraic conventions.

> **Key vocabulary**
>
> **formula**: a general rule written as an equation showing the relationship between unknown quantities; the plural is formulae.

> **Tip**
>
> Formulae often use letters for the variable that relate to the value they represent. For example, in formulae for area, A is often used to represent the area and h to represent height.

> **Key vocabulary**
>
> **subject**: the variable which is expressed in terms of other variables; it is the variable on its own on one side of the equals sign.
> In the formula $s = \frac{d}{t}$, s is the subject.

> **Tip**
>
> For a reminder about variables, constants and coefficients, see Chapter 3.

WORKED EXAMPLE 1

Mary and Peter are sharing half a circular pizza.

Peter cuts himself a slice that makes an angle, a, with the straight edge of the pizza half.

He tells Mary that he will cut himself another slice the same size, and then she can have what is left.

Write a formula for the size of Mary's share of the pizza.

Subject = Size of Mary's share
Variable = Peter's share
Constant = Size of starting slice

List the quantities involved and work out if they are the subject, a variable, a constant or a coefficient.

Continues on next page …

Find answers at: cambridge.org/ukschools/gcsemaths-studentbookanswers

Peter's share = 2a

Angles on a straight line equal 180°.

180° − 2a = size of Mary's share

> Work out the relationship between each quantity. You know that Peter takes two slices with an angle of a, so you can write an expression for the total size of Peter's share.
> You know that angles on a straight line add up to 180° (see Chapter 9). The size of Mary's share is written in terms of the size of the starting slice (half a pizza) and the size of Peter's slice.

Let the size of Mary's share = M

M = 180° − 2a

> Write the formula using the language of algebra.
> It might be useful to draw a diagram to work out this problem.

EXERCISE 14A

1 Write a formula for:

  a S in terms of C and P, where £S is selling price, £C is cost price and £P is profit.

  b D in terms of n, where D is the number of degrees in n right angles.

  c m in terms of h, where m is the number of minutes in h hours.

  d d in terms of m, where d is the number of days in m weeks.

2 When y is the subject and x is an unknown value, write a formula to determine y when y is:

  a three more than x.

  b six less than x.

  c ten times x.

  d the sum of $^-8$ and x.

  e the sum of x and the square of x.

  f twice x more than x plus 1.

3 To cook a chicken you need to allow 20 minutes per $\frac{1}{2}$ kg and another 20 minutes.

  A chicken weighs x kg. Write a formula to show the number of minutes, m, required to cook a chicken.

4 A right-angled triangle has shorter side lengths $9x$ cm and $40x$ cm, a hypotenuse of $41x$ cm, perimeter of p cm.

  What is the formula relating p and x?

5 A gardener has a large rectangular vegetable patch. He wants to put a path around it using paving stones that measure 50 cm × 50 cm.

  The path is to be one paving stone wide. Let n be the number of paving stones required.

  If the vegetable patch measures x metres by y metres, find a formula for n in terms of x and y. (Hint: draw a diagram.)

Section 2: Substituting values into formulae

To find the value of the subject (or any variable) in a formula you need to know the value of all the other variables. The known values are substituted into the formula to work out the unknown value.

Substitute means replace the letters with the numbers you have been given.

Evaluate means calculate the numerical value.

Sometimes a formula will contain only two variables, the subject and one other.

> **Tip**
>
> You learnt about substitution and evaluation in Chapter 3.

WORKED EXAMPLE 2

The perimeter of a square can be found using the formula $P = 4s$, where s is the length of a side.

What is the perimeter of a square with sides of:

a 10 cm?　　**b** 2.5 mm?

a $P = 4s, s = 10$　　You know that $s = 10$ cm and you need to find
　　$P = 4 \times 10$　　P. Substitute the value of s into the formula.
　　$P = 40$ cm　　Remember to include units in the answer.

b $P = 4s, s = 2.5$　　Again, substitute the value of s into the formula
　　$P = 4 \times 2.5$　　and remember to include units in your answer.
　　$P = 10$ mm

Sometimes a formula will contain the subject and more than one other variable. Make sure you substitute in **all** the known values.

WORKED EXAMPLE 3

The volume of an object can be found using the formula $V = \frac{1}{3}Ah$.
Find the volume of an object when $A = 30$ cm² and $h = 6$ cm.

$A = 30$ cm², $h = 6$ cm　　List the all the known values.

$V = \frac{1}{3} \times 30 \times 6$　　Substitute the known values into the formula.

$= \frac{1}{3} \times 180$

$= 60$

The volume is 60 cm³.　　Remember to include the correct units in your answer; volume is measured in **cubic** units.

> **Tip**
>
> It is good practice to show you can correctly substitute values into a formula before calculating the answer. Write down what you need to work out and then calculate the value. Remember to include units as required.

Find answers at: cambridge.org/ukschools/gcsemaths-studentbookanswers

EXERCISE 14B

1 Evaluate these expressions.

   a $2a(a - 3b)$ when:

      i $a = 2$ and $b = {}^-5$.   **ii** $a = 3$ and $b = {}^-2$.   **iii** $a = \frac{1}{3}$ and $b = \frac{1}{2}$.

   b $x^2 - 2y$ when:

      i $x = {}^-7$ and $y = 2$.   **ii** $x = {}^-\left(\frac{1}{3}\right)$ and $y = \frac{5}{6}$.

2 Calculate the value of the subject in each formula.

Where units are given, include the correct units in your answer.
Where appropriate, give your answer to 3 decimal places.

   a $A = lw$, where $l = 6$ m, $w = 9$ m

   b $s = \frac{d}{t}$, where $d = 72$ km, $t = 3$ hours

   c $A = \frac{1}{2}(a + b)h$, where $a = 4$ cm, $b = 7$ cm, $h = 9$ cm

   d $x = \sqrt{ab}$, where $a = 12$, $b = 13$

   e $V = \pi r^2 h$, where $r = 3.5$ cm, $h = 17$ cm

   f $t = a + (n - 1)d$, where $a = 10$, $n = 6$, $d = 2$

   g $a = \sqrt{b^2 - 4cd}$, where $b = {}^-2$, $c = {}^-4$, $d = 5$

   h $w = 3 + \sqrt{y^2 + zy}$, where $y = 7$, $z = {}^-3.5$

> **Tip**
> Remember to write the correct units in your answer.

3 The formula for converting temperature from degrees Fahrenheit (F) to degrees Celsius (C) is

$$C = \frac{5}{9}(F - 32°).$$

What is the value of C when $F = 76°$?

4 The stopping distance of a car once the brakes are applied is given by the formula

$d = 0.2v + 0.005v^2$,

where v km/h is the speed of the car when the brakes are applied.

In how many metres will a car stop if the brakes are applied when $v = 130$ km/h?

5 The Greek mathematician Hero showed that the area of a triangle with sides a, b and c is given by the formula

$A = \sqrt{s(s - a)(s - b)(s - c)}$,

where $s = \frac{1}{2}(a + b + c)$.

Use Hero's formula to find the area of this triangle.

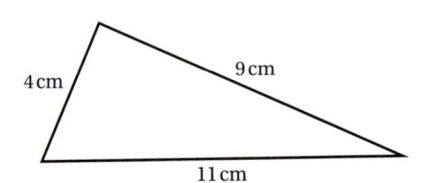

4 cm, 9 cm, 11 cm

> **Tip**
> You will learn about simple and compound interest in Chapter 33.

6 The simple interest payable when £P is invested at a rate of R% per year for T years is given by $I = \frac{PRT}{100}$.

Calculate the simple interest payable when £2000 is invested at 1.5% per year for 6 years.

Section 3: Changing the subject of a formula

You can calculate the value of **any** variable in a formula provided all the other variables are known.

When the value you want to find is not the subject of the formula you are given, you need to rearrange the formula to make the desired value the subject; then you evaluate the formula as normal.

Since a formula is a type of equation, you can use inverse operations to rearrange the formula just as you would an equation; remember to do the same to **both** sides of the formula.

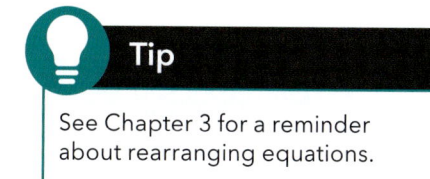

> **Tip**
>
> See Chapter 3 for a reminder about rearranging equations.

WORKED EXAMPLE 4

a Make r the subject of the formula $C = 2\pi r$.

b Given the formula $v^2 = u^2 + 2as$, find the value of s when $u = 8$, $v = 10$ and $a = 3$.

a $C = 2\pi r$ — To make r the subject you need to get it on its own on one side of the equation. Use inverse operations and apply the same to both sides of the formula.

$r = \dfrac{C}{2\pi}$ — Divide both sides by 2π. You would usually write the subject on the left.

b $v^2 = u^2 + 2as$ — s is not the subject of the formula but it is the value you need to calculate.

$v^2 - u^2 = 2as$
$\dfrac{v^2 - u^2}{2a} = s$ — Rearrange the formula to make s the subject using inverse operations: subtract u^2 from both sides, then divide by $2a$.

$s = \dfrac{v^2 - u^2}{2a}$ — Write s on the left-hand side; the subject of the rearranged formula.

$u = 8, v = 10$ and $a = 3$
$s = \dfrac{10^2 - 8^2}{2 \times 3}$
$s = \dfrac{100 - 64}{6}$
$s = \dfrac{36}{6}$
$s = 6$

Substitute in the values you know.
You could alternatively substitute the numbers **before** rearranging and solve the equations for s. Writing:

$v^2 = u^2 + 2as$
$10^2 = 8^2 + 2 \times 3s$
$100 = 64 + 6s$
$100 - 64 = 6s$
$36 = 6s$
$36 \div 6 = s$
$6 = s$
$s = 6$

Find answers at: cambridge.org/ukschools/gcsemaths-studentbookanswers

Tip

You learnt about reciprocals in Chapter 2.

Sometimes the value you need to make the subject of the formula appears twice in the formula, is multiplied by a power or is a reciprocal. Use the same principles as before.

WORKED EXAMPLE 5

a Make r the subject of the formula, $T = \frac{2\pi}{r}$.

b Find a if $3a = ab + 6$.

c Find t if $s = u + \frac{1}{2}vt^2$.

a $T = \frac{2\pi}{r}$
$rT = 2\pi$
$r = \frac{2\pi}{T}$

> Using inverse operations and applying the same to both sides: multiply both sides by r, then divide both sides by T.

b $3a = ab + 6$
$3a - ab = 6$
$a(3 - b) = 6$
$a = \frac{6}{(3 - b)}$

> As before, rearrange the equation using inverse operations and apply the same to both sides of the equation: subtract ab from both sides to get all a terms on the same side. You need to get a on its own. a is a common factor of both terms $3a$ and ab, so you can factorise for a. Divide both sides by $(3 - b)$. a is now the subject of the formula.

c $s = u + \frac{1}{2}vt^2$
$2s = 2u + vt^2$
$2(s - u) = vt^2$
$\frac{2(s - u)}{v} = t^2$
$t = \sqrt{\frac{2(s - u)}{v}}$

> Use inverse operations and apply the same to both sides: multiply both sides by 2, then subtract $2u$ from both sides (factorise by 2). Divide both sides by v.

> You want t not t^2. So, take the square root of both sides.

EXERCISE 14C

1 Rearrange these formulae to make the variable in brackets the subject.

  a $A = \frac{1}{2}bh$ (b) b $V = IR$ (I)

  c $V = \pi r^2 h$ (h) d $A = \frac{1}{2}(a + b)h$ (a)

Tip

You might recognise some of these formulae.

2 Rearrange the formulae to make the variable in brackets the subject.

  a $y = mx + c$ (c) b $V = \frac{1}{3}\pi r^2 h$ (h)

  c $v = u + at$ (t) d $A = 2\pi r^2 + 2\pi rh$ (h)

  e $s = ut + \frac{1}{2}at^2$ (a) f $c^2 = a^2 + b^2$ (b)

3 The formula for the perimeter, P, of a rectangle, l by w, is $P = 2(l + w)$.

If $P = 20$ cm and $l = 7$ cm, what is the length w?

4 The area, A cm², inside an ellipse is given by $A = \pi ab$.

Calculate to one decimal place the length a cm, if $b = 3.2$ and $A = 25$.

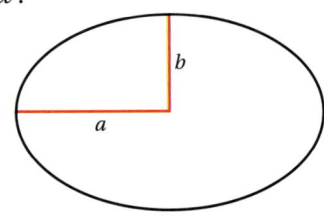

5 When an object is fired into the air at a speed of u metres per second, its height h metres above the ground and time t seconds of flight are related by

$$h = ut - 4.9t^2 \quad \text{(ignoring air resistance)}.$$

Find the speed at which an object was fired if it reached a height of 30 metres after 5 seconds.

6 The kinetic energy, E, joules of a moving object is given by

$$E = \frac{1}{2}mv^2$$

where m kg is the mass of the object and v m/s is its speed.

a Rearrange the formula to make m the subject.

b Use the new formula to calculate the mass of the object when $E = 300$ joules and $v = 10$ m/s.

7 The formula for the sum S of the interior angles in an n-sided polygon is $S = 180(n - 2)$.

Rearrange the formula to make n the subject and use this to find the number of sides of the polygon if the sum of the interior angles is 2160°.

Section 4: Working with formulae

You will use formulae as part of your work in other topics in mathematics, as well as other subjects.

Things to remember when working with formulae:

- Make sure you know what each term represents: the subject, a variable, the constant or a coefficient.
- Make sure you understand the relationship between each value.
- Substitute in the correct values.
- Include appropriate units in your answer.
- When writing a formula try some values to make sure it works.
- You can rearrange a formula to change the subject, but you don't always need to when you are substituting known values.

Writing a formula can be particularly helpful when you are given lots of information and asked to find one value.

Problem-solving framework

A group of sixth form students are planning to run a day conference.

The local university offers conference rooms for hire at a daily rate.

The students think they will have a maximum of 60 delegates and want to offer refreshments costing £4 per delegate.

The largest room they can hire costs £160 for the day.

Continues on next page …

Find answers at: cambridge.org/ukschools/gcsemaths-studentbookanswers

They want to charge each delegate enough to cover the costs of running the conference.

How much should they charge each delegate if there will be 60 delegates attending the conference?

Steps for approaching a problem-solving question	What you would do for this example
Step 1: Identify what you have to do.	Calculate how much to charge each delegate at the conference.
Step 2: Test the problem with what you already know.	You know a formula is a general rule showing the relationship between quantities; writing a formula will help you to calculate the required value.
Step 3: What maths can you do?	1 List the quantities involved and work out if they are the subject, a variable, a constant or a coefficient; use the language of algebra: Number of delegates (d) = 60 (variable, as this can change). Cost of refreshments = £4 per delegate (coefficient, as this value is multiplied by how many delegates there are). Cost of the room = £160 (constant, this is fixed by the university). Cost to charge each delegate = C (subject, this is what you want to find out). 2 Work out what the relationship is between each quantity. The cost to charge each delegate is the same as the cost of having each delegate at the conference (they want to break even not make a profit). So, this is the total cost divided by the number of delegates. The total cost is equal to the cost of refreshments for each delegate and the cost of the room hire. Now put this together using algebra: Cost of conference = $4d + 160$ Cost of one delegate is this value divided by the number of delegates (d). So the formula to calculate how much to charge each delegate is: $C = \dfrac{4d + 160}{d}$ If there are 60 delegates: $d = 60$ $C = \dfrac{4d + 160}{d}$ $C = \dfrac{4 \times 60 + 160}{60}$ $C = \dfrac{400}{60}$ $C = 6.66666666667$ They should charge each delegate £6.67
Step 4: Does your answer seem reasonable? Have you answered the question?	If they charged £6.67 per delegate and there were 60 delegates then they would get £400.20 which would just cover their costs. The answer is reasonable and you have answered the question as you have given a price per delegate.

Kinematics formulae

Kinematics is the study of how objects move; it is studied by mathematicians and physicists. For example, the average speed of an object can be found using the formula,

$$\text{speed} = \frac{\text{distance travelled}}{\text{time taken}}$$

In kinematics there are three important terms:

- **Velocity** – a measure of how fast an object is moving in a direction (in everyday terms this is speed).
- **Acceleration** – the rate at which the velocity of an object changes (in everyday terms this is increasing speed).
- **Displacement** – a change in the position of an object from when it started moving to where it stopped moving (in everyday terms this is like distance travelled).

In science these terms have specific meanings; velocity, acceleration and displacement are vector quantities because they have both size and direction.

You will see questions that involve the following kinematics formulae:

$$\boxed{v = u + at} \qquad \boxed{s = ut + \tfrac{1}{2}at^2} \qquad \boxed{v^2 = u^2 + 2as}$$

where,

v = final velocity   velocity is measured in units of distance and time (m/s – metres per second)

u = initial velocity

a = acceleration   acceleration in units of distance and time (m/s/s or m/s² – metres per second per second)

s = displacement (distance travelled)   displacement (distance travelled) in units of length (m)

t = time taken

> **Tip**
> You will learn more about vectors in Chapter 27.

> **Tip**
> These kinematics equations apply only to an object moving in a straight line at a constant acceleration.

WORK IT OUT 14.1

Two students studying physics were given the equation $v = u + at$ and asked to calculate the value of v when u = 12 metres per second, a = 10 metres per second per second, t = 3 seconds.

Which student has calculated v correctly, and used the correct units?

Student A	Student B
$v = 12 + 10 \times 3$	$v = 12 + 10 \times 3$
$v = 66$ m	$v = 42$ m/s

Common formulae to learn

There are some standard formulae that you will be expected to know and use. Some of these you will already have met in other chapters, others you will come across later. Make sure you know all of these formulae.

Find answers at: cambridge.org/ukschools/gcsemaths-studentbookanswers

Circumference of a circle	$C = \pi d$ or $2\pi r$
	d = diameter, r = radius
Area of a circle	$A = \pi r^2$
	r = radius
Pythagoras' theorem	$a^2 + b^2 = c^2$
	c = hypotenuse of a right-angled triangle
	a and b = two other sides of a right-angled triangle
Trigonometry ratios	$\sin \theta = \dfrac{o}{h}$, $\cos \theta = \dfrac{a}{h}$, $\tan \theta = \dfrac{o}{a}$

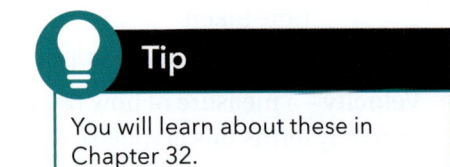

> **Tip**
> You will learn about these in Chapter 32.

EXERCISE 14D

Use these formulae as required to answer the questions in this exercise.

Perimeter of a rectangle	$P = 2l + 2w$ or $P = 2(l + w)$
	l = length, w = width
Area of a rectangle	$A = lw$
	l = length, w = width
Area of a parallelogram	$A = bh$
	b = length of base, h = perpendicular height
Volume of a cuboid	$V = lwh$
	l = length, w = width, h = height
Surface area of a cuboid	$SA = 2lw + 2wh + 2lh$
	l = length, w = width, h = height
Area of a triangle	$A = \dfrac{1}{2}bh$
	b = length of base, h = perpendicular height
Area of a trapezium	$A = \dfrac{1}{2}(a + b)h$
	$a + b$ = sum of lengths of parallel sides, h = height
Volume of a cylinder	$V = \pi r^2 h$
	r = radius, h = height
Volume of a cone	$V = \dfrac{1}{3}\pi r^2 h$
	r = radius, h = height
Converting degrees Celsius into degrees Fahrenheit	$F = \dfrac{9}{5}C + 32$
Converting degrees Fahrenheit into degrees Celsius	$C = \dfrac{5}{9}(F - 32)$

1 Decide whether each statement is true or false. Correct any false statements to make them true.

a If $A = \dfrac{1}{2}bh$, when $b = 4.5$ cm and $h = 8$ cm, then $A = 18$ m².

b When the formula to calculate speed $S = \dfrac{D}{T}$ is rearranged to make T the subject, it becomes $T = \dfrac{D}{S}$.

c A formula to calculate the number n half way between two numbers x and y can be written as $n = \dfrac{x + y}{2}$.

d In the formula to calculate the area of a circle $A = \pi r^2$, π is a constant and A and r are the variables.

2 Use the appropriate formula from the table to complete these problems.

   a Calculate the perimeter P of a rectangle if the length $l = 6.5$ m and width $w = 8$ m.

   b What is the height of a parallelogram that has area $A = 45$ cm² and base $b = 2.5$ cm?

   c What is the surface area of a rectangular solid (cuboid) if the length $l = 20$ cm, the width $w = 3.5$ cm and the height $h = 7.2$ cm?

   d What is the area A of a circle with a radius $r = 12.3$ cm?

   e What is the height h of a cone that has a volume $V = 45$ cm³ and a radius $r = 5$ cm?

3 **a** Find the Fahrenheit temperature F when $C = 8$.

   b Find the Celsius temperature C when $F = 72$.

   c Freezing point is 0 °C. What is the equivalent temperature in Fahrenheit?

4 Given $s = ut + \dfrac{1}{2}at^2$

Find the value of s when $u = 10$, $t = 5$ and $a = 0.27$.

5 Ohm's Law states that the voltage, V, is the product of the current, I, times the resistance, R.

      $V = IR$

   a Calculate the voltage, V, when $I = 25$ milliamps and $R = 330$ ohms.

   b Calculate the current, I, when $V = 9$ volts and $R = 330$ ohms.

   c Calculate the resistance, R, when $V = 9$ volts and $I = 18$ milliamps.

6 Use the formula $A = 4\pi r^2$ to find A correct to 1 decimal place when:

   a $r = 3$ **b** $r = 25.6$

7 Rearrange each of these formulae to make the letter in brackets the subject.

   a $A = 4\pi r^2$ (r)

   b $W = \sqrt{\dfrac{3V}{\pi h}}$ (V)

   c $\dfrac{1}{x} + \dfrac{1}{y} = \dfrac{2}{z}$ (y)

8 A large wooden crate has to be moved by a car. To be moved, the crate has to be placed on its base, which is 150 cm long by 50 cm wide. Which of the following cars could be used and which would be the best one to use? (Hint: calculate the length of each car boot.)

Car	A	B	C
Area of boot (cm²)	11 250	8642	9480
Width (cm)	72	58	62.5

Find answers at: cambridge.org/ukschools/gcsemaths-studentbookanswers

9. Two friends, Shona and Chelsea, are planning to go on holiday together. Shona prefers resorts where the average temperatures are below 27 °C, but at least 20 °C. Convert the following temperatures from Fahrenheit to Celsius for three possible holiday resorts. Which resort would be acceptable to both friends.

   i) Sunshine Beach   84.2 °F
   ii) Palm Tree Bay   77 °F
   iii) Silver Sands   80.6 °F

   The formula for converting Celsius to Fahrenheit is: $F = 1.8\,°C + 32$.

10. Driver A covers a distance of 87 miles in 1.4 hours travelling on a motorway and Driver B covers a distance of 174 miles in 2.4 hours on the same motorway. Work out the average speed of each driver. Which driver is likely to have broken the motorway speed limit of 70 mph?

Checklist of learning and understanding

Writing formulae
- A formula is a general rule or equation showing the relationship between quantities.
- You can use formulae to represent real-life problems as long as you define the subject, any variable(s) you are using, and any constants or coefficients.

Substituting values into formulae
- To evaluate a formula you need to know the value of all but one of its variables.
- Substitute known values into a formula to find the unknown variable.

Changing the subject of a formula
- The subject of a formula is the variable (or quantity) that is being expressed in terms of the other variables in the formula.
- In any formula you can 'change the subject' by rearranging the formula in the same way as you rearrange equations, using inverse operations and performing the same operations to both sides.

Working with formulae
- Formulae are used across many topics in mathematics and other subjects, so make sure you are comfortable using them.
- You will come across kinematic formulae in some questions in science.
- There are some common formulae that you need to learn:
  - circumference of a circle
  - area of a circle
  - Pythagoras' theorem
  - trigonometry ratios

14 Algebraic formulae

Chapter review

> For additional questions on the topics in this chapter, visit GCSE Mathematics Online.

1 Substitute values into these formulae and evaluate:
  a Find v when $v = u + at$ and $u = 50$, $a = 10$ and $t = 2$.
  b Find s when $s = ut + \frac{1}{2}at^2$ and $u = 0$, $a = 6$ and $t = 10$.
  c Find v when $v^2 = u^2 + 2as$ and $u = 5$, $a = 6$ and $s = 12$.

2 Rearrange the formula for the area of a circle, to calculate the radius of a circle with area 25 cm² (leave π in the answer).

> **Learn this formula**
> You will be expected to know that the area of a circle is $A = \pi r^2$.

3 The cost £C of hiring a reception room for a function is given by the formula $C = 12n + 250$, where n is the number of people attending the function.
  a Rearrange the formula to make n the subject.
  b How many people attended the function if the cost of hiring the reception room was:
  i £730?   **ii** £1090?   **iii** £1210?   **iv** £1690?

4 Rearrange the following formulae to make the letter in the brackets the subject.
  a $A = \pi ab$ (a) **b** $P = 2a + 2b$ (a)
  c $\sqrt{ab} = c$ (b) **d** $a\sqrt{b} = c$ (b)
  e $\sqrt{(b+c)} = c$ (b) **f** $\sqrt{(x-b)} = c$ (b)
  g $\sin\theta = \dfrac{o}{h}$ (o) **h** $\dfrac{x}{\sqrt{y}} = c$ (y)

5 Rearrange to make p the subject.
$$C + 5p = a(C - p)$$
(4 marks)
© OCR 2011

Find answers at: cambridge.org/ukschools/gcsemaths-studentbookanswers

15 Perimeter

In this chapter you will learn how to ...
- calculate the perimeter of simple shapes such as rectangles and triangles.
- calculate the circumference of a circle.
- calculate the perimeter of composite shapes, including circles or parts of circles.

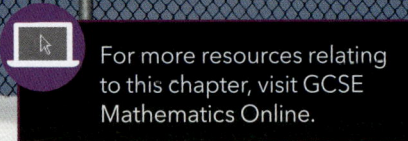

For more resources relating to this chapter, visit GCSE Mathematics Online.

Using mathematics: real-life applications

Working out the amount of fencing needed for a field, the number of tiles needed to edge a swimming pool, or the number of perimeter security cameras needed to secure an area all require the calculation of a perimeter.

"Security cameras in a car park are only effective if they can see all round the perimeter of the car park so I need to know the dimensions of the car park in order to determine how many cameras are needed and where to put them."

(Security camera technician)

Before you start ...

Ch 5	You must be able to recognise and name some common polygons.	**1**	Match each name to the correct shape. Octagon Pentagon Hexagon a b c
Ch 12	You must be able to convert between basic metric units.	**2**	Convert. **a** 5 km into m **b** 12 km into cm **c** 8500 mm into m **d** 4.8 m to mm
Ch 5	You need to know and use the correct names of parts of a circle.	**3**	True or false? **a** The diameter is twice the length of the radius. **b** The diameter is always shorter than the radius. **c** The angles at the centre of a circle add up to 180°.
Ch 14	You should be able to write simple formulae, substitute values into formulae and change the subject of a formula.	**4**	If the side of a square is x cm, write an expression for the sum of all its sides.
		5	Make l the subject of the formula $P = 2(l + w)$.
		6	If $P = \pi r + 2r$, calculate r to two decimal places when $P = 10.28$ (2 DP)

15 Perimeter

Assess your starting point using the Launchpad

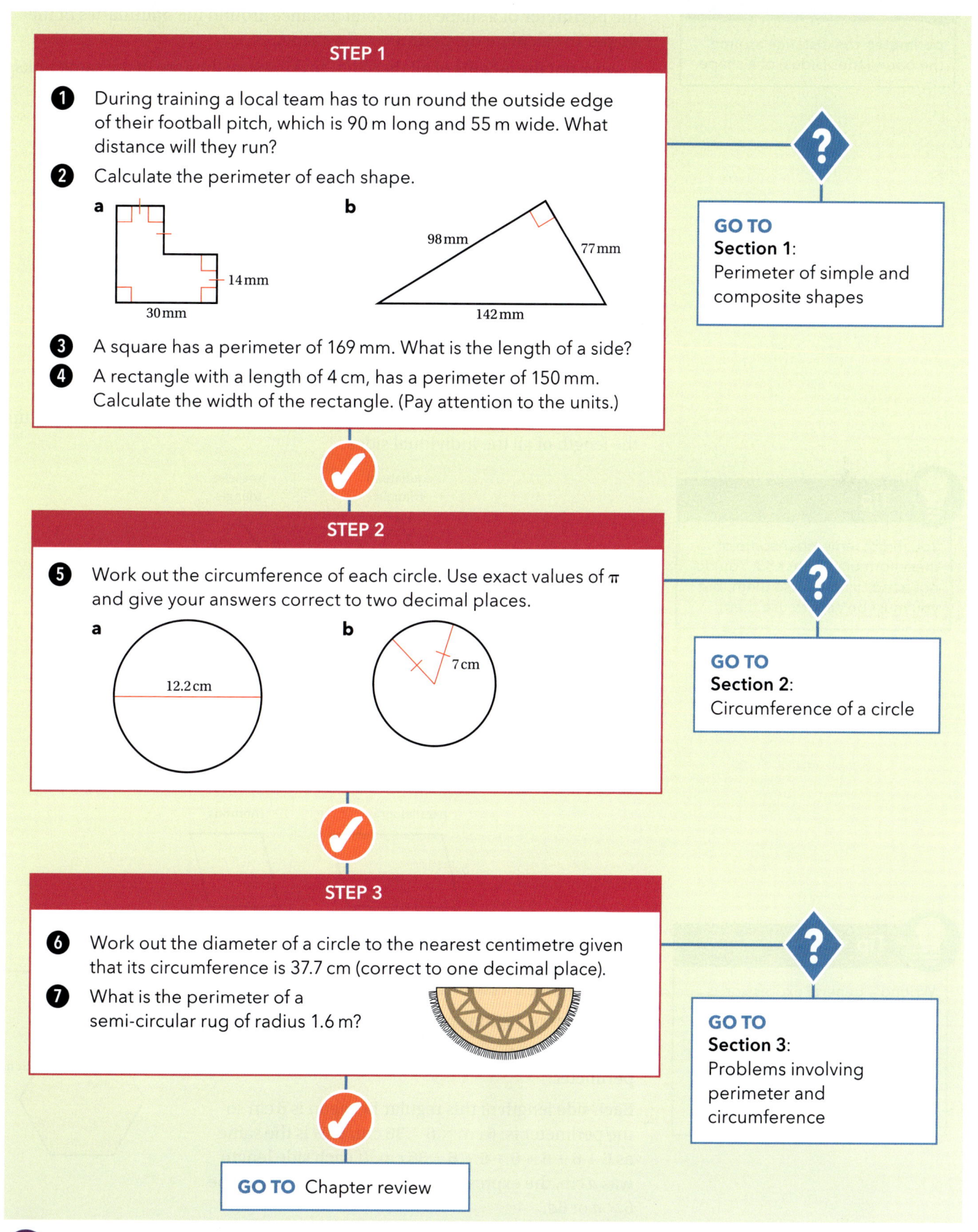

STEP 1

1 During training a local team has to run round the outside edge of their football pitch, which is 90 m long and 55 m wide. What distance will they run?

2 Calculate the perimeter of each shape.

a

b
98 mm, 77 mm, 142 mm

14 mm, 30 mm

3 A square has a perimeter of 169 mm. What is the length of a side?

4 A rectangle with a length of 4 cm, has a perimeter of 150 mm. Calculate the width of the rectangle. (Pay attention to the units.)

GO TO Section 1: Perimeter of simple and composite shapes

STEP 2

5 Work out the circumference of each circle. Use exact values of π and give your answers correct to two decimal places.

a 12.2 cm

b 7 cm

GO TO Section 2: Circumference of a circle

STEP 3

6 Work out the diameter of a circle to the nearest centimetre given that its circumference is 37.7 cm (correct to one decimal place).

7 What is the perimeter of a semi-circular rug of radius 1.6 m?

GO TO Section 3: Problems involving perimeter and circumference

GO TO Chapter review

Find answers at: cambridge.org/ukschools/gcsemaths-studentbookanswers

Key vocabulary

perimeter: the distance around the boundaries (sides) of a shape.

Section 1: Perimeter of simple and composite shapes

The **perimeter** of a shape is the total distance around the boundaries of the shape. To calculate the perimeter of a shape:
- work out the lengths of all the sides, making sure they are in the same units,
- add the lengths together.

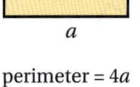

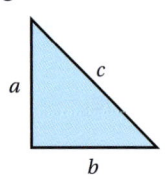

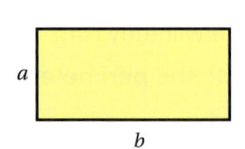

perimeter = $4a$ perimeter = $a + b + c$ perimeter = $2(a + b)$

Using formulae to find the perimeter

The properties of different polygons can be used to derive formulae for calculating the perimeter.

This means that you can substitute in known values without having to add up the length of all the individual sides.

equilateral triangle: $P = 3s$

isosceles triangle: $P = 2a + b$

square: $P = 4s$

rectangle: $P = 2(l + b)$

parallelogram: $P = 2(l + b)$

rhombus: $P = 4s$

Tip

You might remember some of these formulae from KS3. You do not need to memorise them, but you must be able to use them.

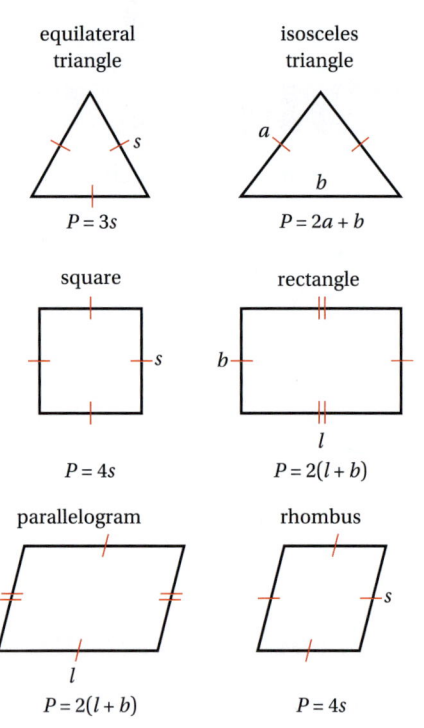

Tip

Writing a general expression is a way of showing the quantity of something when the actual numbers are not known. Numbers can be substituted into the expression to find the quantity required.

The general expression for finding the perimeter of a **regular** polygon is:

perimeter of regular polygon = side length × number of sides.

You only need the length of one side to find the perimeter:

Each side length of this regular hexagon is 6 cm so the perimeter is: 6 cm × 6 = 36 cm. This is the same as 6 + 6 + 6 + 6 + 6 + 6 = 36 cm. If each side length was a cm, the expression for the perimeter would be 6 × a or $6a$.

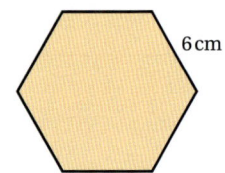

15 Perimeter

WORKED EXAMPLE 1

Calculate the perimeter of this shape if

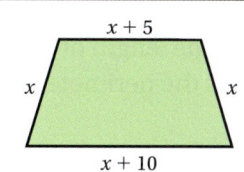

a $x = 5$ cm. **b** $x = 4.5$ cm.

Perimeter $= x + x + 5 + x + x + 10$
$= 4x + 15$

First write an expression for the perimeter in terms of x. Write out the perimeter as a sum of side lengths, and simplify.

a $x = 5$
perimeter $= 4x + 15$
$= 4 \times 5 + 15$
$= 35$ cm²

Substitute the value of x into the formula you wrote for the perimeter.

b $x = 4.5$
perimeter $= 4x + 15$
$= 4 \times 4.5 + 15$
$= 33$ cm²

Substitute the value of x into the formula you wrote for the perimeter.

> **Tip**
>
> Simplifying expressions by collecting like terms was covered in Chapter 3.

EXERCISE 15A

1 What is the perimeter of an equilateral triangle of side length 10 cm?

2 A yard is completely surrounded by a fence of lengths 12 m, 4.7 m, 354 cm and 972 cm. What is the perimeter of the yard?

3 Write expressions for the perimeter of these shapes.

  a An equilateral triangle, side length a.

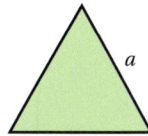

  b A rectangle, width x and length y.

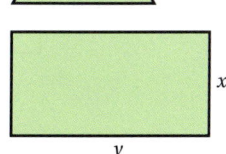

  c A regular octagon, side length z.

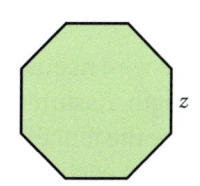

4 Work out the perimeter of this shape when
  a each side length is 10 cm.
  b each side length is 12 cm.

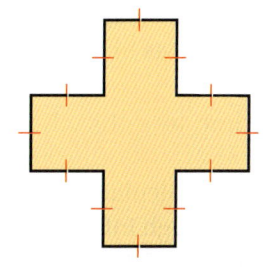

Find answers at: cambridge.org/ukschools/gcsemaths-studentbookanswers

5 A tessellated hexagon creates a pattern for a patchwork quilt.

If the side length of each hexagon is 8 cm, what is the perimeter of this shape?

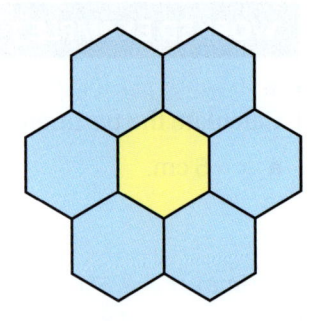

6 Each side length of this tiling pattern measures 15 cm.

Work out its perimeter.

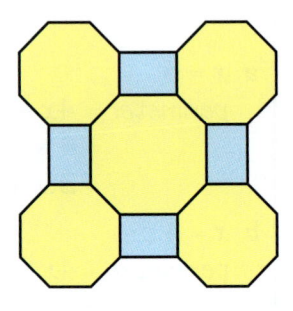

7 a Why are the formulae the same for calculating the perimeter of:
  i a rectangle and a parallelogram?
  ii a square and a rhombus?
b Why is there no formula for finding the perimeter of a trapezium?

8 A field with dimensions shown on the diagram is to be fenced.
The fence is made of of upright posts and four strands of wire (as shown).

Each strand of wire is continuous and is tacked to a post where it passes one.

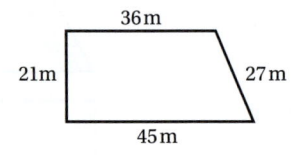

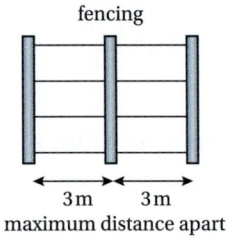

a Find the total length of wire needed for the fencing.

b The wire needs to be tacked to a post every 3 m along its continuous length. Assuming there is no gate to the field (a stile is used to climb over the fence), how many posts would the fence need? There is one post in each corner of the field.

c Calculate the cost of fencing if each post costs £2.39 and the wire costs £1.78 per metre.

Finding lengths when the perimeter is known

You can calculate unknown lengths in a shape if you know the perimeter and have enough information about the shape, by rearranging the formula for the perimeter of that shape.

WORKED EXAMPLE 2

a What is the length of a rectangle of perimeter 20 cm and width 5.5 cm?
b Calculate the length of each side of a rhombus of perimeter 1.8 m.

a $P = 2(l + w)$ $P = 20, w = 5.5$

Think about the information you have. You know the formula for the perimeter of a rectangle is $P = 2(l + w)$.

$20 = 2l + 2(5.5)$
$20 = 2l + 11$
$20 - 11 = 2l$
$9 = 2l$
$l = 4.5$ cm

Substitute the known values into the formula and solve for l. **Alternatively**, you could have rearranged the formula to make l the subject then substituted in the values.

b $P = 4s$

Write down the formula for the perimeter of a rhombus.

$s = \dfrac{P}{4}$

$s = \dfrac{1.8}{4}$

$s = 0.45$ m

Change the subject of the formula and substitute in the values you know to find s. **Alternatively**, you could have substituted the known values in first, and then rearranged to find s.

Perimeter of composite shapes

Composite shapes are formed by combining shapes or by removing parts of a shape.
The shape on the right is made up of a rectangle and a triangle.
You add up the side lengths around the outside boundary of the shape to find the perimeter:
$4 + 3 + 3 + 4 + 3 = 17$ cm
You can use what you know about the properties of shapes to work out any missing lengths.

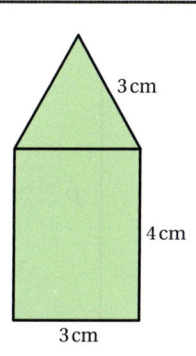

WORKED EXAMPLE 3

Find the perimeter (P) of this composite shape.
All angles are right angles and all dimensions are in centimetres.

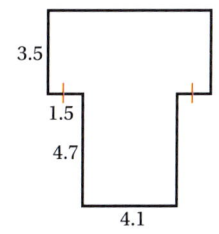

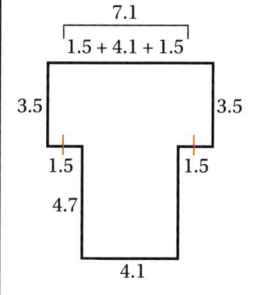

The shape is made of two rectangles. Start by working out the lengths of the missing sides. The top side is made up of the lengths 1.5, 4.1 and 1.5; you know the last bit is 1.5 because it has a mark to show it is the same length as the side labelled 1.5. You know this top shape is a rectangle as it has four right angles (if it was a square all four lengths would be the same). So, you know that opposite sides are equal in length, which gives you the missing length, 3.5. Similarly, the bottom shape is also a rectangle, and so the missing length is 4.7.

$P = 7.1 + 3.5 + 1.5 + 4.7 + 4.1 + 4.7 + 1.5 + 3.5$
$= 30.6$ cm

Add up the side lengths; don't forget to include the correct units in your answer.

Continues on next page …

Find answers at: cambridge.org/ukschools/gcsemaths-studentbookanswers

Alternative solution

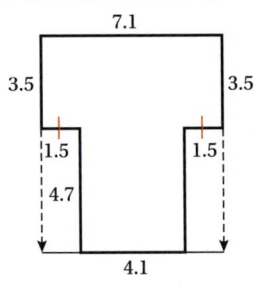

7.1
3.5   3.5
1.5   1.5
4.7
4.1

$P = 2(7.1 + 8.2)$
$= 30.6 \text{ cm}.$

You might have spotted that the composite shape would still have the same perimeter if its two bottom corners were flipped to make a rectangle.
So, instead of adding up all the individual lengths, you could use the formula for calculating the perimeter of a rectangle instead.

The perimeter must include **all** of the shape's boundaries; so be careful when working with composite shapes to include any **inner** boundaries in the perimeter calculation.

WORKED EXAMPLE 4

Calculate the perimeter of this shape.

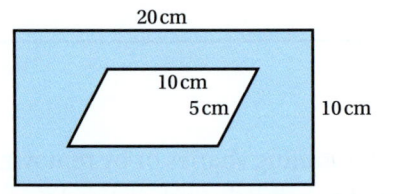

20 cm
10 cm
5 cm
10 cm

$P = 2(20 + 10) + 2(10 + 5)$
$= 2(30) + 2(15)$
$= 60 + 30$
$= 90 \text{ cm}$

The shape is a rectangle with a parallelogram cut out of the middle. The perimeter of the shape is equal to the perimeter of the rectangle **and** the perimeter of the parallelogram inside. Always think carefully about what lengths are included in the perimeter of a shape.

WORK IT OUT 15.1

This shape was made by combining five identical squares with sides of 6.5 cm with four identical equilateral triangles. Which calculation will result in the correct perimeter?

Why?

Option A	Option B	Option C
$P = 16 \times 6.5$	$P = 20 \times 6.5$	$P = 24 \times 6.5$
$= 104 \text{ cm}$	$= 130 \text{ cm}$	$= 156 \text{ cm}$

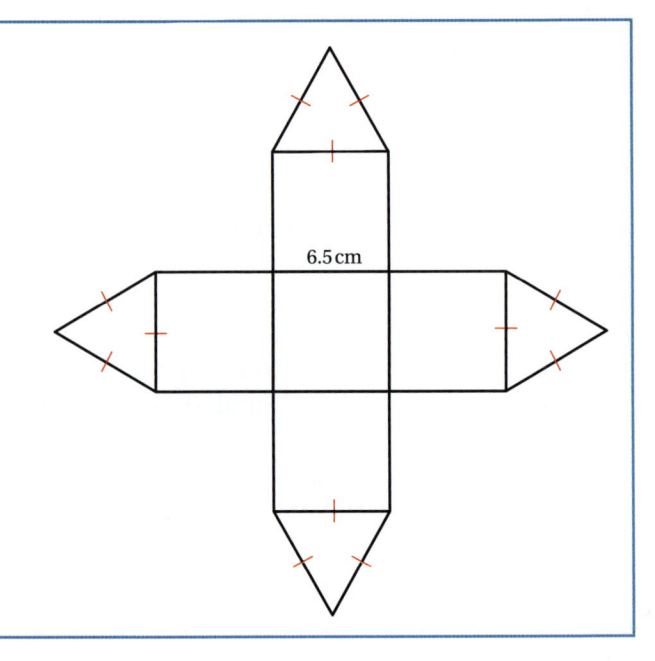

6.5 cm

15 Perimeter

EXERCISE 15B

1 Find the missing values.

Perimeter	Length	Width
Rectangle ABCD $P = 242$ mm	77 mm	
Parallelogram MNOP $P = 200$ mm		55 mm
Rhombus CDEF $P = 12.25$ cm		
Square PQRS $P = 47.28$ cm		

2 Calculate the perimeter of each shape. (Shapes are not drawn to scale.)

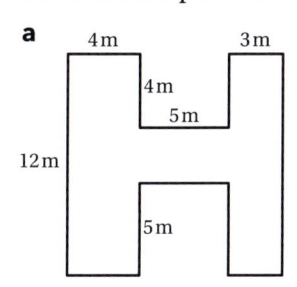

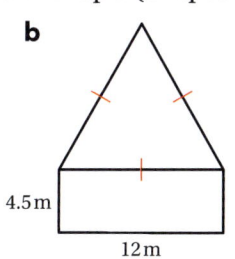

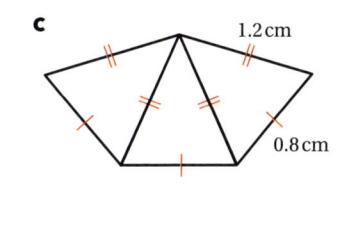

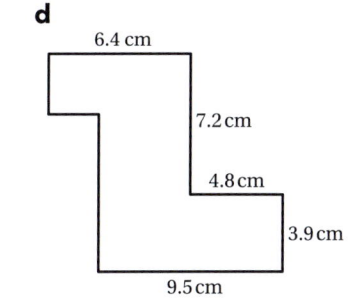

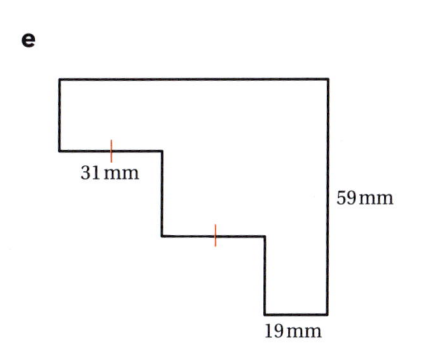

a: 4 m, 3 m, 4 m, 5 m, 12 m, 5 m

b: 4.5 m, 12 m

c: 1.2 cm, 0.8 cm

d: 6.4 cm, 7.2 cm, 4.8 cm, 3.9 cm, 9.5 cm

e: 31 mm, 59 mm, 19 mm

3 Petra has the following mosaic tiles:

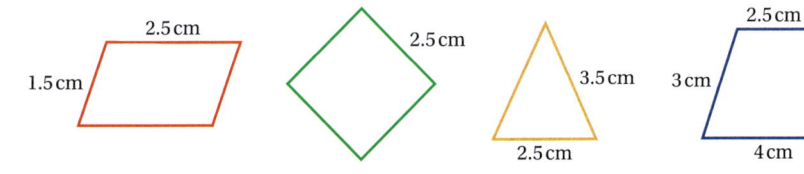

- 2.5 cm, 1.5 cm (parallelogram)
- 2.5 cm (rhombus)
- 3.5 cm, 2.5 cm (triangle)
- 2.5 cm, 3 cm, 3 cm, 4 cm (trapezium)

She arranges the tiles to make these shapes.

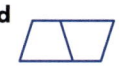

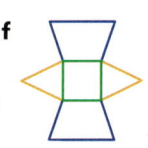

a, b, c, d, e, f

Use the dimensions above to find the perimeter of each shape.

Find answers at: cambridge.org/ukschools/gcsemaths-studentbookanswers

> **Tip**
> If there is no diagram, it is a good idea to draw one to help you think about the problem and the perimeter you need to find.

4 The end of a maze consists of a regular pentagon with side length 5 m.
If a child runs round this 3 times, how far will they run in total?

5 A rectangular allotment has a perimeter of 25 metres.
If the length of one side is 6.8 metres, how wide is the allotment?

Section 2: Circumference of a circle

The perimeter of a circle is called its **circumference (C)**.

The radius (r) is the distance from the centre to the circumference.

The diameter (d) is a line through the centre of a circle. The diameter is twice the radius ($2r$).

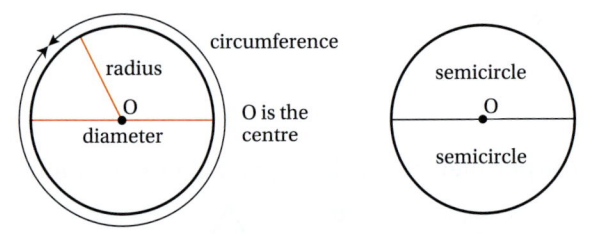

The Ancient Greeks discovered that when you measured the circumference of a circle and divided it by its diameter you got a constant ratio of approximately 3.142.

This ratio is called pi and the symbol π is used to represent it.

$$\pi = \frac{C}{d}$$

This ratio can be rearranged to give two formulae for finding the circumference of any circle.

> **Learn this formula**
>
> $C = \pi d$
> where C = circumference and d = diameter.
> Since the diameter is twice the length of the radius, the formula can also be written in terms of r.
> $C = 2\pi r$
> where r = radius.

Pi has no exact decimal or fractional value (it is an irrational number). So when you do calculations involving pi you might be asked to give rounded or approximate answers.

If you are asked to give an **exact** answer, this means your answer should be a multiple of π, and the π symbol should be in your answer.

Your calculator can work with exact values of pi but sometimes you will be given an approximate value of pi and asked to use that. **Read the question carefully**.

15 Perimeter

WORKED EXAMPLE 5

a Calculate the circumference of a circle with diameter 7 cm.
Give your answer to the nearest cm.

a $C = \pi d$
$= \pi \times 7$
$= 21.991\,149 \approx 22 \text{ cm}$

> Use the π button on your calculator. Check the manual on your calculator to see how to use the π button; for example you might press:
> [π] [×] [7] [=]

$C = 22 \text{ cm}$ (to the nearest cm)

> Round your answer to the requested degree of accuracy; always include the degree of accuracy in your answer when using the '=' sign.

b Calculate the circumference of a circle with radius 4.5 m.
Leave your answer as a multiple of π.

b $C = 2\pi r$
$= 2 \times \pi \times 4.5$
$= 9\pi \text{ m}$

> Simplify the expression as much as possible. The question asks for the answer to be given as a multiple of π, this is the same as being asked to provide an **exact** answer. By leaving π in the answer, you are not giving an approximation of the answer.

c Take the value of π to be 3.142.
What is the circumference of a circle with diameter 20 m? Give your answer to two decimal places.

c $C = \pi d$
$= 3.142 \times 20$
$= 62.84 \text{ m}$

> Use the value for π given to you in the question.

Sometimes questions that require you to calculate the circumference of a circle might not mention it directly. You need to be able to recognise what the question is asking of you.

Problem-solving framework

Racing wheelchairs can travel at speeds of up to 45 mph and can cost up to £20 000.

The rear wheels of a chair have a diameter of 70 cm.

The front wheels have a radius of 20 cm.

Find the number of turns that the rear wheels will make over a 100 m race.

Steps for approaching a problem-solving question	What you would do for this example
Step 1: What have you got to do?	Find the number of turns that the rear wheels will make over 100 m. I need to calculate the circumference of the rear wheels so that I can see how many times the wheel turns in 100 metres.

Continues on next page …

Find answers at: cambridge.org/ukschools/gcsemaths-studentbookanswers

Step 2: What information do you need?	Diameter (d) of rear wheel = 70 cm Circumference of a circle formula: $C = \pi d$ or $2\pi r$ Length of race = 100 m
Step 3: Is there any information you don't need?	I don't need the radius of the front wheel, speed of the wheelchair and its cost.
Step 4: What maths can you do?	Circumference of rear wheel = $\pi d = \pi \times 70 = 219.9$ cm (to 1 dp) Change the units of the distance so that they are the same as the circumference: 100 m = 100 × 100 cm = 10 000 cm Number of turns made by rear wheel = 10 000 ÷ 219.9 = 45.5 (to 1 dp)
Step 5: Have you used all the information? At this point you should check to make sure you have calculated what was asked of you.	All relevant information used ✓ Answered the question ✓
Step 6: Is your answer correct?	Used diameter for rear wheel ✓ Converted cm into m correctly ✓

Knowing the circumference of a circle means that you can calculate the diameter and/or the radius by rearranging the formula for the circumference.

> **Tip**
>
> If you are asked to find r and use $C = \pi d$, remember to divide d by 2 to get r.

WORKED EXAMPLE 6

A circle has a circumference of 200 cm.

Calculate the diameter of the circle to 1 decimal place.

$$C = \pi d$$
$$200 = \pi \times d$$
$$200 \div \pi = d$$
$$d = 63.7 \text{ cm } (1 \text{ dp})$$

Write down the formula for calculating the circumference of a circle. Substitute in the known values, then solve the equation for the unknown value (d). You could also have started by rearranging the formula to make d the subject and then substituting in the known values.

EXERCISE 15C

1 Use the π key on your calculator to calculate the circumference of each circle.

Give your answer correct to two decimal places if necessary.

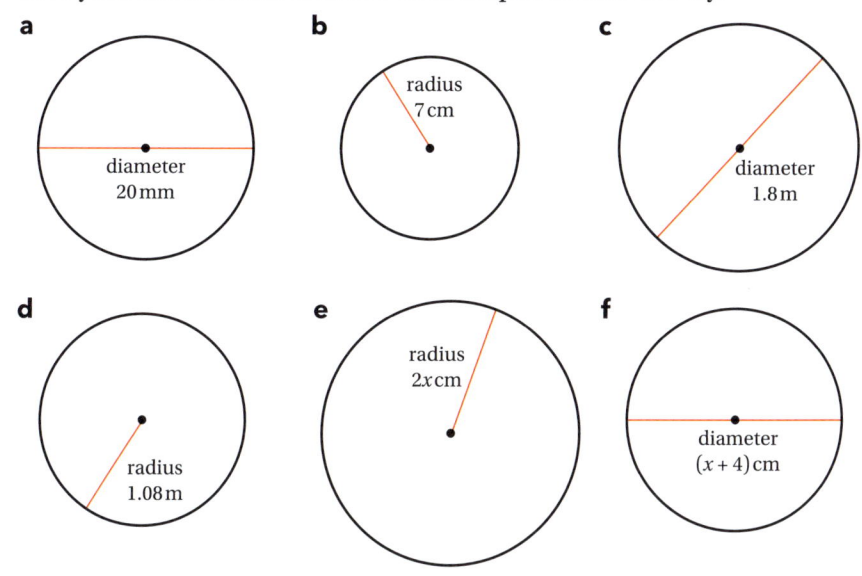

a diameter 20 mm

b radius 7 cm

c diameter 1.8 m

d radius 1.08 m

e radius $2x$ cm

f diameter $(x + 4)$ cm

2 The alloy wheel rims of a car have a diameter of 42 cm.

Calculate the circumference of each rim.

3 A plastic slinky spring consists of 36 coils of plastic.

If the diameter of one coil is 55 mm, what length of plastic is needed to make the spring?

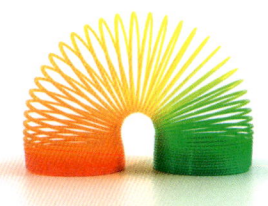

4 Nate has a square piece of metal with sides of 8.5 cm.

He wants to cut out a round disc with a radius of at least 4 cm from the square.

  a Draw a rough sketch to show this situation.

  b Calculate the circumference of the disc if the radius is 4 cm.

  c When he cuts the disc out, Nate finds the diameter is actually 8.3 cm.

  What is the circumference of this disc?

  d What is the perimeter of the piece of metal left after cutting out a disc of:

  i radius 4 cm?   **ii** diameter 8.3 cm?

> **Tip**
> Remember that the perimeter includes both the outer and inner boundaries.

5 Find the diameter, correct to 2 decimal places, of a circle of circumference:

  a 20 mm.   **b** 15.2 cm.

6 Find the radius of a round CD to the nearest mm, if its circumference is 36.33 cm.

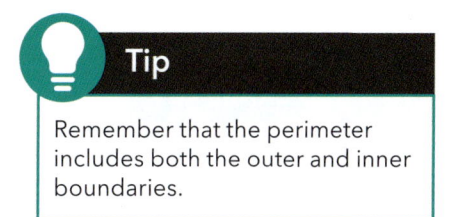

GCSE Mathematics for OCR (Foundation)

7 What is the smallest possible square plate that you can use for a round cake of circumference 77 cm?

8 The minute hand of a clock is 75 mm long.

How far will the tip of the hand travel in one hour?

Give your answer correct to the nearest centimetre.

Sectors of a circle

A **sector** is a 'slice' of a circle.

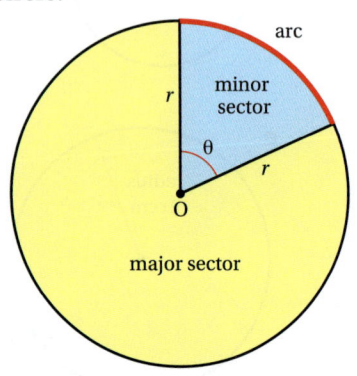

> **Tip**
> You learnt about the parts of a circle in Chapter 5.

> **Tip**
> The term circumference is only used to describe the distance around a whole circle. When you deal with distance around parts of a circle you talk about the **perimeter**.

> **Tip**
> You learnt about the properties of circles in Chapter 5, and about angles in Chapter 9.

The perimeter of a sector is formed by two radii and a section of the circumference called an **arc**.

Perimeter of a sector = radius + radius + arc length.

To work out the length of an arc, you need to use what you know about angles and circles.

Angles around a point add up to 360°; this is true for the angles around the centre of a circle.

The angle formed at the centre of the circle by the two radii in a sector, is therefore a fraction of 360°.

You can write this as $\frac{x}{360}$.

Similarly, the arc length is a fraction of the circumference.

So, to find the length of the arc you multiply the circumference of the circle by the fraction of the full circle that the sector represents:

$$\text{Arc length} = \frac{x}{360} \times \pi d \qquad \text{or} \qquad \text{Arc length} = \frac{x}{360} \times 2\pi r$$

        fraction   circumference   fraction   circumference

WORKED EXAMPLE 7

Find the length of the arc in each of these sectors.

a 30°, 5 m

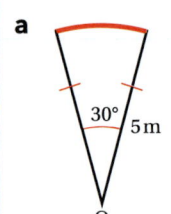

b 65°, 4 cm

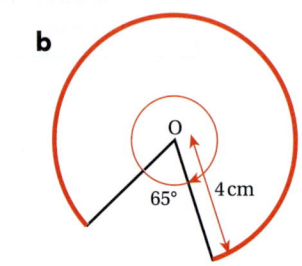

Continues on next page …

a Arc length = $\frac{x}{360} \times 2\pi r$

$= \frac{30}{360} \times 2\pi r$

$= \frac{1}{12} \times 2 \times \pi \times 5$

$= 2.62 \text{ m } (2 \text{ dp})$

> The angle in the sector is 30°, substitute this into the formula for arc length. Use $2\pi r$ here as you have been given the radius.

> If you round your answer, make sure you write what degree of accuracy you used.

b $360° - 65° = 295°$

Arc length $= \frac{295}{360} \times 2 \times \pi \times 4$

$= 20.59 \text{ cm } (2 \text{ dp})$

> The angle inside the sector is not given. Work it out using the angle fact that angles round a point add up to 360°.

> Substitute the angle inside the sector into the formula.

The semicircle and quarter-circle (quadrant) are special examples of a sector.
- In a semicircle, the angle at the centre is 180° and the arc length is half the circumference.
- In a quarter circle, the angle at the centre is 90° and the arc length is a quarter of the circumference.

EXERCISE 15D

1 Find *l* in each of the following circles.

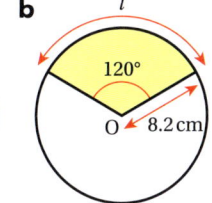

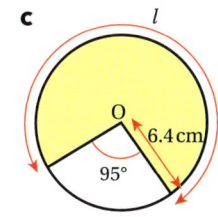

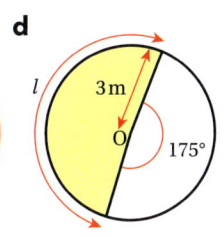

a 70°, 18 cm
b 120°, 8.2 cm
c 95°, 6.4 cm
d 3 m, 175°

2 Find the perimeter of each shape.

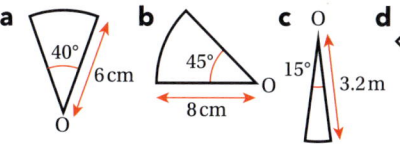

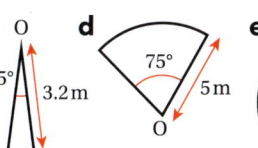

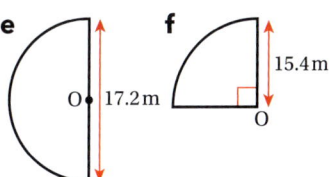

a 40°, 6 cm
b 45°, 8 cm
c 15°, 3.2 m
d 75°, 5 m
e 17.2 m
f 15.4 m

3 The groundskeeper at a school needs to paint a shot put area on the sports field. He uses these official guidelines.

He makes a wooden stop block to sit on the foul line of the throwing circle; the block sits as shown in the diagram. Its inside edge has a curved length of 0.85 m.

Is the size of the throwing circle within the guidelines?

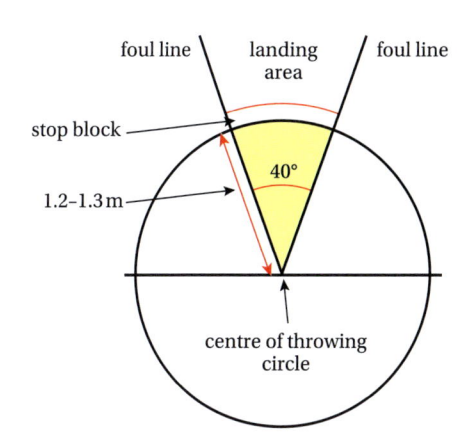

(Diagram labels: foul line, landing area, foul line, stop block, 1.2–1.3 m, 40°, centre of throwing circle)

Find answers at: cambridge.org/ukschools/gcsemaths-studentbookanswers

GCSE Mathematics for OCR (Foundation)

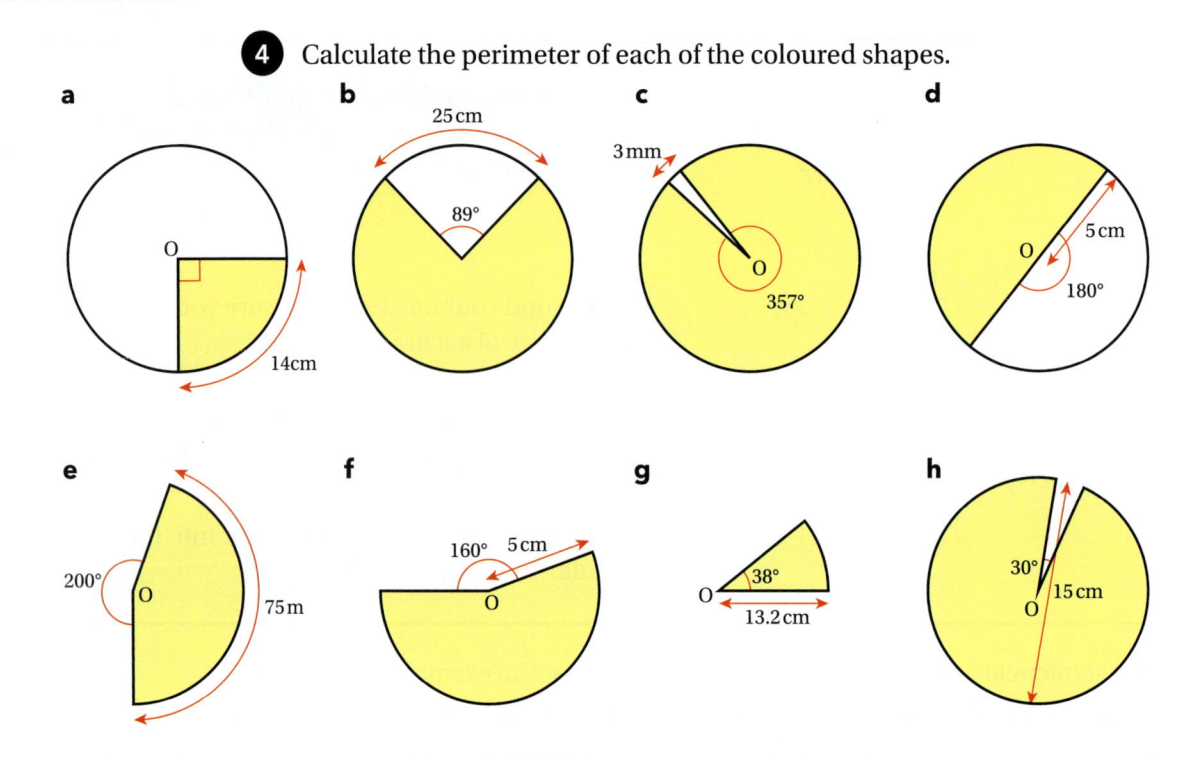

4 Calculate the perimeter of each of the coloured shapes.

a — 14 cm arc, 90° sector
b — 25 cm, 89°
c — 3 mm, 357°
d — 5 cm, 180°
e — 200°, 75 m
f — 160°, 5 cm
g — 38°, 13.2 cm
h — 30°, 15 cm

Section 3: Problems involving perimeter and circumference

You can combine your knowledge of perimeter and circumference to help you calculate the perimeter of irregular and composite shapes.

Remember to divide composite shapes into other shapes whose perimeters can be more easily calculated.

WORKED EXAMPLE 8

Find the outside perimeter of each sporting area to the nearest metre.

a 84.39 m, 73 m

b 28 m; A baseball pitch is $\frac{1}{4}$ of a circle.

a Perimeter = circumference of circle + lengths of straight sides of rectangle.

> The athletics track can be split into a rectangle and two semicircles. Two semicircles make one circle, so you can use this formula to calculate the perimeter.

Circumference of a circle = πd

$= \pi \times 73$

$= 229.336 \ldots$ m

> Substitute the known values into each formula.

Continues on next page …

Perimeter of field = 229.336 … + (2 × 84.39)

= 229.336 … + 168.78

= 398 m (to the nearest metre)

> The three dots here show that the number continues; if you can, always use the exact number in the calculation and only round at the end. Some calculators allow you to store intermediate values.

b Perimeter of a sector = 2r + arc length

Circumference of circle = 2πr = 2 × π × 28.

> The baseball pitch is a sector of a circle; so you can write down the formula for calculating the perimeter of a sector.

Arc length of $\frac{1}{4}$ circle = $\frac{C}{4}$

$= \frac{2 \times \pi \times 28}{4}$

= 43.98 m

> You don't have the angle inside the sector, but you do know that the pitch is $\frac{1}{4}$ of a circle; so you can calculate arc length by dividing the circumference by 4.

Perimeter = 2r + arc length

= 2 × 28 + 43.98

= 56 + 43.98

= 99.98 m

P = 100 m correct to the nearest metre

> Substitute in the known values.

WORK IT OUT 15.2

This is a plan of a children's play area.

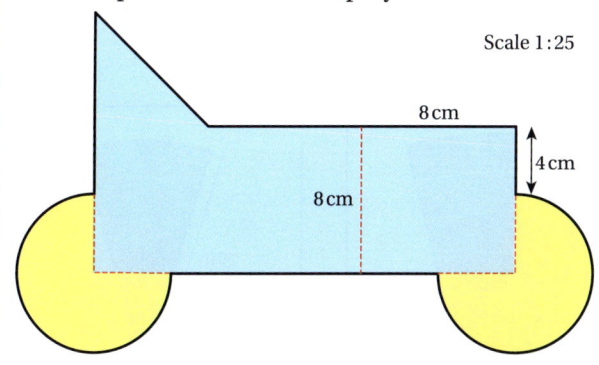

Scale 1 : 25

8 cm

4 cm

8 cm

Tiling is to be placed around the curved edges of the sandpits.

Using π = 3.142, what is the total length of tiling required?

Which of the answers below is the correct answer?

What mistakes have been made in the other workings?

Option A	Option B	Option C
Circumference of a circle = πd = 2πr	Circumference of a circle = πd = 2πr	Circumference of a circle = 2πd = πr
r = 4 cm	r = 4 cm	r = 4 cm
C = 2 × 3.142 × 4	C = 2 × 3.142 × 4	C = 2 × 3.142 × 8
= 3.142 × 8	= 3.142 × 8	= 50.27 cm
= 25.14 cm	= 25.14 cm	

Tip

Perimeter can be worked out by measuring lengths, or by using lengths from a scale diagram. You learnt about scale drawings in Chapter 12.

Continues on next page …

Find answers at: cambridge.org/ukschools/gcsemaths-studentbookanswers

Scale 1 : 25 So, actual circumference of the circle = 25.14 × 25 = 628.5 cm = 6.285 m	Only $\frac{3}{4}$ of the sandpit needs tiling: $\frac{3}{4}$ × 25.14 cm = 18.85 cm	Only $\frac{3}{4}$ of the sandpit needs tiling: $\frac{3}{4}$ × 50.27 cm = 37.7 cm
Two sandpits so total tiling required = 6.285 × 2 = 12.57 m	Two sandpits: 18.85 cm × 2 = 37.7 cm of tiling Scale = 1 : 25 So actual amount of edging required: 37.7 cm × 25 = 942.5 cm = 9.425 m	Two sandpits: 37.7 cm × 2 = 75.4 cm of tiling Scale = 1 : 25 So actual amount of edging required: 75.4 cm × 25 = 1885 cm = 18.85 m

EXERCISE 15E

The diagram shows the shape and dimensions of different throwing event field areas in international competitions; the circles represent the area in which the athlete would stand.

Use the information in these diagrams to answer Questions 1 to 4.

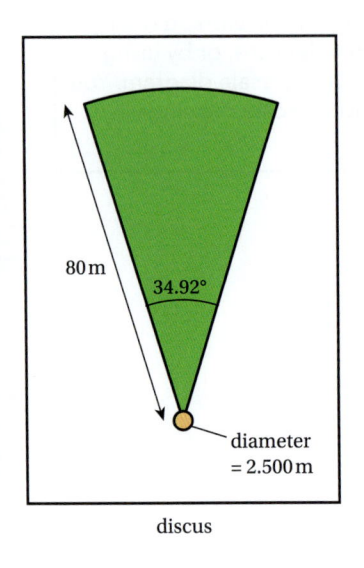

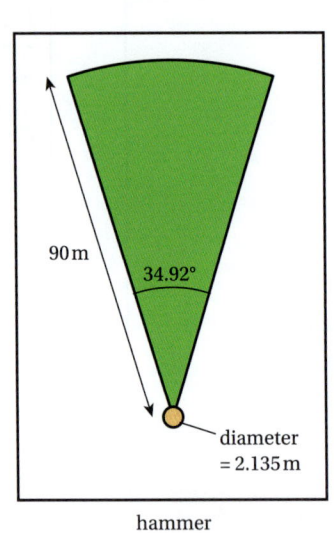

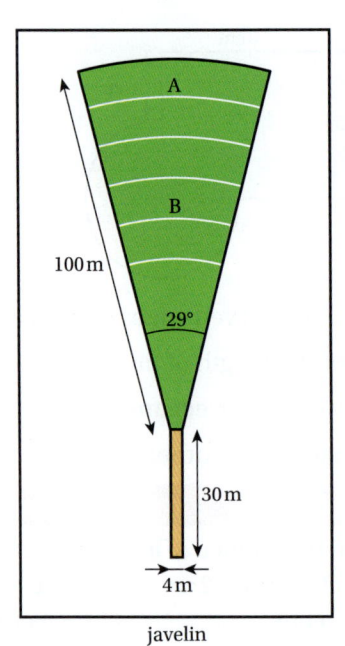

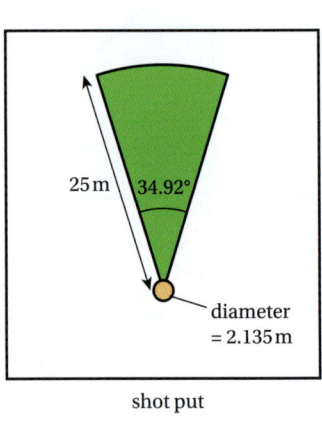

discus: 80 m, 34.92°, diameter = 2.500 m

hammer: 90 m, 34.92°, diameter = 2.135 m

javelin: 100 m, 29°, 30 m, 4 m (sections A and B)

shot put: 25 m, 34.92°, diameter = 2.135 m

1 Calculate the length of the line painted around the outside of:

  a the discus area.

  b the hammer throw area.

2 Competitors in the discus, shot put and hammer throw have to remain inside a marked circle while the equipment is in their hands (before they throw it).

  a Which sport has the largest marked circle?

  b What is the circumference of the standing circle in the discus area?

  c In shot put and hammer throw, a raised edge is built around the circumference of the starting circle. If this edge is 10 cm wide, calculate its inner and outer circumference.

3 Calculate the perimeter of the event space for javelin.

4 The curved measurement lines on each event space are 10 m apart.

Using the javelin field, calculate the length of the lines marked A and B.

5 The radius of the Earth is approximately 6378.1 km at the Equator.

Calculate the approximate distance around the Equator. Give your answer correct to 2 decimal places.

6 A large pizza has a circumference of 94 cm.

What is the side length of the smallest square cardboard box it will fit into?

7 Find the perimeter of this symmetrical logo.

Use a ruler and protractor to measure and find the dimensions you need.

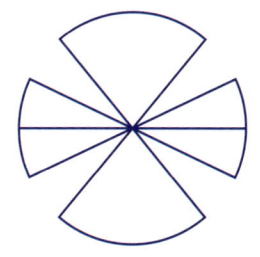

8 Garry is a carpenter who makes wooden abstract art.

He creates a rectangular piece with a sector cut out of the middle.

The sector is part of a circle of radius 5 cm, whose centre is also the centre of the rectangle.

The rectangle's length is 6 times the radius of the circle.

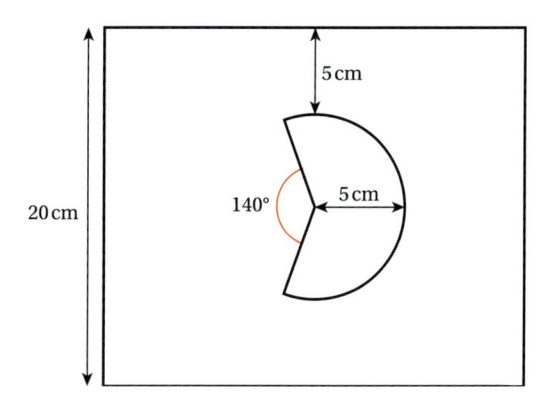

What is the perimeter of Garry's piece of art?

Checklist of learning and understanding

Perimeter

- Perimeter is the total distance around the boundaries of a shape; this includes both inner and outer boundaries.
- You can calculate perimeter by adding the lengths of the sides or by applying a formula based on the properties of the shape.

Circumference

- The perimeter of a circle is called its circumference.
- The formula for calculating the circumference is as follows:
  $C = \pi d$ or $C = 2\pi r$, where d = diameter and r = radius.
- A sector is a part of a circle between two radii and the circumference. You can find the arc length of a sector by working out what fraction of a circle the sector represents and multiplying this by the circumference.

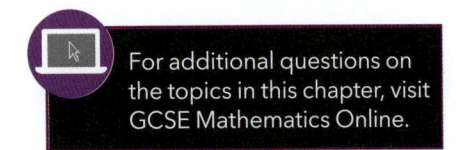

For additional questions on the topics in this chapter, visit GCSE Mathematics Online.

Chapter review

1. The perimeters of the two shapes shown are equal.
   What is the side length of the square?

2. The perimeter of a regular pentagon is 90 cm.
   Work out the length of each side.

3. A rectangular vegetable plot has a perimeter of 50 metres.
   If the width is 6.5 m, what is the length of the plot?

4. A sprinkler in a field can water a circular area of radius 14.5 m.
   What is the circumference of the area that can be watered?
   Use $\pi = 3.142$.

5. A pizza has a circumference of 88 cm. It is put in a cardboard box.
   Calculate the perimeter of the smallest box that it will fit into.

6. Calculate the perimeter of the shape shown.
   Give your answer correct to 1 decimal place.

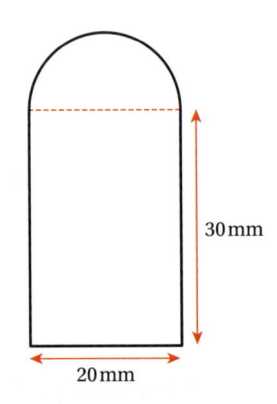

7 The diagram shows some staging for an outdoor concert.

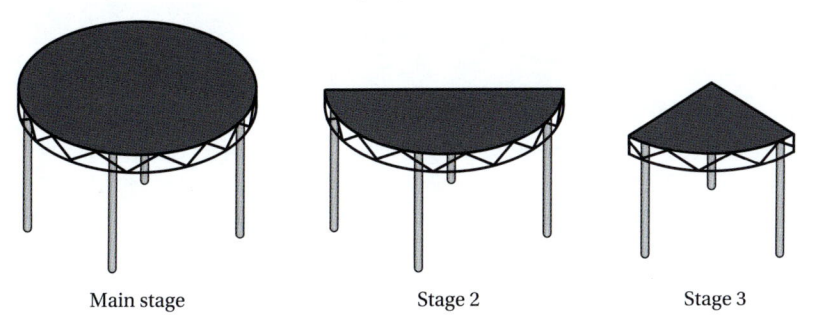

Main stage   Stage 2   Stage 3

The main stage is a circle of diameter 6 m.

There are two smaller stages: stage 2 is half the size of the main stage, and stage 3 is a quarter of the main stage.

Each stage has a patterned strip along its curved edge.

a Work out the length of the patterned edge on each stage.

b A safety rubber strip is to be applied along all the edges of each stage.

Work out the length of strip required for each stage. What is the total amount of rubber strip needed?

8 Natalia is making a pendant out of polymer clay.

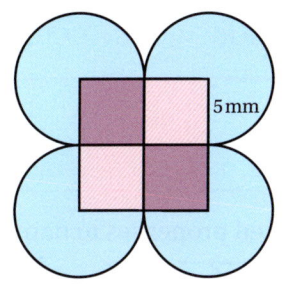

Width of one square = radius of circle

The design is a repeating pattern of a square that shares two sides with two radii of a circle.

a What is the perimeter of the pattern?

b What is the perimeter of the pendant

Natalia decides to make a pair of matching earrings but the earrings will **not** contain the central squares.

c What is the perimeter of each earring?

16 Area

In this chapter you will learn how to …
- use formulae to find the area of different shapes, including circles and parts of circles.
- use appropriate formulae to calculate the area of composite shapes.

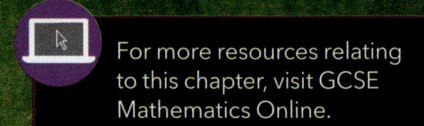

For more resources relating to this chapter, visit GCSE Mathematics Online.

Using mathematics: real-life applications

Ordering the right quantity of turf for a sports field, preparing detailed floor plans, and determining how much fertiliser is needed to treat a field crop all require knowledge and calculation of area.

"Fertiliser application rates are normally given in kilograms per hectare. One hectare is an area of 100 m × 100 m or 10 000 m². Applying too much or too little fertiliser to an area can have disastrous results on the crops." *(Farmer)*

Before you start …

Ch 5	You should know the properties of quadrilaterals.	**1** Use the marked properties to name the quadrilaterals correctly. a b c
Ch 2	You should be familiar with square numbers and square roots.	**2** Calculate. **a** 5^2 **b** 2×10^2 **c** $3^2 + 4^2$ **3** Find the number which is squared to give each of these numbers. **a** 144 **b** 10 000 **c** 0.25
Ch 12	You need to be able to convert between square units of measurement.	**4** Complete these. **a** $5 \text{ m}^2 = \square \text{ cm}^2$ **b** $\square \text{ cm}^2 = 87\,000 \text{ mm}^2$ **c** $4 \text{ km}^2 = \square \text{ m}^2$
Ch 14	You should be able to write simple formulae, substitute values into formulae and change the subject of a formula.	**5** Calculate A if $A = l \times w$, when $l = 2$ cm and $w = 4$ cm. **6** Make r the subject of the formula $A = 2\pi r$.

16 Area

Assess your starting point using the Launchpad

STEP 1

1 The area of each shape can be found using one of the calculations shown below.
Match each figure to the correct calculation.
All dimensions are given in centimetres.

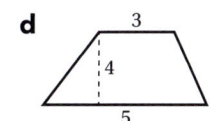

a) triangle with sides 4, 3, 5 (right angle between 4 and 3)
b) rectangle 4 by 3
c) parallelogram with side 5, base 4, height 3
d) trapezium with parallel sides 3 and 5, height 4
e) square of side 4

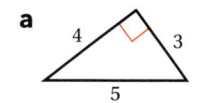

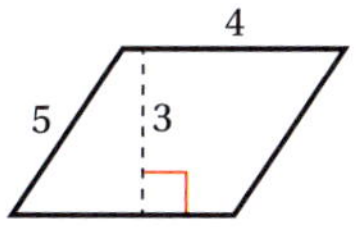

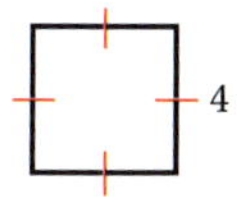

$A = 4 \times 3$ $A = 4 \times 4$ $A = \dfrac{4 \times 3}{2}$

GO TO Section 1: Area of polygons

STEP 2

2 In the formula for the area of a circle:
  a what is the subject of the formula?
  b what does the symbol π represent?
  c what does r represent?

3 Calculate the area of this semicircular rug of diameter 3.2 m.
Use the exact value of π and give your answer correct to three significant figures.

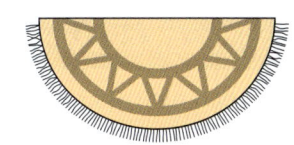

4 Calculate the area of the sector shown.
Use the exact value of π and give your answer to the nearest whole number.

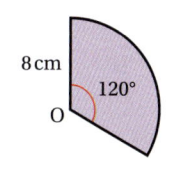

(sector with radius 8 cm and angle 120° at O)

GO TO Section 2: Area of circles and sectors

STEP 3

5 Work out the floor area of this stadium.

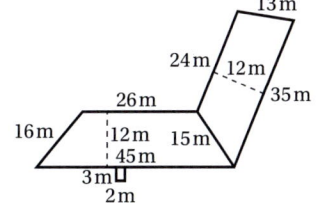

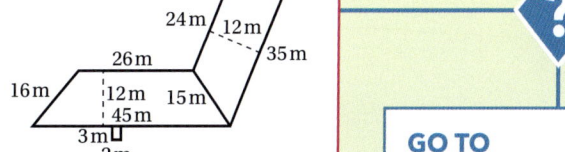

(composite shape with dimensions 13 m, 24 m, 12 m, 35 m, 26 m, 16 m, 12 m, 15 m, 45 m, 3 m, 2 m)

GO TO Section 3: Area of composite shapes

GO TO Chapter review

Find answers at: cambridge.org/ukschools/gcsemaths-studentbookanswers

> **Tip**
>
> You were introduced to plane shapes in Chapter 5; they are flat 2D shapes.

Section 1: Area of polygons

The **area** of a plane shape is the amount of space it takes up. You can think of area as the number of squares (square units) that will fit inside the boundary of a shape.

Area is always given in square units, for example mm² (square millimetres), cm² (square centimetres), m² and km².

Make sure you know the formulae for finding the area of common polygons.

Area of rectangles and squares

The formula for finding the area of a rectangle is

Area = length × width

$A = lw$

In a square, the length and width are equal, so the formula for area is

Area of the square = $l \times l = l^2$

$A = l^2$

Sometimes the side length is written as s (for side) instead of l. In this case the formula for the area is written as $A = s^2$.

If you know the area of a shape and some of the lengths, you can find an unknown length by rearranging the formula for area to make the unknown the subject.

> **Tip**
>
> You were reminded how to change the subject of a formula in Chapter 14.

WORKED EXAMPLE 1

A rectangle of area 45 cm² has one side 9 cm long.

How long is the other side?

$A = l \times w$ — Write down the formula for the area of a rectangle.

$45 = 9 \times w$ — As multiplication is commutative (can be done in any order), you can choose the known length to be l or w.

$\frac{45}{9} = w$ — Divide each side by 9 to get w on its own.

$5 = w$

The other side is 5 cm long.

Area of a triangle

The formula for the area of any triangle is

> **Learn this formula**
>
> Area of a triangle (A) = $\frac{1}{2}$ × base × perpendicular height
>
> $A = \frac{1}{2} \times b \times h$

You can use any side of a triangle as the base. The **perpendicular height** of the triangle **must** be perpendicular to the base. The perpendicular height can be inside the triangle, one of the sides of the triangle or outside the triangle.

> **Tip**
>
> You were reminded about the meaning of perpendicular in Chapter 5.

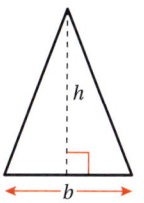

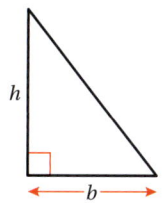

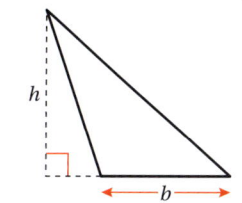

You can prove the formula for the area of any triangle works by showing that the area of a triangle is half the area of a rectangle drawn from the base of the triangle.

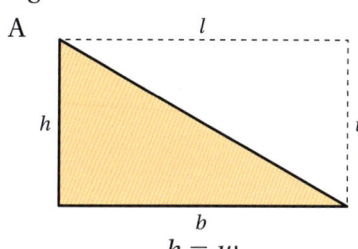

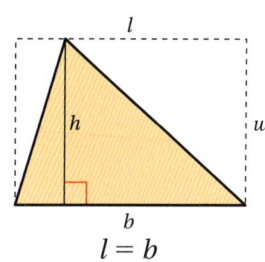

A
$h = w$
$b = l$

B
$l = b$
$h = w$

Figure A shows a right-angled triangle. Figure B shows a scalene triangle.

In both diagrams the area of the shaded part is equal to the area of the unshaded part.

Area of the rectangle = $l \times w$ so the shaded and unshaded areas are equal to $\frac{1}{2} l \times w$. You can see that l is equal to the base of the triangle and w is equal to the perpendicular height of the triangle, so the area of any triangle = $\frac{1}{2} \times$ length of its base $\times$ its perpendicular height.

WORKED EXAMPLE 2

Calculate the area of each triangle.

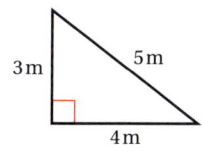

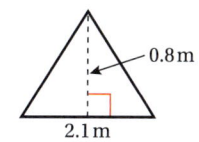

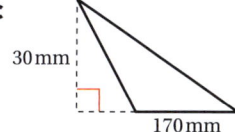

a 3 m, 5 m, 4 m
b 0.8 m, 2.1 m
c 30 mm, 170 mm

a Area = $\frac{1}{2} \times b \times h$

$= \frac{1}{2} \times 4 \times 3$

$= \frac{1}{2} \times 12$

$= 6 \text{ m}^2$

Substitute the values into the formula for the area of a triangle. In a right-angled triangle, either of the two shorter (perpendicular) sides can be used as the base and height.

Remember to include the units in the answer.

> **Tip**
>
> The order of the multiplication is not important so either side can be the base or the height:
>
> $\frac{1}{2} \times 4 \times 3 = \frac{1}{2} \times 12 = 6$
>
> $\frac{1}{2} \times 4 \times 3 = 2 \times 3 = 6$

b Area = $\frac{1}{2} \times b \times h$

$= \frac{1}{2} \times 2.1 \times 0.8$

$= \frac{1}{2} \times 1.68$

$= 0.84 \text{ m}^2$

Use the side marked 2.1 as the base because the height is perpendicular to it.

Continues on next page ...

Find answers at: cambridge.org/ukschools/gcsemaths-studentbookanswers

c Area = $\dfrac{bh}{2}$

= $\dfrac{(170 \times 30)}{2}$

= $\dfrac{5100}{2}$

= 2550 mm²

> This is the same formula written differently. Finding a half is the same as dividing by 2. The dashed line shows you the height perpendicular to the base.

Did you know?

Two triangles that look completely different might still have the same area.

These two triangles are equal in area.

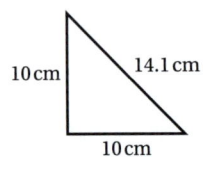

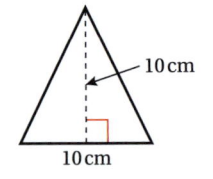

EXERCISE 16A

1. How might each of the following people use area calculations in their jobs? For each one, try to give examples of the shapes they would work with most often and the formulae they might need.

    a House painter   b Mosaic artist   c Gardener
    d Dressmaker   e Carpet layer   f Interior designer

2. Calculate the area of each triangle.

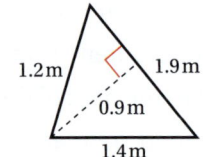

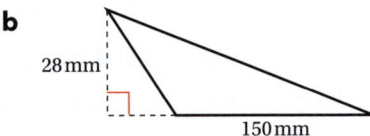

    a   b

3. The area of a triangle is 36 m² and its perpendicular height is 6 m. Work out the length of its base.

4. Work out the total area of this kite.

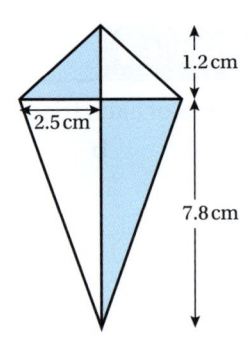

5. A triangle has a base of 3.6 m and a height of 50 cm. What is its area in metres squared?

6. A triangle of area 0.125 m² has a base 25 cm long. What is its height in centimetres?

7. Calculate the total area of the sails on this small boat.

    The mast is 2.7 m tall.

    The smaller sail extends $\dfrac{2}{3}$ of the way up the mast.

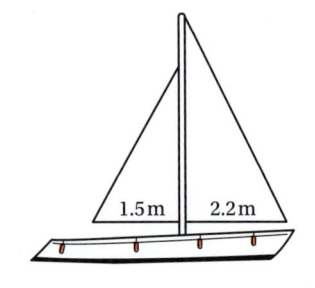

Tip

Use what you know about fractions to help you. See Chapter 10 if you need to.

Area of a parallelogram

The formula for the area of a parallelogram is

> **Learn this formula**
>
> Area of a parallelogram (A) = base × perpendicular height
> $$A = b \times h$$

The base of this parallelogram is b and the **perpendicular height** is h.

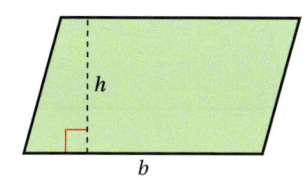

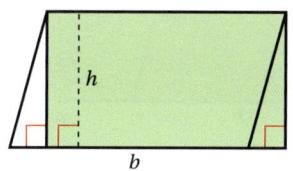

Tip

You must use the perpendicular height and **not** the slant height.

You can see how this formula works by removing a right-angled triangle from one end of the parallelogram and joining it to the other end to form a rectangle. The parallelogram and rectangle have the same area.

WORKED EXAMPLE 3

Calculate the area of the parallelogram.

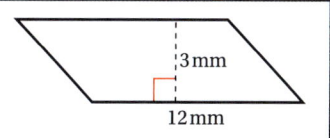

(3 mm, 12 mm)

Area = $b \times h$ — Substitute the known values into the formula.

= 12 × 3 = 36 mm² — Remember to use the correct units!

It might not be immediately obvious what the important values are in a diagram; think carefully about what information you need.

WORK IT OUT 16.1

A parallelogram is made by combining a rectangle and two right-angled triangles.

Which of these options will give the correct area?

Which dimensions are incorrect in the other two? Why?

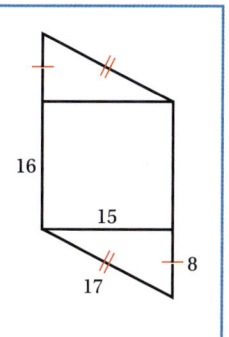

(Diagram dimensions: 16, 15, 17, 8)

Option A	Option B	Option C
$A = bh$	$A = bh$	$A = bh$
$= 16 \times 17$	$= 24 \times 17$	$= 24 \times 15$

Find answers at: cambridge.org/ukschools/gcsemaths-studentbookanswers

Area of a trapezium

The formula for the area of a trapezium is:

Area of a trapezium $(A) = \frac{1}{2} \times (a + b) \times h$,

where a and b are the lengths of the parallel sides.

A trapezium has parallel sides a and b, and **perpendicular height** h.

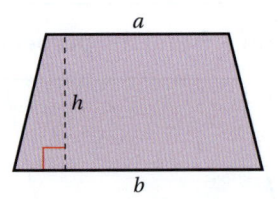

You can see why the formula works by joining two trapezia to form a parallelogram.

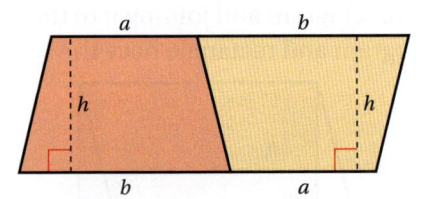

The parallelogram has a base of length $a + b$, and perpendicular height h.

The area of a parallelogram (A) = base × perpendicular height.

$$A = (a + b) \times h$$

Each trapezium is half the area of the parallelogram.

WORKED EXAMPLE 4

Calculate the area of the trapezium.

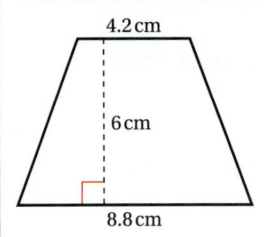

4.2 cm
6 cm
8.8 cm

Area $= \frac{1}{2} \times (a + b) \times h$ Write down the formula for area of a trapezium.

$= \frac{1}{2} \times (4.2 + 8.8) \times 6$ Substitute in the known values, make sure you have the perpendicular height.

$= \frac{1}{2} \times 13 \times 6$

$= 39 \text{ cm}^2$ Don't forget to use the correct units.

When calculating area, make sure you know which shape you are dealing with and be careful to use the correct formula.

WORK IT OUT 16.2

A solar farm is being built in a field. Each solar panel measures 98 cm by 150 cm. If 500 panels can fit onto the field, what is the area of panels being used, in m²?

Which of the options below is correct?

What errors were made in each of the others?

Option A	Option B	Option C
Area of one panel:	Area of one panel:	Area of one panel:
98 × 150 = 14 700 cm²	$\frac{1}{2}$ × (98 × 150) = 7350 cm²	98 × 150 = 14 700 cm²
1 m² = 10 000 cm²	1 m² = 10 000 cm²	1 m² = 100 cm²
1 panel = 14 700 ÷ 10 000 = 1.47 m²	1 panel = 7350 ÷ 10 000 = 0.735 m²	1 panel = 14 700 ÷ 100 = 147 m²
500 panels = 1.47 m² × 500 = 735 m²	500 panels = 0.735 m² × 500 = 367.5 m²	500 panels = 147 m² × 500 = 73 500 m²

EXERCISE 16B

1 Use the formula $A = bh$ to calculate the area of each parallelogram.

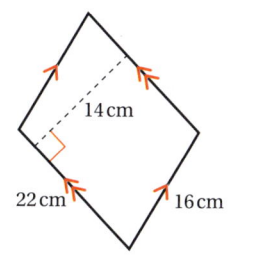

a 12 cm, 5 cm

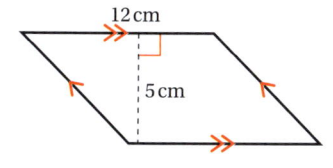

b 37 mm, 19 mm

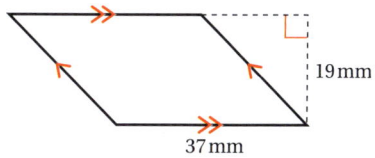

c 22 cm, 14 cm, 16 cm

d 1.2 m, 4.2 m, 0.9 m

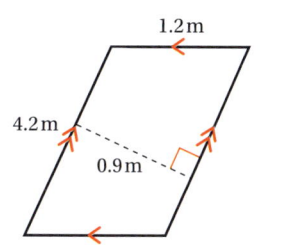

2 Use the formula $A = \frac{1}{2}(a + b)h$ to calculate the area of each trapezium.

a 20 mm, 15 mm, 35 mm

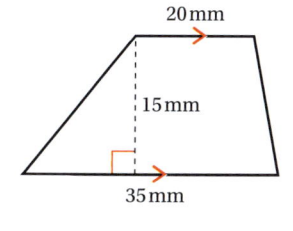

b 2 cm, 7 cm, 5 cm, 7 cm

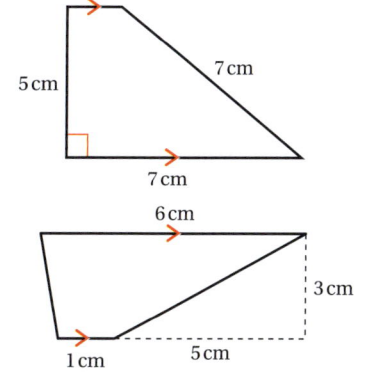

c 16 cm, 3 cm, 5 cm, 19 cm

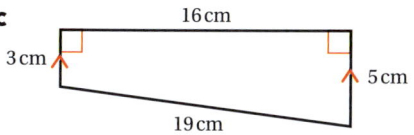

d 6 cm, 3 cm, 1 cm, 5 cm

Find answers at: cambridge.org/ukschools/gcsemaths-studentbookanswers

3. The area of this shape is 96 cm². What is its length?

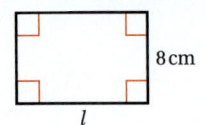

4. The area of a parallelogram is 40 m². If the perpendicular height is 10 cm, what is the length of the base?

5. The area and one other measurement is given for each shape. Find the unknown length in each figure.

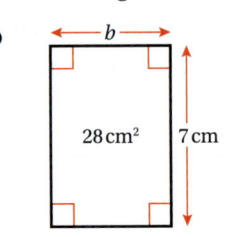

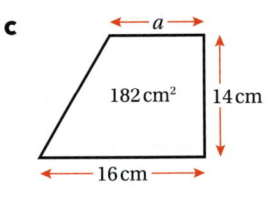

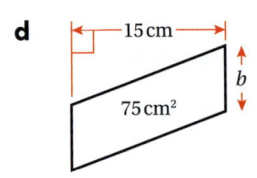

   a Triangle: area 24 cm², base 8 cm, height h
   b Rectangle: area 28 cm², width b, height 7 cm
   c Trapezium: area 182 cm², top a, height 14 cm, bottom 16 cm
   d Parallelogram: 15 cm, area 75 cm², height b
   e Pentagon shape: 6 cm, h, 18 cm, area 153 cm², 6 cm

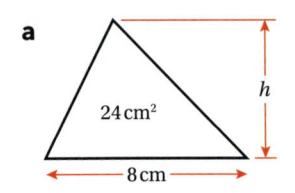

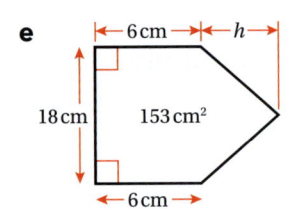

6. The area of a field is shown on the plan.

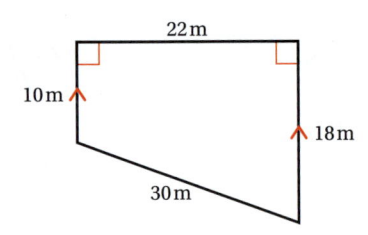

   (22 m, 10 m, 18 m, 30 m)

   a Calculate the area of the field.
   b To prepare the soil, the farmer has to lay down 25 kg of soil and 10 kg of compost per square metre of land. Work out how much soil and compost she will need.
   c There is a gate 2 m wide along the 22 m boundary. The rest of the land needs to be fenced. Work out the total amount of fencing needed.

Tip

Remember that the perimeter of a shape is its boundary. You learnt about perimeter in Chapter 15.

Section 2: Area of circles and sectors

In Chapter 15 you worked with the diameter, radius and circumference of circles and sectors of circles. You also used approximate and exact values of pi in circle calculations. You will meet these terms again in this section.

The area of a circle is calculated using the formula

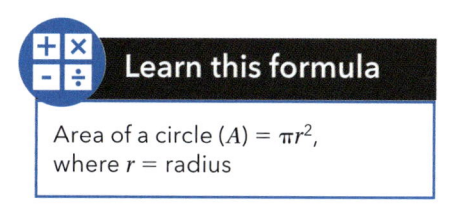

> **Learn this formula**
>
> Area of a circle $(A) = \pi r^2$, where r = radius

> **Tip**
>
> Use the π key of your calculator to find the area and circumference of circles unless you are given an approximate value to use. Leave the value you get on the display for the next step and only round off to the required number of places when you have a final value.

If you are given the diameter, d, you can still use this formula by remembering that:

$r = \frac{1}{2}d$

WORKED EXAMPLE 5

Calculate the area of this circle correct to 3 significant figures.

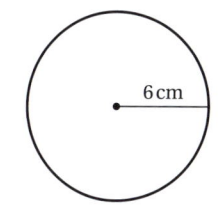

$A = \pi r^2$

Write down the formula for the area of a circle. You will need to know this formula from memory.

6 cm

$= \pi \times 6 \times 6 = 113.0973355 \text{ cm}^2$

$= 113.10 \text{ cm}^2$ (to 2 dp)

Substitute in the known values. Remember to use the π key on your calculator, and to store the values so you only have to round the final answer.

If you know the area of a circle you can find the length of a radius (or the diameter) by rearranging the formula for the area.

WORKED EXAMPLE 6

Calculate the radius of a circle with area 50 cm².

$A = \pi r^2$

Write down the formula for the area of a circle.

$50 = \pi \times r^2$

Substitute in the known values.

$r^2 = \frac{50}{\pi}$

$r = \sqrt{\frac{50}{\pi}} = 3.989422804$

Rearrange the formula to make r the subject using inverse operations and applying the same operation to both sides. (**Alternatively**, you could first rearrange the formula to make r the subject and *then* substitute in the known values.)

$r = 3.99$ cm (to 2 dp)

Use the π key on your calculator, and round your final answer to two decimal places.

Find answers at: cambridge.org/ukschools/gcsemaths-studentbookanswers

Area of a sector

Remember that a sector is a slice of a circle.

The area of a sector can be calculated using the formula,

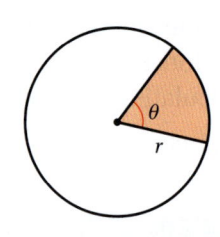

Area of sector $(A) = \dfrac{\theta}{360} \times$ area of circle

$= \dfrac{\theta}{360} \times \pi r^2$

This formula is based on similar principles to those that you used to find the arc length in Chapter 15.

If a sector can be represented as $\dfrac{\theta}{360}$ of a whole circle, and the area of a whole circle $= \pi r^2$ then it follows that the area of sector $= \dfrac{\theta}{360} \times$ area of circle.

Remember the special cases:

- A semicircle is half a circle, so its area is half the area of a circle $\left(\dfrac{\pi r^2}{2}\right)$.
- A quarter-circle is one quarter of a circle, so its area is one quarter of the area of a circle $\left(\dfrac{\pi r^2}{4}\right)$.

WORKED EXAMPLE 7

Calculate the area of the sector shown.

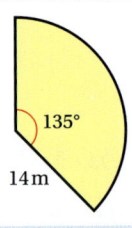

135°
14 m

$A = \dfrac{\theta}{360} \times \pi r^2$ — Write down the area of a sector.

$= \dfrac{135}{360} \times \pi \times r^2$

$= 0.375 \times \pi \times 14^2$ — Substitute in the known values and calculate. Use the π key on your calculator, and only round your answer.

$= 230.90706$

$= 230.91 \text{ m}^2$ (to 2 dp) — Make sure you use the correct units and state the degree of accuracy to which you have rounded.

EXERCISE 16C

1 Find the area of each circle.

Use the exact value of pi and give your answers correct to two decimal places.

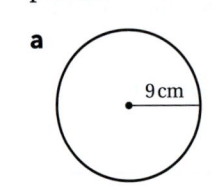

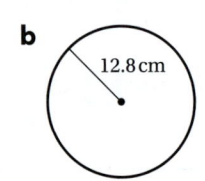

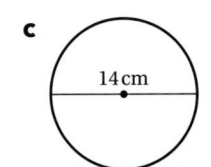

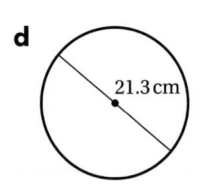

a 9 cm
b 12.8 cm
c 14 cm
d 21.3 cm

2 Use the formula $A = \dfrac{\theta}{360} \times \pi r^2$ to find the area of each sector.

a 53°, 18 mm

b 105°, 2 cm

c 4 m, 28°

d 122°, 19 mm

3 What is the difference in area between these two sectors?

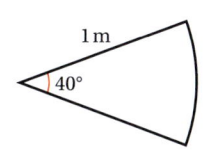

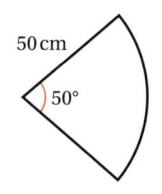

1 m, 40°

50 cm, 50°

4 A pizza has a diameter of 14 cm.

  a Calculate the area of the pizza.

  b Estimate the area of a round plate that the pizza can fit onto with about 1 cm space around the edge.

5 A pair of sunglasses has circular lenses each 8.4 cm in diameter.

What is the total area of the tinted surface of the lenses?

6 The area for discus at an international event has these dimensions.

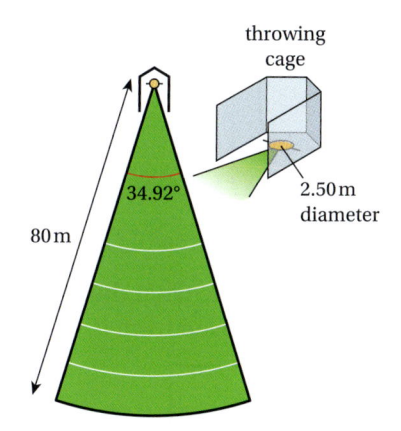

throwing cage

34.92°

80 m

2.50 m diameter

  a Calculate the area of the grass in the landing zone.

  b What is the area of the starting circle in the throwing cage?

7 A circular disc has a circumference of 75.398 mm.

Show clearly how you could use this information to find the area of one side of the disc.

Section 3: Area of composite shapes

Remember that composite shapes are formed by combining shapes or by removing parts of a shape.

You can find the area of composite shapes in different ways.

Tip

You saw how to calculate the perimeter of composite shapes in Chapter 15.

Find answers at: cambridge.org/ukschools/gcsemaths-studentbookanswers

Addition of parts

- Divide the figure into smaller known shapes whose area can be found directly.
- Calculate the area of each part separately.
- Add together the areas of all the parts to find the total area.

For example:

A

B

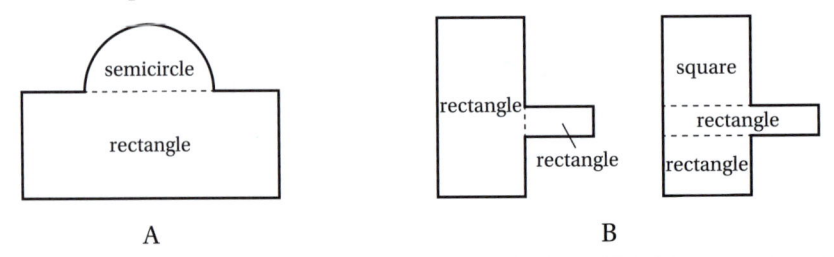

Figure A can be divided into a rectangle and a semicircle.

Figure B can be divided in different ways. The first way requires fewer calculations.

Subtraction of parts

When one figure is 'cut out' of another you have to find the area of the larger figure and subtract the area of the 'cut out' figure.

For example,

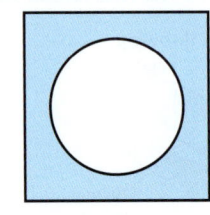

the shaded area = area of square − area of circle

Sometimes you will need to imagine what the larger shape would look like *before* the smaller shape was removed from it.

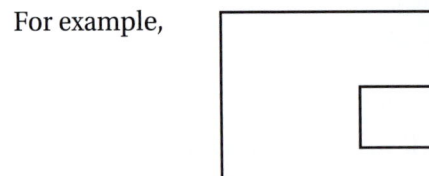

For example,

Drawing in a broken line helps to see the shape as a large rectangle with a smaller rectangle cut out of it. Then,

the area of the shape = area of larger rectangle − area of smaller rectangle.

For example, you could have also found the area of the shape above by splitting the shape into three rectangles and adding each area, but this would require more calculations.

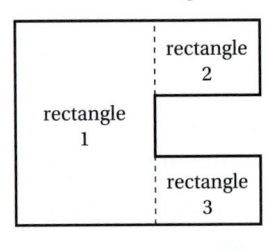

> **Tip**
> Some problems can be solved using either the 'addition of parts' or the 'subtraction of parts' method. Think carefully about which method will be easier before you decide which one to use.

> **Tip**
> Copy diagrams into your exercise book so you can draw on them and mark dimensions. This helps you keep track of your working.

WORKED EXAMPLE 8

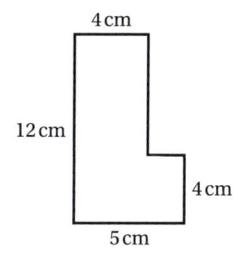

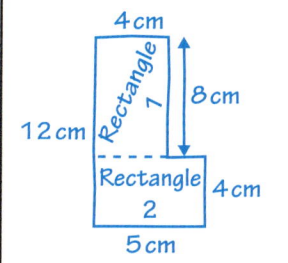

Calculate the area of this shape.

[Shape: L-shape with dimensions 4 cm (top), 12 cm (left side), 4 cm (inner right), 5 cm (bottom)]

[Split shape: Rectangle 1 (4 cm × 8 cm) on top, Rectangle 2 (4 cm × 5 cm) on bottom, with 12 cm total height on left]

Use the 'addition of parts' method and split the shape into Rectangle 1 (4 cm × 8 cm) and Rectangle 2 (4 cm × 5 cm).

> **Tip**
>
> This shape can also be split into:
> Rectangle 1: 12 cm × 4 cm
> Rectangle 2: 4 cm × 1 cm

Area of Rectangle 1 = 4 × 8 = 32 cm²
Area of Rectangle 2 = 4 × 5 = 20 cm²
Area of shape = 32 + 20 = 52 cm²

Calculate the area of each rectangle.

Add the areas together to find the total area of the original shape.

Sometimes questions on area might also require you to calculate the perimeter or circumference of a shape. Think carefully about what is being asked of you and what information you need.

WORKED EXAMPLE 9

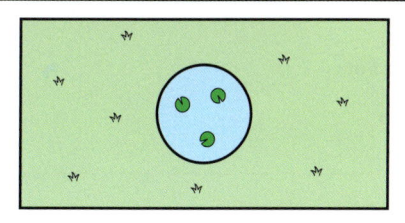

Gwen has a rectangular garden of width 15 m and length 20 m.
She plans for her garden to be all grass except for a circular pond in the middle.
The pond has a radius of 5 m to its inside edge.

a The pond needs a flat layer of netting across its surface.
The netting will be fixed to a circular wire that is pinned to the inside rim of the pond.
How much netting and wire will Gwen need?
Take the value of π to be 3.142.

b Gwen has 15 kg of grass seed.
What area must she sprinkle the grass seed over?

Continues on next page …

Find answers at: cambridge.org/ukschools/gcsemaths-studentbookanswers

GCSE Mathematics for OCR (Foundation)

a Area of circle = πr^2
            = 3.142 × 5 × 5
            = 78.55 m²

   Circumference of circle = $2\pi r$
                       = 2 × 3.142 × 5
                       = 31.42 m

   Gwen needs 78.55 m² of netting and 31.42 m of wire.

> You are told the netting sits flat on the pond's surface and is fixed to the inside rim, so you can assume that the netting is a circle with radius of 5 m. You are also told that the wire is circular and is pinned to the inside rim of the pond; ignoring the width of the wire which you are not given, you can assume that the length of the wire is the circumference of a circle with radius 5 m. Use the appropriate formulae for the area and circumference of a circle, and substitute in the value given for the radius.

b Area to be seeded = area of garden − area of pond's surface

> You are told that all of Gwen's garden, except for the pond, will be grass. So, the area you need to calculate is the area of the rectangular garden minus the area of the pond's surface.

   Area of rectangle = length × width
                   = 15 × 20 = 300 m²
   Area of pond = 78.55 m²
   Area to be seeded = 300 − 78.55
                   = 221.45 m²

> Use the formula for the area of a rectangle and substitute in the known values. Then substitute this value and the answers to part **a** into your formula for calculating the area to be seeded.

Sometimes questions that require area calculations might not ask directly for an area, but instead require you to apply the knowledge you have to find a different value. You need to recognise what information is being asked for and what knowledge you need to apply.

Problem-solving framework

Jose wants to paint the side of his house.

He chooses paint that costs £25.99 for a 2.5 litre tin.

If each tin of paint can cover an area of 12 m², how many tins of paint will Jose need?

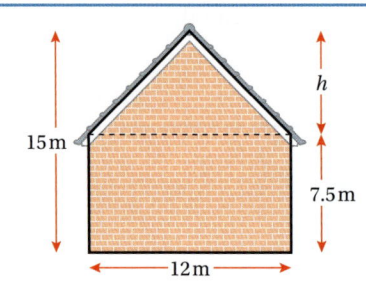

Steps for approaching a problem-solving question	What you would do for this example
Step 1: What have you got to do?	You need to find out how many tins of paint are needed.
Step 2: What information do you need?	Number of tins of paint = area to be painted ÷ area each tin of paint can cover. So you need to calculate the area of the side of the house. Use the 'addition of parts' method and split the side of the house into a rectangle and triangle. Area of rectangle = $l \times w$ l = 12 m, w = 7.5 m Area of triangle = $\frac{1}{2} \times b \times h$ b = 12 m, h = perpendicular height Each tin of paint covers an area of 12 m².

Continues on next page …

Step 3: What information don't you need?	The price and volume of each tin of paint is not relevant.
Step 4: What maths can you do?	Area of rectangle = $l \times w$ $= 12 \times 7.5 = 90 \, m^2$ Area of triangle = $\frac{1}{2} \times b \times h$ Perpendicular height, h, of triangle = $15 - 7.5 = 7.5 \, m$ Area of triangle = $\frac{1}{2} \times 12 \times 7.5$ $= 45 \, m^2$ Area to be painted = $90 + 45$ $= 135 \, m^2$ Number of tins of paint = $135 \div 12 = 11.25$ Jose needs 12 tins of paint.
Step 5: Have you used all the relevant information? Have you answered the question?	All relevant information used ✓ The question asked for the number of tins of paint needed ✓
Step 6: Does your answer seem reasonable?	Check answer: $12 \times 12 = 144 \, m^2$ which is enough paint to cover the side of the house; $11 \times 12 = 132 \, m^2$ which would not be enough paint. The question asked for the number of tins, not the volume of paint used; as you can't have 11.25 tins, Jose would need to round up to 12 tins in order to have enough paint. The answer of 12 tins is reasonable.

EXERCISE 16D

1 Find the total area of each of these shapes. Show all your working.

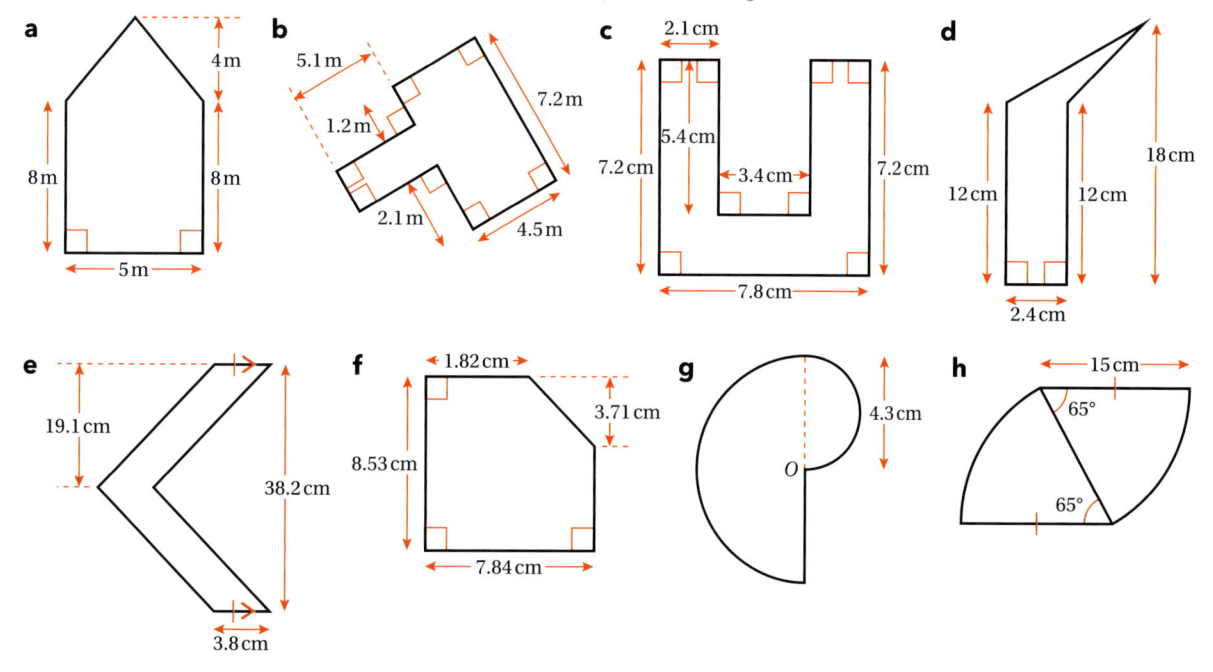

a. 4 m, 8 m, 8 m, 5 m

b. 5.1 m, 1.2 m, 7.2 m, 2.1 m, 4.5 m

c. 2.1 cm, 5.4 cm, 7.2 cm, 3.4 cm, 7.2 cm, 7.8 cm

d. 18 cm, 12 cm, 12 cm, 2.4 cm

e. 19.1 cm, 38.2 cm, 3.8 cm

f. 1.82 cm, 3.71 cm, 8.53 cm, 7.84 cm

g. 4.3 cm, O

h. 15 cm, 65°, 65°

Find answers at: cambridge.org/ukschools/gcsemaths-studentbookanswers

2 Find the area of the shaded part of each figure.

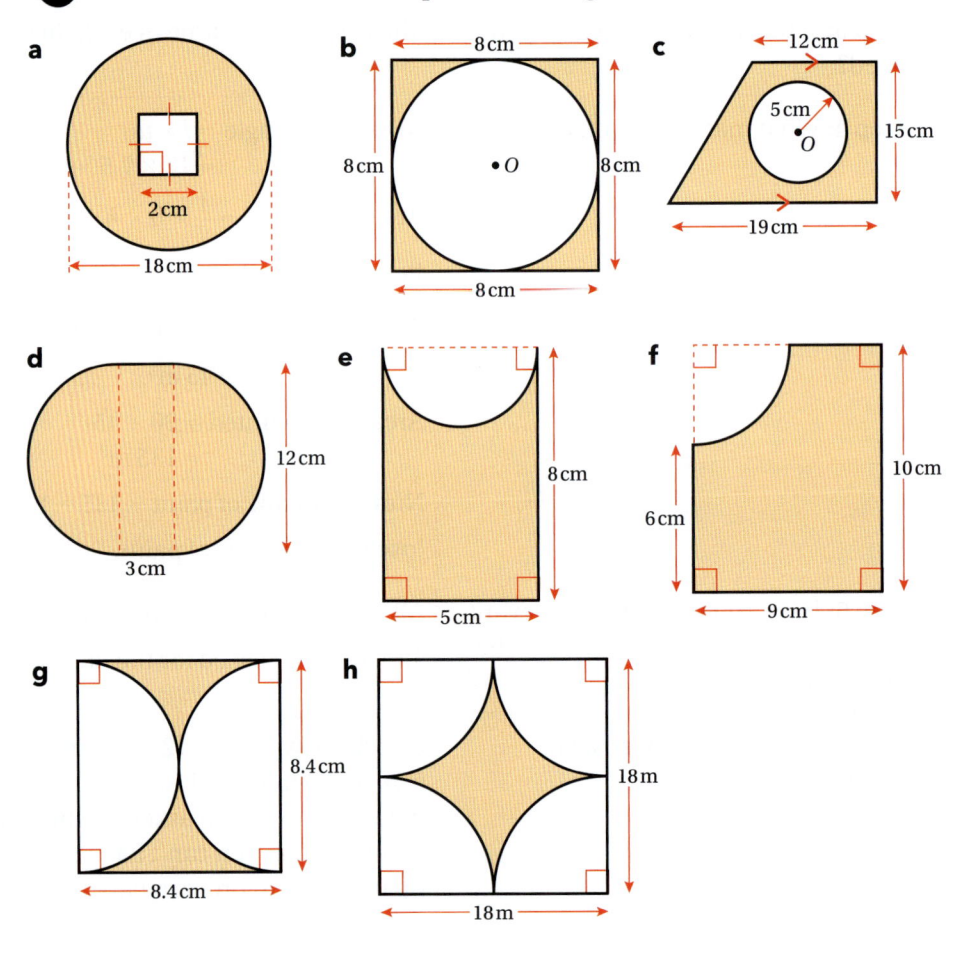

a (circle diameter 18 cm with a 2 cm square removed)

b (8 cm × 8 cm square with inscribed circle, centre O)

c (trapezium: top 12 cm, right side 15 cm, bottom 19 cm, with circle of radius 5 cm centred at O removed)

d (shape: circle of diameter 12 cm with a 3 cm wide rectangle... 12 cm height, 3 cm width marker)

e (rectangle 5 cm wide, 8 cm tall with semicircle removed from top)

f (rectangle 9 cm × 10 cm with quarter circle of radius 6 cm... 6 cm marked on left side)

g (8.4 cm × 8.4 cm square with two semicircles removed from left and right sides)

h (18 m × 18 m square with four quarter circles removed from corners, leaving a star shape)

3 How many rectangular tiles 20 cm by 30 cm would you need to tile the area shown?

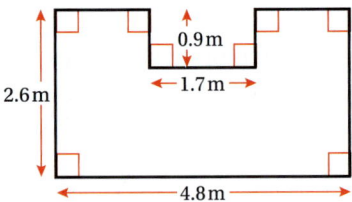

(L-shaped region: 4.8 m wide, 2.6 m tall, with a 1.7 m × 0.9 m notch cut from the top)

Tip
A net is a 2D shape that can be folded to create a 3D solid.

4 The net of a cylinder is shown below.

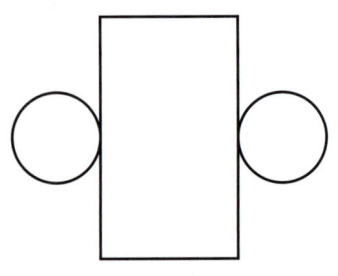

(net of cylinder: rectangle with two circles)

The rectangle has dimensions 10 cm × 16 cm, and each circle has radius 2.55 cm.

Using 3.142 as an approximate value of π, calculate the surface area of the cylinder.

Tip
Remember that the surface area of a solid is the total area of each of its faces.

5 The diagram shows a circular mirror with a decorative frame.

The frame is 12 cm wide all the way round.

The frame width is $\frac{4}{5}$ of the radius of the **whole** piece.

  a Calculate the area of the whole piece. Use 3.142 as an approximate value of π.

  b Calculate the area of just the frame surrounding the mirror.

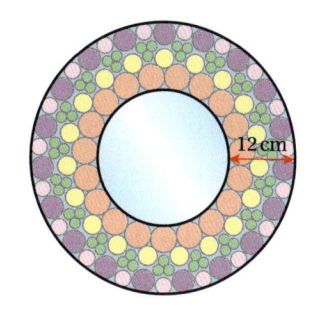

> **Tip**
>
> If 12 cm is $\frac{4}{5}$ of the radius, then what is the radius? Look back at Chapter 10 on fractions if you need to.

6 A piece of fondant icing is rolled out into the shape of a square.

A circle with radius 11 cm is cut out from the square.

Given that the largest circle possible is cut out, find the difference between the area of the circular icing and the area of the square.

7 A semicircular sandpit sits at the end of a lawn.

A cover is to be placed over the sandpit.

What is the area that needs to be covered?

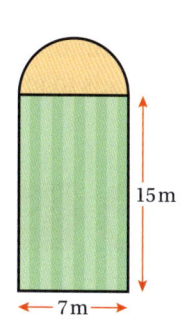

8 A circular photo frame has a plastic surround.

The width of the plastic surround is 8 cm.

The diameter of the complete photo frame is 28 cm.

Calculate the area available for the photo.

9 The blue shapes have the same area.

The second shape is a square.

What is the side length of the square?

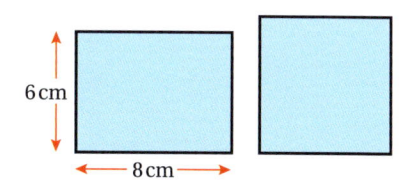

Checklist of learning and understanding

Area of polygons

- Area is the amount of surface covered by a plane shape. Area is always given in square units.
- Area can be calculated using formulae. Some common formulae are:

Rectangle	Square	Triangle	Parallelogram	Trapezium
$A = lw$	$A = l^2$	$A = \frac{1}{2}bh$	$A = bh$	$A = \frac{1}{2}(a+b)h$

Find answers at: cambridge.org/ukschools/gcsemaths-studentbookanswers

Area of circles

- Area of a circle = πr^2.
- Area of a sector is a fraction of the area of the whole circle.
- Area of a sector = $\dfrac{\theta}{360} \times \pi r^2$.

Composite shapes

- The area of composite shapes can be found by splitting them into known shapes.
- You can use the 'addition of parts' method to calculate the areas of smaller shapes separately and then add them together to find the total area.
- You can use the 'subtraction of parts' method to calculate the area of a shape with a 'cut out' section by finding the area of the larger shape and subtracting the area of the 'cut out' shape. Sometimes this will require you to imagine what the larger shape would look like *before* the smaller shape had been cut out.
- The area of some composite shapes can be calculated using either the 'addition of parts' or the 'subtraction of parts' method; use whichever one leads to fewer calculations.

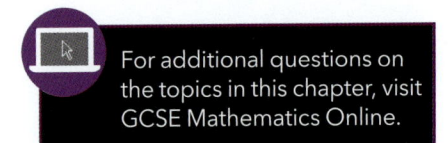

For additional questions on the topics in this chapter, visit GCSE Mathematics Online.

Chapter review

1. A rectangular vegetable plot has an area of 100 m².
   If the width is 6.5 m, what is the length of the plot?

2. The net of a square-based pyramid is shown.
   The square has sides of length 5 cm.
   The triangles have a perpendicular height of 4.3 cm.

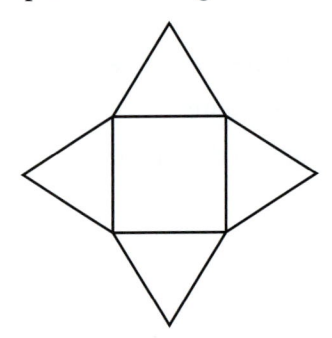

   Calculate the surface area of the square-based pyramid.

3. A square flower bed of side length 3 m sits exactly in the middle of a rectangular grassed area of side length 5 m and width 450 cm.
   Calculate the area of grass.

4. A sprinkler in a field can water a circular crop within a radius of 14.5 m.
   What is the total area of field that can be watered?

5 Calculate the area of the shape shown.
Give your answer in cm².

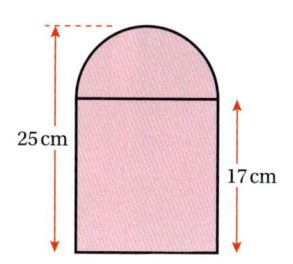

25 cm
17 cm

6 A kite has dimensions as shown in the diagram.

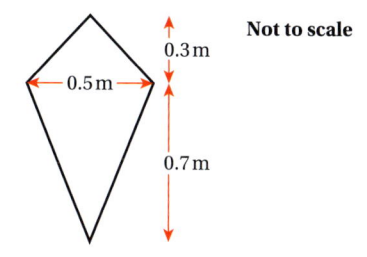

Not to scale
0.3 m
0.5 m
0.7 m

   a Work out the area of the kite. *(4 marks)*
   b Convert your answer in part **a** to cm². *(1 mark)*
                                                                                        © OCR 2013

7 Calculate the area of the shape below.

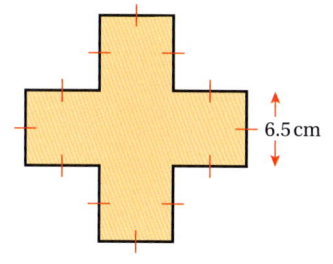

6.5 cm

8 Guy is paid £0.15 for every square metre of grass he cuts.
How much would he be paid for cutting the grass in this garden?

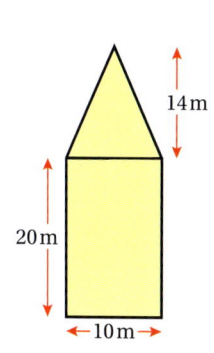

14 m
20 m
10 m

9 A stained glass window is a semicircle with radius 30 cm. Calculate:
   a the perimeter of the window.
   b the area of glass.

Find answers at: cambridge.org/ukschools/gcsemaths-studentbookanswers

17 Approximation and estimation

In this chapter you will learn how to ...
- approximate values by rounding them to different degrees of accuracy or truncating.
- use approximations to estimate and check the results of calculations.
- understand and apply limits of accuracy in numbers and measurements.

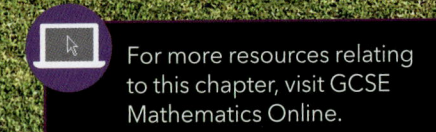

For more resources relating to this chapter, visit GCSE Mathematics Online.

Using mathematics: real-life applications

When you estimate what you spent over the weekend, or look at an object and guess it is about $2\frac{1}{2}$ m long, or say things like "I live about 15 kilometres from school" you are estimating and using approximate values.

"I round off the prices to the nearest pound and keep a mental running total of the costs of things I put in my trolley so I know that I am not over-spending."
(Consumer)

Before you start ...

KS3	You should be able to use rounding to quickly estimate the answers to calculations.	**1** Use rounded values to estimate and decide if each answer is correct. **Do not do the calculation.** **a** $312 - 56 = 256$ **b** $479 \times 17 = 3142$ **c** $350 + 351 - 96 = 798$
Ch 11	You should be able to calculate with decimals and estimate to decide whether an answer is reasonable.	**2** Say whether each statement is true or false. **a** $5.8 \times 6.72 \approx 42$ **b** $3.789 + 234.6 \approx 4 + 230$ **c** $0.00432 + 3.55 \approx 4$ **d** $4 \times \pi \approx 12$
Ch 11	You need to be able to work confidently with decimals and place value.	**3** Write the number halfway between: **a** 3.0 and 5.0 **b** 3.5 and 3.6 **c** 0.02 and 0.07

17 Approximation and estimation

Assess your starting point using the Launchpad

STEP 1

1 Round each value to the degree of accuracy specified.
  a 86 to the nearest 10.
  b 1565 to the nearest 1000.
  c 134.1234 to 2 decimal places.
  d 19.999 to 1 decimal place.
  e 1235.26 to 1 significant figure.
  f 234 650 034 to 3 significant figures.

2 The length of a piece of metal is found to be 0.937 cm. What is its length to the nearest millimetre?

3 The cost of an international call on a phone bill is given as £5.159 32.
  a What is this amount truncated to the nearest penny?
  b What is this amount rounded to two decimal places?

GO TO
Section 1: Rounding

STEP 2

4 Estimate the cost of 12 packets of seeds at £1.36 each.

5 Approximately how many litres of petrol can you get for £20 if each litre costs £1.89?

6 Use rounding to find an approximate answer to each calculation.
  a $\dfrac{784 + 572}{109}$
  b $(2.099)^2$
  c $\sqrt{\dfrac{3.803 + 7.52}{3.29}}$

GO TO
Section 2: Approximation and estimation

STEP 3

7 A piece of wire is 10 m long, correct to the nearest metre.
If the actual length of the wire is x, complete the following statement to show the longest and shortest possible lengths that this wire could be.

  $\square \leq x < \square$

GO TO
Section 3: Limits of accuracy

GO TO Chapter review

Find answers at: cambridge.org/ukschools/gcsemaths-studentbookanswers

Section 1: Rounding

Approximation lets you give numbers in a more convenient form by writing them in a simpler, but less accurate way. For example, you might tell your friends that you pay £10 a month for your mobile phone contract when really you pay £10.32.

Approximate values are created by **rounding**.

Rounding a number means writing it with fewer non-zero digits to make it less precise.

Numbers can be rounded to different **degrees of accuracy**, such as 'to the nearest whole number' or to 'three significant figures'.

To round a number to a given degree of accuracy, find the digit in the specified place and look at the next digit to the right. It helps to think of its position on a number line.
- If it is **less than 5**, you keep the digit in the specified place the same; this results in the original number being rounded **down**.
- If it is 5 or greater than 5, you increase the digit in the specified place by 1; this results in the original number being rounded **up**.

The 'specified place' will vary depending on the degree of accuracy used.

Rounding to the nearest …

You might be asked to round a number to the nearest ten, hundred or thousand and so on.

If the number you are rounding is:
- an **integer**, after rounding you need to replace each digit to the right of the specified place with a zero.
- a **decimal number**, after rounding you replace each digit to the right of the specified place with a zero up to the decimal point, but you **do not** include the decimal point or any digits after the decimal point; the resulting approximate value will be an integer.

Rounding 456 189 to the nearest ten:

456 1**8**9   Find the specified place, this is the digit in the 'tens' place.

456 190   Look at the digit to its right. 9 > 5 (over half way) so 8 is increased by 1. To keep the approximate value a six-digit number, the digit to the right of the specified value is replaced with a placeholder zero. 456 189 has been **rounded up**.

Rounding 456 189 to the nearest hundred:

456 **1**89   Find the digit in the 'hundreds' place and look at the digit to its right. 8 > 5, so the 1 is increased by 1 and the next two digits to the right are replaced by zero.

456 200   456 189 has been **rounded up**.

Rounding 456 189 to the nearest thousand:

45**6** 189   Find the digit in the 'thousands' place and look at the digit to its right.
1 < 5, (less than half way) so the 6 stays the same and the next three digits to the right are replaced by zero.

456 000   456 189 has been **rounded down**.

Key vocabulary

rounding: writing a number with fewer non-zero digits by replacing some digits with zeroes.

degree of accuracy: the number of places to which you round a number, for example to the nearest whole number, 2 decimal places, 3 significant figures.

Tip

The zeros act as placeholders to make sure that the approximate value is the appropriate size in terms of place value. For example, ensuring that 232 is rounded to 200, not 2! If asked to round a number to the nearest hundred then your answer must be a number in its hundreds.

If you are asked to round a decimal number to the **nearest whole number**, the specified value is the digit in the units/ones place and the digit to the right will be the first digit after the decimal place.

WORKED EXAMPLE 1

a Round these numbers to the nearest whole number.
   i 0.5   **ii** 23.1   **iii** 0.034 235   **iv** 2 583 943.34

b Round 415.75 to
   i the nearest ten.   **ii** the nearest hundred.

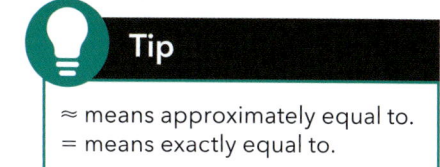

> **Tip**
> ≈ means approximately equal to.
> = means exactly equal to.

a i 0.5

The specified place is in the units/ones place. Look at the digit to the right (i.e., after the decimal place). It is 5, so the digit in the specified place increases by 1.

0.5 ≈ 1 (to the nearest whole number)

Because you are rounding to the nearest **whole number**, you **do not** include the decimal point or replace the digits after it with zeros. State the degree of accuracy used in your answer.

ii 23.1 ≈ 23 (to the nearest whole number)

You use the same approach as for part **a i**, except that 1 < 5 so the digit in the specified place stays the same.

iii 0.034235 ≈ 0 (to the nearest whole number)

Same approach as parts **a i** and **ii**.

iv 2583943.34 ≈ 2583943 (to the nearest whole number)

Same approach as parts **a i** and **ii**.

b i 415.75
415.75 ≈ 420 (to the nearest ten)

Same approach as for part **a**, except the specified place is in the tens place. Replace all digits to the right of the specified place up to the decimal point with zeros but **do not** include the decimal point or digits after it.

ii 415.75 ≈ 400 (to the nearest hundred)

Same approach as for part **b i**, except the specified place is in the hundreds place.

EXERCISE 17A

1 Choose the correct approximation of each animal's mass.

	Mass of animal	Rounded to	Identify the correct one	
a	Cow 635 kg	Nearest 10 kg	A 630 kg	B 640 kg
b	Horse 526 kg	Nearest 100 kg	A 500 kg	B 600 kg
c	Sheep 96 kg	Nearest 10 kg	A 90 kg	B 100 kg
d	Dog 32 kg	Nearest 10 kg	A 30 kg	B 40 kg
e	Cat 5.2 kg	Nearest 10 kg	A 0 kg	B 10 kg

2 a Round each value to the nearest whole number.
   i 54.8   **ii** 10.6   **iii** 9.4   **iv** 12.3

b Round each value to the nearest 10.
   i 26   **ii** 57.5   **iii** 111.1   **iv** 35 814

Find answers at: cambridge.org/ukschools/gcsemaths-studentbookanswers

c Round each value to the nearest 100.
  i 458   ii 5732   iii 2389   iv 35 814
d Round each value to the nearest 1000.
  i 2590   ii 176   iii 35 814   iv 66 876
e Round the following to the nearest hundred thousand.
  i 123 456   ii 1 234 567   iii 12 354 642   iv 123 456 789
f Round the following to the nearest million.
  i 545 000   ii 555 000   iii 14 354 642   iv 546 267 789

3 a A food bill is £27.60. How much is this to the nearest pound?
b There are 27 students in a class. What is this to the nearest ten students?
c I have £175 saved up. What is this to the nearest £100?
d You need 167 cm of material to make a kite. Approximately how many metres do you need?
e Sue says that the population of the United Kingdom is 63 793 234 which is 63.7 million to the nearest hundred thousand people. Is she correct?

Rounding to a decimal place

A **decimal place (dp)** is the position of a digit to the right of the decimal point.

The number of decimal places relates to place value:

Place value after decimal point	.	tenths	hundredths	thousandths	...
Number of decimal places	.	1	2	3	...

When rounding to a specified decimal place you must:
- include the decimal point in your answer.
- include any digits after the decimal point up to and including the specified decimal place.
- **not** include digits to the right of the specified place.

Key vocabulary

decimal place (dp): place value position of a digit to the right of the decimal point.

WORKED EXAMPLE 2

Round:
a 54.149 to one decimal place.
b 0.8751 to two decimal places.
c 0.100 24 to three decimal places.

a 54.1<u>4</u>9   The first decimal place is the first digit after the decimal point. Look at the digit to its right;
  54.1   4 < 5 so the specified value stays the same. Delete the digits to the right of the specified place.

b 0.87<u>5</u>1   The second decimal place is two digits after the decimal point, round as normal. Remember
  0.88   to include the decimal point and any digits after the decimal point up to and including the specified place, and take off the digits to the right.

c 0.100<u>0</u> 24 Round as in part **b**, except the specified place is the third digit after the decimal. Although
  0.100   0.100 is the same as 0.1, you include the two placeholder zeros to show that the number is rounded to 'or accurate to' 3 decimal places.

17 Approximation and estimation

Suitable levels of accuracy

The level of accuracy that is suitable for rounding depends on the situation. If you are not given a degree of accuracy to work to, you need to decide whether it is sensible to use a rounded value or whether it needs to be an exact value. You also need to consider whether a rough whole number is good enough or whether you should use decimals.

Here are some example answers from calculations, the appropriate degree of accuracy chosen for the answer, and the reasoning for choosing that accuracy.

> **Tip**
>
> In some situations you have to round up or down to answer a particular question. In this case, you use common sense rather than the rules of rounding.

Answer		
Before rounding	**After rounding**	**Reasoning**
Number of tins of paint needed = 9.15	10 tins	You can only buy whole numbers of tins so you round to the nearest whole number. Following the rules of rounding, you would round down to 9 tins. **However,** if you bought 9 tins you wouldn't have enough paint, so actually it is more appropriate here to round up.
Cost of repairs = £4.568 96	£4.57	The smallest denomination of pounds sterling is 1p (1p = £0.01), so round to two decimal places. Using the rules of rounding, you would round up.
Driving distance to Kent = 133.7364864 km	134 km	It's not reasonable to give the answer to 1 or 2 decimal places because that's more accurate than anyone would need to know (2 dp would give the distance to the nearest 10 m). As driving distances are generally recorded in kilometres, the nearest kilometre seems the most reasonable degree of accuracy. Using the rules of rounding, you would round up.
Temperature for weather forecast = 36.895 79°	37°	Most people want to have a general idea of the weather: is it hot, cold, warm, raining and so on, so rounding to the nearest whole number is appropriate. Using the rules of rounding, you would round up.

When you calculate with decimals or significant figures and there isn't an obvious degree of accuracy to work to, then you normally round to no more than the degree of accuracy given in the original values.

When providing a rounded answer, **always state the degree of accuracy used**.

WORKED EXAMPLE 3

Calculate 4.13×2.07.

4 . 1 3 × 2 . 0 7 =   Key the calculation into your calculator.

8.5491   Given the size of the values in the question, the answer seems too precise.

8.55 (2 dp)   As the question uses values to 2 decimal places, round your answer to 2 decimal places. Write the degree of accuracy you have used.

Find answers at: cambridge.org/ukschools/gcsemaths-studentbookanswers

EXERCISE 17B

1 Round each number to:
   i 1 dp.   **ii** 2 dp.   **iii** 3 dp.

   a 4.526 38   **b** 25.256 37   **c** 125.617 38

   d 0.537 921   **e** 32.3972   **f** 0.8993

2 Write each value correct to two decimal places.

   a 19.869 03   **b** 302.0428   **c** 0.292

   d 0.205 28   **e** 21 245.8449   **f** 0.0039

   g 0.0972   **h** 0.999 999 9   **i** 99.997

3 Round each value to a suitable level of accuracy. Explain your decisions.

   a A large dog weighs 24.4872 kg.

   b To calculate a circumference I use the value pi = 3.141 592 653 589 793 238 46...

   c Dan's car can travel 13.7895 km per 1.000 098 7 litres of petrol.

   d My share of a phone bill is £14.098 76.

Key vocabulary

significant figure: the most significant figure (digit) in a number is the first non-zero digit when reading the number from left to right.

Significant figures

The first **significant figure (sf)** in a number is the first non-zero digit when you read the number from left to right. It is the most **significant** figure because it tells you the number's overall size in terms of place value, that is, if it is in the millions, thousands, hundreds or tenths and so on.

All digits that follow the first significant figure are significant, including any zeros. For example:

first significant figure	**1**20 000 000	**2**08.130	**1**.000 87	0.000 **5**60 3
second significant figure	1**2**0 000 000	2**0**8.130	1.**0**00 87	0.000 5**6**0 3
third significant figure	12**0** 000 000	20**8**.130	1.0**0**0 87	0.000 56**0** 3

When rounding to a given number of significant figures,

- replace each digit to the right of the specified place with a zero (using zero as a placeholder).
- if the original number is a **decimal**, and the specified place is
  - **before** the decimal point, do not include the decimal point or any digits after it.
  - **after** the decimal point, include the decimal point and all digits (zero or non-zero) between the decimal point and the specified place but delete any digits to the right of the specified place.

Tip

One significant figure does not mean that you will have only one digit in the answer. 18 756 is 20 000 correct to 1 significant figure, not 2. Always think of the size of the original number you are rounding. Think of its position on a number line.

17 Approximation and estimation

WORKED EXAMPLE 4

Write each figure correct to the given degree of accuracy.

a 308 000 000 (2 sf)   **b** 476.372 (4 sf)
c 2531.8 (2 sf)   **d** 0.004 36 (1 sf)

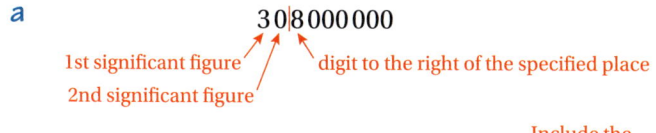

a

30|8 000 000
- 1st significant figure
- 2nd significant figure
- digit to the right of the specified place

30|8 000 000 ≈ 310 000 000 (2 sf)
- 1st sf
- >5
- round to 2sp
- round up
- state the level of accuracy
- Include the zeros. 31 is not the same as 310 000 000.

Read the number from left to right to find the first non-zero digit; this is the first significant figure. You need the second significant figure, so count on 1 digit. '0' is the second significant figure. Look at the digit to the right of the specified place; it is 8.

308 000 000 ≈ 310 000 000 (2 sf)

8 > 5 so you increase the digit in the specified place by 1. Remember to replace all digits to the right with zero as placeholders (31 is not the same as 310 000 000!). Don't forget to include the degree of accuracy in your answer.

b 476.3̲72 ≈ 476.4 (4 sf)

The fourth significant figure is '3'. As the specified place is after the decimal point, you **do not** include any digits after the specified place.

c 25̲31.8 ≈ 2500 (2 sf)

The second significant figure is '5'. Replace digits to the right with placeholder zeros. As the specified place is before the decimal point, do not include the decimal point or any digits to the right of it.

d 0.004̲36 ≈ 0.004 (1 sf)

The first significant figure is '4'. As the specified place is after the decimal place, you include the decimal point and any digits between it and the specified place but **do not** include any digits after the specified place.

Significant figures are particularly useful for scientific or medical calculations where you deal with either very small or very large values.

Imagine that having 0.0001 ml or more of substance x in the bloodstream was dangerous. If the machine that measured the volume of the substance in the blood only measured to 2 decimal places, the following result would come back negative: 0.000345 ml ≈ 0.00 (2 dp). However, if the machine rounded to 2 sf, you would get a positive result: 0.000345 ml ≈ 0.00035 ml (2sf).

The moon is about 384 400 km from the Earth. Say the precise measurement was 384 400.434563 km, rounding to a decimal place would give a much more detailed value than would make sense for such a large distance. Rounding to a significant figure would mean you could use a value that is accurate to the nearest km, or hundred km or thousand km, which is more appropriate for such a large distance.

Tip

Rounding numbers to a given number of decimal places means that you start the rounding at the specified place after the decimal point. Rounding numbers to significant figures means you start at the specified significant figure, which can be before or after the decimal point.

Find answers at: cambridge.org/ukschools/gcsemaths-studentbookanswers

EXERCISE 17C

1 **a** Round each value to 1 sf.
   i 789 **ii** 3874 **iii** 69 356 **iv** 0.0456

b Write correct to 2 sf.
   i 789 **ii** 3145 **iii** 0.003 325 **iv** 0.000 749 9

c Express each number correct to 3 sf.
   i 789 **ii** 46 712 **iii** 0.004 214 **iv** 753 413

d Round each value to 2 sf.
   i 37.673 **ii** −4127 **iii** 3.0392 **iv** 1 999 000

e Write correct to 3 sf.
   i 37.673 **ii** −4127 **iii** 3.0392 **iv** 1 999 000

2 Explain why it is more useful to round a value such as 0.000 134 567 to two significant figures than to two decimal places.

3 **a** Pi ≈ 3.141 592 6. What is this to 3 sf?
   b The density of a gas is 1.234 kg/m^3. What is this to 2 sf?
   c The speed of light is 299 792 458 m/s. What is this to 2 sf?
   d The strength of gravity at the Earth's surface is 9.806 65 m/s^2. What is this to 3 sf?

Key vocabulary

truncation: cutting off all digits after a certain point without rounding.

Tip

$2 \div 3 = \frac{2}{3} = 0.\dot{6}$; you learnt about recurring decimals in Chapter 11.

Tip

When you use rounded or truncated values during calculations, your results will not be completely accurate. You will learn more about this in Section 3.

Did you know?

Truncation is used in statistics. A truncated mean is an average worked out by discarding (cutting off) very high or very low values in the data.

Truncation

Truncation is when all the digits past a given point are cut off **without** rounding.

You need to be aware that your calculator display might give you a truncated value rather than a rounded value.

Test your calculator by entering [2] [÷] [3], the precise answer is the recurring decimal $0.\dot{6}$.

If your calculator display shows:
- 0.6666666666 your calculator has **truncated** the value to 10 decimal places.
- 0.6666666667 your calculator has **rounded** the value to 10 decimal places.

EXERCISE 17D

1 Truncate each number to 2 decimal places.
   a 37.673 **b** −4.1275 **c** 3.0392 **d** 0.997

2 Truncate each number after the third significant figure.
   a 4.526 38 **b** 25.256 37 **c** 125.617 38
   d 0.537 921 **e** 32.397 **f** 200.6127

3 Consider splitting a bill of £20 equally between three people. What would each person pay?
   What method of approximation is most useful for deciding?

17 Approximation and estimation

Section 2: Approximation and estimation

Approximate values are useful for checking the results of calculations are sensible.

If your **estimate** and your actual answer are not similar, then you might have made a mistake in your calculation.

When estimating an approximate answer, you can generally round to 1 sf.

> **Key vocabulary**
>
> **estimate**: an approximate value or rough calculation.

WORKED EXAMPLE 5

Estimate then calculate the value of $\frac{8.3 \times 536}{2.254 \times 9.612}$.

$$\frac{8.3 \times 536}{2.254 \times 9.612} \approx \frac{8 \times 500}{2 \times 10}$$

$$\approx \frac{4000}{20}$$

$$\approx 200$$

Round each number to 1 sf, then do the calculation.

$$\frac{8.3 \times 536}{2.254 \times 9.612} = 205.3407804$$

Key the calculation into your calculator to get the precise answer. Comparing this with your estimate tells you that your calculated answer is reasonable.

Estimating is also useful for giving you an idea of what to expect.

> "I estimate measurements and prices to quote an approximate cost so that customers have an idea of what a building job will cost them." *(Builder)*

WORK IT OUT 17.1

A group of four friends are travelling to a festival.

They want to split the cost of everything between them.

The costs are: tent hire, £86.50; travel, 140 km round trip with petrol costing roughly 20p per kilometre, and camping entry tickets at £44 per night for three nights.

They decide to estimate how much they will each have to pay.

Which is the best estimate? Why is it better than the others?

Estimate A	Estimate B	Estimate C
The cost of tent hire is roughly £88, which is £22 per person split between four.	The tent hire is roughly £100, which is £25 per person.	The tent hire is roughly £80, which is £20 each.
Petrol costs roughly £28 (140 × 0.2) which is £7 per person.	The petrol is roughly £150 × 0.2, which is £30, so split four ways is £7.50.	Petrol is about £100 × 0.2 = £20 so £5 per person.
The camping ticket costs are £44 × three nights, which is roughly £120 which is £30 per person.	The camping costs about £50 × 3 = £150, which is about £40 each.	Camping cost is about £40 × 3 = £120 for three nights, so about £30 each.
So total cost per person is approximately £22 + £7 + £30 = £59.	Total cost per person is approximately £25 + £7.50 + £40 = £72.50.	Total cost per person is approximately £20 + £5 + £30 = £55.

Find answers at: cambridge.org/ukschools/gcsemaths-studentbookanswers

271

EXERCISE 17E

1 Estimate the following by rounding each number to 1 sf.

a 111.11×3.6
b 378×1.07
c 0.99×16.7
d 13.6×0.48
e $\pi \times (5.3)^2$
f 4.8×12.5
g $\dfrac{192}{17.2}$
h $\dfrac{58.38}{0.5185}$

2 Which calculation would provide the best estimate (A, B or C)?

a 186×9.832 A 200×10 B 190×9 C 190×10
b $15.76 \div 7.6$ A $15 \div 7$ B $16 \div 8$ C $16 \div 7$

3 Estimate the following by rounding each number to 1 sf.

a $\dfrac{82.65 \times 0.4654}{42.4 \times 2.43}$
b $\dfrac{16.96 + 3.123}{16.96 - 6.432}$
c $\dfrac{979 \div 43.6}{2.36 \times 0.23}$
d $\dfrac{979 \div 492.9}{21.6 \div 43.87}$

4 Estimate the following.

a $\sqrt{\dfrac{3.2 \times 4.05}{0.39 \times 0.29}}$
b $\sqrt{\dfrac{4.1 \times 11.9}{7.9 \times 0.25}}$

5 Shafiek runs a cross country race at an average speed of 6.25 m/s.

a Estimate how far he will have run after 6 minutes.

b Estimate how long it takes him to cover 1467 m.

6 Look at the calculator display answers for each calculation. Use your estimation skills to say whether the answer is sensible or not without actually doing the calculation.

a $3 \times \pi \times 5^2$ 125.6637061

b 5×8.9 445

c 50×8.9 445

d 3×192.5 57.75

e $\dfrac{\sqrt{86}}{2.8 \times 16.18}$ 0.204697565

f $0.0253 \div 0.45$ 56.222222222

7 A parallelogram has an area of 54.67 cm². The base of the parallelogram is 7.9 cm long.

a When a student tries to find the height on his calculator, he gets a result of 69 202 531.

This is clearly wrong.

Give the height correct to 2 significant figures.

b Estimate the perimeter of the parallelogram to the nearest cm.

Section 3: Limits of accuracy

All measurements of mass, height, length, area and capacity are given to a certain level of accuracy. Even with very accurate measuring instruments, these quantities cannot be measured exactly because they are **continuous variables**.

When you are given a measurement you assume it is accurate except for the last digit as this has been rounded. The rules of rounding mean the measurement has to fall within certain limits. The limits are determined by the degree of accuracy used to round.

The smallest value a measurement can take is called the **lower bound** of the measurement.

The largest value it can take is called the **upper bound**.

The difference between the upper and lower bounds is called the **error interval**. This indicates the range of values in which the precise value could fall.

For example, a piece of wood is measured and its length recorded as 47 cm **to the nearest cm**.

Use what you know about rounding to determine the upper and lower bounds:

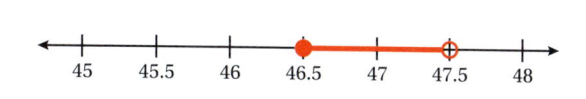

If the length was less than 46.5 cm, rounding to the nearest cm would give 46 cm.

If the length was 47.5 cm or more, rounding to the nearest cm would give 48 cm.

If we let l represent the length of the piece of wood, the error interval can be expressed as

$46.5 \text{ cm} \leq l < 47.5 \text{ cm}$

This is called **inequality notation** and it means the length of the wood is greater than or equal to 46.5 cm and less than 47.5 cm.

For any measurement correct to a given level of accuracy, the exact values lie in a range half a unit below and half a unit above the measurement.

Look at the following examples and note the rules that apply for decimals and significant figures:

Example	Lower and upper bounds	Error interval (let the value be x)
0.5 rounded to 1 dp	0.645 and 0.655	$0.45 \leq x < 0.55$
0.65 rounded to 2 dp	0.645 and 0.655	$0.645 \leq x < 0.655$
0.7663 rounded to 4 dp	0.76625 and 0.76635	$0.76625 \leq x < 0.76635$
15 rounded to 2 sf	14.5 and 15.5	$14.5 \leq x < 15.5$
320 to 2 sf	315 and 325	$315 \leq x < 325$
2.32 rounded to 2 dp	2.315 and 2.325	$2.315 \leq x < 2.325$

Find answers at: cambridge.org/ukschools/gcsemaths-studentbookanswers

Key vocabulary

continuous variable: data that can take any numerical value within a range; it can be measured.

lower bound: the smallest value that a number (given to a specified accuracy) can be.

upper bound: the largest value that a number (given to a specified accuracy) can be.

error interval: the difference between the upper and lower bounds.

Tip

You will learn more about continuous and discrete data in Chapter 35.

Tip

It is helpful to draw a number line to work out the upper and lower bounds of a value. The closed circle means the value **is** included, the open circle means it is **not** included.

Tip

$\leq$ means less than or equal to
$\geq$ means greater than or equal to
$<$ means less than
$>$ means greater than

GCSE Mathematics for OCR (Foundation)

For a **truncated** value, the upper and lower bounds are **not** ± half a unit because the value is cut off not rounded; this means that the digit to the right of the specified place is irrelevant, and it is only the digit in the specified place that is considered.

For example, if 6.6 is a value truncated to 1 dp, then the error interval is

$6.6 \leqslant x < 6.7$

WORKED EXAMPLE 6

Use inequality notation to write down the error interval for:

a 10 cm correct to the nearest cm.

b 22.5 kg to one decimal place.

c 128 000 correct to 3 sf.

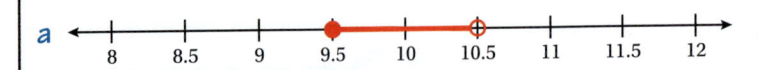

a ⟵───┼───┼───●━━━○───┼───┼───⟶
      8   8.5 9 9.5 10 10.5 11 11.5 12

The degree of accuracy is 'to the nearest cm' so half a unit is 0.5 cm. The error interval is half a unit above and below, so it is 10 cm ± 0.5 cm. 9.5 cm would be rounded to 10 cm, and 10.5 cm would be rounded to 11 cm. Check using a number line; use a solid circle for the lower bound and an open circle for the upper bound.

Let the length be x.

$9.5 \text{ cm} \leqslant x < 10.5 \text{ cm}$

Write the error interval using inequality notation, don't forget to include the correct symbols: 'greater than or equal to' and 'less than'.

b ⟵───┼───●───┼───○───┼⟶
      22.4 22.45 22.5 22.55 22.6

Let the mass be x.

$22.45 \text{ kg} \leqslant x < 22.55 \text{ kg}$

The degree of accuracy is 'to one decimal place'; so half a unit is 0.05 kg. The error interval will be 22.5 kg ± 0.05 kg. Draw a number line to check.

c ⟵───●───┼───○───┼⟶
    127 000 127 500 128 000 128 500 129 000

Let the value be x.

$127\,500 \leqslant x < 128\,500$

The degree of accuracy is '3 sf', so half a unit is 500. The error interval is 128 000 ± 500. Draw a number line to check.

Sometimes you will need to be able to identify when a question is asking for upper and lower bounds.

WORKED EXAMPLE 7

The healthy mass of a male labrador is between 27 kg and 34 kg to the nearest kilogram.

Sophia's dog has a mass of 34.34 kg. In terms of his mass, is he healthy?

Let m be the mass in kg.

$26.5 \leqslant m < 34.5$

Yes, the dog is healthy.

The question requires you to calculate the upper bound. Half a unit of 1kg is 0.5kg. Write the error interval. The mass is less than the upper bound.

274

EXERCISE 17F

1 Find the lower and upper bound of each value.
   a 96 rounded to 2 sf
   b 96.0 rounded to 3 sf
   c 96.00 rounded to 4 sf
   d 0.6 rounded to 1 dp
   e 0.06 rounded to 1 dp
   f 0.60 rounded to 2 dp
   g 3.142 rounded to 3 dp
   h 9.9 rounded to 2 sf

2 The following lengths were measured to the nearest millimetre.
Write down an error interval for each one using inequality notation.
Let the length be L in each case.
   a 4.9 cm
   b 12.520 m
   c 43.0 cm
   d 29 mm

3 a There are 36 litres of petrol in a car's tank, to the nearest litre.
What is the least possible volume of petrol in the tank?
   b A length of wood is 1.4 m to the nearest cm.
Is it possible for the wood to be 137 cm long?
   c The weight of a stone is 43.4 kg to the nearest tenth of a kg.
What is the least and greatest weight it could be?

4 A calculator has truncated the following number to 4 decimal places.
$$34.5638$$
Write down the error interval for this number.

Checklist of learning and understanding

Approximate values

- Approximate values are created by rounding a value to a given degree of accuracy.
- When you round to a specified place, if the digit to the right is 5 or more (half way or more), then the original number is rounded up. If it is less than 5 (less than half way), then the original number is rounded down.
- Rounding to a given number of decimal places means that you start the rounding at the specified place after the decimal point. Rounding to significant figures means you start rounding at the specified significant figure, which can be before or after the decimal point.
- Truncating a number means removing all digits after a specified place without rounding.

Estimation

- Complex calculations can be estimated without using a calculator by using approximations of each term in the calculation to make a simple calculation.
- Estimating the answer first can help you to spot when the answer to a calculation is incorrect.

Find answers at: cambridge.org/ukschools/gcsemaths-studentbookanswers

Level of accuracy

- Measurement of continuous variables is really an approximation of the value within an upper and lower bound. Therefore, the measurement of a continuous variable can be expressed as an error interval using inequality notation (≤, <).

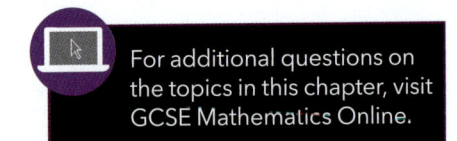

For additional questions on the topics in this chapter, visit GCSE Mathematics Online.

Chapter review

1 Are the following true or false?

	Original number	Approximation	Answer
a	123.456	Rounded to 2 dp (2 decimal places)	123.456
b	123.456	Rounded to 1 sf (1 significant figure)	120.000
c	123.456	Rounded to 1 dp (1 decimal place)	123.5
d	123.456	Rounded to 4 sf (4 significant figures)	123.5
e	123 456.789	Truncated to 1 dp (1 decimal place)	123 456.8

2 Elizabeth says she is 24 years old to the nearest year.
What is the youngest age she could be and the oldest age she could be?

3 Round the following numbers to the degree of accuracy given.
   a 34.3643 to 3 sf   b 578403 to 1 sf   c 3.543 1 dp

4 The population of a town is given as 425 000 to the nearest 1000.
What is the largest the population could be?

5 Estimate.
   a $\sqrt{8.67} + \sqrt{99.9}$ b $\dfrac{(7.6)^2}{1.98}$ c $\sqrt{\dfrac{124.62}{0.252 \times 19.9}}$

6 If there are 140 people at party, to the nearest 10 people, what is the maximum number of people that could be there?

7 If a length of rope has been rounded to the nearest centimetre and it measures 90 cm, what is the possible range of values for its length?

8 Dipak spends £45.67 per month on his mobile phone bill at a fixed rate, plus an additional £0.99 for every 10 minutes over his internet limit.
If Dipak goes over his internet limit by 28 minutes one month, what will be the approximate cost of his bill for that month?

18 Straight-line graphs

In this chapter you will learn how to ...

- use a table of values to plot graphs of linear functions.
- identify the main features of straight-line graphs and use them to sketch graphs with equations in the form $y = mx + c$.
- find the equation of a straight line using the gradient and points on the line.
- identify parallel lines from the equation of the line in the form $y = mx + c$.

For more resources relating to this chapter, visit GCSE Mathematics Online.

Usng mathematics: real-life applications

This is a building in London nicknamed *The Gherkin*. The curves and lines of the building were designed using complex equations and their graphs. Architecture is just one of many professions in which people plot and use graphs in their work.

"When designing a new building, I use graphs to help identify and describe the structural properties the building needs to have." *(Architect)*

Before you start ...

Ch 4	You should remember how to generate terms in a sequence using a rule.	1 Use the rule $T(n) = 3n - 2$ to complete this table. | n | 1 | 3 | 5 | 10 | |---|---|---|---|---| | $T(n)$ | | | | |
KS3	You should be able to give the coordinates of points on a grid.	2 **a** Write down the coordinates of points A, D and E. **b** What point has the following coordinates? 　**i** $(-2, 2)$　**ii** $(0, -6)$ **c** What is the name given to the point $(0, 0)$?
Ch 8	You must be able to rearrange and solve equations.	3 Solve for x. **a** $4 - 3x = 13$　**b** $\dfrac{x}{7} = 6$　**c** $-3(5x + 2) = 0$ 4 If $y = 2x + 5$: **a** find y when $x = -2$.　**b** find x when $y = 8$.
Ch 14	You should remember how to change the subject of a formula.	5 Make y the subject of each equation. **a** $-2x - y + 1 = 0$　**b** $2x + 3y = 6$　**c** $x - 2y = -2$

Find answers at: cambridge.org/ukschools/gcsemaths-studentbookanswers

GCSE Mathematics for OCR (Foundation)

Assess your starting point using the Launchpad

STEP 1

1 Copy and complete the table of values for each function.

a $x - y = 2$

x	-2	-1	0	1
y				

b $x + y = 4$

x	-2	-1	0	1
y				

c $2x + y + 2 = 0$

x	-2	-1	0	1
y				

d $x - 2y + 2 = 0$

x	-2	-1	0	1
y				

2 The graphs of two of the functions from Question **1** are shown here.

Match each graph to its equation.

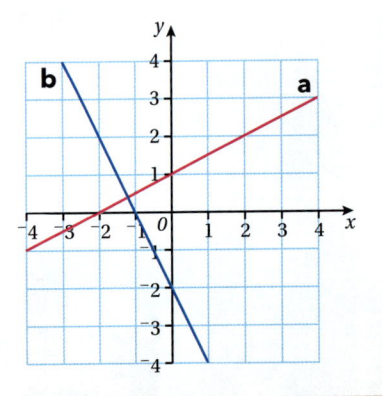

GO TO Section 1: Plotting graphs

STEP 2

3 a Sketch the graph of $y = 2x + 4$ without plotting a table of values.
   b Find the gradient and y-intercept of the resulting straight line.

4 Find the equation of the straight line that passes through the points (1, 4) and (3, 7).

5 A line cuts the x-axis at 4 and the y-axis at 5. What is its gradient?

GO TO Section 2: Using the features of straight-line graphs

GO TO Step 3: The Launchpad continues on the next page …

Launchpad continued ...

STEP 3

6 Which of these lines are parallel to each other?
- **a** $y = {}^-3x + 3$
- **b** $y = 7 - 3x$
- **c** $y = 3x + 7$
- **d** $y = \frac{1}{3}x + 3$
- **e** $y = 7 - 2x$

7 A line is parallel to the line $y = \frac{1}{2}x$ and passes through the point (2, 4). What is its equation?

GO TO
Section 3: Parallel lines

GO TO
Section 4: Working with straight-line graphs

Section 1: Plotting graphs

Graphs can be used to show the relationship between two variables.

You can think of a graph as a picture of a **function**. The line of the graph shows what happens when you apply a rule to x to get a value of y.

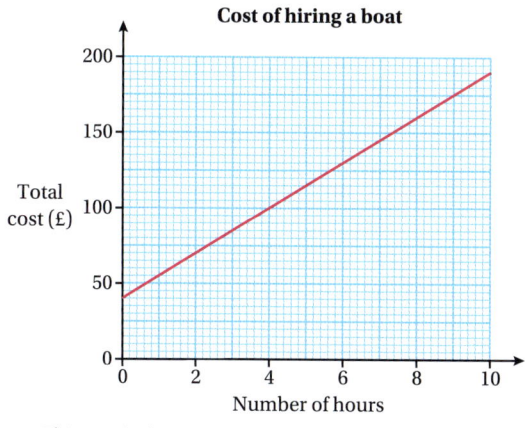

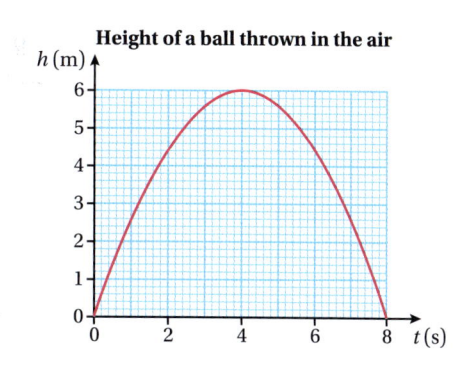

> **Tip**
> You learnt about functions in Chapter 4.

Cost of hiring a boat

Height of a ball thrown in the air

This graph shows the relationship between the cost of hiring a boat and the time the boat is hired for.

This graph shows the height of a projectile from the time it is released to the time it falls to the ground.

For every value of x on the graph there is a corresponding value of y. Each pair of x and y values form the **coordinates**, (x, y), of a point on the line.

Functions that produce straight lines when you plot their x- and y-values are called **linear functions**. You know from Chapter 8 on equations, that a linear function or equation is one where the highest power of x is 1.

Plotting linear functions

The graphs of a linear function are called straight-line graphs.

You can **plot** the graph by first drawing up a table of values.

> **Key vocabulary**
> **coordinates**: an ordered pair (x, y) identifying position on a grid.
> **plot**: draw a graph accurately by marking points on a grid using coordinates.

Find answers at: cambridge.org/ukschools/gcsemaths-studentbookanswers

Tip

When you worked with functions and sequences in Chapter 4 you used a rule to find the terms in a pattern or sequence. You will apply these skills again in this section.

Tip

When you draw a graph, continue the line in both directions through the points, as far as you can. Don't just join the three plotted points together; they are just three of the infinite number of points on the line.

Make sure you have at least three or four values of x. It is usually simpler to use small values such as -1, 0, 1 and 2.

Substitute each value of x into the function to find the corresponding values of y. Then plot the (x, y) coordinates on a set of axes.

WORKED EXAMPLE 1

Draw up a table of values and plot the graph of $y = 2x + 1$.

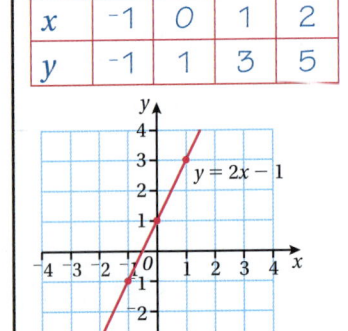

x	-1	0	1	2
y	-1	1	3	5

Choose some values for x. Substitute each x-value into the function to find the corresponding y-value.

Plot at least three points using the coordinates. Points (-1, -1), (0, 1) and (1, 3) have been plotted here.

Use a ruler to draw a straight line through the points. Label the graph with the equation.

EXERCISE 18A

1 Complete a table of values for each function. Then plot the graphs.

   a $y = x$ **b** $y = x + 2$ **c** $y = 3x - 5$
   d $y = 6 - x$ **e** $y = 2x + 1$ **f** $y = x - 1$
   g $y = -2x + 3$ **h** $y = 4 - x$ **i** $y = 3x - 2$

2 What is the minimum number of points you need to plot a straight line accurately? Why?

Section 2: Using the features of straight-line graphs

The main characteristics of a straight-line graph are:
- the **gradient**, or slope of the graph
- the ***x*-intercept** (where it crosses the x-axis)
- the ***y*-intercept** (where it crosses the y-axis)

Gradient

Key vocabulary

gradient: a measure of the steepness of a line.
$$\text{Gradient} = \frac{\text{change in } y}{\text{change in } x}.$$
***x*-intercept**: the point where a line crosses the x-axis when $y = 0$.
***y*-intercept**: the point where a line crosses the y-axis when $x = 0$.

The gradient is a measure of how steep a line is.

It is the **vertical** distance travelled divided by the **horizontal** distance travelled as you move from left to right along the line.

$$\text{Gradient} = \frac{\text{vertical 'rise'}}{\text{horizontal run}} = \frac{\text{difference in } y\text{-values}}{\text{difference in } x\text{-values}}$$

If the 'rise' is upward, the gradient will be positive.
If the 'rise' is downward, the gradient will be negative.

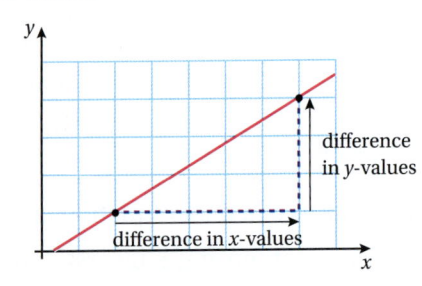

18 Straight-line graphs

Calculating the gradient from a graph

The graph of the linear equation $y = 2x + 4$ has been plotted using the coordinates (1, 6), (0, 4), (−4, −4).

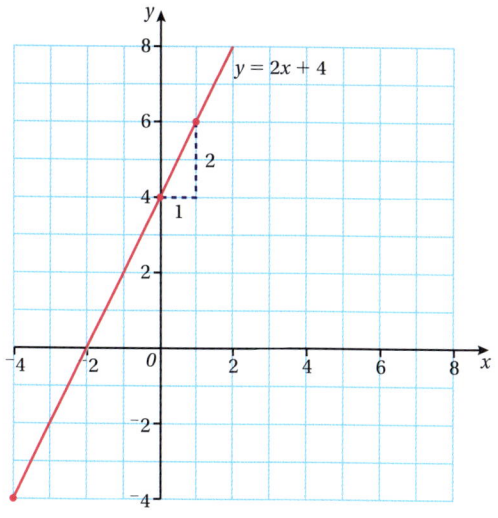

A right-angled triangle has been drawn between the points (1, 6) and (0, 4); the vertical height of the triangle is the same as the difference in y-values and the horizontal length of the triangle is the same as the difference in x-values. You can use these to calculate the gradient.

$$\text{Gradient} = \frac{\text{difference in } y\text{-values}}{\text{difference in } x\text{-values}} = \frac{2}{1} = 2.$$

A gradient of 2 means that for every one unit the graph moves to the right, it moves up two units; when a graph slopes **up** as you move from left to right it is said to have a **positive** gradient.

When a graph slopes **down** as you move from left to right, it has a **negative** gradient.

WORKED EXAMPLE 2

Calculate the gradient of each line.

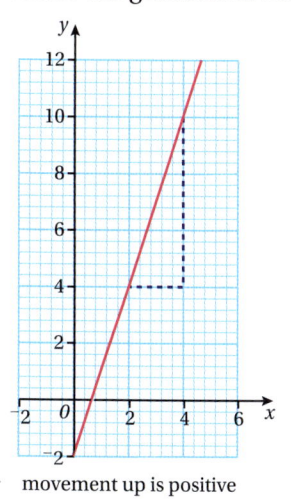

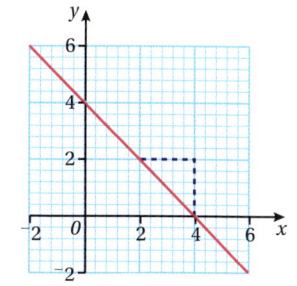

a movement up is positive

b movement down is negative

> **Tip**
>
> **Be careful** to check the scale on each axis when calculating the difference in x- and y-values. The vertical rise might be two squares but if each square represents two units, then the rise is four units, not two.

a $\text{Gradient} = \frac{\text{difference in } y\text{-values}}{\text{difference in } x\text{-values}}$
$= \frac{6}{2}$
$= 3$

Using the scale on the y-axis, work out the length of the vertical line of the right-angled triangle; this is the difference in y-values. Using the scale on the x-axis, work out the horizontal length of the triangle; this is the difference in x-values. As you move from the first point to the second, the graph is moving up so the gradient is positive.

Continues on next page …

Find answers at: cambridge.org/ukschools/gcsemaths-studentbookanswers

b Gradient = $\dfrac{\text{difference in } y\text{-values}}{\text{difference in } x\text{-values}}$

$= \dfrac{-2}{2}$

$= -1$

> Use the right-angled triangle to work out the differences as before. As you move from the first point to the second point, the graph is moving down, so the gradient is negative.

Calculating the gradient using two points

You can represent any two points on the line algebraically as (x_1, y_1) and (x_2, y_2).

If you look at the graph, you can see

difference in y-values $= y_2 - y_1$

difference in x-values $= x_2 - x_1$

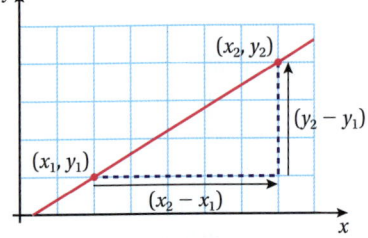

This means the gradient can be calculated as follows

Gradient $= \dfrac{\text{difference in } y\text{-values}}{\text{difference in } x\text{-values}} = \dfrac{(y_2 - y_1)}{(x_2 - x_1)}$

In turn, this means that if you know the coordinates of two points on a straight-line graph you can use them to find the gradient without drawing the graph.

WORKED EXAMPLE 3

Find the gradient of the straight line that passes through the points (1, 4) and (3, 8).

gradient $= \dfrac{(y_2 - y_1)}{(x_2 - x_1)}$

> Substitute the x- and y-values from the coordinates into the formula.

$= \dfrac{(8 - 4)}{(3 - 1)} = \dfrac{4}{2}$

$= 2$

The gradient of the line that passes through the points (1, 4) and (3, 8) is 2.

EXERCISE 18B

1 Calculate the gradient of each line.

a

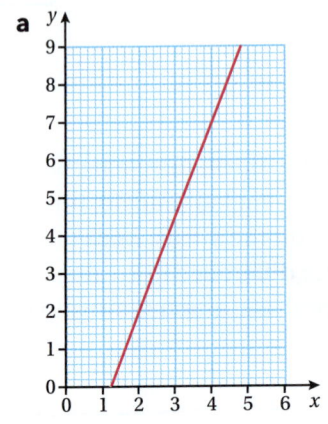

b

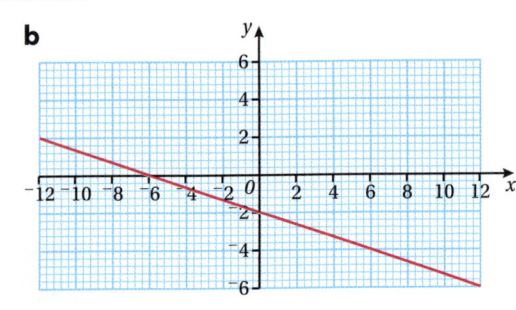

c, **d** (graphs)

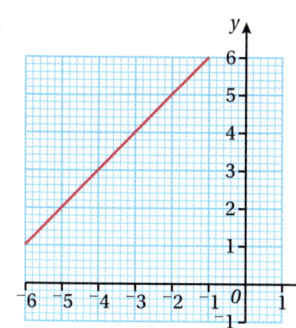

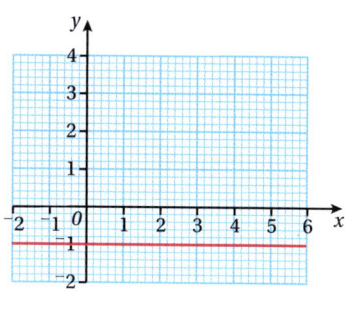

2 Plot the graph of $y = 2x + 3$ and calculate its gradient.

3 Calculate the gradient of each line.

Leave your answer as a fraction in lowest terms if necessary.

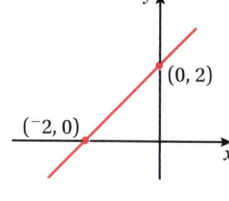

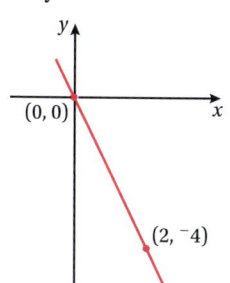

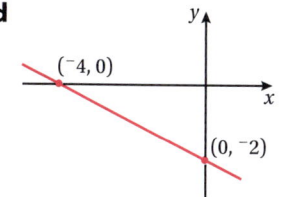

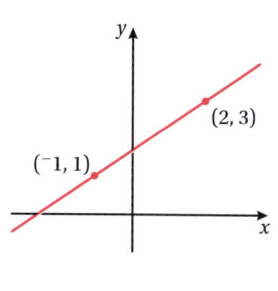

a (0, 0) and (1, 3)

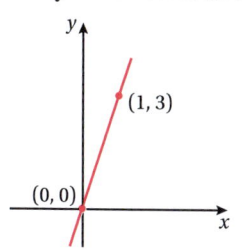

b (−2, 0) and (0, 2)

c (0, 0) and (2, −4)

d (−4, 0) and (0, −2)

e (−1, 1) and (2, 3)

f (−1, 3) and (3, −2)

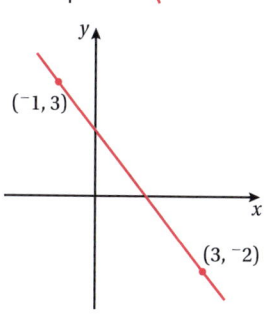

4 Find the gradient of the line that passes through points A and B in each case.

a A(1, 2) and B(3, 8)
b A(0, 6) and B(3, 9)
c A(−1, −4) and B(−3, 2)
d A(3, 5) and B(7, 12)

The x-intercept and y-intercept

The **x-intercept** is where the line crosses the x-axis, and the **y-intercept** is where the graph crosses the y-axis.

Look at the coordinates of these points.

All points on the x-axis have a y-value of 0. All points on the y-axis have an x-value of 0.

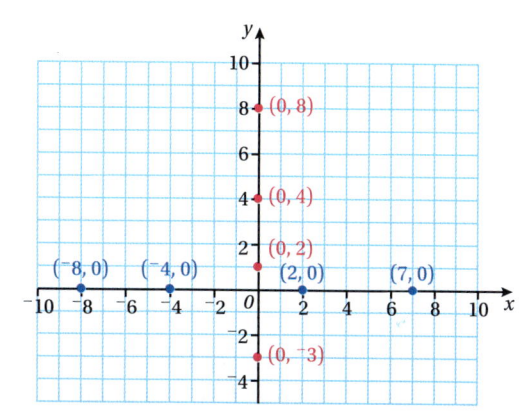

Find answers at: cambridge.org/ukschools/gcsemaths-studentbookanswers

Now consider these two lines.

Line A has an *x*-intercept at (2, 0) and a *y*-intercept at (0, -1).

Line B has an *x*-intercept at (-1, 0) and a *y*-intercept at (0, 1).

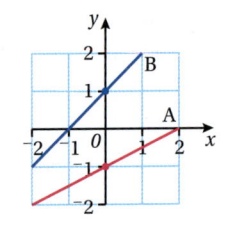

This shows that you can identify an *x*- or *y*-intercept from its (*x*, *y*) coordinates:

- when the *x*-value is zero, the corresponding *y*-value is the *y*-intercept.
- when the *y*-value is zero, the corresponding *x*-value is the *x*-intercept.

These points are important and you will use them to sketch graphs and to find the equation of a graph.

The general form of a linear equation

When a linear equation is in the general form $y = mx + c$, it is known as the **gradient-intercept** form.

> **Tip**
>
> If a linear equation is not written in the gradient-intercept form you can rearrange it so that it is; see Chapter 8 if you need a reminder on how to rearrange equations.

Tip

You learnt about coefficients and constants in Chapter 7.

This form tells us the value of the:

- **gradient** – the **coefficient** *m* is the gradient of the graph.
- ***y*-intercept** – the **constant** *c* is the *y*-intercept.

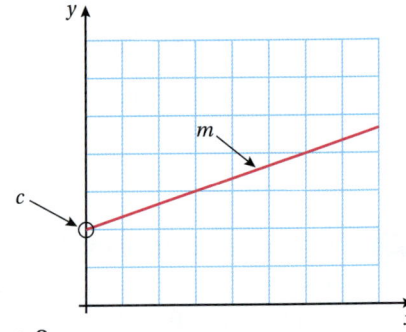

To demonstrate, look at the graph of $y = -x + 2$.

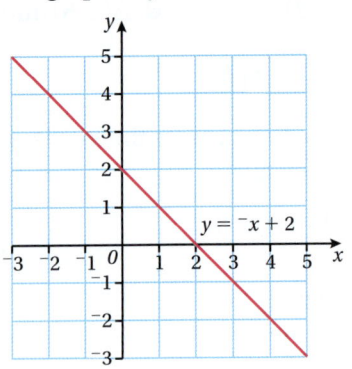

Tip

A gradient of -1 means that for every one unit the graph moves to the right it moves one unit down.

From the graph, the gradient of the line is $\frac{1}{-1} = -1$.

The *y*-intercept is 2.

In the equation $y = -x + 2$, the coefficient of *x* is -1 and the constant is 2.

This means that for any straight-line graph you can write its equation in the form $y = mx + c$ if you know the gradient and the *y*-intercept.

WORKED EXAMPLE 4

Write the equation of each line.

a

b A straight line with a gradient of -2 and a y-intercept of 3.

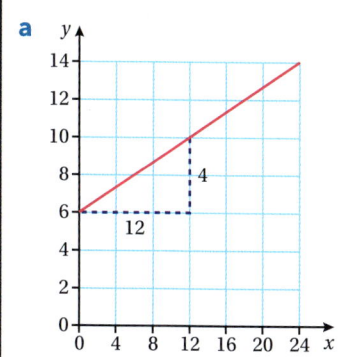

a

> Draw in the right-angled triangle to work out the difference in y-values and the difference in x-values.

$$\text{Gradient} = \frac{\text{difference in } y\text{-values}}{\text{difference in } x\text{-values}}$$

$$= \frac{4}{12} = \frac{1}{3}$$

$c = 6$

y-intercept = (0, 6) so $c = 6$.

The equation of the line is $y = \frac{1}{3}x + 6$

> Calculate the gradient (m) and read off the y-intercept (c).

> Substitute the values into the gradient-intercept form of the equation: $y = mx + c$

$x = 24$

$y = \frac{1}{3}x + 6$

$= 8 + 6$

$= 14$ ✓

> You can use some points on the line to check your equation works. Substitute the value of x from the coordinate of the point into the equation and see if the resulting y-value matches the coordinate of the point.

b $y = mx + c$

$m = -2, c = 3$

$y = -2x + 3$

> Substitute the given values of m and c into the gradient-intercept form of the equation.

The gradient-intercept form also lets you identify the gradient and y-intercept without having to plot the graph.

GCSE Mathematics for OCR (Foundation)

WORK IT OUT 18.1

Find the gradient and y-intercept of the linear function $y = {}^-2x + 4$.
Do not plot a graph.
Think about which direction the line moves across the page.
Which of the answers below is correct?

Option A	Option B	Option C
$y = {}^-2x + 4$ 2 is the coefficient of x. 4 is the constant. So, the gradient is 2 and the y-intercept is 4. The graph goes up to the right.	$y = {}^-2x + 4$ ${}^-2$ is the coefficient of x. 4 is the constant. So, the gradient is ${}^-2$ and the y-intercept is 4. The graph goes down to the right.	$y = {}^-2x + 4$ ${}^-2$ is the coefficient of x. 4 is the constant. So, the gradient is ${}^-2$ and the y-intercept is 4. The graph goes down to the left.

Finding the equation of the line from points on the line

If you know the gradient and at least one point on the line, you can find the y-intercept of a straight-line graph and therefore write its equation. Substitute the gradient and the x- and y-values of the point into the gradient-intercept form and solve for c.

This also means that you can write the equation if you only know two points on the line; you can use those points to calculate the gradient of the line and then use the gradient and one of the points to solve for c as before.

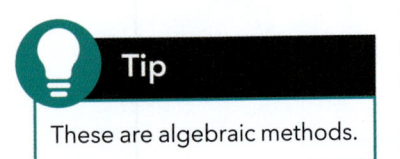

Tip
These are algebraic methods.

WORKED EXAMPLE 5

a Find the equation of the line passing through points $(3, 11)$ and $(6, 7)$.
b Find the equation of a line that has the same gradient as the line $y = \frac{1}{2}x - 3$ and passes through the point $({}^-1, 2)$.

a Gradient $= \dfrac{y_2 - y_1}{x_2 - x_1}$

$= \dfrac{7 - 11}{6 - 3} = \dfrac{{}^-4}{3}$

So, $y = \dfrac{{}^-4}{3}x + c$. *Substitute the calculated gradient into the gradient-intercept form.*

$(6, 7)$ is a point on the line.
So, $7 = \dfrac{{}^-4}{3} \times 6 + c$ *Pick one of the points and substitute the values of x and y into the equation. Solve for c.*
$7 = {}^-8 + c$
$15 = c$
The equation is $y = \dfrac{{}^-4}{3}x + 15$. *Write the equation of the line.*

b $y = mx + c$ *You are told that the line has the same gradient as the line $y = \frac{1}{2}x - 3$, so you know that the equation you are trying to find will contain $m = \frac{1}{2}$. Substitute the values you know into the equation to find the value of c.*
$y = \dfrac{1}{2}x + c$
$2 = (\dfrac{1}{2} \times {}^-1) + c$
$c = \dfrac{5}{2}$
The equation is $y = \dfrac{1}{2}x + \dfrac{5}{2}$. *Write the equation of the line.*

286

Using the gradient-intercept form to sketch a graph

You can use the gradient-intercept form of a linear equation to **sketch** its graph without plotting values from a table.

Key vocabulary

sketch: draw a basic graph showing the direction, gradient and y-intercept; it is not drawn by plotting a table of values.

WORKED EXAMPLE 6

Sketch the graph of $y = 4x + 4$

$y = 4x + 4$
y-intercept = 4
$m = 4 = \frac{4}{1}$

From the equation you know that the gradient, m, is 4 and the y-intercept is 4.

You know that the gradient = $\frac{\text{vertical rise}}{\text{horizontal run}}$ so you can use m to work out the rise and run.

Draw a pair of axes and plot the y-intercept at (0, 4). Then use the rise of 4 and run of 1 to plot another point at (1, 8). Join the two points and draw a line that passes through them.

Using the x-intercept and y-intercept to sketch a graph

If you know where the graph cuts the axes you can sketch the graph of the line. You can find the x-intercept by substituting $y = 0$ into the equation and you can find the y-intercept by substituting $x = 0$ into the equation.

WORKED EXAMPLE 7

Find the x- and y-intercepts and use them to sketch the graph of $y + 2x = 6$.

First find the intercepts.
when $x = 0$
$y + 2(0) = 6$
The y-intercept is (0, 6).
when $y = 0$
$0 + 2x = 6$
$2x = 6$
$x = 3$
The x-intercept is (3, 0).

Plot the two points and join them to draw the graph. Label the line.

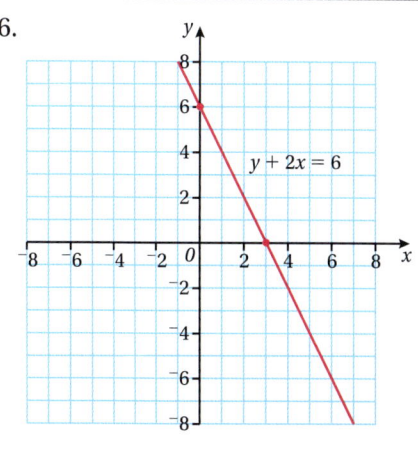

Find answers at: cambridge.org/ukschools/gcsemaths-studentbookanswers

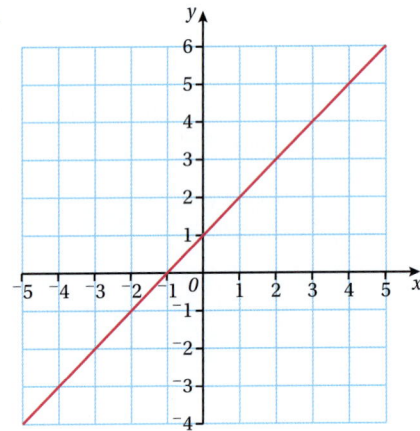

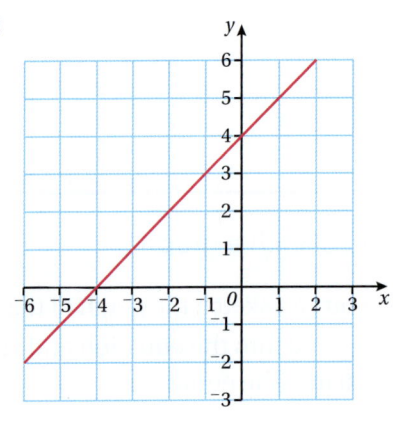

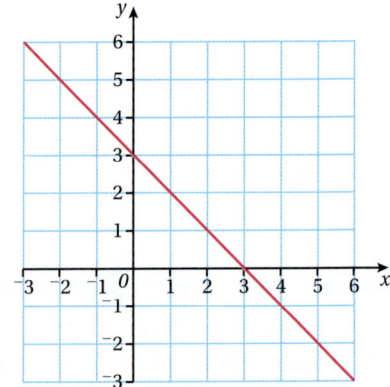

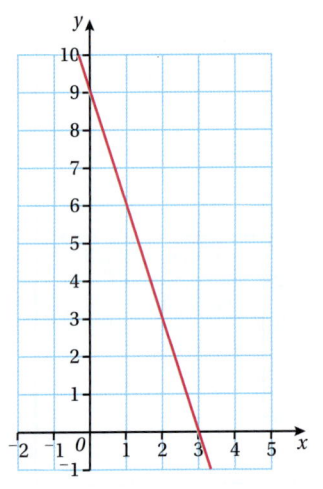

This method of sketching graphs is called the intercept-intercept method. It is useful when the equation is in the general form $ax + by = c$. You don't need to rearrange the equation to find the intercepts.

EXERCISE 18C

1 **Plot** the graph of each function.

Write a description of each one, giving the y-intercept and gradient, and stating if the gradient is positive or negative.

a $y = 3x - 2$
b $y = {}^-2x + 3$
c $y = \frac{1}{2}x - 1$
d $y = x - 1$

2 Rearrange each equation so it is in the gradient-intercept form $(y = mx + c)$.

Sketch each of the lines.

a $3x - 2y = 6$
b $6x + 2y + 10 = 0$
c $3y - 6x + 12 = 0$
d $2y - x + 18 = 0$
e $6y - 2x + 18 = 0$
f $2x - 3y + 12 = 0$

3 Match each graph to the correct linear equation.

a $y = x + 1$
b $y = 3 - x$
c $y = 9 - 3x$
d $y = x + 4$
e $y = {}^-2x + 20$

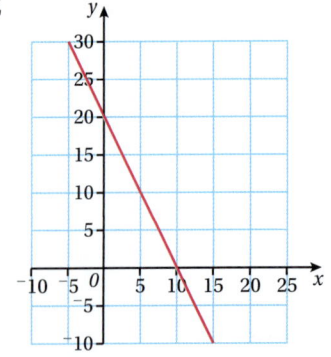

4 Sketch the graph of each line by calculating the coordinates of the x- and y-intercepts.

Write down the gradient of each graph.

   a $2x + y = 4$ **b** $3x + 4y = 12$ **c** $x + 2y = 1$ **d** $3x + y = 2$

   e $x - y = 4$ **f** $x - y = 1$ **g** $4x - 2y = 8$ **h** $3x - 4y = 12$

5 For each equation, find c if the given point is on the line.

   a $y = 3x + c$ (1, 5)   **b** $y = 6x + c$ (1, 2)

   c $y = {}^-2x + c$ ($^-3$, $^-3$)   **d** $y = \frac{3}{4}x + c$ (4, $^-5$)

6 Find the equation of the line passing through each pair of points.

   a (0, 0) and (6, $^-2$)   **b** (0, 0) and ($^-2$, $^-3$)

   c ($^-2$, $^-5$) and ($^-4$, $^-1$)   **d** ($^-2$, 9) and (3, $^-1$)

7 **a** A line passes through the point (2, 4) and has gradient 2. Find the y-coordinate of the point on the line when $x = 3$.

   b A line passes through the point (4, 8) and has gradient $\frac{1}{2}$. Find the y-coordinate of the point on the line when $x = 8$.

   c A line passes through the point ($^-1$, 6) and has gradient $^-1$. Find the y-coordinate of the point on the line when $x = 4$.

> **Tip**
>
> Find the equation of the line before you try to find the coordinates of points on it.

Section 3: Parallel lines

These three graphs are parallel to each other.

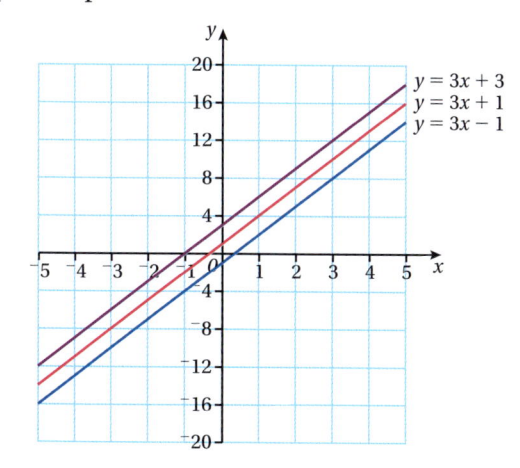

> **Tip**
>
> You learnt about parallel and perpendicular lines in Chapter 5.

If you look at the equations of each line you can see that they all have the same gradient.

Lines with equal gradients are parallel to each other.

These graphs are members of a family of parallel lines with a gradient of positive 3. Each line in the family can be defined by the equation $y = 3x + c$.

If equations written in the form $y = mx + c$ have identical values for m, they have the same gradient and therefore they are parallel lines.

Find answers at: cambridge.org/ukschools/gcsemaths-studentbookanswers

Problem-solving framework

Lucia is helping her classmates by checking their work.
Who has correctly grouped together 2 sets of parallel lines and who hasn't?

Tip

In mathematics one way to prove a statement is true is to follow a series of statements that end in a valid conclusion. You can use this method to prove that lines are parallel.

Carlos
$y = 4 - 2x$
$y + 2x = 5$
$y = {}^-2x + 1$

$y = 3x + 1$
$y - 3x = {}^-1$
$y = 2 + 3x$

Jonathan
$y = \frac{1}{3}x + 1$
$3y + x = 1$
$y = 3x + 1$

$2y = x + 1$
$2y - x = 3$
$y = \frac{1}{2}x - 1$

Monika
$y = x - 1$
$y + x = 1$
$y = 1 - x$

$x = y + 1$
$x - y = 1$
$x = 1 - y$

Steps for approaching a problem-solving question	What you would do for this example
Step 1: Draw a diagram?	A diagram might take too long, especially if you are working with many different lines.
Step 2: Identify what you have to do.	Determine who has and hasn't correctly grouped parallel lines.
Step 3: Test the problem with what you know.	If lines are parallel they will have an identical value for the gradient. The gradient is the coefficient of x in the equation (the value of m).
Step 4: What maths can you do?	Rearrange the equations so they are all in the form $y = mx + c$ to compare the gradients (m). If there are identical values for m then Lucia's classmates have correctly shown/proved the lines are parallel.
Step 5: Set your working and solutions out clearly. Check your working and make sure your answer is reasonable.	**Carlos** In $y = mx + c$ form Gradient $y = 4 - 2x$ ${}^-2$ $y + 2x = 5$ $y = 5 - 2x$ ${}^-2$ $y = {}^-2x + 1$ ${}^-2$ Gradient of each line is ${}^-2$. $y = 3x + 1$ 3 $y - 3x = {}^-1$ $y = 3x - 1$ 3 $y = 2 + 3x$ 3 Gradient of each line is 3. Carlos has correctly grouped parallel lines as each group has the same gradient.

Continues on next page …

	Jonathan In $y = mx + c$ form Gradient
	$y = \frac{1}{3}x + 1$ $\frac{1}{3}$
	$3y + x = 1$ $y = \frac{1}{3} - \frac{1}{3}x$ $-\frac{1}{3}$
	$y = 3x + 1$ 3
	The lines do not all have the same gradient.
	Gradient
	$2y = x + 1$ $y = \frac{1}{2}x + \frac{1}{2}$ $\frac{1}{2}$
	$2y - x = 3$ $y = \frac{3}{2} + \frac{1}{2}x$ $\frac{1}{2}$
	$y = \frac{1}{2}x - 1$ $\frac{1}{2}$
	The lines do have the same gradient of $\frac{1}{2}$.
	Jonathan correctly grouped one group but not the other.
	Monika In $y = mx + c$ form Gradient
	$y = x - 1$ 1
	$y + x = 1$ $y = 1 - x$ $^-1$
	$y = 1 - x$ $^-1$
	$x = y + 1$ $y = x - 1$ 1
	$x - y = 1$ $y = x - 1$ 1
	$x = 1 - y$ $y = 1 - x$ $^-1$
	Monika did not correctly group either group.
	Checked answers are accurate ✓
	They are reasonable because it is easy to see where her classmates could have gone wrong, mistakenly thinking that a positive and negative gradient of the same number is the same gradient.
Step 6: Check that you have answered the question.	Yes. You state who has and hasn't grouped the lines correctly and have proved your answer.

EXERCISE 18D

1 Identify the parallel lines in each set.

   a $y = 3x - 5$ $y = x - 5$ $3x + 7 = y$ $6x - 2y = {}^-1$

   b $y = 2x + 3$ $y = 3x + 2$ $2x - y = {}^-6$ $2y = x + 3$ $y = 2x - 3$

   c $y + 3 = x$ $x + y = 3$ $y = 3x - 1$ $y + x = 8$

2 **a** If $y = (2a - 3)x + 1$ is parallel to $y = 3x - 4$, find the value of a.

    b If $y = (3a + 2)x - 1$ is parallel to $y = ax - 4$, find the value of a.

GCSE Mathematics for OCR (Foundation)

③ Find the equation of the blue line.

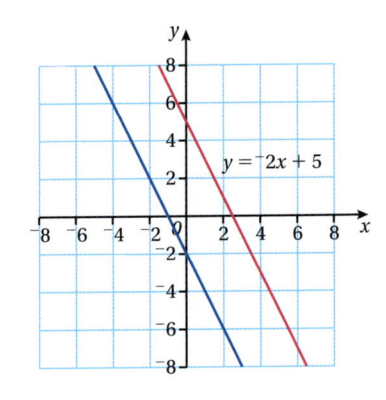

(graph showing $y = -2x + 5$ in red and a blue line)

④ The vertices (corners) of a quadrilateral have coordinates A(1, 6), B(3, 14), C(15, 16) and D(13, 8).
   a Find the gradient of the line AB.   b Find the equation of the line AB.
   c Prove that ABCD is a parallelogram.

⑤ Investigate lines that are parallel to the axes.
   How are the equations for these graphs different to those for slanted graphs? Why?

Section 4: Working with straight-line graphs

You need to be able to interpret straight-line graphs.

Interpreting graphs means you can:
- determine the equation of the graph.
- calculate the gradient of a line using given information.
- use graphs to model and solve problems, including solving simultaneous equations. This means that you can answer questions by reading the correct information off a graph and know what it means.

> **Tip**
> You learnt about the properties of quadrilaterals in Chapter 5.

> **Tip**
> You learnt how to solve simultaneous equations in Chapter 8; remember that the point of intersection between two graphs is the simultaneous solution to the equation of each line.

> **Tip**
> You will learn more about interpreting graphs in Chapter 34 in the context of direct and indirect proportion.

WORKED EXAMPLE 8

a Sketch the graphs of $x + 3y = 6$ and $y = 2x - 5$.
b What are the coordinates of the point of intersection of the two graphs?
c Show by substitution that these values are the simultaneous solution to the equations $x + 3y = 6$ and $y = 2x - 5$.

a $x + 3y = 6$
$y = 2 - \frac{1}{3}x$
Let $x = 0$
$y = 2 - \left(\frac{1}{3} \times 0\right)$
$y = 2$
y-intercept $(0, 2)$
Let $y = 0$
$0 = 2 - \frac{1}{3}x$
$\frac{1}{3}x = 2$
$x = 6$

Sketch the graphs using your preferred method.

Here, the first graph has been sketched by plotting the intercepts and drawing a straight line through them. Rearrange the first equation into the form $y = mx + c$. For both equations: substitute $x = 0$ into the equation to find the y-intercept; then substitute $y = 0$ into the equation to find the x-intercept.

Continues on next page …

x-intercept (6, 0)
y = 2x − 5
y-intercept = −5
gradient = 2

Here, the graph has been sketched using the gradient and the y-intercept.

b The point of intersection is (3, 1).

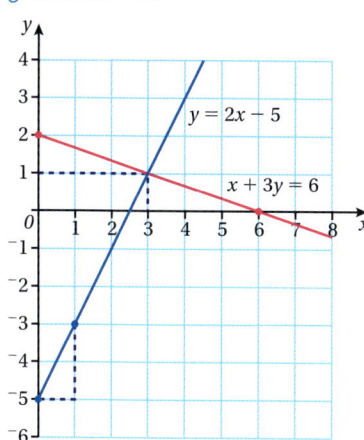

Read this from the graph; the point of intersection is the point at which the two graphs cross each other.

c Let x = 3 and y = 1
Substitute in x + 3y = 6:
3 + 3(1) = 6.
Substitute in y = 2x − 5:
1 = 2(3) − 5
1 = 6 − 5
1 = 1

Use the substitution method to solve the simultaneous equation. See Chapter 8 for a reminder if you need to.

The solutions work for both equations.

EXERCISE 18E

1 This table of values has been generated from a function.

x	−2	−1	0	1	2	3
y	−4	−3	−2	−1	0	1

a Which of these functions would produce the values in the table?
   $y = -x + 2$ $y = 2x - 1$ $y = -2x + 4$ $y = x - 2$
b Plot the graph of this function.
c Draw a line parallel to your graph which crosses the y-axis at (0, 3) and write its equation.

2 Find and write in gradient-intercept form $y = mx + c$ equations which satisfy the following statements.

a A linear equation that does not pass through the first quadrant.
b Two lines whose gradients differ by 2.
c An equation of a straight line that passes through (2, 3) and has a gradient of 3.

Find answers at: cambridge.org/ukschools/gcsemaths-studentbookanswers

3   Calculate the gradient of the line shown in the diagram and write down the equation of the line.

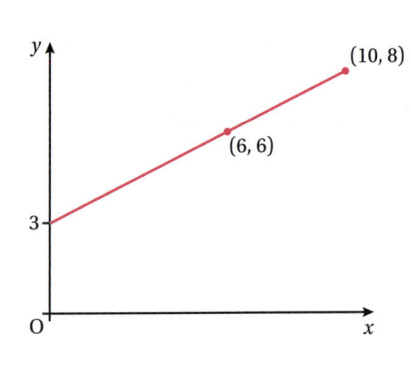

4   Sketch each of the following graphs.
    a $y = 3x + 2$
    b $y = -2x - 1$
    c $2y = x + 8$
    d $x - y = -3$
    e $y + 4 = x$
    f $3x + 4y = 12$

5   Find the equation of the line that passes through each pair of points.
    a (5, 6) and (−4, 10)
    b (3, 4) and (−2, 8)
    c (−2, 6) and (1, 10)

6   a Find the equation of the line with gradient −4 that passes through the point (0, −6).
    b Find the equation of the line with gradient −4 that passes through the point (3, 8).
    c Find the equation of the line that passes through the points (−4, 8) and (−6, −2).

7   The line passing through the points (−1, 6) and (4, b) has gradient −2. Find the value of b.

8   a Is the gradient of this straight line 2 or −2? Write down the equation of the line.

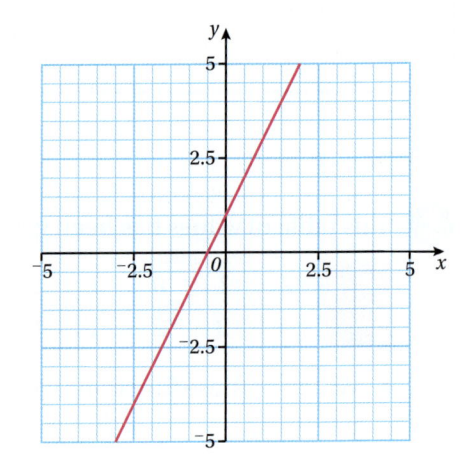

    b Write the equation of this line.

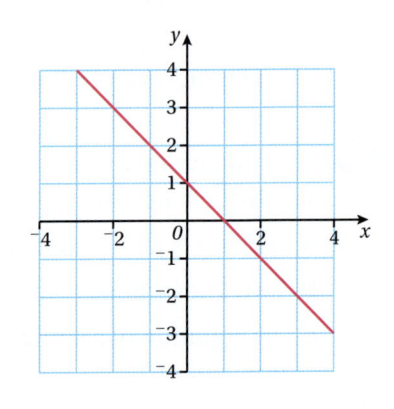

9 Find the equations of the four straight lines that would intersect to make this rhombus.

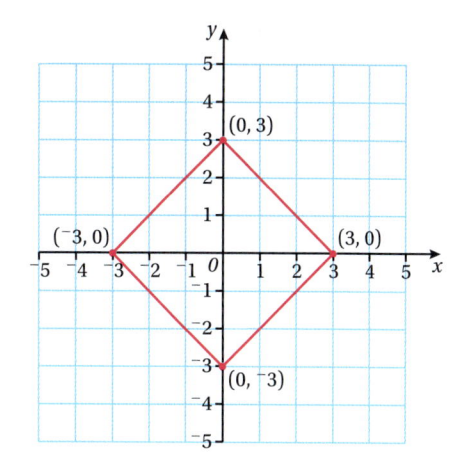

Checklist of learning and understanding

Plotting linear functions
- The graph of a linear function is a called a straight-line graph.
- You can use the equation of a line to generate a table of x- and y-values.
- Choose any three (x, y) values, plot them and join the points to draw the graph.

Features of straight-line graphs
- When a linear equation is in the general form $y = mx + c$, it is known as the **gradient-intercept** form, where m is the gradient and c is the point where the line cuts the y-axis.
- You can find the equation of a straight line if you have one of the following:
  ○ the gradient and the y-intercept
  ○ two points on the line
  ○ one point and the gradient.
- You can sketch graphs using the gradient and y-intercept or using the x- and y-intercepts.

Parallel lines
- Parallel lines have the same gradient so the value of m is equal when the equations are written in the form $y = mx + c$.

Chapter review

1 Draw these lines on the same grid.
  a $y = x + 1$
  b $y = 2x + 5$
  c $y + 2 = 4x$

2 Write the equation of each line.
  a
  b

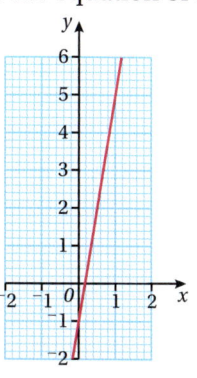

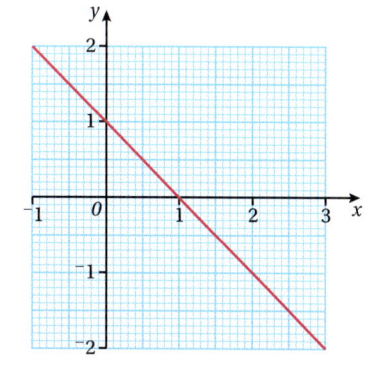

For additional questions on the topics in this chapter, visit GCSE Mathematics Online.

Find answers at: cambridge.org/ukschools/gcsemaths-studentbookanswers

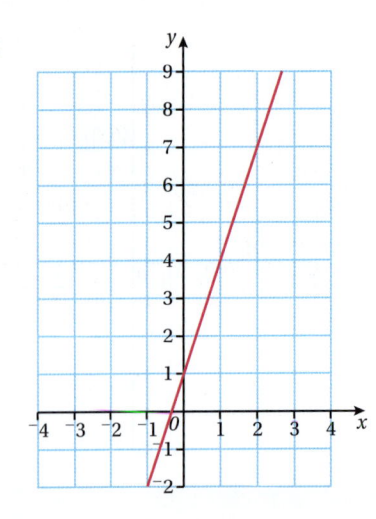

c   d

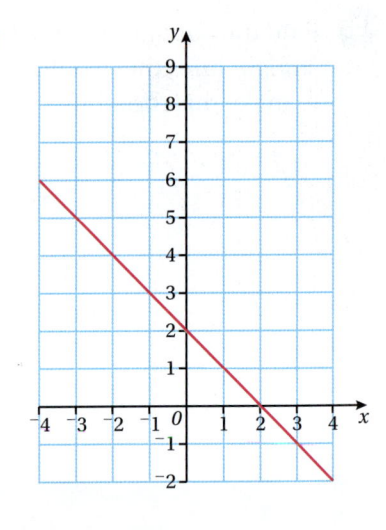

3. Which of the following lines are parallel to each other?

   a $y = \frac{1}{2}x + 1$ b $2y - x = 4$ c $y = 2x - 5$ d $y = 0.5x + 3$

4. Here are six equations of straight lines, each labelled with a letter.

A	B	C
$y = 4x - 7$	$y = 3x + 14$	$y = 2x + 5$

D	E	F
$y = {}^-3x + 1$	$y = 14x - 7$	$y = 4x + 3$

   Choose the correct letters to make each statement true.

   Line _____ is the steepest line.

   Lines _____ and _____ are parallel.

   Lines _____ and _____ meet on the y-axis. *(3 marks)*

   © OCR 2013

5. Find the equation of a line parallel to $y = \frac{1}{2}x + 1$ passing through the point $(^-1, 2)$.

6. Find the equation of the line that passes through the two points $(2, 4)$ and $(6, {}^-12)$.

7. a Plot a graph of the two lines $y = 3x - 2$ and $y + 2x = 3$ and find their point of intersection.

   b Show by substitution that this is the simultaneous solution to the two equations.

19 Graphs of equations and functions

In this chapter you will learn how to …
- plot and sketch graphs of quadratic functions.
- identify the main features of graphs of quadratic functions and equations.
- plot and sketch other polynomials and reciprocal functions.

For more resources relating to this chapter, visit GCSE Mathematics Online.

Using mathematics: real-life applications

Graphs are used to process information, make predictions and generalise patterns from sets of data. The nature of the data and the relationship between values determines the shape and form of the graph.

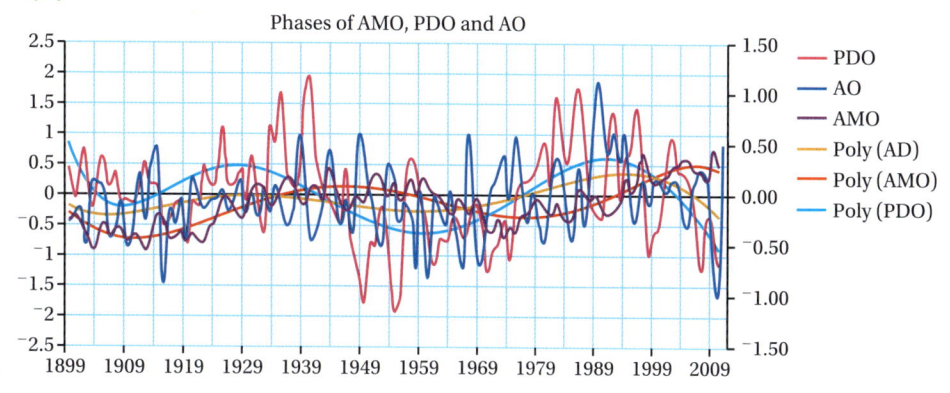

Phases of AMO, PDO and AO
— PDO
— AO
— AMO
— Poly (AD)
— Poly (AMO)
— Poly (PDO)

"I study the earth using gravity, magnetic, electrical, and seismic methods. I used this graph in a study of the Pacific and Atlantic Oceans. I need to be able to understand equations and recognise the features of graphs to understand and interpret it."

(Geophysicist)

Before you start …

Ch 18	You should be able to interpret equations of linear graphs.	**1** For the graph $y = 3x + 1$: **a** identify the gradient of the graph. **b** give the coordinates of the y-intercept. **c** find the value of x when $y = {-}14$. **d** show that it is parallel to the graph $2y - 6x = {-}4$.
Ch 4, 18	You must be able to generate a table of values from a function.	**2** Given $y = 3x^2 + 1$, complete the table of values. | x | -2 | -1 | 0 | 1 | 2 | |---|---|---|---|---|---| | y | | | | | |
Ch 8	You need to be able to find the roots of a quadratic equation algebraically.	**3** What are the roots of: **a** $x^2 + 2x - 8 = 0$? **b** $x^2 + 5x = {-}4$?
Ch 2	You should be able to work with cubed numbers and cube roots.	**4** Evaluate. **a** 2^3 **b** 4^3 **c** $\sqrt[3]{125}$ **d** $\sqrt[3]{-27}$

Find answers at: cambridge.org/ukschools/gcsemaths-studentbookanswers

GCSE Mathematics for OCR (Foundation)

Assess your starting point using the Launchpad

STEP 1

① How many points do you need to plot the graph of a linear equation?

② Sketch the graph of $y = 2x + 1$.

GO TO
Section 1:
Review of linear graphs

STEP 2

③
a Is this the graph of $y = x^2 + 1$ or $y = {}^-x^2 + 1$?
b How can you tell?
c Is the turning point a maximum or a minimum?
d What are the coordinates of the vertex?
e For what values of x is $y = 0$?

GO TO
Section 2:
Graphs of quadratic functions

STEP 3

④
a What type of equation is $y = x^3$?
b How many points do you need to plot the graph of $y = x^3$?

GO TO
Section 3:
Graphs of other polynomials and reciprocals

STEP 4

⑤ Given $y = \dfrac{1}{x}$:
a explain what happens when $x = 0$.
b what happens to the value of y as the value of x increases?
c when $x = 60$ what is the value of y?

GO TO
Section 4:
Plotting, sketching and recognising graphs

GO TO
Chapter review

19 Graphs of equations and functions

Section 1: Review of linear graphs

In Chapter 18 you learnt how to plot, sketch and interpret linear graphs. You also learnt that the general form of a linear function is $y = mx + c$, where m is the gradient of the graph and c is the y-intercept.

In this section you will review some of that work and learn to recognise line graphs when the general equation looks slightly different from the form $y = mx + c$.

Graphs in the form of $y = mx$

In the equation $y = mx + c$, the value of c tells you where the graph cuts the y-axis. When there is no value of c in the equation you get a graph in the form of $y = mx$.

These graphs pass through the origin (0, 0) because when $y = 0$, x must be 0. Any linear equation of the form $y = mx$ passes through the origin with a gradient of m.

The graphs of $y = mx$ and $y = {}^-mx$ are shown here.

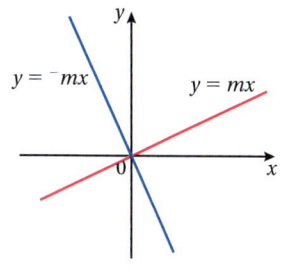

If $m = 1$ the equation is written as $y = mx$. If $m = {}^-1$, the equation is written as $y = {}^-x$.

$y = x$ is the line that passes through the origin going up from left to right at an angle of 45°.

$y = {}^-x$ is the line that passes through the origin going down from left to right making an angle of 45°.

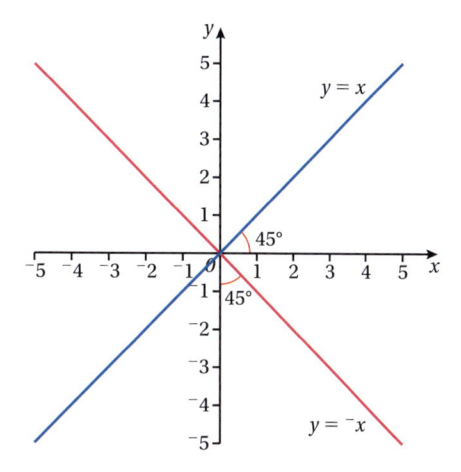

Sketching $y = mx$ ...	Examples	Notes
If m is greater than 1.	$y = 3x$, $y = 7x$	The line still passes through the origin but is steeper than $y = x$.
If m is a value between 0 and 1.	$y = \frac{1}{2}x$, $y = \frac{1}{5}x$	The line still passes through the origin but is less steep than $y = x$.
If m is a negative value.	$y = {}^-3x$, $y = {}^-\frac{1}{2}x$ $y = {}^-3x$, $y = {}^-\frac{1}{2}x$	The line still passes through the origin, but will go down from left to right like $y = {}^-x$.

Find answers at: cambridge.org/ukschools/gcsemaths-studentbookanswers

Vertical and horizontal lines

The equations of some lines are in the form of $x = a$ or $y = b$. (Where a and b are constant values.) Equations in this form tell you that there is only one value of x or y for each graph.

Consider the equation $x = 7$.

The graph of this equation passes through the point (7, 0). It also passes through all points on the grid with an x-coordinate of 7. For example: (7, ⁻4), (7, ⁻1), (7, 3), (7, 50).

Now consider the equation $y = 7$.

This graph would need to pass through the point (0, 7) and all other points with a y-coordinate of 7. For example: (3, 7), (⁻2, 7), (7, 7) and (50, 7).

The graphs of $x = 7$ and $y = 7$ are shown here.

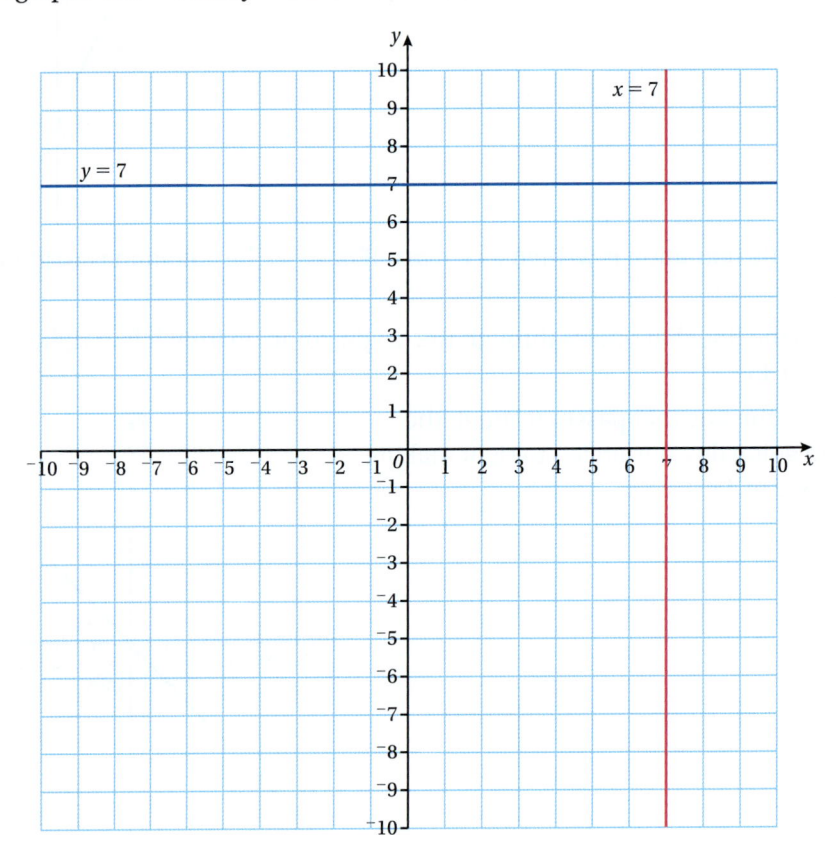

In general:
- Any graph in the form of $x = a$ is parallel to the y-axis and passes through a on the x-axis.
- Any graph in the form of $y = b$ is parallel to the x-axis and passes through b on the y-axis.
- The values of a and b can be positive or negative.

Tip

You should be able to recognise and sketch the graphs of any line in the form $x = a$ or $y = b$.

The axes themselves can be described using equations.

The x-axis is the line $y = 0$ and the y-axis is the line $x = 0$.

EXERCISE 19A

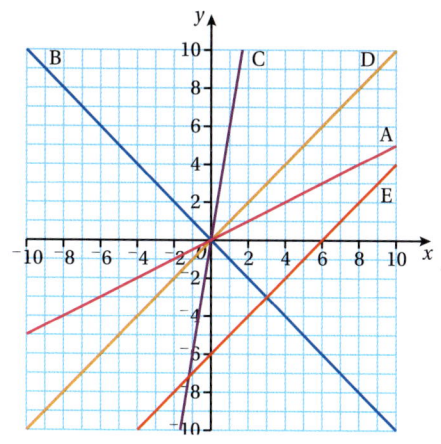

1

Write down which of the graphs on the grid above can be described in each of the following ways. There may be more than one correct answer.

a The x-coordinate of each point is equal to the y-coordinate.

b The gradient is negative.

c The general form of the graph is $y = mx$.

d The y-coordinate is 6 times the x-coordinate.

e The y-coordinate is 6 less than the x-coordinate.

2 Give the equation of each line on the grid in Question **1**.

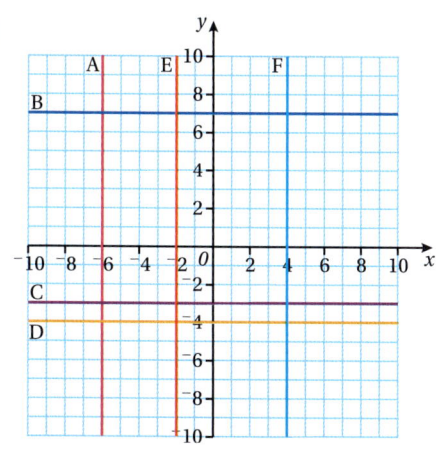

3

a Write down the equation of each line A to F.

b Determine the equation of the line parallel to D which passes through point (0, 2).

4 Draw the following graphs on a grid numbered from $^-6$ to 6 on each axis.

a $x = ^-3$ **b** $y = 5$ **c** $y = ^-3$ **d** $x = 5$

5 What type of quadrilateral is enclosed by the four lines you drew in Question **4**.

Give reasons for your answer.

6 a Write the equations of two lines that would divide the quadrilateral formed in Question **4** into two identical rectangles.

Find answers at: cambridge.org/ukschools/gcsemaths-studentbookanswers

GCSE Mathematics for OCR (Foundation)

b What is the mathematical name for lines that divide shapes into two identical halves?

c It is possible to draw two other lines that divide the quadrilateral into two equal halves.
  i Draw these lines on your diagram.
  ii Determine the equation of each line.

7 Plot the graphs of
a $y + 2x = 6$
b $3x - 9y = 21$
c $x - y = {}^-4$

Section 2: Graphs of quadratic functions

You saw in Chapters 7 and 8 that a quadratic expression has the form $ax^2 + bx + c$, where $a \neq 0$.

The graph of a quadratic function is a curve called a **parabola**.

The simplest equation of a parabola is $y = x^2$.

This is the graph of $y = x^2$.

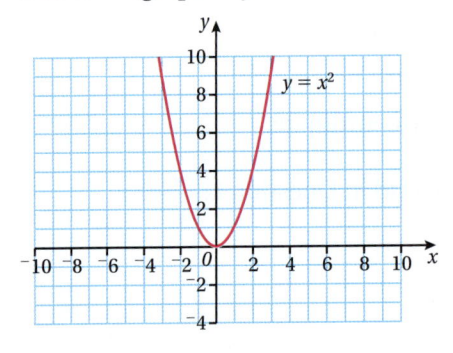

You can plot the graph of a quadratic function by drawing up a table of values.

> **Tip**
>
> Equations in the form $ax + by = c$ can be rearranged into the general form $y = mx + c$ to help you calculate the (x, y) points and plot the linear graph.

> **Key vocabulary**
>
> **parabola**: the symmetrical curve produced by the graph of a quadratic function.

> **Did you know?**
>
> The path of moving objects, such as this basketball, can be modelled by a parabola.

> **Tip**
>
> Remember that the square of a negative number is positive. For example, when $x = {}^-3$: $({}^-3)^2 + 2 = 9 + 2 = 11$.

WORKED EXAMPLE 1

Plot the graph of the function $y = x^2 + 2$.

x	-3	-2	-1	0	1	2	3
y	11	6	3	2	3	6	11

Draw up a table of x- and y-values by substituting values of x into the equation. To make the graph as accurate as possible, include at least five points (the more the better), and both positive and negative values of x.

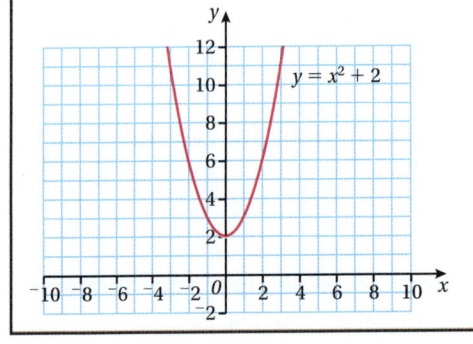

Plot all the points on a grid and join them to produce a smooth curved graph that extends through and beyond the points you have plotted. Label the graph.

302

EXERCISE 19B

1 **a** Complete a table of values of x from -3 to 3 for each equation.
Draw the graphs on the same grid.
   i $y = x^2$ **ii** $y = -x^2$

b How are the graphs different?

c Look at the equation of each graph.
What is the impact of the negative sign on the graph $y = -x^2$?

2 **a** Complete a table of values of x from -3 to 3 for each function.
Draw the graphs on the same grid.
   i $y = 3x^2$ **ii** $y = \frac{1}{3}x^2$ **iii** $y = 4x^2 + 1$ **iv** $y = -2x^2 + 3$

b Look at the equation of each graph.
What does the constant value in the equations of graphs **iii** and **iv** tell you about the graphs?

Features of parabolas

Quadratic graphs have characteristics that you can use to sketch and interpret them.

The main features of a parabola are:

- the turning point or vertex of the graph – this is the point at which the graph changes direction.
- the axis of symmetry – a line which divides the parabola into two symmetrical halves; this line passes through the turning point.
- the y-intercept – a parabola can only have one y-intercept.
- the x-intercepts – a parabola can have 0, 1 or 2 x-intercepts depending on the position of the graph.

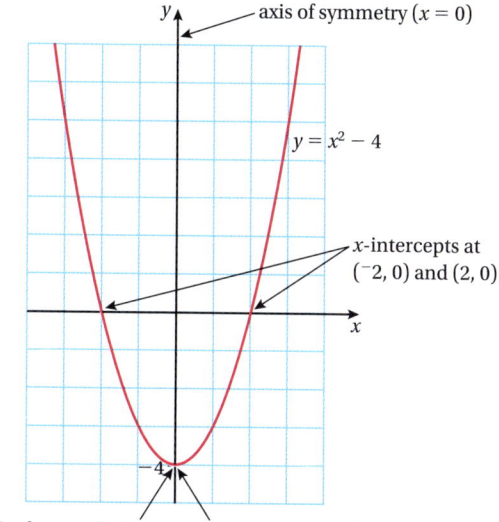

axis of symmetry ($x = 0$)

$y = x^2 - 4$

x-intercepts at $(-2, 0)$ and $(2, 0)$

in this graph the turning point is a minimum (lowest point on graph)

turning point at $(0, -4)$ which is also the y-intercept

When a quadratic equation is in the general form $y = ax^2 + c$, a is the coefficient of x, $b = 0$ and c is the y-intercept of the curve. In this form the following is always true:

- the axis of symmetry is always the y-axis, that is, the line $x = 0$.
- the y-intercept and the turning point have the same coordinates, that is, they are the same point.

For any form of a quadratic equation, the parabola can extend upwards to a maximum turning point or downwards to a minimum turning point. The equation of the graph tells you which of these shapes it will be:

If a is positive, the turning point will be a minimum (this is the lowest point of the graph).

If a is negative, the turning point will be a maximum (this is the highest point of the graph).

> **Tip**
> At GCSE, you will only learn about parabolas with equations in the form $y = ax^2 + c$.

> **Tip**
> The value of x^2 will always be positive, so it is the sign of the coefficient a that determines if the turning point is a maximum or minimum.

Find answers at: cambridge.org/ukschools/gcsemaths-studentbookanswers

WORKED EXAMPLE 2

For each parabola determine:
  i the turning point and whether it is a minimum or maximum.
 ii the axis of symmetry.
iii the y-intercept.
 iv the x-intercepts.

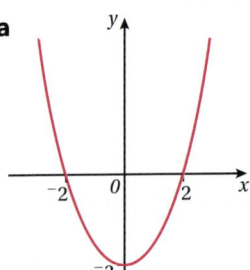

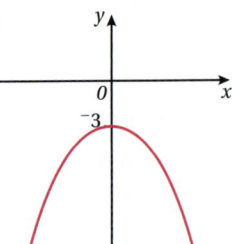

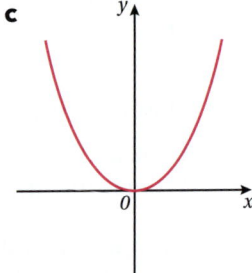

a i Turning point at $(0, -3)$ is a minimum

> If you follow the curved line from left to right, it moves downwards; when it reaches $(0, -3)$ it changes direction and moves upwards. It is the lowest point on the graph.

   ii Axis of symmetry: $x = 0$

> The axis of symmetry is the straight line that divides the curve into two equal halves that are mirror images of each other. Here it is the y-axis.

  iii y-intercept at $(0, -3)$

> This is the point where the curve cuts the y-axis.

   iv x-intercepts at $(-2, 0)$ and $(2, 0)$

> These are the points where the curve cuts the x-axis.

b i Turning point at $(0, -3)$, maximum
   ii Axis of symmetry: $x = 0$
  iii y-intercept at $(0, -3)$

> $(0, -3)$ is the point where the graph changes direction; it is the highest point on the curve.

   iv There are no x-intercepts.

> The curve does not touch or cross the x-axis.

c i Turning point at $(0, 0)$, minimum
   ii Axis of symmetry: $x = 0$
  iii y-intercept at $(0, 0)$
   iv one x-intercept at $(0, 0)$

> Even though the curve doesn't cross the x-axis to the other side, it touches the x-axis and is therefore counted as the x-intercept.

x-intercepts and roots of a quadratic equation

The x-intercepts of a parabola are the roots (or solution) of the quadratic equation that defines the graph. You can find the roots graphically by reading their value off the graph.

You can also solve the quadratic equation algebraically to find its roots and therefore work out the points at which its curve crosses the x-axis. This is useful when you have to sketch the graph.

Tip

> In Chapter 8 you learnt how to solve quadratic equations algebraically. Revise that chapter if you have forgotten how to do this.

A parabola will have no x-intercepts if the quadratic equation cannot be solved.

19 Graphs of equations and functions

EXERCISE 19C

1 For each parabola determine:
  i whether the turning point is a minimum or maximum.
  ii the axis of symmetry.
  iii the y-intercept.
  iv the x-intercept(s).

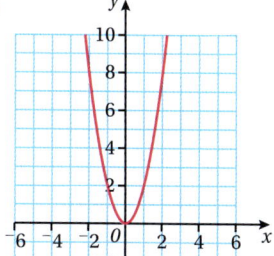

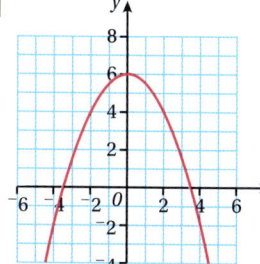

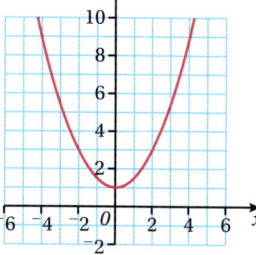

a [graph] **b** [graph] **c** [graph]

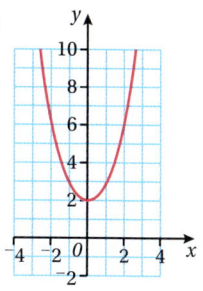

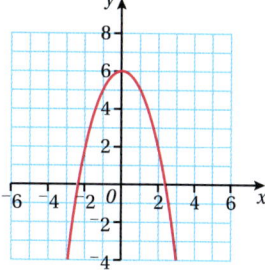

d [graph] **e** [graph] **f** [graph]

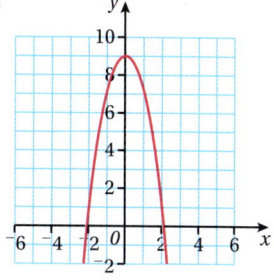

2 Graphs A to E are shown on the same grid.

Use the diagram to determine whether each statement is true or false.

a Graph A has two x-intercepts.

b Graphs A and B have minimum turning points.

c Graph B has y-intercepts at $(-2, 0)$ and $(2, 0)$.

d Graphs B and C have the same x-intercepts.

e The equation of graph D will have a positive x^2 term.

f Graph E has a maximum turning point at $(0, -2)$.

g The equation of graph D has a constant of 2. This tells you the y-intercept is $(0, 2)$.

h All of these graphs are symmetrical about the line $x = 0$.

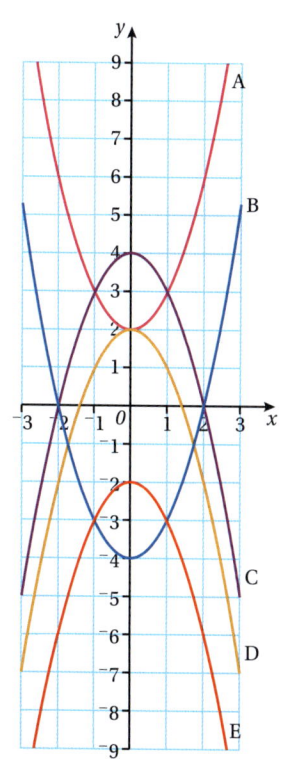

Sketching quadratic graphs

You can use the characteristics of a parabola to sketch graphs without drawing up a table of values:

- Write the equation in the general form $y = ax^2 + c$.
- Use the sign of a to determine if the graph goes up to a maximum turning point or down to a minimum turning point.
- Work out the y-intercept (this is given by c in the equation).

Find answers at: cambridge.org/ukschools/gcsemaths-studentbookanswers

305

- Calculate the x-intercepts by substituting $y = 0$ and solving for x. If the x-intercept is at the origin ($x = 0$) or there are no x-intercepts (no solution), find the coordinates of one point on the graph.
- Mark the y-intercept and x-intercepts (or single point) and use the shape and symmetry of the graph as a guide to draw a smooth curve.
- Label your graph.

WORKED EXAMPLE 3

Sketch the graph of $y = 3x^2$.

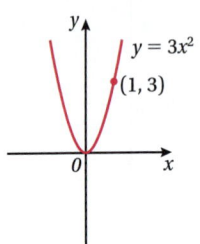

$a = 3$ so the graph goes down to a minimum turning point.

There is no constant, so $c = 0$ and the y-intercept is at the point (0, 0).

When $y = 0$ then $x = 0$, so the x-intercept is at (0, 0); find one point on the curve.

When $x = 1$
$y = 3(1)^2 = 3$
So, (1, 3) is a point on the curve.

Sketch the graph by marking the y-intercept and the point (1, 3). As the graph is in the form $y = ax^2 + c$, you know that the turning point has the same coordinate at the y-intercept and the axis of symmetry is the line $x = 0$, use this and the point (1, 3) to create a curve.

Label the graph.

Tip

Draw a smooth curve to join the points and try to make your graph as symmetrical as possible.

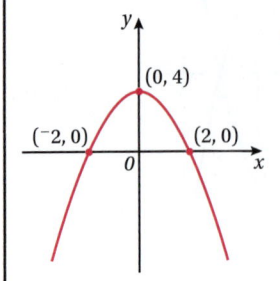

WORKED EXAMPLE 4

Sketch the graph of $y = {}^-x^2 + 4$.

$a = {}^-1$, so the graph goes up to a maximum turning point. $c = 4$, so y-intercept is (0, 4).

x-intercepts when $y = 0$

$0 = {}^-x^2 + 4$

$\therefore x^2 - 4 = 0$

This is a difference of squares

$(x + 2)(x - 2) = 0$

$x + 2 = 0$ or $x - 2 = 0$

$x = {}^-2$ or $x = 2$

So, intercepts are (${}^-2$, 0) and (2, 0).

Sketch: mark the intercepts; the turning point is the same as the y-intercept; the axis of symmetry is $x = 0$. Add labels.

EXERCISE 19D

1 Sketch and label these graphs on the same grid.
   a $y = x^2$
   b $y = -x^2$
   c $y = 2x^2$
   d $y = \frac{1}{2}x^2$
   e $y = -2x^2$
   f $y = -\frac{1}{2}x^2$

2 What do you notice about the width of the parabola as the value of the coefficient of x^2 changes?

3 Solve each equation algebraically to find the x-intercepts of each graph. Do not draw the graphs.
   a $y = x^2 - 4$
   b $y = x^2 - 9$

4 Sketch the following graphs on the same grid.
   a $y = x^2 - 3$
   b $y = 3x^2 - 4$
   c $y = -x^2 - 2$
   d $y = -3x^2 + 12$

5 Noor sketched these graphs but she didn't write the equations on them. Use the features of each graph to work out what the correct equations are.

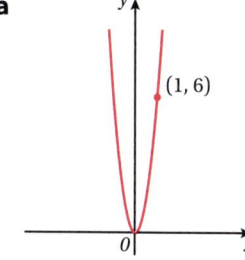

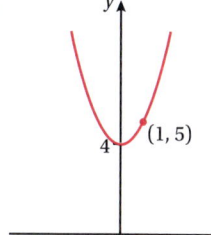

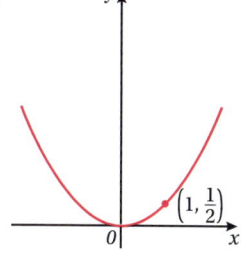

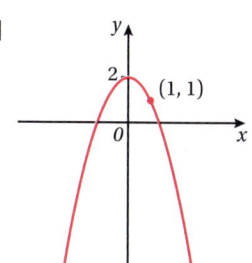

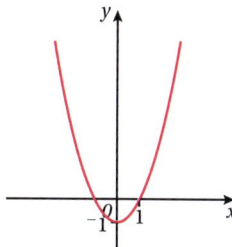

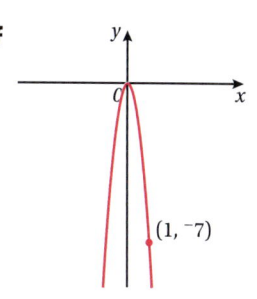

Section 3: Graphs of other polynomials and reciprocals

A **polynomial** is an expression with many unlike terms; all the variables have positive powers.

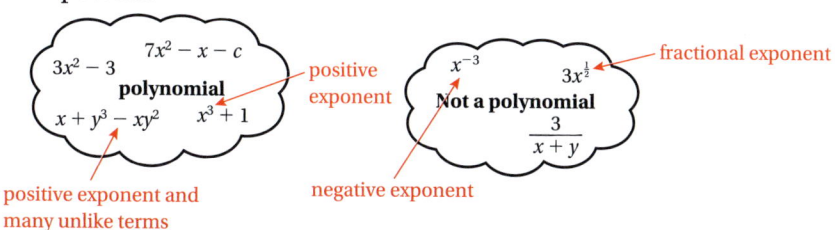

$3x^2 - 3$, $7x^2 - x - c$, $x + y^3 - xy^2$, $x^3 + 1$ — **polynomial** (positive exponent and many unlike terms)

x^{-3} (negative exponent), $3x^{\frac{1}{2}}$ (fractional exponent), $\frac{3}{x + y}$ — **Not a polynomial**

If the highest power of x is 3, the expression is called a cubic expression.

For example, $2x^3$ and $2x^3 + x^2 + 3$ are both cubics.

The simplest equation of a cubic graph is $y = x^3$.

Find answers at: cambridge.org/ukschools/gcsemaths-studentbookanswers

Key vocabulary

polynomial: an expression made up of many unlike terms with positive powers for the variables.

Tip

You saw in Chapter 7 that a **binomial** is an expression with **two** unlike terms.

> **Tip**
>
> In both graphs, c = 0 and so has not been included in the written equation.

All cubic graphs have a similar shape. The diagram shows the basic shape of cubic graphs in the form of $y = ax^3 + c$.

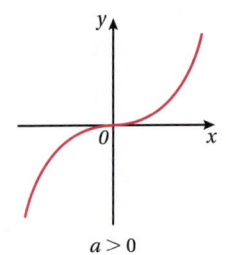

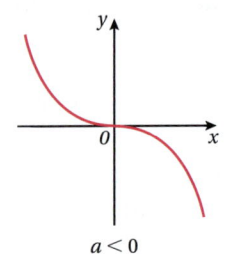

a > 0   a < 0

The shape on the left occurs when a is positive. We call this an increasing curve.

The shape on the right occurs when a is negative. We call this a decreasing curve.

The larger the value of a, the steeper the curve.

The constant, c, is the y-intercept.

To draw an accurate graph of a cubic equation, you plot at least five points including both positive and negative values of x, then draw a smooth curve through and beyond them.

This is a table of values for $y = x^3$.

x	−3	−2	−1	0	1	2	3
y	−27	−8	−1	0	1	8	27

> **Tip**
>
> Remember that when you cube a negative number you will get a negative result. For example, $(-1)^3 = -1 \times -1 \times -1 = -1$.

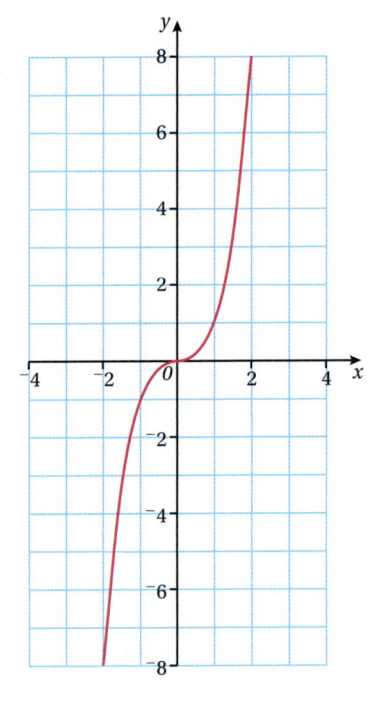

Note that the curve passes through the origin but it is not symmetrical.

When you **sketch** a cubic graph you need to show its general shape and its important features; you would use the value of a to determine if it is a decreasing or increasing curve, and the value of c to determine the y-intercept. You still use a table of values, but you don't need to work out as many points as you need for an accurate graph.

19 Graphs of equations and functions

EXERCISE 19E

1 Complete a table of values for whole number values of x from $^-3$ to 3 for $y = {}^-x^3$.

How does this graph differ from the graph of $y = x^3$?

2 Use a table of values to sketch the following pairs of cubic graphs.

Plot each pair on the same grid, but use a separate grid for each pair.

a $y = {}^-2x^3$ and $y = 2x^3$ **b** $y = \frac{1}{2}x^3$ and $y = {}^-\frac{1}{2}x^3$

3 Work with a partner to compare the pairs of graphs you drew in Question **2**.

Discuss how you could sketch the graph of $y = {}^-4x^3$ if you were given the graph of $y = 4x^3$.

4 Complete a table of values for whole number values of x from $^-3$ to 3 for these equations and draw a graph of each curve.

a $y = x^3 + 1$ **b** $y = x^3 - 2$

5 Look at the graphs and their equations in Question **4**.

What is the y-intercept in each graph?

6 The red line is the graph $y = x^3$.

What are the equations of graphs A and B?

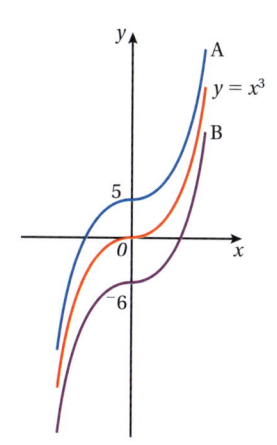

Reciprocal functions

Every number has a **reciprocal** except for 0, as $\frac{1}{0}$ cannot be defined.

A **reciprocal function** relates x to its reciprocal, and has the general equation $y = \frac{a}{x}$, where a is a constant value. You might also see this expressed as $xy = a$.

The graphs of reciprocal functions have a characteristic shape called a **hyperbola**. Each graph is made of two non-connected curves which are mirror images in opposite quadrants of the grid.

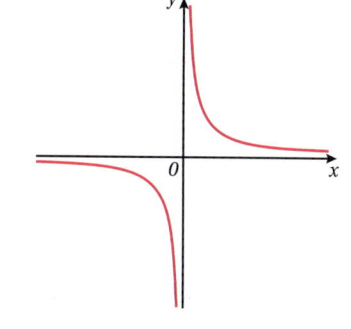

> **Key vocabulary**
>
> **hyperbola**: the curved graph(s) formed by a reciprocal function; the curve of $y = \frac{1}{x}$ gets increasingly close to the x-axis and y-axis but never touches them.

Find answers at: cambridge.org/ukschools/gcsemaths-studentbookanswers

This is the table of values for the equation $y = \frac{1}{x}$.

x	-3	-2	-1	$\frac{-1}{2}$	$\frac{-1}{3}$	0	$\frac{1}{2}$	$\frac{1}{3}$	1	2	3
y	$\frac{-1}{3}$	$\frac{-1}{2}$	-1	-2	-3	N/A	2	3	1	$\frac{1}{2}$	$\frac{1}{3}$

In order to draw a reciprocal graph accurately you need many points that include integer and some non-integer values of x.

Note that there is no y-value when $x = 0$ or x-value when $y = 0$ because division by 0 is undefined.

To draw the graph:

- Plot the (x, y) values from the table.
- Join the points with a smooth curve.
- Write the equation on both parts of the graph.

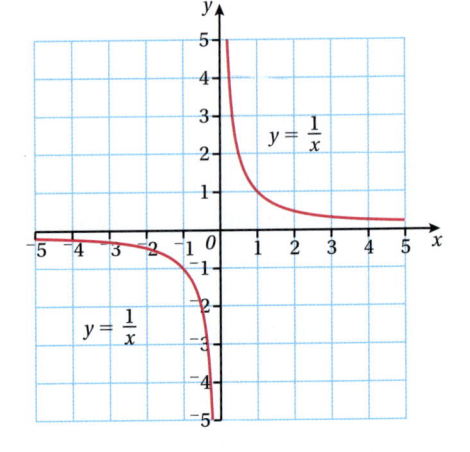

Its curves are in quadrants 1 and 3.

The graph of $y = \frac{-1}{x}$ has its curves in quadrants 2 and 4.

Note that as the digit for x (ignoring the sign) gets bigger the value for y gets closer and closer to 0 but the graph never actually meets the x-axis.

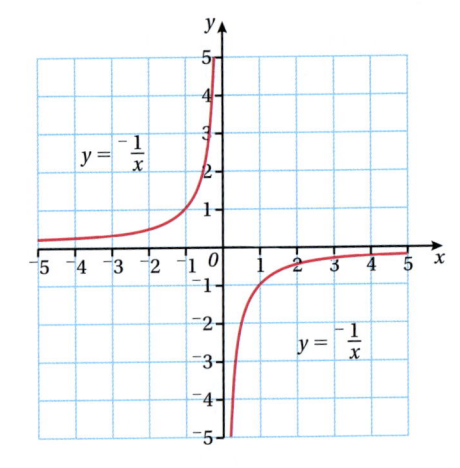

EXERCISE 19F

1. Plot each of the following graphs on the same grid using x-values from -5 to 5.

   a $y = \frac{1}{x}$ **b** $y = \frac{1}{x} + 1$ **c** $y = \frac{1}{x} + 3$ **d** $xy = 1$

2. Use your graphs from Question 1 to describe how the constant c in the equation $y = \frac{1}{x} + c$ changes the reciprocal graph of $y = \frac{1}{x}$.

3. Plot each of the following reciprocal functions.

   a $y = \frac{1}{x} + x$ **b** $y = \frac{1}{x} - x$ **c** $y = \frac{1}{x} + 2x$

4. Neo says that the line $y = x$ is the line of symmetry of the graph $y = \frac{1}{x}$. Is he correct? Explain your answer.

5 a Copy and complete each table for the given values of x. Plot the graphs on the same grid.

  i $y = \frac{2}{x}$

x	-4	-2	-1	1	2	4
y						

  ii $y = \frac{6}{x}$

x	-6	-3	-1	1	3	6
y						

  iii $xy = -12$

x	-10	-8	-6	-4	-2	2	4	6	8
y									

  iv $y = \frac{8}{x}$

x	-8	-6	-4	-2	1	2	4	6	8
y									

  b Compare the graphs that you have drawn in part **a**.
  How does the value of the constant in the equation affect the graph?

6 Here are four reciprocal graphs.

  a Without doing any calculation, match each of these equations to a graph.

  $y = \frac{2}{x}$ $y = \frac{4}{x}$

  $y = \frac{8}{x}$ $y = \frac{10}{x}$

  b Explain how you worked out which equation belonged with each graph.

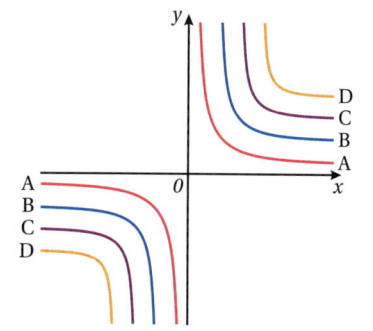

Section 4: Plotting, sketching and recognising graphs

Equations in different forms produce different types of graphs.

You have seen that you can use the characteristics of different types of graphs to work out what they will look like and how to sketch them:

- $y = mx + c$ will produce a straight line, or linear graph.
- $y = ax^2 + c$ will produce a quadratic graph called a parabola.
- $y = ax^3 + c$ will produce a cubic curve.
- $y = \frac{a}{x}$ and $xy = a$ will produce a reciprocal curve.

Work through Exercise 19G to apply what you have learnt about graphs.

Find answers at: cambridge.org/ukschools/gcsemaths-studentbookanswers

EXERCISE 19G

1 Determine whether each statement is true or false. Correct any false statements.

  a The points (3, 7) (0, 1), (⁻1, ⁻1) all lie on the line $y = 2x + 1$.

  b The graph of the equation $y = \dfrac{5}{x}$ cannot be evaluated for $x = 0$.

  c This diagram shows a graph of a quadratic equation which has roots 1 and ⁻1.

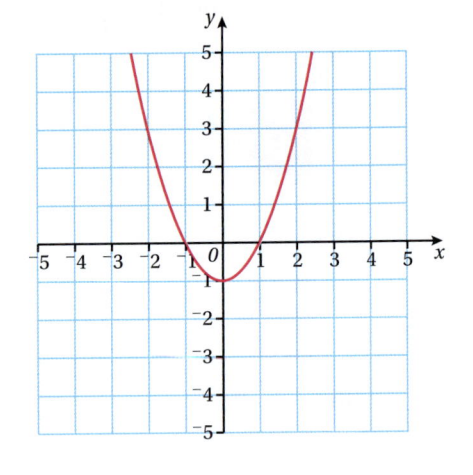

  d $xy = 5$ is the same function as $y = \dfrac{5}{x}$.

  e $y = {}^-2x^2 + 4$ goes down to a minimum turning point with a y-intercept at (0, ⁻2)

  f The line $y = {}^-x$ is a line of symmetry of $xy = 4$.

2 Sketch each of the following graphs.

  a $y = x + 2$
  b $y = 3x - 4$
  c $y = 7 - 3x$
  d $y = 3$
  e $x = {}^-5$
  f $2x + 3y = {}^-12$

3 Draw up a table of values and plot each graph.

  a $y = 2x^2$
  b $y = x^2 - 3$
  c $y = {}^-x^2 + 5$
  d $y = x^3 + 4$
  e $y = \dfrac{1}{x}$
  f $y = \dfrac{1}{x} + 1$

4 Solve the following equations algebraically and hence write down the x-intercepts of each graph.

  a $y = x^2 - 16$
  b $y = x^2 - 2x$

5 If a quadratic equation has roots $x = {}^-3$ and $x = 5$, give the coordinates of the points of intersection with the x-axis.

6 Match each of the following graphs with the appropriate equation from the list.

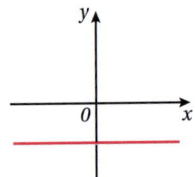

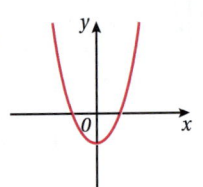

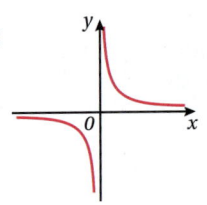

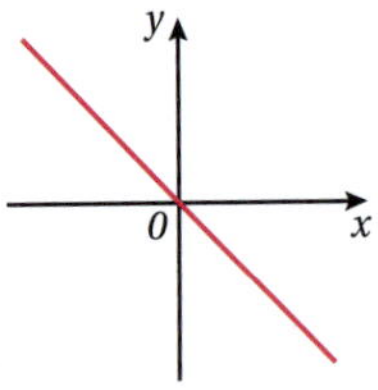

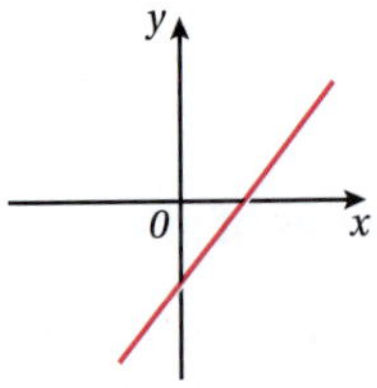

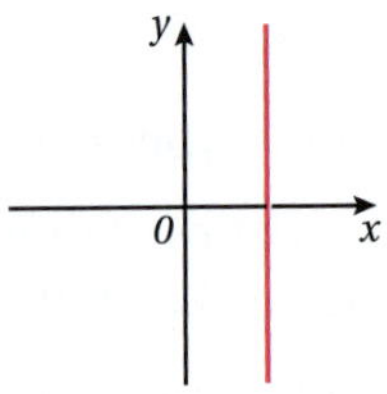

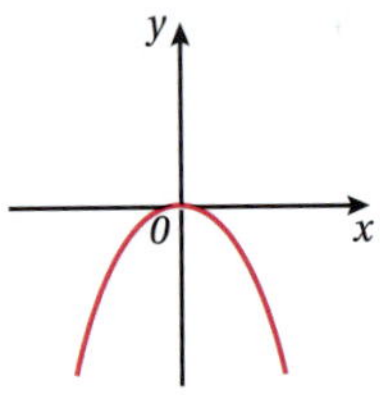

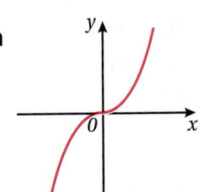

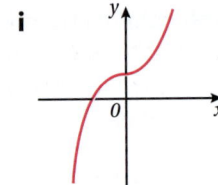

Equations:

$y = x^2 - 2$

$y = {}^-x$

$x = 4$

$y = 3x - 4$

$y = 2x^3$

$y = {}^-4$

$xy = 1$

$y = 3x^3 + 3$

$y = {}^-x^2$

19 Graphs of equations and functions

Checklist of learning and understanding

Linear functions
- Linear functions produce straight-line graphs.
- The general form of the linear function is $y = mx + c$.
- Graphs $x = a$ are vertical lines parallel to the y-axis.
- Graphs $y = a$ are horizontal lines parallel to the x-axis.
- Lines of the form $y = mx$ go through the origin.

Quadratic functions
- The graphs of quadratic equations such as $y = ax^2$ and $y = ax^2 + c$ are called parabolas.
- When a is positive the graph goes down to a minimum point. When a is negative the graph goes up to a maximum point. The y-intercept is given by c.
- Parabolas have a turning point which can be a minimum or maximum depending on the shape of the graph. The axis of symmetry has the same x-value as the turning point $x = 0$.

Polynomials and reciprocals
- To draw graphs of polynomials first calculate a table of values that satisfy the equation for a range of values for x.
- A cubic function is a curve defined by $y = ax^3 + c$.
- A reciprocal function is a graph made of two non-connected curves in opposite quadrants defined by $y = \dfrac{a}{x}$ or $xy = a$.

Chapter review

For additional questions on the topics in this chapter, visit GCSE Mathematics Online.

1 **a** Complete this table for $y = 2x + 1$ and plot the points to draw a straight-line graph.

x	-2	-1	0	1	2	3
y						

   b Use the graph to find:

   i the value of y when $x = -1.5$.   **ii** the value of x when $y = 6$.

2 **a** Complete this table for $y = x^2 - 3$ and plot the points to draw the curve of the parabola

x	-2	-1	0	1	2	3
y		-3	-2			

   b Give the coordinate of the minimum point of the curve (the turning point).

   c What line is the axis of symmetry for this graph?

   d Estimate the roots of the equation $x^2 - 3 = 0$.

Find answers at: cambridge.org/ukschools/gcsemaths-studentbookanswers

3. Each statement below is sometimes true and sometimes false.

Statement	True	False
A straight line graph goes through the origin.	(graph through origin)	(graph not through origin)
The gradient of a straight line graph is positive.		
A quadratic equation $ax^2 + bx + c = 0$ has two positive solutions.		

For each statement sketch a graph to show an example where it is true and an example where it is false.

The first one has been done for you.

(3 marks)

© OCR 2013

4. Match the equations $y = x^3$ and $y = \dfrac{1}{x}$ with the correct graph.

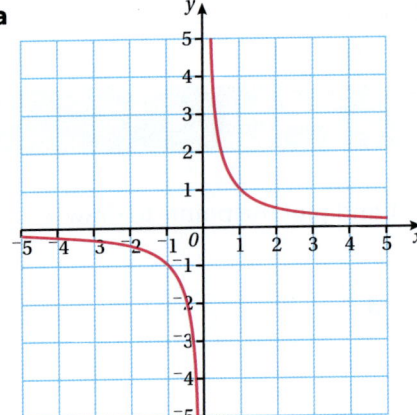

a

b

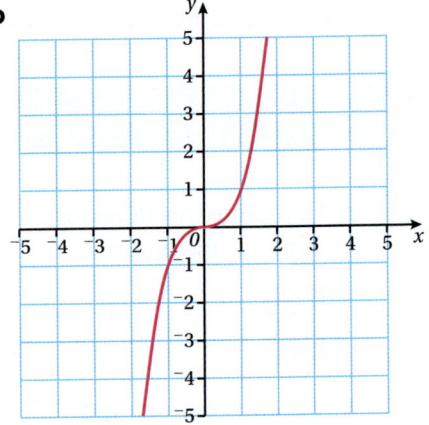

5. Draw a sketch diagram of $y = x^3 - 5$ and $y = \dfrac{1}{x} + 2$.

6. If the roots of the quadratic equation $x^2 + 2x - 3 = 0$ are $x = 1$ and $x = -3$, what are the coordinates of the points at which the equation $y = x^2 + 2x - 3$ cuts the x-axis?

20 Three-dimensional shapes

In this chapter you will learn how to …
- work with 2D representations of 3D objects.
- construct and interpret plans and elevations of 3D objects.

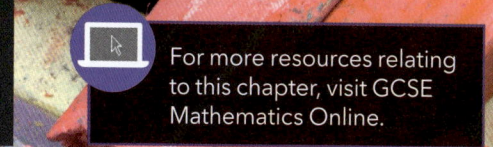

For more resources relating to this chapter, visit GCSE Mathematics Online.

Using mathematics: real-life applications

Buildings, engine parts, vehicles and packaging are all carefully planned and designed before they are built. Most design work starts on paper or screen using two-dimensional images to represent the final three-dimensional objects.

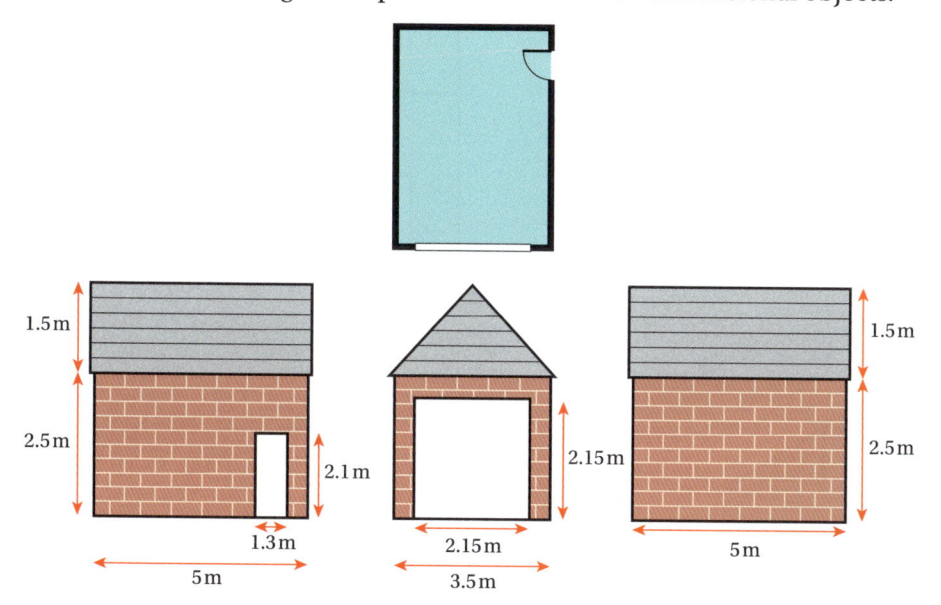

"No one will buy an apartment that isn't built yet if they don't know what it is going to look like! When we sell a development we show people floor plans as well as elevations from all four sides. Sometimes we also have a 3D scale model of the development." *(Estate agent)*

Before you start …

Ch 5	You must be able to identify and name some common 3D solids.	1	Name each of these 3D solids. 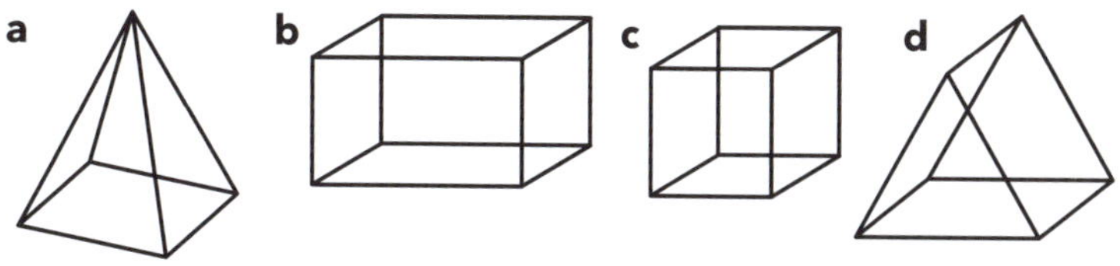 a b c d
Ch 5	You should know the basic properties of polygons and other 3D solids.	2	True or false? Correct the false statements. a A cube has 4 faces. b A cube has 12 edges. c A cuboid has 8 vertices.
Ch 6	You must be able to accurately construct lines and angles using your ruler and a pair of compasses.	3	Construct and bisect a right angle ABC.

Find answers at: cambridge.org/ukschools/gcsemaths-studentbookanswers

315

GCSE Mathematics for OCR (Foundation)

Assess your starting point using the Launchpad

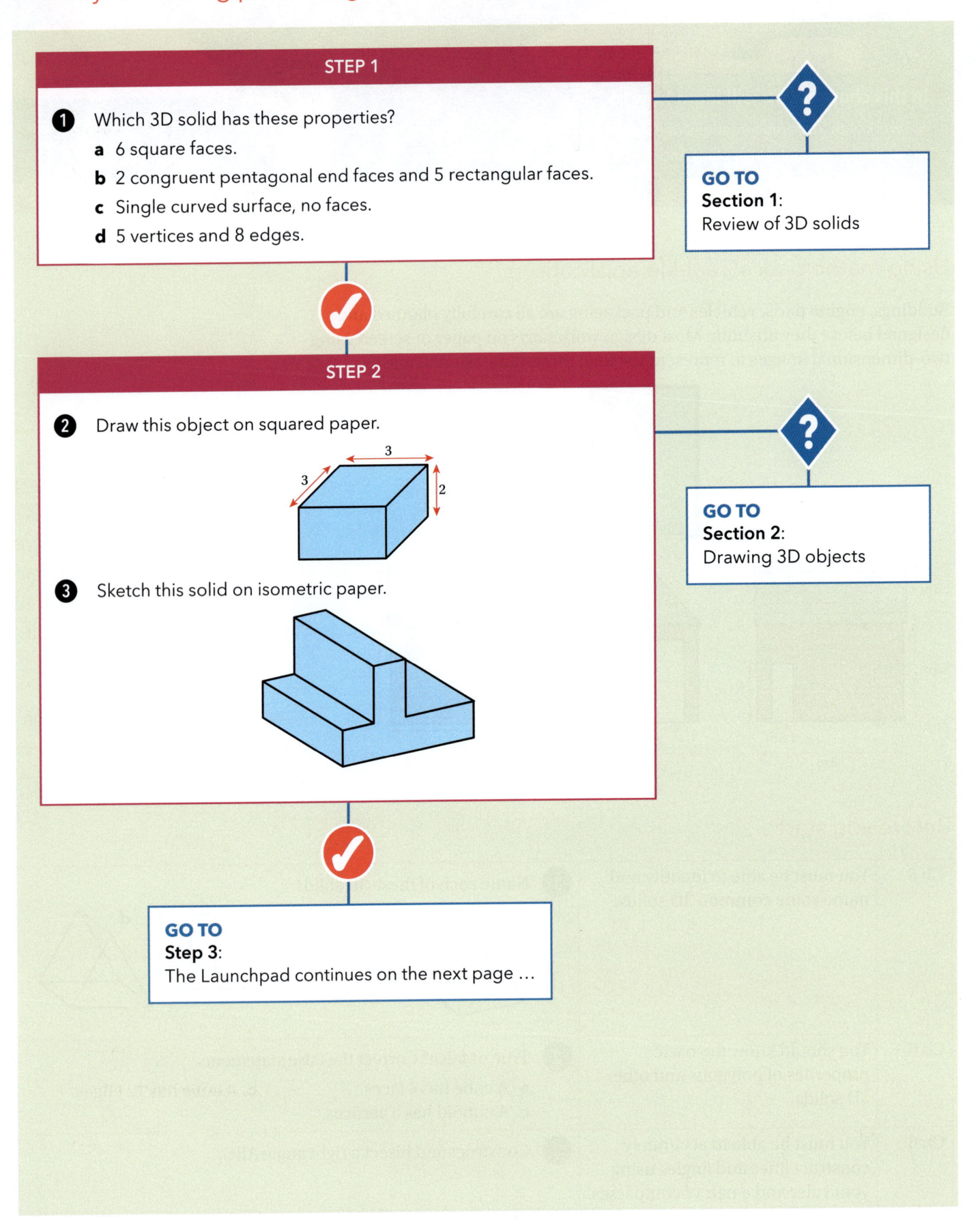

STEP 1

1 Which 3D solid has these properties?
  a 6 square faces.
  b 2 congruent pentagonal end faces and 5 rectangular faces.
  c Single curved surface, no faces.
  d 5 vertices and 8 edges.

GO TO Section 1: Review of 3D solids

STEP 2

2 Draw this object on squared paper.

3 Sketch this solid on isometric paper.

GO TO Section 2: Drawing 3D objects

GO TO Step 3: The Launchpad continues on the next page …

20 Three-dimensional shapes

Launchpad continued ...

STEP 3

4 Which is the plan view for this square-based pyramid?

a b c d

GO TO
Section 3:
Plan and elevation views

5 Draw the plan view, front and right side elevation of each shape on squared paper.

a   b

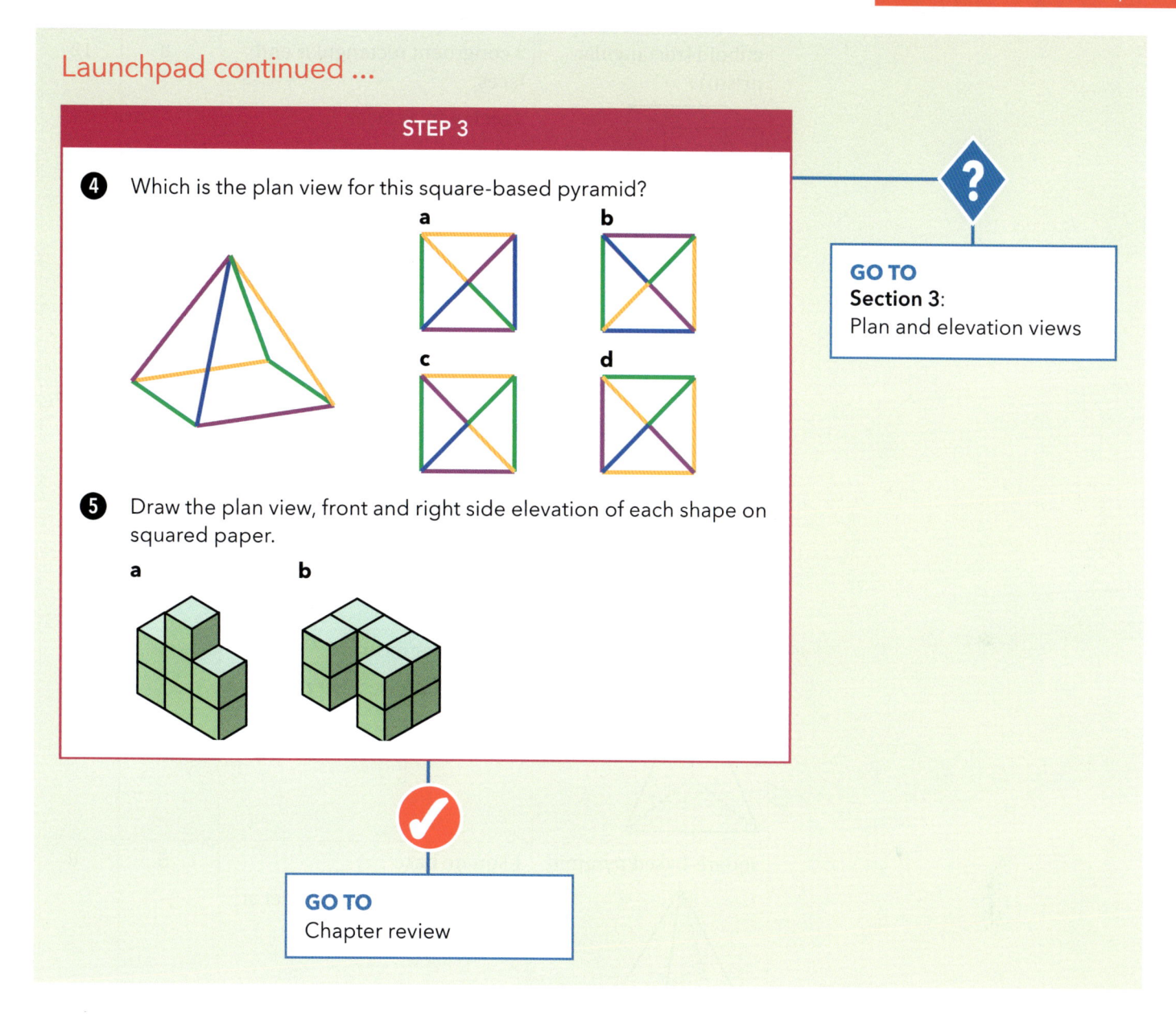

GO TO
Chapter review

Section 1: Review of 3D solids

In Chapter 5 you saw that polyhedra are solid shapes with flat faces that are polygons.

The table summarises the main properties of different polyhedra.

Polyhedron	Faces	Vertices	Edges
cube (square prism)	6 square faces	8	12

Tip

The cross section of a prism is the same shape along the entire length of the prism. If the cross section is a regular polygon, the prism is named after it. For example, hexagonal prism. If you need reminding about properties of 2D shapes, see Chapter 5.

Find answers at: cambridge.org/ukschools/gcsemaths-studentbookanswers

317

cuboid (rectangular prism)	2 congruent rectangular end faces 4 rectangular faces	8	12
triangular prism	2 congruent triangular end faces 3 rectangular faces	6	9
pentagonal prism	2 congruent pentagonal end faces 5 rectangular faces	10	15
triangular pyramid	1 triangular base 3 triangular faces that meet at an apex	4	6
square-based pyramid	1 square base 4 triangular faces that meet at an apex	5	8

Cylinders, cones and spheres are also 3D shapes but they are **not** polyhedra; they do not have flat faces that are polygons.

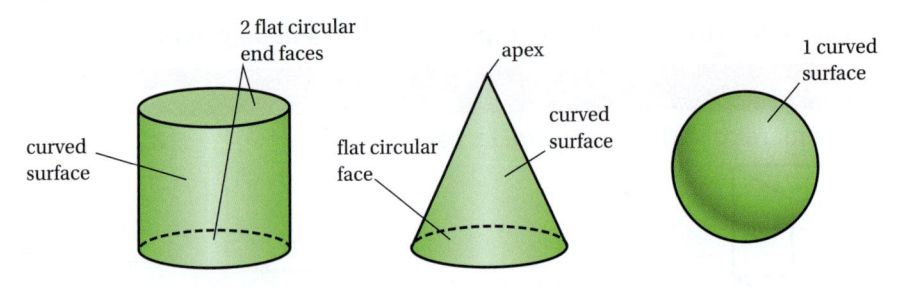

20 Three-dimensional shapes

WORKED EXAMPLE 1

Describe each object fully by referring to its properties.

Say if it is a polyhedron or not, giving a reason for your decision.

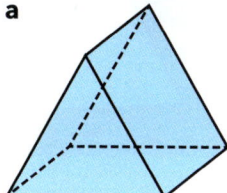

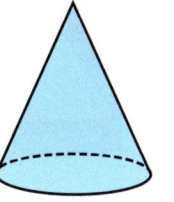

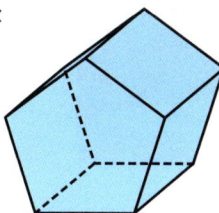

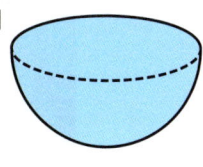

a   b   c   d

a Two end faces are congruent triangles. There are also three rectangular faces. It has 6 vertices and 9 edges. Its cross-section is a regular polygon. It is a polyhedron because all of its faces are polygons.

b The shape has one end face that is a circle. It has one vertex and a single curved face. It is not a polyhedron because not all of its faces are polygons.

c It has two congruent pentagon faces and 5 rectangular faces. It has 15 edges and 10 vertices. It has a regular cross-section. It is a polyhedron because all its faces are polygons.

d The shape has a flat circle face and a single curved face. It has no vertices. It is not a polyhedron because not all of its faces are polygons.

> Make sure you use the correct vocabulary. Don't forget to include how many vertices and edges it has.

EXERCISE 20A

1. What is the mathematical name for each of the following shapes?
   a A solid with 6 faces; the 2 end faces are congruent rectangles.
   b There are 4 vertices and 6 edges. At one of the vertices, 3 triangular faces meet. The base of the shape is a triangle.
   c A solid with 6 vertices and 2 congruent triangular end faces.
   d A regular solid with 6 identical faces, 8 vertices and 12 edges.

2. Which solid or solids does each photo remind you of?
   a
   b

Find answers at: cambridge.org/ukschools/gcsemaths-studentbookanswers

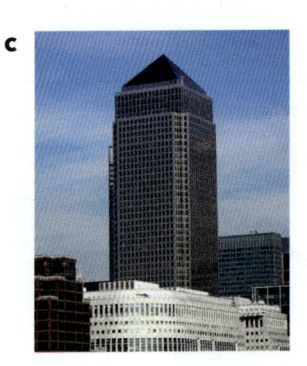

3 Where might you find the following in real life?

    a A sphere.   **b** A cube.

    c A cone.   **d** A cylinder.

Section 2: Drawing 3D objects

You need to be able to make drawings of 3D objects, and to interpret drawings of 3D objects from different perspectives.

It can be challenging to draw a 3D object because you are trying to show three dimensions on a two-dimensional plane (your paper or computer screen).

There are a number of ways of drawing 3D objects to show their features in 2D. As you read through each method, try it out on rough paper.

Prisms and cylinders using end faces

You can make fairly realistic drawings of prisms and cylinders by imagining the position of their end faces.

Cuboid

a

A cuboid is a rectangular prism. Imagine where the rectangular end faces would be and draw those first. Draw two rectangles, positioning one above the other, with one of them further over to one side.

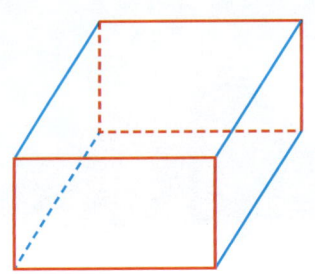

b

Then join the two rectangles together by drawing a line from each vertex on one rectangle to the corresponding vertex on the other rectangle. For any edges that you wouldn't be able to see, use a broken line.

20 Three-dimensional shapes

Cylinder

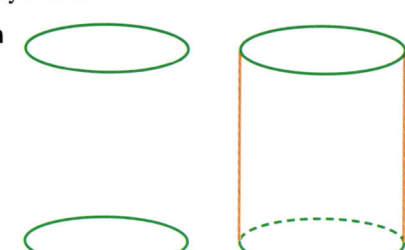

a

First draw the two circular end faces. Draw them as **ovals** to get a more realistic drawing. Then draw in two lines to join the end faces.

b

Shading can make a drawing look more realistic.

Triangular prism

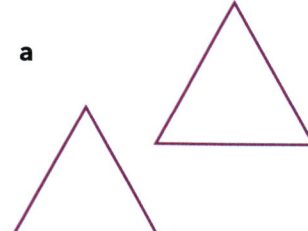

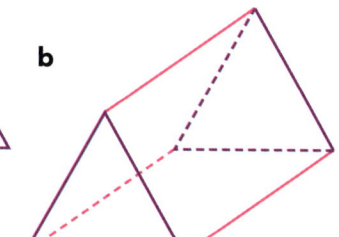

a   b

First draw the two triangular end faces. Then draw in lines to join the vertices. For any edges that you wouldn't be able to see, use a broken line.

The same process can be used for any shaped prism, just make sure you remember:
- start with the two end faces
- join all corresponding vertices
- shading can help make the shape look more realistic.

WORKED EXAMPLE 2

Draw an L-shaped prism.

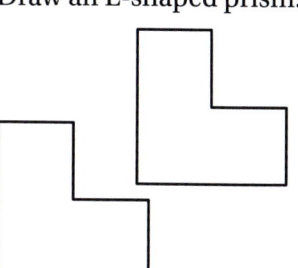

Start by drawing the two end faces, one above the other and one over to one side.

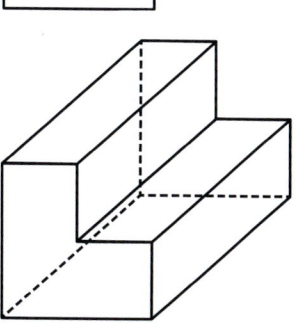

Then join each vertex on one of the faces to the corresponding vertex on the other face.

Continues on next page …

Find answers at: cambridge.org/ukschools/gcsemaths-studentbookanswers

Use shading to make the shape look more realistic.

Prisms and pyramids from parallel lines

You can draw square and rectangular prisms and square-based pyramids using two pairs of parallel lines as a starting point.

Prism

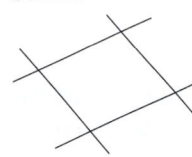

Begin by drawing two pairs of parallel lines that intersect (cross each other).

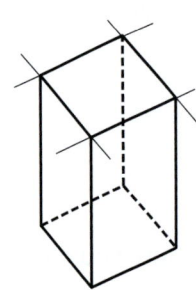

Then draw vertical lines of equal length down (or up) from each intersection. Complete the shape by joining the ends to make a prism.

Square-based pyramid

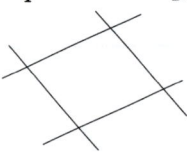

Start by drawing two pairs of parallel lines that intersect.

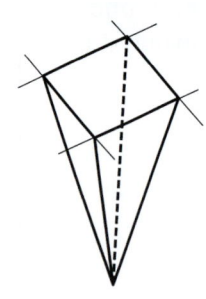

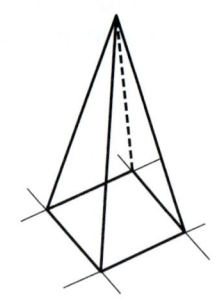

Mark a point above, below or to the side, of the parallel lines. Draw lines from the intersections of the parallel lines to the point.

Tip

Parallel lines were covered in Chapter 5.

Tip

'Viewpoints' means that you could look at a shape from the front, the back, the side, or from one of its edges. The viewpoint from which you look at a shape will determine which of its faces/edges/vertices you can see and which would be hidden.

Drawing shapes on squared or isometric grids

3D objects can be drawn on squared or isometric grids to show the object from different viewpoints.

The vertical lines on each type of grid are used to represent the vertical edges of the 3D object. You draw along the lines at an angle on the paper to represent the horizontal edges of the 3D object.

The diagram below shows a cube and a cuboid drawn on a square grid. The shapes are drawn as if viewed 'face-on'.

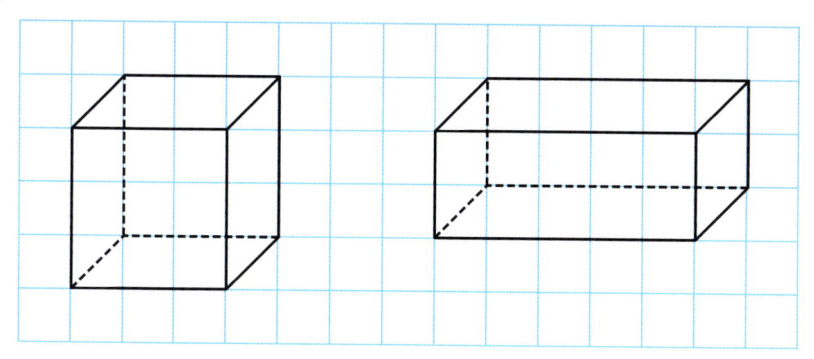

This diagram shows the same objects drawn on an **isometric grid**. The shapes are drawn as if viewed from one of their edges.

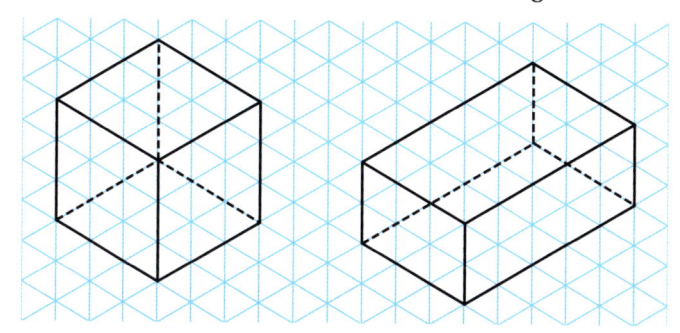

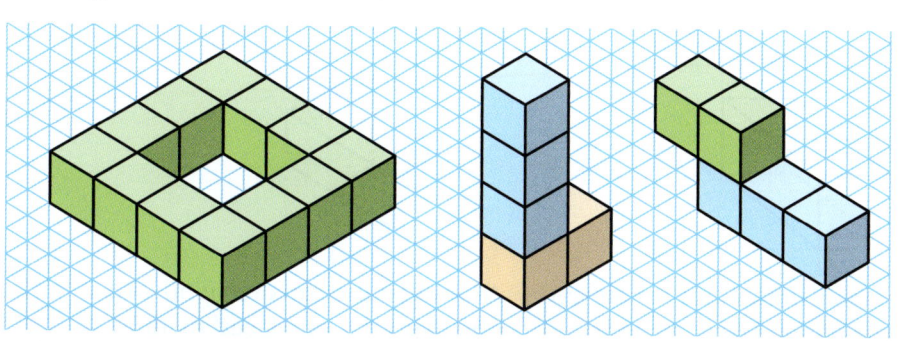

> **Key vocabulary**
>
> **isometric grid**: special drawing paper based on an arrangement of triangles.

Remember that when you draw 3D shapes you use broken lines to show the edges that would **not** be seen from that viewpoint.

Isometric drawings

Isometric drawings are used to represent three-dimensional objects in two dimensions in technical and engineering drawings.

This diagram shows the design of an engineering component on isometric paper.

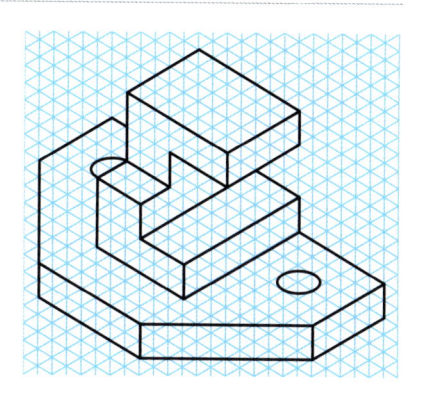

Isometric paper is very useful for drawing solids built from cubes.

Find answers at: cambridge.org/ukschools/gcsemaths-studentbookanswers

GCSE Mathematics for OCR (Foundation)

WORKED EXAMPLE 3

Draw this shape on an isometric grid.

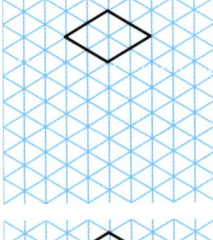

> Use the lines on the grid to help you draw the horizontal face of one of the cubes; here, the top-most yellow cube is the starting point

> Use that face to draw in the other horizontal faces.

> Use the vertical lines on the grid to draw in the vertical edges.

> Use the angled lines to draw in the bottom horizontal edges.

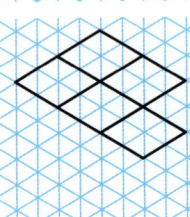

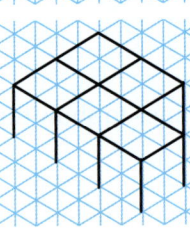

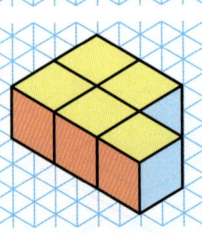

You can use the 'end faces' or 'parallel lines' methods you saw earlier in the chapter on square and isometric grids. The grid makes it easier for you to make sure that the end faces are the same size.

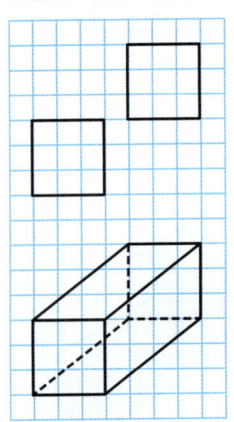

A cuboid drawn on a square grid using the 'end faces' method.

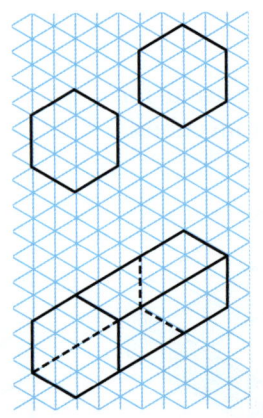

A hexagonal prism drawn on an isometric grid using the 'end faces' method.

Tip

Be very careful to join up corresponding vertices. Remember to use a sharp pencil and a ruler to make your diagrams look professional.

324

20 Three-dimensional shapes

WORK IT OUT 20.1

Students were asked to draw this view of a shape on an isometric grid.

This is how they started their sketches.

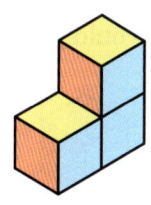

Student A	Student B	Student C

Which student is likely to end up with the correct view of the shape?

What are the others doing incorrectly?

EXERCISE 20B

1 Draw the following objects without using a grid.

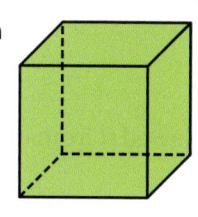

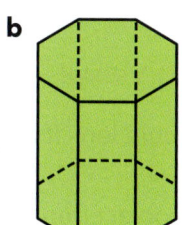

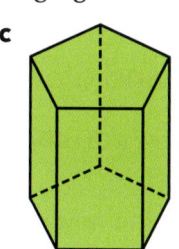

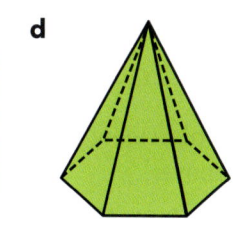

a b c d

2 One of the parallel end faces of three different prisms is shown here.

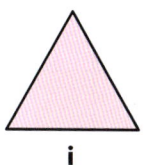

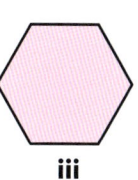

i   ii   iii

   a Sketch each prism on squared paper.

   b Sketch each prism on isometric paper.

   c Compare the two drawings. How does the grid affect what your drawing looks like?

3 Draw the following shapes on an isometric grid.

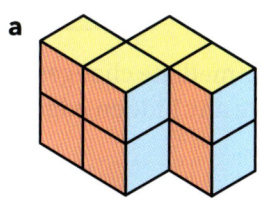

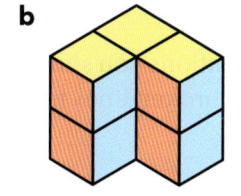

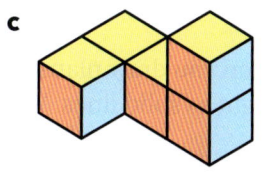

a   b   c

Find answers at: cambridge.org/ukschools/gcsemaths-studentbookanswers

4. The diagrams show different shapes made from cubes.
   If there are no cubes missing from the layers you cannot see, how many cubes would you need to build each shape?

   a

   b

   c

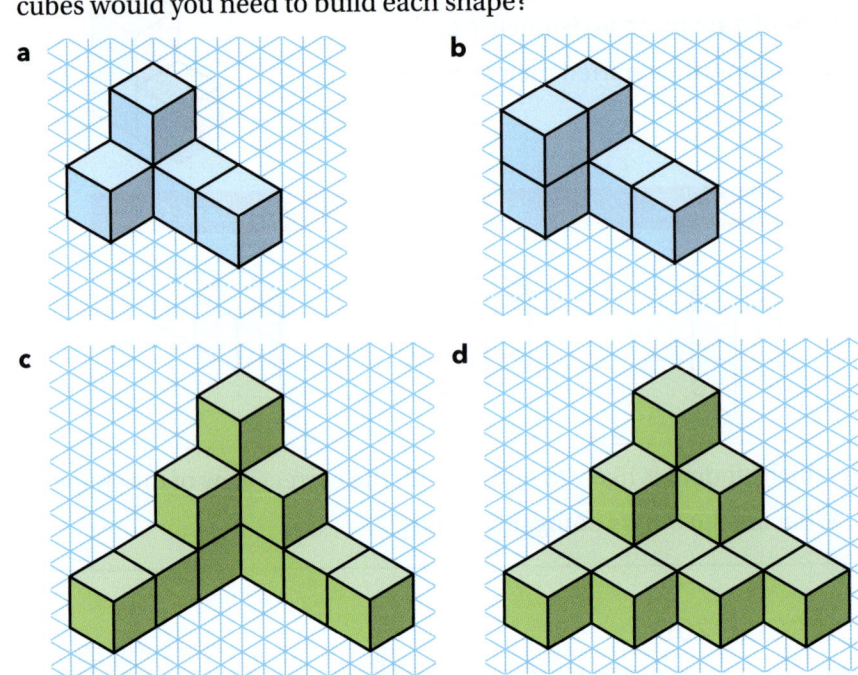

   d

Section 3: Plan and elevation views

A **plan** view shows how a 3D object would look if you viewed it from directly above.

The front **elevation** is the view of a 3D object from its front.

The side elevation is the view from the side.

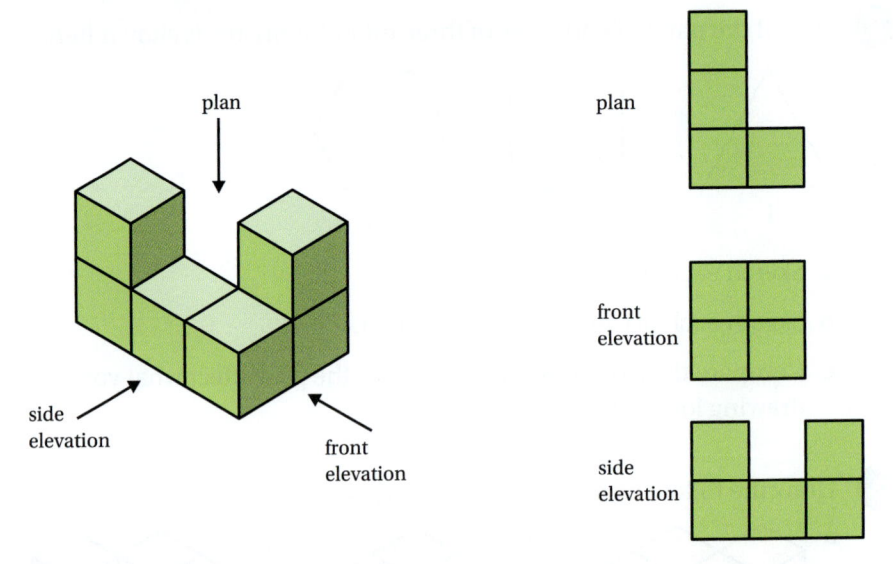

Key vocabulary

plan view: the view of an object from directly above.

elevation: a view of an object from the front, side or back.

When you draw plans or elevations you show any immediate changes in height as solid lines. You use broken lines to indicate any hidden edges.

Think carefully about what the parts of the shape you cannot see will look like. For example, the shape below must have a fourth (hidden) cube in order to support the top cube; you would need to include this cube when drawing the back and side elevations.

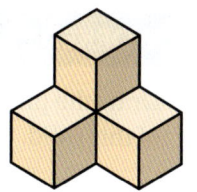

Look at the shape opposite. You can think of it as a prism with trapezium-shaped end faces. The front is higher than the back.

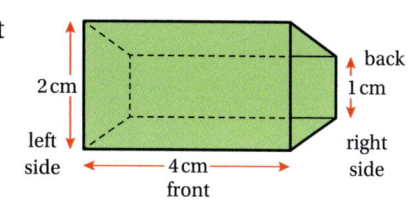

The plan view is a rectangle. Even though the top of the object slopes down to the back, if you look at it from above, it will look like a rectangle. The plan view is normally drawn above the front view because the two views will be the same width.

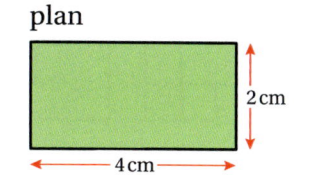

The left and right elevations are reflections of each other. They are drawn on the left and right side of the front elevation.

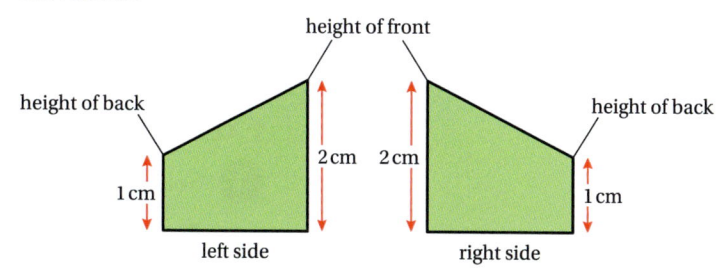

The front and back elevations look the same except that on the back elevation there is a solid line to show that the height of the back face is shorter than the front; you can see the same line in the front elevation but here it is broken to indicate that it is a hidden height. From these elevations, you would not be able to tell that the change in height from the front and back is not immediate, it is sloping; you need the side views to know this.

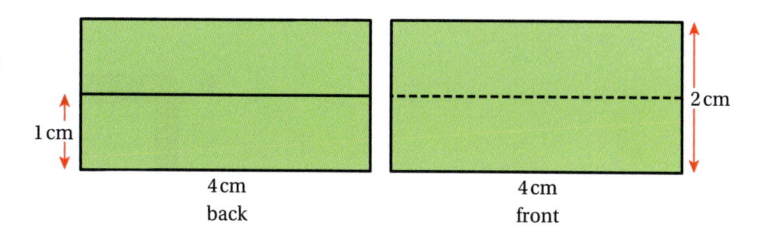

You get different information from different views because each one shows two of the three dimensions of the solid:

- The plan view shows the length and width of the solid.
- The front view shows the length and height of the solid.
- The side views show the width and height of the solid.

GCSE Mathematics for OCR (Foundation)

WORKED EXAMPLE 4

Draw the plan, front and side elevations of this solid.

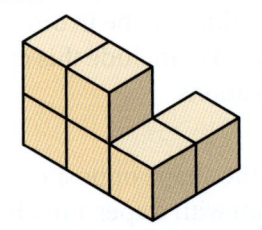

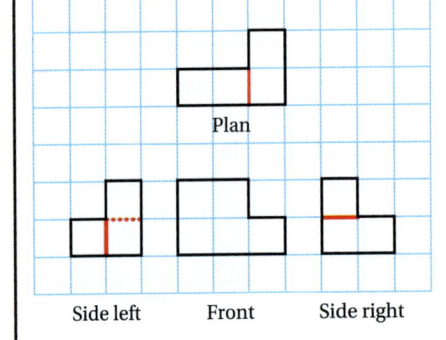

Start by drawing the plan view

Next, draw the front view below it. It will be the same width as the plan view.

Work out what the right side will look like if you view it face on. Draw it next to the front view. It will be the same height.

You can't see the left view, so you have to imagine it. Draw it in the correct place.

EXERCISE 20C

1. Select the correct plan view of each object.

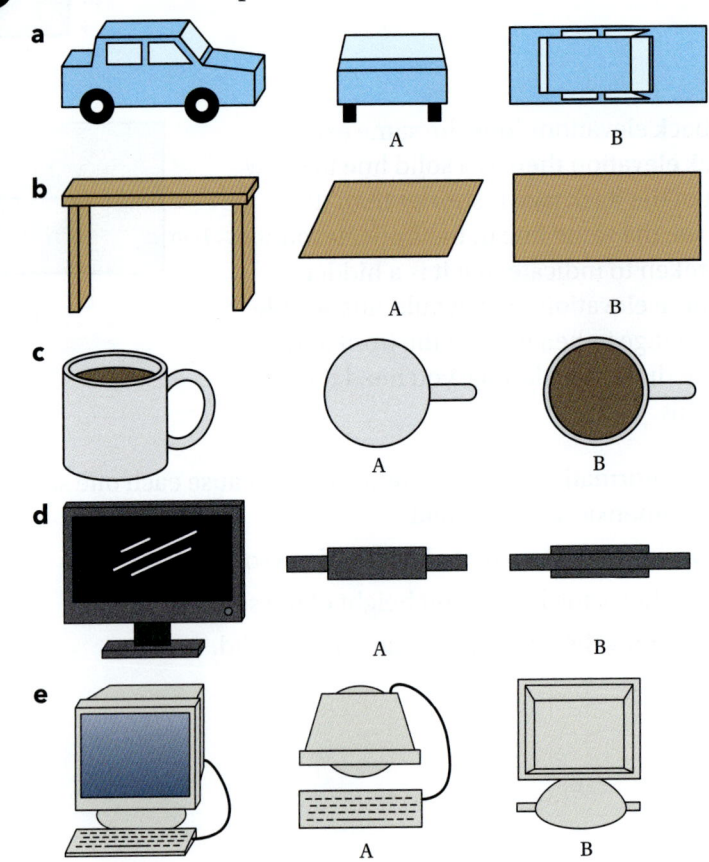

   a

   b

   c

   d

   e

328

2 a Match each shape to its plan and elevation.

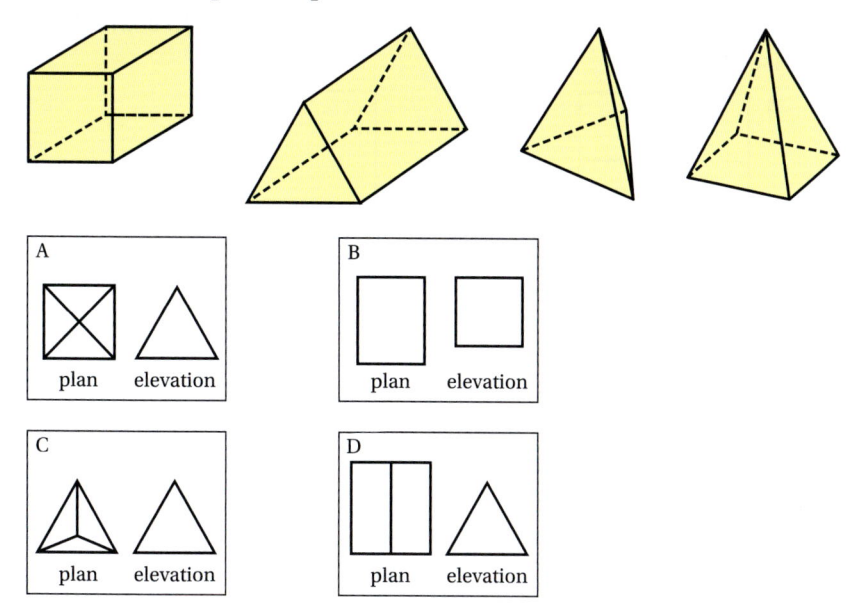

	A	B
	plan elevation	plan elevation
	C	D
	plan elevation	plan elevation

b Sketch and label the elevations that are not shown for each shape.

3 For each set of differently coloured cubes, draw:

a a plan.

b a front elevation.

c a right side elevation (from the right-hand side).

4 Draw the plan, the front elevation and the side elevation of the shape below.

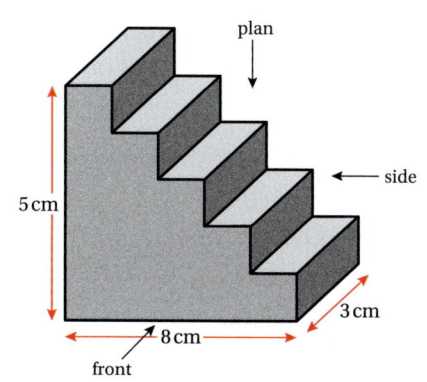

5 cm, 8 cm, 3 cm

front, side, plan

5 The plan view and elevations of different solids are shown.

Use these views to work out what each solid looks like and draw it on an isometric grid.

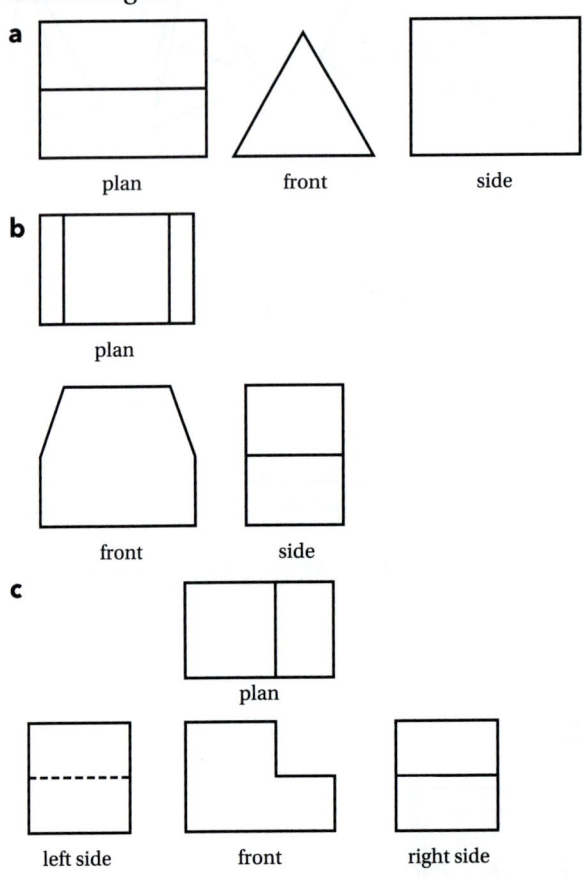

a

plan   front   side

b

plan

front   side

c

plan

left side   front   right side

Checklist of learning and understanding

Review of 3D solids
- The number and shape of the faces, and the number of edges and vertices can be used to identify and name 3D solids.
- Prisms are shapes with two end faces that are congruent polygons, and they have a regular cross-section.
- Pyramids have a polygon base, and triangular sides that meet at an apex.
- Cylinders, cones and spheres are 3D shapes, but they are not polyhedra (polyhedra have faces that are polygons and no curved sides).

2D representations of 3D shapes
- 3D shapes can be represented by 2D drawings on squared or isometric grids.
- Hidden edges are shown as broken lines.

Plans and elevations
- A plan is a view from above a shape.
- An elevation is a view from the front, sides or back of a shape.
- Immediate changes in height are shown using a solid line; hidden edges are shown using a broken line.

Chapter review

1 a Which solid is being described?
  i It has a square cross-section and 12 edges.
  ii A solid with two identical circular bases.
  iii 12 vertices, two congruent hexagon faces.
  iv Circular flat face and one vertex.
  v Three triangular faces meet at an apex.

b Draw each solid.

2 a Match each block of cubes to the correct plan and elevation.

b Identify any missing elevations and draw them for each shape.

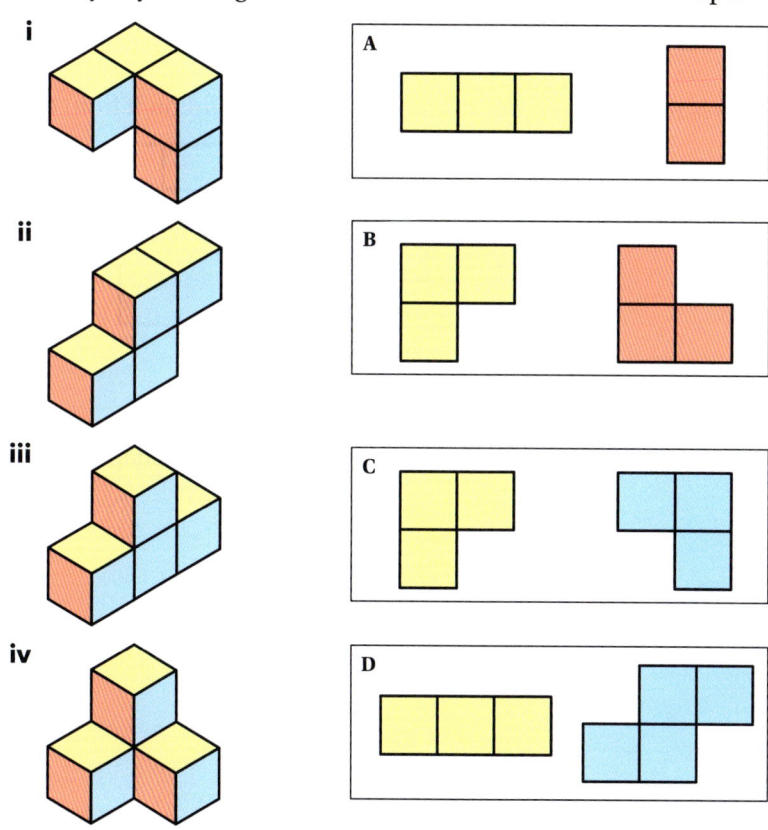

3 The plan and elevation of a solid built from cubes are shown here.

Work out what the solid looks like and sketch it accurately on an isometric grid.

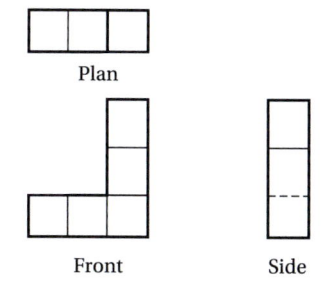

> 20 Three-dimensional shapes
>
> For additional questions on the topics in this chapter, visit GCSE Mathematics Online.

Find answers at: cambridge.org/ukschools/gcsemaths-studentbookanswers

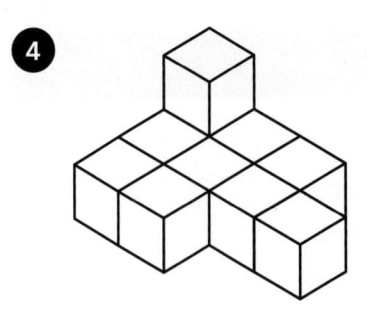

4. Draw this shape:
   a on square paper.
   b on isometric paper.

5. Draw each of the following onto isometric paper.
   a a cube
   b a 3D shape with 4 rectangular faces
   c a triangular-based pyramid.

6. This is the front and right side elevation of a solid built from cubes.

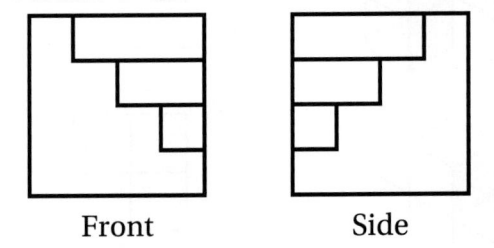

   Front   Side

   a Draw one possible plan view of this shape.
   b How many cubes would be needed to build this shape?

21 Volume and surface area

In this chapter you will learn how to …

- calculate the volume and surface area of cuboids and other prisms.
- calculate the volume and surface area of cylinders.
- solve volume and surface area problems involving composite shapes.

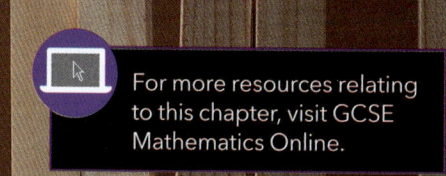

For more resources relating to this chapter, visit GCSE Mathematics Online.

Using mathematics: real-life applications

Freight costs are dependent upon the volume of material being transported. Freight rates are calculated using the container volume measured against the length of the container. The longer the container the higher the freight cost.

"To transport a container full of apples from Felixstowe, England to Le Havre in France I have to let the freight operator know the volume of apples I have to transport as well as the dimensions of the crates. I am then quoted a transport cost."

(Apple farmer)

Before you start …

Ch 5, 20	You need to be able to recognise and identify solid objects, and understand and use their properties	1	Name each object as accurately as possible from the description. a A 3D object with 6 identical square surfaces. b A 3D solid with 2 parallel circular faces. c An object with a square base and triangular side faces that meet at an apex. d A 3D object with a circular base and 1 vertex. e A 3D object with many flat surfaces that are polygons. f A polyhedron with 2 triangular and 3 rectangular faces. 2 A shape has 6 faces, 8 vertices and 12 edges. a What could it be? b What additional information do you need to name the shape more accurately?
Ch 16	You must be able to calculate the area of plane shapes.	3	What is the formula for the area of a circle?
		4	What is the area of a right-angled triangle with sides of 3 cm, 4 cm and 5 cm?

Find answers at: cambridge.org/ukschools/gcsemaths-studentbookanswers

333

GCSE Mathematics for OCR (Foundation)

Assess your starting point using the Launchpad

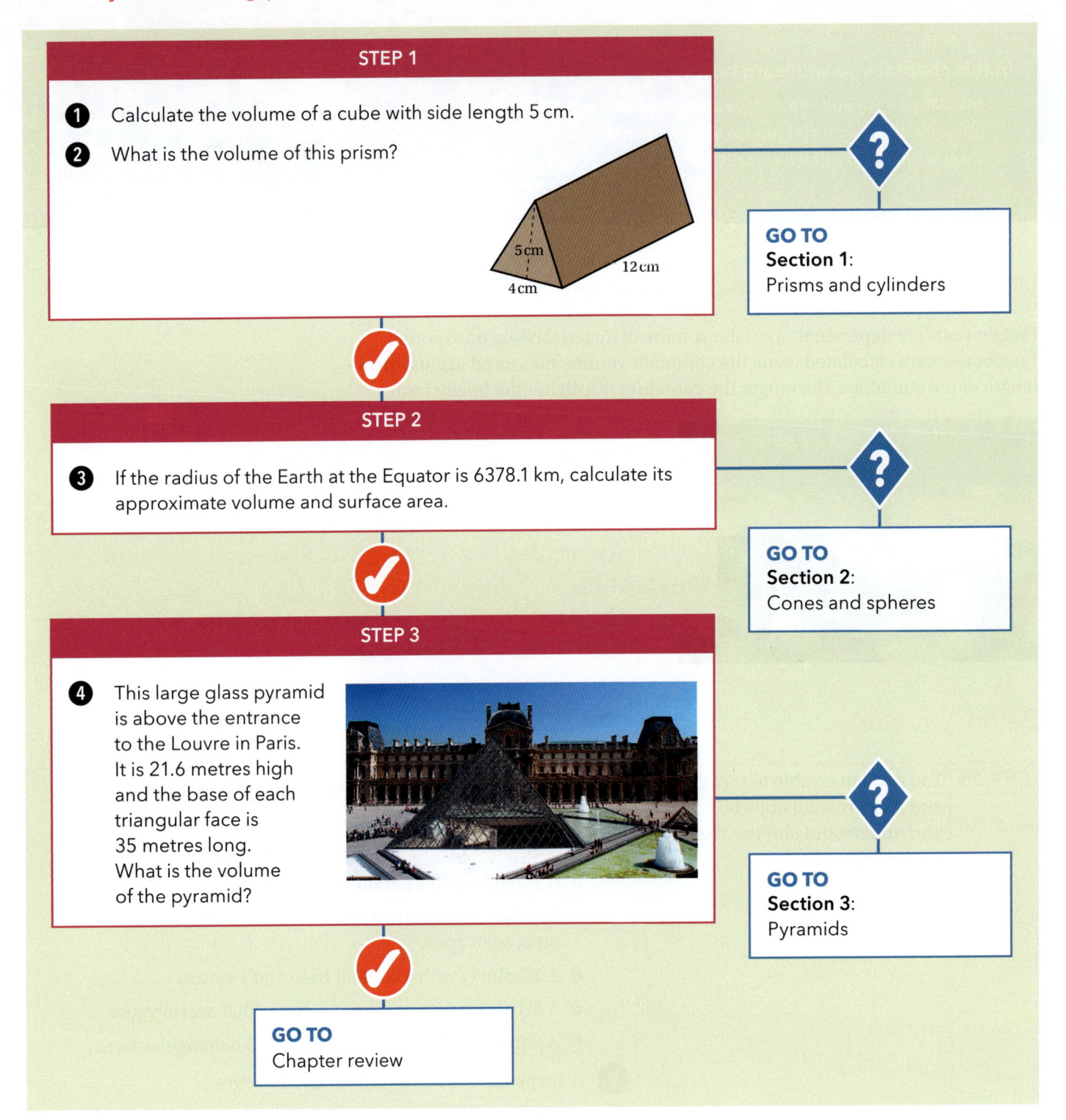

STEP 1

1 Calculate the volume of a cube with side length 5 cm.

2 What is the volume of this prism?

(5 cm, 4 cm, 12 cm)

GO TO
Section 1: Prisms and cylinders

STEP 2

3 If the radius of the Earth at the Equator is 6378.1 km, calculate its approximate volume and surface area.

GO TO
Section 2: Cones and spheres

STEP 3

4 This large glass pyramid is above the entrance to the Louvre in Paris. It is 21.6 metres high and the base of each triangular face is 35 metres long. What is the volume of the pyramid?

GO TO
Section 3: Pyramids

GO TO
Chapter review

Section 1: Prisms and cylinders

In Chapter 5 you learnt that a prism is a 3D object with two parallel and congruent polygonal end faces and a uniform cross-section along its length.

You also learnt that a cylinder is not a prism because the circular end faces of a cylinder are not polygons. However, it is very similar: a cylinder also has a uniform cross-section and two parallel and congruent end faces.

This shape sorter is really a prism sorter. You should be able to name the shapes sticking out of it.

The diagram below shows examples of **right prisms**. One of the end faces is known as the base of the object. The other faces are rectangles perpendicular to the base.

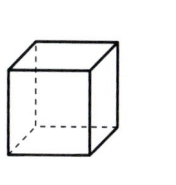

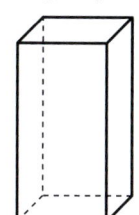

cube (square prism) rectangular prism triangular prism

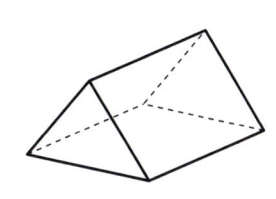

> **Key vocabulary**
>
> **right prism**: a prism with sides perpendicular to the end faces (base).

Volume

The volume of an object is the three-dimensional space that it takes up. Volume is given in cubic units, such as mm^3, cm^3 and m^3 (for solids).

You can find the volume of any right prism by finding the area of one end face (base) and multiplying this by its length.

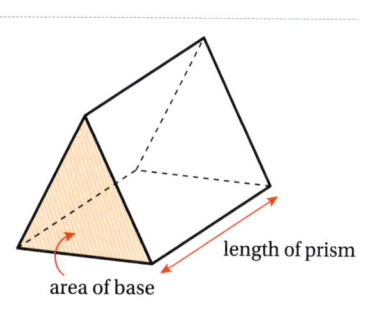

Surface area

Surface area is the total area of the faces of a three-dimensional object.

Sketching a rough net of the object can help you to see what faces to include when you calculate the surface area.

The net of a cuboid shows that the surface area includes the area of six faces.

> **Tip**
>
> You learnt about nets of solids in earlier school years; a net is a 2D shape that can be folded to make a 3D solid.

The surface area of the cuboid is calculated by adding the area of each of its faces. The opposite faces match, so

Surface area = 2(area of side A) + 2(area of side B) + 2(area of base).

A cube has six identical square faces. You can use the following formulae for volume and surface area:

Volume of a cube = x^3

Surface area of a cube = $6x^2$

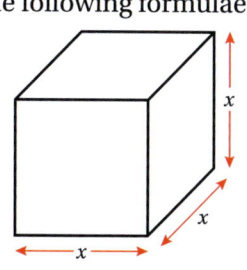

Find answers at: cambridge.org/ukschools/gcsemaths-studentbookanswers

WORKED EXAMPLE 1

Calculate the volume and surface area of this cuboid.

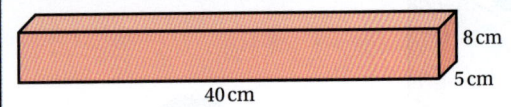

Volume = area of base × length
       = 40 × 5 × 5 = 1000 cm³

> Use the formula for volume of a cuboid and substitute in the known values. Use the correct units for volume.

Surface area = 4 × (40 × 5) + 2 × (5 × 5)
             = 800 + 50
             = 850 cm²

> The two end faces are the same, and the four other sides are the same. Write a formula and substitute in the values. Use the correct units for area.

Prisms with bases of other shapes

The same general formula is used to find the volume and the surface area of any prism.

This is a triangular prism. The base is a triangle and the side faces are rectangles.

Area of a triangular base = $\frac{1}{2}bh$

Volume of triangular prism = $\frac{1}{2} \times b \times h \times l$

Surface area of prism = 2(area of triangular base) + area of three side faces

$= 2\left(\frac{1}{2} \times b \times h\right) + (a \times l) + (c \times l) + (b \times l)$

Tip

Remember that the triangular base could be isosceles, equilateral or scalene; this will determine if the rectangular faces have the same or different area.

WORKED EXAMPLE 2

Find the volume and surface area of this triangular prism.

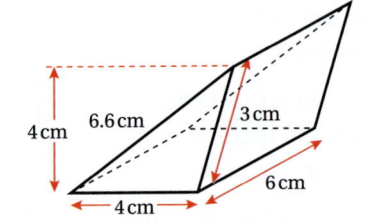

Area of the base = $\frac{1}{2} \times b \times h$

$= \frac{1}{2} \times 4 \times 4 = 8$ cm²

> Remember to use the perpendicular height of the triangle to calculate its area.

Volume of prism = area of base × length
                = 8 × 6 = 48 cm³

> Remember to use the correct units for volume.

Surface area of base triangles = 8 + 8 = 16 cm²
Surface area of side face 1 = 3 × 6 = 18 cm²
Surface area of side face 2 = 4 × 6 = 24 cm²
Surface area of side face 3 = 6.6 × 6 = 39.6 cm²
Total surface area = 97.6 cm²

> Notice that the triangular base is a scalene triangle. This means that each rectangular face will have a different area. Remember to use the correct units for area.

Rearranging the formulae

You can change the subject of the formula to find the length of a prism if you know the volume and area of the base. You can also find the area of the base if you know the volume and length.

For example, the volume of a triangular prism is 100 cm³ and the area of the end face is 25 cm². How long is the prism?

V = area of the triangle × length

$v = al$ so $v \div a = l$

$100 \div 25 = l = 4$ cm.

Other prisms

Prisms with bases that are trapeziums are quite common. Rubbish skips, wheelbarrows, planters and many other containers take this shape.

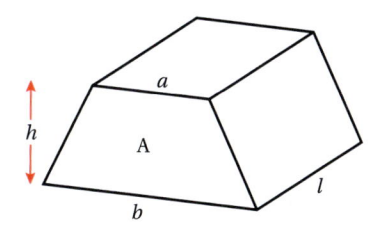

Area of the trapezium base = $\frac{1}{2}(a + b) \times h$.

Volume of prism = area of the trapezium × length

WORK IT OUT 21.1

What is the volume of soil that can be contained in this skip?

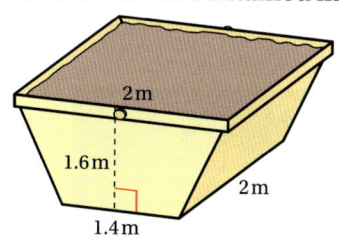

Which of the following is the correct calculation?

Calculation A	Calculation B	Calculation C
Area of the trapezium	Area of the trapezium	Area of the trapezium
Area = $\frac{1}{2}(a + b) \times h$	Area = $\frac{1}{2}(a - b) \times h$	Area = $\frac{1}{2} \times b \times h$
Area = $\frac{1}{2} \times 3.4 \times 1.6 = 2.72$ m²	Area = $\frac{1}{2} \times 0.6 \times 1.6 = 0.48$ m²	Area = $\frac{1}{2} \times 1.4 \times 1.6 = 1.12$ m²
Volume = area of the trapezium × length	Volume = area of the trapezium × length	Volume = area of the trapezium × length
Volume = 2.72 × 2 = 5.44 m³	Volume = 0.48 × 2 = 0.96 m³	Volume = 1.12 × 2 = 2.24 m³

Find answers at: cambridge.org/ukschools/gcsemaths-studentbookanswers

Cylinders

Cylinders are not prisms, but you can find their volume and surface area in the same way as you do with prisms.

The net of a cylinder shows that the curved surface forms a rectangle when it is flattened out. The length of the rectangle is equivalent to the circumference of the circular base.

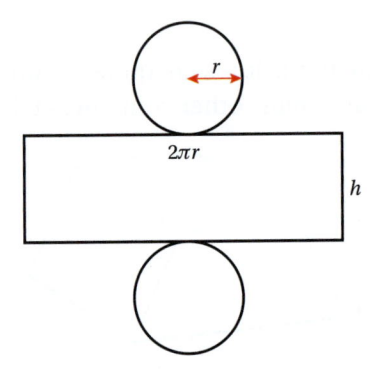

The surface area of a cylinder is calculated using the formula:

Surface area = area of curved surface + 2(area of circular base)

$$S = 2\pi rh + 2\pi r^2$$

WORKED EXAMPLE 3

A road roller has a roller on the front which is filled with water to make it heavy. The tank of water in the roller has a radius of 0.95 m and a width of 2.4 m.

What volume of water is needed to fill the tank?

Volume of water = area of the circle × length
$= \pi r^2 \times l$
$= 3.14 \times 0.95 \times 0.95 \times 2.4$
$= 6.801\,24$ m³
$= 6.8$ m³ (1 dp)

> Round your answer to a suitable degree of accuracy. (See Chapter 17 if you need a reminder.)

21 Volume and surface area

Problem-solving framework

You are painting a room and it needs 2 coats of paint. The room is 10 m long, 7 m wide and 3 m high. There is a door which is 2 m high and 1.5 m wide and a window that is 2.6 m high and 2.2 m wide. You want to colour the room blue and it should take 5 days to paint it.

A litre of paint covers 5 m² and you can buy it in 5-litre tins. Each tin costs £14.99. How many 5-litre paint tins will you need to buy?

You should add 10% into your calculations for special circumstances.

Steps for approaching a problem-solving question	What you would do for this example
Step 1: What have you got to do?	Paint a room with 2 coats of paint. Work out how many 5-litre tins of paint are needed.
Step 3: What information do you need?	Room dimensions are needed for surface area calculations. Door and window dimensions need to be taken away from the coverage area. It is useful to estimate before you start. The room is roughly 100 m² and the door and window are roughly 10 m². So coverage is 2 × 90 m² = 180 m². Plus 10% takes it roughly to 200 m². This means 200 ÷ 5 = 40 litres. Eight 5-litre tins are needed.
Step 4: What information don't you need?	The colour of paint, the length of time taken and the cost of the paint are not needed.
Step 5: What maths can you do?	Calculate the surface area of the room: Walls 1 & 3: 10 × 3 = 30 m² Walls 2 & 4: 7 × 3 = 21 m² Total surface area = 30 + 30 + 21 + 21 = 102 m² Door area = 2 × 1.5 = 3 m² Window area = 2.6 × 2.2 = 5.72 m² Total surface area for painting 102 − 3 − 5.72 = 93.28 m². Two coats required = 93.28 × 2 = 186.56 m² 10% = 18.656 m² Total paint coverage required 18.656 + 186.56 = 205.216 m² 1 litre = 5 m² coverage of paint 205.216 ÷ 5 = 41.0432 litres of paint are required. 5-litre tins of paint can be bought: 41.0432 ÷ 5 = 8.208 64 You will need to buy 9 tins.
Step 6: Have you done it all?	Room size less the door and window sizes ✓ 2 coats of paint + 10% ✓ Litres divided by 5 for the number of 5-litre tins required Total divided by the coverage of 1 tin of paint ✓
Step 7: Is it correct?	Checked against estimate ✓

Find answers at: cambridge.org/ukschools/gcsemaths-studentbookanswers

EXERCISE 21A

1 Calculate the volume and surface area of each object. (Each object is a closed object.)

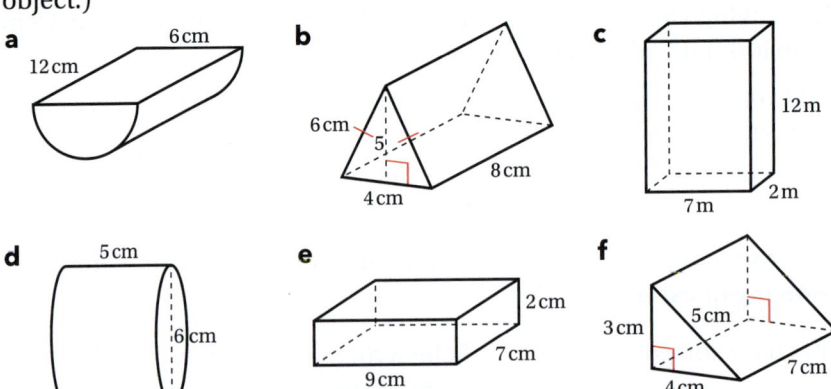

a 12 cm, 6 cm

b 6 cm, 5, 4 cm, 8 cm

c 12 m, 7 m, 2 m

d 5 cm, 6 cm

e 2 cm, 7 cm, 9 cm

f 3 cm, 5 cm, 4 cm, 7 cm

2 If 1 litre = 1000 cm³ what is the volume, in litres of the aquarium below?

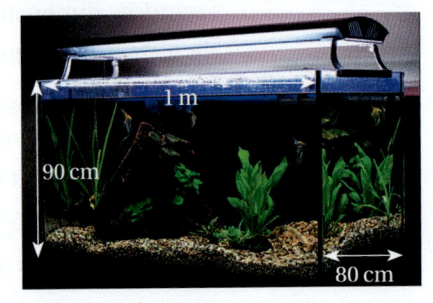

1 m, 90 cm, 80 cm

3 The volume of a cube is 144 m³. What is the length of each side?

4 An Olympic-sized swimming pool is 50 m long, 25 m wide, and the water is 2 m deep. What is the volume of water in an Olympic-sized swimming pool?

5 What is the volume of this triangular prism?
Give your answer correct to 2 dp.

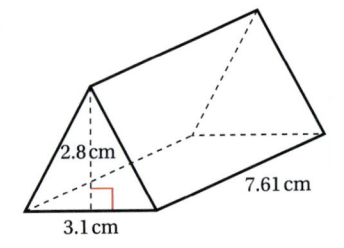

2.8 cm, 3.1 cm, 7.61 cm

6 What is the surface area of one side of this roof, for the solar panel calculations?

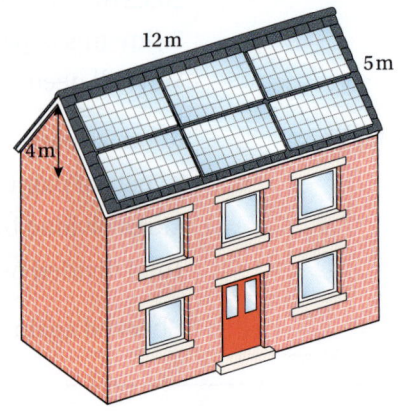

12 m, 5 m, 4 m

7 Calculate the volume of the object below.

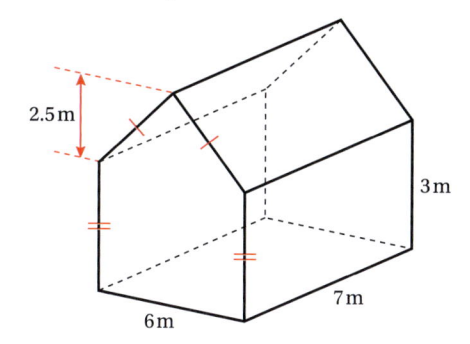

8 Calculate the volume of this solid piece of wood with a cylindrical hole drilled through the middle.

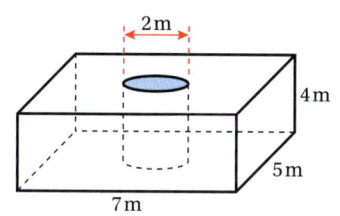

> **Tip**
> Think back to how you calculated the area of composite 2D shapes in Chapter 16; subtract the volume of the 'cut out' shape from the volume of the larger shape.

Section 2: Cones and spheres

Cones

The formula for the volume of a cone is,
$\frac{1}{3}$ × area of circular base × h,
where h is the **perpendicular height** from the base to the apex of the cone.

The area of the base can be found using the formula for the area of a circle, πr^2.

So, the volume of a cone = $\frac{1}{3}\pi r^2 h$

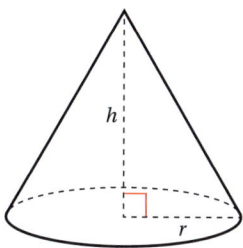

> **Tip**
> You don't need to learn these formulae. The formulae will be given if you need to use them in a test or exam. Investigate on the internet if you want to find proofs of these formulae.

> **Tip**
> In some problems involving cones you might need to use Pythagoras' theorem to find the perpendicular height using the radius and the slant height.

WORKED EXAMPLE 4

Find the volume of a cone of radius 12 cm with a perpendicular height of 14 cm.

Volume = $\frac{1}{3}(\pi r^2)h = \frac{1}{3}(3.14 \times 12 \times 12) \times 14$

= 2110.08 cm³

You are given all the values you need. Substitute them into the formula.

The area of the curved surface of a cone is πrs, where r is the radius of the base, and s is the **slant height** of the cone. To find the total surface area of a solid cone you need to include the curved surface area as well as the circular base.

Find answers at: cambridge.org/ukschools/gcsemaths-studentbookanswers

Therefore, the total surface area (S) of the cone is:

S = area of curved surface + area of base

= $\pi rs + \pi r^2$

Spheres

A sphere is any perfectly round object.

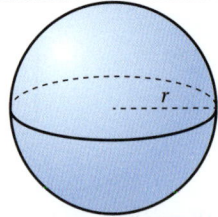

The volume of a sphere is equal to $\frac{4}{3}\pi r^3$ where r is the radius of the sphere.

The surface area of a sphere is equal to $4\pi r^2$, where r is the radius of the sphere.

Many objects include spheres or parts of spheres in their structure.

WORKED EXAMPLE 5

Find the surface area and volume of a sphere of radius 3 cm.
Use 3.142 as an approximation of pi.

Surface area = 4 × 3.14 × 3 × 3 = 113.04 cm²
Volume = $\frac{4}{3}$ × 3.14 × 3 × 3 × 3 = 113.04 cm³

Substitute known values into the relevant formula. Don't forget to use the correct units!

WORKED EXAMPLE 6

The radius of the Earth is approximately 6378.1 km.

a Find the approximate volume and surface area of the Earth.
  Use exact values of pi.

b 70% of the surface of the Earth is covered with water.
  What is the surface area of land?

a $V = \frac{4}{3} \times \pi \times 6378.1^3 \approx 1\,086\,832\,412\,000$ km³

Surface area = 4 × π × 6378.1² ≈ 511 201 962.3 km²

b 30% of the Earth's surface area is land.
  0.3 × 511 201 962.3 = 153 360 588.7 km²

If 70% is water then 30% is land. Refer back to Chapter 13 for a reminder on percentages if you need to.

Tip

In calculations with such large values you would normally give your answers in standard form. You will deal with this in Chapter 26.

EXERCISE 21B

1 Calculate the volume and surface area of each object.

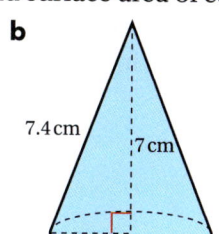

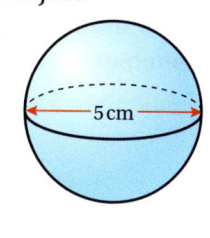

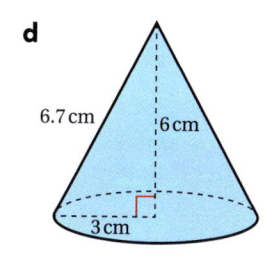

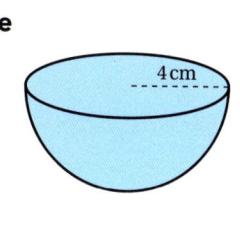

a. cone: 3 cm (radius), 11.6 cm, 12 cm
b. cone: 7.4 cm, 7 cm, 2.5 cm
c. sphere: 5 cm
d. cone: 6.7 cm, 6 cm, 3 cm
e. hemisphere: 4 cm

2 Earth's moon has a mean radius of 1738 km. Use the exact value of pi to find its approximate volume.

3 The table below gives some standard diameters of spherical balls used in different sports. Calculate the surface area of each ball. Assume they are round and ignore any dimples on the surface.

	Sport	Standard diameter
a	snooker	52.5 mm
b	tennis	6.35 cm
c	football	15 cm
d	golf	42.7 mm
e	bowling	21.6 cm
f	basketball	25.4 cm
g	hockey	3 cm
h	baseball	74 mm
i	cricket	7 cm

4 A factory needs to calculate the volume and surface area of plastic cones which have the dimensions given in centimetres in the table. Calculate each volume and surface area.

	Radius (r)	Slant height (s)	Perpendicular height (h)
a	5	10	8.7
b	18	34	28.8
c	7	21	19.8
d	16	22	15.1
e	60	64	22.3
f	9	26	24.4
g	30	52	42.5

5 A conical tent has a circular base with a diameter of 3 m, a perpendicular height of 2.6 m and a slant height of 3 m.

What is its volume?

Find answers at: cambridge.org/ukschools/gcsemaths-studentbookanswers

Composite solids

Objects in real life are very rarely made up of just one kind of geometric object. Most buildings involve a combination of solid shapes, and modern buildings often use unusual shapes in their designs.

This is the winning design for the air traffic control tower at Newcastle airport. The design uses cut-off conical shapes around a cuboid-shaped cement tower.

This is the North Gate Bus Station in Northampton. Many different solids have been used in the design.

When you worked with area in Chapter 16 you split composite shapes into known shapes and found the area of each shape separately. You can use the same technique to find the volume of composite solids.

To find the total surface area of a composite solid you need to find the area of each section separately. However, you cannot just automatically use the formula for this because the area of some faces will overlap and not form part of the 'outside' or surface area of the solid.

Tip

It is useful to develop a system for checking that you have included all the surfaces when you are finding the surface area of a composite shape.

WORKED EXAMPLE 7

Calculate the total volume and surface area of the object.

Use exact values of π in your calculations and give final answers correct to 2 decimal places.

Volume	Surface area
Volume of cone = $\frac{1}{3}(\pi r^2) \times h$ $= \frac{1}{3} \times \pi \times (8)^2 \times 9$ $= 603.19 \text{ cm}^3$	Conical top is a cone without a base. Curved surface area = πrs $= \pi \times 8 \times 12$ $= 301.59 \text{ cm}^2$
Volume of cylinder = $\pi r^2 h$ $= \pi \times (8)^2 \times 25$ $= 5026.55 \text{ cm}^3$	Cylinder with one base only. S = area of base + area of curved side $= \pi \times (8)^2 + 2 \times \pi \times 8 \times 25$ $= 1457.70 \text{ cm}^2$
Total volume = 5629.74 cm^3	Total surface area = 1759.29 cm^2

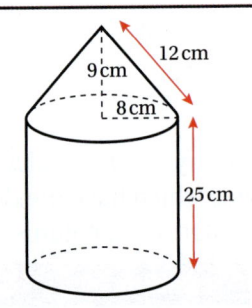

The object consists of a cone and a cylinder. The base of the cone is not included in the surface area because this is **inside** the shape.

The top end of the cylinder is not included in the surface area because it is **inside** the shape.

When the composite shape is made of a shape with another shape cut out of it, you subtract the volume of the 'cut out' shape from the volume of the larger shape.

21 Volume and surface area

EXERCISE 21C

1 Find the surface area of each solid. Give your answers correct to the nearest cm² or mm².

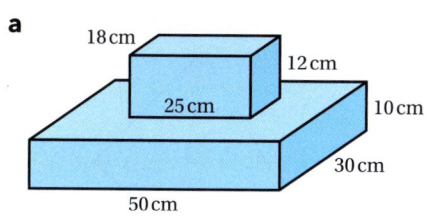

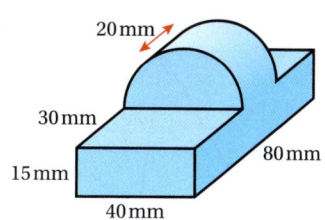

  a (18 cm, 12 cm, 25 cm, 10 cm, 30 cm, 50 cm)

  b (20 mm, 30 mm, 15 mm, 40 mm, 80 mm)

2 Calculate the volume of each solid.

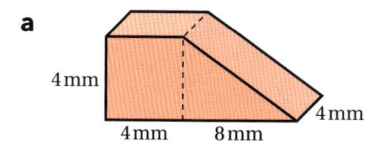

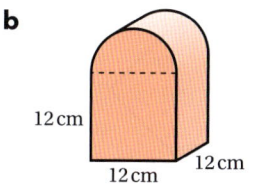

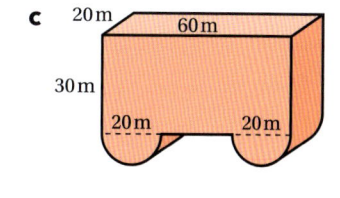

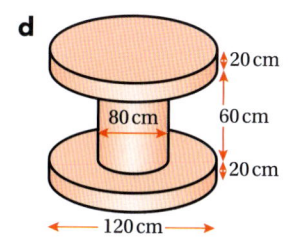

  a (4 mm, 4 mm, 8 mm, 4 mm)

  b (12 cm, 12 cm, 12 cm)

  c (20 m, 60 m, 30 m, 20 m, 20 m)

  d (20 cm, 80 cm, 60 cm, 20 cm, 120 cm)

3 A sphere of diameter 1.6 m is cut through the centre to form two hemispheres. What is the surface area of each hemisphere?

Section 3: Pyramids

Pyramids are named according to the shape of their base.

The volume of a pyramid is $\frac{1}{3}$ of the volume of a prism with the same base area and height.

Volume of a pyramid = $\frac{1}{3}$ area of base × perpendicular height.

The surface area of a pyramid is the total area of the base plus the area of each triangular side.

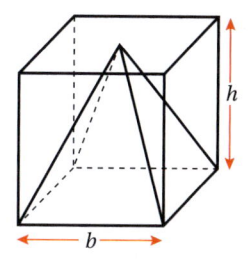

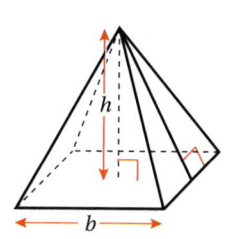

WORKED EXAMPLE 8

Calculate the volume and the surface area of the square-based pyramid.

Volume = $\frac{1}{3}$ × area of base × h

= $\frac{1}{3} \times 9 \times 9 \times 9 = 243 \text{ cm}^3$

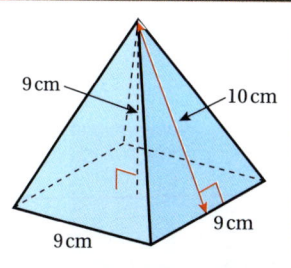

Surface area = $b \times b + 4 \times \left(\frac{1}{2} \times \text{slant height} \times b\right)$

= $(9 \times 9) + 4 \times \left(\frac{1}{2} \times 10 \times 9\right)$

= $81 + 180 = 261 \text{ cm}^2$

Surface area = area of square base + 4 × area of triangular sides. The height of the triangular side is the slant height.

Find answers at: cambridge.org/ukschools/gcsemaths-studentbookanswers

EXERCISE 21D

1 The six pyramids below have either square or triangular bases.
Calculate the volume and the surface area of each one.

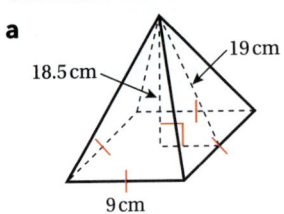

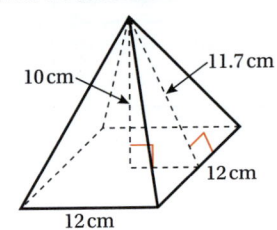

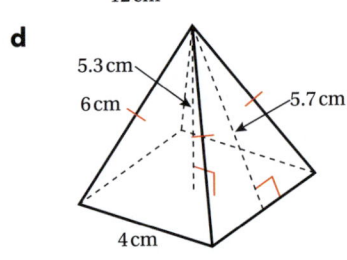

a) 18.5 cm, 19 cm, 9 cm

b) 10 cm, 11.7 cm, 12 cm, 12 cm

c) 4 cm, 5 cm, 3 cm, 9 cm

d) 5.3 cm, 6 cm, 5.7 cm, 4 cm

2 What is the volume of the Great Pyramid in the photograph? It has a square base.

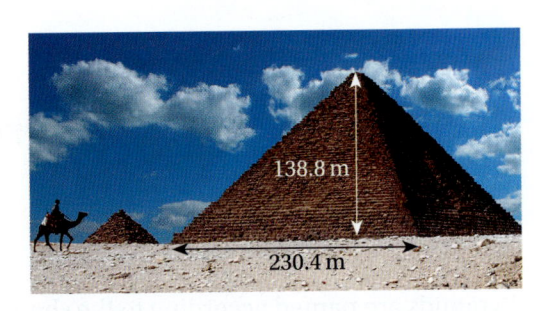

138.8 m
230.4 m

> **Tip**
> The perpendicular height of a 6 m equilateral triangle is 5.2 m.

3 What is the difference in the volumes of a pyramid with a square base of side 6 m and a pyramid with an equilateral triangle with side 6 m as a base, if both have a perpendicular height of 8 m?

> **Tip**
> The perpendicular height of a 1 m equilateral triangle is 0.87 m.

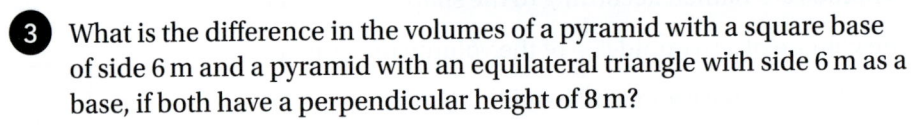

4 The wooden sculpture below is a triangular-based pyramid.
The base is an equilateral triangle with sides of 1 m. The height of the sculpture is 2 m.
Calculate the volume of wood used to make the sculpture.

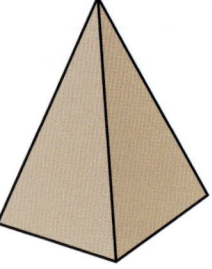

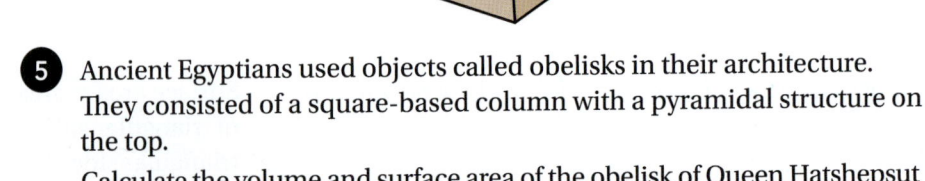

5 Ancient Egyptians used objects called obelisks in their architecture. They consisted of a square-based column with a pyramidal structure on the top.
Calculate the volume and surface area of the obelisk of Queen Hatshepsut in the photograph (exclude the base from the surface area). The obelisk is 30 m high, the square base has an area of 5 m² and the pyramid itself is 1.5 m high. The slant height of the pyramid is 1.87 m.

21 Volume and surface area

Checklist of learning and understanding

Volume

- Volume is the amount of space a 3D object occupies.
- Volume is calculated in cubic units.
- The volume of a prism and a cylinder = area of base × length.
- Volume of a cone = $\frac{1}{3}$ × area of base × height.
- Volume of a sphere = $\frac{4}{3}\pi r^3$.
- Volume of a pyramid = $\frac{1}{3}$ × area of base × height.

Surface area

- The surface area of a solid is the combined areas of all the external faces.
- You will need to apply what you know about calculating the area of 2D shapes to find the surface area of a solid.

Tip

Remember length, area and volume represent very different measurements. 1 cm, 1 cm² and 1 cm³. What do these look like?

Chapter review

For additional questions on the topics in this chapter, visit GCSE Mathematics Online.

1 How much canvas is in this tent, including the ground sheet on the floor? (Assume the shape is a triangular prism.)

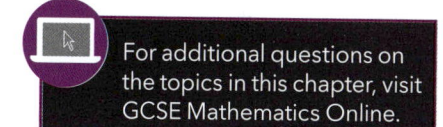

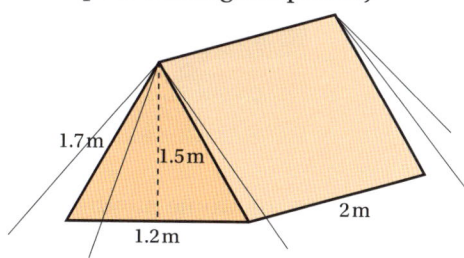

1.7 m, 1.5 m, 2 m, 1.2 m

2 These solids have been built from cubes with side length 2 cm.
Find the total surface area of each solid.

a   b   c

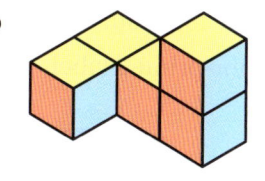

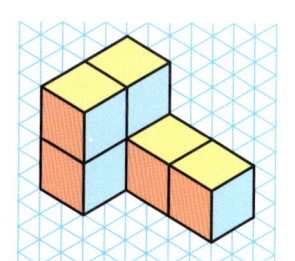

3 What is the volume of this model house?

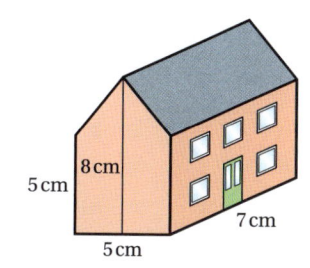

5 cm, 8 cm, 5 cm, 7 cm

Find answers at: cambridge.org/ukschools/gcsemaths-studentbookanswers

347

4 A cheese is a cylinder of radius 7 cm and depth 5 cm.

The cheese is totally covered with a thin coating of wax.

A slice of the cheese is cut so that the top is the sector of the circle of angle 34°.

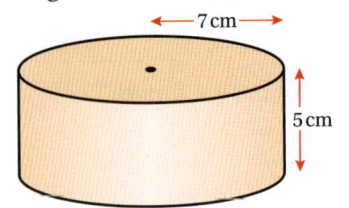

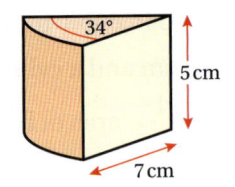

Work out the area of the wax coating this slice of cheese. *(6 marks)*

© OCR 2013

5 What is the volume of this piece of art sculpture?

It is made of a cube with a cylinder cut out through the middle of it.

6 The dimensions of a cube are whole numbers. If the volume of this cube is 64 cm³ which of the following whole numbers could be a side length?

A 4   B 10   C 8   D 16   E 5

7 Calculate:

a the volume of a tin of dog food.

b the surface area of the printed label.

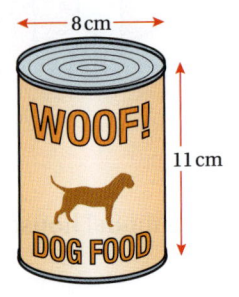

22 Calculations with ratio

In this chapter you will learn how to …

- work with equivalent ratios.
- divide quantities in a given ratio.
- identify and work with fractions in ratio problems.
- apply ratio to real contexts and problems, such as those involving conversion, comparison, scaling, mixing and concentrations.

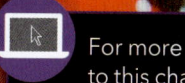

For more resources relating to this chapter, visit GCSE Mathematics Online.

Using mathematics: real-life applications

Converting between different currencies, working out which packet of crisps is the best value for money, mixing large quantities of cement and scaling up a recipe to cater for more people all involve reasoning using ratios.

"Every day customers bring me paints to match. I have to understand how changing the ratio of base colours affects the colour of the paint and how to scale the quantities up and down for larger or smaller amounts of paint. If I get it wrong, customers will have patches of different colours and their walls would look quite strange." *(Paint technician)*

Before you start …

Ch 10	You need to be able to identify and simplify fractions.	**1**	**a** In a class of 35 pupils 21 are boys. What fraction of the class are girls? **b** What fraction of this shape is shaded? Write your answer in its simplest form.
Ch 10	You need to be able to find a fraction of a quantity.	**2**	Find $\frac{2}{3}$ of 42.
Ch 10	You need to be able to find an original amount given a fraction.	**3**	There are 51 parents of students in the audience at a school play. These parents make up $\frac{3}{4}$ of the audience. How many people are in the audience?

Find answers at: cambridge.org/ukschools/gcsemaths-studentbookanswers

349

GCSE Mathematics for OCR (Foundation)

Assess your starting point using the Launchpad

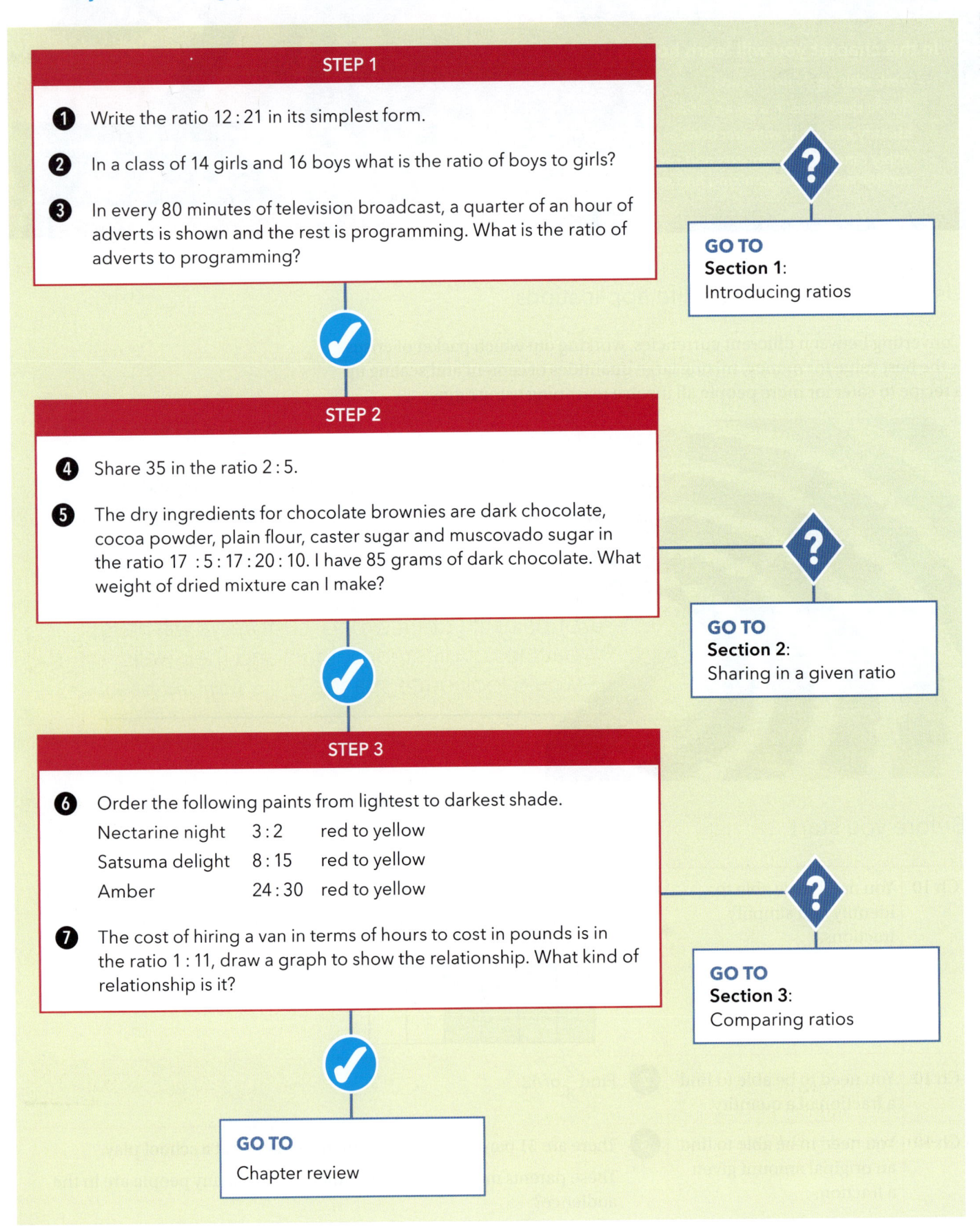

STEP 1

1. Write the ratio 12 : 21 in its simplest form.

2. In a class of 14 girls and 16 boys what is the ratio of boys to girls?

3. In every 80 minutes of television broadcast, a quarter of an hour of adverts is shown and the rest is programming. What is the ratio of adverts to programming?

GO TO
Section 1: Introducing ratios

STEP 2

4. Share 35 in the ratio 2 : 5.

5. The dry ingredients for chocolate brownies are dark chocolate, cocoa powder, plain flour, caster sugar and muscovado sugar in the ratio 17 : 5 : 17 : 20 : 10. I have 85 grams of dark chocolate. What weight of dried mixture can I make?

GO TO
Section 2: Sharing in a given ratio

STEP 3

6. Order the following paints from lightest to darkest shade.

Nectarine night	3 : 2	red to yellow
Satsuma delight	8 : 15	red to yellow
Amber	24 : 30	red to yellow

7. The cost of hiring a van in terms of hours to cost in pounds is in the ratio 1 : 11, draw a graph to show the relationship. What kind of relationship is it?

GO TO
Section 3: Comparing ratios

GO TO
Chapter review

22 Calculations with ratio

Section 1: Introducing ratios

Many colours of paint can be mixed from the four base colours: blue, yellow, red and white.

Think about mixing green paint. You would need to know which base colours to mix. You would also need to know how much of each colour to mix to get dark green or light green. The amount of each colour is important for getting the same shade of green each time you make it.

Paint technicians can mix the same shade of green over and over by mixing yellow and blue paints in a particular **ratio**.

Artists and designers use a special chart with thousands of numbered shades of colours to make sure they get the exact shade they want. The number allows the colour to be mixed using the correct ratio of base colours.

Ratio describes how parts of equal size relate to each other. A ratio of yellow to blue paint of 1 : 3 means one unit of yellow for every three units of blue. This would give a very dark green. The order in which a ratio is written is important. A ratio of 2 : 5 means 2 parts to 5 parts. Each part is equal in size.

A ratio of yellow to blue paint of 5 : 1 means five units of yellow for every one unit of blue. This would give a much lighter green.

The diagram shows a ratio of yellow to blue of 3 : 9.

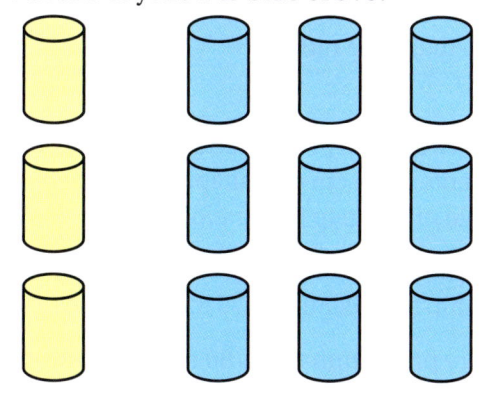

Dividing by three simplifies the ratio of 3 : 9 to give 1 : 3.

$$\div 3 \begin{pmatrix} 3 & : & 9 \\ 1 & : & 3 \end{pmatrix} \div 3$$

Mixing paint in the ratio 3 : 9 would give the same colour as mixing it in the ratio 1 : 3 because the colours are mixed in the same ratio. The yellow paint makes up the same **proportion** of the mix in both cases.

The ratios 3 : 9 and 1 : 3 are **equivalent** ratios.

The difference between ratio and proportion

A ratio compares two or more quantities with each other. A proportion compares a quantity to the 'whole' of which it is a part.

For example, in the dark green paint mixture, the ratio of yellow paint to blue paint is 3 : 9 or 1 : 3. The proportion of yellow paint in the dark green paint mixture is $\frac{3}{12}$, $\frac{1}{4}$ or 25%.

> **Key vocabulary**
>
> **ratio**: a comparison of two or more different parts, or amounts, in relation to each other.

> **Tip**
>
> With many ratio questions, drawing a picture of the situation can help you work it out.

> **Key vocabulary**
>
> **proportion**: a comparison of a part, or amount, to the whole; often expressed as a fraction, percentage or ratio.
>
> **equivalent**: having the same value; two ratios or fractions are equivalent if one is a multiple of the other because they will cancel to the same simplest term.

> **Tip**
>
> The 'whole' of a ratio 3 : 9 is 3 + 9 = 12; the 'whole' of the ratio 1 : 3 is 1 + 3 = 4.

Find answers at: cambridge.org/ukschools/gcsemaths-studentbookanswers

EXERCISE 22A

1 36 girls, 45 boys and 9 teachers went on a school trip.
   a What is the ratio of boys to girls?
   b What is the ratio of pupils to teachers?
   c What is the ratio of pupils to people on the trip?
   d The school policy is that each teacher can be responsible for no more than 10 pupils. Does this trip meet this requirement?

2 Look at each diagram. What is the ratio of shaded squares to unshaded squares in each? Write the answers in simplest form.

   a 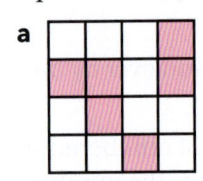   **b** 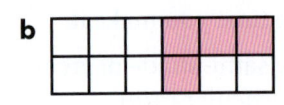   **c**

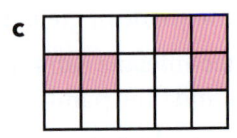

3 Look at each diagram. What is the ratio of shaded squares to total squares in each? Write the answers in simplest form.

   a 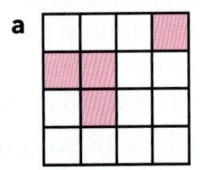   **b** 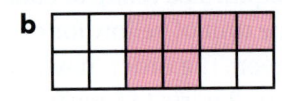   **c**

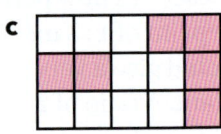

> **Tip**
> Think about what the ratio would have been **before** it was simplified to 1 : 3, and how many parts there are in the whole.

4 The ratio of shaded to unshaded squares in this diagram is 1 : 3. How many more squares need to be shaded to make the ratio 2 : 3?

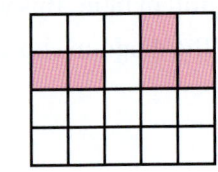

> **Tip**
> Ratios do not include units. To compare measured amounts you need to make sure they are written in the same units.

5 The distance between the post office and the bank on the local high street is represented as 5 cm on a map. In real life this distance is 20 m. What is the scale of the map (as a ratio)?

6 On a scale drawing of a cruise ship a cabin is 8 cm from the restaurant. On the actual ship the distance is 76 m. Write the distances as a ratio.

7 A natural history programme lasts 90 minutes. The crew recorded 60 hours of footage. What is the ratio of footage used to footage recorded?

8 a Use the diagram to find the ratio of:
   i side AB to side AC.   **ii** side EB to side DC.   **iii** side AE to side AD.

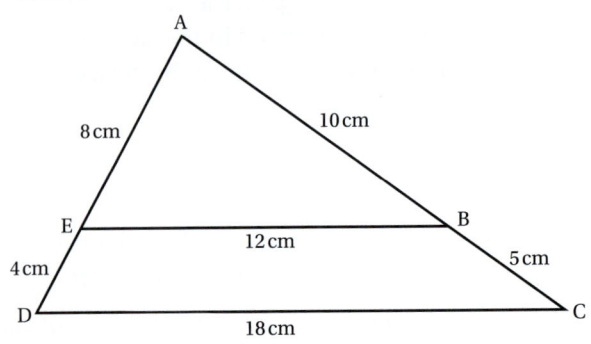

> **Tip**
> You will learn more about similarity in Chapter 29 but for now think back to work you have done in earlier school years.

   b What does this tell you about triangles ABE and ACD?
   c On this basis, what is the ratio of the angle AEB to angle EDC?

9 A jam recipe uses 55 g of fruit for every 100 g of jam. The rest is sugar. What is the ratio of fruit to sugar?

10 An adult ticket for the cinema is one and a half times the price for a child's ticket. What is the ratio of the price of an adult ticket to the price of a child's ticket? Write the ratio in its simplest form.

11 According to recent statistics $\frac{3}{5}$ of 16 year olds have a mobile phone. What is the ratio of 16 year olds with mobiles to those without?

> **Tip**
>
> Ratios can include decimal numbers but not when they are written in their simplest form; the simplest form always uses integers.

Section 2: Sharing in a given ratio

Often you will be given a ratio and asked to share an amount using that ratio.

For example, a group of three office workers form a lottery syndicate. Together they buy eight lottery tickets a week.

Simon pays £1 a week, Oliver £3 and Lucy £4. They win £32 000.

Should they each get an equal share of the winnings? If not, how should they share their winnings? What is the fairest way?

The fairest way would be for each member to receive winnings in the same ratio as they bought tickets.

The winnings should therefore be distributed between Simon, Oliver and Lucy in the ratio 1 : 3 : 4. This can be represented using a diagram, where each box represents the number of parts of the whole each individual should receive.

Every box has to have the same quantity in it. In total we have 8 boxes (1 + 3 + 4), in which we have to share £32 000.

Each box gets £32 000 ÷ 8 = £4000.

So:
Simon receives £4000.
Oliver receives 3 × £4000 = £12 000
Lucy receives 4 × £4000 = £16 000

> **Tip**
>
> The box method shown in the example is useful for working out shares in a given ratio problems.

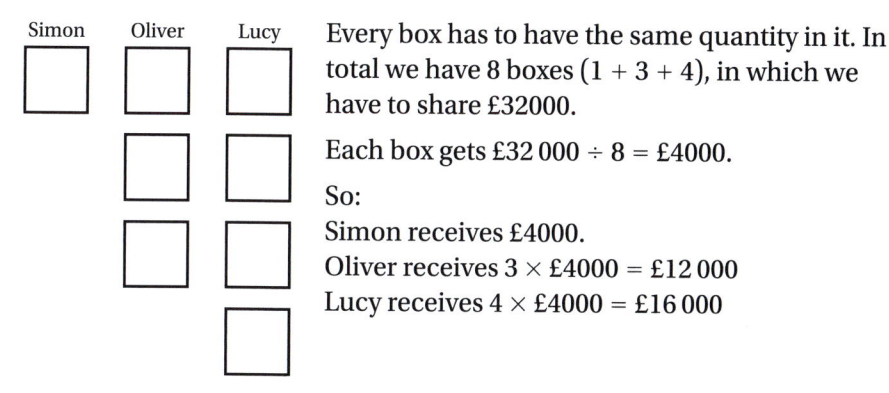

You can also think in terms of fractions and use what you know about finding fractions of a quantity:

1 : 3 : 4 gives 8 parts, so each person gets the following:

Simon receives $\frac{1}{8} \times 32\,000 = £4000$

Oliver receives $\frac{3}{8} \times 32\,000 = £12\,000$

Lucy receives $\frac{4}{8} \times 32\,000 = \frac{1}{2} \times 32\,000 = £16\,000$

> **Tip**
>
> You learnt how to find a fraction of a quantity in Chapter 10.

The final step is to check that the shared quantities sum to the original amount:

£4000 + £12 000 + £16 000 = £32 000

Find answers at: cambridge.org/ukschools/gcsemaths-studentbookanswers

EXERCISE 22B

1 Share 144 in each of the given ratios.

   a 1 : 3   **b** 4 : 5   **c** 11 : 1

   d 2 : 3 : 1   **e** 1 : 2 : 5   **f** 2 : 7 : 5 : 4

2 To make mortar you mix sand and cement in the ratio of 4 : 1.

   a How much sand is needed to make 25 kilograms of mortar?

   b What fraction of the mix is cement?

3 The first bi-colour £2 coin was issued in 1998. The inner circle is made of cupronickel. This is copper and nickel in the ratio 3 : 1. The inner circle weighs 6 grams. How much copper is used to make the centres of ten £2 coins?

4 Flaky pastry is made by mixing flour, margarine and lard in the ratio 8 : 3 : 3 and then adding a drizzle of cold water.

   a How much of each ingredient is needed to make 350 g of pastry?

   b What fraction of the pastry does the margarine and lard make together?

5 The sides of a rectangle are in the ratio of 2 : 5. Its perimeter is 112 cm.

   a What are the dimensions of the rectangle?

   b Use these dimensions to calculate its area.

6 Orange squash is made by mixing one part cordial to five parts of water. How much squash can you make with 750 ml of cordial?

7 Two-stroke fuel is used to power small engines. It is produced by mixing oil and petrol in the ratio of 1 : 20. How much oil needs to be mixed with 10 litres of petrol to make two-stroke fuel?

8 Tiffin is a sweet made by crushing biscuits and mixing them with dried fruit, butter and cocoa powder. The ratio of biscuit to dried fruit to butter to cocoa powder is 5 : 6 : 2 : 2. How much of each ingredient is needed to make 600 g of tiffin?

9 In a music college the ratio of flute to oboe to string to percussion players is 7 : 2 : 15 : 1. If the college has 175 students. How many play an oboe?

10 The ratio of red to green to blue to black to white pairs of socks in a drawer is 2 : 3 : 7 : 1 : 4. If there are 8 pairs of white socks, how many pairs are there altogether?

11 Potting compost is made by mixing loam, peat and sand in the ratio of 7 : 3 : 2. If a gardener has 4.5 kg of peat and plenty of loam and sand, how much potting compost can she make?

Section 3: Comparing ratios

It is often useful to write ratios in the form $1:n$ (where n represents a number) so that they are in the same form and you can compare them directly by size.

> **Did you know?**
>
> The scale of maps is given as a ratio in the form of $1:n$. For example $1:25\,000$.

WORKED EXAMPLE 1

Red and white paints can be mixed to make pink paint.

Which of the mixes below will give the lightest shade of pink?

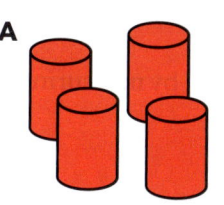

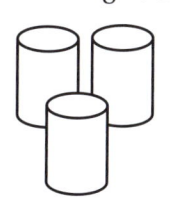

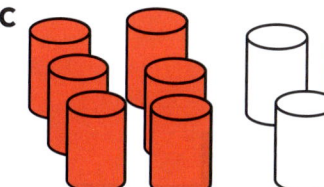

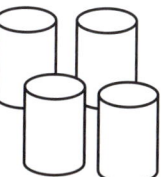

A

B

C

The ratios of red to white paint are:

A $4:3$ B $3:2$ C $6:4$

A $\dfrac{4}{4}:\dfrac{3}{4} = 1:0.75$ B $\dfrac{3}{3}:\dfrac{2}{3} = 1:0.67$ C $\dfrac{6}{6}:\dfrac{4}{6} = 1:0.67$.

Paint A has the greatest amount of white paint per unit of red paint, that is, 0.75 tins of white for 1 tin of red, so this will be the lightest shade of pink.

First, work out the ratio of red to white paint in each diagram.

Change these to form $1:n$. For each diagram, divide both parts of the ratio by the first part. Give the answers as decimals to make the comparison simpler.

Ratios in the form of $1:n$ are also useful for converting from one unit to another.
For example, the ratio of inches to centimetres is $1:2.54$.

This means that 1 inch is equivalent to 2.54 cm.

So, 2 inches = 2×2.54 cm and
12 inches = 12×2.54 cm.

This is a **linear** relationship and it can be shown as a straight-line graph. The equation of the line is $y = 2.54x$. Notice that the ratio of inches to centimetres (the ratio of $x:y$) is $1:2.54$. The equation $y = 2.54x$ and the ratio $1:2.54$ both state that for every value of x, y is 2.54 times larger.

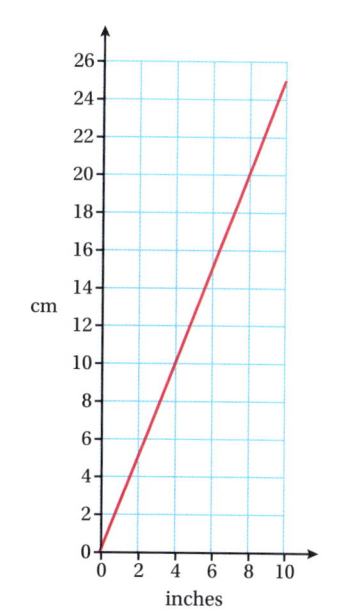

> **Tip**
>
> Ratios in the form of $1:n$ can also be written as $n:1$.

> **Tip**
>
> You learnt about linear graphs in Chapter 18.

Golden ratio

The golden ratio, $1:\dfrac{1+\sqrt{5}}{2} = 1:1.618$, has been studied and used for centuries. Artists including Leonardo Da Vinci and Salvador Dali often produced work using this ratio. The ratio can also be seen in buildings, such as the Acropolis in Athens. The golden ratio is said to be the most attractive way to space out facial features.

Find answers at: cambridge.org/ukschools/gcsemaths-studentbookanswers

The diagram shows how the golden ratio can be worked out using the dimensions of a 'golden' rectangle. The large rectangle ACDF is similar to BCDE. Therefore the ratio of $a : a + b$ is equivalent to $b : a$.

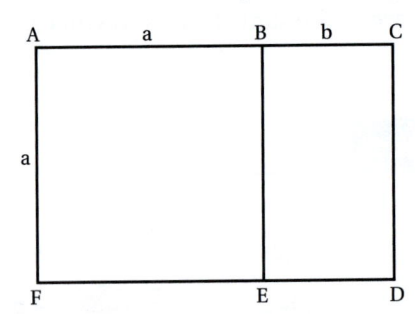

An approximate numerical value for this ratio can be found by measuring.

WORKED EXAMPLE 2

How golden are your hands?

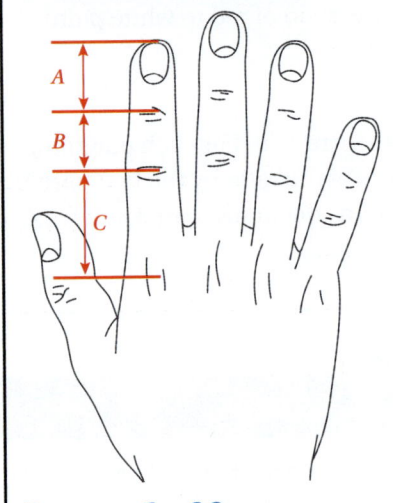

Measure the distances *A*, *B* and *C* on your hand.

Distance B = 22 mm
Distance C = 40 mm
Distance A = 13 mm
Length of hand = 170 mm
Wrist to elbow = 240 mm
B : C = 22 : 40 = 1 : 1.81
A : B = 13 : 22 = 1 : 1.69
Hand : wrist-elbow = 170 : 240 = 1 : 1.41
All the ratios are close to 1 : 1.618 which is the golden ratio.

Now calculate these ratios and write them in the form $1 : n$.
Distance *B* : Distance *C*
Distance *A* : Distance *B*
Length of your hand : Distance from your wrist to your elbow
Can you see anything special about these ratios?

The closer your results are to 1.1618 the more golden your hand!

You worked with the sequence of Fibonacci numbers in Chapter 4. This sequence follows the golden ratio. If you calculate the ratio of consecutive numbers in the Fibonacci sequence you will find that the ratio gets closer and closer to the actual golden ratio $1 : \dfrac{1 + \sqrt{5}}{2}$ as you get further along the sequence.

22 Calculations with ratio

EXERCISE 22C

1 Different types of coffee are made by mixing espresso shots, hot water and milk in specified ratios.

Espresso	1 : 0 : 0
Double espresso	2 : 0 : 0
Flat white	1 : 2 : 1
Cappuccino	1 : 0 : 2
Latte	1 : 0 : 4

Put the drinks in order of strength, weakest first.

Tip: The weakest coffee has the least espresso by volume.

2 When Jon was going on holiday he used this graph to convert between pounds and euros.

  a What is the ratio of pounds to euros? Express this in the form $1 : n$.
  b What is the ratio of euros to pounds? Express this in the form $1 : n$.

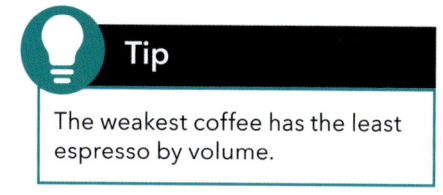

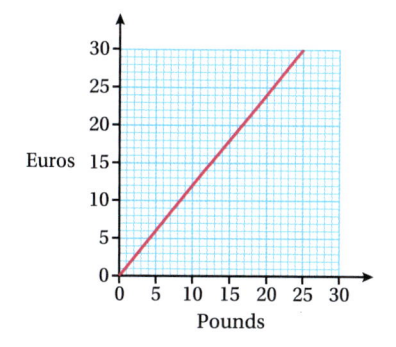

3 This graph shows the relationship between ounces and grams.

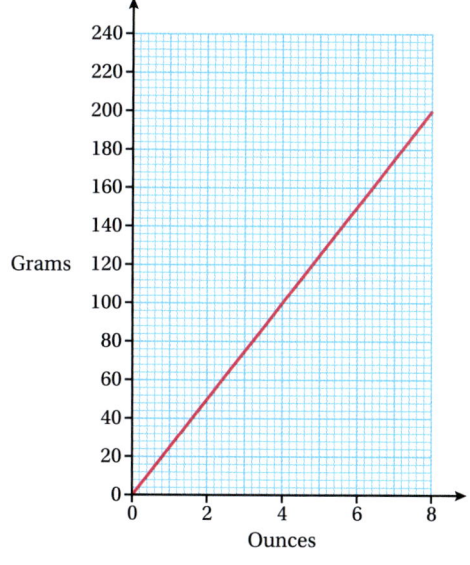

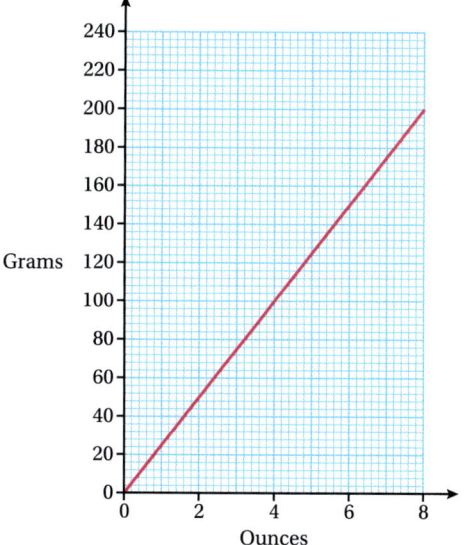

Tip: Ounces is an imperial measurement of mass; you worked on metric units in Chapter 12.

  a What is the ratio of ounces to grams? Express this in the form $1 : n$.
  b What is the ratio of grams to ounces? Express this in the form $1 : n$.

4 The ratio of litres to gallons is $1 : 1.8$.
  a Draw a conversion graph to show this relationship.
  b What is the ratio of gallons to litres in the form $1 : n$?

5 Three siblings; Daisy, aged 5, Patrick, 8, and Imogen, 12, share sweets in the same ratio as their ages. Imogen gets 21 more sweets than Daisy.
  a How many sweets were there to begin with?
  b What fraction of the sweets did Patrick get?

Find answers at: cambridge.org/ukschools/gcsemaths-studentbookanswers

6 The ratio of kilometres to miles is approximately 8 : 5. A car travels at 60 miles per hour for 30 minutes. Approximately how many kilometres does it travel?

7 This recipe for sausage casserole serves 6.

Find the quantities of ingredients needed to serve 4 people.
Show all the steps in your answer.

> **Sausage casserole (serves 6)**
> 12 sausages
> 3 tins of tomatoes
> 450 g potatoes
> 9 tsp mixed herbs
> 600 ml vegetable stock

8 Gill and her sister Bell share a box of chocolate. Bell gets $\frac{1}{3}$ of the box.
Gill shares her chocolates with her best friend Katy in the ratio 4 : 3. Katy gets 12 chocolates. How many chocolates were there in the box?

9 A quarter of a box of chocolates are white chocolate. The ratio of dark to milk chocolates is 2 : 5. There are 7 white chocolates. How many more milk chocolates than dark chocolates are there?

Checklist of learning and understanding

Notation
- A ratio compares two or more quantities with each other.
- The order in which a ratio is written is important. A ratio of 2 : 5 means 2 parts to 5 parts. Each part is equal in size.
- A proportion compares a quantity to the 'whole' of which it is a part; this can be written as a fraction, percentage or ratio.

Simplifying ratios
- Ratios can be simplified by dividing both parts of the ratio by a common factor.
- Two ratios are equivalent if one is a multiple of another; that is, if they can be cancelled to the same simplest terms.
- Expressing ratios in the form 1 : n makes it easy to compare ratios. If three different ratios of $a : b$ were converted to 1 : n and compared, then the ratio with the highest value of n has the greatest amount of b per amount of a.
- Ratios can be useful for converting from one unit to another where the relationship is **linear**. The relationship can be represented by a straight-line graph.

Sharing in a given ratio
- The box method can be used to tackle problems that involve sharing a quantity in a given ratio. To share quantity Q in the ratio $a : b : c$, divide the quantity evenly into $a + b + c$ boxes.
- You can also work out the fraction each part is of the whole, and multiply the quantity by the fraction.

22 Calculations with ratio

Chapter review

1 What is the ratio of the side length of a square to its perimeter in the form $1:n$?

2 What is the ratio of the diameter of a circle to its circumference in the form $1:n$?

3 The three angles of a triangle are in the ratio $3:3:4$. What information can you give about the triangle?

4 The ratio of the five angles in a pentagon are $1:1:1:1:1$. What information does this tell you about the pentagon? How do you know this?

5 The ratio of the angles in a triangle is $1:2:1$. What information can you give about the triangle?

6 Gareth and John share a box of chocolates. Gareth gets $\frac{3}{5}$ of the box.

The ratio of white to milk to dark chocolates in John's share is $1:2:1$, he gets 4 white chocolates. The ratio of milk to dark to white chocolates in Gareth's share is $2:1:5$. How many types of each type of chocolate were in the box?

7 Debi makes Chocolate Courgette Cake.

Her recipe uses 480 g of grated courgettes.

The total weight of the other ingredients is 1.1 kg.

    a Find the ratio of the weight of grated courgettes to the total weight of the other ingredients.

    Give your answer in its simplest form. *(3 marks)*

    b Debi wants to make a larger Chocolate Courgette Cake.

    She wants to use 600 g of grated courgettes.

    Calculate the total weight of the other ingredients that she will need to use.

    Give the units of your answer. *(3 marks)*

    © OCR 2013

8 What is the ratio of vowels to consonants in the English alphabet?

9 What is the ratio of prime numbers to square numbers between (and including) 1 and 20 in its simplest form?

10 Share 360 in the ratio $3:5:1$.

Find answers at: cambridge.org/ukschools/gcsemaths-studentbookanswers

> For additional questions on the topics in this chapter, visit GCSE Mathematics Online.

> **Tip**
> To answer the questions about circles, triangles, pentagons and rectangles you may need to look again at Chapter 5.

11 Using the graph below express the ratio of miles to kilometres in the form $1 : n$.

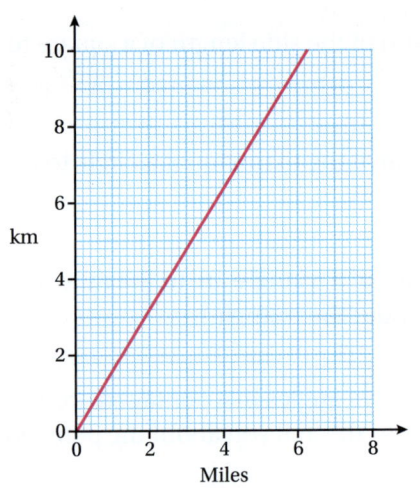

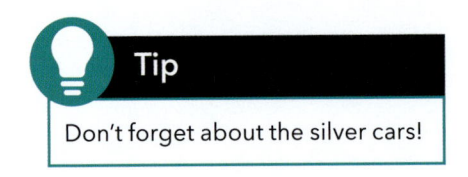

12 In a car park, three-quarters of the cars are not silver, but are blue, red, black or yellow. The proportion of blue to red to black to yellow cars is $6 : 2 : 3 : 1$. There are 6 more black cars than yellow cars. How many cars of each colour are in the car park?

Tip

Don't forget about the silver cars!

23 Basic probability and experiments

In this chapter you will learn how to …
- use the language of probability and the 0 to 1 probability scale.
- calculate the probability of events happening or not happening.
- carry out experiments, record outcomes and use results to predict future probabilities.

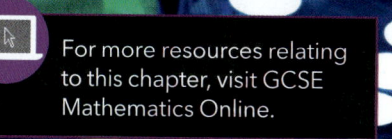

For more resources relating to this chapter, visit GCSE Mathematics Online.

Using mathematics: real-life applications

Data is collected by many professionals and used to find the probability of particular things happening. For example, in a fertility clinic data collected over a period of many years can be used to draw a graph that shows the probability that a woman of a certain age will be successful at falling pregnant.

> "A 20-year-old woman has an 86% chance of falling pregnant and only a 3% chance of being infertile. This means there is a high probability that she will get pregnant if she is trying to have a baby." *(Fertility doctor)*

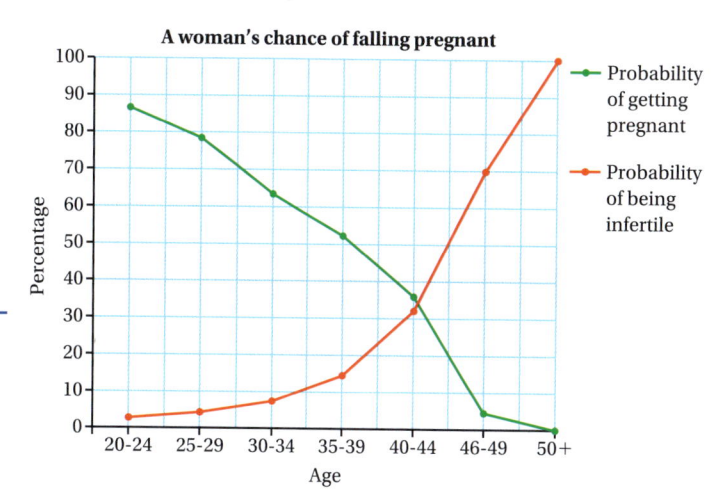

A woman's chance of falling pregnant

Before you start …

Ch 10, 11, 13	You need to be able to calculate with fractions, decimals and percentages	1	Choose the correct answer without doing the calculations. a $\frac{1}{2} + \frac{1}{4}$ A $\frac{2}{3}$ B $\frac{2}{6}$ C $\frac{3}{4}$ b 0.2×0.3 A 0.5 B 0.06 C 0.6 c 20% of 40 A 0.8 B 8% C 8
Ch 17	You need to be able to round decimals to 1, 2 or 3 places.	2	Which answers are rounded incorrectly? Why? a $0.705\,882\,352 \approx 0.706$ b $0.316\,666\,6 \approx 0.316$ c $0.989\,087 \approx 1.09$
Ch 10, 11, 13	You should be able to find equivalent fractions, decimals and percentages.	3	Choose the correct sign: <, = or > a $\frac{12}{25}$ ☐ 8% b 0.8 ☐ 8% c $\frac{24}{50}$ ☐ 0.5

Tip

In probability calculations you will need to work with fractions, decimals and percentages, often changing between them. Remember:
- a fraction is a number in the form of $\frac{a}{b}$.
- you can change fractions to decimals and decimals to fractions (see Chapter 11).

Find answers at: cambridge.org/ukschools/gcsemaths-studentbookanswers

GCSE Mathematics for OCR (Foundation)

Assess your starting point using the Launchpad

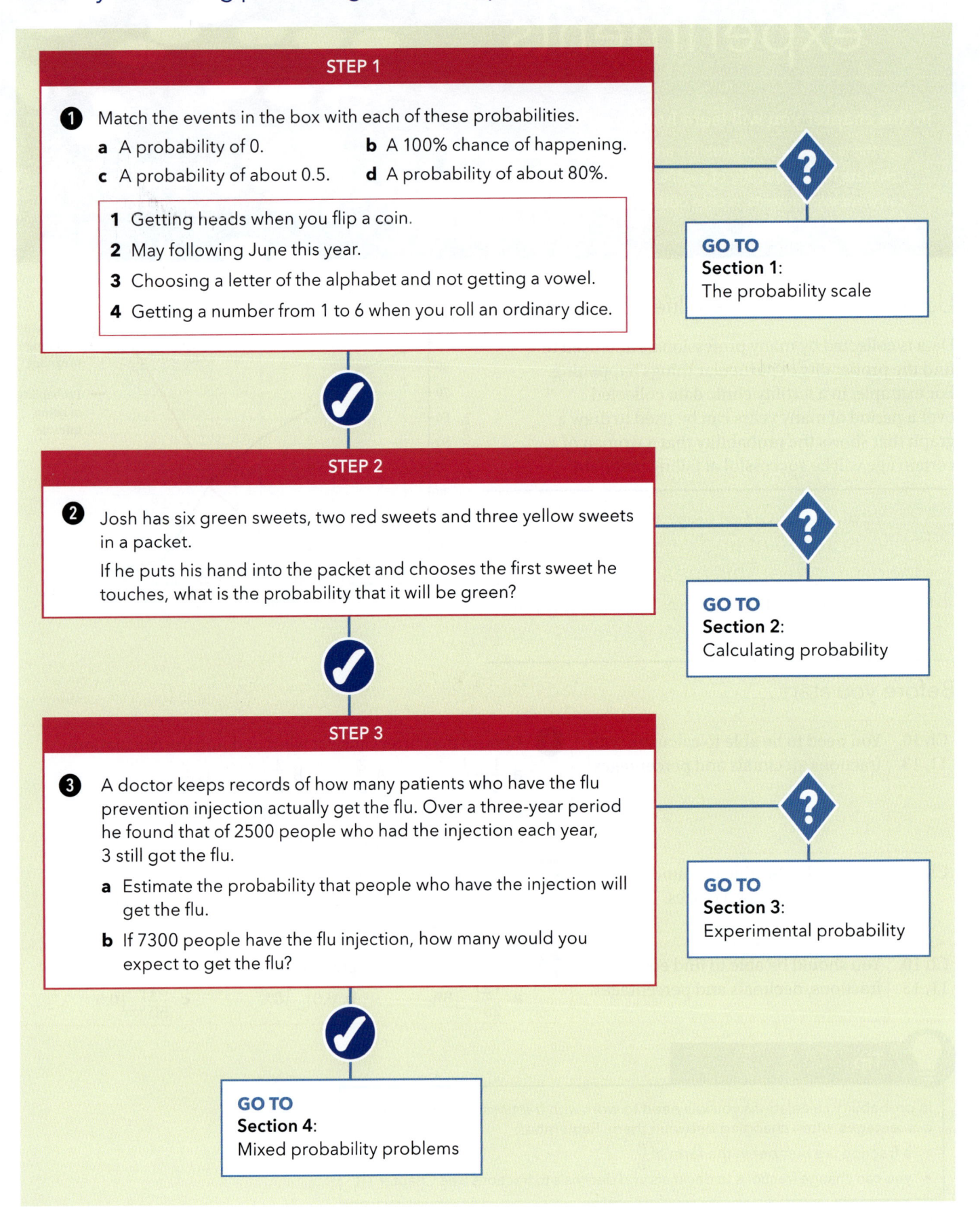

STEP 1

1 Match the events in the box with each of these probabilities.
  a A probability of 0.
  b A 100% chance of happening.
  c A probability of about 0.5.
  d A probability of about 80%.

  1 Getting heads when you flip a coin.
  2 May following June this year.
  3 Choosing a letter of the alphabet and not getting a vowel.
  4 Getting a number from 1 to 6 when you roll an ordinary dice.

GO TO
Section 1:
The probability scale

STEP 2

2 Josh has six green sweets, two red sweets and three yellow sweets in a packet.
If he puts his hand into the packet and chooses the first sweet he touches, what is the probability that it will be green?

GO TO
Section 2:
Calculating probability

STEP 3

3 A doctor keeps records of how many patients who have the flu prevention injection actually get the flu. Over a three-year period he found that of 2500 people who had the injection each year, 3 still got the flu.
  a Estimate the probability that people who have the injection will get the flu.
  b If 7300 people have the flu injection, how many would you expect to get the flu?

GO TO
Section 3:
Experimental probability

GO TO
Section 4:
Mixed probability problems

Section 1: The probability scale

You often hear people saying things like:

- There is a good chance it will rain tomorrow.
- I'm certain that it's going to rain tomorrow.
- It is impossible for Arsenal to win the league this year.
- There's a fifty-fifty chance that she will make the team.

These statements describe the chance, or likelihood, of something happening (or not happening). This is known as **probability**.

Impossible means there is no chance that something will happen, while **certain** means it will definitely happen. A **fifty-fifty chance** means that it is just as likely to happen as it is to not happen.

Talking probability

An **outcome** is the mathematical word for the result of an experiment. An **event** is the thing to which you give a probability, it is a set of outcomes.

For example, in the event 'flipping a coin' there are two possible outcomes:

Outcome 1: heads   Outcome 2: tails.

The particular outcome you are calculating the probability for is called the **favourable outcome**. So, if the event is 'flipping a coin' and you want to know the probability of getting a head, the favourable outcome is 'a head'. You can write this as P(head) or P(H). This is the general notation used in probability calculations, where the favourable outcome is written inside the brackets.

You can write this as P(favourable outcome).

Expressing probability in numbers

Probability can be described in numbers using a scale from 0 to 1.

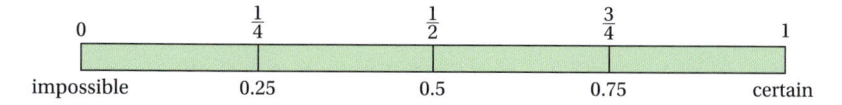

0	$\frac{1}{4}$	$\frac{1}{2}$	$\frac{3}{4}$	1
impossible	0.25	0.5	0.75	certain

A probability of 0.5 means having the same chance of happening or not happening. For example:

- the probability that the day immediately after a Friday will be a Tuesday is 0.
- the probability that the day immediately after a Sunday will be a Monday is 1.
- the probability of getting heads when you flip a coin is 0.5; you have an equal chance of getting heads or tails.

The smaller the fraction, the less likely it is that the favourable outcome will happen. A favourable outcome with a probability of 0.5 ($\frac{1}{2}$) is more likely to happen than a favourable outcome with a probability of 0.25 ($\frac{1}{4}$) or 0.1 ($\frac{1}{10}$).

Find answers at: cambridge.org/ukschools/gcsemaths-studentbookanswers

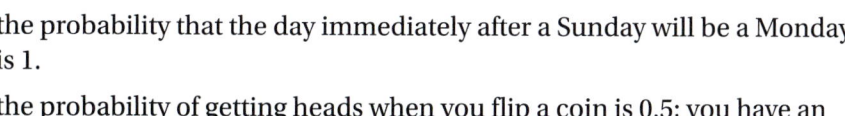

> **Tip**
> The terms 'likely', 'not likely', 'more likely', 'less likely', 'least likely' and 'most likely' are often used in probability.

> **Key vocabulary**
> **outcome**: a single result of an experiment or situation.
> **event**: a set of possible outcomes in an experiment or situation, to which you give a probability.

> **Tip**
> The favourable outcome can also be referred to as a successful outcome.

> **Tip**
> You cannot get a negative number or an answer greater than 1 when you calculate probability. If you do, then you know you have made an error.

Probability as a percentage

Probability can be given as a decimal, fraction or percentage.

For example an evens probability can be expressed as 0.5, $\frac{1}{2}$ or 50%.

In different situations, probabilities can be easier to imagine when given in a particular form.

For example, decimal values can be quickly compared on the probability scale because you don't have to work with different denominators.

The probability of winning the jackpot on a three barrel slot machine is given as 0.00038%. Although this is clearly a very small percentage, it doesn't really give a sense of size. But, if the probability was given as the fraction $\frac{1}{266\,144}$ you can see the probability means that in about a quarter of a million goes on the slot machine, you're only likely to win once.

> **Tip**
> In real life people often say things like "I have a 1 in 5 chance of getting the job". You should not give mathematical probabilities in the form of '1 in 5 chance', '1 to 5' or '1 : 5' in your answers.

In reality, someone might win from playing just five times and another time nobody might win even after playing a million times. This is because the frequency of favourable outcomes is not the same as the calculated probability of that outcome (see Section 3: Experimental probability).

EXERCISE 23A

1. Jane has three red scarves, two yellow scarves and a black scarf. It's dark when she gets dressed, so she grabs a scarf from her drawer hoping for the black one.
   a. What is the event in this example?
   b. What are the possible outcomes?
   c. Does Jane have a high or low probability of a favourable outcome? Why?
   d. Which outcome has the highest probability? Why?

2. Estimate and then write the probability of each of these events as a fraction, a decimal and a percentage.
   a. You'll get heads when you flip a coin.
   b. You'll get a 7 when you roll a normal dice.
   c. You'll win the lotto when you haven't bought a ticket.
   d. A newborn baby will be a girl.
   e. You'll get an odd number when you roll a dice.
   f. You will see a famous person this week.
   g. It will rain tomorrow.

> **Tip**
> In probability questions sometimes you have to make assumptions about the event. So, unless you are **told otherwise**, you should: assume a coin has a head on one side and a tail on the other; a dice is a cube with faces numbered 1-6; and there is an evens chance of being male or female at birth.

> **Tip**
> Is there enough information to answer parts **f** and **g**?

3 Work with a partner. Discuss whether the following statements are true, false or you can't say and give reasons for your answers.

  a The lotto grand prize has rolled over for three weeks now, so someone is certain to win the grand prize this week.

  b If a woman has already given birth to three boys, she has an excellent chance of having a girl next time round.

  c It is impossible to go back to last night and do my homework.

  d Two football teams playing against each other have an equal chance of winning.

  e It can either rain or be sunny, so there is a 50% chance of rain tomorrow.

Section 2: Calculating probability

There are two ways of calculating probability:

- Theoretical probability – where you calculate a probability based on fairness and symmetrical properties of results.
- Experimental probability – where you do an experiment, observe the outcome and record the results.

Equally likely, random outcomes

When you flip a fair coin there are two possible outcomes: head and tails.

You have the same chance of getting heads as you have of getting tails so we say the outcomes are **equally likely**.

This does not mean that if you flip a coin six times in a row you will get three heads and three tails. Although the outcomes are equally likely, they are also **random**.

So, you could get six heads in a row, six tails in a row or four heads in a row, followed by one tail and then one head.

However, the more often you flip the coin, the closer you will get to an equal number of heads and tails.

Theoretical probability

When the outcomes of an event are equally likely you can calculate the **theoretical probability** of each event using the formula:

$$\text{probability of a favourable outcome} = \frac{\text{number of favourable outcomes}}{\text{total number of outcomes}}$$

The probability of an event not happening

The sum of all the possible outcomes of an event is 1.

If the probability of a given outcome is P(E), then the probability of that outcome **not** happening is 1 − P(E).

> **Tip**
> A fair, or unbiased, coin, spinner or dice is one that is symmetrical, not damaged or unbalanced in ways that make it fall more often on one side than the other. Each outcome is equally likely to occur.

> **Key vocabulary**
> **equally likely**: having the same probability of happening.
> **random**: not predetermined.

> **Tip**
> Remember, the probability scale goes from 0 to 1.

Find answers at: cambridge.org/ukschools/gcsemaths-studentbookanswers

For example, if a fair dice is rolled what is the probability of rolling any number except 6?

P(*not* 6) = 1 − (probability of rolling a 6)

$= 1 - \frac{1}{6}$ (there are six equally likely outcomes of rolling a dice)

$= \frac{5}{6}$ (there are five possible outcomes that would result in 'not 6')

WORK IT OUT 23.1

A teacher puts the names of six students: Anna, Basil, Candy, David, Eliza and Fatimah into a container and chooses one at random to decide which student is going to give the answers to a homework task.

Calculate the probability that the teacher draws the following:

a Basil. **b** a girl's name. **c** a name other than Basil.

Which of these solutions is correct? Why are the others incorrect?

Solution A	Solution B	Solution C
a P(Basil) $= \frac{1}{5} = 0.2$	**a** P(Basil) $= \frac{1}{6} = 0.17$	**a** P(Basil) $= \frac{1}{6} = 1.7\%$
b P(Girl) $= \frac{3}{6} = \frac{1}{2} = 0.5$	**b** P(Girl) $= \frac{4}{6} = \frac{2}{3} = 0.67$	**b** P(Girl) $= \frac{4}{6} = 6.7\%$
c P(*not* Basil) $= 1 - 5 = {}^-4$	**c** P(*not* Basil) $= 1 - \frac{1}{6} = \frac{5}{6} = 0.83$	**c** P(*not* Basil) $= \frac{5}{6} = 8.3\%$

Mutually exclusive events

What is the probability that the teacher in Work it out 23.1 chooses either Anna or Basil?

In this situation, the two events cannot take place at the same time. The teacher has to pick either Anna **or** Basil. In this event there are two favourable outcomes: Anna is favourable and so is Basil.

Events that cannot happen at the same time, are known as **mutually exclusive**.

For example:

- When you roll a normal dice, you cannot roll a six **and** a four at the same time.
- When you flip a coin you cannot get heads **and** tails.

If you drew one card from a standard pack of playing cards:

- drawing a card that is a king and a queen is mutually exclusive.
- drawing a card that is red and the number two is possible so is **not** mutually exclusive.

To find the probability of a favourable outcome from mutually exclusive events, we add the probabilities of each of the possible favourable outcomes.

Two favourable outcomes out of six possible outcomes means a probability of $\frac{2}{6}$ or $\frac{1}{3}$.

We add together the probabilities of the two outcomes:

P(Anna) + P(Basil) = P(Anna *or* Basil)

$\frac{1}{6} + \frac{1}{6} = \frac{2}{6} = \frac{1}{3}$

> **Key vocabulary**
>
> **mutually exclusive**: events that cannot happen at the same time.

> **Tip**
>
> You expressed fractions in their simplest form in Chapter 10.

EXERCISE 23B

1 For each of the following events:
  i identify all the possible outcomes.
  ii say whether the outcomes are equally likely. Explain why.

  a A fair dice is rolled.
  b 100 raffle tickets are placed in a barrel and one is drawn at random.
  c A drawing pin is dropped to see whether it lands point up or point down.
  d A coin is drawn from a bag containing twelve £1 coins and twenty-five 50p coins.
  e A student from your class is chosen to speak at a school assembly.
  f Flipping two coins at the same time.

2 A couple plan to have three children.

Given that they have an equal chance of having a boy or a girl, what is the probability that their first child will be a girl?

3 A wallet contains three £1 coins and four £2 coins.

What is the probability that the first coin taken at random from the wallet is:

  a £1   **b** not £1   **c** 50p

4 In a game at a school fete, a dart is equally likely to hit any of the numbers from 1 to 20 when thrown at a game board.

What is the probability that the dart will land on:

  a an even number?
  b a number < 13?
  c a multiple of 6?
  d 26?
  e a number that is not 19?

5 Scrabble® tiles with one each of the 26 letters of the alphabet are placed in a bag and a tile is drawn at random.

What is the probability of getting:

  a a vowel?
  b a consonant?
  c a letter in the word square?
  d a letter from the name John or a letter from the name Ali?
  e a letter from the name Nicky or a letter from the name Sue?

6 When two people are competing in a quiz competition there are three possible outcomes: win, draw or lose.

Does this mean that the probability of one person winning is $\frac{1}{3}$?

Explain your answer.

Find answers at: cambridge.org/ukschools/gcsemaths-studentbookanswers

Section 3: Experimental probability

Predicting outcomes

The probability of getting heads when you flip a coin is $\frac{1}{2}$, but think about what really happens if you flip a coin twice. It doesn't always land once on heads and once on tails.

Similarly, if you roll a dice it can land on any of the numbers from 1 to 6, but if you rolled the dice six times, you probably wouldn't get 1, 2, 3, 4, 5 and 6.

If you do an experiment with coins, counters, dice, spinners or playing cards involving a number of trials, and for each trial you record the outcome, you can see how often the favourable outcome occurs. You can use this to calculate the **relative frequency**, also known as the **experimental probability**.

The relative frequency (or experimental probability) is the number of times you get a favourable outcome (e.g. 'heads') out of all the outcomes. It is useful for estimating probability.

$$\text{Relative frequency} = \frac{\text{number of favourable outcomes recorded}}{\text{total number of trials}}$$

If you flipped a coin 80 times and the favourable outcome 'head' was recorded 32 times, then the relative frequency of 'head' is:

$$\text{relative frequency (H)} = \frac{32}{80} = 0.4$$

A head came up 40% of the time.

You can use the relative frequency (or experimental probability), to predict that in 120 flips of a coin you would get H 48 times (0.4 × 120).

Increasing the number of trials gives a relative frequency that is closer to the **theoretical probability** of the event.

Predictions based on empirical evidence

People collect data (empirical evidence) about all sorts of things to make predictions about what might happen in the future.

For example, an insurance company might collect data about the age of drivers who have car accidents and find that drivers aged from 17 to 23 years have a higher relative frequency of being involved in accidents than people aged from 30 to 37.

The insurance company estimates the probability of these drivers getting into an accident and uses this to calculate their premiums.

Probabilities based on empirical evidence are used:

- in weather forecasting.
- in market research to predict what people might buy.
- by medical professionals to work out the risk of different people contracting a disease.
- by sports teams and betting agencies to work out the chance of a team or player winning their match.

Key vocabulary

relative frequency: the ratio of the number of times a favourable outcome is recorded to the total number of trials conducted.

WORK IT OUT 23.2

A laboratory tested 500 batches of tablets and found 4 to be contaminated. What is the probability that a batch of tablets produced in this laboratory would be:

a contaminated?   **b** not contaminated?

Which of these answers is the correct answer to the following question? Why is the other one wrong?

Option A	Option B
a P(contaminated) $= \frac{4}{500} = 0.8\%$ **b** P(*not* contaminated) $= \frac{496}{500} = 92\%$	**a** P(contaminated) $= \frac{4}{500} = 0.008$ **b** P(*not* contaminated) $= 1 - 0.008 = 0.992$

EXERCISE 23C

1 Work in pairs. You will need two identical coins and a small container. Shake the coins in the container and then drop them onto your desk. Do this 40 times each (80 in total).

a Copy this table, which shows the three possible outcomes in this event.

Possible outcomes	Predicted frequency	Tally	Actual frequency
Heads, Heads (HH)			
Heads, Tails (HT) or Tails, Heads (TH)			
Tails, Tails (TT)			

Tip

Here two events are happening at the same time: 'flipping coin A' and 'flipping coin B'; this is a combined event. The outcome could be a head on both coins, a tail on both coins or a head on one and a tail on the other. You will learn more about combined events in Chapter 24.

b **Before** you start, use theoretical probability to predict how many times you think each outcome will occur in 80 throws. Write your prediction in the table.

c Do the experiment. Take turns to drop the coins and use tallies to record the outcomes.

d Total the tallies and write the actual frequency of each outcome (in other words, how many times each outcome happened).

e How do your results compare with your predictions?

f How many times would you expect to get two heads if you dropped the coins 10 000 times? Why?

g Will your results be the same if you do the experiment again (or will they be the same as another pair)? Why?

2 What is the experimental probability of getting heads with a coin if you have done an experiment with the coin and it has landed heads up on 35 out of 60 flips?

3 Nick rolled up balls of paper and threw them from his desk into the bin. The paper balls landed in the bin 175 out of 200 throws.

What is the experimental probability that the paper will land in the bin the next time Nick throws?

Find answers at: cambridge.org/ukschools/gcsemaths-studentbookanswers

4. Paul has six red T-shirts, a green T-shirt and a yellow T-shirt.
   He says the probability of picking a red T-shirt at random is $\frac{6}{3}$ because there are three possible colours and six red T-shirts to choose from.
   Paul's reasoning is incorrect. How would you explain this to him?

5. Mrs Noonan drives a taxi on the same route every morning. Over a period of 290 days in a year, she has been stopped by a train crossing the road 58 times.
   Calculate the experimental probability that she will be stopped by the train crossing on her morning route.

6. A pharmacist kept a record of which painkiller brand was bought by 80 customers in a month. These are her results:

Brand	Stopthepayne	Make-it-go-away	Painless	Generic
Frequency	27	22	20	11

   a Based on this data, what is the experimental probability of a customer buying:
   i a generic painkiller? ii a 'Stopthepayne' painkiller?
   b Do you think this data is sufficient to predict what brand of painkiller would be chosen by most customers in Britain? Give a reason for your answer.

Tip

You will learn more about sampling in Chapter 35.

7. Another pharmacist only stocks the 'Make-it-go-away' brand and the generic brand. He estimates that three times as many customers choose the 'Make-it-go-away' brand over the generic brand.

   a If 381 customers chose the 'Make-it-go-away' brand, estimate how many chose the generic.
   b Copy and complete the table on the right.
   c Use the data in your table to estimate the probability that the next person who buys a painkiller will choose:
   i the 'Make-it-go-away' brand.   ii the generic brand.

Brand	Number sold	Relative frequency
Make-it-go-away	381	
Generic		
Total		

8. Amira kept a record of the weather forecast for ten days and compared it with the actual weather on each day. These are her results:

Day	Forecast	Actual weather	Was the forecast correct?
1	Rain	Rain	Yes
2	Some showers	Sunny and warm	No
3	Cloudy	Cloudy	Yes
4	Sunny and warm	Sunny and warm	Yes
5	Some showers	Sunny and warm	No
6	Some showers	Some showers	Yes
7	Cloudy and windy	Cloudy and windy	Yes
8	Rain	Rain	Yes
9	Sunny and warm	Some showers	No
10	Sunny and warm	Sunny and warm	Yes

a Calculate the experimental probability that the weather forecast is correct.

b What is the chance that the weather forecast is wrong?

c You plan to go for a hike the next day. The weather forecast for that day is rain. Would you take rain gear with you? Explain why or why not.

9 Mica is a film-maker based in Edinburgh. She needs to know what the weather is going to be like in advance because bad weather can cause delays in her schedule and this is very expensive. She uses predictions from a specialist weather website because she finds its forecasts to be accurate 99% of the time. This is the meteogram she downloaded on 24 March.

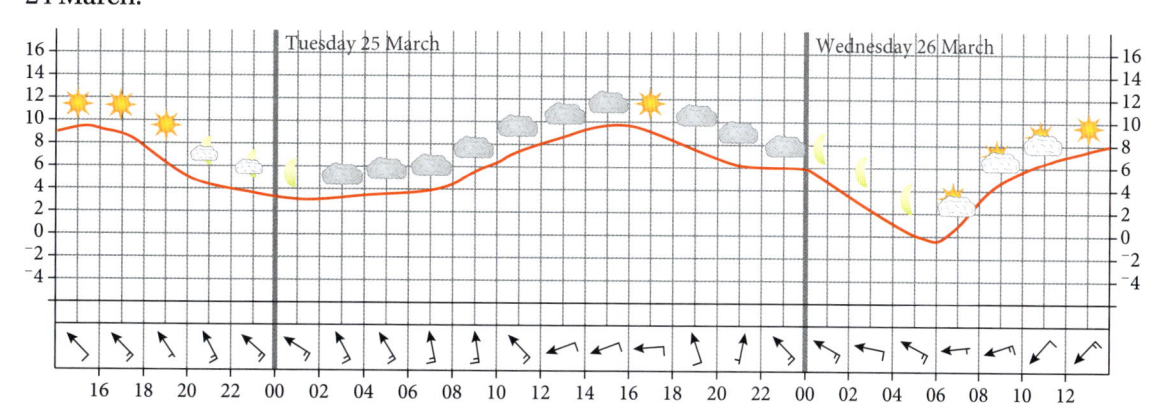

a What information is shown on the graph?

b Mica can only film when it is not raining. Should she schedule a shoot for Tuesday?

c Is Mica right to trust this website? Access a site to download the meteogram or long-term forecast for your area. Decide how you will test the reliability of the data and work out how accurate it is for your area.

Tip

You can do this activity using any weather forecasting site, and you could compare two or more to see which one has the highest probability of being correct for your area.

Organising outcomes – tables and frequency trees

With probabilities it is important to find ways of recording and organising the information to show how many favourable outcomes there are, how many outcomes there are in total and to find the figures you need to make decisions and calculate probabilities. Tables and simple diagrams called frequency trees are used to do this.

A doctor was interested in whether patients knew the difference between having a cold and having the flu. He collected data one winter and kept track of 42 patients. He organised his data as follows.

Two-way table

	Actual diagnosis	
Self-diagnosis	**Cold**	**Flu**
Cold	7	4
Flu	12	19

Frequency tree

Find answers at: cambridge.org/ukschools/gcsemaths-studentbookanswers

Frequency trees

A frequency tree shows the actual frequency of different outcomes.

The branches of the tree show the paths or decisions and the 'leaves' show the actual number of data for each path. Both the two-way table and the frequency tree on the previous page show the same information, but the frequency tree is clearer because it shows how many patients thought they had a cold or flu without you having to interpret the data in the table.

Frequency trees allow you to understand and make sense of complicated probabilities. For example, if a woman is screened for breast cancer and her test results come back positive she is likely to assume that she has breast cancer. But research has shown that there are many false-positive results.

The frequency tree below shows how many women who test positive for breast cancer will really have cancer.

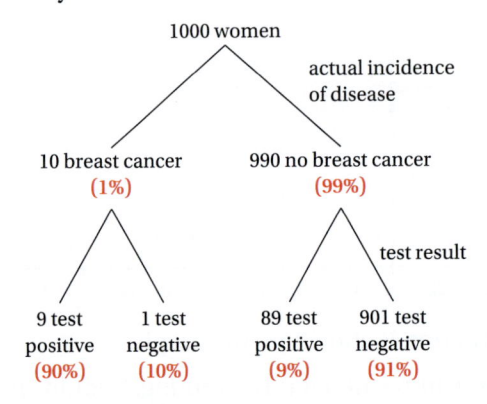

```
                    1000 women
                                        actual incidence
                                        of disease
          10 breast cancer      990 no breast cancer
              (1%)                   (99%)
                                                test result
      9 test    1 test         89 test    901 test
     positive  negative        positive   negative
      (90%)    (10%)            (9%)      (91%)
```

Tip

Frequency trees are organisational tools and they are often used in computer programming (they are sometimes called binary trees). They are not the same as probability tree diagrams which you will deal with in Chapter 24.

The frequency tree shows that 98 women test positive on the screening test.

Of these, only 9 actually have breast cancer.

$\frac{9}{98} = 0.09 \ldots = 9\%$ (1 sf)

So only 9 out of every 98 women (around 1 out of every 10) who get a positive screening test for breast cancer will actually have cancer.

EXERCISE 23D

1 A hotel chain keeps track of which customers use its spa. Here are its results.

Gender	Use the spa	Don't use the spa
Female	780	232
Male	348	640

a Complete this frequency tree to show this data.

b Are male or female guests more likely to use the spa?

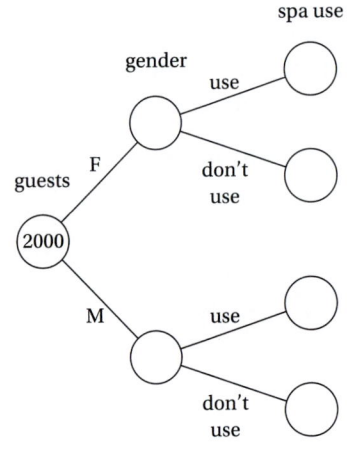

> 23 Basic probability and experiments

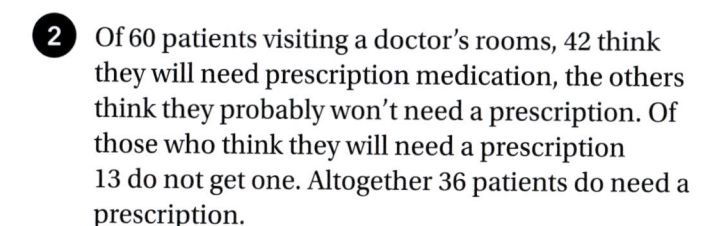

2 Of 60 patients visiting a doctor's rooms, 42 think they will need prescription medication, the others think they probably won't need a prescription. Of those who think they will need a prescription 13 do not get one. Altogether 36 patients do need a prescription.

Complete the frequency tree to show the actual numbers.

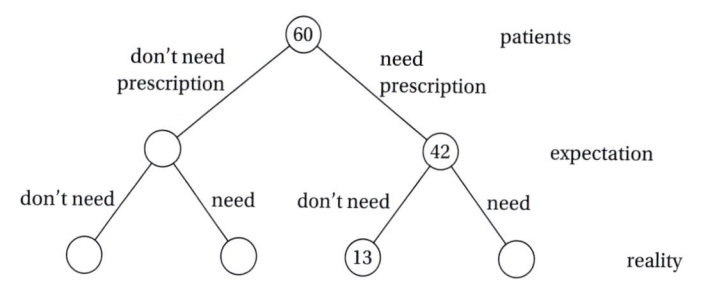

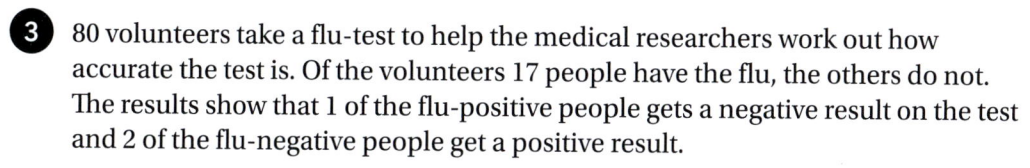

3 80 volunteers take a flu-test to help the medical researchers work out how accurate the test is. Of the volunteers 17 people have the flu, the others do not. The results show that 1 of the flu-positive people gets a negative result on the test and 2 of the flu-negative people get a positive result.

Draw a frequency tree to show the actual results.

Section 4: Mixed probability problems

In real life, people often use probability quite informally to explain things and to predict what will happen in the future. You might have heard people say things like:
- It is never sunny here in February.
- Most people prefer to wear sandals in summer.
- There is a very high risk of HIV among intravenous drug users.
- We are only selling 10 000 tickets so you have an excellent chance of winning the car.
- Young people who haven't had a driving licence for very long have more accidents than older drivers.

Understanding probability allows you to think more critically about statements like those above and to work out more accurately the likelihood of different events.

WORKED EXAMPLE 1

Zunaid read on a travel website that September was a good time to holiday in Italy because there was little chance of rain and the chance of sunny weather was highly likely, whereas in August it was 67.8%.

He went on the internet and found the average weather for the first four weeks (28 days) of September.

Sunny days	Cloudy days	Rainy days
11	9	8

Zunaid decided to go in August. Calculate the relative frequency for each outcome to justify his choice.

The relative frequency of rainy days was $\frac{8}{28} = \frac{4}{14}$ or 28.6%. — This is not such a low chance of rain.

The relative frequency of sunny days was $\frac{11}{28} = 39.3\%$. — This is less than an even 50% chance of sun.

The percentage chance of sunny days in September was less than in August. — In reality, it rained more than 1 out of every 4 days and there were far more cloudy and rainy days than sunny days.

Find answers at: cambridge.org/ukschools/gcsemaths-studentbookanswers

Sometimes the way a problem is worded can be confusing, but the actual calculations in probability generally use the same principles. When you have to solve word problems involving basic probability you can generally do this by organising your work and following the steps in the problem-solving framework.

Problem-solving framework

Nick is throwing a ball randomly at a wall on the side of a building. The side of the building is 2 m high and 10 m wide. There are three windows on the side of the building, each window is 2 m wide and 1 m high. What is the probability that Nick will hit a window when he throws the ball at the wall?

Express your answer as a percentage.

Steps for approaching a problem-solving question	What you would do for this example
Step 1: What are you trying to work out?	The probability of hitting any of the windows.
Step 2: What information do you need?	The area of the wall and the area of the windows.
Step 3: What maths can you do?	Area of wall = 10 m × 2 m = 20 m² Area of windows = 3 × (2 m × 1 m) = 3 × 2 m² = 6 m² Apply this information to the formula for calculating relative probability: P(hits window) = $\frac{6}{20}$ = $\frac{3}{10}$ (Convert to a percentage) $\frac{3}{10}$ × 100 = 30% There is a 30% probability that Nick will hit a window.

EXERCISE 23E

1 Calculate the theoretical probability of each outcome. Order the outcomes from most likely to least likely.

  a Flipping a coin and getting tails.

  b Rolling a dice labelled 1 to 6 and getting 2.

  c Randomly picking a red counter from a bag that contains 3 green, 1 red and 5 blue counters.

  d Rolling two dice and getting seven as the total score.

2 Zara has 10 black, 5 white, 6 red and 3 green sweets in a packet. She offers the packet to her friend Anna who takes a sweet without looking.

  a What colour is Anna most likely to pick?

  b Which colour has the lowest chance of being picked?

  c What is the probability that she picks a red sweet?

  d What is the probability that the sweet is white or green?

3 Nina and Maria made up a game with an eight-sided dice. The sides of the dice are labelled 6, 24, 9, 29, 15, 7, 18 and 12. The chance of rolling each number is equally likely.

They take turns to roll the dice. Nina wins the roll if the dice shows a multiple of 2. Maria wins the roll if the dice shows a multiple of 3.

   a Is this a fair game? Give a reason for your answer.

   b What is the theoretical probability that the dice will show a multiple of 3?

4 During a netball competition, the same coin was flipped 20 times. Busi claimed the coin was unfair because it landed on tails only 5 out of the 20 times.

She says the probability of getting tails when you flip a coin is 0.5, so if you flip the coin 20 times you should get 20 × 0.5 = 10 tails.

Was she correct? Explain your answer.

5 Grey College has a sports tournament against St George's College every year. The weather on the day of the tournament can be described as sunny and dry, cloudy and humid, or rainy. Grey College keeps a record of the weather on the day and whether it won or drew the tournament.

Here are its results for the past 30 years.

Weather	Wins	Draws	Tournaments played
Sunny and dry	4	1	7
Cloudy and humid	3	2	10
Rainy	3	3	13
Total	10	6	30

   a What is the relative frequency of rain on tournament days?

   b A student from Grey College says they have a better chance of winning if it is sunny. Is that a correct statement? Support your answer.

   c A student from St George's says they have an almost even chance of winning the tournament, no matter what the weather. Is that a correct statement? Support your answer.

   d Calculate the experimental probability that Grey College will draw a tournament. Write this as a probability in words.

6 The chart below is a 10-day weather forecast in April for Cardiff.

Today	Sun 8	Mon 9	Tue 10	Wed 11	Thu 12	Fri 13	Sat 14	Sun 15	Mon 16
Rain	Showers	Sunny	Sunny	Sunny	Sunny	Partly cloudy	Mostly sunny	Cloudy	Scattered showers

Chance of rain:

| 100% | 80% | 10% | 0% | 0% | 0% | 0% | 0% | 10% | 30% |

   a What is the probability that it will rain on:

   i Sunday, 8 April?   **ii** Sunday, 15 April?

   b What does a 100% chance of rain mean?

Find answers at: cambridge.org/ukschools/gcsemaths-studentbookanswers

c Rhys wants to go hiking on Monday 9 April. Should he pack rain clothes? Give a reason for your answer.

d The 10-day forecast for Plymouth for this period shows a 0% chance of rain every day. Does this mean it definitely won't rain in Plymouth in this period? Give a reason for your answer.

7 A local educational authority wants to introduce random drug testing in secondary schools. It claims the tests have a very small false-positive rate of one half of one per cent.

a Write one half of one per cent as a decimal.

b The parents at a school with 800 students object to the test. They claim that 4 students could incorrectly test positive for drug use.

Are the parents' concerns valid? Give a reason for your answer.

c There were 3 831 937 secondary school students under this authority in the year they wanted to do the drug testing.

If they were all tested for drug use, how many of them would you expect to be incorrectly identified as using drugs?

> **Tip**
>
> A false-positive in a drug test means that a person who is not using drugs tests positive for drug use.

8 Professional athletes are routinely tested for banned performance enhancing substances. The testing authority estimates only 1% of the athletes tested are actually using banned substances. If an athlete is using banned substances, 90% of the time he or she will test positive in the test (in other words, fail the drug test). But, 10% of the athletes who are not using banned substances will also test positive (in other words, fail the drug test even though they are not using banned substances).

a Complete this table to show how many athletes will pass or fail the drug test for every 1000 athletes tested.

Status	Test positive (i.e. fail drug test)	Test negative (i.e. pass drug test)	Total
Athletes who are using banned substances			10
Athletes who are not using banned substances			990
Total			1000

b Represent the same information on a frequency tree.

c If an athlete tests positive for the banned substance, what is the chance that he or she is not actually using the substance? Give your answer as a percentage.

d If an athlete tests negative for the substances is it certain that he or she is not using them? Explain your answer.

9 80 people are asked if they can tell the difference between butter and margarine. 37 say they can, 24 say no and 19 say they are not sure.

The interviewer then carries out a blind taste test. Of those who said they could tell the difference, 14 got it wrong, of those who said no, 9 got it right and 14 of those who said they were not sure got it wrong.

Draw a frequency tree to show the outcomes of this experiment.

10 Lee and Haroon want to know what the probability is of getting two heads when you flip two coins one after the other. Lee says it is 25% and Haroon says it is $33\frac{1}{3}$%. They decide to do an experiment in which they flip five different sets (to be fair) of two coins and record the outcomes.

   a List all the possible outcomes when you flip two coins.

   b Copy and complete this table to show the results of Lee and Haroon's experiment.

Set of coins	Number of flips	Number of times we got two heads	Running total of two heads	Percentage of two heads (running total)
Two 10p coins	25	6	6	$\frac{6}{25} \times 100 = 24$
Two 50p coins	25	8		
Two £1 coins	25	5		
Two £2 coins	25	7		
Two 20p coins	25	9		

   c What type of probability have they recorded?

   d What is the relative frequency of getting two heads according to their results?

   e Do their results settle their argument? Give a reason for your answer.

11 Lee finds a computer program that simulates coin flips. He does a trial flipping the two coins 1000 times.

The computer produces this graph of his results.

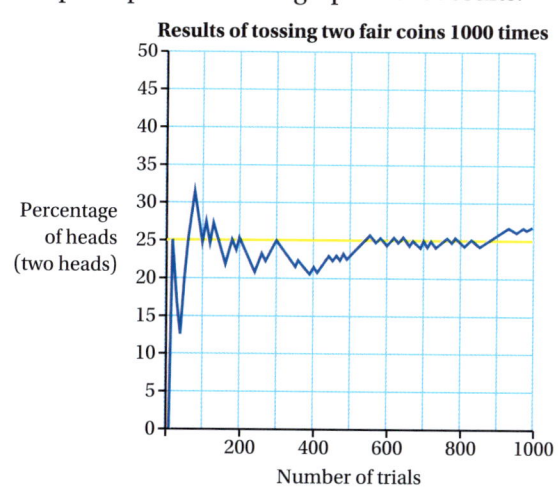

   a What does the graph show?
   b What does the yellow line on the graph represent?
   c Why does the other line vary up and down?
   d What happens to the line showing the results as the number of flips increases?
   e How does this graph help to settle the argument between Lee and Haroon?

Find answers at: cambridge.org/ukschools/gcsemaths-studentbookanswers

Checklist of learning and understanding

Probability

- Probability is a measure of how likely something is to happen.
- The probability scale ranges from 0 to 1. Impossible events have a probability of 0 and certain events have a probability of 1. It is not possible to have a negative probability (< 0) or a probability greater than 1.
- Probabilities between 0 and 1 can be expressed as fractions, decimals or percentages.
- A favourable outcome is the particular outcome of an event for which you are calculating the probability.
- The sum of probabilities will always total 1.
  The probability of a favourable outcome happening is equal to 1 minus the probability of it not happening. So, P(E) = 1 − P(*not* E)

Theoretical probability

- Probability of a favourable outcome = $\dfrac{\text{number of favourable outcomes}}{\text{number of possible outcomes}}$

Experimental probability

- Relative frequency or experimental probability, tells you how often a favourable outcome occurs in an experiment as a fraction of the number of trials in that experiment.

Relative frequency/experimental probability = $\dfrac{\text{frequency of a favourable outcome}}{\text{number of trials}}$

- Tables and frequency trees can be used to organise the outcomes of different experiments.
- Statistical data (empirical evidence) can also be used to find relative frequency of particular events.
- The relative frequency of an event can be used to predict future outcomes.

Mutually exclusive events

- Mutually exclusive events cannot happen at the same time. For example, you cannot throw a 1 and a 5 at the same time when you roll a dice. We **add** together the probabilities of mutually exclusive outcomes.

For additional questions on the topics in this chapter, visit GCSE Mathematics Online.

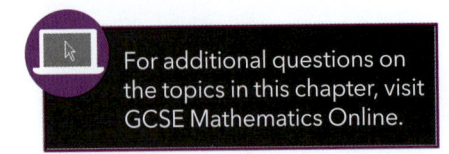

Chapter review

1. Choose the correct answer. Sharon is playing a game and she needs to roll a six to start. What is the probability of her rolling a six on her first go?

   A $\dfrac{1}{6}$ B $\dfrac{5}{6}$ C $\dfrac{6}{6}$ D 0

2. I have 30 red, 40 white, 2 brown and 8 green beads in a container. If I choose one at random, what is the probability that it will be:

   a white?   b not green?   c brown or green?

3 Nina rolled a dice 200 times and recorded her results in a table.

Result	1	2	3	4	5	6
Frequency	28	20	20	40	36	56
Experimental probability						

   a Calculate the experimental probability of each result.
   b What is the relative frequency of rolling an odd number?
   c The theoretical probability of rolling a 4 is $\frac{1}{6}$. Compare this with

4 Jill interviews 64 people to get their opinions about sending texts when in company. 44 of those interviewed say it is rude to send texts in company. Jill then observes the people at a large event. Of those who said it was rude to send texts in company 13 sent texts when at the table with others. Of those who said it was acceptable, 9 did not send texts when in company. Complete the frequency tree to show this data.

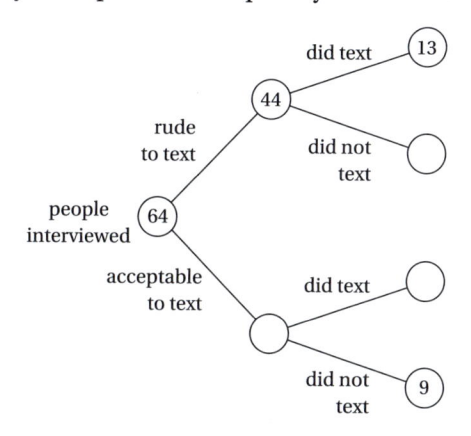

5 A company tests a new brand of soap and produces the following data.

Number of participants	Developed a rash	Did not develop a rash
2500	180	2320

   a Use these results to determine the probability of using this soap and developing a rash.
   b The company decides to print the following warning statement on the soap: '7% of people who use this soap may develop a rash.'
      i Is the statement correct?
     ii Why would the company use a percentage rather than giving the number of people who developed a rash?
    iii If 100 people used this soap, how many of them would you expect to develop a rash?
    iv Why is the word 'expect' used in part **iii** above?

Find answers at: cambridge.org/ukschools/gcsemaths-studentbookanswers

24 Combined events and probability diagrams

In this chapter you will learn how to …
- use a range of sample space diagrams to list outcomes of combined events.
- apply the addition rule and use various representations to solve probability problems.

For more resources relating to this chapter, visit GCSE Mathematics Online.

Using mathematics: real-life applications

Medical researchers have developed a range of tests to detect drug use, blood-alcohol levels, disease markers and genetic and birth defects in unborn children. The probability that the test results are accurate is very high, but it is not often 100%.

> "An incorrect test result can be devastating. People can be convicted of drink-driving, be expelled from competitive sports, risk surgery or decide to terminate a pregnancy based on test results, so it is really important to understand the probability of a good test giving a bad result." *(Medical statistician)*

Before you start …

Ch 10, 11	You'll need to be able to calculate effectively with fractions and decimals.	**1** These calculations are all incorrect. What should the answers be? **a** $\frac{1}{8} + \frac{1}{4} = \frac{1}{12}$ **b** $\frac{2}{3} + \frac{1}{5} = \frac{2}{15}$ **c** $1 - \frac{3}{5} = -\left(\frac{2}{5}\right)$ **d** $\frac{2}{3} \times \frac{2}{5} = \frac{2}{15}$ **e** $0.3 \times 0.6 = 1.8$
Ch 23	You should be familiar with the vocabulary of basic probability.	**2** Select the correct term from the box for each definition. event outcomes random equally likely relative frequency **a** The number of times an event is recorded divided by the total number of trials conducted. **b** The set of results of an experiment. **c** Something of interest, such as getting heads when you flip a coin. **d** Things that have the same chance of happening are … **e** Not predetermined.

Ch 23	Check that you can list all the possible outcomes of an experiment.	**3** Complete each list of possible outcomes.
		a Two students are to be chosen at random from a group of males and females:
		    FF, FM, …
		b Two coins are to be flipped at the same time:
		    HH, …
		c Two cards are selected from a set of three cards labelled A, B and C and placed next to each other in the order they are drawn:
		    AB, AC, …

24 Combined events and probability diagrams

Assess your starting point using the Launchpad

STEP 1

1 The Venn diagram shows the different sports chosen by students from one particular class. T represents students who play tennis and S represents those who take swimming.

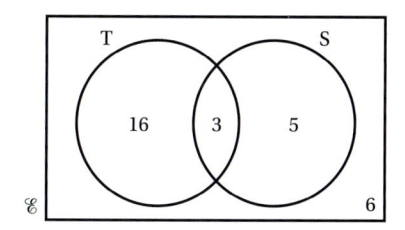

a How many students are in the class?
b How many students play tennis?
c How many students play tennis and swim?
d If a student is chosen at random from the class, what is the probability that he or she will take swimming?

2 Complete the tree diagram to show all the possible outcomes if you spin this spinner twice in a row. Add the probability of landing on each colour to the tree diagram.

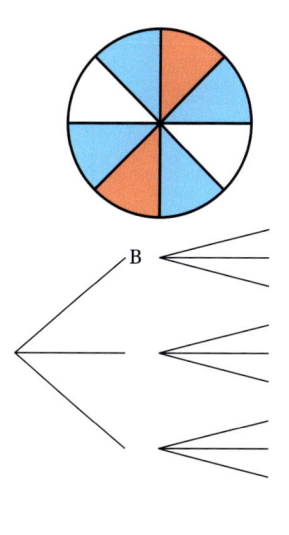

GO TO
Section 1: Representing combined events

GO TO
Step 2: The Launchpad continues on the next page …

Find answers at: cambridge.org/ukschools/gcsemaths-studentbookanswers

381

Launchpad continued ...

STEP 2

3 The diagram gives the probability of drawing hearts or twos at random from a normal pack of 52 playing cards.

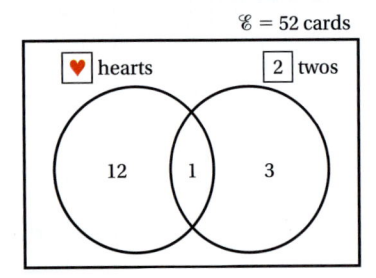

ℰ = 52 cards

♥ hearts   2 twos

12   1   3

What is the probability that a card drawn at random will be:

a both a heart and a two?

b either a heart or a two?

c neither a heart nor a two?

4 A black (B) or white (W) counter is drawn at random from a box containing both black and white counters. The counter is replaced before a second counter is drawn. The possible outcomes and the probabilities of each outcome are shown below.

1st counter	2nd counter	outcome
B ($\frac{5}{9}$)	B ($\frac{5}{9}$)	B B
	W ($\frac{4}{9}$)	B W
W ($\frac{4}{9}$)	B ($\frac{5}{9}$)	W B
	W ($\frac{4}{9}$)	W W

What is the probability of:

a drawing a black counter on the first draw?

b drawing two counters the same colour?

c drawing a white counter first and a black counter second?

GO TO
Section 2: Theoretical probability of combined events

GO TO
Chapter review

24 Combined events and probability diagrams

Section 1: Representing combined events

Two or more events can happen at the same time. For example, if you flip a coin and roll a dice then you get heads (H) or tails (T) and a number from 1 to 6. These are called **combined events** because there is a combination of outcomes.

For combined events you have to find efficient ways of identifying all the possible outcomes so that you can find the probability of different combinations of outcomes.

The picture shows the **sample space** for flipping a coin and rolling a dice at the same time. The sample space must include **all** possible outcomes of the combined events.

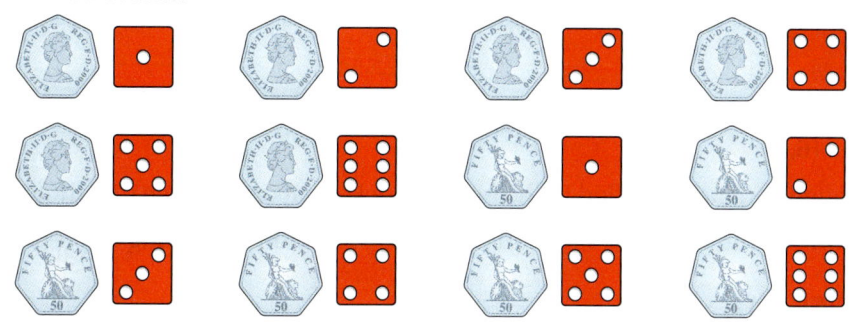

> **Key vocabulary**
>
> **combined events**: one event followed by another event producing two or more outcomes.
>
> **sample space**: a list or diagram that shows all possible outcomes from two or more events.

The sample space in the diagram can be represented as an ordered list like this:

H, 1   H, 2   H, 3   H, 4   H, 5   H, 6   T, 1   T, 2   T, 3   T, 4   T, 5   T, 6

Tables and grids

Listing the sample space takes a long time and you might make mistakes. Two-way tables and grids let you work faster and also let you see quickly whether you have left out, or repeated any outcomes.

WORKED EXAMPLE 1

Represent the sample space for flipping a coin and rolling a dice using:

a a table.   **b** a grid.

a

Dice / Coin	1	2	3	4	5	6
Heads	H1	H2	H3	H4	H5	H6
Tails	T1	T2	T3	T4	T5	T6

Make the header of each column a different score for one roll of a dice, and the header of each row one result from flipping a coin. Fill in the table to find all the possible combinations.

b 12 possible outcomes

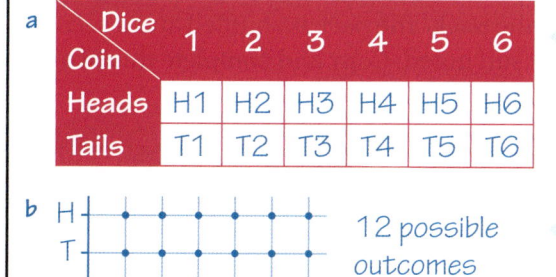

Use a similar process to creating the two-way table but here use a set of axes to list each result and match them by drawing dots.

Find answers at: cambridge.org/ukschools/gcsemaths-studentbookanswers

Using tables to list probabilities of favourable outcomes

In some cases you don't have to list all the possible outcomes. For example, let's say you want to know how many ways there are to get a total score of 7 when you roll two ordinary dice. You can draw up a table like this one:

Number on dice	1	2	3	4	5	6
1	2	3	4	5	6	7
2	3	4	5	6	7	
3	4	5	6	7		
4		4	6	7		
5		6	7			
6		7				

Once you get to a sum of 7 you can stop because the next sum will be greater than that.

The table shows there are six ways of getting a score of 7: (1, 6), (2, 5), (3, 4), (4, 3), (5, 2) and (6, 1).

Even though you haven't filled in the empty blocks, you can still see that there are 36 possible outcomes (it is a 6 × 6 table). So the probability of getting 7 is $\frac{6}{36}$ or $\frac{1}{6}$.

EXERCISE 24A

1. Use a grid to represent the sample space for:
   a. flipping two coins.
   b. choosing a letter at random from the word CAT and flipping a coin.
   c. drawing one counter each from two bags containing red, blue and yellow counters.

2. a. Draw a table to show:
      i. all possible combinations of scores when you roll two dice.
      ii. the sample space for flipping a coin and spinning a spinner with sectors A, B, C and D.
   b. For each table above, make up five probability questions that could be answered from the tables. Exchange questions with a partner and try to answer each other's questions.

3. A card is drawn from a standard pack of 52 cards. Its colour and suit are noted and then it is returned to the pack. The pack is shuffled and a second card is drawn and its colour and suit noted. Copy and complete this two-way table to show the possible outcomes.

First card / Second card	Diamonds (red)	Hearts (red)	Clubs (black)	Spades (black)
Diamonds (red)	RR			
Hearts (red)	RR			
Clubs (black)	RB			
Spades (black)	RB			

   a. How many possible outcomes are there?
   b. What is the probability of drawing two black cards?
   c. What is the most likely probability?

24 Combined events and probability diagrams

Venn diagrams

Venn diagrams show the mathematical relationships between sets of data. Different events (sets of outcomes) are represented by circles inside a rectangular frame. The rectangular frame represents all the possible outcomes, that is, the sample space (this is called the universal set).

Look at the Venn diagram and read through the information to revise the main features of Venn diagrams.

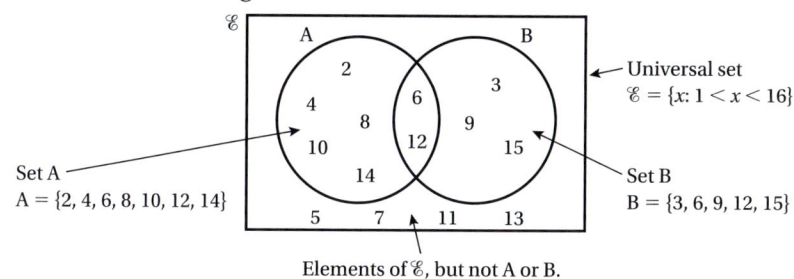

- Universal set $\mathcal{E} = \{x: 1 < x < 16\}$
- Set A: A = {2, 4, 6, 8, 10, 12, 14}
- Set B: B = {3, 6, 9, 12, 15}
- Elements of $\mathcal{E}$, but not A or B.

$\mathcal{E}$ is the universal set. In this case this is the whole numbers between 1 and 16.

$\mathcal{E}$ = {set of numbers between 1 and 16}.

This can also be written in set notation as: $\mathcal{E} = \{x: 1 < x < 16\}$.

The circles A and B represent sets.

Set A is the set of even numbers between 1 and 16 and it can be listed as: A = {2, 4, 6, 8, 10, 12, 14}.

Set B is the set of multiples of three between 1 and 16 and it can be listed as B = {3, 6, 9, 12, 15}.

There are seven elements in Set A. This can be written as n(A) = 7, which means 'the number of elements in set A is 7'.

There are five elements in Set B, so n(B) = 5.

Set A and Set B have two elements in common. The numbers 6 and 12 are written in the overlapping section of the circles to show that they are elements of both sets.

The numbers 5, 7, 11 and 13 are not elements of A or B but they are elements of the universal set so they are written inside the rectangle, but outside the circles.

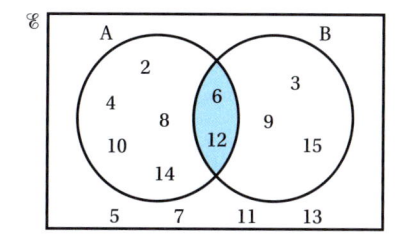

> **Tip**
> The curly brackets { } are used to show that you are describing a set. The numbers between the brackets are elements of the set.

Intersection, union and complement of sets

Venn diagrams can also represent operations between sets. The three important operations for probability work are intersection, union and complement.

The shaded area in the diagram represents the **intersection** between A and B.
The intersection of two sets is the elements that are common to (shared by) both sets.

A ∩ B = {6, 12}

n(A ∩ B) = 2

Find answers at: cambridge.org/ukschools/gcsemaths-studentbookanswers

The shaded area here represents the **union** of A and B. This is the **combined elements** of both sets with no elements repeated.

A ∪ B = {2, 3, 4, 6, 8, 9, 10, 12, 14, 15}

n(A ∪ B) = 10

The **complement** of a set refers to all the elements in the universal set other than the ones in the given set. The complement of Set A is shaded in the diagram.

A′ = {3, 5, 7, 9, 11, 13, 15}

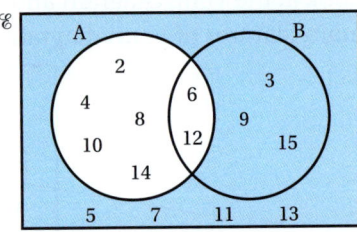

You will learn more about how to solve probability problems using Venn diagrams in Section 2.

> **Tip**
> You might be given the elements of the different sets and asked to draw a Venn diagram.

Set notation

Sometimes the information about sets is described in a specific way using set notation.

Think about the following set.

A = {integers greater than zero but less than 20}

This is quite a lot to write out, so it makes sense to find a shorter notation.

A = {$x: x$ is an integer, $0 < x < 20$}

The element symbol, ∈, ('is an element of') might also appear in set notation. For example:
C = {$x: x \in$ primes, $10 < x < 20$}

You read this as C is the set of prime numbers greater than 10 but less than 20. This information allows you to work out that C = {11, 13, 17, 19}.

> **Tip**
> The symbol ∉ means 'not an element of a set'. For example, 3 ∉ C means that 3 is not an element of the set C.

WORKED EXAMPLE 2

Given that ℰ = {$x: x$ is a letter from a to h inclusive}, A = {a, b, c, e} and B = {c, d, e, f, g}, draw a Venn diagram to represent this information.

ℰ = {a, b, c, d, e, f, g, h}
A = {a, b, c, e}
B = {c, d, e, f, g}

Start by comparing the sets to find the intersection and any elements which are in the universal set but which are not in A or B (the complement of A and B or (A ∪ B)′.)

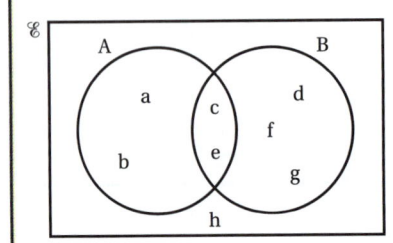

c and e are elements of A and B, so
A ∩ B = {c, e}
h is not in A or B, so (A ∪ B)′ = h (in other words, h is outside the two circles)
Draw the diagram and label it.

24 Combined events and probability diagrams

In some problems you might be given information and have to define the sets yourself. In some cases you can't list the separate elements of the sets so you write the number of elements in each set.

WORKED EXAMPLE 3

In a survey of 25 people it was found that they all liked either chocolate or ice cream. 15 people said they liked ice cream and 18 said they liked chocolate.

Draw a Venn diagram and use it to work out the probability that a person chosen at random from this group will like both chocolate and ice cream.

$\mathcal{E}$ = {number of people surveyed}, so, $n(\mathcal{E})$ = 25
C = {people who like chocolate}, so, $n(C)$ = 18
I = {people who like ice cream}, so, $n(I)$ = 15

Start by defining the sets and writing the information in set language.

Tip

You don't know the names of the people, so you can't list them in the diagram. You do know how many of each response there was, so you can just write the number of people in the diagram.

$n(C) + n(I) = 15 + 18 = 33$
$n(C \cap I) = 8$

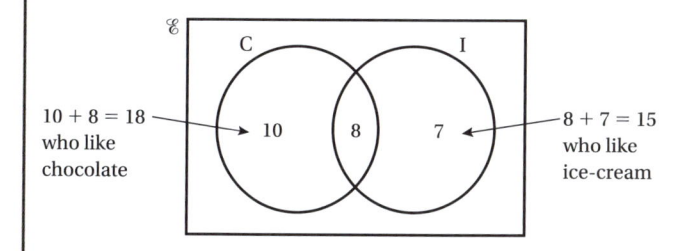

Only 25 people were surveyed, so 8 people must have said they liked both chocolate and ice cream (since 33 − 25 = 8).

10 + 8 = 18 who like chocolate — 10, 8, 7 — 8 + 7 = 15 who like ice-cream

Use the figures to draw your Venn diagram. There are 18 people in total who liked chocolate and 8 of these also like ice cream, so the number who just like chocolate: 18 − 8 = 10; enter this value in the left circle of your diagram and label this circle 'C'. Similarly, of the 15 who liked ice cream, 8 also liked chocolate so ice cream only: 15 − 8 = 7.

$$P(\text{person likes both}) = \frac{\text{number of people who like both}}{\text{number of people surveyed}}$$

Finally calculate the probability

$$= \frac{8}{25} = 0.32$$

EXERCISE 24B

1 $\mathcal{E} = \{x: 1 \leq x \leq 20\}$, $A = \{x: 5 < x \leq 12\}$ and $B = \{x: x \text{ is a factor of } 24\}$.

  a Draw a Venn diagram to show this information.

  b Use your Venn diagram to find:

  i $A \cap B$.   **ii** $A \cup B$.   **iii** $n(A)$.   **iv** $n(A')$.   **v** $n(B')$.

2 Nadia has 20 pairs of shoes. Six pairs are sports shoes, four pairs are red and only one of the pairs of sports shoes is red.

Draw a Venn diagram to show this information and work out the probability that a pair of shoes chosen at random from her shoe collection will be neither red nor sports shoes.

Find answers at: cambridge.org/ukschools/gcsemaths-studentbookanswers

3. A factory employs 100 people. 47 of the employees have to work with moving machinery so if they have long hair they have to tie it back. 35 employees have long hair, and of these, some work with moving machinery. 23 employees neither have long hair nor work with moving machinery.

Draw a Venn diagram to show this information and use it to work out the probability of a random employee having to tie his or her hair back at work.

4. Of the first 20 students to walk into a classroom, 13 were wearing headphones and 15 were sending texts. Four students were not wearing headphones or sending texts.

Represent this information on a Venn diagram and say how many students were wearing headphones while sending texts when they walked into class.

Tip

Tree diagrams show probabilities, not actual responses. This is the main difference between them and the frequency trees you worked with in Chapter 23.

Tree diagrams

A tree diagram is a branching diagram that shows all the possible outcomes (sample space) of one or more activity.

To draw a tree diagram:

1. Make a dot to represent the first activity.
2. Draw branches from the dot to show all possible outcomes of that activity only.
3. Write the outcomes at the end of each branch.
4. Repeat the same process for the next activity except that the starting dot is drawn at the end of **each** outcome from the previous activity.

These two diagrams both show the possible outcomes for throwing a dice and flipping a coin at the same time. Both diagrams are correct.

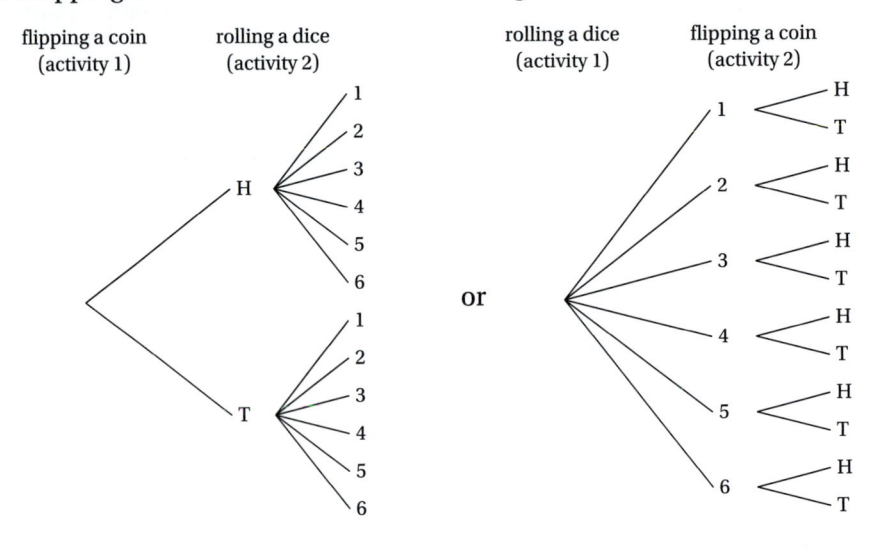

Once you've drawn a tree diagram you can list the possible outcomes by following the paths along the branches. Listing the combinations lets you work out the probability of different events.

24 Combined events and probability diagrams

WORKED EXAMPLE 4

a Draw a tree diagram to show that when the probability of having a boy or a girl is equal, there are eight possible combinations of boys and girls in a three-child family. Using the sample space, calculate the probability of:

  i having three girls.

  ii having three children of the same gender.

> **Tip**
>
> You should remember how to calculate theoretical probability from Chapter 23.

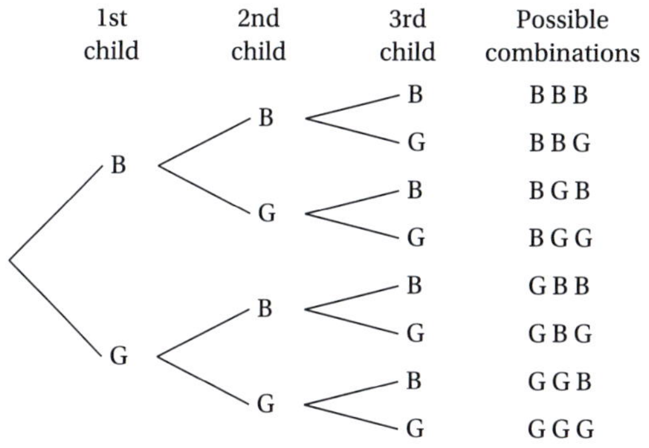

1st child	2nd child	3rd child	Possible combinations
B	B	B	BBB
B	B	G	BBG
B	G	B	BGB
B	G	G	BGG
G	B	B	GBB
G	B	G	GBG
G	G	B	GGB
G	G	G	GGG

1. Draw a dot for the first-born child.
2. Draw two branches as there are only two possible outcomes.
3. Label the outcomes (one B and one G).
4. Repeat this at the end of each branch for the second and third child.

List the possible combinations.

You can see from the diagram there are eight possible combinations of boys and girls.

$P(3 \text{ girls}) = \frac{1}{8}$.

You can use the diagram to find different probabilities. There is only one outcome that produces three girls.

$P(\text{all the same gender}) = \frac{2}{8} = \frac{1}{4}$.

There are two outcomes that produce three children of the same gender.

Did you know?

This tree diagram assumes that a boy or a girl is equally likely for each pregnancy. In reality the probability of having a boy or a girl varies by family and by country. Worldwide the probability of having a boy is a little higher than having a girl. The UN, for example, estimates that in 2013 there were 107 boys born for every 100 girls born.

EXERCISE 24C

1 Here are two groups of jelly beans.

Ahmed is allowed to pick one jelly bean from each group.

Draw a tree diagram to show the sample space for taking a jelly bean at random from each group of jelly beans.

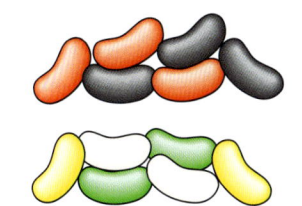

2 Sandy has a bag containing a red, a blue and a green pen.

Complete this tree diagram to show the sample space when she takes a pen from the bag at random, replaces it, and then takes another pen.

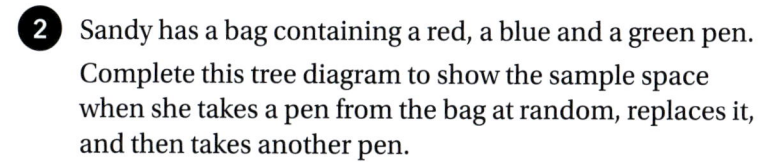

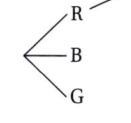

3 Draw a tree diagram to show the sample space when three coins are flipped one after the other.

How many ways are there to get two heads and a tail?

Find answers at: cambridge.org/ukschools/gcsemaths-studentbookanswers

4 Andrew offers a gift-wrapping service in a large department store. Customers can choose striped, checked, metallic, spiral or plain brown wrapping paper and white, silver, black or pink ribbon.

   a Draw a tree diagram to show all the possible combinations of paper and ribbon.

   b How many possible combinations are there?

5 In a knockout quiz, the winner goes on to the next round. Naresh takes part in a four-round quiz and he estimates that he has an equal chance of winning or losing each round.

   a Using W to represent win and L to represent loss, draw a tree diagram to show all possible outcomes for Naresh.

   b How many possible outcomes are there?

   c What is the probability that he will win the first round given his own estimate of his chances?

Section 2: Theoretical probability of combined events

You can use sample space diagrams (tables, grids, tree diagrams and Venn diagrams) to find the probability of getting a favourable outcome from probabilities of combined events.

Use the sample space diagram to calculate the number of favourable outcomes and the total number of possible outcomes, then use the formula for calculating theoretical probability that you saw in Chapter 23.

Once you have identified all the possible outcomes you can mark the ones that are favourable and use these to find the probability of different outcomes. The formula

$$P(\text{event with favourable outcome}) = \frac{\text{number of favourable outcomes}}{\text{total number of possible outcomes}}$$

can still be used to work this out.

WORKED EXAMPLE 5

Jay has six cards with the numbers 0, 0, 2, 2, 3 and 7 on them. He picks a card, returns it and then picks another at random.

a Draw a grid to show the sample space.

b Use the grid to find the probability that Jay will pick:

   i two numbers that are the same.   **ii** two numbers that add up to 7.

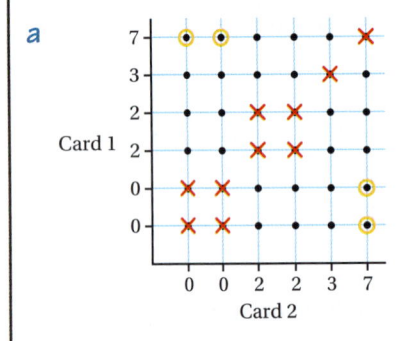

a

Draw the sample space. Use this to mark all the combinations where the two numbers are the same (here a cross has been used). Then mark all the combinations where the two numbers sum to 7 (here, a circle has been used).

Continues on next page …

b **i** P(two numbers the same) = $\frac{10}{36}$

= $\frac{5}{18}$

or 0.28 (correct to 2 dp)

> The grid shows there are 36 possible outcomes. The successful outcomes are marked with a cross on the grid.

ii P(sum of 7) = $\frac{4}{36}$

= $\frac{1}{9}$

> The successful outcomes are circled on the grid.

EXERCISE 24D

1 One box contains a red, a yellow and a blue marble, the other box contains a red, a green and a purple marble.

  a Draw up a table to show the sample space if you choose one marble at random from each box.

  b What is the probability of choosing two red marbles?

  c What is the probability of choosing a red and a purple marble?

  d Is it possible to end up with one yellow marble and one blue marble? Why?

2 Linda and Annie each take a coin at random out of their pockets and add the totals together to get an amount. Linda has two £1 coins, a 50p coin, a £2 coin and three 20p coins in her pocket. Annie has three £2 coins, one £1 coin and three 50p coins.

  a Draw up a two-way table to show all the possible outcomes for the sum of the two coins.

  b What is the probability that the coins will add up to exactly £2.50?

  c What is the probability of the coins adding up to less than £2?

  d What is the probability that the coins will add up to £3 or more?

3 The diagram shows picture cards from a normal deck (J, Q or K). Just the picture cards are shuffled, a card is drawn, the type of card is noted and it is replaced before another card is drawn.

  a Draw a tree diagram to show the possible results (J, Q or K) when you draw three cards at random from this set.

  b What is the probability of drawing three cards with the same letter?

  c What is the probability that all three cards will have a different letter?

  d What is the probability of getting at least one king?

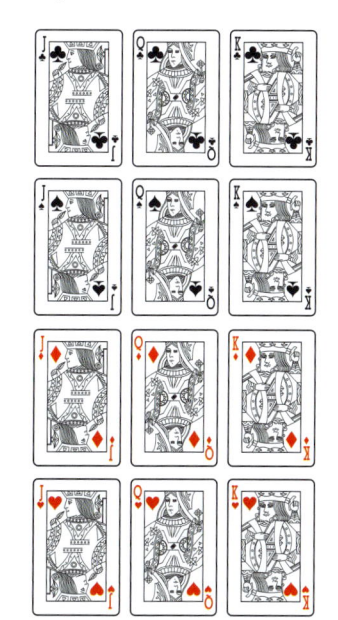

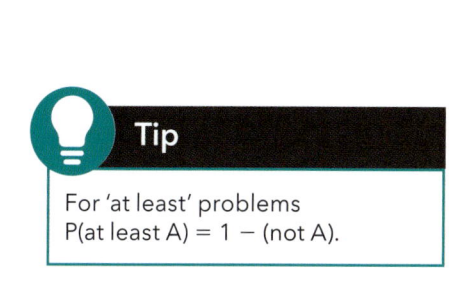

> **Tip**
>
> For 'at least' problems P(at least A) = 1 − (not A).

Different types of events

The type of event determines whether you add or multiply the probabilities.

Mutually exclusive events and the addition rule

> **Tip**
>
> You should remember from Chapter 23 that mutually exclusive events cannot happen at the same time.

Imagine you have a bag with 3 red, 2 yellow and 5 green sweets in it and you are allowed to choose one sweet at random. You cannot pick a red sweet and a yellow sweet at the same time, so the events P(red) and P(yellow) are mutually exclusive.

You can work out the probability of choosing *either* a red *or* a yellow sweet.

There are 3 red and 2 yellow sweets, so $\frac{5}{10}$ of the sweets are either red or yellow.

$$P(\text{red or yellow}) = P(\text{red}) + P(\text{yellow}) = \frac{3}{10} + \frac{2}{10} = \frac{5}{10} = \frac{1}{2}$$

> **Tip**
>
> Questions involving 'either-or' events normally involve mutually exclusive events so they can usually be solved by adding the probabilities.

We can say that P(A or B) = P(A) + P(B) where A and B are mutually exclusive events.

This is called the **addition law** for mutually exclusive events.

Events that are not mutually exclusive

When you list the elements in the union of sets you do not repeat shared elements (those in the intersection).

In set language, we can write this as $n(A \cup B) = n(A) + n(B) - n(A \cap B)$. The elements in the intersection of sets are **not** mutually exclusive and this affects your probability calculations.

WORKED EXAMPLE 6

The Venn diagram shows the possible outcomes when a six-sided dice is rolled. Set A = {prime numbers} and Set B = {odd numbers}. Use the diagram to find the probability of rolling a number that is either odd or prime.

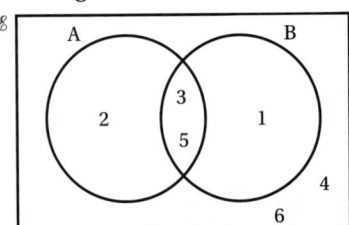

> **Tip**
>
> The word 'or' means it belongs in one set or the other, so you need to deal with the union of the sets.

P(A or B) = P(A) + P(B) − P(A and B)

$P(A) = \frac{3}{6}$

$P(B) = \frac{3}{6}$

The total number of outcomes is the denominator, and it's easier to add and subtract the fractions if you don't simplify the fractions first. Remember that the P(A) includes the values in the intersection so there are 3 outcomes out of 6 that are in set A.

$P(A \text{ and } B) = \frac{2}{6}$

So, $P(A \text{ or } B) = \frac{3}{6} + \frac{3}{6} - \frac{2}{6} = \frac{4}{6} = \frac{2}{3}$

You can see this is true by looking at the diagram. The combined elements of A and B are 1, 2, 3 and 5, giving you $\frac{4}{6}$ numbers falling into one or the other of these sets. We don't want to add the numbers that fall into the intersecting part twice which is why we subtract $n(A \cap B)$ in the formula.

24 Combined events and probability diagrams

Independent events

When the outcome of one event does not affect the outcome of the others, we say they are **independent events**.

Rolling a dice and flipping a coin are independent events. The score on the dice doesn't affect whether you get heads or tails.

Tree diagrams are useful for solving problems involving independent events if you write the probabilities of the events on the branches.

Here is the tree diagram showing possible outcomes for throwing a dice and flipping a coin at the same time (H is used for heads and T is used for tails).

This is the same diagram as in the previous section but now the probability of each outcome is written at the side of each branch.

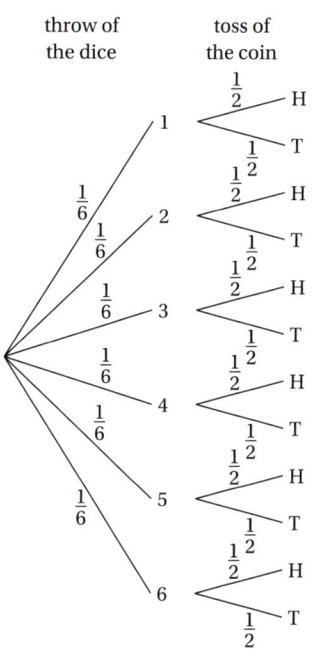

> **Key vocabulary**
>
> **independent events**: events that are not affected by what happened before.

The probability of combined events on a tree diagram

To find the probability of one particular combination of outcomes multiply the probabilities on consecutive branches, for example, the probability of throwing a 5 **and** getting heads is $\frac{1}{6} \times \frac{1}{2} = \frac{1}{12}$.

This is called the **multiplication law**.

$P(A \text{ and } B) = P(A) \times P(B)$

> **Tip**
>
> It can be helpful to use a colour to mark the route along the branches to show which events you are dealing with.

Combining the laws

To find the probability when you have independent events and there is more than one favourable combination, or when the combinations are mutually exclusive:

- multiply the probabilities on consecutive branches for each favourable outcome
- add the probabilities.

For example,

P(rolling 1 or 2 and getting an H) = P(rolling a 1 and getting an H) + P(rolling a 2 and getting an H)

$$= \left(\frac{1}{6} \times \frac{1}{2}\right) + \left(\frac{1}{6} \times \frac{1}{2}\right)$$

$$= \frac{1}{12} + \frac{1}{12} = \frac{2}{12} = \frac{1}{6}.$$

Find answers at: cambridge.org/ukschools/gcsemaths-studentbookanswers

GCSE Mathematics for OCR (Foundation)

WORKED EXAMPLE 7

Two coins are flipped together. Draw a tree diagram to find the probability of getting:

a two tails.

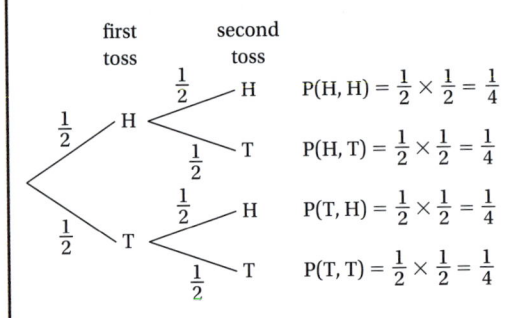

b one head and one tail.

first toss — second toss

$\frac{1}{2}$ H $\to$ $\frac{1}{2}$ H P(H, H) = $\frac{1}{2} \times \frac{1}{2} = \frac{1}{4}$

$\frac{1}{2}$ H $\to$ $\frac{1}{2}$ T P(H, T) = $\frac{1}{2} \times \frac{1}{2} = \frac{1}{4}$

$\frac{1}{2}$ T $\to$ $\frac{1}{2}$ H P(T, H) = $\frac{1}{2} \times \frac{1}{2} = \frac{1}{4}$

$\frac{1}{2}$ T $\to$ $\frac{1}{2}$ T P(T, T) = $\frac{1}{2} \times \frac{1}{2} = \frac{1}{4}$

> Draw a tree diagram and label each branch with the probability of that particular outcome. List all the possible outcomes.

a P(TT) = P(T on 1st flip) × P(T on 2nd flip)

$= \frac{1}{2} \times \frac{1}{2} = \frac{1}{4}$

> Follow the branches to find the probability of getting a T **and** another T; multiply the probabilities along the branches.

b P(HT or TH) = P(HT) + P(TH)

$= \left(\frac{1}{2} \times \frac{1}{2}\right) + \left(\frac{1}{2} \times \frac{1}{2}\right)$

$= \frac{1}{4} + \frac{1}{4} = \frac{1}{2}$

> There are two different ways that you could get a head and a tail: HT **or** TH. The two different combinations are mutually exclusive. Calculate the probability of each outcome first by multiplying the probabilities along the branches, then add the two probabilities together.

Key vocabulary

dependent events: events in which the outcome is affected by what happened before.

Dependent events

When the outcome of one event affects the outcome of the other events, we say they are **dependent events**.

Here are 4 red and 2 yellow sweets.

Suppose you choose one sweet at random and eat it before you select a second sweet. What is the probability of the second sweet being red?

The answer to this depends on what colour the first sweet was. If the first sweet was red then the probability that the second sweet is red is $\frac{3}{5}$ because there are only 5 sweets left and only 3 of those are red.

1 red eaten

If the first sweet was yellow then the probability that the second one is red is $\frac{4}{5}$. There are still only five sweets left to choose from, but this time four of them are red.

1 yellow eaten

For dependent events you can find the probability by adapting the multiplication rule to accommodate the dependent event.

P(A and then B) = P(A) × P(B given that A has occurred)

You can use tree diagrams to help work this out.

24 Combined events and probability diagrams

WORKED EXAMPLE 8

A box contains three yellow, four red and two purple marbles. A marble is chosen at random and not replaced before choosing the next one. If three marbles are chosen (without replacement) what is the probability of choosing:

a three red marbles?

b a yellow, red and purple marble in that order?

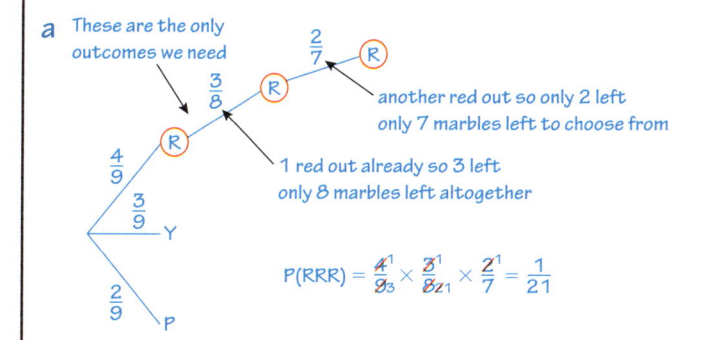

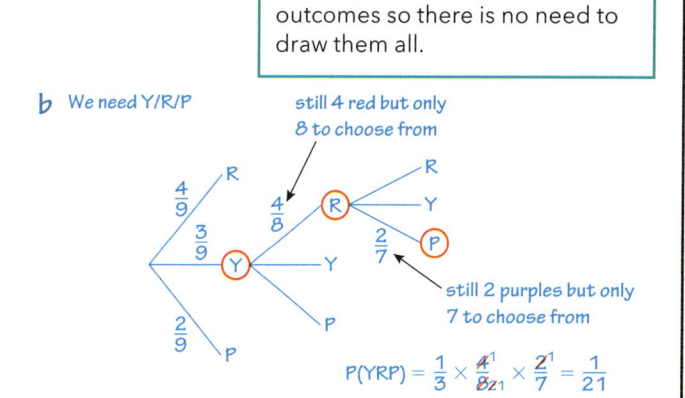

> **Tip**
> Notice in both parts only a partial tree diagram was drawn; you are only interested in certain outcomes so there is no need to draw them all.

a These are the only outcomes we need

- another red out so only 2 left only 7 marbles left to choose from
- 1 red out already so 3 left only 8 marbles left altogether

$$P(RRR) = \frac{4^1}{9_3} \times \frac{3^1}{8_{2\,1}} \times \frac{2^1}{7} = \frac{1}{21}$$

b We need Y/R/P

- still 4 red but only 8 to choose from
- still 2 purples but only 7 to choose from

$$P(YRP) = \frac{1}{3} \times \frac{4^1}{8_{2\,1}} \times \frac{2^1}{7} = \frac{1}{21}$$

Probability using a Venn diagram

When you use Venn diagrams to solve problems it is important to choose the correct operation (union, intersection or complement) to solve the problem. The wording of the problem normally gives you clues about which operation you need.

For example, if you have Set A = {x: x is an even number} and Set B = {x: x is a multiple of 3} you might be asked questions like the ones in the first column of the table.

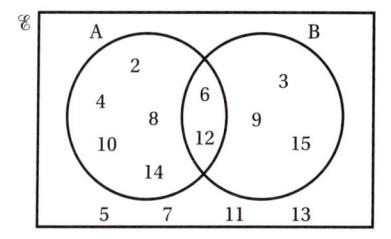

Question: What is the probability of a number ...	Which operation is involved in finding the solution?	Why?
... being even and not a multiple of 3	No operations	The probability will involve all the elements in circle A, including those in the intersection with circle B.
... being even **and** a multiple of 3	Intersection	The word 'and' tells you are looking for numbers that are elements of both sets (i.e. those in the overlapping section).
... being even **or** a multiple of 3	Union	The word 'or' tells you it can be in either of the two sets, so you need to include all the elements of both sets – without repeating any in the intersection.
... **not** being even	Complement	All the numbers that are outside the set of even numbers must be included. This means all the numbers outside circle A: the numbers outside both circles, and the numbers inside circle B, but not in the intersection.
... being **neither** even **nor** a multiple of 3	Complement	'Neither, nor' tells you that two sets have to be excluded, you are looking for the elements outside the circles in this case.

Find answers at: cambridge.org/ukschools/gcsemaths-studentbookanswers

395

EXERCISE 24E

1 In a class of 28 students, 12 take physics, 15 take chemistry and 8 take neither physics nor chemistry.

  a Draw a Venn diagram to represent this information.

  b What is the probability that a student chosen at random from this class:

   i takes physics but not chemistry?

   ii takes physics or chemistry?

   iii takes physics and chemistry?

2 Nico is on a bus. He amuses himself by choosing a consonant and a vowel at random from the names of towns on road signs. The next road sign is DUNDEE.

  a Draw up a sample space diagram to list all the options that Nico has.

  b Calculate P(D and E).

  c Calculate P(D and E or U).

  d Calculate P(not N and U).

3 A bag contains 3 red counters, 4 green counters, 2 yellow counters and 1 white counter. Two counters are drawn from the bag one after the other, without being replaced.

Calculate:

  a P(2 red counters).

  b P(2 green counters).

  c P(2 yellow counters).

  d P(white and then red).

  e P(white or yellow in any order, but not both).

  f P(white or red in any order, but not both).

  g P(white or yellow first and then red or green).

4 Mohammed has four Scrabble® tiles with the letters A, B, C and D on them. He draws a letter at random and places it on the table, then he draws a second letter and a third, placing them down next to the previously drawn letter.

  a What is the probability that the letters he has drawn spell the words:

   i cad?   **ii** bad?   **iii** dad?

  b What is the probability that he will not draw the letter B?

  c What is Mohammed's chance of drawing the letters in alphabetical order?

5 In a standard pack of cards, A = {hearts} and B = {kings}.

If a card is picked at random, determine:

  a P(A).   **b** P(B).   **c** P(A and B).   **d** P(A or B).

6 Maria has a bag containing 18 fruit drop sweets. 10 are apple flavoured and 8 are blackberry flavoured. She chooses a sweet at random and eats it. Then she chooses another sweet at random.

  a Calculate the probability that:

  i both sweets are apple flavoured.

  ii both sweets are blackberry flavoured.

  iii the first is apple and the second is blackcurrant.

  iv the first is blackberry and the second is apple.

  b Add up your answers from part **a**. Explain why you should get an answer of 1 if you worked out the probabilities correctly.

7 Amira has a colour wheel with four colours on the inside and five colours on the outside as shown. She turns the wheel to find possible colour combinations to use in her clothing designs.

  a Draw a sample space to show all the possible colour combinations on this wheel.

  b Determine P(blue and brown).

  c Determine P(yellow and orange).

  d Amira doesn't really like green or orange. If she picks a combination at random, what is the chance that she will get a combination with at least one of those colours?

8 A cleaner accidentally knocked the name labels off three students' lockers. The labels say Raju, Sam and Kerry. The tree diagram shows the possible ways of replacing the labels.

  a Copy the diagram and write the probabilities next to each branch.

  b Are these events dependent or independent? Why?

  c How many correct ways are there to match the name labels to the lockers?

  d How many possible ways are there for the cleaner to label the lockers?

  e If the cleaner randomly stuck the names back onto the lockers, what is the chance of getting the names correct?

  f What is the probability of getting the labels on Lockers 2 and 3 correct given that the first one is correctly labelled Kerry?

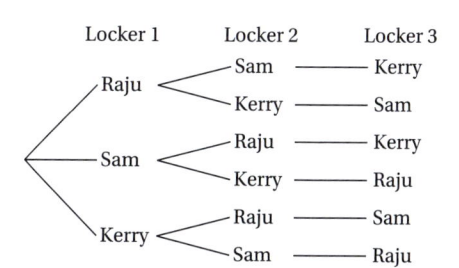

Checklist of learning and understanding

Representing combined events
- The sample space of an event is all the possible outcomes of the event.
- When an event has two or more stages it is called a combined event.
- Lists, tables, grids, tree diagrams and Venn diagrams can be used to represent combined events.

Calculating probabilities for combined events
- For mutually exclusive events P(A or B) = P(A) + P(B).
- For independent events P(A and then B) = P(A) × P(B).
- When the combined outcome of independent events are mutually exclusive, you need to add the probabilities after you have obtained the probability of each event using multiplication.
- For dependent events P(A and then B) = P(A) × P(B given that A has happened).
- For 'at least' problems P(at least A) = 1 − (not A).

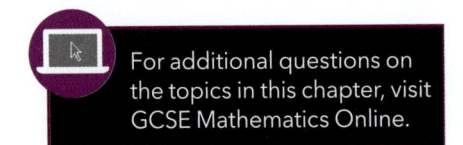

For additional questions on the topics in this chapter, visit GCSE Mathematics Online.

Chapter review

1. Choose the most appropriate method and use it to represent the sample space in each of the following.

   a A coin is flipped and an octagonal dice with faces numbered 0 to 7 is rolled at the same time.

   b Boxes A, B and C contain pink and yellow tickets. A box is selected at random and a ticket is drawn from it.

   c The number of ways in which three letters P, A and N can be arranged to form a three letter sequence.

   d In a class of 24 students, 10 take art, 12 take music and 5 take neither.

2. Two normal six-sided dice are rolled simultaneously. Draw a sample space for this information and hence calculate the probability of rolling:

   a double 2.

   b at least one 4.

   c a total greater than 9.

   d a total of 6 or 7.

3. The letters from the word MANCHESTER are written on cards and placed in a bag.

   a What is the probability of drawing a vowel if one letter is drawn at random?

   b Copy and complete this tree diagram to show all probabilities for when a letter is drawn from the bag, noted and replaced and then another letter is drawn.

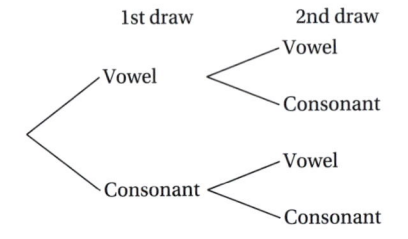

c Use the tree diagram to determine the probability of drawing:
  i two vowels.
  ii two consonants.
  iii a vowel and a consonant.
  iv at least one consonant.

d Explain why drawing the letters can be considered independent events in this case.

e How could you change the experiment to make the events dependent?

4 Amir sells laptops.

Before selling each laptop, he checks the hard drive and the screen.

The probability that the hard drive is faulty is $\frac{1}{10}$.

The probability that the screen is faulty is $\frac{1}{5}$.

These probabilities are independent.

a Complete the tree diagram to represent this information. *(2 marks)*

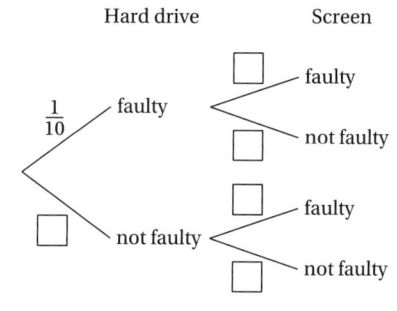

b Amir tests a laptop at random.

Find the probability that both the hard drive and the screen are **not** faulty. *(2 marks)*

© OCR 2012

5 There are 50 students in a year group. 30 have brown eyes, 9 have fair hair and 3 have both brown eyes and fair hair. Represent this information on a Venn diagram and use it to determine the probability that a student chosen at random from this group:

a has neither brown eyes nor fair hair.

b has brown eyes but not fair hair.

6 An unbiased cubical dice has six faces numbered 4, 6, 10, 12, 15 and 24. The dice is thrown twice and the highest common factor (HCF) of the scores is recorded.

a Draw a possibility diagram to show the possible outcomes.

b Calculate the probability that:
  i the HCF is 2.
  ii the HCF is greater than 2.
  iii the HCF is not 7.
  iv the HCF is 3 or 5.

25 Powers and roots

In this chapter you will learn how to …

- use positive and negative powers to represent numbers in index notation.
- calculate with powers and roots.
- apply the rules for multiplying and dividing indices.

For more resources relating to this chapter, visit GCSE Mathematics Online.

Using mathematics: real-life applications

Powers and roots are used in many different jobs. Builders, painters and decorators need to work out areas using square units (powers of 2 and square roots). Bankers and accountants who do calculations involving growth rates or decay rates use different powers and roots, and many scientific formulae rely on being able to work with powers and roots.

Calculator tip

Make sure you know which buttons to use to evaluate different powers and find different roots of numbers.

"I'm pretty good at estimating. I can usually look at a room and guess the area of the floor and walls quite accurately. Tiles are harder, I do rough sketches on squared paper to help me work out how many tiles of a particular size are needed to cover a floor area." (Interior designer)

Before you start …

Ch 1	You should be able to quickly add and subtract pairs of integers mentally.	**1** Choose the correct sign: <, = or >. a $^-3 + {^-3}\ \square\ 4 + 2$ b $6 - 7\ \square\ 3 - 4$ c $4 - (^-5)\ \square\ ^-3 + {^-6}$ d $^-2 + 6\ \square\ 9 - 5$

Ch 1	You need to be able to find the squares, cubes, square roots and cube roots of numbers.	**2** Choose the correct answer.
		a The area of a square with sides of 3 cm.
		  A $6\,cm^2$ B $9\,cm^2$ C $12\,cm^2$
		b $\sqrt[3]{27}$
		  A 9 B 5.2 C 3
		c $\sqrt{810000}$
		  A 9 B 90 C 900

Ch 10	You need to be able to find the reciprocal of a number or fraction.	**3** Find the reciprocal of each number. Choose from the values in the box. a $\frac{3}{4}$ b 12 c $1\frac{2}{5}$ $\dfrac{12}{1}\quad \dfrac{4}{3}\quad \dfrac{1}{12}\quad \dfrac{7}{5}\quad \dfrac{5}{7}$

400

25 Powers and roots

Assess your starting point using the Launchpad

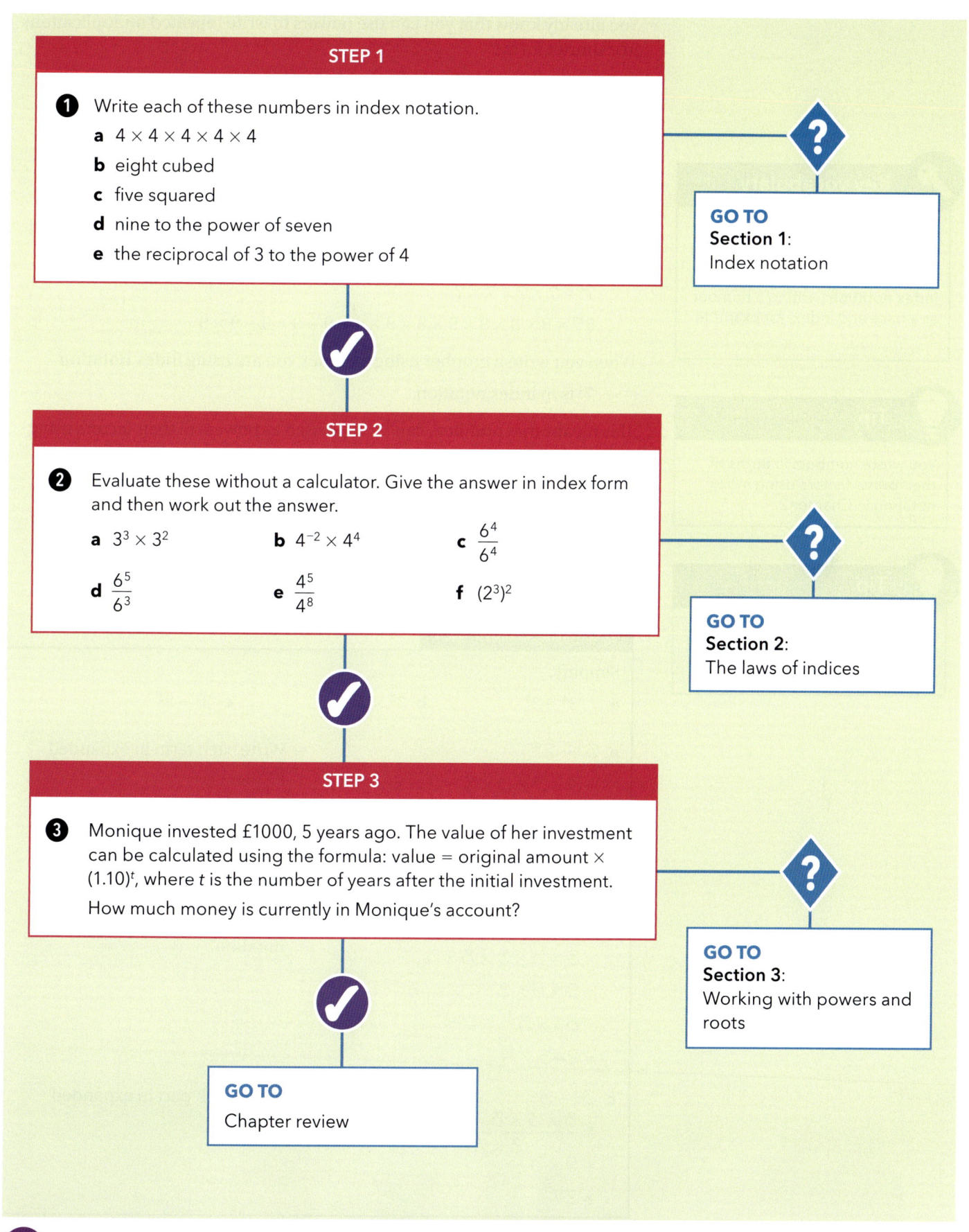

STEP 1

1 Write each of these numbers in index notation.
  a $4 \times 4 \times 4 \times 4 \times 4$
  b eight cubed
  c five squared
  d nine to the power of seven
  e the reciprocal of 3 to the power of 4

GO TO
Section 1:
Index notation

STEP 2

2 Evaluate these without a calculator. Give the answer in index form and then work out the answer.
  a $3^3 \times 3^2$
  b $4^{-2} \times 4^4$
  c $\dfrac{6^4}{6^4}$
  d $\dfrac{6^5}{6^3}$
  e $\dfrac{4^5}{4^8}$
  f $(2^3)^2$

GO TO
Section 2:
The laws of indices

STEP 3

3 Monique invested £1000, 5 years ago. The value of her investment can be calculated using the formula: value = original amount × $(1.10)^t$, where t is the number of years after the initial investment. How much money is currently in Monique's account?

GO TO
Section 3:
Working with powers and roots

GO TO
Chapter review

Find answers at: cambridge.org/ukschools/gcsemaths-studentbookanswers

401

Section 1: Index notation

You already know that you can use powers to write repeated multiplications in a shorter form.

For example: $6 \times 6 = 6^2$ and $5 \times 5 \times 5 = 5^3$

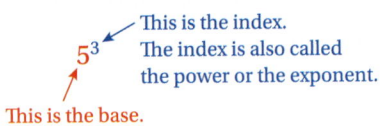

5^3 — This is the index. The index is also called the power or the exponent.

This is the base.

The **index** tells you how many times the base number is multiplied by itself.

$4^3 = 4 \times 4 \times 4$

$7^4 = 7 \times 7 \times 7 \times 7$

$9^{12} = 9 \times 9 \times 9 \times 9 \times 9 \times 9 \times 9 \times 9 \times 9 \times 9 \times 9 \times 9$

When you write a number using an index you are using **index notation**.

7^4 is in index notation.

This means that numbers can be expressed as powers of their factors using index notation.

When you write the multiplication out in full you are using expanded form.

$7 \times 7 \times 7 \times 7$ is in expanded form.

The plural of index is indices.

> **Key vocabulary**
>
> **index**: a power or exponent indicating how many times a base number is multiplied by itself.
>
> **index notation**: writing a number as a base and index, for example 2^3.

> **Tip**
>
> You wrote numbers in terms of their prime factors using index notation in Chapter 2.

> **Tip**
>
> Any number to the power of 1 stays the same number so you don't write powers of 1.

WORKED EXAMPLE 1

Simplify.

a $\quad 3^4 - 2^4$ 	b $\quad 3^2 \times 3^3$ 	c $\quad 3^5 \div 3^2$

a $\quad 3^4 - 2^4$
$= 3 \times 3 \times 3 \times 3 - 2 \times 2 \times 2 \times 2$
$= 9 \times 9 - 4 \times 4$
$= 81 - 16$
$= 65$

Write each term in expanded form.
Multiply mentally. It is easier to do this in pairs.

b $\quad 3^2 \times 3^3$
$= 3 \times 3 \times 3 \times 3 \times 3$
$= 9 \times 9 \times 3$
$= 81 \times 3$
$= 243$

Write each part in expanded notation.

c $\quad 3^5 \div 3^2$
$= \dfrac{3 \times 3 \times 3 \times \cancel{3} \times \cancel{3}}{\cancel{3} \times \cancel{3}}$
$= 9 \times 3$
$= 27$

Write each part in expanded notation.

25 Powers and roots

EXERCISE 25A

1 Write each of the following in index notation. You do not need to work out the value.

a $4 \times 4 \times 4$
b $3 \times 3 \times 3 \times 3 \times 3 \times 3$
c $7 \times 7 \times 7 \times 7$
d $9 \times 9 \times 9$
e $5 \times 5 \times 5 \times 5 \times 5$
f $12 \times 12 \times 12$
g $18 \times 18 \times 18 \times 18 \times 18 \times 18 \times 18$
h $11 \times 11 \times 11 \times 11 \times 11 \times 11 \times 11 \times 11 \times 11$
i nineteen to the power of eight
j 23 to the power of 6
k eleven multiplied by itself 14 times
l nine multiplied by itself 8 times

> **Tip**
>
> Here, simplifying is the same as evaluating. In Section 2 you will learn how to use the laws of indices to simplify expressions in index form without having to expand them.

2 Write in expanded form. Don't work out the answers.

a 3^4
b 9^3
c 4^5
d 8^3
e 5^6
f 3^8
g 23^5
h 51^4
i 72^5
j 203^3
k 121^4
l 100^5

3 Evaluate each expression without using a calculator.

a 2^3
b 6^2
c 1^8
d 8^3
e 10^4
f 10^6
g $2^3 - 1^5$
h $1^6 + 7^2$
i $2^4 \times 2^2$
j $2^4 + 4^2$
k $2^3 \times 2^4$
l $3^3 \times 3^3$
m $2^4 \div 2^3$
n $4^5 \div 4^3$
o $7^2 \times 10^3$
p 7×10^6
q $2 \times 10^2 + 3 \times 10^3$
r $6^2 \times 10^6$

Index notation on your calculator

Most calculators have one key to square a number: $\boxed{x^2}$.

Your calculator is also likely to have a key that allows you to enter any other powers quickly and easily. It may be $\boxed{y^x}$ or $\boxed{x^y}$ or $\boxed{a^b}$.

To enter 13^4, you press: $\boxed{1}\ \boxed{3}\ \boxed{y^x}\ \boxed{4}\ \boxed{=}$.

You will get a result of 28 561.

> **Calculator tip**
>
> Check your calculator to see which button(s) you have.

EXERCISE 25B

1 Use your calculator to evaluate the following.

a 4^6
b 12^3
c 8^5
d 7^4
e 15^3
f 10^4
g 28^2
h 25^3

2 Use a calculator to find the value of each expression.

a $12^3 - 2^8$
b $20^4 - 15^2$
c $15^3 \times 15^2$
d $3^{12} + 3^4$
e $3^6 + 2^8$
f $35^3 \div 5^3$

Find answers at: cambridge.org/ukschools/gcsemaths-studentbookanswers

3 Fill in < or > to make each statement true. You can use your calculator to help.

a $4^6 \square 6^4$　　b $10^3 \square 3^{10}$　　c $4^9 \square 9^4$

d $15^2 \square 2^{15}$　　e $9^8 \square 8^9$　　f $2^{10} \square 10^2$

Zero and negative indices

Look at this table of powers of 10.

Index notation	Expanded form	Value
10^6	$10 \times 10 \times 10 \times 10 \times 10 \times 10$	1 000 000
10^5	$10 \times 10 \times 10 \times 10 \times 10$	100 000
10^4	$10 \times 10 \times 10 \times 10$	10 000
10^3	$10 \times 10 \times 10$	1 000
10^2	10×10	100
10^1	10	10

If you look at the table you can see that each value is $\frac{1}{10}$ of the value above it. (In other words $10^6 \div 10 = 10^5$).

If you continue dividing by 10 you get this pattern for smaller and smaller indices:

Index notation	Expanded form	Value
10^6	$10 \times 10 \times 10 \times 10 \times 10 \times 10$	1 000 000
10^5	$10 \times 10 \times 10 \times 10 \times 10$	100 000
10^4	$10 \times 10 \times 10 \times 10$	10 000
10^3	$10 \times 10 \times 10$	1 000
10^2	10×10	100
10^1	10	10
10^0	$10 \div 10 = 1$	1
10^{-1}	$1 \div 10 = \frac{1}{10}$	$\frac{1}{10}$
10^{-2}	$\frac{1}{10} \div 10 = \frac{1}{100}$	$\frac{1}{100}$
10^{-3}	$\frac{1}{100} \div 10 =$	$\frac{1}{1000}$
10^{-4}	$\frac{1}{1000} \div 10$	$\frac{1}{10000}$

The pattern in the table gives us two very important facts about indices.

Any number with an index of 0 is equal to 1: $a^0 = 1$ (except for 0^0 which is undefined).

So, for example: $5^0 = 1$ and $7^0 = 1$.

Any number with a negative index is equal to its reciprocal with a positive index: $a^{-m} = \frac{1}{a^m}$.

So, for example: $4^{-2} = \frac{1}{4^2}$ and $5^{-3} = \frac{1}{5^3}$.

> **Tip**
>
> Remember that we use the reciprocals to change fraction divisions into multiplications.
>
> $\frac{1}{10} \div 10 = \frac{1}{10} \times \frac{1}{10} = \frac{1}{100}$

25 Powers and roots

EXERCISE 25C

1 Write each of the following using positive indices only.

  a 2^{-1} **b** 3^{-1} **c** 4^{-1}
  d 3^{-2} **e** 4^{-3} **f** 3^{-5}
  g 3^{-4} **h** 6^{-6} **i** 34^{-5}

2 Express the following with negative indices.

  a $\frac{1}{3}$ **b** $\frac{1}{5}$ **c** $\frac{1}{7}$ **d** $\frac{1}{3^2}$
  e $\frac{1}{4^5}$ **f** $\frac{1}{2^6}$ **g** $\frac{1}{7^2}$ **h** $\frac{1}{10^5}$
  i $\frac{1}{2^2}$ **j** $\frac{1}{12^3}$ **k** $\frac{1}{10^4}$ **l** $\frac{1}{3(2)^2}$

3 Fill in $=$ or $\neq$ in each of these statements.

  a $10^{-1}\ \square\ \frac{1}{10}$ **b** $6^0\ \square\ 1$ **c** $6^{-1}\ \square\ \frac{1}{6}$
  d $10^{-2}\ \square\ \frac{2}{10}$ **e** $6^{-3}\ \square\ \frac{1}{6^3}$ **f** $10^0\ \square\ 1$
  g $6^{-4}\ \square\ \frac{1}{6^4}$ **h** $\frac{1}{10^4}\ \square\ 10^{-4}$ **i** $\frac{1}{6^3}\ \square\ \frac{3}{6}$

Section 2: The laws of indices

Calculators cannot deal with powers and variables in algebra, for example $x^2 \times 2x^3$, and it takes a long time to simplify expressions like these by first writing them in expanded form.

The laws of indices are a set of rules that allow you to multiply and divide powers without writing them out in expanded form.

Multiplying numbers in index notation

Look at these examples:

$3^4 \times 3^2 = (3 \times 3 \times 3 \times 3) \times (3 \times 3) = 3^6$ Can you see a short-cut?

$3^4 \times 3^2 = 3^{4+2} = 3^6$

$2^3 \times 2^5 = (2 \times 2 \times 2) \times (2 \times 2 \times 2 \times 2 \times 2) = 2^8$

$2^3 \times 2^5 = 2^{3+5} = 2^8$

To multiply two numbers in index notation you add the indices.

$a^m \times a^n = a^{m+n}$

This law works for all indices, including negative indices.

For example $2^3 \times 2^{-2} = 2^{3+(-2)} = 2^1 = 2$.

Dividing numbers in index notation

Look at these examples to find the short-cut for division.

$2^5 \div 2^2 = \dfrac{2 \times 2 \times 2 \times 2 \times 2}{2 \times 2} = 2^3$

$3^4 \div 3^2 = \dfrac{3 \times 3 \times 3 \times 3}{3 \times 3} = 3^2$

Find answers at: cambridge.org/ukschools/gcsemaths-studentbookanswers

You should notice that

$2^5 \div 2^2 = 2^{5-2} = 2^3$ and $3^4 \div 3^2 = 3^{4-2} = 3^2$.

To divide two numbers in index notation you subtract the indices.

$a^m \div a^n = a^{m-n}$

This law works for all indices, including negative indices.

$2^2 \div 2^4 = 2^{2-4} = 2^{-2}$

You can understand how this works by looking at the expanded notation:

$2^2 \div 2^4 = \dfrac{2 \times 2}{2 \times 2 \times 2 \times 2}$ and if you cancel you get $\dfrac{1}{2 \times 2}$.

$\dfrac{1}{2^2}$ is equal to 2^{-2}.

Powers of a power

$(3^2)^3$ means 3^2 to the power of 3 which is $3^2 \times 3^2 \times 3^2$.

$3^2 \times 3^2 \times 3^2 = 3^6$ (When you multiply powers, you add them.)

This means that $(3^2)^3 = 3^6$.

To find the power of a power you multiply the indices.

$(a^m)^n = a^{mn}$

This law works for all indices, including negative indices.

$(4^3)^{-4} = 4^{(3)(-4)} = 4^{-12}$

You will use these laws of indices over and over in algebra, so it is important to know them well. Here is a summary:

Law of indices for ...	
multiplication	$a^m \times a^n = a^{m+n}$
division	$a^m \div a^n = a^{m-n}$
powers of indices	$(a^m)^n = a^{mn}$

> **Tip**
>
> The laws of indices also help to show that $a^0 = 1$
> $4^3 \div 4^3 = 4^{3-3} = 4^0$
> You already know that any number divided by itself is 1, so $4^3 \div 4^3 = 1$.
> But this is also equal to 4^0 so 4^0 must equal 1.

EXERCISE 25D

1 Simplify. Leave the answers in index notation.

   a $2^4 \times 2^3$ **b** $10^2 \times 10^5$ **c** $4^3 \times 4^3$

   d 5×5^6 **e** $2^4 \times 2^7$ **f** $3^2 \times 3^{-4}$

   g $2^{-2} \times 2^5$ **h** $3^0 \times 3^2$ **i** $2 \times 2^3 \times 2^{-5}$

   j $3^2 \times 3^2 \times 3$ **k** $10^2 \times 10^{-3} \times 10^2$ **l** $10^0 \times 10^{-2} \times 10^2$

2 Simplify. Leave the answers in index notation.

   a $6^4 \div 6^2$ **b** $10^5 \div 10^2$ **c** $6^5 \div 6^3$

   d $6^3 \div 6^5$ **e** $10^3 \div 10^5$ **f** $3^{10} \div 3^0$

   g $3^8 \div 3$ **h** $10^4 \div 10^4$ **i** $\dfrac{5^4}{5^{-2}}$

   j $\dfrac{10^6}{10^{-4}}$ **k** $\dfrac{3^{-2}}{3^{-3}}$ **l** $\dfrac{2^0}{2^3}$

3. Simplify each expression. Give the answers in index notation.
   a $(2^2)^3$
   b $(2^3)^3$
   c $(2^4)^2$
   d $(10^2)^2$
   e $(10^2)^3$
   f $(10^4)^2$
   g $(2^4)^{-3}$
   h $(10^{-2})^2$
   i $(10^2)^{-3}$
   j $(3^4)^{-2}$
   k $(2^3)^0$
   l $(2^2 \times 2^3)^2$

4. Say whether each statement is true or false. If it is false, write the correct answer.
   a $3^3 \times 3^5 = 3^8$
   b $3^8 \div 3^2 = 3^4$
   c $10^8 \div 10^2 = 10^6$
   d $(3^3)^2 = 3^6$
   e $121^0 = 1$
   f $4^5 \times 4^2 = 4^7$
   g $3^{10} \div 3^2 = 3^5$
   h $(4^2)^4 = 4^8$
   i $(3^2)^0 = 1$

Section 3: Working with powers and roots

Powers and roots are used every day in many different jobs, not to mention throughout mathematics.

Powers of 2, 3, 4 and 5

It is useful to recognise the first few powers of 2, 3, 4 and 5. This can help you to work out their roots as well.

EXERCISE 25E

1. Draw up a table like this one.

Base \ Index	−3	−2	−1	0	1	2	3	4	5
2	$2^{-3} = \frac{1}{8}$	$2^{-2} =$	$2^{-1} = \frac{1}{2}$	$2^0 = 1$	$2^1 = 2$	$2^2 = 4$	$2^3 =$	$2^4 = 16$	$2^5 =$
3									
4									
5									

   a Use a calculator to work out the missing values in the table. Some powers of two have been done as an example.
   b Compare the positive and negative values for the same index. What do you notice?
   c Compare the powers of 2 with the powers of 4. What do you notice?
   d How can you decide quickly that a number is *not* a power of 5?

Roots

You know that $5^2 = 25$ and $\sqrt{25} = 5$ and that $2^3 = 8$ and $\sqrt[3]{8} = 2$.

Finding the square root of a number involves working out what number multiplied by itself gives you the value under the root sign. For any other roots, the little number in front of the root sign tells you how many times the number has to be multiplied by itself.

Find answers at: cambridge.org/ukschools/gcsemaths-studentbookanswers

Calculator tip

You can find the square root or cube root of a number with your calculator using the √ and ∛ buttons. The √ button allows you to find any root (fourth root, fifth root, and so on). On some calculators you would enter 1 6 √ 4 = to find $\sqrt[4]{16}$. Check how your calculator works.

Mathematically, finding the root of a number is the inverse of working out the powers of the number.

Look at your table from Exercise 25E. You can see that $2^4 = 16$.

So, $\sqrt[4]{16} = 2$. You know this is correct because $2 \times 2 \times 2 \times 2 = 16$.

EXERCISE 25F

1 Use the table that you completed in Exercise 25E to decide whether each statement is true or false.

a $2^4 = 4^2$
b $2^5 > 3^5$
c $2^0 = 5^0$
d $2^1 = 2^{-1}$
e $3^4 > 4^3$
f $4^4 < 3^4$
g $5^2 = 2^5$
h $3^5 > 5^3$
i $2^{-3} > 3^{-2}$
j $3^{-3} = \dfrac{1}{27}$
k $5^{-1} = 4^{-1}$
l $2(2^{-1}) = 1$

2 Use your table to work these out **without** using a calculator.

a $\sqrt{25}$
b $\sqrt[3]{8}$
c $\sqrt[4]{256}$
d $\sqrt[3]{125}$
e $\sqrt[5]{243}$
f $\sqrt[3]{64}$
g $\sqrt[3]{8} + \sqrt[4]{625}$
h $\sqrt{2500}$
i $\sqrt[5]{32} + \sqrt[4]{81}$
j $\sqrt[3]{27\,000}$
k $\sqrt[4]{160\,000}$
l $\sqrt[5]{3125} \times \sqrt[4]{625}$

Solving problems involving powers and roots

Knowing that squaring or cubing numbers and finding their roots are inverse operations can help you to solve problems involving area and volume.

WORKED EXAMPLE 2

Mr Jones wants to pave a courtyard 4 m long and 4 m wide with square paving slabs. The label on the box of paving slabs says that each slab covers an area of 0.25 m².

a What are the dimensions (length and width) of the slabs?
b How many slabs will he need for his courtyard?

Courtyard: 4 m × 4 m
Paving slab: 0.25 m²

In problems like this it helps to make a sketch and to label it with the information you are given.

a Slab length = L; L² = 0.25 m²
   Length of each side = $\sqrt{0.25}$ m² = 0.5 m

b Courtyard area = 4 × 4 = 16 m²
   Area of one paving slab = 0.25 m²
   16 ÷ 0.25 = 64 paving slabs

Once you've made sense of the problem, present your solution clearly.

EXERCISE 25G

1 Find the lengths of the sides of each of these square areas:

a Area = 64 cm²
b Area = 0.09 cm²
c Area = 0.16 m²
d Area = 1600 mm²

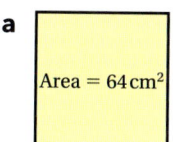

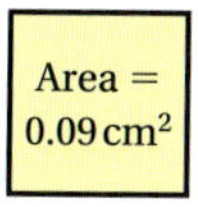

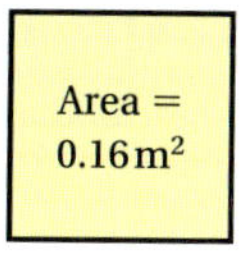

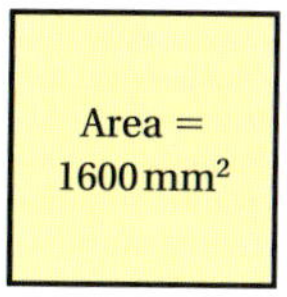

2 Jane has 900 square mosaic tiles.

Is it possible to arrange them to make a perfect square?

3 Sandy has a square piece of plastic with sides of 140 cm.

Is this big enough to cover a table with an area of 1.69 m²?

4 Mr Khan wants to tile a square floor of length 3.5 m. The square tiles he plans to use each have an area of 1024 cm².

a What is the area of the floor?

b What is the length of one side of each tile?

c How many tiles will he need to tile the floor? Show your working.

d Mr Khan knows from experience that he needs to buy 15% more than he needs in case of breakages. How many boxes of tiles should he buy if they come in boxes of eight?

e The tiles cost £23.50 per box. How much will it cost Mr Khan to buy the tiles he needs (including the 15% extra)?

> **Tip**
> You learnt about calculating percentage increases and decreases in Chapter 13

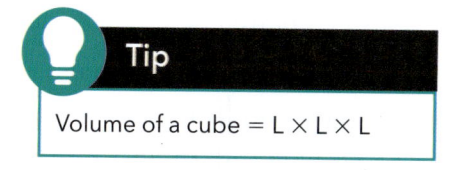

5 Nisha and Sandy want to buy pizzas. The pizzas come in small or large size.

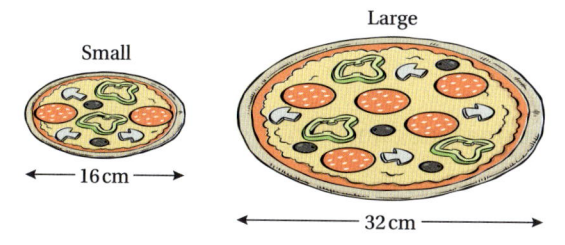

Small — 16 cm
Large — 32 cm

The small pizza has a diameter of 16 cm and the large one has a diameter of 32 cm. Nisha says that two small pizzas will give the same amount of pizza as one large one. Sandy disagrees.

a Use the formula Area = $3.14 \times (\frac{1}{2} \times \text{diameter})^2$ to work out the area of each pizza correct to 2 decimal places. Is Nisha correct?

b What happens to the area of the pizza when you double the diameter?

6 Work out the length of the sides of each of these cubes.

a volume = 125 cm³
b volume = 64 cm³
c volume = 0.125 m³

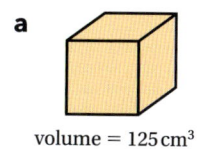

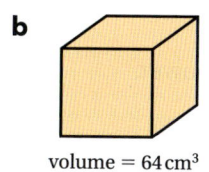

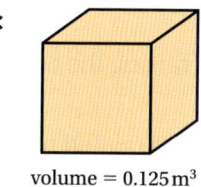

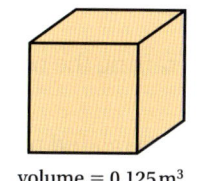

> **Tip**
> Volume of a cube = L × L × L

Find answers at: cambridge.org/ukschools/gcsemaths-studentbookanswers

GCSE Mathematics for OCR (Foundation)

7 Nick uses small boxes like the one shown to store electronic components. Each box is 4 cm long and 4 cm wide with a volume of 24 cm³.

How deep are the boxes?

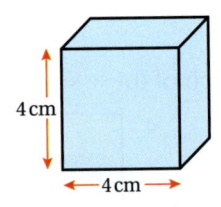

8 Shamila receives £2500. She wants to invest it for 10 years in an account that offers 5% growth but she wants to know how much money she will have after the 10-year period. There is a formula to work this out quickly:

value of future investment = original amount × $(1.05)^{10}$

  a Work out how much money Shamila will have in the investment after 10 years.

  b How much will she have if she decides to spend £500 and put the rest of the money into this investment?

9 Pam took a mortgage of £55 000 to buy a flat. She can use this formula for working out how much she will repay over a 20-year period:

total amount paid = mortgage amount × $(1.04)^{20}$

  a Work out how much her mortgage will cost if she takes 20 years to repay it.

  b The power of 20 in the formula represents the number of years over which it is repaid. Work out what the total amount paid would be if Pam paid her mortgage off in 15 years.

  c How much would she save by paying over the shorter period?

Checklist of learning and understanding

Index notation
- Numbers can be expressed as powers of their factors using index notation.
  - $2 \times 2 \times 2 \times 2$ can be written in index notation as 2^4.
  - The 4 is the index (also called the power or the exponent) and it tells us how many times the base (2) must be multiplied by itself.
- Any number to the power of 0 is equal to 1: $a^0 = 1$.
- A negative index is the reciprocal of a positive index: $a^{-m} = \dfrac{1}{a^m}$

Laws of indices
- Multiplication: $a^m \times a^n = a^{m+n}$
- Division: $\dfrac{a^m}{a^n} = a^{m-n}$
- Raising a power: $(a^m)^n = a^{mn}$

Working with powers and roots
- Finding the root of a number is the inverse of raising the number to a power. For example $4^2 = 16$ and $\sqrt{16} = 4$.
- Powers and roots are useful for solving problems related to area, volume and future value of investments.

25 Powers and roots

Chapter review

For additional questions on the topics in this chapter, visit GCSE Mathematics Online.

1 Write each number in index form.
  a $8 \times 8 \times 8 \times 8 \times 8$
  b three cubed
  c nine squared
  d fourteen to the power of five

2 Write each expression in expanded form and work out the answer.
  a 4^4
  b 9^3
  c $(4^3 - 3^3) \times 13^2$

3 Put these expressions in order from smallest to greatest.
  a $3^4, \sqrt{81}, 10^2, 4^3, 2 \times \sqrt{121}$
  b $4^5, 5^4, 10^3, 96^0, 3^2, 20^2$

4 Write these numbers with positive indices.
  a 3^{-3}
  b 2^{-10}
  c 5^{-2}

5 Use the laws of indices to simplify each expression and write it as a single power of 4.
  a $4^2 \times 4^2$
  b $4^6 \times 4^{-3}$
  c $4^7 \div 4^3$
  d $4^3 \div 4^5$
  e $(4^3)^2$
  f $(4^{-2})^2$

6 Evaluate. Check your answers with a calculator.
  a $\sqrt{121}$
  b $\sqrt{0.25}$
  c $\sqrt[3]{125}$
  d $\sqrt[5]{32}$
  e $\sqrt[4]{81}$
  f $\sqrt{\dfrac{1}{4}}$

7 Find the length of each side of a cube of volume 0.027 m³.

8 $\dfrac{V}{30} = \sqrt{h}$. Find V when $h = 25$.

9 $P - y = x^2$. Find P when $x = 2$ and $y = 8$.

10 Electricians use the formula $V = \sqrt{PR}$ to work out voltage (V) when P is the power in watts and R is the resistance in ohms. Calculate the voltage when $P = 2000$ and $R = 24.2$.

11 a Evaluate
  i 17^0 *(1 mark)*
  ii 4^{-3} *(2 marks)*

  b The distance, d, in miles to the horizon is given by the formula
  $$d = \left(\dfrac{3h}{2}\right)^{\frac{1}{2}}$$
  where h is the height, in feet, of an observer's eyes above sea level.
  i How far away is the horizon from a man whose eyes are 6 feet above sea level? *(2 marks)*
  ii From the top of a cliff, Samira can see the horizon 12 miles away. Find the height above sea level of Samira's eyes. *(3 marks)*

© OCR 2011

Find answers at: cambridge.org/ukschools/gcsemaths-studentbookanswers

26 Standard form

In this chapter you will learn how to ...
- convert numbers to and from standard form.
- use a calculator to solve problems with numbers in standard form.
- apply the index laws to add, subtract, multiply and divide numbers in standard form with and without using a calculator.

For more resources relating to this chapter, visit GCSE Mathematics Online.

Using mathematics: real-life applications

The study of stars, moons and planets involves huge numbers. Astronomers use standard form to make it easier to write or type very large quantities, to make them easier to compare and to allow them to calculate with and without calculators. The Sun has a mass of 1.988×10^{30} kg. This is a number with 27 zeros and it would be clumsy and impractical to have to write it out each time you wanted to use it.

> **Calculator tip**
> Make sure you know how your calculator deals with exponents and that you have it in the correct mode to do calculations involving exponents.

> "In astronomy we work with very large and very small numbers. There are 100 000 000 000 000 000 000 000 known stars alone! Imagine having to write this number out in full every time you wanted to use it! It is much easier to write 1×10^{23}."
> *(Astronomy student)*

Before you start ...

Ch 11	You should be able to calculate efficiently with decimals.	**1** Evaluate these without using a calculator. **a** $2.9 + 5.8$ **b** $12.5 - 3.8$ **c** 4.5×1.5 **d** $4.5 \div 0.3$

Ch 17	You need to be able to round numbers to a given number of significant figures.	**2** Choose the correct answer.
		a 507 000 000 rounded to 2 sf.
		    A 50 700 B 510 000 000
		b 1.098 rounded to 3 sf.
		    A 1.10 B 1.09
		c 0.006 25 rounded to 1 sf.
		    A 0.6 B 0.006

Ch 25	You should know how to apply the laws of indices.	**3** State whether the following are true or false. **a** $3^2 \times 3^3 = 3^6$ **b** $x^5 \times x^3 = x^8$ **c** $x^{-3} \times x^4 = x$ **d** $\dfrac{x^4}{x^5} = x$ **e** $\dfrac{x^{-4}}{x^2} = x^{-6}$

26 Standard form

Assess your starting point using the Launchpad

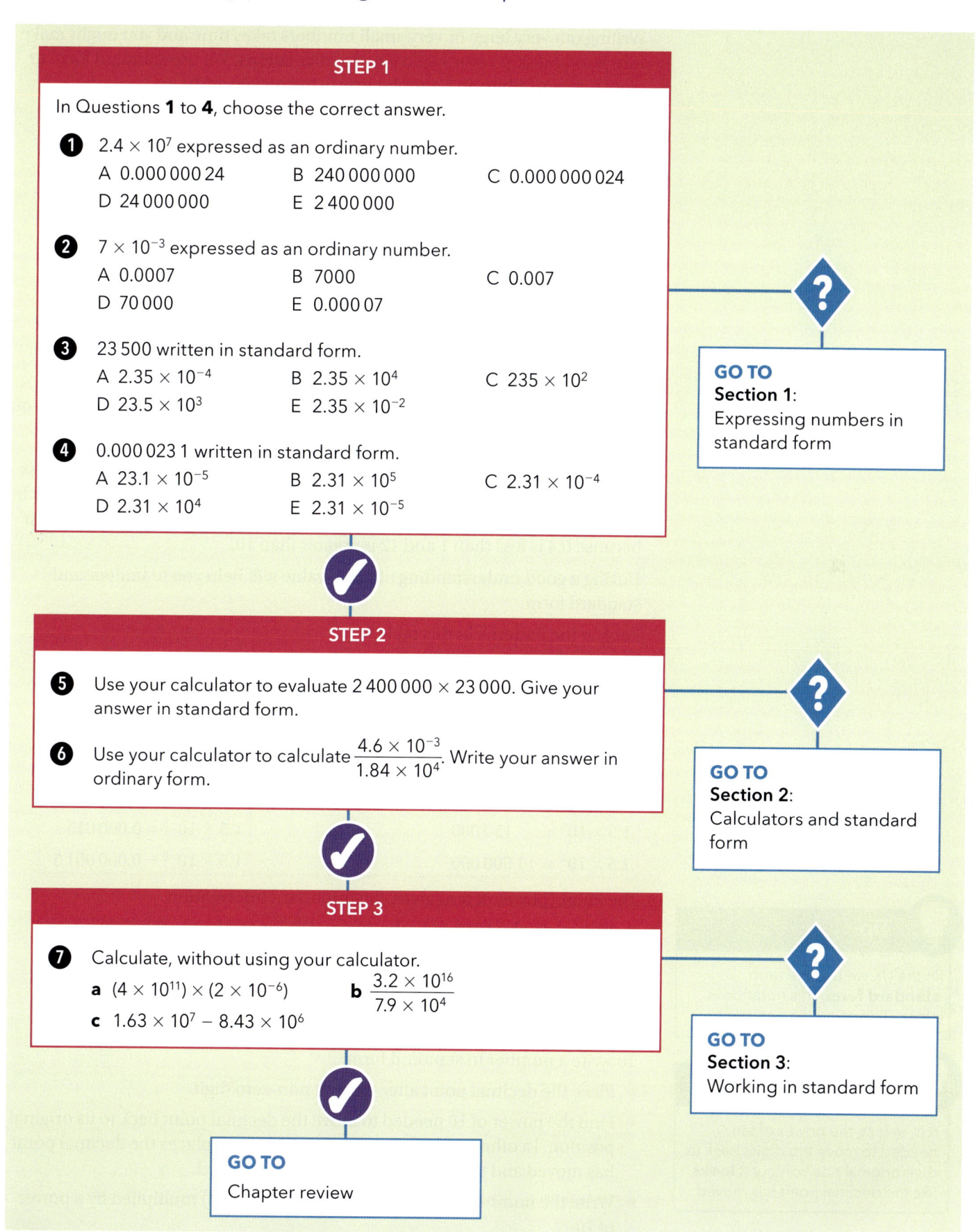

STEP 1

In Questions **1** to **4**, choose the correct answer.

1 2.4×10^7 expressed as an ordinary number.
- A 0.000 000 24
- B 240 000 000
- C 0.000 000 024
- D 24 000 000
- E 2 400 000

2 7×10^{-3} expressed as an ordinary number.
- A 0.0007
- B 7000
- C 0.007
- D 70 000
- E 0.000 07

3 23 500 written in standard form.
- A 2.35×10^{-4}
- B 2.35×10^4
- C 235×10^2
- D 23.5×10^3
- E 2.35×10^{-2}

4 0.000 023 1 written in standard form.
- A 23.1×10^{-5}
- B 2.31×10^5
- C 2.31×10^{-4}
- D 2.31×10^4
- E 2.31×10^{-5}

GO TO Section 1: Expressing numbers in standard form

STEP 2

5 Use your calculator to evaluate $2\,400\,000 \times 23\,000$. Give your answer in standard form.

6 Use your calculator to calculate $\dfrac{4.6 \times 10^{-3}}{1.84 \times 10^4}$. Write your answer in ordinary form.

GO TO Section 2: Calculators and standard form

STEP 3

7 Calculate, without using your calculator.
- **a** $(4 \times 10^{11}) \times (2 \times 10^{-6})$
- **b** $\dfrac{3.2 \times 10^{16}}{7.9 \times 10^4}$
- **c** $1.63 \times 10^7 - 8.43 \times 10^6$

GO TO Section 3: Working in standard form

GO TO Chapter review

Find answers at: cambridge.org/ukschools/gcsemaths-studentbookanswers

GCSE Mathematics for OCR (Foundation)

Section 1: Expressing numbers in standard form

Writing out very large or very small numbers takes time and you might make mistakes and skip zeros when you do calculations. We use standard form to write these numbers in a simpler way using powers of 10.

Remember

$10^2 = 100$	one hundred
$10^3 = 1000$	one thousand
$10^4 = 10\,000$	ten thousand
$10^5 = 100\,000$	one hundred thousand
$10^6 = 1\,000\,000$	one million

A number is in standard form when it is written as a product (×) of a factor and a power of 10. The factor must be greater than or equal to 1 and smaller than 10.

Algebraically, we can say that any number (x) can be expressed in the form of:

$x \times 10^n$, where $1 \leq x < 10$ and n is an integer.

For example, 2×10^2 and 1.2×10^{-2} are both in standard form. If the factor is smaller than 1 or if it is greater than (or equal to) 10 then the number is not in standard form. For example, 0.4×10^5 and 12×10^3 are not in standard form because 0.4 is less than 1 and 12 is greater than 10.

Having a good understanding of place value will help you to understand standard form.

Look at the patterns in this table.

$1.5 \times 10^0 =$	1.5	Remember $n^0 = 1$	$1.5 \times 10^{-1} = 0.15$
$1.5 \times 10^1 =$	15		$1.5 \times 10^{-2} = 0.015$
$1.5 \times 10^2 =$	150		$1.5 \times 10^{-3} = 0.001\,5$
$1.5 \times 10^3 =$	1500		$1.5 \times 10^{-4} = 0.000\,15$
$1.5 \times 10^4 =$	15 000		$1.5 \times 10^{-5} = 0.000\,015$
$1.5 \times 10^5 =$	150 000		$1.5 \times 10^{-6} = 0.000\,001\,5$
$1.5 \times 10^6 =$	1 500 000		

The index (power of ten) gives you important information.

- Multiplying by 10^4 moves the decimal point 4 places to the right.
- Multiplying by 10^{-4} moves the decimal point 4 places to the left.

Writing a number in standard form

To write a number in standard form:

- Place the decimal point after the first non-zero digit.
- Find the power of 10 needed to move the decimal point back to its original position. In other words, work out the number of places the decimal point has moved and the direction in which it has moved.
- Write the number as a decimal (between 1 and 10) multiplied by a power of 10.

Tip

In the UK we use the term **standard form**; this notation is also called scientific notation.

Tip

It is, in fact, the power of ten needed to move the digits back to their original position but it **looks** like the decimal point has moved.

26 Standard form

WORKED EXAMPLE 1

Express these numbers in standard form.
 a 416 000   b 0.0037

a 416 000
   4.16

   4.1 6 0 0 0

   416 000 = 4.16 × 10⁵

Find the number between 1 and 10 and insert the decimal point after the first non-zero digit.
Work out how many decimal places the point needs to move to get back to the original number.

The decimal point needs to move five places to the right (+), so the power of ten is 5.

b 0.0037
   3.7

   0.0 0 3.7

   0.0 0 3.7 = 3.7 × 10⁻³

Find the number between 1 and 10.
Work out how many decimal places the point needs to move to get back to the original number.

The decimal point needs to move three places to the left (−), so the power of 10 is ⁻3.

$0.0037 = \dfrac{37}{10\,000}$

$= \dfrac{3.7}{1000}$

$= 3.7 \times 10^{-3}$

Alternatively, you could convert the decimal to a fraction first.
Divide the top and bottom by 10 to get a numerator between 1 and 10.

Look at the number of zeros in the denominator to find the index. As the original number is less than 1, the index must be negative.

EXERCISE 26A

1 Express each of the following in standard form.
   a 321 000   b 1340   c 40 050
   d 3 010 000   e 0.08   f 0.0001
   g 32 000 000   h 910 000   i 0.000 031 255
   j 0.000 000 241 52 k 0.003 05   l 0.201
   m 34 000   n 0.000 34   o 0.009
   p 2.45   q 0.000 426   r 0.426

2 Express each of the following quantities in standard form.
   a In 2011 the population of the Earth reached 7 000 000 000.
   b The distance from the Earth to the Moon is approximately 240 000 miles.
   c There are about 100 000 000 000 000 (a hundred trillion) cells in your body.
   d Some cells are about 0.000 000 2 metres in diameter.
   e The surface area of the Earth's oceans is about 140 million square miles.
   f An angstrom is a unit of measure. One angstrom is equivalent to 0.000 000 000 1 metre.
   g Humans blink on average about 6 250 000 times per year.
   h A dust particle has a mass of about 0.000 000 000 753 kg.

Find answers at: cambridge.org/ukschools/gcsemaths-studentbookanswers

GCSE Mathematics for OCR (Foundation)

Converting from standard form to ordinary numbers

To convert numbers from standard form to ordinary numbers or decimals you need to look at the power of ten and move the decimal point this number of places to the left or right.

WORKED EXAMPLE 2

Write as ordinary numbers.

a 3.25×10^5 b 2.07×10^{-5}

a 3.25×10^5

3.2 5 0 0 0 — The power of ten is 5. Move the decimal point 5 places to the right (positive direction).

3 2 5 0 0 0 — Fill in the correct number of zeros; notice that the digits '2' and '5' count as two of the 5 places so only three zeros are needed.

$3.25 \times 10^5 = 325\,000$

b 2.07×10^{-5}

2.0 7 — Move the decimal point 5 places to the left (negative direction).

.0 0 0 0 2 0 7 — Fill in the correct number of zeros; notice that the '2' counts as one of the 5 places (it is the first significant figure), so only four zeros are needed before the decimal point.

$2.07 \times 10^{-5} = 0.000\,020\,7$ — Remember to write the 0 before the decimal point as well.

EXERCISE 26B

1 Express each of the following as a basic numeral.

a 1.4×10^2 b 4.8×10^4 c 2.9×10^3

d 3.25×10^2 e 3.25×10^{-1} f 3.67×10^5

g 4.5×10^7 h 2.13×10^{-2} i 3.209×10^4

j 3.46×10^{-3} k 1.89×10^{-4} l 7×10^{-7}

m 1.03×10^{-2} n 1.025×10^{-3} o 2.09×10^{-5}

2 Write each quantity out in full as an ordinary number.

a The area of the Atlantic Ocean is 3.18×10^7 square miles.

b The space between tracks on a DVD disk is 7.4×10^{-4} mm.

c The diameter of the silk used to weave a spider's web is 1.24×10^{-6} mm.

d There are 3×10^9 possible ways to play the first four moves in a game of chess.

e A sheet of paper is about 1.2×10^{-4} m thick.

f The distance between the Sun and Jupiter is about 7.78×10^8 km.

g The Earth is about 1.5×10^{11} km from the Sun.

h The mass of an electron is about $9.109\,382\,2 \times 10^{-31}$ kg.

3 Order these numbers from smallest to largest.

1.75×10^2 3×10^{-3} 9.9×10^1 5.7×10^{-2} 3.654645×10^{20} 1.75×10^4

Section 2: Calculators and standard form

You can use a scientific calculator to enter calculations in standard form. The calculator will also give you an answer in standard form if it has too many digits to display on the screen.

Entering standard form calculations

You will need to use the 10^x, Exp or EE button on your calculator. These are known as the exponent keys and they all work in the same way, even though they might look different on different calculators.

When you are using the exponent function key of your calculator you don't enter the × 10 part of the calculation because the calculator function automatically includes that part.

Use your own calculator to work through this example. You should get the same result even if your function key is different to the one in the example.

WORKED EXAMPLE 3

Calculate:

a 2.134×10^4 **b** 3.124×10^{-6}

a 2.134×10^4

[2][.][1][3][4][10^x][4][=]

$2.134 \times 10^4 = 21\,340$

Enter the digits into your calculator, and write down the answer.

b 3.124×10^{-6}

[3][.][1][2][4][Exp][+/−][6][=]

$3.124 \times 10^{-6} = 0.000\,003\,123$

Use the correct key for your calculator to enter the negative 6.

Calculator tip

Calculators work in different ways and you need to understand how your own calculator works. Make sure you know what buttons to use to enter standard form calculations, how to read and make sense of the display and how to convert your calculator answer into decimal form.

Making sense of the calculator display

The answer your calculator displays will depend on the calculator you use. Here are two ways in which calculators display answers in standard form:

5.98 −06

This is 5.98×10^{-6}

2.56ᴇ24

This is 2.56×10^{24}

To give the answer in standard form read the display and write the answer correctly.

To give the answer as an ordinary number, apply the rules you know to convert it from standard form to ordinary form.

Find answers at: cambridge.org/ukschools/gcsemaths-studentbookanswers

EXERCISE 26C

1. Enter each of these numbers into your calculator using the correct function key and write down what appears on the display.

   a 4.2×10^{12}
   b 1.8×10^{-5}
   c 2.7×10^{6}
   d 1.34×10^{-2}
   e 1.87×10^{-9}
   f 4.23×10^{7}
   g 3.102×10^{-4}
   h 3.098×10^{9}
   i 2.076×10^{-23}

2. Here are ten different calculator displays giving answers in exponential form. Write each answer correctly in standard form.

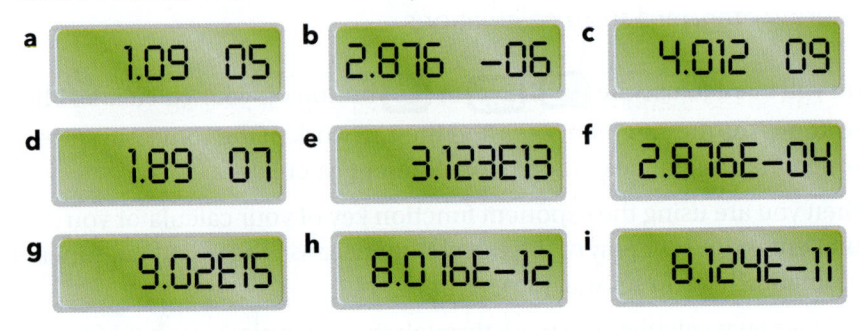

   a 1.09 05
   b 2.876 −06
   c 4.012 09
   d 1.89 07
   e 3.123E13
   f 2.876E−04
   g 9.02E15
   h 8.076E−12
   i 8.124E−11

Significant figures

When you work with standard form, you will often be asked to give the answers in standard form correct to a given number of significant figures.

You already know how to round answers to a given number of significant figures (refer to Chapter 17 if you have forgotten). When you are working with decimal values, you need to remember that none of the zeros before a non-zero digit are significant.

- 0.003   is correct to 1 significant figure.
- 0.01   is correct to 1 significant figure.
- 0.10   is correct to 2 significant figures.

A zero after a non-zero digit **is** significant.

EXERCISE 26D

1. Use your calculator to do these calculations. Give your answers in standard form correct to 3 sf.

   a 4216^6
   b $(0.00009)^4$
   c $0.0002 \div 2500^3$
   d $65\,000\,000 \div 0.000\,0045$
   e $(0.0029)^3 \times (0.003\,65)^5$
   f $(48 \times 987)^4$
   g $\dfrac{4525 \times 8760}{0.000\,020}$
   h $\dfrac{9500}{0.0005^4}$
   i $\sqrt{5.25} \times 10^8$
   j $\sqrt[3]{9.1} \times 10^{-8}$

26 Standard form

Section 3: Working in standard form

Writing numbers in standard form allows you to use the laws of indices to calculate quickly without using a calculator.

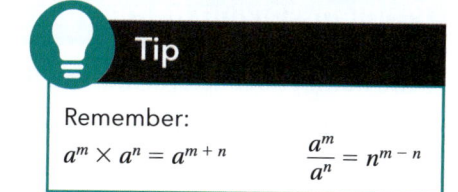

> **Tip**
>
> Remember:
> $a^m \times a^n = a^{m+n}$ $\quad \dfrac{a^m}{a^n} = n^{m-n}$

Multiplying and dividing numbers in standard form

When you multiply powers of ten, you add the indices.

When you divide powers of ten, you subtract the indices.

WORKED EXAMPLE 4

Do these calculations without using a calculator. Give your answers in standard form.

a $(3 \times 10^5) \times (2 \times 10^6)$ b $(2 \times 10^{-3}) \times (3 \times 10^{-7})$ c $(2 \times 10^3) \times (8 \times 10^7)$ d $\dfrac{2.8 \times 10^6}{1.4 \times 10^4}$ e $\dfrac{4 \times 10^8}{9 \times 10^5}$

a $(3 \times 10^5) \times (2 \times 10^6)$
$\quad 3 \times 2 \times 10^5 \times 10^6$ Remove the brackets and group like terms. Using the multiplication law of indices, add the indices.
$\quad = 6 \times 10^{5+6}$
$\quad = 6 \times 10^{11}$ Write the answer in standard form.

b $(2 \times 10^{-3}) \times (3 \times 10^{-7})$
$\quad 2 \times 3 \times 10^{-3} \times 10^{-7}$ Remove the brackets and group like terms. Using the multiplication law of indices, add the indices.
$\quad = 6 \times 10^{-3+-7}$
$\quad = 6 \times 10^{-10}$ Write the answer in standard form.

c $(2 \times 10^3) \times (8 \times 10^7)$
$\quad 2 \times 8 \times 10^3 \times 10^7$
$\quad = 16 \times 10^{3+7}$
$\quad = 16 \times 10^{10}$
$\quad = 1.6 \times 10 \times 10^{10}$ But 16 is greater than 10 so this is not in standard form.
$\quad = 1.6 \times 10^{11}$ If you think of 16 as 1.6×10 you can change it to standard form.

d $\dfrac{2.8 \times 10^6}{1.4 \times 10^4} = \dfrac{2.8}{1.4} \times \dfrac{10^6}{10^4}$
$\quad = 2 \times 10^{6-4}$ Subtract the indices to divide the powers.
$\quad = 2 \times 10^2$

e $\dfrac{4 \times 10^8}{9 \times 10^5} = \dfrac{4}{9} \times \dfrac{10^8}{10^5}$ Rewrite so that like terms are grouped.
$\quad = 0.44 \times 10^3$
$\quad = 4.4 \times 10^{-1} \times 10^3$ 0.44 is smaller than 1 so this is not standard form. If you think of 0.44 as 4.4×10^{-1} you can change it to standard form.
$\quad = 4.4 \times 10^2$

You need to be able to solve problems involving numbers in standard form. Although the problems might seem complicated when you read them, you will be able to solve them easily once you work out what operation you need to do.

Find answers at: cambridge.org/ukschools/gcsemaths-studentbookanswers

GCSE Mathematics for OCR (Foundation)

Problem-solving framework

The number of bacteria that can fit onto a piece of skin of area 1 mm² is approximately 1.5×10^{14}.

If your index fingertip has an approximate area of 3.75×10^2 mm, how many bacteria could fit onto it?

Give your answer in standard form and as an ordinary number.

Steps for approaching a problem-solving question	What you would do for this example
Step 1: Work out what you need to do.	Find the number of bacteria that will fit onto a larger area than the one given.
Step 2: Look for information that will help you.	The area of a fingertip is 3.75×10^2 mm. The number of bacteria that can fit onto 1 mm² = 1.5×10^{14}.
Step 3: What maths can you do?	Multiply the number of bacteria by the area: $1.5 \times 10^{14} \times 3.75 \times 10^2 = 1.5 \times 3.75 \times 10^{14} \times 10^2$ $= 5.625 \times 10^{16}$
Step 4: Set out the solution clearly, making sure you have answered the original question.	5.625×10^{16} = 56 250 000 000 000 000 bacteria

EXERCISE 26E

1 Simplify, giving the answers in standard form.

  a $(2 \times 10^{13}) \times (4 \times 10^{17})$
  b $(1.4 \times 10^8) \times (3 \times 10^4)$
  c $(1.5 \times 10^{13}) \times (1.5 \times 10^{13})$
  d $(0.2 \times 10^{17}) \times (0.7 \times 10^{16})$
  e $(9 \times 10^{17}) \div (3 \times 10^{16})$
  f $(8 \times 10^{17}) \div (4 \times 10^{16})$
  g $(1.5 \times 10^8) \div (5 \times 10^4)$
  h $(2.4 \times 10^{64}) \div (8 \times 10^{21})$

2 Simplify, giving the answers in standard form.

  a $(2 \times 10^{-4}) \times (4 \times 10^{-16})$
  b $(1.6 \times 10^{-8}) \times (4 \times 10^{-4})$
  c $(1.5 \times 10^{-6}) \times (2.1 \times 10^{-3})$
  d $(11 \times 10^{-5}) \times (3 \times 10^2)$
  e $(9 \times 10^{17}) \div (4.5 \times 10^{-16})$
  f $(7 \times 10^{-21}) \div (1 \times 10^{16})$
  g $(4.5 \times 10^8) \div (0.9 \times 10^{-4})$
  h $(11 \times 10^{-5}) \times (3 \times 10^2) \div (2 \times 10^{-3})$

3 Carry out these calculations without using your calculator. Leave the answers in standard form.

  a $(3 \times 10^{12}) \times (4 \times 10^{18})$
  b $(1.5 \times 10^6) \times (3 \times 10^5)$
  c $(1.5 \times 10^{12})^3$
  d $(1.2 \times 10^{-5}) \times (1.1 \times 10^{-6})$
  e $(0.4 \times 10^{15}) \times (0.5 \times 10^{12})$
  f $(8 \times 10^{17}) \div (3 \times 10^{12})$
  g $(1.44 \times 10^8) \div (1.2 \times 10^6)$
  h $(8 \times 10^{-15}) \div (4 \times 10^{-12})$

26 Standard form

4 The speed of light is approximately 3×10^8 metres per second.
How far will the light travel in:

a 10 seconds? **b** 20 seconds? **c** 10^2 seconds? **d** 2×10^3 seconds?

5 A human being blinks approximately 6.25×10^6 times per year.

a How often will you blink in 5 years? Give the answer in standard form and as an ordinary number.

b If there were 7.2×10^9 people on the planet, how many blinks would there be in a year?

6 A sheet of paper is 1.2×10^{-4} m thick.

a Work out the height (in metres) of a stack of 500 sheets of this paper, giving your answer in standard form and as an ordinary number.

b How many millimetres high is the stack of paper?

Adding and subtracting in standard form

When you have to add or subtract numbers in standard form it is usually easier to rewrite them both as ordinary numbers to do the calculation. You then convert your answer back to standard form.

> **Calculator tip**
>
> If you are using a calculator you don't need to rewrite the numbers. You just need to enter the calculation correctly.

WORKED EXAMPLE 5

Calculate

a $6 \times 10^{-3} - 3 \times 10^{-4}$. **b** $6 \times 10^{-4} + 7 \times 10^{-4}$.

a Using a calculator

[6] [10ˣ] [−] [3] [−] [3] [10ˣ] [−] [4] [=]

$= 0.0057$
$= 5.7 \times 10^{-3}$

Using a written method

0.0060
-0.0003
$\overline{0.0057}$
$= 5.7 \times 10^{-3}$

Convert each value to an ordinary number. Write the numbers so the place values line up. Remember to convert your answer into standard form.

b Using a written method

0.0006
$+0.0007$
$\overline{0.0013}$
$= 1.3 \times 10^{-3}$

By factorising

$6 \times 10^{-4} + 7 \times 10^{-4}$
$= 10^{-4}(6 + 7)$
$= 10^{-4}(13)$
$= 1.3 \times 10^{-3}$

Alternatively, because the powers of ten are the same, you could factorise for the power of ten, then add like terms. 13×10^{-4} is not in standard form so write the answer correctly.

EXERCISE 26F

1 Carry out these calculations without using a calculator. Give your answers in standard form.

a $(3 \times 10^8) + (2 \times 10^8)$
b $(3 \times 10^{-3}) - (1.5 \times 10^{-3})$
c $(1.5 \times 10^5) + (3 \times 10^6)$
d $(6 \times 10^7) - (4 \times 10^6)$
e $(4 \times 10^{-4}) + (3 \times 10^{-3})$
f $(5 \times 10^{-3}) - (2.5 \times 10^{-2})$

Find answers at: cambridge.org/ukschools/gcsemaths-studentbookanswers

2 The Pacific Ocean has a surface area of approximately 1.65×10^8 km^2 and the Atlantic Ocean has a surface area of approximately 1.06×10^8 km^2.

    a Which ocean has the greater surface area?

    b How much larger is it?

    c If the total surface area of the world's oceans is 361 000 000 km^2, work out the combined surface area of the other three oceans (the Indian, Southern and Arctic), giving the answer in standard form.

3 The Earth is approximately 9.3×10^7 miles from the Sun and 2.4×10^5 miles from the Moon. How much further is it from Earth to the Sun than from the Earth to the Moon?

Checklist of learning and understanding

Standard form

- Very large and very small numbers can be written in standard form by expressing them as the product of a value greater than or equal to 1 and less than 10, and a power of 10.
- Any number can be expressed in the form $x \times 10^n$, where $1 \leq x < 10$ and n is an integer. Positive powers of ten indicate large numbers and negative powers of ten indicate small numbers.

Using a calculator

- The exponent function of the calculator allows you to enter calculations in standard form without entering the $\times 10$ part of the calculation.
- When a number has too many digits to display, the calculator will give the answer in standard form.

Calculations in standard form

- You can multiply and divide numbers in standard form by applying the laws of indices; you can manipulate expressions to group like terms so that you can do the calculations with standard form without a calculator.
- When adding and subtracting numbers in standard form without a calculator, it can be easier to first convert them to an ordinary number to do the calculation and then convert your answer to standard form. If you are using a calculator, then you can enter the calculation directly using the appropriate keys. If the powers of ten are the same, then you can also use factorising.

For additional questions on the topics in this chapter, visit GCSE Mathematics Online.

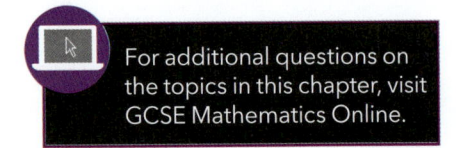

Chapter review

1 Express the following numbers in standard form.

    a 45 000   **b** 80   **c** 2 345 000

    d 32 000 000 000   **e** 0.0065   **f** 0.009

    g 0.000 45   **h** 0.000 000 8   **i** 0.006 75

26 Standard form

2 Write the following as ordinary numbers.
   a 2.5×10^3
   b 3.9×10^4
   c 4.265×10^5
   d 1.045×10^{-5}
   e 9.15×10^{-6}
   f 1.0×10^{-9}
   g 2.8×10^{-5}
   h 9.4×10^7
   i 2.45×10^{-3}

3 Use a calculator and give the answers in standard form.
   a $5 \times 10^4 + 9 \times 10^6$
   b $3.27 \times 10^{-3} \times 2.4 \times 10^2$
   c $5(8.1 \times 10^9 - 2 \times 10^7)$
   d $(3.2 \times 10^{-1}) - (2.33 \times 10^{-3})$ (to 3 sf)

4 Simplify the following without using a calculator and give the answers in standard form.
   a $(1.44 \times 10^7) + (4.3 \times 10^7)$
   b $(4.9 \times 10^5) \times (3.6 \times 10^9)$
   c $(3 \times 10^4) + (4 \times 10^3)$
   d $(4 \times 10^6) \div (3 \times 10^5)$

5 The Sun has a mass of approximately 1.998×10^{27} tonnes. The planet Mercury has a mass of approximately 3.302×10^{20} tonnes.
   a Which has the greater mass?
   b How many times heavier is the greater than the smaller mass?

6 The UK has an approximate area of 2.4×10^5 km². Australia has an area of approximately 7.6×10^6 km².
   a What is the difference in the areas of the two countries? Give the answer in standard form.
   b What is the combined area of the two countries? Give the answer in standard form.
   c How many times could the map of the UK fit onto the map of Australia if they were drawn at the same scale?

7 The table shows the areas of some countries.

   a The area of Brazil is 8 459 417 square kilometres.
   Complete the table to show the area of Brazil.
   Give the area in standard form, correct to three significant figures.
   (1 mark)

   b Complete the following sentences.
   The area of _____ is about twice the area of Turkey.
   The area of China is about three times the area of _____.
   (2 marks)

   c The population of India in 2011 was approximately 1.19×10^9.
   Estimate the population density of India in people per square kilometre.
   (2 marks)

   © OCR 2013

Country	Area (square kilometres)
Brazil	
China	9.33×10^6
India	2.97×10^6
Mongolia	1.55×10^6
Tunisia	1.55×10^5
Turkey	7.70×10^5

Find answers at: cambridge.org/ukschools/gcsemaths-studentbookanswers

27 Plane vector geometry

In this chapter you will learn how to …
- represent vectors as a diagram or column vector.
- add and subtract vectors.
- multiply vectors by a scalar.

For more resources relating to this chapter, visit GCSE Mathematics Online.

Using mathematics: real-life applications

Vectors have huge applications in the physical world. For example, mathematical modelling of objects sliding down slopes with varying amounts of friction, working out how far objects can tilt before they tip over and making sure two ships don't crash in the night. All these problems involve the use of vectors.

"When landing at any airport I have to consider how the wind will blow me off course. Over a set amount of time I expect to travel through a particular vector but I have to add on the effect the wind has on my flight path. If I don't do this accurately I would struggle to land the plane safely." *(Pilot)*

Before you start …

Ch 18	You need to be able to plot coordinates in all four quadrants.	**1** Draw a set of axes going from $^-6$ to 6 in both directions. Plot the points A(2, 3), B($^-$3, 4) and C($^-$2, $^-$3).
Ch 2	You need to be able to add, subtract and multiply negative numbers.	**2** Calculate. **a** $3 - 7$ **b** $^-4 + 11$ **c** $^-5 - 18$ **d** $^-4 \times 7$ **e** $^-3 \times ^-9$
Ch 8	You need to be able to solve simple linear equations.	**3** Solve. **a** $12 = 4m - 36$ **b** $2k + 15 = 7$ **c** $^-6 + 5d = ^-41$
Ch 8	You need to be able to solve simultaneous linear equations.	**4** Solve. $3x + 2y = 8$ and $4x - 3y = 5$

424

27 Plane vector geometry

Assess your starting point using the Launchpad

STEP 1

1 Give the column vector for $\overrightarrow{HG}$.

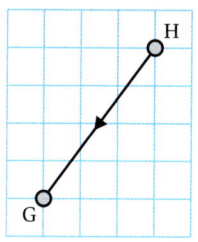

2 Draw the triangle ABC where $\overrightarrow{AB} = \begin{pmatrix} 3 \\ -5 \end{pmatrix}$ and $\overrightarrow{CA} = \begin{pmatrix} 2 \\ 7 \end{pmatrix}$.

GO TO
Section 1: Vector notation and representation

STEP 2

3 $\mathbf{j} = \begin{pmatrix} -1 \\ 3 \end{pmatrix}$ $\quad \mathbf{k} = \begin{pmatrix} 2 \\ 1 \end{pmatrix}$ $\quad \mathbf{l} = \begin{pmatrix} -4 \\ -2 \end{pmatrix}$

Write the following as single vectors.
a $\mathbf{j} + \mathbf{k}$ **b** $2\mathbf{k} - \mathbf{l}$

4 Find the values of f and g.
$\begin{pmatrix} 10 \\ g \end{pmatrix} - 4 \begin{pmatrix} f \\ -3 \end{pmatrix} = \begin{pmatrix} -2 \\ 18 \end{pmatrix}$.

5 In the diagram $\overrightarrow{AC} = \begin{pmatrix} 14 \\ 2 \end{pmatrix}$ and $\overrightarrow{AB} = \begin{pmatrix} 9 \\ 12 \end{pmatrix}$.

Find.
a $\overrightarrow{CA}$
b $\overrightarrow{CA} + \overrightarrow{AB}$

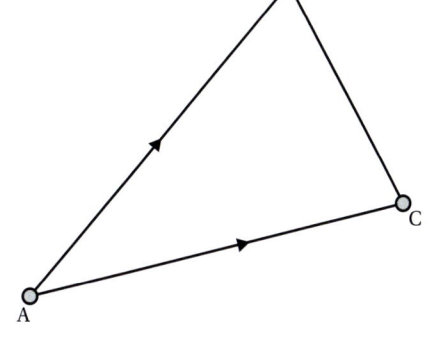

GO TO
Section 2: Vector arithmetic

6 Which of these vectors are parallel?

$\begin{pmatrix} -3 \\ 4 \end{pmatrix} \begin{pmatrix} 9 \\ 16 \end{pmatrix} \begin{pmatrix} 15 \\ -20 \end{pmatrix} \begin{pmatrix} -3 \\ 2 \end{pmatrix}$

GO TO
Section 3: Mixed practice

Find answers at: cambridge.org/ukschools/gcsemaths-studentbookanswers

GCSE Mathematics for OCR (Foundation)

Section 1: Vector notation and representation

A **vector** describes movement from one point to another, it has a direction and a magnitude (size).

Vectors can be used to describe many different kinds of movement. For example: **displacement** of a shape following translation, displacement of a boat during its journey, the velocity of an object, and the acceleration of an object.

Key vocabulary

vector: a quantity that has both magnitude and direction.

displacement: a change in position.

A vector that describes the movement from A to B can be represented by:

- an arrow in a diagram

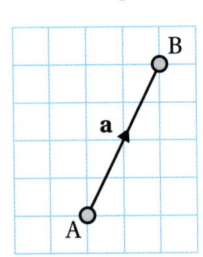

- $\overrightarrow{AB}$ (arrow indicates direction)
- **a** (if handwritten this would be underlined, a)
- a column vector $\begin{pmatrix} x \\ y \end{pmatrix}$

If you were to travel along this vector in the opposite direction, from B to A, you would represent this vector as:

- $\overrightarrow{BA}$
- $^-$**a**
- $\begin{pmatrix} -x \\ -y \end{pmatrix}$

Tip

You include the negative sign because we are now moving in the opposite direction.

Column vectors

In a column vector x represents the **horizontal** movement; y represents the **vertical** movement.

	Movement	
	x	y
positive	right	up
negative	left	down

In the diagram, $\overrightarrow{AB} = \begin{pmatrix} 2 \\ 4 \end{pmatrix}$.

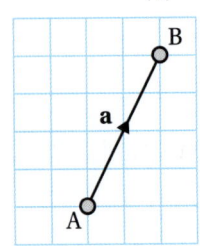

426

27 Plane vector geometry

EXERCISE 27A

1 Match up equivalent representations of the vectors.

1 (G to H, down-right)	2 (H to G, right)	3 (F to E, up-right)	4 (F to E, down)	5 (E to F, down-left)
A $\begin{pmatrix} -4 \\ -2 \end{pmatrix}$	**B** $\begin{pmatrix} 4 \\ 2 \end{pmatrix}$	**C** $\begin{pmatrix} 2 \\ -4 \end{pmatrix}$	**D** $\begin{pmatrix} 3 \\ 0 \end{pmatrix}$	**E** $\begin{pmatrix} 0 \\ -4 \end{pmatrix}$
i $\overrightarrow{FE}$	**ii** $\overrightarrow{HG}$	**iii** $\overrightarrow{EF}$	**iv** $\overrightarrow{GH}$	**v** $\overrightarrow{FE}$

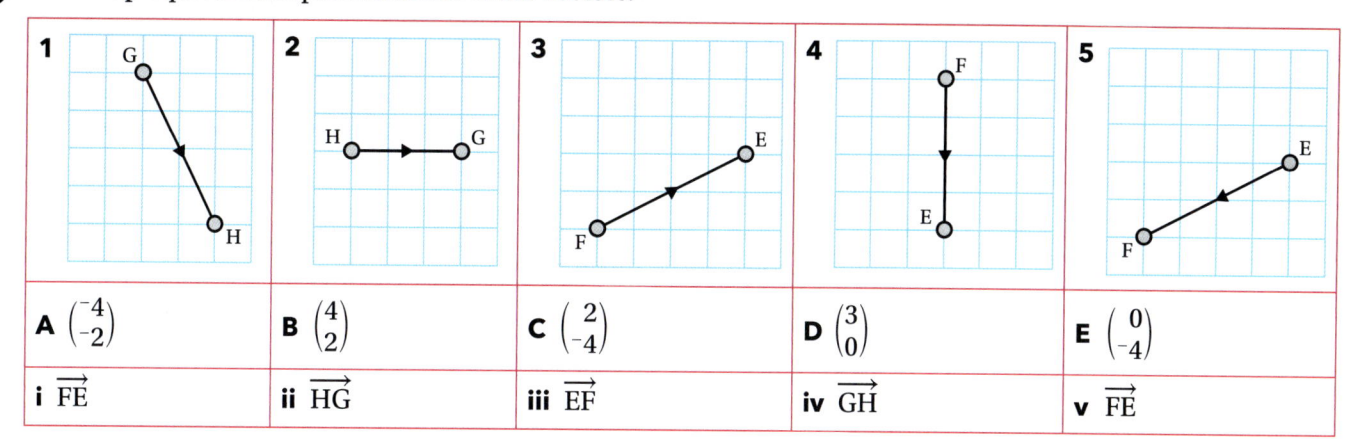

2 Use the diagram to answer the following questions.

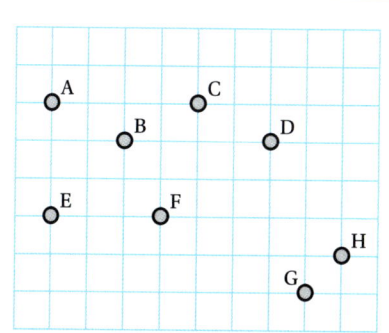

Find:

a $\overrightarrow{AB}$ **b** $\overrightarrow{DC}$ **c** $\overrightarrow{BC}$ **d** $\overrightarrow{DF}$ **e** $\overrightarrow{HF}$ **f** $\overrightarrow{BH}$

g What do you notice about $\overrightarrow{AB}$ and $\overrightarrow{DC}$?

h What do you notice about $\overrightarrow{AB}$ and $\overrightarrow{BH}$?

3 Draw a pair of axes where x and y vary from ⁻8 to 8.

Plot the point A (2, ⁻1).

Then plot points B, C, D, E, F and G where:

$\overrightarrow{AB} = \begin{pmatrix} 2 \\ 7 \end{pmatrix}$ $\overrightarrow{AC} = \begin{pmatrix} -3 \\ 7 \end{pmatrix}$ $\overrightarrow{AD} = \begin{pmatrix} -6 \\ 3 \end{pmatrix}$

$\overrightarrow{AE} = \begin{pmatrix} 5 \\ 3 \end{pmatrix}$ $\overrightarrow{AF} = \begin{pmatrix} -3 \\ -1 \end{pmatrix}$ $\overrightarrow{AG} = \begin{pmatrix} 2 \\ -1 \end{pmatrix}$

4 a Find the vector from point A with coordinates (3, ⁻4) to point B with coordinates (⁻1, 2).

b Give the coordinates of two more points E and F where the vector from E to F is the same as $\overrightarrow{AB}$.

5 a Find the vector from point K with coordinates (⁻2, ⁻1) to point L with coordinates (⁻8, 9).

b Use your answer to find the coordinates of the midpoint of KL.

> **Tip**
> The midpoint of the line KL is halfway along the line from K to L.

6 These vectors describe how to move between points A, B, C and D.

$\overrightarrow{AB} = \begin{pmatrix} 2 \\ 1 \end{pmatrix}$ $\overrightarrow{BC} = \begin{pmatrix} 1 \\ 0 \end{pmatrix}$ $\overrightarrow{DA} = \begin{pmatrix} -1 \\ 2 \end{pmatrix}$

Draw a diagram showing how the points are positioned to form the quadrilateral ABCD.

7 The vector $\begin{pmatrix} 12 \\ -8 \end{pmatrix}$ describes the displacement from point A to point B.

a What is the vector from point B to point A?

b Point A has coordinates (3, 5). What are the coordinates of point B?

Find answers at: cambridge.org/ukschools/gcsemaths-studentbookanswers

Section 2: Vector arithmetic

Addition and subtraction

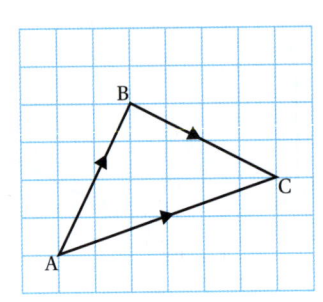

The diagram shows $\overrightarrow{AB} = \begin{pmatrix} 2 \\ 4 \end{pmatrix}$, $\overrightarrow{BC} = \begin{pmatrix} 4 \\ -2 \end{pmatrix}$, and $\overrightarrow{AC} = \begin{pmatrix} 6 \\ 2 \end{pmatrix}$

Moving from A to B and then from B to C is the same as moving directly from A to C. In other words, you can take a 'shortcut' from A to C by adding together $\overrightarrow{AB}$ and $\overrightarrow{BC}$.

$\overrightarrow{AC}$ is known as the **resultant** of $\overrightarrow{AB}$ and $\overrightarrow{BC}$.

$$\overrightarrow{AB} + \overrightarrow{BC} = \overrightarrow{AC}$$

$$\begin{pmatrix} 2 \\ 4 \end{pmatrix} + \begin{pmatrix} 4 \\ -2 \end{pmatrix} = \begin{pmatrix} 6 \\ 2 \end{pmatrix}$$

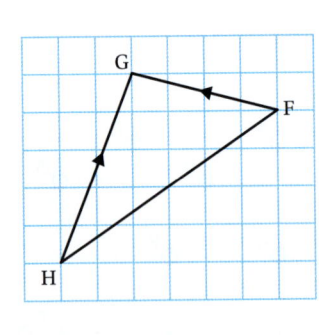

The diagram shows $\overrightarrow{FG}$ and $\overrightarrow{HG}$.

To find $\overrightarrow{FH}$ you need to travel along $\overrightarrow{FG}$, then travel along $\overrightarrow{HG}$ in the opposite direction.

So, **subtract** $\overrightarrow{HG}$.

$$\overrightarrow{FG} - \overrightarrow{HG} = \overrightarrow{FH}$$

$$\begin{pmatrix} -4 \\ 1 \end{pmatrix} - \begin{pmatrix} 2 \\ 5 \end{pmatrix} = \begin{pmatrix} -4 - 2 \\ 1 - 5 \end{pmatrix} = \begin{pmatrix} -6 \\ -4 \end{pmatrix}$$

Key vocabulary

scalar: a numerical quantity (it has no direction).

Multiplying by a scalar

Multiplying a vector by a **scalar** results in repeated addition.

This is the same as multiplying the *x*-component by the scalar, *k*, and the *y*-component by the same scalar, *k*.

$\overrightarrow{AB} = \begin{pmatrix} 4 \\ -1 \end{pmatrix}$ and $\overrightarrow{CD} = \begin{pmatrix} 12 \\ -3 \end{pmatrix}$.

$\overrightarrow{CD} = 3\overrightarrow{AB}$

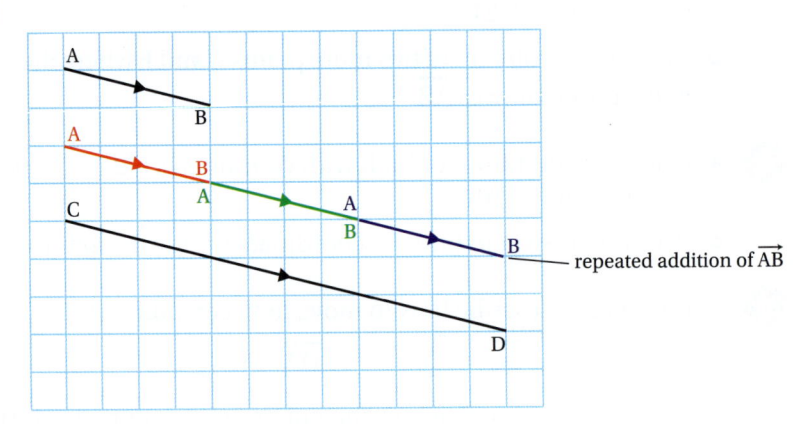

repeated addition of $\overrightarrow{AB}$

$$3 \times \begin{pmatrix} 4 \\ -1 \end{pmatrix} = \begin{pmatrix} 4 \\ -1 \end{pmatrix} + \begin{pmatrix} 4 \\ -1 \end{pmatrix} + \begin{pmatrix} 4 \\ -1 \end{pmatrix}$$ —— repeated addition

$$= \begin{pmatrix} 3 \times 4 \\ 3 \times -1 \end{pmatrix}$$ —— multiplying the *x*-component by the scalar 3

—— multiplying the *y*-component by the scalar 3

$$= \begin{pmatrix} 12 \\ -3 \end{pmatrix}$$

Multiplying a vector by a scalar, *k*, results in a **parallel vector** with a magnitude multiplied by *k*.

Vectors are parallel if one is a multiple of the other.

> **Key vocabulary**
>
> **parallel vectors**: occur when one vector is a multiple of the other.

WORK IT OUT 27.1

Which of the following vectors are parallel?

$$\mathbf{a} = \begin{pmatrix} 3 \\ -1 \end{pmatrix} \quad \mathbf{b} = \begin{pmatrix} 4 \\ -3 \end{pmatrix} \quad \mathbf{c} = \begin{pmatrix} 9 \\ -3 \end{pmatrix} \quad \mathbf{d} = \begin{pmatrix} 6 \\ 2 \end{pmatrix} \quad \mathbf{e} = \begin{pmatrix} -6 \\ 2 \end{pmatrix}$$

Option A	Option B	Option C
Vectors **a** and **c**	Vectors **d** and **e**	Vectors **a**, **c** and **e**

EXERCISE 27B

1 $\mathbf{p} = \begin{pmatrix} -3 \\ 2 \end{pmatrix} \quad \mathbf{q} = \begin{pmatrix} 5 \\ -1 \end{pmatrix} \quad \mathbf{r} = \begin{pmatrix} -3 \\ -2 \end{pmatrix} \quad \mathbf{s} = \begin{pmatrix} 4 \\ -7 \end{pmatrix}$

Write each of these as a single vector.

- **a** $\mathbf{p} + \mathbf{q}$
- **b** $\mathbf{s} - \mathbf{r}$
- **c** $4\mathbf{p}$
- **d** $-3\mathbf{s}$
- **e** $\mathbf{p} + \mathbf{q} + \mathbf{r}$
- **f** $2\mathbf{p} + \mathbf{q} - 2\mathbf{s}$
- **g** Which of the results from parts **a** to **f** are parallel to the vector $\begin{pmatrix} 3 \\ -2 \end{pmatrix}$?

2 Give three vectors parallel to $\begin{pmatrix} 2 \\ -3 \end{pmatrix}$.

3 Find *x, y, s* and *t* in each of the following vector calculations.

- **a** $\begin{pmatrix} x \\ 3 \end{pmatrix} + \begin{pmatrix} 5 \\ y \end{pmatrix} = \begin{pmatrix} 9 \\ 3 \end{pmatrix}$
- **b** $\begin{pmatrix} 10 \\ y \end{pmatrix} - \begin{pmatrix} x \\ -3 \end{pmatrix} = \begin{pmatrix} -2 \\ 8 \end{pmatrix}$
- **c** $\begin{pmatrix} x \\ -3 \end{pmatrix} + \begin{pmatrix} -6 \\ y \end{pmatrix} = \begin{pmatrix} 11 \\ -8 \end{pmatrix}$
- **d** $s\begin{pmatrix} x \\ 12 \end{pmatrix} = \begin{pmatrix} 7 \\ -24 \end{pmatrix}$
- **e** $s\begin{pmatrix} -12 \\ y \end{pmatrix} = \begin{pmatrix} 3 \\ -8 \end{pmatrix}$
- **f** $\begin{pmatrix} 2 \\ -4 \end{pmatrix} + s\begin{pmatrix} 5 \\ y \end{pmatrix} = \begin{pmatrix} 17 \\ 14 \end{pmatrix}$
- **g** $\begin{pmatrix} x \\ -4 \end{pmatrix} - s\begin{pmatrix} -5 \\ -3 \end{pmatrix} = \begin{pmatrix} 20 \\ 5 \end{pmatrix}$
- **h** $s\begin{pmatrix} 3 \\ 4 \end{pmatrix} + t\begin{pmatrix} 2 \\ -2 \end{pmatrix} = \begin{pmatrix} 18 \\ 10 \end{pmatrix}$

4 In the diagram, $\overrightarrow{AB} = \begin{pmatrix} 20 \\ 16 \end{pmatrix}$.

The ratio of AC : CB is 1 : 3.

- **a** Find $\overrightarrow{AC}$.
- **b** Find $\overrightarrow{BC}$.

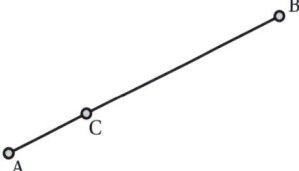

> **Tip**
>
> You can multiply a vector by a fractional scalar if you need to divide. If you need a reminder on fractions see Chapter 10; if you need a reminder of how to calculate ratios, see Chapter 22.

5 These vectors describe how to move between points E, F, G and H, which are four vertices of a quadrilateral.

$$\overrightarrow{EF} = \begin{pmatrix} 3 \\ -1 \end{pmatrix} \quad \overrightarrow{HG} = \begin{pmatrix} 6 \\ -2 \end{pmatrix} \quad \overrightarrow{EH} = \begin{pmatrix} 0 \\ -1 \end{pmatrix}$$

- **a** What can you say about sides EF and HG?
- **b** Predict what kind of quadrilateral EFGH is.
- **c** Draw the quadrilateral and find $\overrightarrow{GF}$.

6 ABCD is a quadrilateral. $\overrightarrow{AB} = \overrightarrow{DC}$ and $\overrightarrow{DA} = \overrightarrow{CB}$.

What kind of quadrilateral is ABCD? How do you know this?

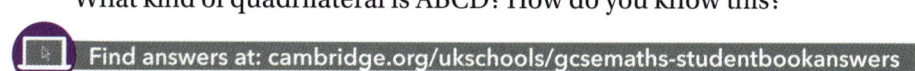

Find answers at: cambridge.org/ukschools/gcsemaths-studentbookanswers

Section 3: Mixed practice

It is important that you understand what calculations are needed when given a problem involving vectors.

Test your knowledge using the exercise.

EXERCISE 27C

Tip

Remember that the line CM is half the length of the line CB. What does this mean about the journey from C to M?

1. In the diagram, $\vec{AC} = \begin{pmatrix} 10 \\ 2 \end{pmatrix}$ and $\vec{AB} = \begin{pmatrix} 8 \\ 14 \end{pmatrix}$.

   M is the midpoint of BC.

   Find:

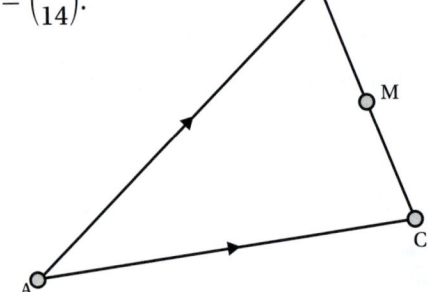

   a $\vec{CA}$.

   b $\vec{CA} + \vec{AB}$.

   c $\vec{CM}$

2. Two triangles have vertices A, B, C and D, E, F.

   The coordinates of the vertices are A(0, 0), B(3, 2), C(2, 5) and D(1, 1), E(7, 5), F(5, 11).

   Compare the vectors.

   a $\vec{AB}$ and $\vec{DE}$

   b $\vec{AC}$ and $\vec{DF}$

   c What does this tell you about the triangles ABC and DEF?

3. In a game of chess different pieces move in different ways.
   - A king can move one square in any direction (including diagonals).
   - A knight moves two squares horizontally and one square vertically or two squares vertically and one horizontally (in an L-shape).

   A chessboard is eight squares wide and eight squares long.

   What vectors can the following pieces move?

   a King   b Knight

4. A ship travels 8 km east and 10 km north. What vector has it travelled?

5. The vector from E to F is $\begin{pmatrix} -6 \\ 2 \end{pmatrix}$ and the vector from F to G is $\begin{pmatrix} 5 \\ 1 \end{pmatrix}$.

   What is the vector from:

   a E to G?   b G to F?

   c E to the midpoint of EF?   d G to the midpoint of EF?

6. The vector from A to B is $\begin{pmatrix} 1 \\ -2 \end{pmatrix}$.

   The vector joining C to D is parallel to AB, D is five times the distance from C as B is from A.

   What is the vector from C to D?

27 Plane vector geometry

Checklist of learning and understanding

Notation
- Vectors can be written in a variety of ways: $\overrightarrow{AB}$, **a**, $\begin{pmatrix} 1 \\ 2 \end{pmatrix}$.

Addition and subtraction
- To add or subtract vectors simply add or subtract the x- and y-components.

$$\begin{pmatrix} 3 \\ 2 \end{pmatrix} + \begin{pmatrix} 2 \\ -4 \end{pmatrix} = \begin{pmatrix} 5 \\ -2 \end{pmatrix} \qquad \begin{pmatrix} -1 \\ 4 \end{pmatrix} - \begin{pmatrix} 5 \\ -6 \end{pmatrix} = \begin{pmatrix} -6 \\ 10 \end{pmatrix}$$

Multiplication by a scalar
- To multiply by a scalar you can use repeated addition, or multiply the x-component by the scalar and the y-component by the scalar.

$$3\begin{pmatrix} -2 \\ 1 \end{pmatrix} = \begin{pmatrix} -2 \\ 1 \end{pmatrix} + \begin{pmatrix} -2 \\ 1 \end{pmatrix} + \begin{pmatrix} -2 \\ 1 \end{pmatrix} = \begin{pmatrix} -6 \\ 3 \end{pmatrix} \qquad 3\begin{pmatrix} -2 \\ 1 \end{pmatrix} = \begin{pmatrix} -6 \\ 3 \end{pmatrix}$$

- Multiplying a vector by a scalar quantity produces a parallel vector; you can identify that vectors are parallel if one vector is a multiple of the other. Parallel vectors can be part of the same line and described using a ratio.

Chapter review

For additional questions on the topics in this chapter, visit GCSE Mathematics Online.

1 What is the difference between coordinate $(-2, 3)$ and vector $\begin{pmatrix} -2 \\ 3 \end{pmatrix}$?

2 Match the parallel vectors.

$\mathbf{a} = \begin{pmatrix} -6 \\ 2 \end{pmatrix}$ $\quad \mathbf{b} = \begin{pmatrix} 1 \\ 3 \end{pmatrix}$ $\quad \mathbf{c} = \begin{pmatrix} 3 \\ -1 \end{pmatrix}$ $\quad \mathbf{d} = \begin{pmatrix} 7 \\ 21 \end{pmatrix}$ $\quad \mathbf{e} = \begin{pmatrix} -2 \\ 4 \end{pmatrix}$ $\quad \mathbf{f} = \begin{pmatrix} -6 \\ 12 \end{pmatrix}$ $\quad \mathbf{g} = \begin{pmatrix} -1 \\ 2 \end{pmatrix}$

3 Calculate.

a $\begin{pmatrix} 1 \\ -2 \end{pmatrix} + \begin{pmatrix} -2 \\ -1 \end{pmatrix}$ $\qquad$ **b** $\begin{pmatrix} 0 \\ -3 \end{pmatrix} - \begin{pmatrix} -2 \\ 4 \end{pmatrix}$ $\qquad$ **c** $-3\begin{pmatrix} 2 \\ -1 \end{pmatrix}$

4 The ratio of $\overrightarrow{AB} : \overrightarrow{BC}$ is $2 : 3$.

If $\overrightarrow{AB} = \begin{pmatrix} -6 \\ 4 \end{pmatrix}$ what is the column vector of $\quad$ **a** $\overrightarrow{BC}$? $\quad$ **b** $\overrightarrow{AC}$?

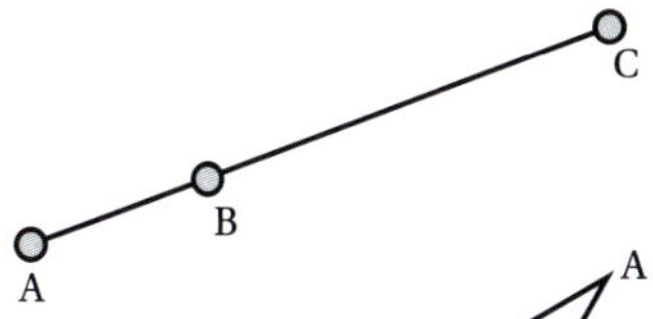

5 In the diagram, M is the midpoint of AB. Find:
a $\overrightarrow{AB}$. $\qquad$ **b** $\overrightarrow{AM}$. $\qquad$ **c** $\overrightarrow{MO}$.

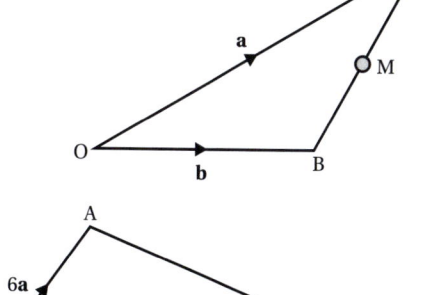

6 In triangle OAB, $\overrightarrow{OA} = 6\mathbf{a}$ and $\overrightarrow{OB} = 6\mathbf{b}$.

M is the midpoint of OB and N is the midpoint of AB.
In this question give your answers in their simplest form in terms of **a** and **b**.

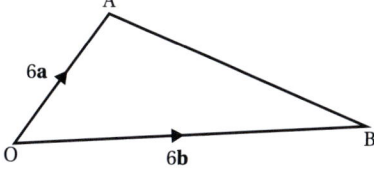

a Find $\overrightarrow{AB}$. $\hfill$ (1 mark)
b Find $\overrightarrow{ON}$. $\hfill$ (2 marks)

G is a point on AM such that $AG = \frac{2}{3}AM$.

c **i** Find $\overrightarrow{AM}$. $\hfill$ (1 mark)
$\quad$ **ii** Find $\overrightarrow{OG}$. $\hfill$ (2 marks)
d What do your answers tell you about the points O, G and N? $\hfill$ (1 mark)

© OCR 2012

Find answers at: cambridge.org/ukschools/gcsemaths-studentbookanswers

431

28 Plane isometric transformations

In this chapter you will learn how to …
- carry out rotations, reflections and translations.
- identify and describe rotations, reflections and translations.
- describe translations using column vectors.

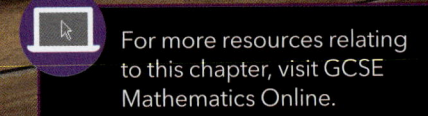

For more resources relating to this chapter, visit GCSE Mathematics Online.

Using mathematics: real-life applications

You can see examples of reflections, rotations and translations all around you. Patterns in wallpaper and fabric are often translations, images reflected in water are reflections and the blades of a wind turbine are a good example of rotation.

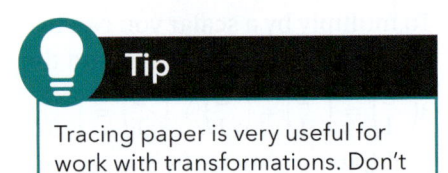

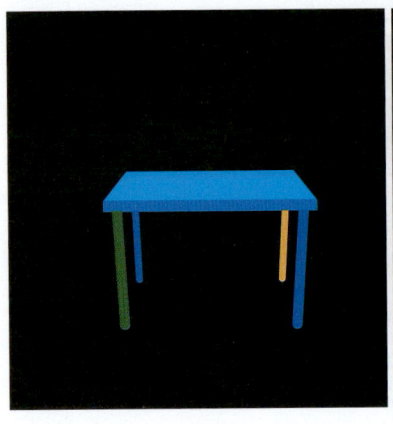

Tip
Tracing paper is very useful for work with transformations. Don't be afraid to ask for it in an exam.

"I use transformations all the time when I program computer graphics. Transformations allow me to position objects, shape them and change the view I have of them. I can even change the type of perspective that is used to show something." *(Computer programmer)*

Before you start …

Ch 9	You need to know what angles of 90°, 180° and 270° look like and also the directions clockwise and anti-clockwise.	1	How many degrees is each angle? State whether each arrow is showing clockwise or anti-clockwise movement. a 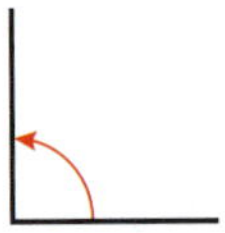 b 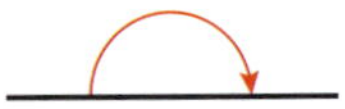 c 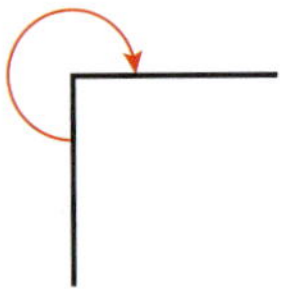
Ch 18, 19	You need to know how to plot straight-line graphs in the form $x = a$, $y = a$ and $y = x$.	2	Draw the graph for each equation. a $y = 2$ b $y = x$ c $x = {}^-1$ d $y = {}^-x$
Ch 27	You need to know what a vector is and how they describe movement.	3	a What is the difference between the coordinate (3, 2) and the vector $\begin{pmatrix} 3 \\ 2 \end{pmatrix}$? b What is the relationship between the vectors $\begin{pmatrix} -1 \\ 3 \end{pmatrix}$ and $\begin{pmatrix} 3 \\ 1 \end{pmatrix}$?

28 Plane isometric transformations

Assess your starting point using the Launchpad

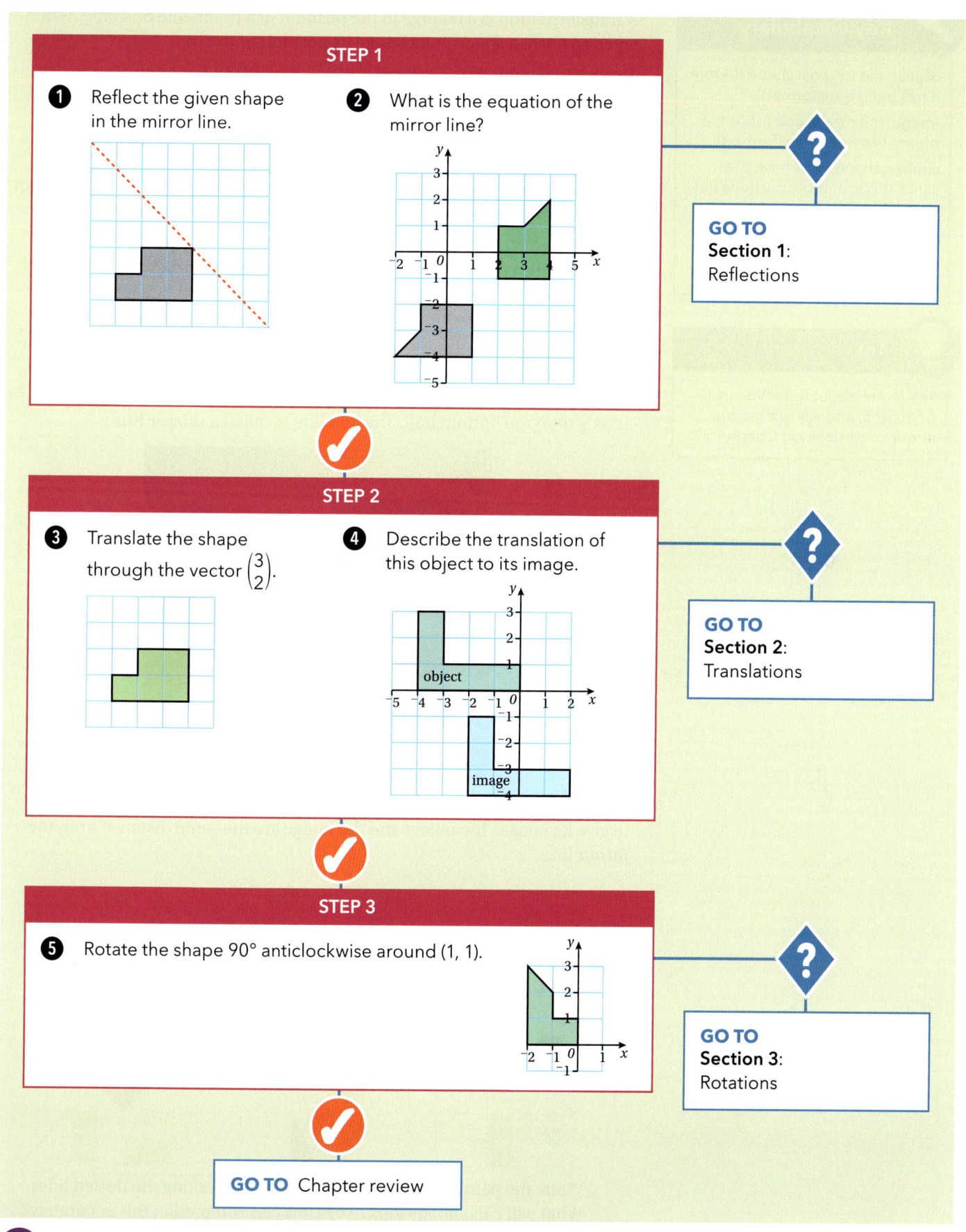

STEP 1

1 Reflect the given shape in the mirror line.

2 What is the equation of the mirror line?

GO TO Section 1: Reflections

STEP 2

3 Translate the shape through the vector $\begin{pmatrix} 3 \\ 2 \end{pmatrix}$.

4 Describe the translation of this object to its image.

GO TO Section 2: Translations

STEP 3

5 Rotate the shape 90° anticlockwise around (1, 1).

GO TO Section 3: Rotations

GO TO Chapter review

Find answers at: cambridge.org/ukschools/gcsemaths-studentbookanswers

433

Key vocabulary

object: the original shape (before it has been transformed).

image: the new shape (once the object has been transformed).

similar: shapes that have the same shape and proportions but are a different size.

mirror line: a line equidistant from all corresponding points on a shape and its reflection.

Tip

You learnt about reflection in Chapter 5, and will learn more about congruency in Chapter 29.

Section 1: Reflections

A transformation is a change in the position of a point, line or shape. When you transform a shape you change its position or its size.

The original point, line or shape is called the **object**. For example, the triangle ABC.

The transformation is called the **image**. The symbol ′ is used to label the image. For example, the image of triangle ABC is A′B′C′.

Reflection, rotation and translation change the position of an object, but not its size. Under these three transformations an object and its image will be **congruent**, that is, identical in size and shape.

Enlargement is also a transformation. Enlargement changes the position of an object and also its size. Under enlargement an object and its image are **similar**. You will learn about similarity in more detail in Chapter 30.

Mirrors, windows and water surfaces all reflect objects. You can see the reflection of clouds and trees clearly in the photograph below. If you draw a line horizontally across the centre of the image and fold it, the top half will fit exactly onto the bottom half. The fold line is called a **mirror line**.

Mathematically, when a shape is reflected it is flipped over a mirror line to give its image. The object and the image are the same distance from the mirror line.

EXERCISE 28A

1. Suppose the following images are painted on three pieces of square paper:

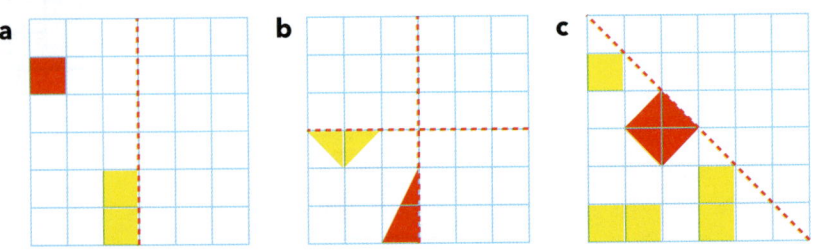

   a   b   c

   While the paint is still wet, the paper is folded along the dotted lines. What will each image look like? How can you predict this accurately?

2 Look at this picture. Its mirror line has been marked. Join corresponding points in the two halves of the diagram. What do you notice?

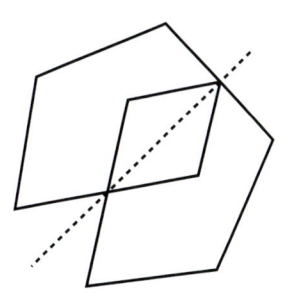

3 Reflect each shape in the given mirror line.

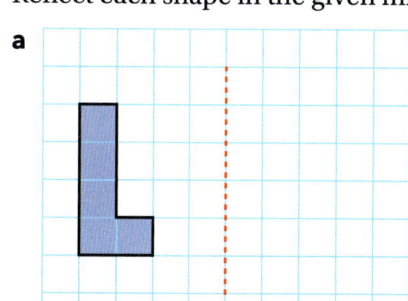

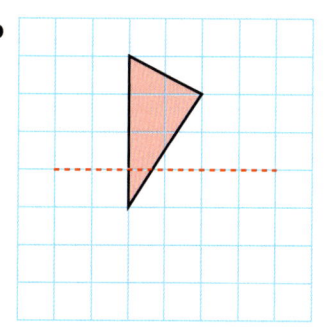

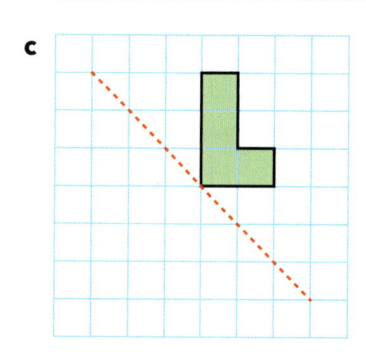

a

b

c

Under reflection, corresponding points on the object and the image are the same distance from the mirror line. If you join a pair of corresponding points, the line formed is cut in half by the mirror line and the lines meet at 90°. The mirror line is the **perpendicular bisector** of any pair of corresponding points.

Tip
You learnt about the perpendicular bisector in Chapter 6.

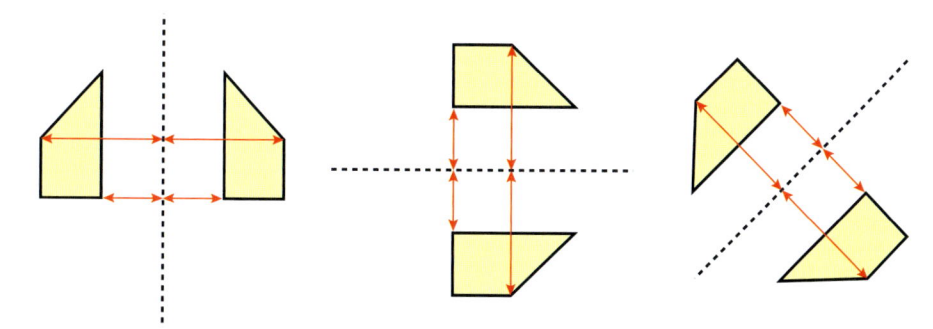

Tip
You can turn your book around so that diagonal mirror lines look vertical or horizontal. Often our brains find this easier than working diagonally.

Find answers at: cambridge.org/ukschools/gcsemaths-studentbookanswers

GCSE Mathematics for OCR (Foundation)

WORK IT OUT 28.1

This shape is reflected in the line $y = {}^-1$. What is its image?

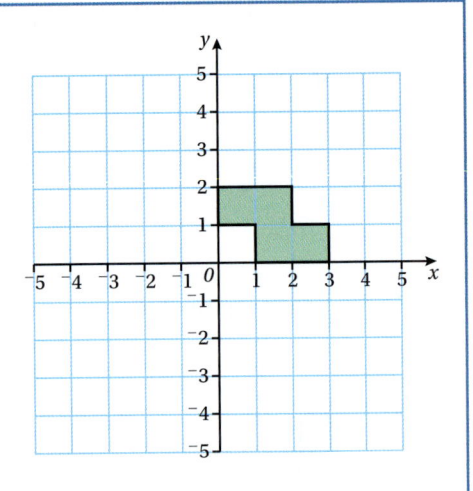

Which one of these answers is correct?

What has gone wrong in each of the others?

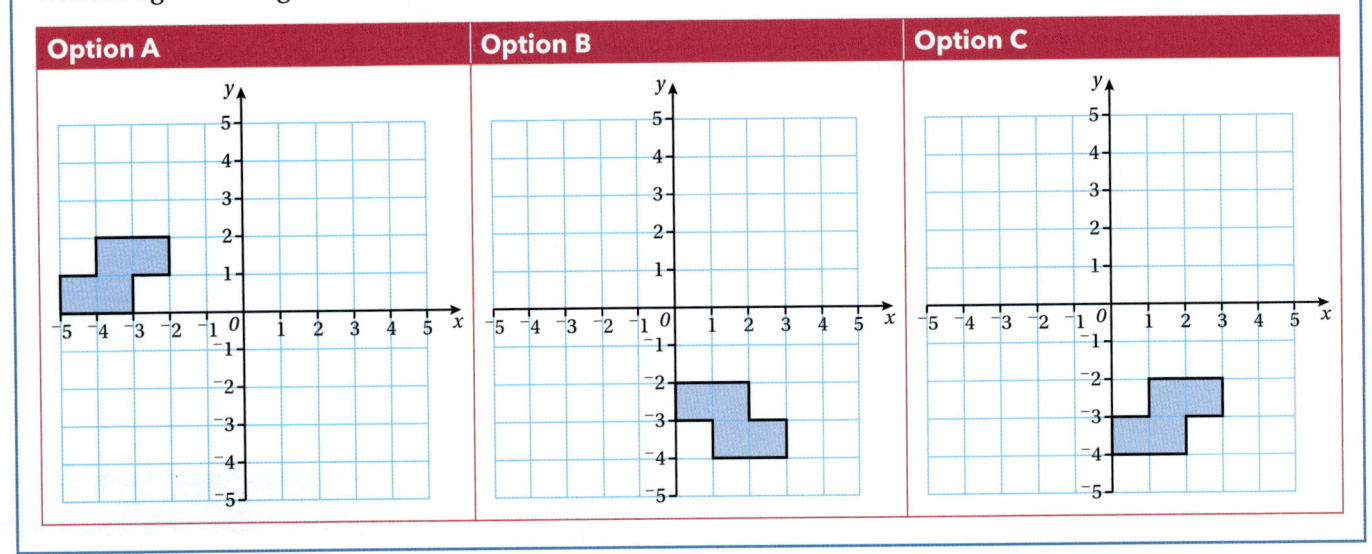

Option A	Option B	Option C

EXERCISE 28B

1. Reflect the triangle in the line $x = 1$, and then reflect the triangle and the resultant image in the line $y = {}^-1$.

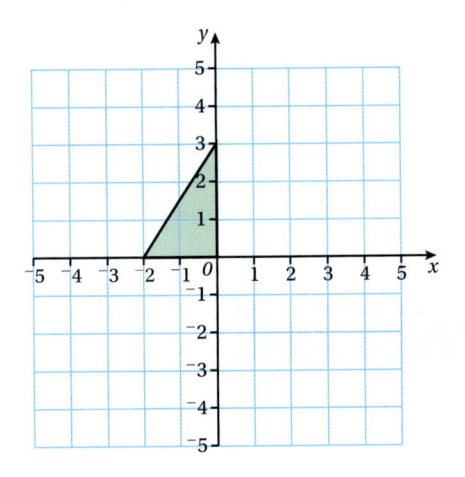

28 Plane isometric transformations

2 Reflect this shape in the line $y = x$, and then reflect the shape and the resultant image in the line $y = -x$.

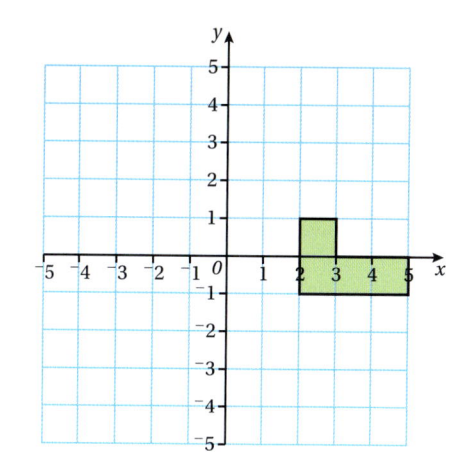

3 Carry out the ten reflections on the grid to reveal the word.
Shape **A** in the line $y = x$
Shape **B** in the x-axis
Shape **C** in the line $y = -2$
Shape **D** in the line $y = 4$
Shape **E** in the line $x = 7$
Shape **F** in the line $y = -x$
Shape **G** in the line $x = -4$
Shape **H** in the line $x = 1.5$
Shape **I** in the line $y = 6$
Shape **J** in the line $y = x$

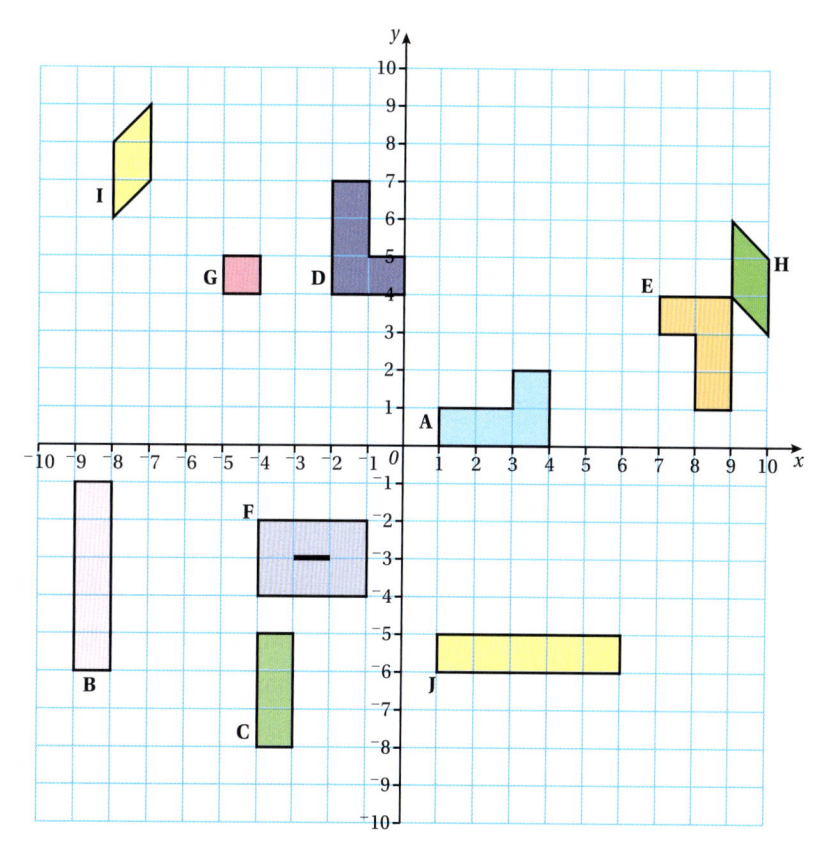

Describing reflections

You need to be able to draw a mirror line on a diagram. You must also be able to give the equation of the mirror line when the reflection is shown on a coordinate grid. This is known as describing the reflection.

The mirror line is the perpendicular bisector of two corresponding points in a reflection. So if you can't 'spot' a mirror line, you can join two corresponding points and construct the perpendicular bisector to find it.

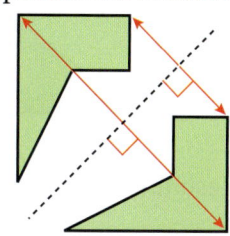

> **Tip**
>
> To check a reflection, trace the **object**, the **image** and the mirror line. Fold the tracing paper along the mirror line; the shapes should match up exactly.

Find answers at: cambridge.org/ukschools/gcsemaths-studentbookanswers

437

EXERCISE 28C

1 Find the equation of the mirror line in each reflection.

a

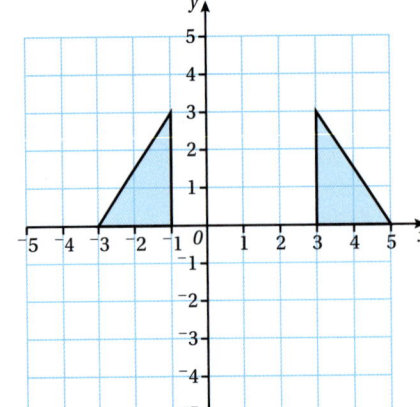

b

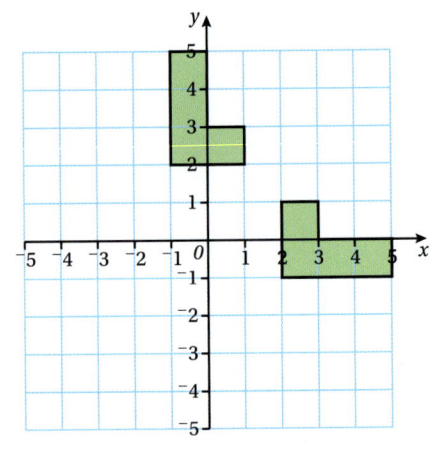

c

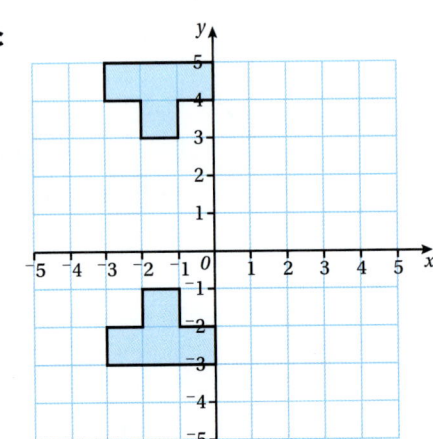

d

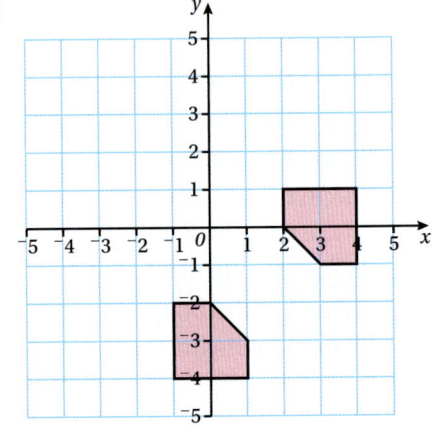

2 a Fully describe each of the following reflections.

   i Shape **A** to shape **E**.

   ii Shape **C** to shape **G**.

   iii Shape **A** to shape **C**.

   iv Shape **H** to shape **D**.

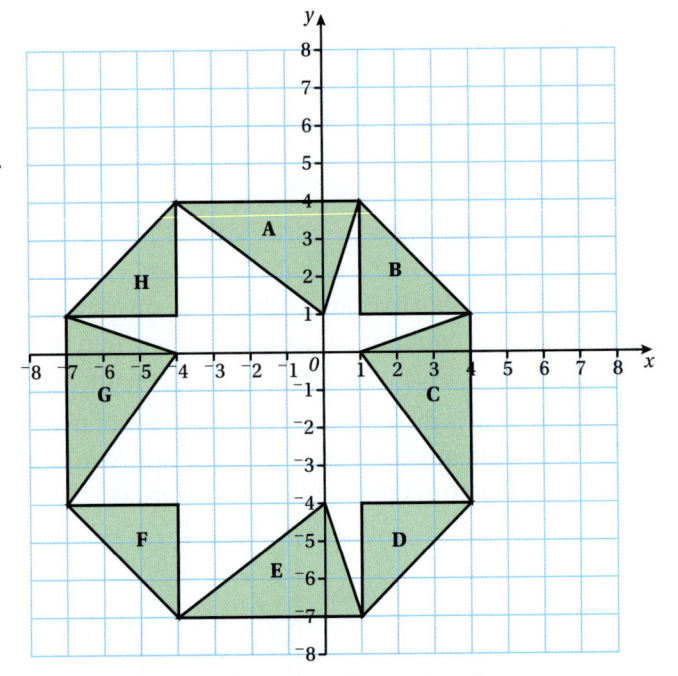

b Challenge another student to describe a reflection of two triangles you choose.

3. Trace each pair of shapes and construct the mirror line for the reflection.

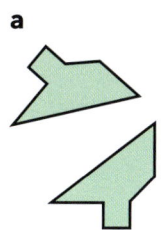

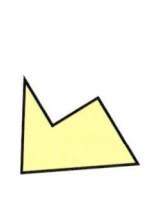

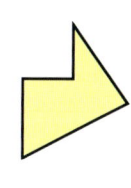

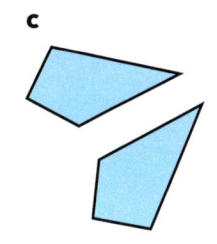

a   b   c

Section 2: Translations

A translation is a slide along a straight line. (Think about pushing a box across a floor.) The translation can be from left to right (horizontal), up or down (vertical) or both (horizontal and vertical).

The image is in the same **orientation** as the object and every point on the shape moves exactly the same distance in exactly the same direction. Translated shapes are congruent to each other.

You can describe translations on a coordinate grid using column vectors. Remember a column vector shows horizontal displacement over vertical displacement.

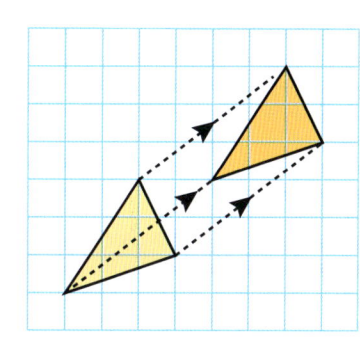

Key vocabulary

orientation: the position of a shape relative to the grid.

Tip

You learnt about vectors in Chapter 27.

WORKED EXAMPLE 1

Describe the translation ABC to A'B'C' by means of a column vector.

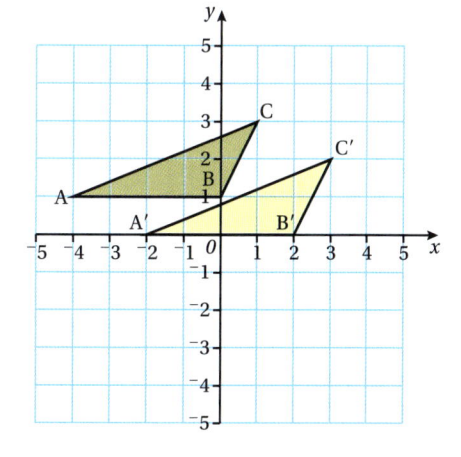

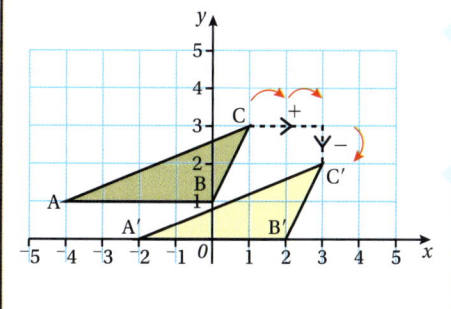

Take any point on the object and find the corresponding point on the image. Look at point C and point C'.

Work out how the point has been translated horizontally and vertically. To get from C to C' you move
2 units to the right = +2
1 unit down = ⁻1

The translation is $\begin{pmatrix} 2 \\ -1 \end{pmatrix}$

Write this as a column vector.

Tip

Drawing on the grid to show the movements can help you to avoid unnecessary mistakes.

Find answers at: cambridge.org/ukschools/gcsemaths-studentbookanswers

GCSE Mathematics for OCR (Foundation)

WORK IT OUT 28.2

This shape is translated through a vector of $\begin{pmatrix} -2 \\ 4 \end{pmatrix}$. Draw its image.

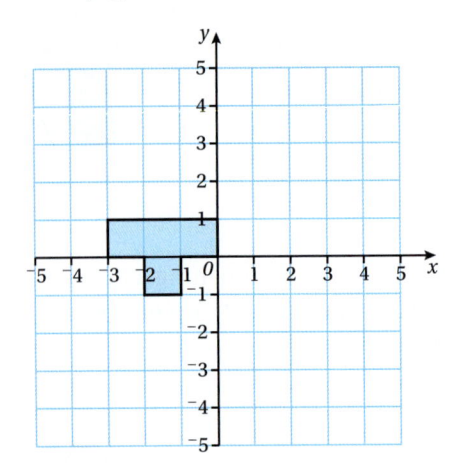

Which one of these answers is correct?

What has gone wrong in each of the others?

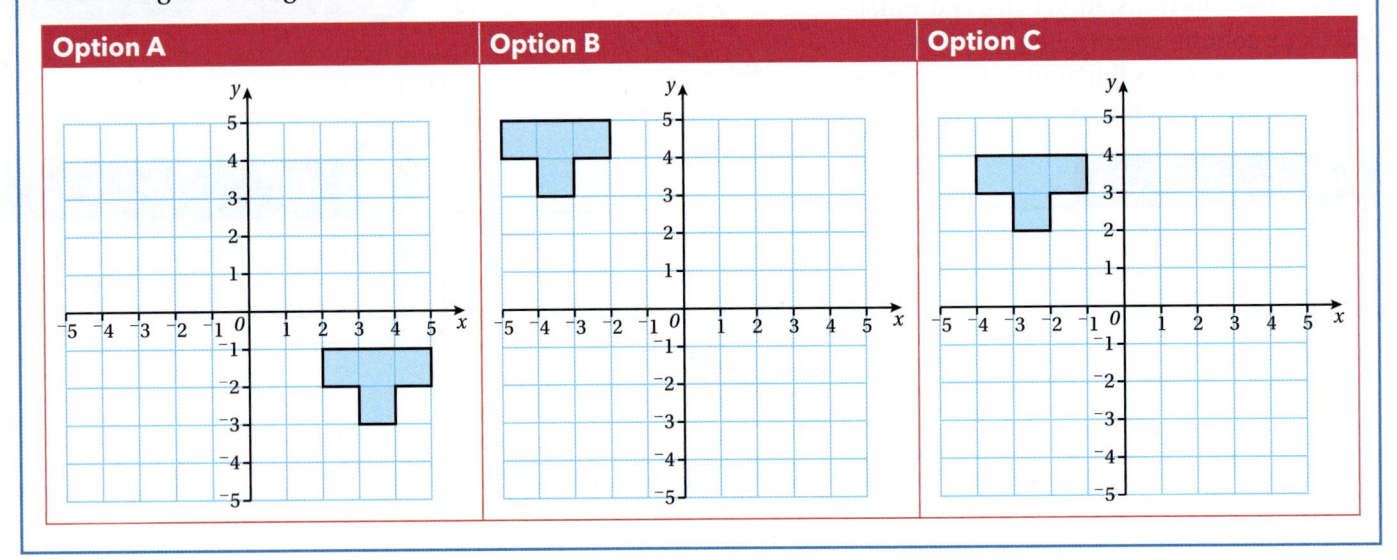

Option A	Option B	Option C

EXERCISE 28D

1. Translate each shape as directed.

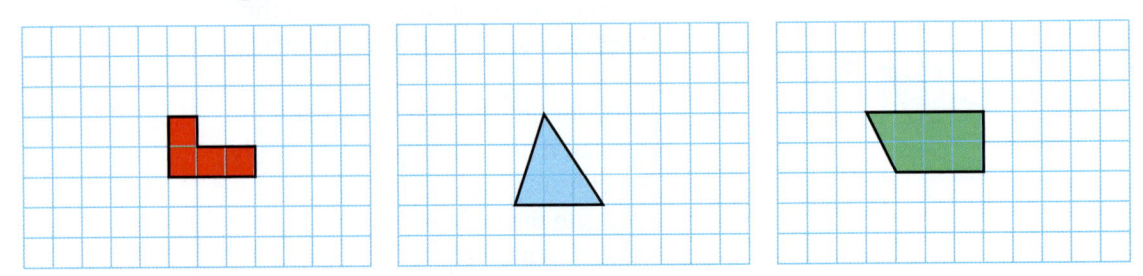

   a Translate 6 right and 2 up.   b Translate 3 left and 1 down.   c Translate 2 down and 4 right.

28 Plane isometric transformations

2 Translate each shape using the given vector.

a $\begin{pmatrix} 3 \\ -1 \end{pmatrix}$
b $\begin{pmatrix} -1 \\ 2 \end{pmatrix}$
c $\begin{pmatrix} 0 \\ 4 \end{pmatrix}$

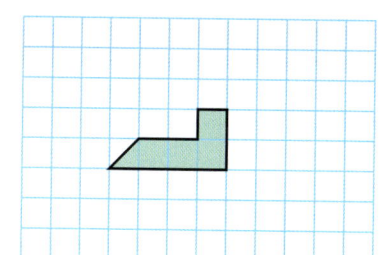

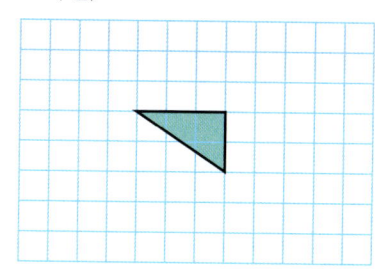

3 Translate each shape by the given vector then give the name of the shape you have put together;

a Translate shape **A** by $\begin{pmatrix} -1 \\ -3 \end{pmatrix}$.

b Translate shape **B** by $\begin{pmatrix} 1 \\ 5 \end{pmatrix}$.

c Translate shape **C** by $\begin{pmatrix} 1 \\ -1 \end{pmatrix}$.

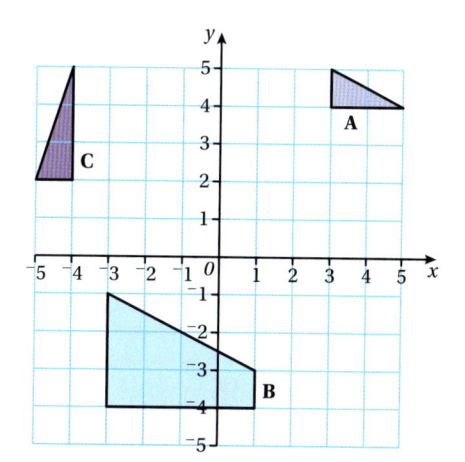

4 Translate each piece of this jigsaw using the vectors below.

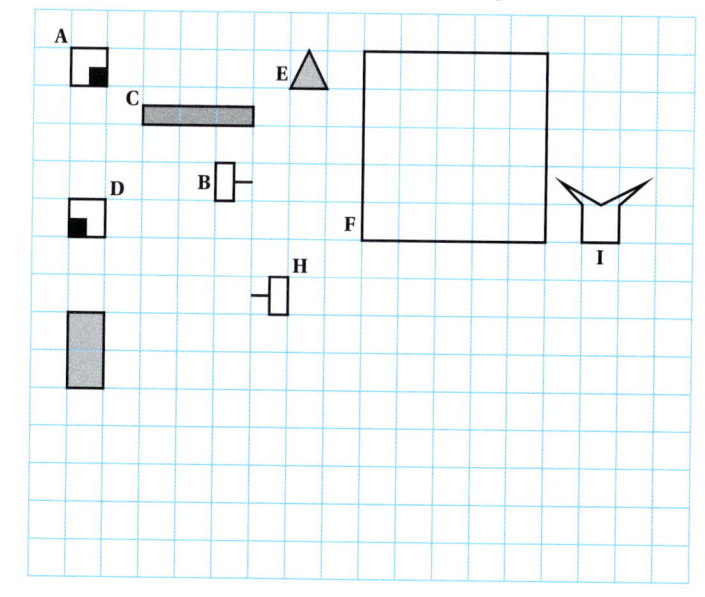

A $\begin{pmatrix} 12 \\ -8 \end{pmatrix}$ B $\begin{pmatrix} 12 \\ -5 \end{pmatrix}$ C $\begin{pmatrix} 10 \\ -9 \end{pmatrix}$ D $\begin{pmatrix} 14 \\ -4 \end{pmatrix}$ E $\begin{pmatrix} 7 \\ -9 \end{pmatrix}$

F $\begin{pmatrix} 3 \\ -7 \end{pmatrix}$ G $\begin{pmatrix} 13 \\ -5 \end{pmatrix}$ H $\begin{pmatrix} 5 \\ -2 \end{pmatrix}$ I $\begin{pmatrix} -1 \\ -2 \end{pmatrix}$

Describing translations

You should be able to use vectors to describe a translation. Remember to count between corresponding points on the two shapes.

Tip

Make sure you count from the object to the image and to write this as a column vector (not a coordinate)!

Find answers at: cambridge.org/ukschools/gcsemaths-studentbookanswers

441

GCSE Mathematics for OCR (Foundation)

WORK IT OUT 28.3

Which transformations below are reflections and which are translations? How did you make your decision?

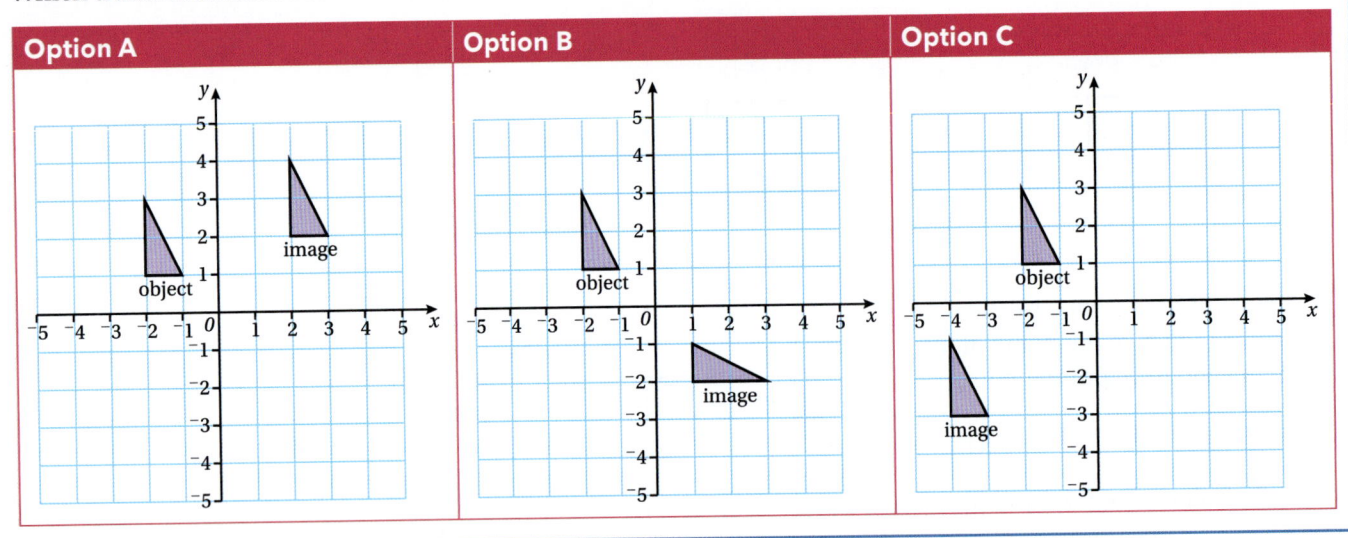

Option A	Option B	Option C

EXERCISE 28E

1. Here are some completed translations. The objects (**A** to **E**) are shown in colour and the images are in grey.

   Write column vectors to describe the translation from each object to its image.

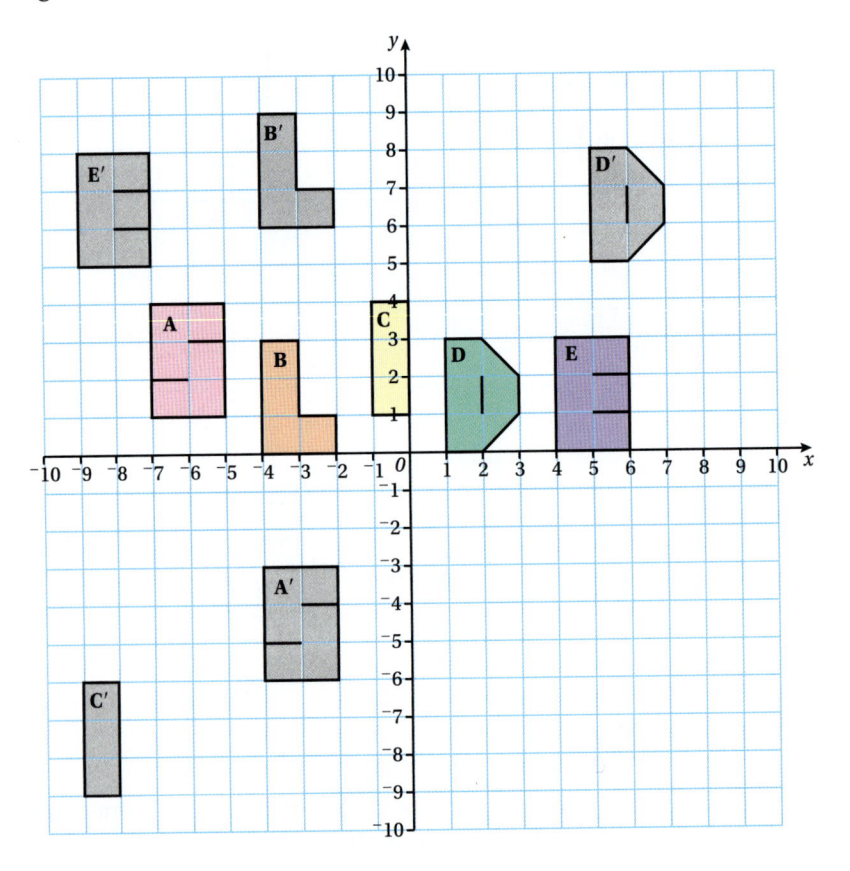

442

2 Work on a square grid. Draw the four objects (**A** to **D**) used to make this image in any position on the grid.

Make up translation instructions for moving the four objects to form the image.

Exchange with a partner and perform the translations to make sure their instructions are correct.

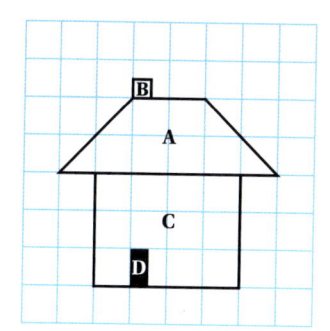

Section 3: Rotations

A rotation is a turn. An object can turn clockwise or anti-clockwise around a fixed point called the **centre of rotation**. The centre of rotation may be inside, on the edge of, or outside the object.

A rotation changes the orientation of a shape, but the object and its image remain congruent.

When you rotate a shape, the distance from the centre of rotation to any point on the object remains the same. Each point travels in a circle around the centre. Think about the tip of a blade on a wind turbine or a child sitting on a roundabout. When they rotate, the paths they trace out are circles.

To carry out a rotation you need to know the centre of rotation as well as the angle and direction of rotation. At this level, all rotations will be in multiples of 90°.

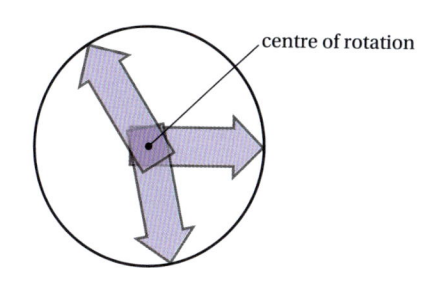

WORK IT OUT 28.4

This shape is rotated anti-clockwise, with centre of rotation (0, 1) through an angle of 90°. What is its image?

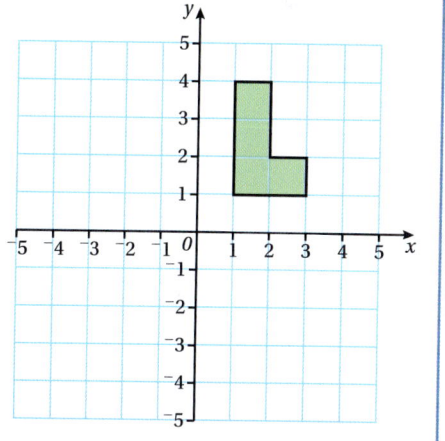

Which one of these answers is correct?
What has gone wrong in each of the others?

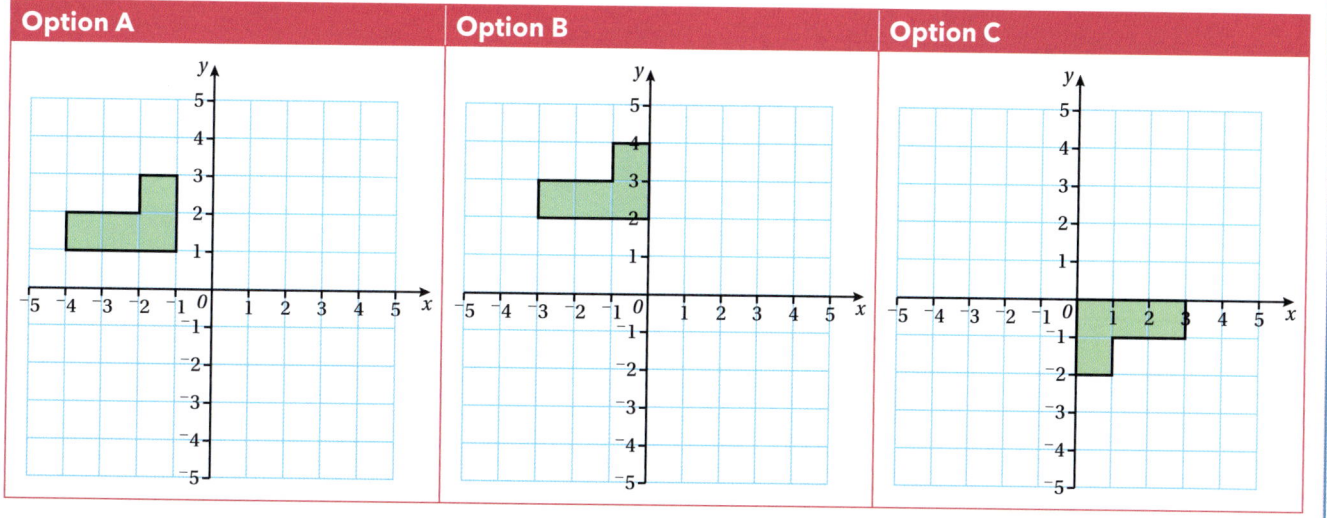

| Option A | Option B | Option C |

Find answers at: cambridge.org/ukschools/gcsemaths-studentbookanswers

EXERCISE 28F

1 Rotate each shape as directed. Use the centre of the shape as the centre of rotation.

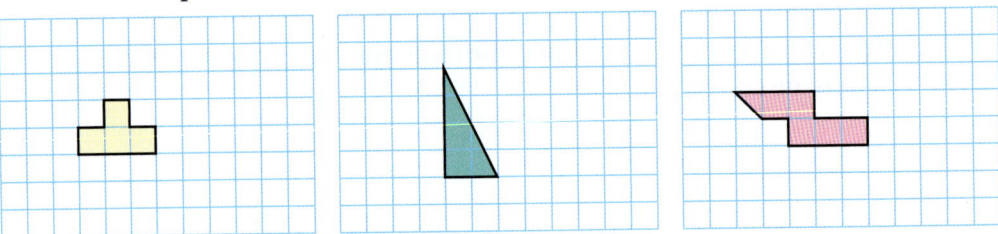

    a Rotate 90° clockwise.   **b** Rotate 180°.   **c** Rotate 90° anti-clockwise.

2 Rotate each shape as directed about the marked centre

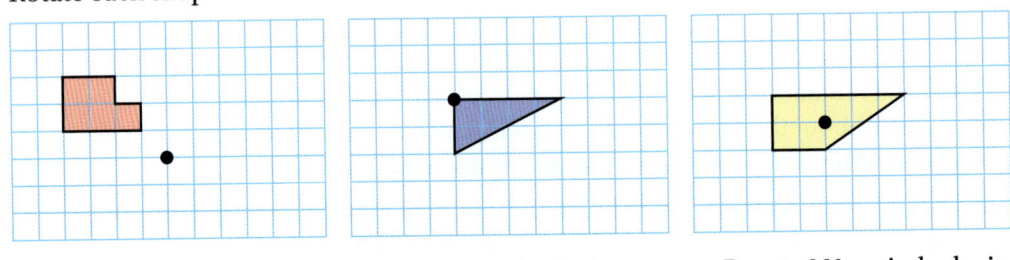

    a Rotate 180°.   **b** Rotate 90° clockwise.   **c** Rotate 90° anti-clockwise.

3 Rotate the triangle 180° about the origin.

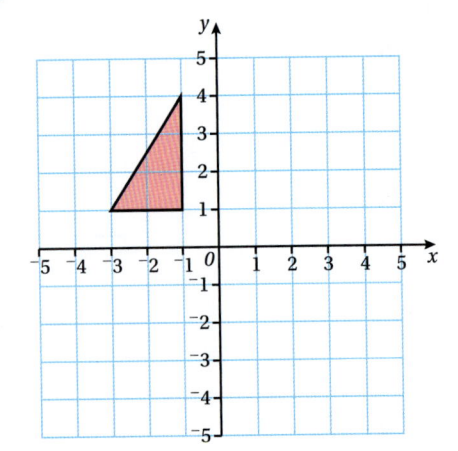

4 Rotate the shape 90° clockwise around the point (1, 1).

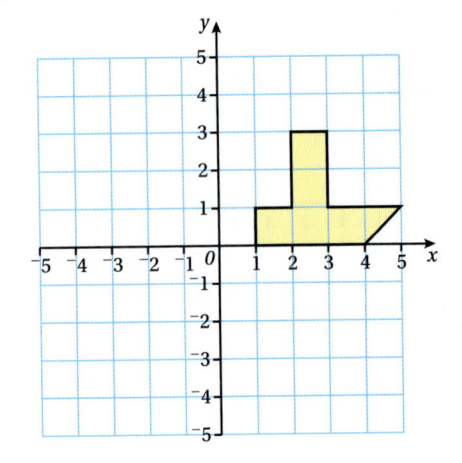

28 Plane isometric transformations

5 Rotate the shape 90° anti-clockwise around the point (−2, 1).

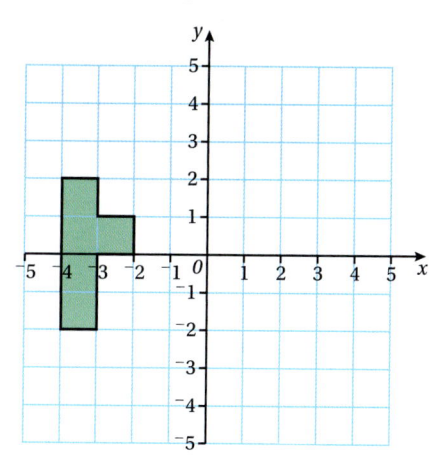

6 Rotate the shape 90°, anti-clockwise, around the point (2, 1).

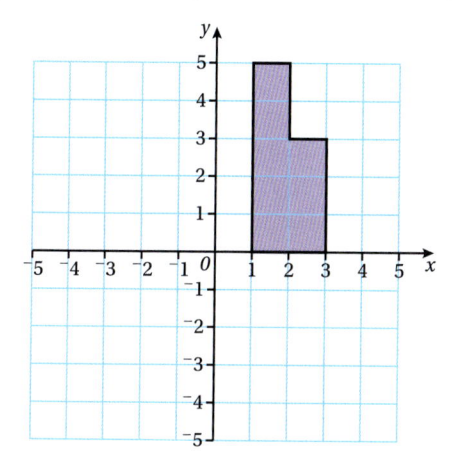

7 Rotate each shape as directed.
Shape **A**: 90° anti-clockwise around the point (−1, −1).
Shape **B**: 180° around the point (2, 3).
Shape **C**: 90° clockwise around the point (1, 0). Label this D.
Shape **D**: 180° around the point (−3.5, 2).
Shape **E**: 180° around the point (3, 1).

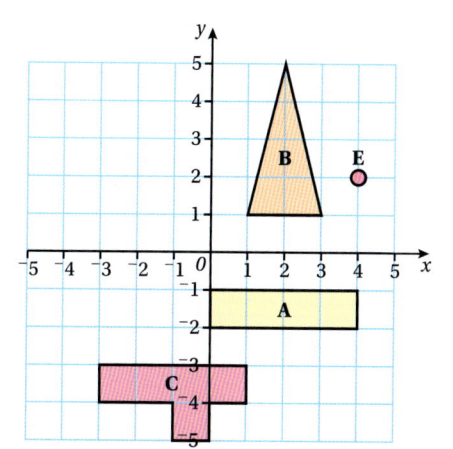

Find answers at: cambridge.org/ukschools/gcsemaths-studentbookanswers

GCSE Mathematics for OCR (Foundation)

8 The following image was designed by drawing a triangle and rotating this around the origin in multiples of 90°.

What do you notice about the coordinates of the vertices of the triangle? Would this work if you rotated an image around a different point? Why?

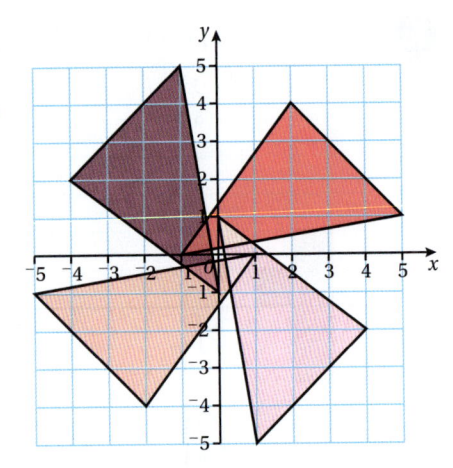

Describing rotations

To describe a rotation you give a centre, angle and direction. Very often you can find the centre using tracing paper and trial and error. Trace the object and rotate the tracing paper using different centres of rotation. Spotting the centres improves with practice.

Tip

Always give the direction and angle of the rotation from the object to the image.

WORK IT OUT 28.5

Which of these transformations are reflections, which are rotations and which are translations? How did you make your decision? Were there any transformations you couldn't identify?

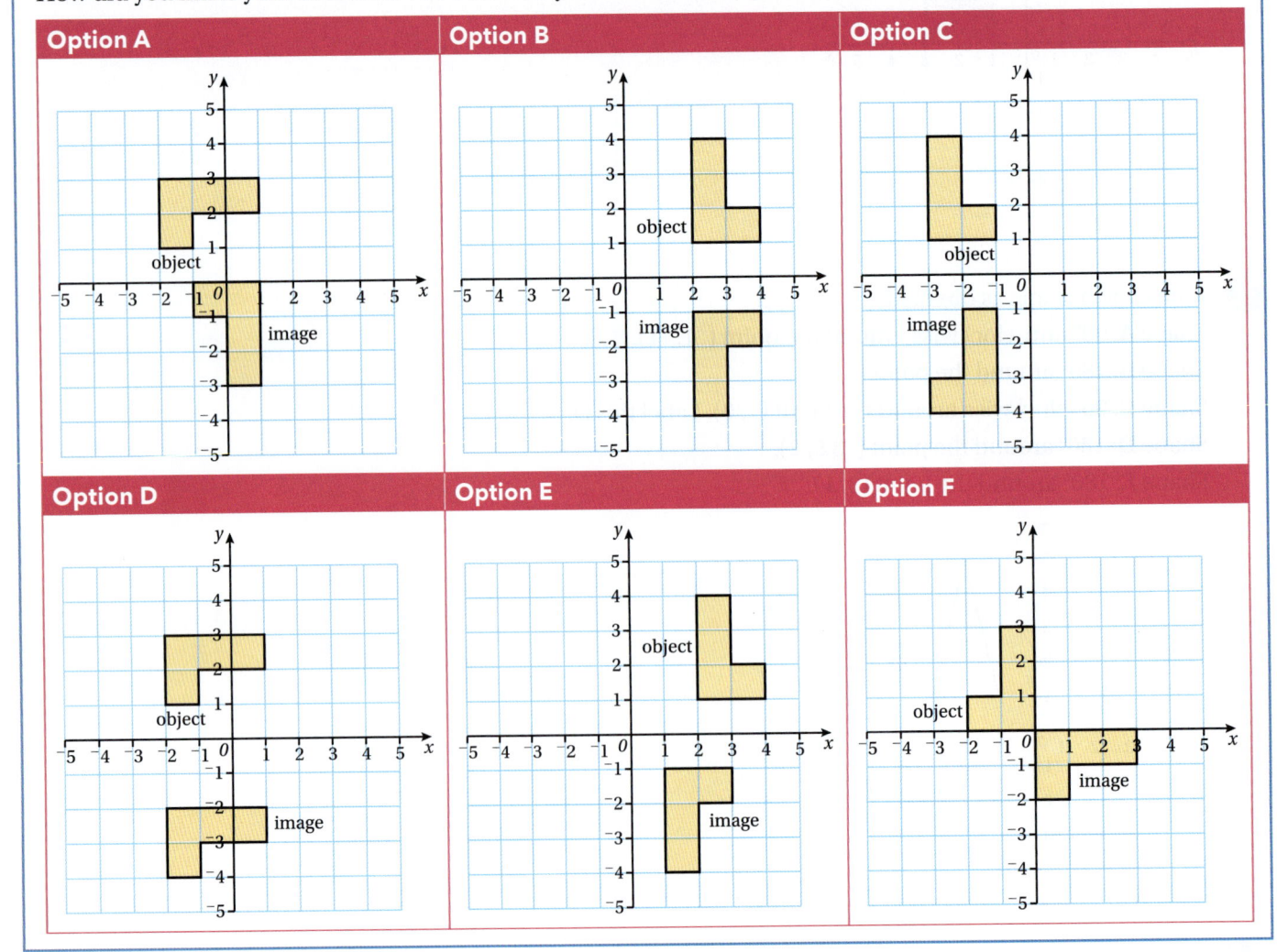

Option A

Option B

Option C

Option D

Option E

Option F

446

EXERCISE 28G

1 Describe each of the following rotations.

a, **b**, 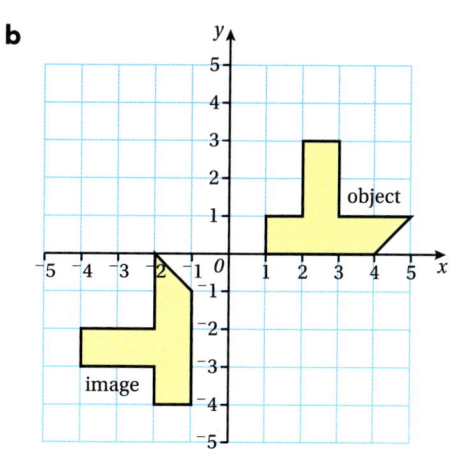 **c**, 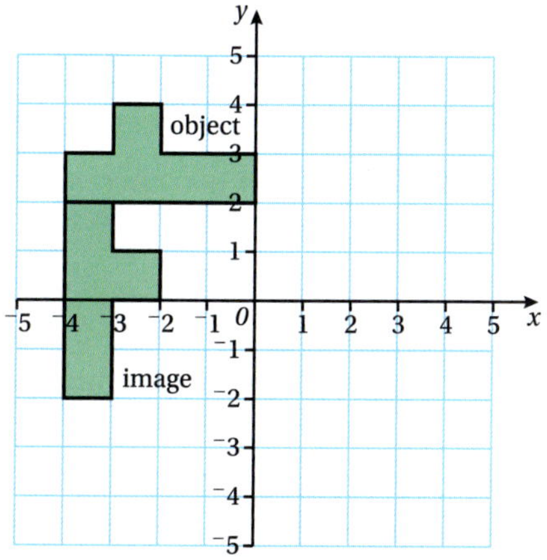 **d** (coordinate grid diagrams showing objects and images)

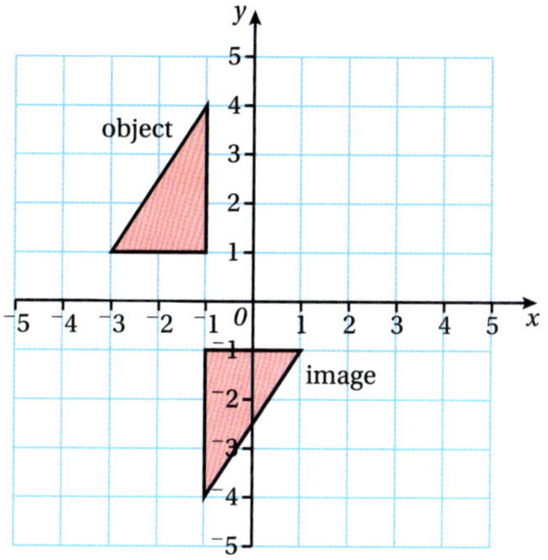

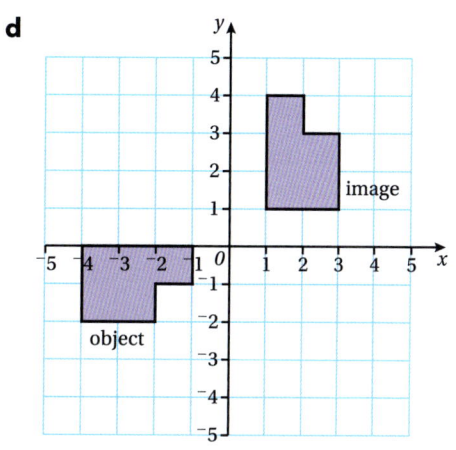

2 This section of wallpaper has been designed using rotations. A **coordinate** grid has been overlaid.

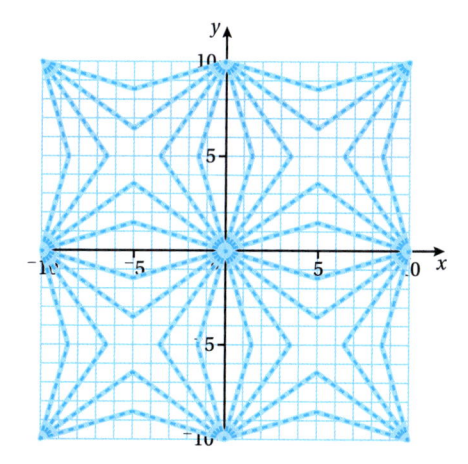

Identify as many different rotations as you can.

Find answers at: cambridge.org/ukschools/gcsemaths-studentbookanswers

Checklist of learning and understanding

Transformations

- A transformation is a change in the position of a point, line or shape. When you transform a shape you change its position or its size.
- The original point, line or shape is called the **object**. For example, the triangle ABC.
- The transformation is called the **image**. The symbol ′ is used to label the image. For example, the image of triangle ABC is A′B′C′.
- Different types of transformation include reflections, translations and rotations.

Reflections

- Reflections change the orientation of a shape but the image remains congruent.
- To describe a reflection the equation of the mirror line needs to be given.
- The mirror line is the perpendicular bisector of any two corresponding points on the image and object.

Translations

- Translations leave the orientation of the shape unchanged but move it horizontally and/or vertically.
- Translations are described using vectors.

Rotations

- A rotation is a turn around a centre. Rotations are described by giving the coordinates of the centre of rotation, angle and direction of the rotation.

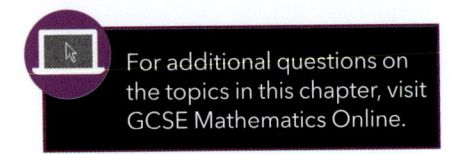

For additional questions on the topics in this chapter, visit GCSE Mathematics Online.

Chapter review

1 Which of the following statements are true? Explain your reasoning

a The images constructed by reflecting, rotating or translating are congruent to the objects you started with.

b The images constructed by reflecting, rotating or translating are similar to the objects you started with.

c The images constructed by reflecting, rotating or translating are in the same orientation to the objects you started with.

d The images constructed by reflecting, rotating or translating have the same angles as the objects you started with.

28 Plane isometric transformations

2 Describe fully the transformation from:
   a shape **A** to shape **B**.
   b shape **B** to shape **C**.
   c shape **C** to shape **A**.

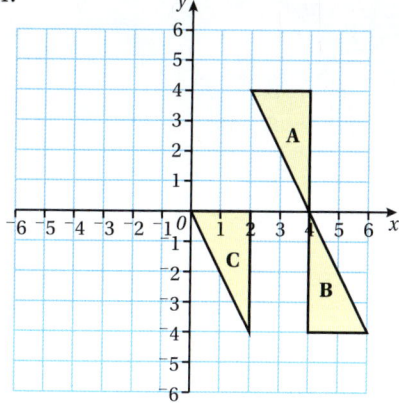

3 This triangle is used to create a tessellating pattern. This is produced using multiple translations and one rotation. Explain how this could be done.

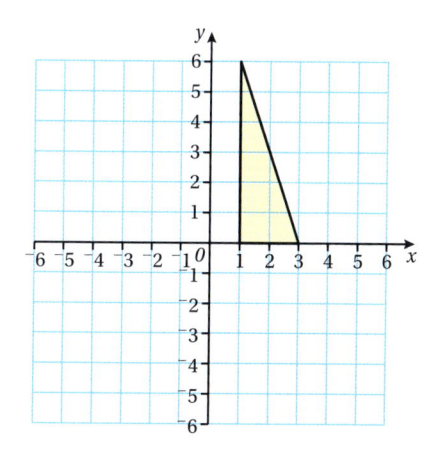

> **Tip**
>
> Tessellation is a pattern of shapes that fit together perfectly, with no gaps or overlaps.

4 Rotate shape **A** 90° clockwise around the point (1, 2). Label it **B**.

Reflect shape **B** in the line $y = x$. Label it **C**.

Translate shape **C** through the vector $\begin{pmatrix} -1 \\ 1 \end{pmatrix}$. Label it **D**.

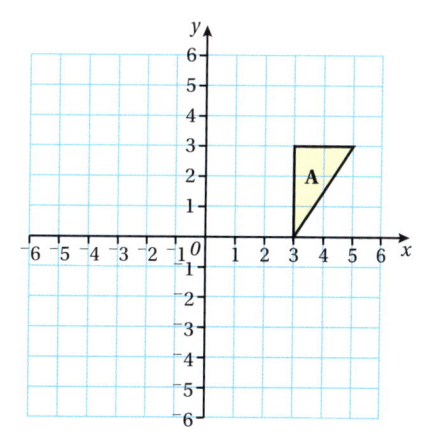

5 Look at the dancing figure. Describe how the figure can be drawn using only transformations of shapes **A**, **B**, **C** and **D**.

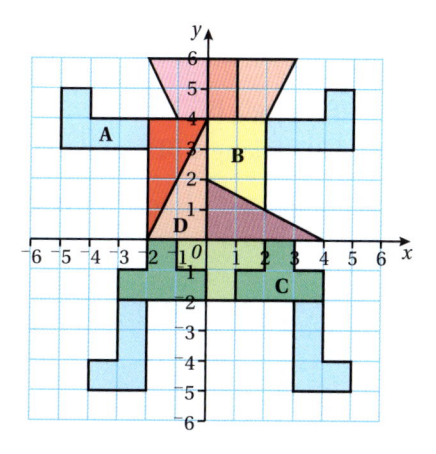

Find answers at: cambridge.org/ukschools/gcsemaths-studentbookanswers

29 Congruent triangles

In this chapter you will learn how to ...
- prove that two triangles are congruent using the cases SSS, ASA, SAS, RHS.
- apply congruency in calculations and simple proofs.

For more resources relating to this chapter, visit GCSE Mathematics Online.

Using mathematics: real-life applications

Congruent triangles are used in construction to reinforce structures that need to be strong and stable.

"When designing any bridge I have to allow for reinforcement. This ensures that the bridge doesn't collapse under heavy traffic. Any bridge I design has many congruent triangles." (Structural engineer)

Before you start ...

Ch 5	You need to know how to label angles and shapes that are equal.	**1** Here are two identical triangles. a Write down a pair of sides that are equal in length. b What angle is equal in size to angle BAC? c Write down another pair of angles that are equal in size.	
Ch 9	You need to know basic angle facts.	**2** Match up the correct statement with the correct diagram. a Vertically opposite angles are equal. b Alternate angles are equal. c Corresponding angles are equal.	
Ch 5, 9	You should be able to apply angle facts to find angles in figures and to justify results in simple proofs.	**3** Decide whether each statement is true or false. a Angle DBE = 40° (alternate to angle ADB). b Angle BEC = 50° (complementary to angle ADB). c Angle BDE = angle BED = 70°. d Triangle ABD, triangle BDE and triangle BCE are congruent.	
Ch 5	You need to know and be able to apply the properties of triangles and quadrilaterals.	**4** What is the value of x? Choose the correct answer. A 60° B 30° C 45° D 50°	

450

29 Congruent triangles

Assess your starting point using the Launchpad

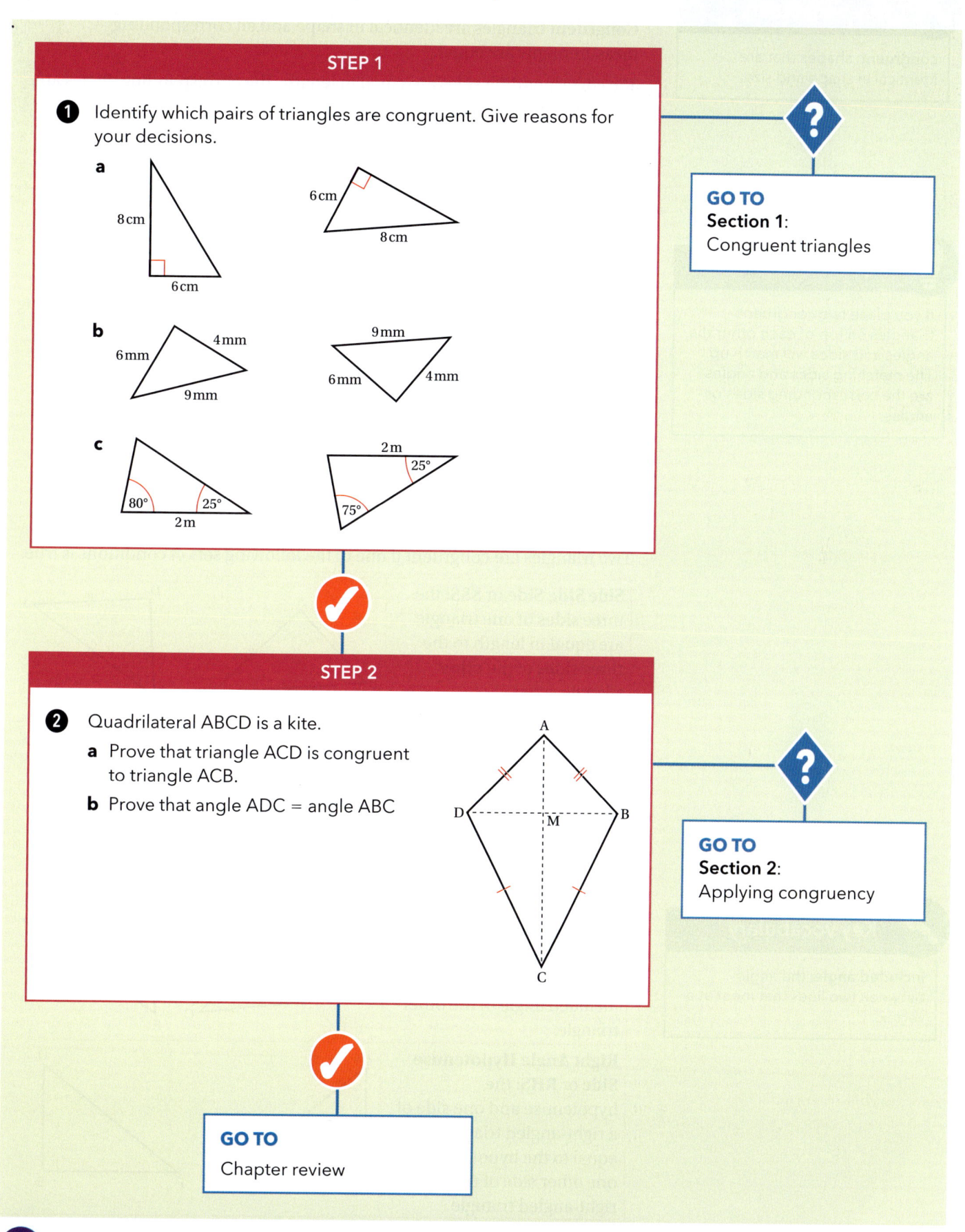

STEP 1

1 Identify which pairs of triangles are congruent. Give reasons for your decisions.

a Triangle with sides 8 cm, 6 cm and right angle; triangle with sides 6 cm, 8 cm and right angle.

b Triangle with sides 6 mm, 4 mm, 9 mm; triangle with sides 9 mm, 4 mm, 6 mm.

c Triangle with angles 80°, 25° and side 2 m; triangle with angles 25°, 75° and side 2 m.

GO TO
Section 1: Congruent triangles

STEP 2

2 Quadrilateral ABCD is a kite.
  a Prove that triangle ACD is congruent to triangle ACB.
  b Prove that angle ADC = angle ABC

GO TO
Section 2: Applying congruency

GO TO
Chapter review

Find answers at: cambridge.org/ukschools/gcsemaths-studentbookanswers

451

GCSE Mathematics for OCR (Foundation)

Key vocabulary

congruent: shapes that are identical in shape and size.

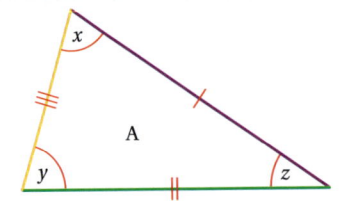

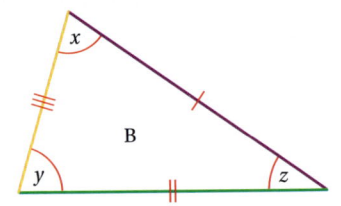

Tip

If you place two congruent triangles on top of each other the angles and sides will match up. The matching sides and angles are the corresponding sides or angles.

Section 1: Congruent triangles

Congruent triangles are identical in shape and all corresponding measurements are equal.

The corresponding sides are equal in length. The corresponding angles are the same size.

Congruent triangles can have different orientations. When the triangles are in different orientations you need to think carefully about the corresponding sides and angles.

This diagram shows triangle A and B from the example above in different orientations.

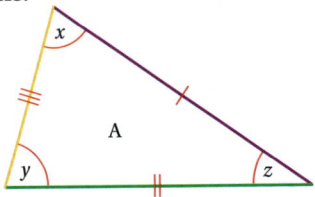

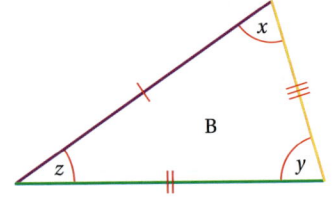

Two triangles are congruent if one of the following sets of conditions is true.

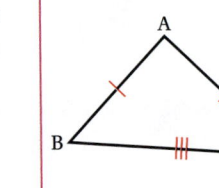

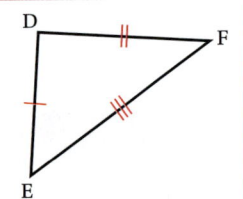

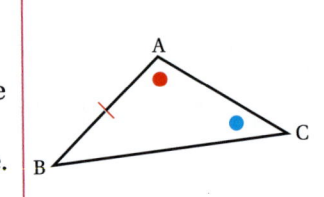

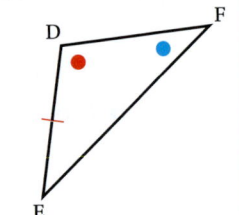

Side Side Side or **SSS**: the three sides of one triangle are equal in length to the three sides of the other triangle.	
Angle Side Angle or **ASA**: two angles and one side of one triangle are equal to the corresponding two angles and side of another triangle.	
Side Angle Side or **SAS**: two sides and the **included angle** of one triangle are equal to two sides and the included angle of the other triangle.	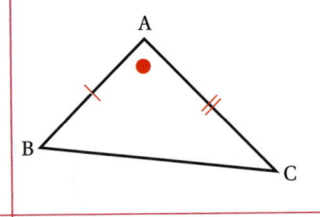
Right Angle Hypotenuse Side or **RHS**: the hypotenuse and one side of a right-angled triangle are equal to the hypotenuse and one other side of the other right-angled triangle.	

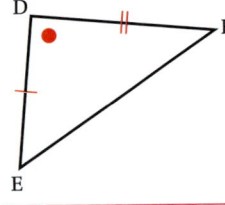

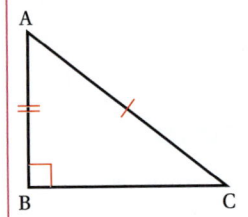

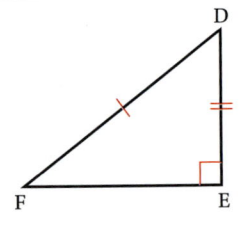

Key vocabulary

included angle: the angle between two lines that meet at a vertex.

29 Congruent triangles

> **Tip**
>
> It is important to write the letters of the vertices of the two triangles in the correct order. When we write that triangle ABC is congruent to triangle DEF, it means that:
> $\hat{A} = \hat{D}$
> $\hat{B} = \hat{E}$
> $\hat{C} = \hat{F}$
> and
> AB = DE
> AC = DF and
> BC = EF.

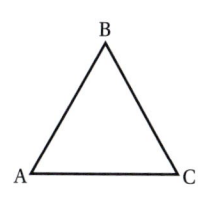

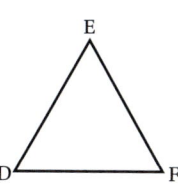

The conditions in the table are the minimum conditions for proving that triangles are congruent. No other combinations of side and angle facts are sufficient to tell us whether a triangle is congruent or not.

For example:

Two triangles with all their angles equal can still be very different sizes.

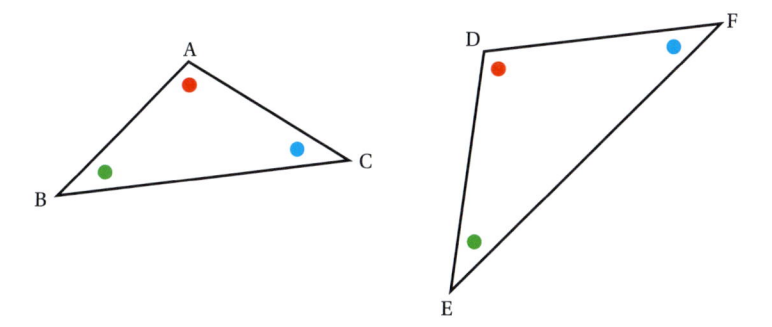

If you are given two triangles that have two equal sides and one equal angle, but where the equal angle is not included (between the two given sides), you do not know if the triangles are congruent or not. The third side might have a different length in the two triangles.

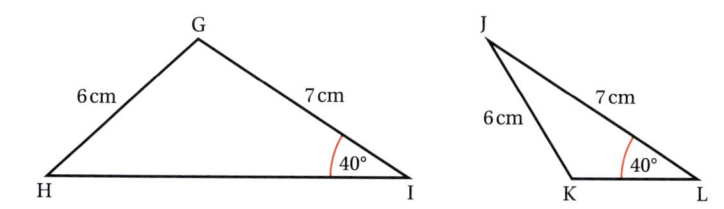

Although a pair of triangles with one of these sets of information could still be congruent, the conditions given are not sufficient to **prove** that they are.

> **Tip**
>
> If two congruent shapes are drawn in different orientations it is sometimes hard to see which angles and sides match each other. To help you, trace one shape onto tracing paper and label its vertices, then rotate and/or flip the paper over to help see which sides and angles match up.

Find answers at: cambridge.org/ukschools/gcsemaths-studentbookanswers

GCSE Mathematics for OCR (Foundation)

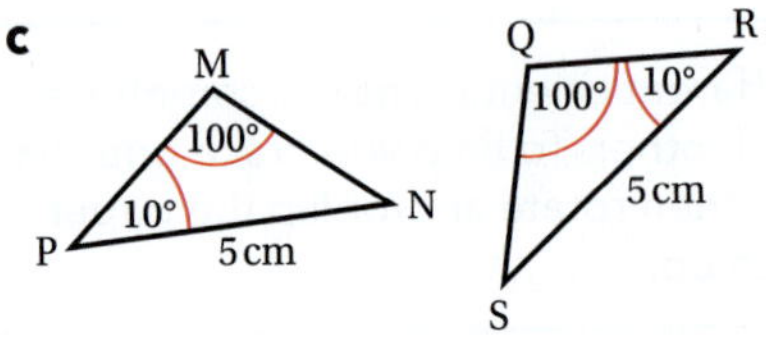

WORK IT OUT 29.1

Here are three proofs for congruence for the pair of triangles.

Which one uses the correct reasoning?

Why are the others incorrect?

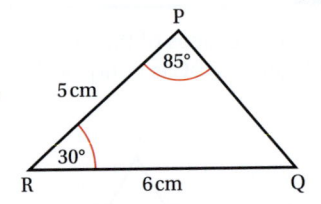

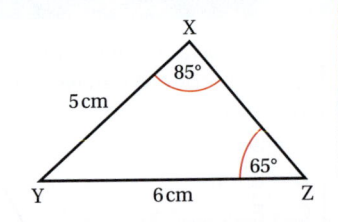

Option A	Option B	Option C
In triangle PQR and triangle XYZ: PR = XY = 5 cm angle P = angle X = 85° RQ = YZ = 6 cm so triangle PQR is congruent to triangle XYZ (SAS).	In triangle PRQ and triangle XYZ: In triangle PRQ, angle Q = 65° (sum of angles in a triangle) angle Q = angle Z = 65° RQ = YZ so the triangles are congruent.	In triangle PRQ and triangle XYZ: PR = XY = 5 cm RQ = YZ = 6 cm In triangle XYZ, angle Y = 30° (sum of angles in a triangle) so triangle PRQ is congruent to triangle XYZ (SAS).

EXERCISE 29A

1. Match up each of the congruency descriptions (SSS, ASA, SAS, RHS) with each pair of triangles below:

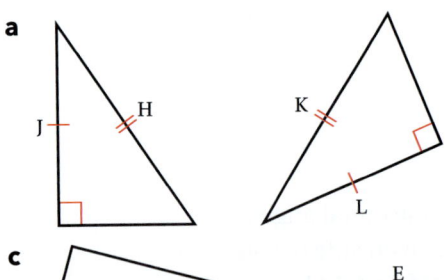

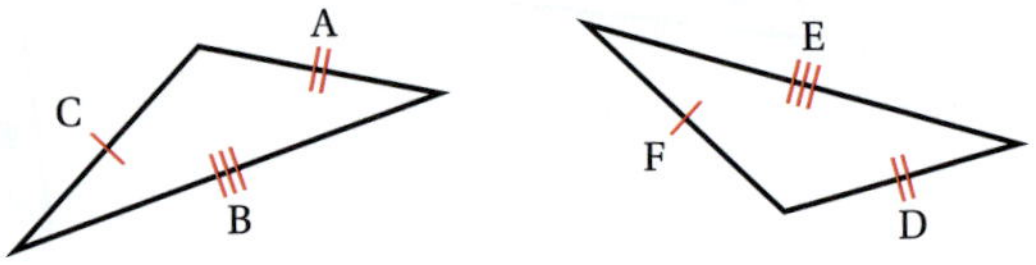

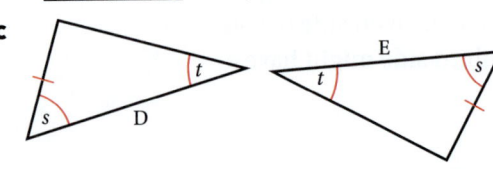

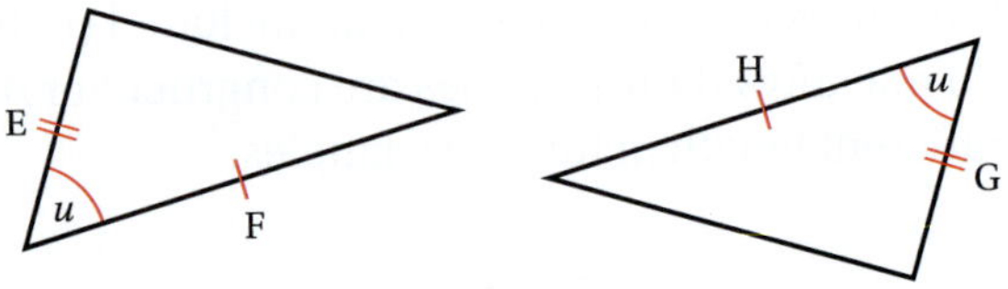

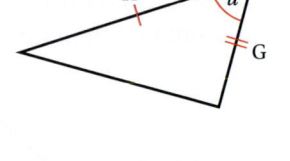

2. Which of the following figures show a pair of congruent triangles? In your answer, state whether the triangles are congruent or not, or whether there is insufficient information. Write the triangles with the vertices in the correct order and give the reasons as SSS, SAS, ASA or RHS.

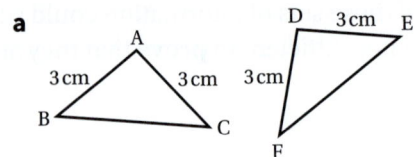

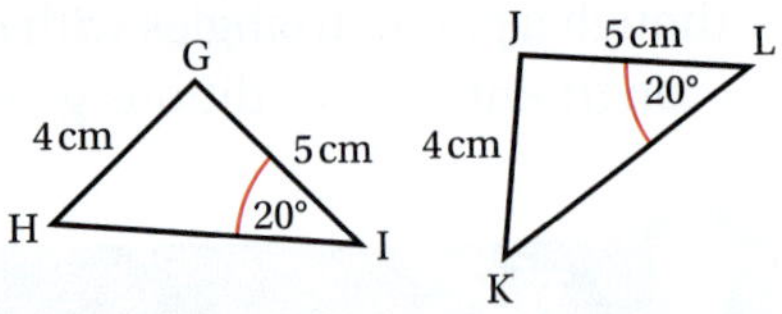

454

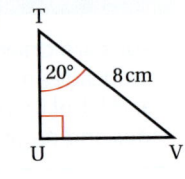

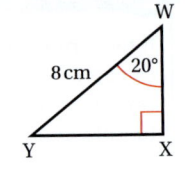

3 Prove that triangle ABC is congruent to triangle DEC.

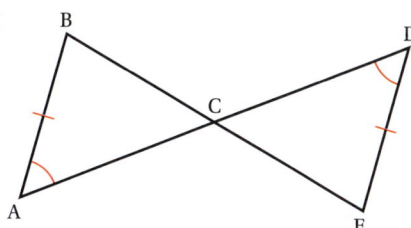

4 Write down two different proofs for congruence of triangles DEF and DGF.

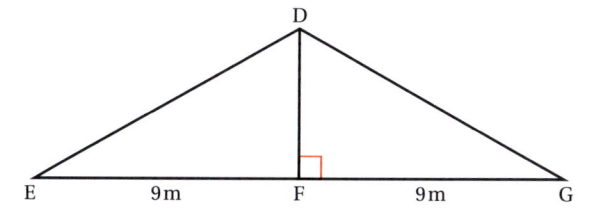

5 In the diagram, PQ is parallel to SR and QT = TR = 2 cm.

Prove that triangle PQT is congruent to triangle SRT.

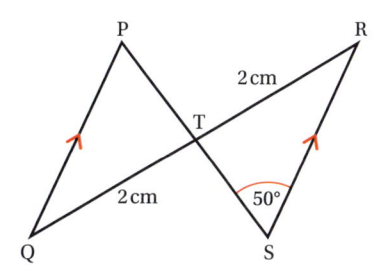

6 Prove that triangles ABE and CBD in the figure are congruent, giving full reasons.

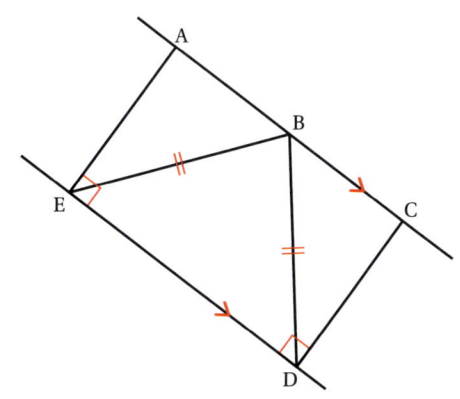

7 Triangle ABD is isosceles. AC is the perpendicular height. Prove that triangle ABC is congruent to triangle ADC.

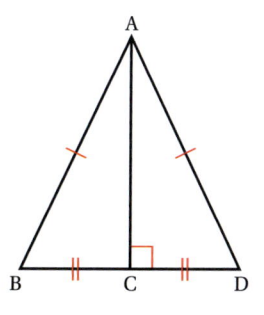

Tip

What do we know about line AC in an isosceles triangle?

Find answers at: cambridge.org/ukschools/gcsemaths-studentbookanswers

8 In the figure below, PR = SU and RTUQ is a kite.

Prove that triangle PQR is congruent to triangle SQU.

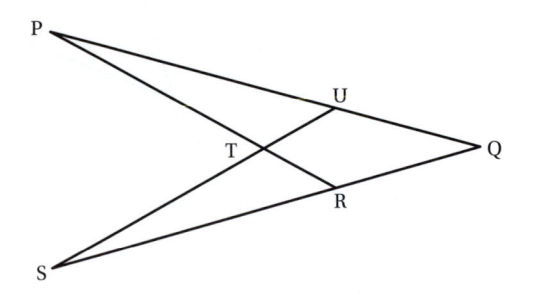

9 ABCD in the figure is a kite.

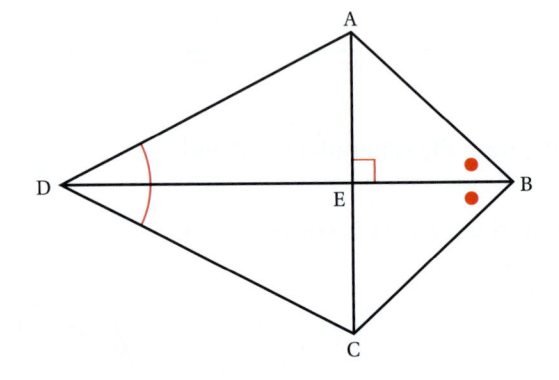

Prove that:

a triangle ADB is congruent to triangle CDB.

b triangle AED is congruent to triangle CED.

10 Quadrilateral ABCD is a rhombus.

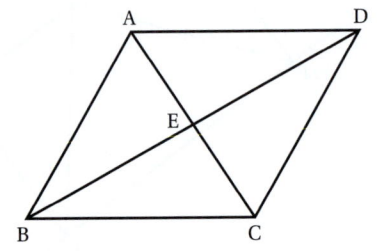

Prove that:

a triangle AED is congruent to triangle CEB.

b triangle AEB is congruent to triangle CED.

Section 2: Applying congruency

Whenever you learn new skills and concepts in geometry, you add them to your toolbox and use them in problem-solving. So you will need to combine what you've learnt previously with your new skills to solve problems.

The steps in the following framework are useful for solving geometry problems.

29 Congruent triangles

Problem-solving framework

In the diagram, AM = BM and PM = QM.

a Prove that triangle AMP is congruent to triangle BMQ.

b Prove that AP // QB.

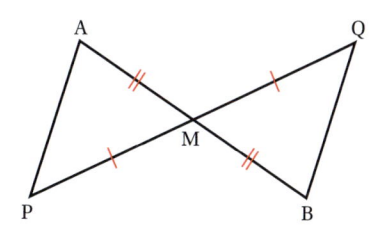

> **Tip**
>
> You saw in Chapter 5 that the symbol // means 'is parallel to'.

Steps for approaching a problem-solving question	What you would do for this example
Step 1: Read the question carefully to decide what you have to find.	Find mathematical evidence to show that the triangle AMP is congruent to triangle BMQ; look for SSS, SAS, RHS or ASA. Find evidence to show that lines AP and QB are parallel.
Step 2: Write down any further information that might be useful.	Lines AB and PQ intersect, so the two triangles also have vertically opposite angles. Vertically opposite angles are equal (see Chapter 9 if you need to).
Step 3: Decide what method you'll use.	We are given two equal sides and we can see that the included angle is also equal, so use SAS to prove congruence.
Step 4: Set out your working clearly.	a In triangles AMP and BMQ: AM = BM (given). PM = QM (given). angle AMP = angle BMQ (vertically opposite angles at M). So triangle AMP is congruent to triangle BMQ (SAS). b Angle APM = BQM (matching angles of congruent triangles). So AP // QB (alternate angles are equal).

WORKED EXAMPLE 1

Triangle DEF is divided by GF into two smaller triangles.

Prove that FG is perpendicular to DE in the diagram.

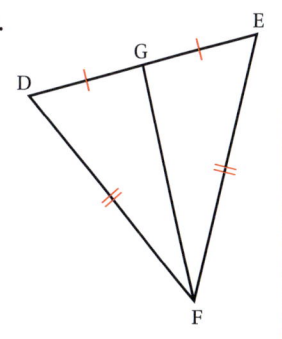

In triangle FGD and triangle FGE:

Side FG is common to both triangles.

DG = EG (given)

DF = EF (given)

So the triangles are congruent (SSS).

Angle DGF = angle EGF and the two angles lie on a straight line (angles on a straight line add up to 180°).

So each angle = 90°, and FG is perpendicular to DE.

Find answers at: cambridge.org/ukschools/gcsemaths-studentbookanswers

EXERCISE 29B

1 In the diagram, prove that KL = ML.

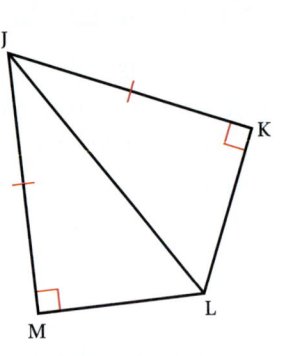

2 Use the facts given in the diagram to:

　a prove that angle ABE = angle EDC.

　b prove that quadrilateral ABCD is a parallelogram.

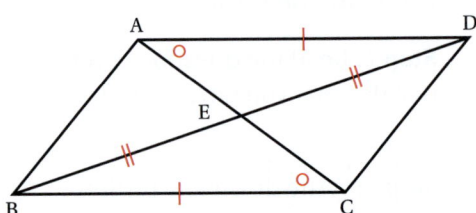

3 In the quadrilateral, SP = SR and QP // RS. Angle QRP = 56°.

　a Calculate the size of angle PQR and give reasons.

　b Find the size of angle PSR and give reasons.

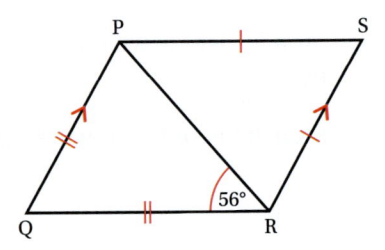

4 In the diagram, PQ = PT, QR = ST and angle PQR = angle PTS. Prove that triangle PRS is isosceles.

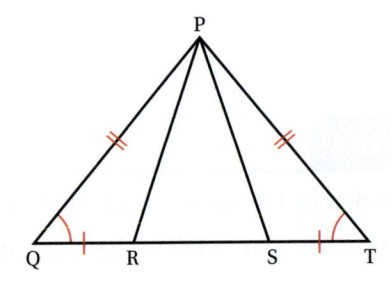

5 In the figure below, prove that:

　a triangle AEB is congruent to triangle CEB.

　b angle EAD = angle ECD.

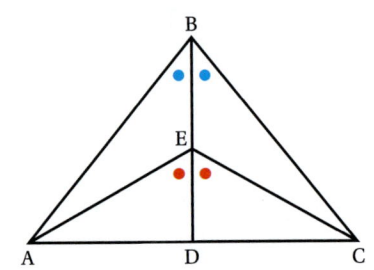

6 In quadrilateral ABCD, AD = BC and AD // BC.

Prove that angle ABC = angle ADC.

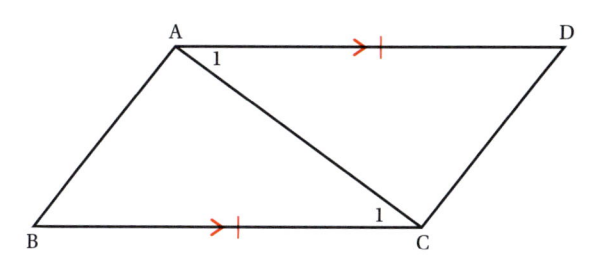

Checklist of learning and understanding

Congruent triangles

- You can prove that two triangles are congruent using one of the four cases of congruence:
  - Side Side Side or SSS: the three sides of one triangle are equal in length to the three sides of the other triangle.
  - Angle Side Angle or ASA: two angles and one side of one triangle are equal to the corresponding two angles and side of another triangle.
  - Side Angle Side or SAS: two sides and the included angle of one triangle are equal to two sides and the included angle of the other triangle.
  - Right Angle Hypotenuse Side or RHS: the hypotenuse and one side of a right-angled triangle are equal to the hypotenuse and one other side of the other right-angled triangle.
- You can apply your knowledge of congruency to help prove other geometrical features such as parallel and perpendicular lines.

Chapter review

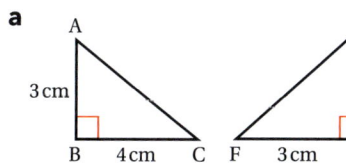

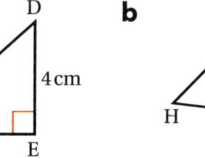

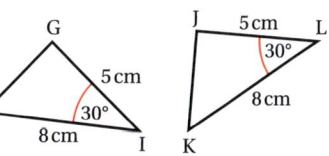

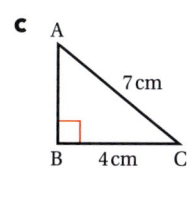

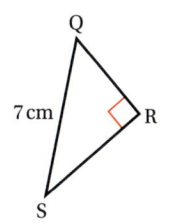

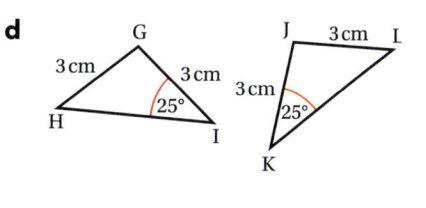

For additional questions on the topics in this chapter, visit GCSE Mathematics Online.

1 State whether each pair of triangles is congruent or not. Give a reason for your answer and give the vertices of the triangles in the correct order.

a, **b**, **c**, **d**

Find answers at: cambridge.org/ukschools/gcsemaths-studentbookanswers

2. In the figure below, prove that angle T = angle R.

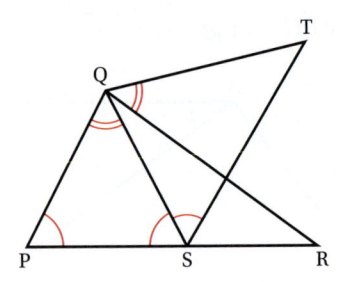

3. Show that angle EBC = angle ECB in the figure below.

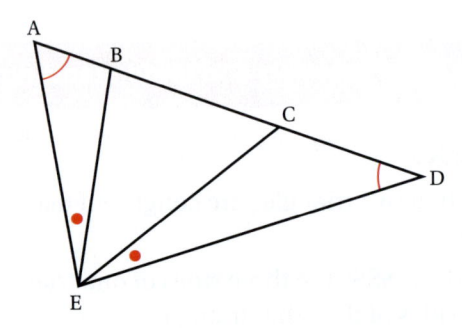

4. In the figure below, triangle ABD lies between two parallel lines. BC = CA = AD. Prove that angle EAD = 2 × angle ABC.

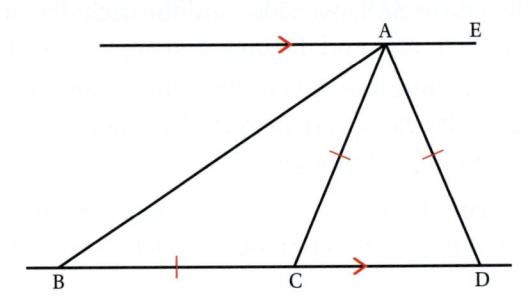

5. Prove that WX = XV in the diagram.

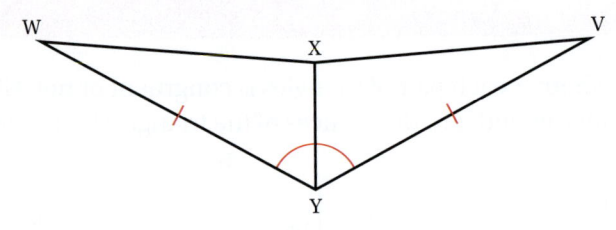

30 Similarity

In this chapter you will learn how to ...
- identify similar triangles and prove that two triangles are similar.
- work with positive and fractional scale factors to enlarge shapes on a grid.
- find the scale factor and centre of enlargement of a transformation.
- apply the concept of similarity to calculate unknown lengths.

For more resources relating to this chapter, visit GCSE Mathematics Online.

Using mathematics: real-life applications

When you enlarge a photo, project an image onto a screen or make scaled models you are dealing with similarity. Many toys and other objects are scaled, similar, versions of larger objects from real life.

"I work with scale drawings and scale models all the time. The models are mathematically similar to the real planes so the clients can see what they are buying. We made these scaled models to display at an international air show." *(Aircraft designer)*

Before you start ...

Ch 9	You need to be able to label angles correctly.	**1**	**a** Which angle is a right angle? **b** What size is angle DOA? **c** What size is angle BOD?
Ch 29	You need to be able to prove that two triangles are congruent.	**2**	Prove that the triangles below are congruent, giving reasons.
Ch 8	You need to know how to solve simple equations using inverse operations.	**3**	Solve **a** $3x = 24$ **b** $15 = 6h$ **c** $6.25 = 25k$
Ch 22	You need to be able to recognise numbers in equivalent ratios.	**4**	Which pair of numbers is in the same ratio as $3:2$? A $6:5$ B $4:6$ C $0.15:0.1$
		5	Given that $\dfrac{4}{15} = \dfrac{x}{90}$, find x.

Find answers at: cambridge.org/ukschools/gcsemaths-studentbookanswers

GCSE Mathematics for OCR (Foundation)

Assess your starting point using the Launchpad

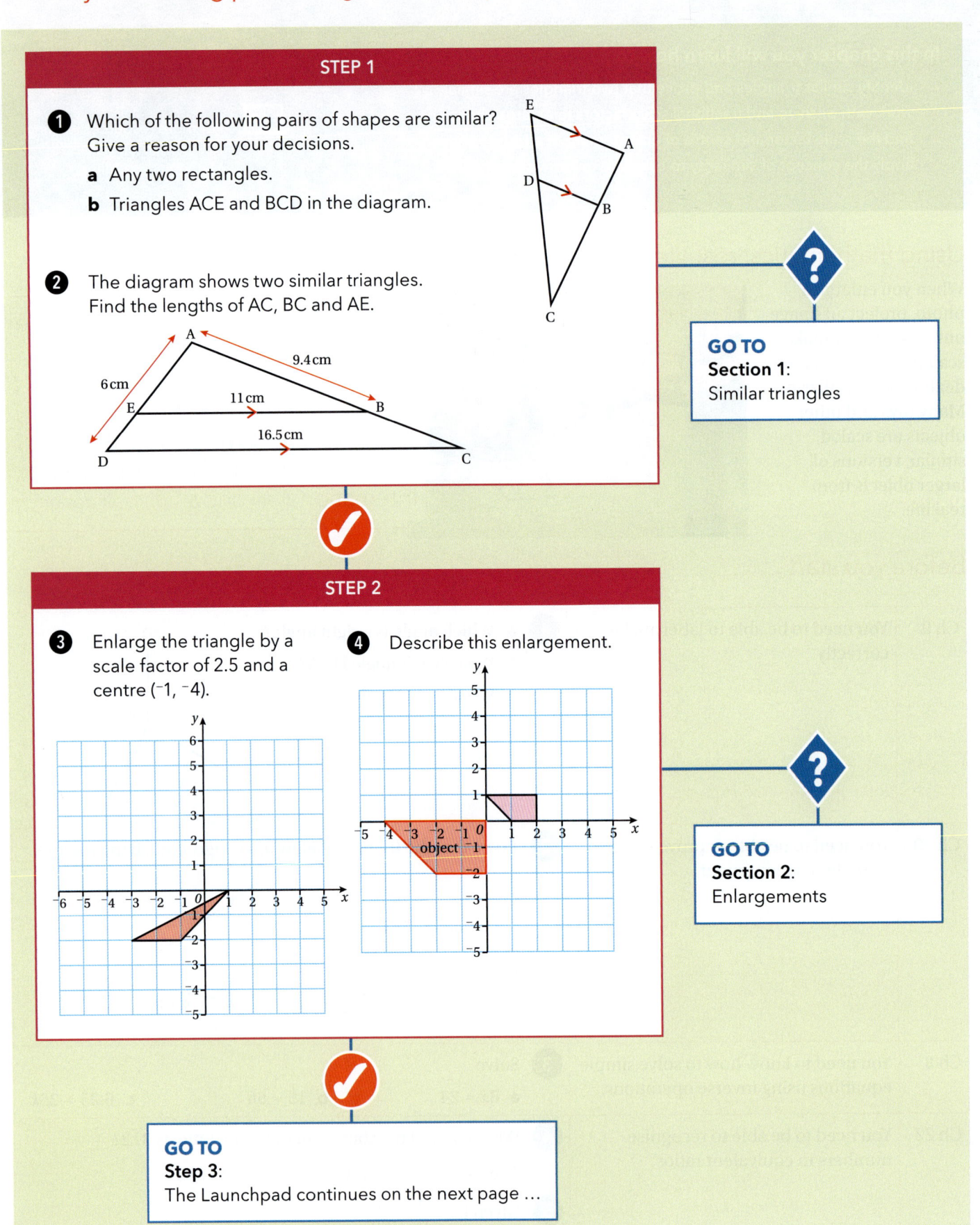

STEP 1

1 Which of the following pairs of shapes are similar? Give a reason for your decisions.

   a Any two rectangles.

   b Triangles ACE and BCD in the diagram.

2 The diagram shows two similar triangles. Find the lengths of AC, BC and AE.

GO TO Section 1: Similar triangles

STEP 2

3 Enlarge the triangle by a scale factor of 2.5 and a centre (−1, −4).

4 Describe this enlargement.

GO TO Section 2: Enlargements

GO TO Step 3: The Launchpad continues on the next page …

462

30 Similarity

Launchpad continued ...

STEP 3

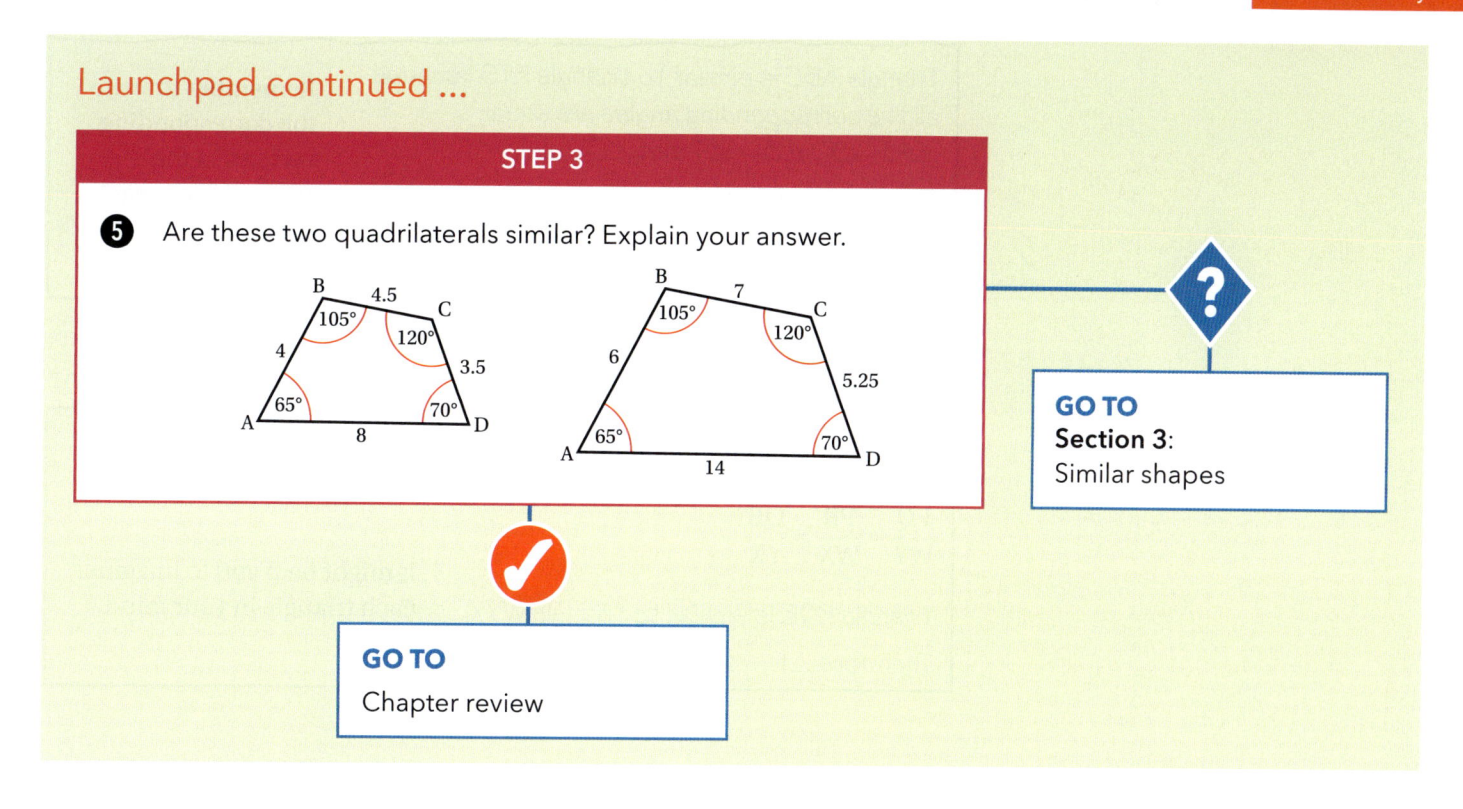

5 Are these two quadrilaterals similar? Explain your answer.

[Two quadrilaterals ABCD shown:
First: AB = 4, BC = 4.5, CD = 3.5, AD = 8; angles B = 105°, C = 120°, A = 65°, D = 70°
Second: AB = 6, BC = 7, CD = 5.25, AD = 14; angles B = 105°, C = 120°, A = 65°, D = 70°]

GO TO Section 3: Similar shapes

GO TO Chapter review

Section 1: Similar triangles

Two shapes are mathematically similar if they have the same shape and proportions but are different in size.

If the corresponding angles in two triangles are equal, then the corresponding sides will be in proportion, and the triangles will be similar.

To prove that two triangles are similar, we have to show that one of these statements is true:

- All the corresponding angles are equal.
- The three sides are in the same proportion.
- Two sides are in proportion and the included angles (between these two sides) are equal.

You must name triangles with the corresponding vertices in the correct order when you state facts about similarity.

WORKED EXAMPLE 1

Prove that the triangles ABC and RTS are similar.

Say which angles are equal and which sides are in proportion.

[Two triangles shown: triangle ABC with angle markers (dot at A, star at B, tick at C) and triangle RTS with corresponding markers (dot at R, tick at S, star at T)]

Continues on next page ...

Find answers at: cambridge.org/ukschools/gcsemaths-studentbookanswers

463

Triangle ABC is similar to triangle RTS because all the corresponding angles are equal:
$\angle A = \angle R$, $\angle B = \angle T$ and $\angle C = \angle S$.
This means that the three sides are in the same proportion, so $\frac{AB}{RT} = \frac{AC}{RS} = \frac{BC}{TS}$

> Remember to write the corresponding vertices in the same order in each triangle.

WORKED EXAMPLE 2

Given that the following relationship exists between the sides of triangle PQR and triangle WYX, write down which angles are equal.

$$\frac{PQ}{WY} = \frac{PR}{WX} = \frac{QR}{YX}$$

Triangle PQR is similar to triangle WYX.

Therefore $\angle P = \angle W$; $\angle Q = \angle Y$ and $\angle R = \angle X$.

> It might help you to imagine each triangle in your mind.

Finding unknown lengths using proportional sides

In similar triangles the ratio of the lengths of any pair of corresponding sides is equal. You can therefore use the ratio of corresponding sides to find the lengths of unknown sides in similar figures.

Problem-solving framework

In the figure, triangle ABC is similar to triangle QRP. Find the length of x.

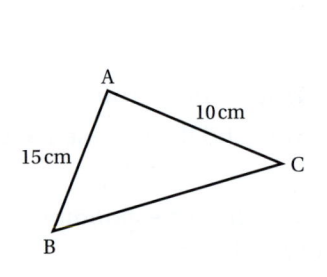

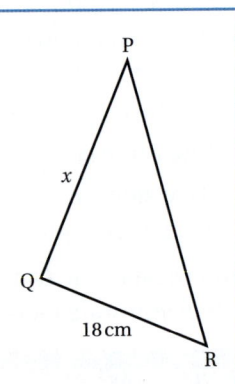

Steps for approaching a problem-solving question	What you would do for this example
Step 1: What do you have to do?	Use the fact that two triangles are similar to calculate an unknown length in one of the triangles.
Step 2: Write down what you know.	That the triangles are similar. Check that the vertices are written in the correct order: ABC is similar to QRP. You know the length of two sides of triangle ABC and one side of triangle QRP.

Continues on next page ...

Step 3: What maths can you do?	Find the ratio between the sides: AB corresponds to QR so the ratio is 15 : 18. AC corresponds to QP so $\frac{AC}{QP} = \frac{AB}{QR}$ Write a proportion with the unknown side. $\frac{10}{x} = \frac{AB}{QR}$ so $\frac{10}{x} = \frac{15}{18}$ Solve for x $x = \frac{18 \times 10}{15} = 12$ cm $x = 12$ cm
Step 4: Have you answered the question?	Yes, you have used the principle of similarity between the two triangles to find the unknown length.

EXERCISE 30A

1 Each diagram below contains a pair of similar triangles.
Identify the matching angles and the sides that are in proportion.
Explain your reasoning using the correct angle vocabulary.

a, b, 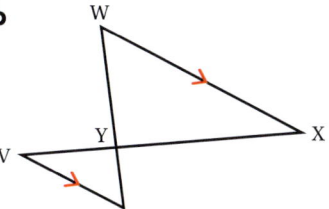 c, 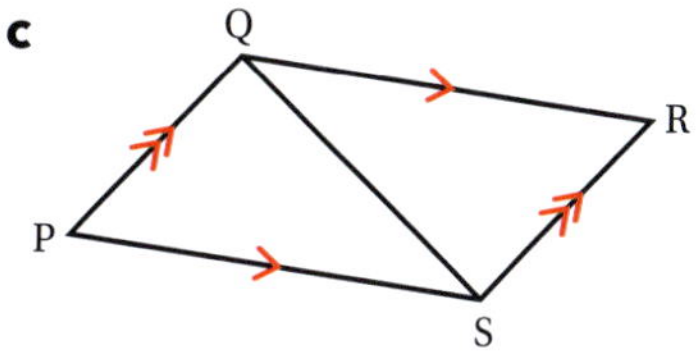 d

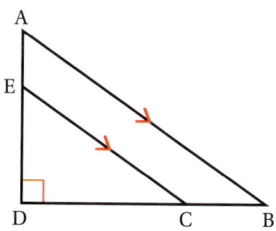

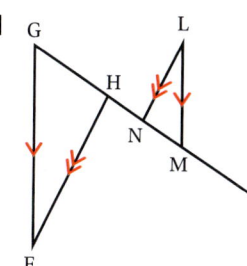

2 Are the following pairs of triangles similar? Explain your answers.

a

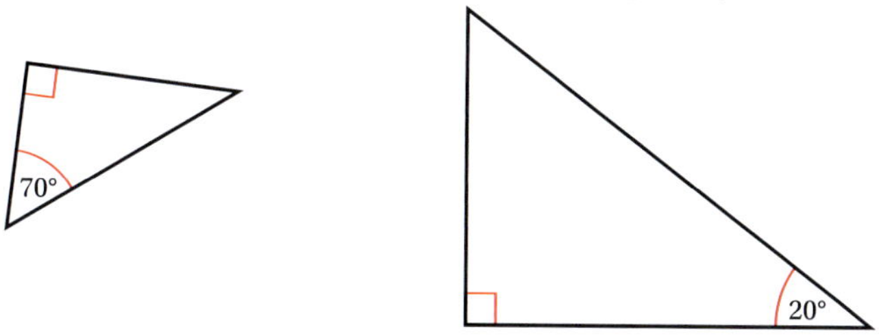

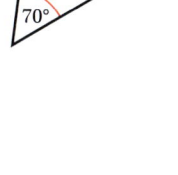

b

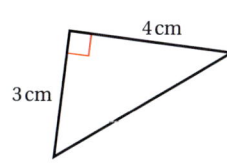

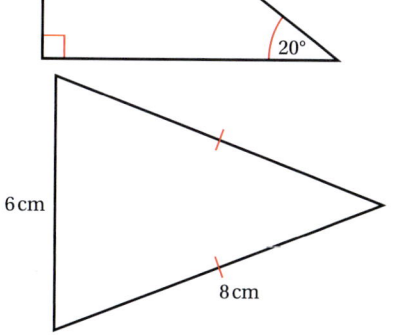

c

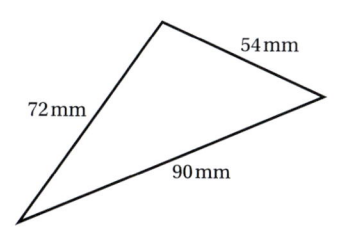

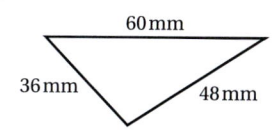

3. Are the statements below true or false? Explain your reasoning, give a counter-example for any statement you believe is false.
   a. All isosceles triangles are similar.
   b. All equilateral triangles are similar.
   c. All right-angled triangles are similar.
   d. All right-angled triangles with an angle of 30° are similar.
   e. All right-angled isosceles triangles are similar.
   f. No two scalene triangles are ever similar.

4. Each diagram below contains three similar triangles. Identify the matching angles and sides in each group of triangles, explaining your reasoning.
   a. 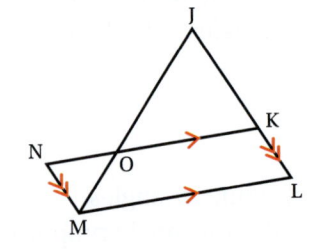
   b.

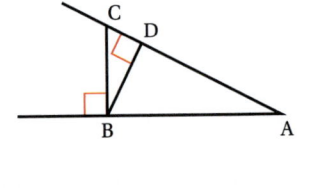

5. The two shapes below are similar. Find the missing lengths c and d.

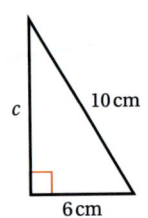

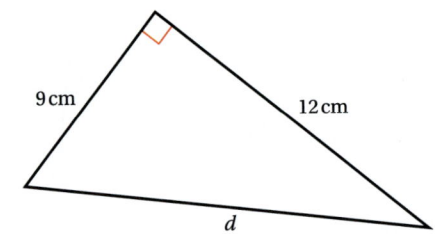

6. The two shapes below are similar. Find the missing lengths e and f.

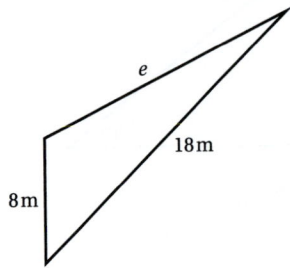

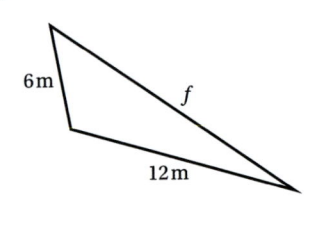

7. Find the lengths of AE, CE and AD.

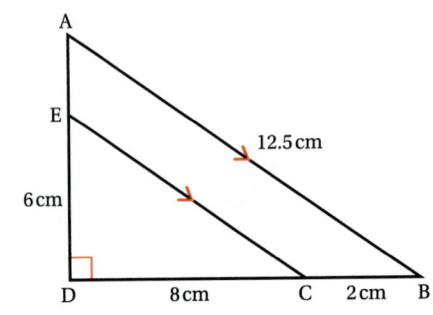

8 Find the lengths of YZ and XY.

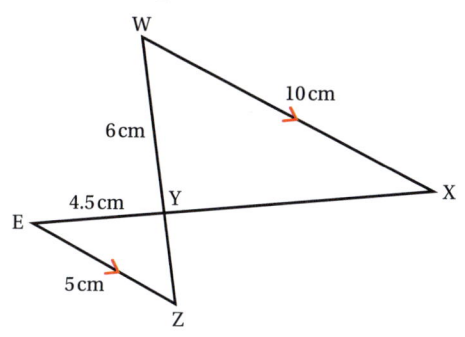

9 Arrange the lengths in the correct positions to label the sides of the similar shapes.

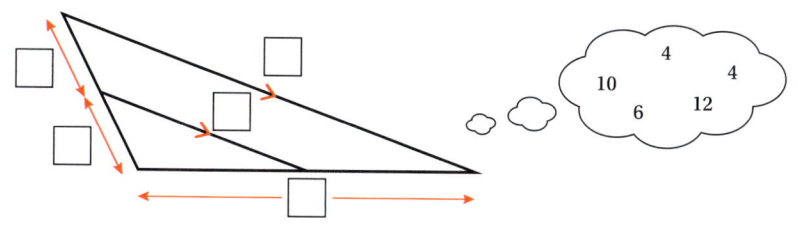

10 Arrange the lengths in the correct positions to complete the similar shapes.

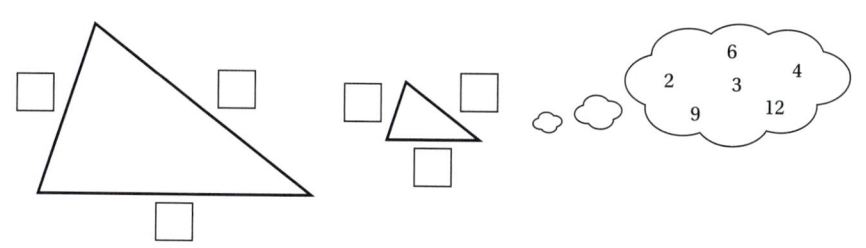

Section 2: Enlargements

An enlargement is a transformation that changes the position of a shape as well as its size. Under enlargement, an object and its image are similar shapes.

When your teacher projects an image onto a whiteboard, you see an enlargement of whatever is on the computer screen. In mathematics, we use the word enlargement for all transformations that produce similar images even if the image is smaller than the original object. When you take a photo the image you see on your screen is considered to be an enlargement of the scene in front of you even though it is smaller.

To construct an enlargement of a shape, you multiply the length of each side by the **scale factor**. You saw scale factors when you learnt about maps and scale drawings in Chapter 12.

Enlarged shapes are mathematically similar to each other, because their angles remain unchanged.

Before you enlarge a shape, consider its new dimensions.

Find answers at: cambridge.org/ukschools/gcsemaths-studentbookanswers

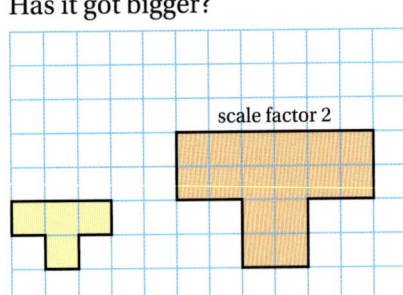

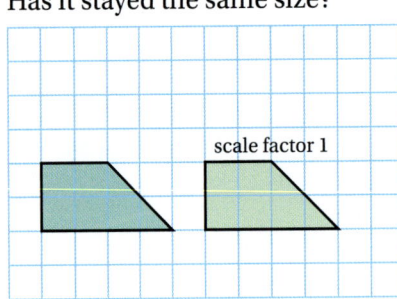

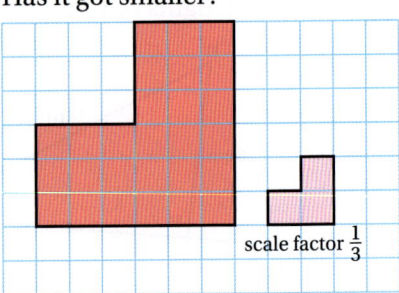

Has it got bigger? | Has it stayed the same size? | Has it got smaller?

scale factor 2 | scale factor 1 | scale factor $\frac{1}{3}$

WORKED EXAMPLE 3

Draw an enlargement of triangle ABC by a scale factor of 2.

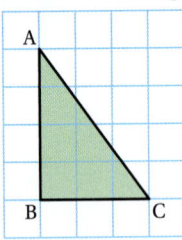

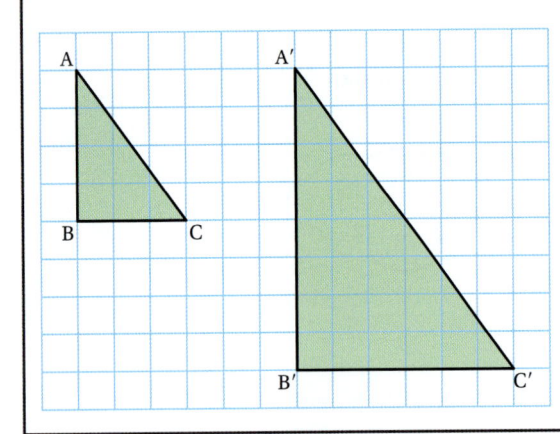

To increase triangle ABC by a scale factor of 2, increase each length by the scale factor:

A'B' = AB × 2 = 8

B'C' = BC × 2 = 6

A'C' = AC × 2 = $\begin{pmatrix} 3 \\ -4 \end{pmatrix}$ × 2 = $\begin{pmatrix} 6 \\ -8 \end{pmatrix}$

The image of triangle ABC is triangle A'B'C'.

Notice that triangle ABC is similar to triangle A'B'C' and that the sides are in proportion.

EXERCISE 30B

1 Enlarge each shape as directed.

   a Enlarge **A** by a scale factor of 3.   **b** Enlarge **B** by a scale factor of 0.5.

   c Enlarge **C** by a scale factor of $1\frac{1}{2}$.

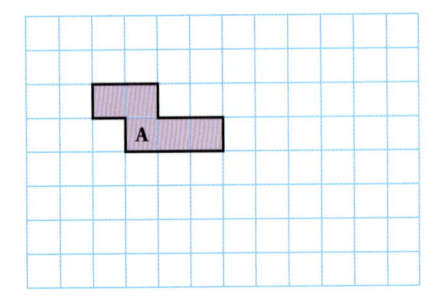

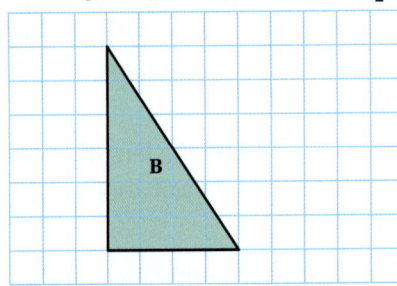

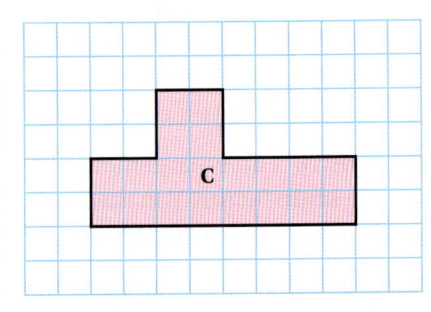

   d What do you notice about the enlargement when the scale factor, x, is $0 < x < 1$?

The centre of enlargement

You need two pieces of information to accurately draw an enlargement.
- The scale factor.
- The centre of enlargement.

The centre of enlargement is the point from where the enlargement is measured. In Worked example 3, you drew the enlargements on another position on the grid. When we use a centre of enlargement, we draw the enlargement in a certain position in relation to the original object.

The table below shows how to enlarge a shape from a given centre of enlargement by a scale factor 2.

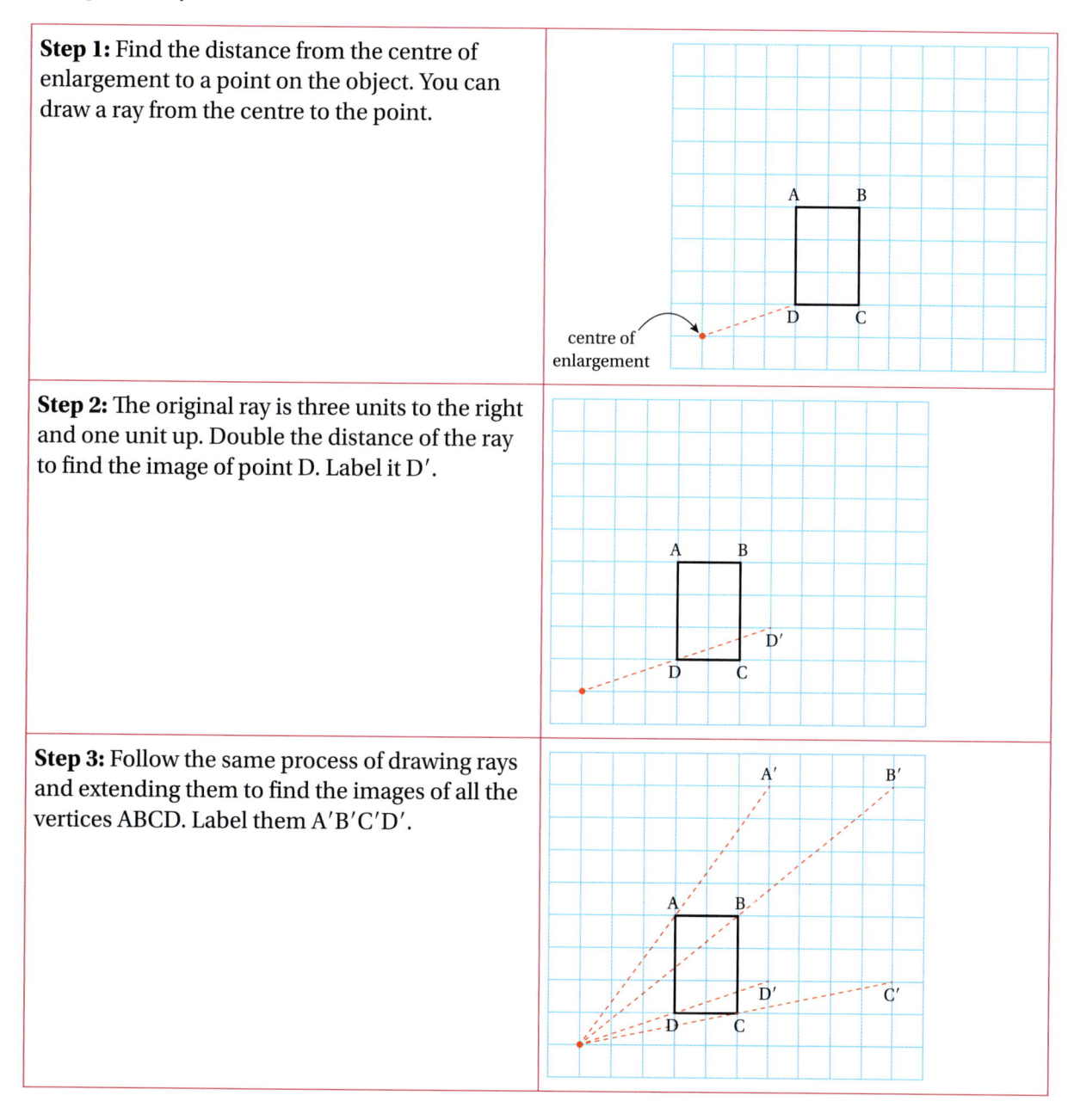

Step 1: Find the distance from the centre of enlargement to a point on the object. You can draw a ray from the centre to the point.	
Step 2: The original ray is three units to the right and one unit up. Double the distance of the ray to find the image of point D. Label it D′.	
Step 3: Follow the same process of drawing rays and extending them to find the images of all the vertices ABCD. Label them A′B′C′D′.	

Find answers at: cambridge.org/ukschools/gcsemaths-studentbookanswers

Step 4: Draw in the image. Check that the lengths of the image are correct. Note that lines from the corresponding vertices of the object and its image will **meet at the centre of enlargement**.

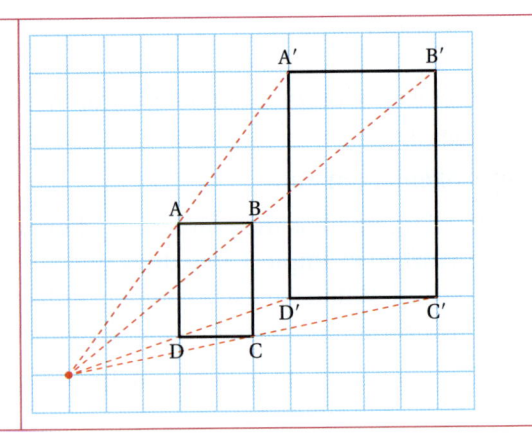

The steps are the same for a centre of enlargement in any position, even for a centre of enlargement inside the shape itself.

WORK IT OUT 30.1

This triangle is enlarged from centre (−3, 4) scale factor 2. Draw its image.

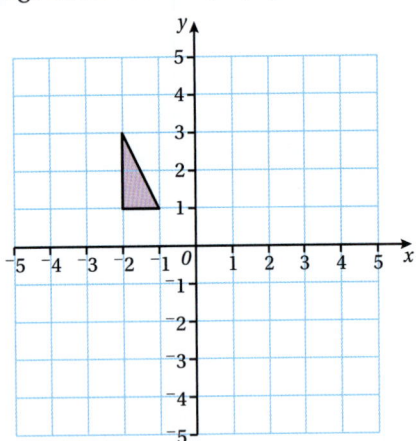

Tip

Sketch the new shape before you construct the enlargement. Draw one ray to identify the new position of the shape. After drawing the enlargement add in additional rays to check that it is in the correct position.

Which one of these answers is correct? Why are the others wrong?

How many marks would you give the incorrect answers if you were the teacher? Why?

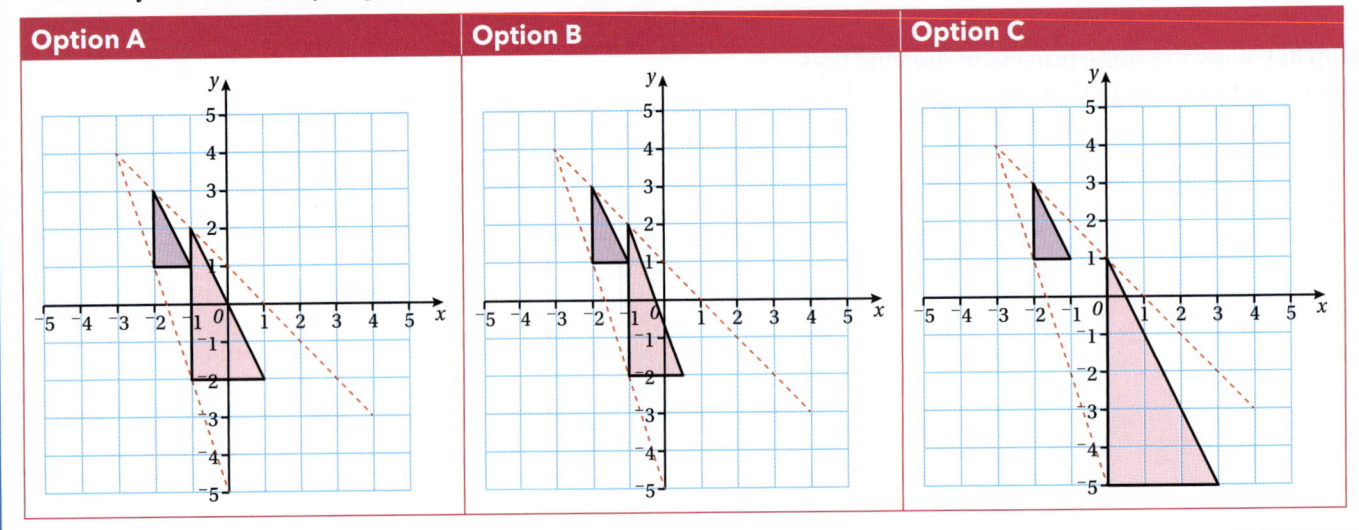

Option A	Option B	Option C

A fractional scale factor

If the scale factor is a fraction **less than one but greater than zero**, the image will be smaller than the object.

WORKED EXAMPLE 4

Enlarge the triangle on the grid by a scale factor of $\frac{1}{2}$ through the given centre of enlargement.

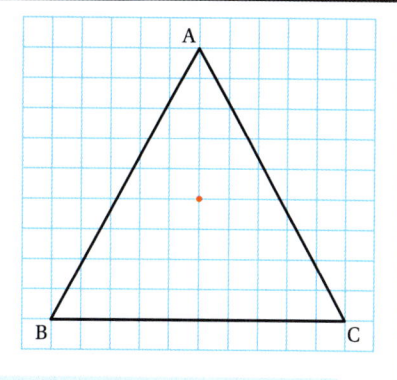

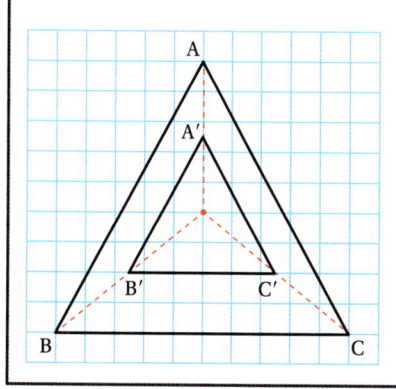

In this case, the rays from each vertex of the object are halved to find the position of the image.

EXERCISE 30C

1 Enlarge each shape as directed using the point C as the centre of enlargement.

  a Enlarge shape **R** by a scale factor of 3.
  b Enlarge shape **S** by a scale factor of 2.
  c Enlarge shape **T** by a scale factor of $\frac{1}{2}$.

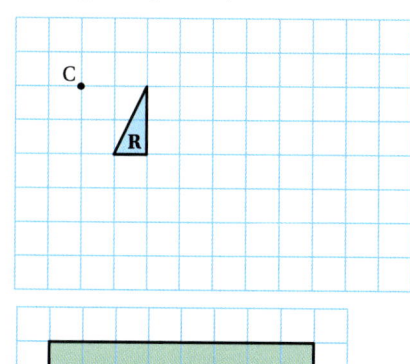

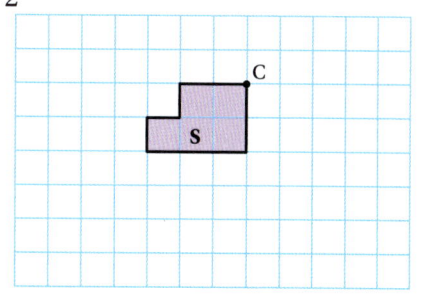

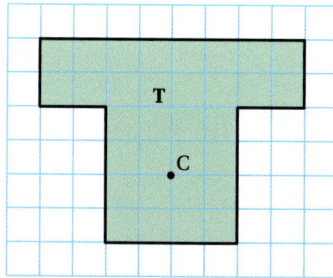

Find answers at: cambridge.org/ukschools/gcsemaths-studentbookanswers

2. Enlarge the given shape by a scale factor of 3, using the origin as the centre of enlargement.

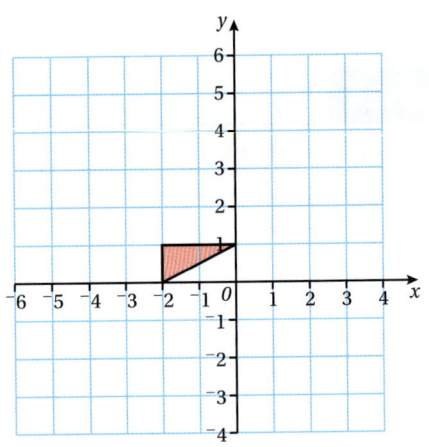

3. Enlarge the given shape by a scale factor of 2 using (−4, 3) as the centre of enlargement.

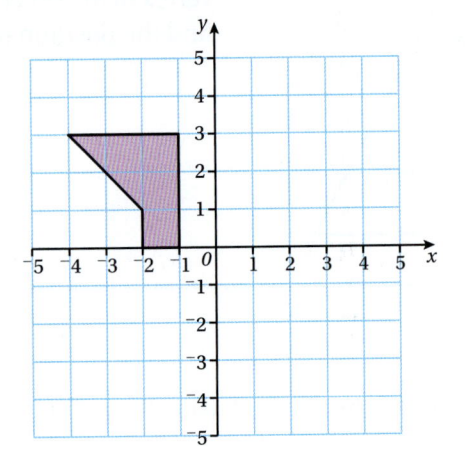

4. Enlarge the given shape by a scale factor of $\frac{1}{3}$ using (−5, 2) as the centre of enlargement.

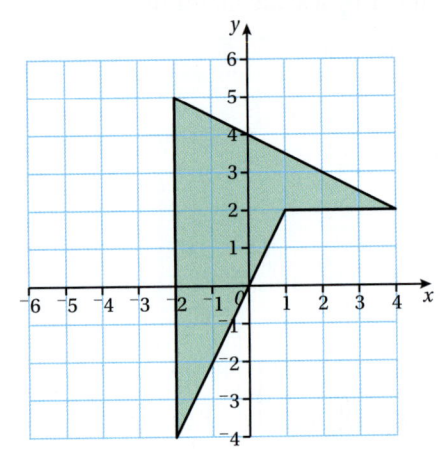

5 Enlarge the given shape by a scale factor of $1\frac{1}{2}$ using (0, 1) as the centre of enlargement.

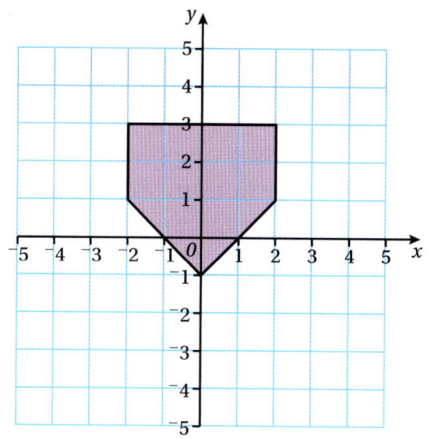

Properties of enlargements

The centre of enlargement can be anywhere: inside the object, on a vertex or side of the object or outside the object.

A scale factor greater than 1 will enlarge the object. A scale factor smaller than 1 will reduce the size of the object, but this is still called an enlargement.

The object and its image are **similar under enlargement**.
- Sides are in the ratio $1 : k$, where k is the scale factor.
- The area of an object and its image will be in the ratio $1 : k^2$, where k is the scale factor.
- An object and its image have the same angles.
- For **positive** scale factors ($x > 0$), an object and its image have the same orientation.

Describing enlargements

To describe an enlargement you need to give:
- the scale factor
- the centre of enlargement.

To find the centre of enlargement you need to draw lines from corresponding vertices of the object and its image to find the point where they meet.

WORK IT OUT 30.2

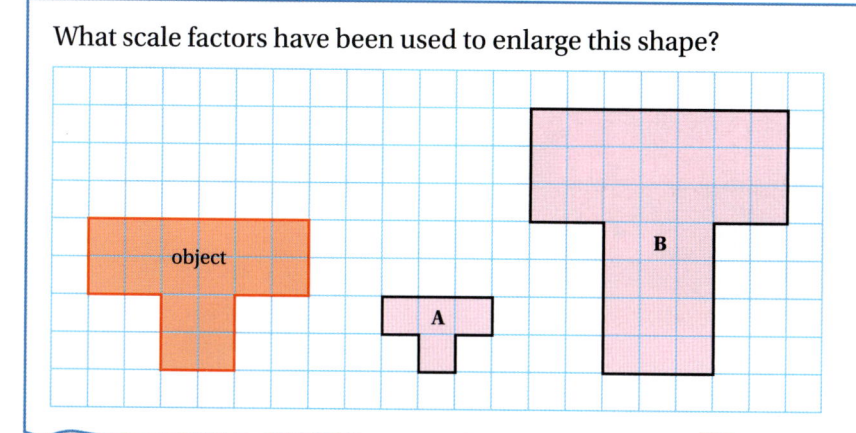

What scale factors have been used to enlarge this shape?

Continues on next page ...

Find answers at: cambridge.org/ukschools/gcsemaths-studentbookanswers

Which one of these students' answers is correct?

What feedback would you give each student to make sure they don't make the same mistakes again?

Ben	Ellie	Rosie
A scale factor of 2 has been used to produce shape **A**.	Since the sides have halved in length to get **A**, the scale factor is $\frac{1}{2}$.	To get shape **A** you have to take away one square along the bottom and along each side edge. So the scale factor is $^-1$.
The top of shape **A** is 3 squares across, multiply this by 2 to get 6, the length of the top of the object.	Shape **B** isn't an enlargement. Each side has been increased by different numbers of squares.	Shape **B** is a scale factor of $1\frac{1}{2}$ because 2 squares have become 3 squares.
B can't be an enlargement. Its top is 7 squares and the object is 6. You can't do that using multiplication. Maybe it's $^-1$?		

EXERCISE 30D

1 Which of the photos below show an enlargement of the original? How can you tell?

Original

A

B

C

30 Similarity

2 Which of the following houses are enlargements of house **A**? For each enlargement state the scale factor.

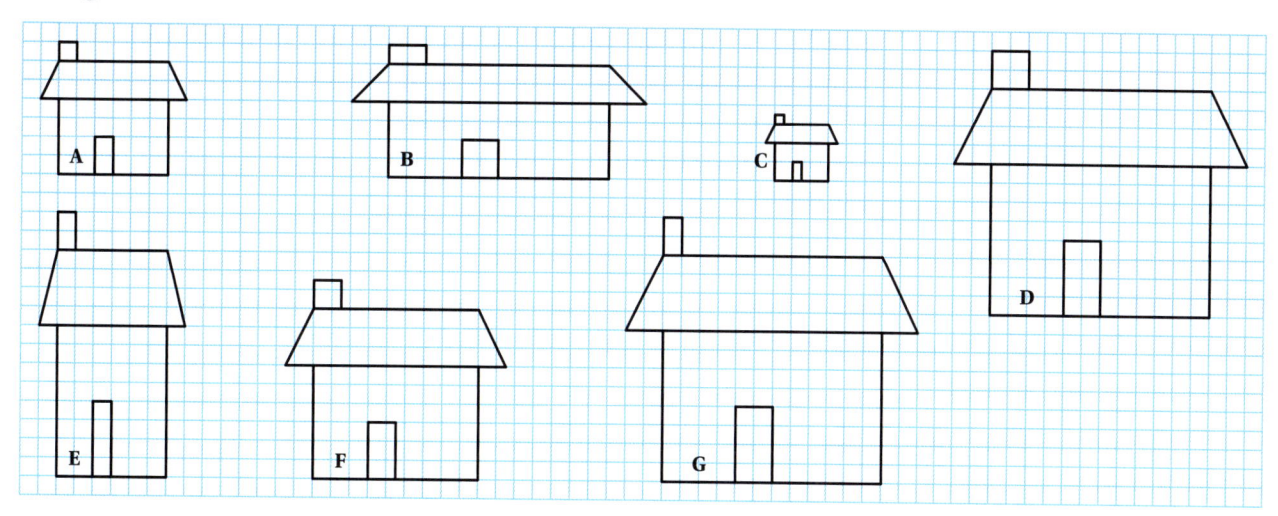

3 These diagrams each show an object and its image after an enlargement.
Describe each of these enlargements by giving both the scale factor and the coordinates of the centre of enlargement. In each case the object is labelled.

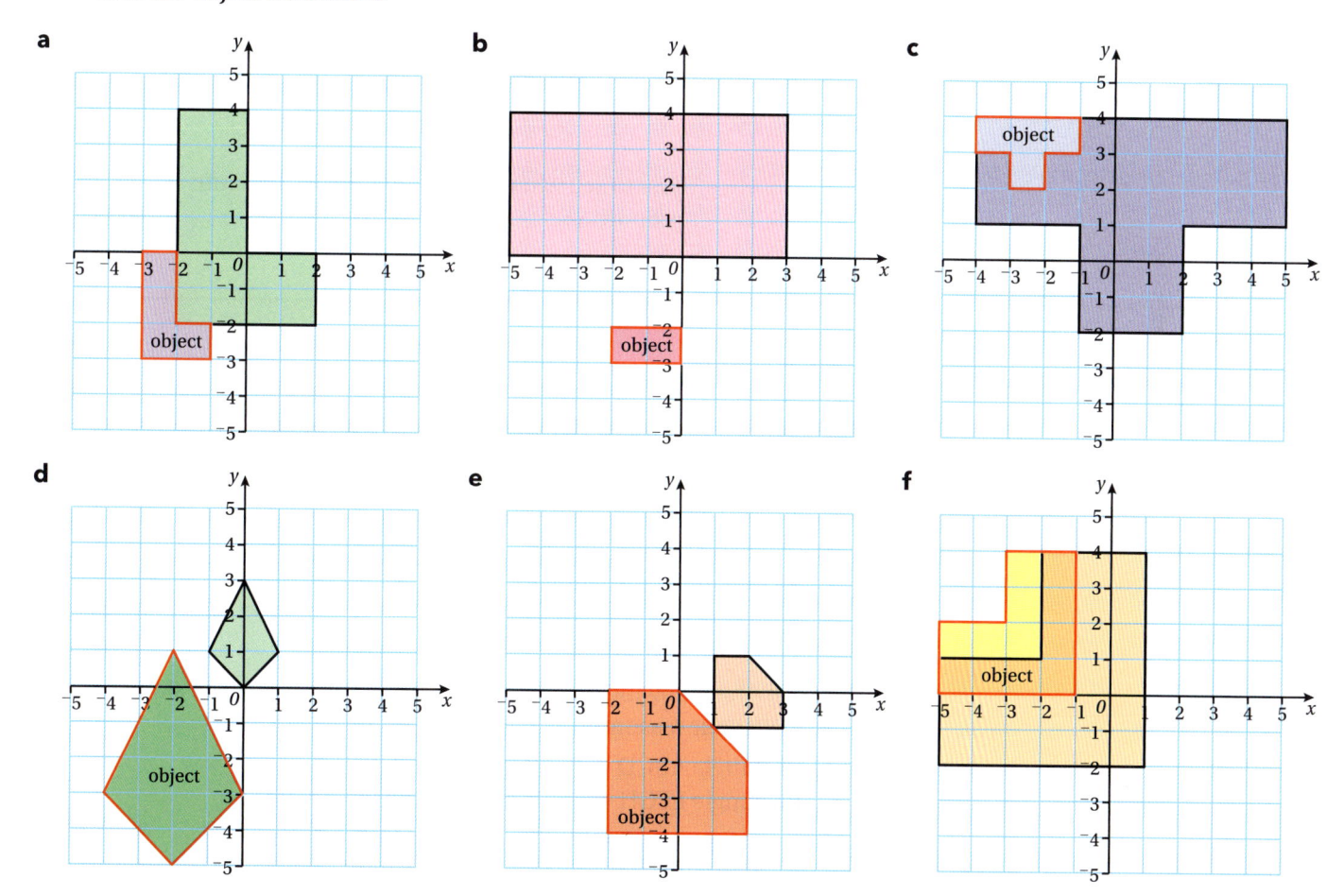

a   b   c

d   e   f

Find answers at: cambridge.org/ukschools/gcsemaths-studentbookanswers

475

Section 3: Similar shapes

A polygon is similar to another polygon if it is an enlargement of the original polygon. So two polygons will be similar if the angles in one polygon are equal to the angles in the other polygon, **and** the ratio of the sides from the one polygon to the other are kept the same.

For polygons other than triangles, equal angles alone are not sufficient to prove similarity.

WORKED EXAMPLE 5

Compare each of the quadrilaterals B to D below to the first quadrilateral, A.

Which of them are similar to A?

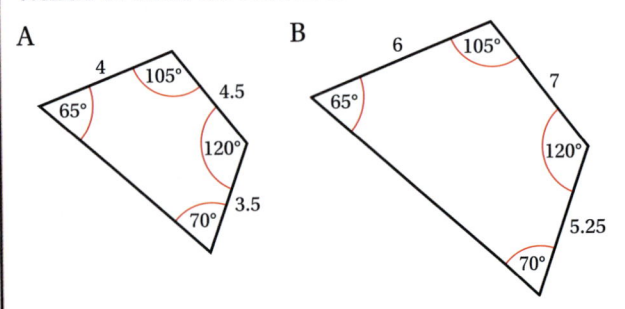

$\frac{4}{6} \neq \frac{4.5}{7}$. So B is not similar to A

> B has the same size angles as A, but the sides are not in proportion.

The angles in C are different to the angles in A, so C is not similar to A.

D has corresponding angles equal to those in A.

$\frac{4}{6} = \frac{4.5}{6.75} = \frac{3.5}{5.25}$. D is similar to A.

> Test to see whether the sides are in the same proportion.

D is an enlargement of A with a scale factor of 1.5.

EXERCISE 30E

1. Decide whether each statement below is true or false. Explain your reasoning.

   a All squares are similar.

   b All hexagons are similar.

   c All rectangles are similar.

   d All regular octagons are similar.

2. Sketch the following pairs of shapes and decide if they are similar. Explain your reasoning.

   a Rectangle ABCD with AB = 5 cm and BC = 3 cm.
   Rectangle EFGH with EF = 10 cm and FG = 6 cm.

   b Rectangle ABCD with AB = 5 cm and BC = 3 cm.
   Rectangle EFGH with AB = 10 cm and BC = 9 cm.

   c Square ABCD with AB = 4 cm.
   Square EFGH with EF = 6 cm.

3 The two shapes below are similar.

Find the missing lengths a and b.

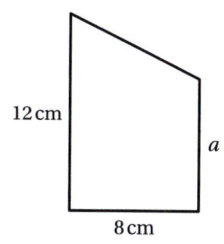

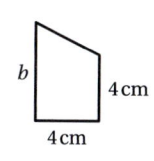

4 The two shapes below are similar.

Find the lengths of the missing sides in the second shape.

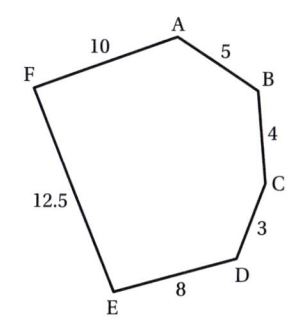

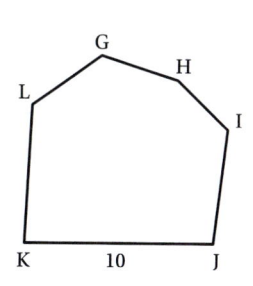

5 The first shape below has been enlarged by a scale factor of 1.5 to create the image GHIJKL.

AB = 5 cm and BC = 7 cm.

Find the lengths of the sides in the second shape.

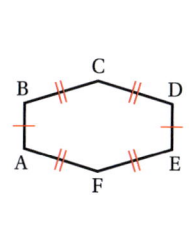

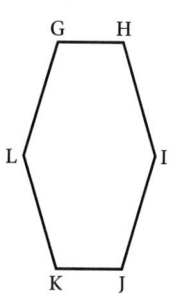

6 Emily drew the diagram below as a plan for a mass display at an athletics stadium. The actual size of each side will be 10 m.

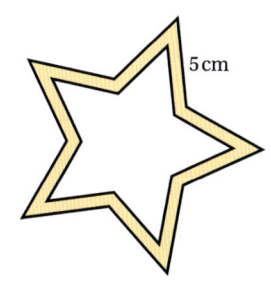

a What is the scale factor of enlargement required to create the display?

b Write the scale as a ratio.

Find answers at: cambridge.org/ukschools/gcsemaths-studentbookanswers

Checklist of learning and understanding

Similar triangles

- Two triangles are similar if all three corresponding angles are equal. Similar triangles are the same shape, and their corresponding sides are in proportion.
- The proportion between corresponding sides of similar triangles can be used to solve problems in geometry.

Enlargements

- An enlargement is a transformation that changes the position and size of a shape.
- Enlargements are described by a scale factor and centre of enlargement.
- A fractional scale factor that is less than one will make the image smaller than the object but is still called an enlargement.

Similar shapes

- If shapes are enlarged by a scale factor, similar shapes are created with all their sides in proportion. The proportionality between lengths can be used to solve geometry problems.

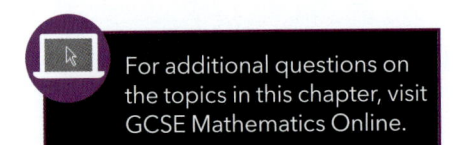

For additional questions on the topics in this chapter, visit GCSE Mathematics Online.

Chapter review

1 a Prove that triangle VWX is similar to triangle VYZ.

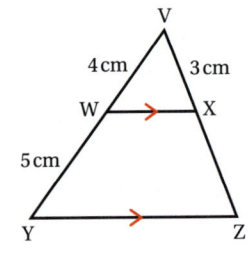

b Find the length of XZ.

2 A tree which is 3 m high has a shadow length of 7.5 m. At the same time of day, a building casts a shadow that is 16.25 m long.
Use similar triangles to calculate the height of the building.

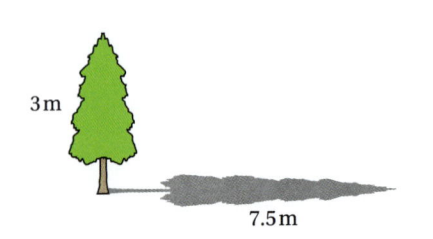

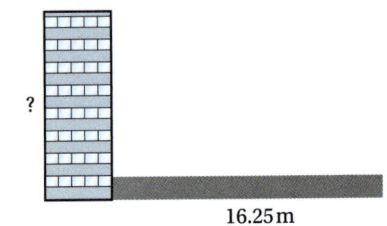

30 Similarity

3 Triangles ABC and DEF are similar.

All lengths are in centimetres.

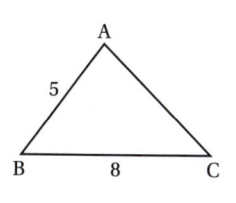

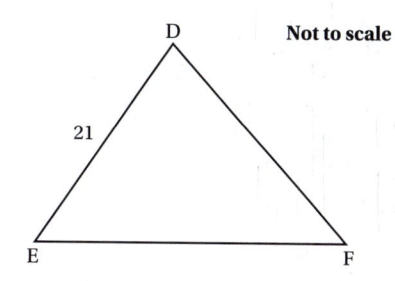

Not to scale

Calculate EF.

(3 marks)

© OCR 2012

4 Draw an enlargement of ABCD by $\frac{1}{2}$, using the given point as the centre of enlargement.

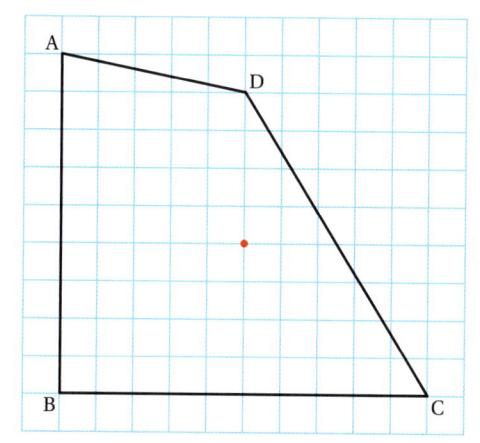

5 Draw an enlargement of this shape by 1.5, using the origin as the centre of enlargement.

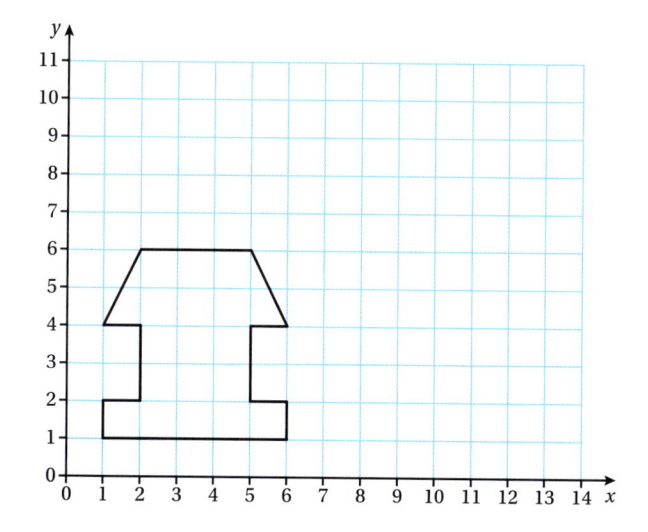

6 Are any two regular hexagons similar shapes? Explain.

7 Are any two rhombuses similar shapes? Explain.

Find answers at: cambridge.org/ukschools/gcsemaths-studentbookanswers

479

31 Pythagoras' theorem

In this chapter you will learn how to ...
- develop full knowledge and understanding of Pythagoras' theorem.
- apply Pythagoras' theorem in 2D problems.
- link the maths to real-life skills for industry.

For more resources relating to this chapter, visit GCSE Mathematics Online.

Using mathematics: real-life applications

Builders, carpenters, garden designers and navigators all use Pythagoras' theorem in their jobs. It is a method based on right-angled triangles which helps them to work out unknown lengths and check for right angles.

"I use Pythagoras' theorem to help me prepare floor plans and do calculations for footings and heights of buildings. Any building surveyor will have a range of tools to help them make check calculations on site." *(Building surveyor)*

Calculator tip
Make sure you know how to square a number and calculate a square root on your calculator.

Before you start ...

Ch 1, 2	You need to work confidently with squares and square roots.	**1** a Which are correct? 　i $\sqrt{100} = \sqrt{10}$　　ii $\sqrt{100} = 10$　　iii $\sqrt{100} = \pm 10$　　iv $10^2 = 100$ b Which are correct? 　i $4^2 = 4 \times 2 = 8$　　ii $3^3 = 3 \times 3 \times 3 = 27$
Ch 9	You need to recognise different angle types and define them.	**2** a Which is a right angle? Identify the other angles. 　i　　　ii　　　iii 　iv　　　v b How many degrees are there in three right angles?
Ch 5	You'll need to apply the properties of different types of triangles to solve problems.	**3** What is the area of this triangle? **4** What do you know about angles x and y in this triangle?

Tip
When answering questions about Pythagoras' theorem it might be useful to draw a diagram if one isn't provided.

31 Pythagoras' theorem

Assess your starting point using the Launchpad

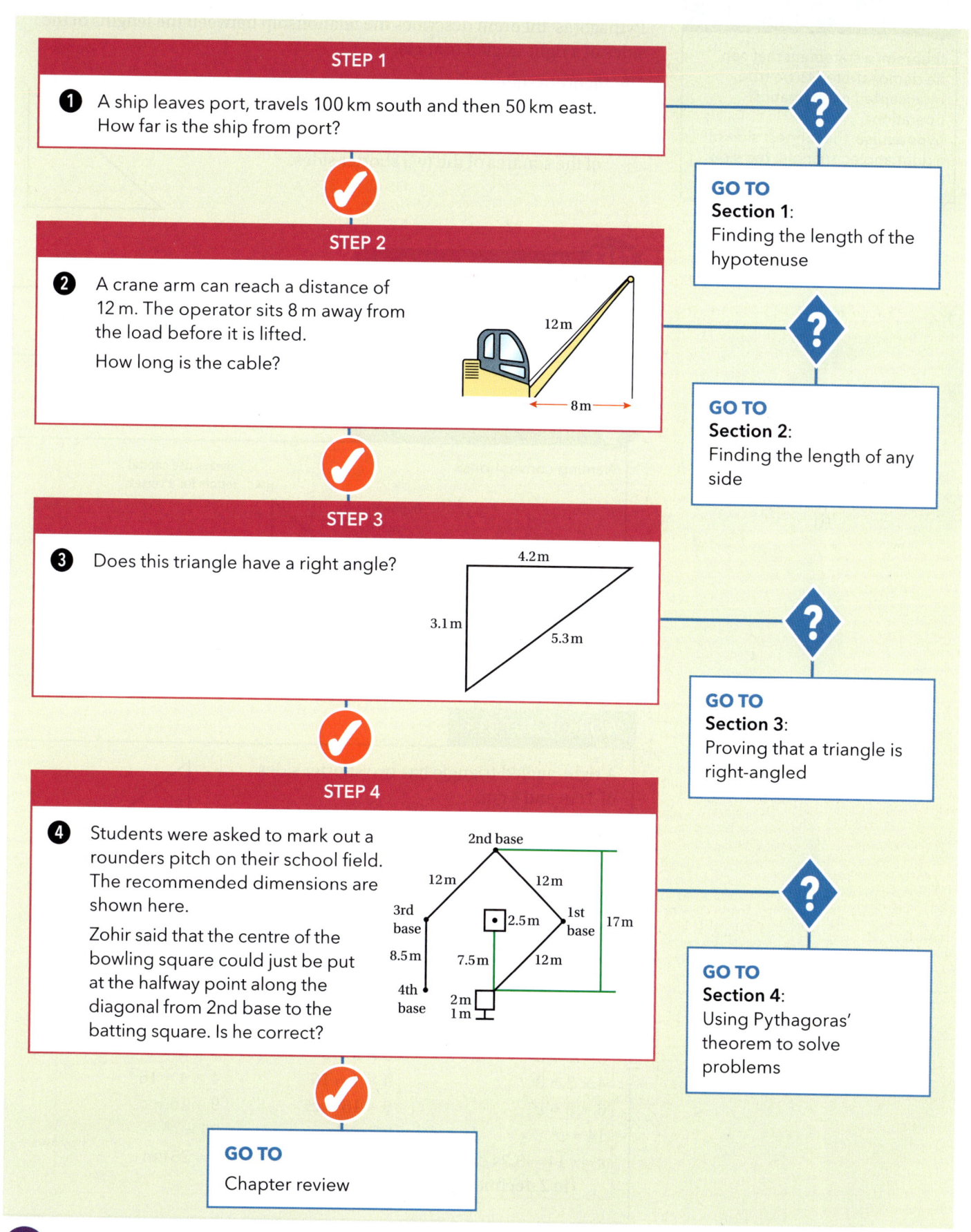

STEP 1

1 A ship leaves port, travels 100 km south and then 50 km east. How far is the ship from port?

GO TO Section 1: Finding the length of the hypotenuse

STEP 2

2 A crane arm can reach a distance of 12 m. The operator sits 8 m away from the load before it is lifted.

How long is the cable?

GO TO Section 2: Finding the length of any side

STEP 3

3 Does this triangle have a right angle?

(Triangle with sides 4.2 m, 3.1 m, 5.3 m)

GO TO Section 3: Proving that a triangle is right-angled

STEP 4

4 Students were asked to mark out a rounders pitch on their school field. The recommended dimensions are shown here.

Zohir said that the centre of the bowling square could just be put at the halfway point along the diagonal from 2nd base to the batting square. Is he correct?

GO TO Section 4: Using Pythagoras' theorem to solve problems

GO TO Chapter review

Find answers at: cambridge.org/ukschools/gcsemaths-studentbookanswers

481

GCSE Mathematics for OCR (Foundation)

Key vocabulary

theorem: a statement that can be demonstrated to be true by accepted mathematical operations.

hypotenuse: the longest side of a right-angled triangle; the side opposite the 90° angle.

Section 1: Finding the length of the hypotenuse

Pythagoras' theorem describes the relationship between the lengths of the sides of a right-angled triangle.

The **theorem** states:

In a right-angled triangle, the square of the length of the **hypotenuse** is equal to the sum of the squares of the two shorter sides.

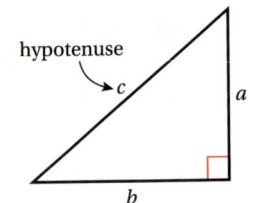

Learn this formula

For this triangle, the theorem can be expressed using the formula:
$a^2 + b^2 = c^2$

Tip

Naming conventions:
- always use capital letters for a vertex
- hypotenuse is called c
- side b is opposite angle B

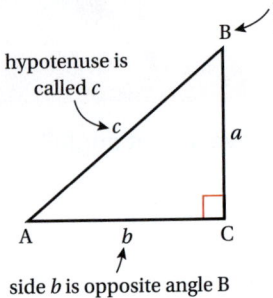

WORK IT OUT 31.1

A right-angled triangle has two shorter sides of 3 cm and 4 cm.

Calculate the length of the hypotenuse.

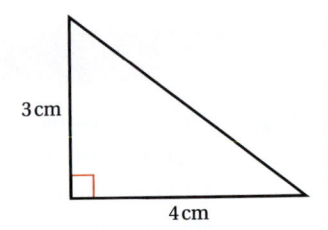

Which of these builders has got the correct answer to the question?

Why are the others wrong?

Builder A	Builder B	Builder C
$a^2 + b^2 = c^2$	$a^2 + b^2 = c^2$	$a^2 + b^2 = c^2$
$3 \times 2 = 6$	$3 \times 3 = 9$	$3 \times 3 = 9$
$4 \times 2 = 8$	$4 \times 4 = 16$	$4 \times 4 = 16$
$6 + 8 = c^2$	$9 + 16 = c^2$	$9 + 16 = c^2$
$14 = c^2$	$25 = c^2$	$25 = c^2$
$c = \sqrt{14} = 3.74$ cm (to 2 decimal places)	$c = \sqrt{25} = 5$ cm	$c = 25$ cm

482

You can find squares and square roots on your calculator.

You can use your calculator to work out what the square of a number is by pressing the x^2 button. To find 3^2 press 3 x^2 $=$ and you get 9.

The reverse of squaring is finding the square root. The square root of 9 is 3. This is written as $\sqrt{9} = 3$. You can use the $\sqrt{}$ button on your calculator to work out a square root.

To find $\sqrt{9}$ press $\sqrt{}$ 9 $=$ and you get 3.

> **Tip**
>
> See Chapter 25 if you need a reminder about powers and roots.

> **Tip**
>
> **The four rules when working with Pythagoras' theorem:**
> - Always write the formula.
> - Always include a sketch of the problem.
> - Show full workings.
> - Show the final answer to a given degree of accuracy. This could be 2 decimal places or several significant figures, depending on the detail of the problem.

EXERCISE 31A

1 In this diagram, three squares have been drawn on the sides of a right-angled triangle.

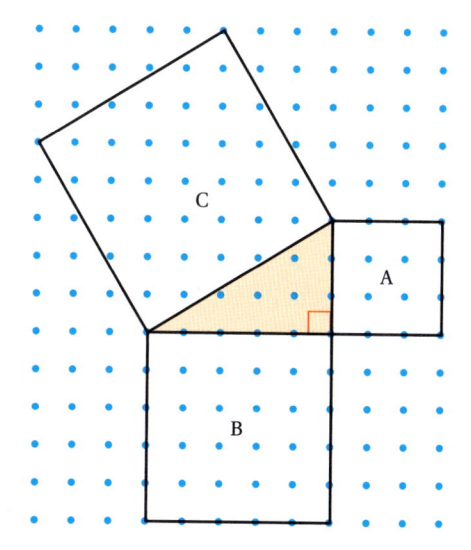

> **Tip**
>
> One of these is a tilted square. One way to find the area of a tilted square is by dividing the square into right-angled triangles and a square, and adding the areas together to find the area of the square. For example, 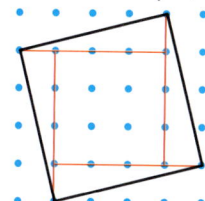
>
> The area of the tilted square is $8 + 9 = 17$ squares. (8 is the combined area of the 4 triangles and 9 is the area of the central square.)

Find and record the area of each square in a table like the one below.

Draw some different right-angled triangles and repeat the process.

Make sure that the square labelled C is opposite the right angle.

Area of square A	Area of square B	Area of square C
...	...	...

What do you notice about the relationship between the different areas?

This shows that Pythagoras' theorem works.

Find answers at: cambridge.org/ukschools/gcsemaths-studentbookanswers

GCSE Mathematics for OCR (Foundation)

2 a Calculate:

  i 25^2 **ii** 5.3^2 **iii** 167^2 **iv** 136^2 **v** 14.5^2

  b Calculate, working to 2 decimal places:

  i $\sqrt{3}$ **ii** $\sqrt{7}$ **iii** $\sqrt{4}$ **iv** $\sqrt{17}$ **v** $\sqrt{61}$

3 Find the length of the hypotenuse in each of the following triangles:

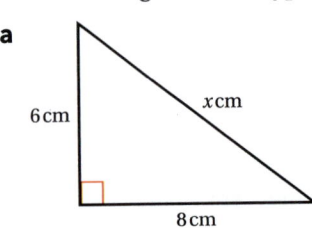

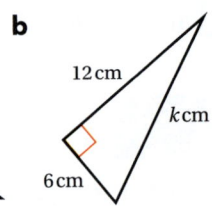

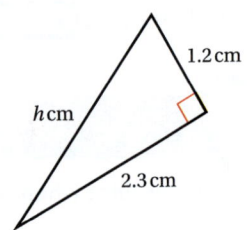

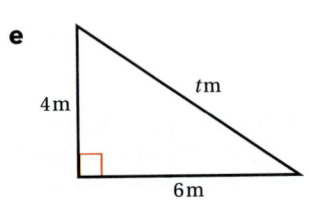

a 6 cm, 8 cm, x cm

b 12 cm, 6 cm, k cm

c 1.2 cm, 2.3 cm, h cm

d 1.5 cm, 0.6 cm, p cm

e 4 m, 6 m, t m

4 a Jamie calculates that the hypotenuse of this triangle is 14 cm. Without calculating the length yourself, explain why this must be wrong.

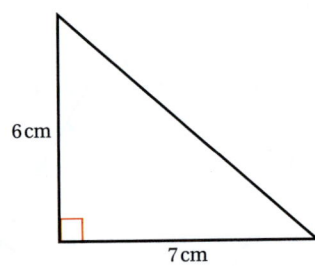

(Triangle: 6 cm, 7 cm)

  b He recalculates and gets 7 cm for the length of the hypotenuse. How do you know that this is wrong?

  c What range of answers could Jamie have given where you wouldn't know straight away that his answer was wrong?

Section 2: Finding the length of any side

If you know the lengths of any two sides of a right-angled triangle, you can use them to find the length of the third side.

In the formula $a^2 + b^2 = c^2$, c is the hypotenuse and a and b are the two shorter sides.

The formula can be rearranged to make a^2 or b^2 the subject of the formula:

$$a^2 = c^2 - b^2$$
$$b^2 = c^2 - a^2$$

Tip

You changed the subjects of formulae in Chapter 14.

484

WORK IT OUT 31.2

This is the design of an access ramp for the front entrance to a building.
What is the vertical height of the ramp?

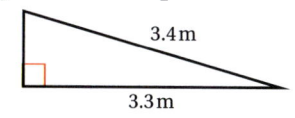

3.4 m
3.3 m

Which of these calculations is correct for this design? Why are the others wrong?

Option A	Option B	Option C
$c^2 - b^2 = a^2$	$c^2 - b^2 = a^2$	$c^2 - b^2 = a^2$
$3.4^2 - 3.3^2 = a^2$	$3.3^2 + 3.4^2 = c^2$	$3.4^2 - 3.3^2 = a^2$
$3.4 \times 2 = 6.8$	$3.3 \times 3.3 = 10.89$	$3.4 \times 3.4 = 11.56$
$3.3 \times 2 = 6.6$	$3.4 \times 3.4 = 11.56$	$3.3 \times 3.3 = 10.89$
$6.8 - 6.6 = a^2$	$10.89 + 11.56 = c^2$	$11.56 - 10.89 = a^2$
$0.2 = a^2$	$22.45 = c^2$	$a^2 = 0.67$
$a = 0.2 \div 2$	$a = \sqrt{22.45}\text{ m} = 4.74\text{ m}$	$a = \sqrt{0.67}\text{ m} = 0.82\text{ m}$
$a = 0.1$ m	(to 2 decimal places)	(to 2 decimal places)

Tip

Always think about whether the answers are realistic and reasonable. Being able to recognise whether values are reasonable will help you to spot mistakes.

EXERCISE 31B

1 Find the length of the missing side in each of these triangles:

a 8 cm, k cm, 6 cm

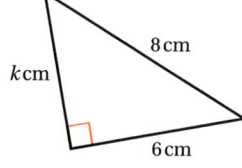

b x cm, 2.3 cm, 3.25 cm

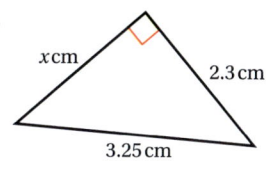

c 12 cm, 10 cm, j cm

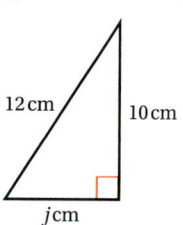

d 1.2 cm, y cm, 3.3 cm

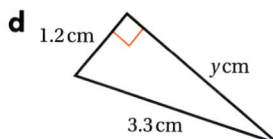

e 10.5 cm, 4.5 cm, z cm

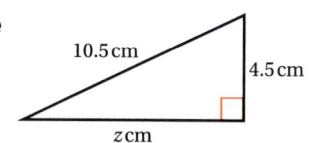

f p km, 3 km, 8 km

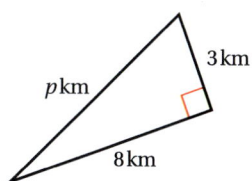

g k cm, 6 cm, 12 cm

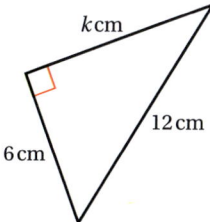

h 9 cm, h cm, 8 cm

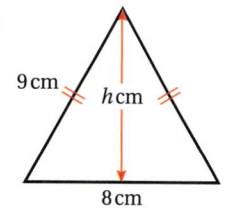

i 8 m, d m, 6 m, 3 m

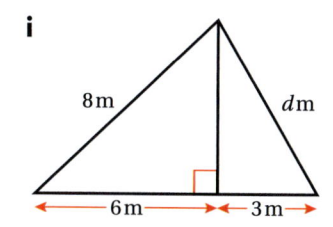

j 12 m, f m, 4 m, 3 m

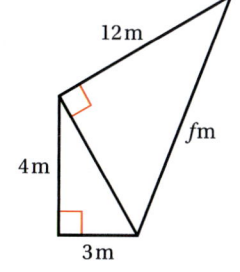

Tip

There are different types of right-angled triangle.

Scalene right-angled triangles have:
- one right angle
- two other unequal angles
- no equal sides.

Isosceles right-angled triangles have:
- one right angle
- two other equal angles, always 45°
- two equal sides.

You can apply Pythagoras' theorem to both types of right-angled triangle.

Find answers at: cambridge.org/ukschools/gcsemaths-studentbookanswers

2 Jamil says that the missing side in this triangle is 5.5 cm long.

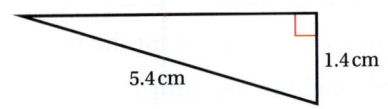

Without calculating the length, explain why this must be wrong.

3 In this kite, the dimensions of the two isosceles triangles that make it are given.

Using what you know about different types of triangles, work out how long the rod is that holds the kite together from top to bottom.

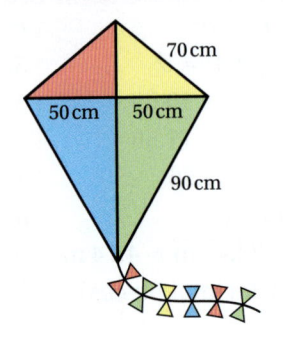

4 The front of the tent is a scalene triangle.

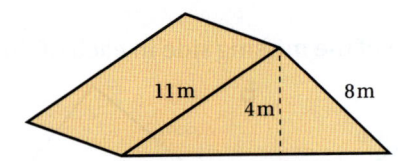

The perpendicular height of the tent is 4 m.

What is the length of the base?

5 Which length, A–D, gives the correct value of x in each triangle?

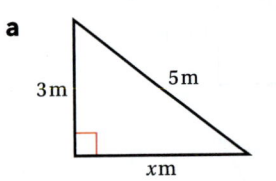

a

A $2.56 + 0.25 = 2.81$
$$x = \sqrt{2.81}$$

B $x^2 = 6^2 + 2.5^2$

C $6^2 - 4^2 = x^2$

D $x = 4\,\text{m}$

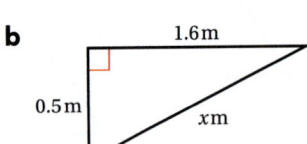

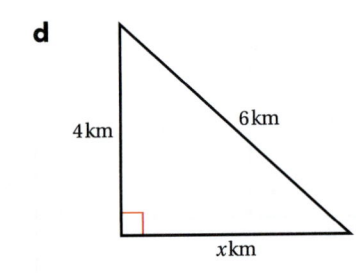

b

c

d

486

6 A girl swims across a river.

The distance she swims is 20 m from one shore to the other.

The distance along the bank she has travelled is 10 m.

The banks are parallel.

How far apart are they?

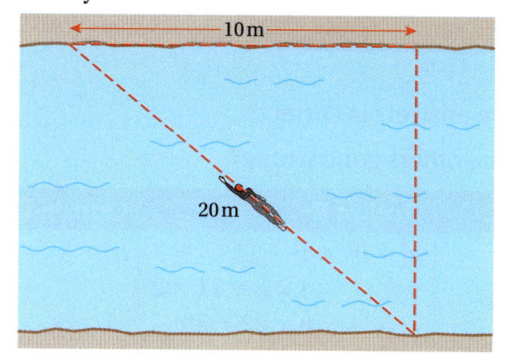

Section 3: Proving that a triangle is right-angled

If a triangle contains a right angle, then both sides of Pythagoras' theorem will be true ($a^2 + b^2$ will equal c^2). This fact is crucial to many people in their jobs.

Carpenters need to make rectangular window frames. If the frames don't have right angles at the corners then the window won't fit. If the sides of the triangle at the corner of the frame have lengths in the ratio of 3, 4 and 5, then the carpenter knows the angle is a right angle because $3^2 + 4^2 = 5^2$. Carpenters know this as the '3, 4, 5 rule'.

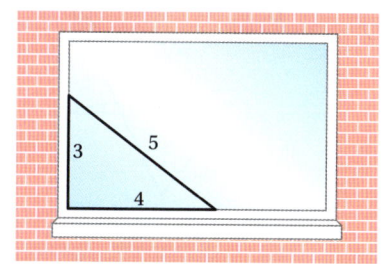

The side lengths 3, 4, 5 are known as a **Pythagorean triple**. There are a number of Pythagorean triples to explore.

> "I use 'Pythagorean triples' in my job – using the 3, 4, 5 rule I know whether the window frame is a true right angle or not. It means the window will fit properly."
>
> *(Window fitter)*

Key vocabulary

Pythagorean triple: three non-zero numbers (a, b, c) for which $a^2 + b^2 = c^2$.

Find answers at: cambridge.org/ukschools/gcsemaths-studentbookanswers

WORK IT OUT 31.3

Is this triangle right-angled?

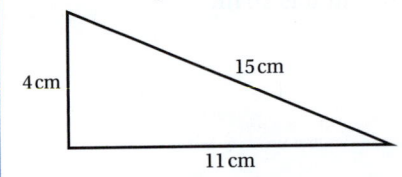

4 cm, 15 cm, 11 cm

Which of these answers is correct?

Where have the others gone wrong?

Option A	Option B	Option C
$4 + 11 = 15$ So $a^2 + b^2 = c^2$ Yes, the triangle is right-angled!	$a^2 + b^2 = 4^2 + 11^2$ $= 4 \times 2 + 11 \times 2$ $= 8 + 22 = 30$ $c^2 = 15^2 = 15 \times 2 = 30$ $a^2 + b^2 = c^2$ Yes, the triangle is right-angled!	$a^2 + b^2 = 4^2 + 11^2$ $= 16 + 121 = 137$ $c^2 = 15 \times 15 = 225$ $a^2 + b^2 \neq c^2$ No, the triangle is not right-angled!

EXERCISE 31C

1 Use Pythagoras' theorem to help you decide which of the following triangles are right-angled.

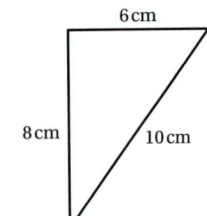

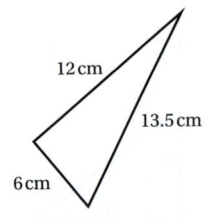

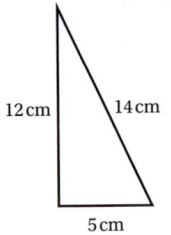

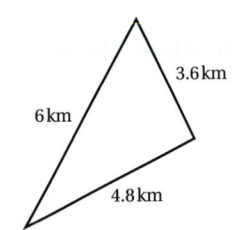

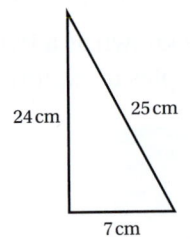

a 6 cm, 8 cm, 10 cm

b 12 cm, 13.5 cm, 6 cm

c 12 cm, 14 cm, 5 cm

d 3.6 km, 6 km, 4.8 km

e 24 cm, 25 cm, 7 cm

2 The lengths of the sides of a number of different triangles are given below. Determine whether each triangle is right-angled.

a 1, 1, 1

b 1, 1, 2

c 5, 7, 9

d 5, 12, 13

e 8, 10, 6

f 1, 2, 2

3 A builder uses 3, 4, 5 triangles to make right angles.

  a Write down the dimensions of three other right-angled triangles where the sides are in the ratio 3 : 4 : 5.

  b Some other Pythagorean triples occur regularly. Carry out an investigation to find at least five common triples.

4 A field has straight sides of length 25 m and width 15 m.

There is a 35 m long drainage pipe lying diagonally across the field from corner to corner.

Is the field a rectangle with right angles at the corners? Explain your reasoning.

Section 4: Using Pythagoras' theorem to solve problems

You know Pythagoras' theorem and you know how to apply it to calculate missing lengths and to test whether or not a triangle is right-angled. You will use these skills regularly in geometry and trigonometry, particularly where you need to find missing sides in figures with right angles.

WORKED EXAMPLE 1

Find the length of side x and then calculate the perimeter of this composite shape.

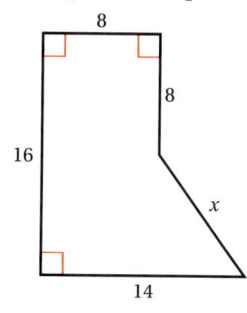

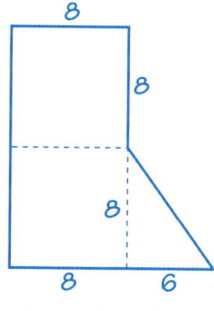

[Diagram of composite shape with dimensions 8, 8, 16, 14 and side x]

[Diagram showing shape divided into rectangle and right-angled triangle with sides 8, 8, 8, 8, 6]

Divide the shape to make a right-angled triangle.

$8^2 + 6^2 = x^2$
$100 = x^2$
$x = 10 \text{ cm}$

The broken lines show you that the composite shape is made up of a rectangle with dimensions 8 × 16, and a right-angled triangle with sides 6 and 8. The unknown, x, is the hypotenuse of the triangle. Use Pythagoras to find x.

Perimeter = 16 + 14 + 8 + 8 + 10 = 56 cm.

Find answers at: cambridge.org/ukschools/gcsemaths-studentbookanswers

Pythagoras' theorem is also very useful for solving a range of problems involving real-life contexts.

Shortest and longest route problems are a good example.

Problem-solving framework

To get home, you normally cross a 100 metre by 60 metre rectangular football field diagonally from one corner to the other as it is the quickest route.

Today there is a game playing so you have to go round the edge.

Calculate how much further you have to walk.

Steps for approaching a problem-solving question	What you would do for this example
Step 1: If it is useful to have a diagram sketch one and add the information. This may help you visualise the problem.	A rectangle 100 m by 60 m with a diagonal drawn from one corner to the opposite corner.
Step 2: Identify what you have to do.	Find the difference between the length of the diagonal and the length of the two sides added together.
Step 3: Test the problem with what you know. Can I use a ruler? What type of angle is it?	You could use a ruler, but you would have to draw a very accurate diagram to scale. As you have a right-angled triangle and side lengths you can use Pythagoras' theorem.
Step 4: What maths can I do?	Use Pythagoras' theorem to work out the length of the diagonal: $100^2 + 60^2 = c^2$ $10\,000 + 3600 = c^2$ $13\,600 = c^2$ $c = \sqrt{13\,600} = 116.6\,m$ If you walked straight across the diagonal the distance would be 116.6 m. You have to go round the outside which is 160 m (100 + 60), so you must walk 43.4 m further.
Step 5: Check your workings and that your answer is reasonable.	A diagonal pitch length of 116.6 m seems reasonable given the sides are 60 m and 100 m.
Step 6: Have you answered the question?	You were asked to find how much further you would have to walk. You have found this to be 43.4 m.

EXERCISE 31D

In each of the following show your working and give reasons where necessary.
Figures are **not to scale** and all dimensions are in centimetres.

1 Find the length of x in this figure.

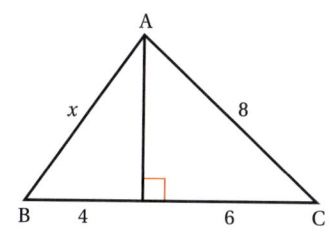

2 Determine the length of:
   a BE.
   b BD.
   c BC.

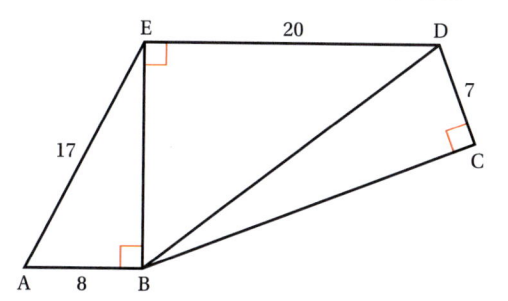

3 Find the length of AD in this figure.

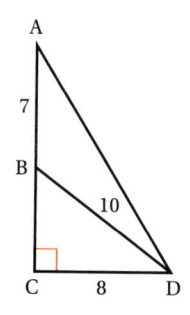

4 Calculate the length of:
   a AC.
   b BC.
   c EC.

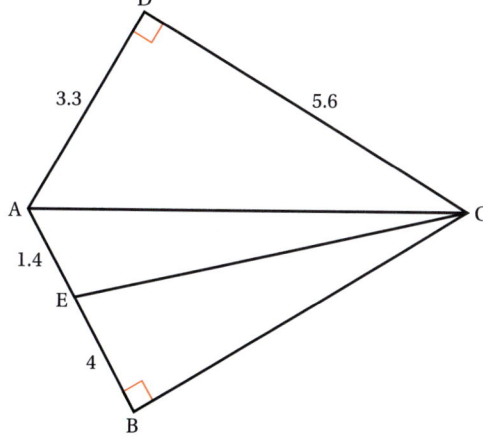

5 For trapezium ABCD, calculate the perpendicular height EB and then find the area of the figure.

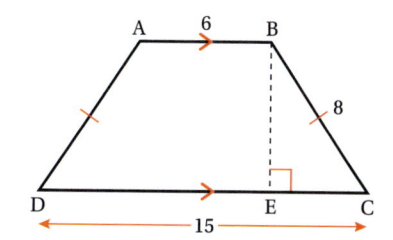

Find answers at: cambridge.org/ukschools/gcsemaths-studentbookanswers

6 Find the length of side AD and calculate the perimeter of this shape.

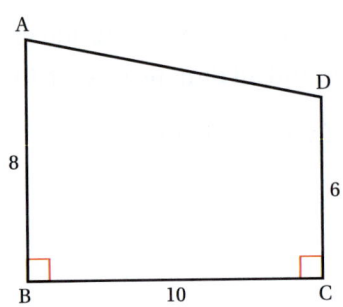

7 Computer game designers use x- and y-coordinates to place characters or objects in a game. They need to know distances between characters or how far players are apart.

If one player is at coordinate (30, 10) and the other at (15, 4), how far apart are they?

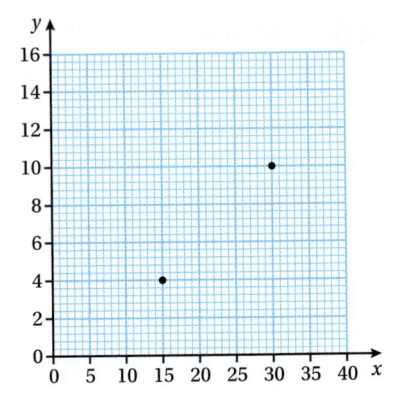

8 When you buy a television or computer, the size of the screen (for example, 15 inches) is actually the length of the diagonal. The diagram shows the length and width of a screen.

How would this screen be described?

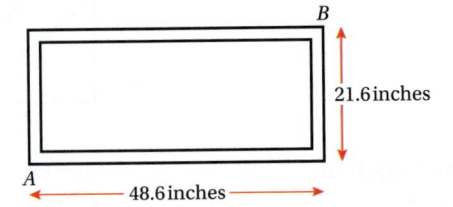

9 You are going to buy a new television. It is an 80 inch television (measured along its diagonal length).

Your current television is a 52 inch.

Both are the same height, 40 inches.

a How much wider is your new television than your current one?

b More importantly, will it fit in the 58 inch gap between the chimney and wall?

10 The diagram shows the side view of a shed.

Calculate the height from the ground to the top of the roof of the shed.

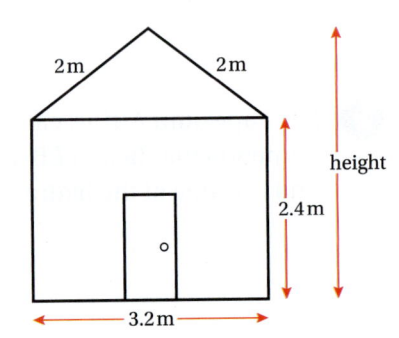

11 Show how you could use Pythagoras' theorem to find the length of side BD in this trapezium.

> **Tip**
>
> Think of the trapezium as a composite shape. How can you divide it up to solve the problem?

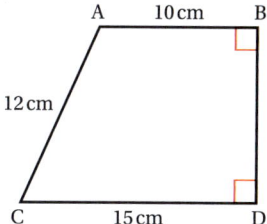

12 The height of a mast is 8 m. The longest side of the main sail is 11.4 m.

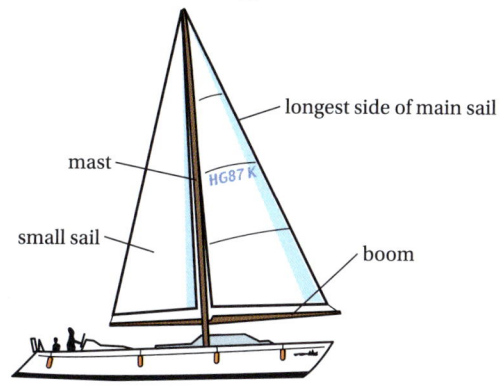

How far does the boom of the sail swing out?

The smaller sail has a boom length of 1.5 m.

How long is the longest side of the smaller sail?

Checklist of learning and understanding

Pythagoras' theorem

- Pythagoras' theorem only applies to right-angled triangles.
- The theorem is that the square of the hypotenuse of a right-angled triangle equals the sum of the squares of the other two sides. It can be written as
$a^2 + b^2 = c^2$
- Rearrange the formula to find the square of either of the other two sides:
$a^2 = c^2 - b^2$
$b^2 = c^2 - a^2$
- You can use the theorem to find the length of the hypotenuse, the longest side. The theorem can also be used to prove there is a right angle within a triangle or to find a missing length within a right-angled triangle.
- Always draw a diagram and label it; also write out the formula you are using to fully explain what you have done.
- Pythagorean triples are three lengths that satisfy the formula and therefore prove you have a right angle; learn the common ones, such as 3, 4, 5 and 5, 12, 13.
- If you need to find an unknown length in a composite shape, see if it is possible to divide the shape up so that it contains one or more right-angled triangles so that you can use Pythagoras' theorem to calculate the unknown length.

Find answers at: cambridge.org/ukschools/gcsemaths-studentbookanswers

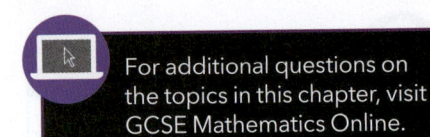

Chapter review

1. Which of the following statements are true?

   A Using Pythagoras' theorem you can find any angle within a right-angled triangle.

   B If you know one length in a right-angled triangle you can find the other two.

   C You can show that 3, 4, 5 is a Pythagorean triple using Pythagoras' theorem.

   D The hypotenuse is always the longest side in a triangle.

2. ABC is a right-angled triangle.

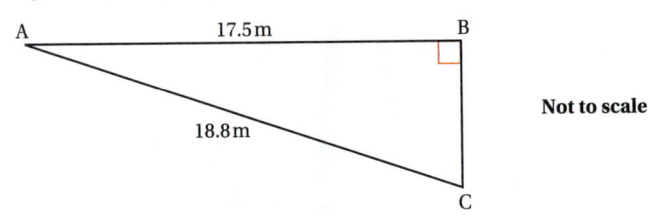

   AB = 17.5 m, AC = 18.8 m, right angle at B.

   Not to scale

   Calculate BC.

   Give your answer correct to 2 decimal places.   *(4 marks)*

   © OCR 2012

3. What is the perimeter of this kite?

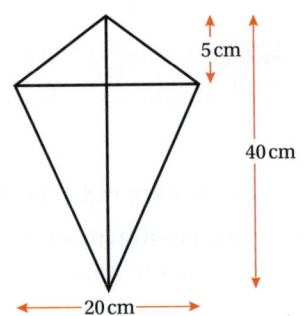

   5 cm, 40 cm, 20 cm

4. A five-bar gate measures 4 m wide and 1.5 m high at its highest point where the diagonal pieces of wood meet.

   What is the length of each diagonal piece of wood used in the gate?

32 Trigonometry

In this chapter you will learn how to …

- use trigonometric ratios to find lengths and angles in right-angled triangles.
- find and memorise exact values of important trigonometric ratios.

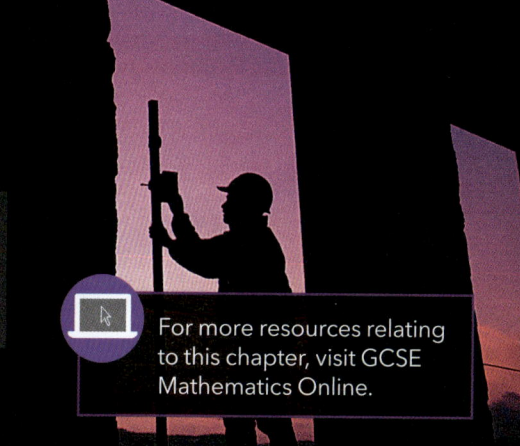

For more resources relating to this chapter, visit GCSE Mathematics Online.

Using mathematics: real-life applications

Trigonometry means 'triangle measurements' and it is very useful for finding the lengths of sides and sizes of angles. Trigonometry is used to determine lengths and angles in navigation, surveying, astronomy, engineering, construction and even in the placement of satellites and satellite receivers.

"I use a theodolite to work out the height of mountains. You basically point it at the top of the mountain. The theodolite uses the principles of trigonometry to measure angles and distances."
(Geologist)

Before you start …

Ch 31	You should be able to use Pythagoras' theorem to find lengths in triangles.	1	Find the length of x in each triangle: a (7, 16, x) b (x, 7, 5)
Ch 17	You must be able to work with approximate values and round to a specified number of places.	2	What is $\sqrt{53}$ correct to 2 decimal places?
		3	If $c^2 = 94.34$, what is c correct to 3 significant figures?
Ch 22, 30	You need to be able to use ratio and proportion to calculate sides in similar triangles.	4	Find the length of AC if the ratio of sides $\dfrac{AB}{AC} = \dfrac{5}{3}$ and AB = 35 cm.

Find answers at: cambridge.org/ukschools/gcsemaths-studentbookanswers

Assess your starting point using the Launchpad

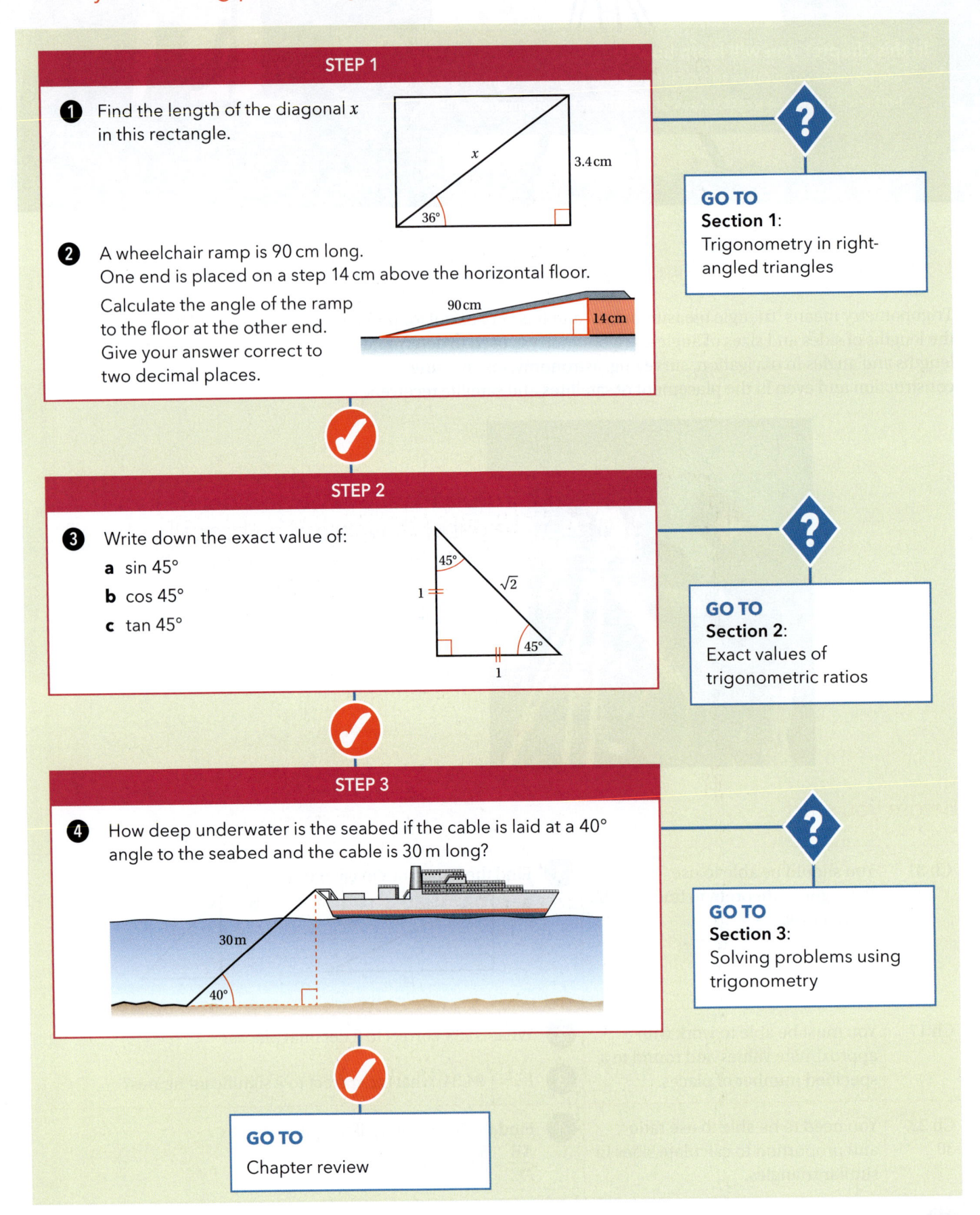

STEP 1

1 Find the length of the diagonal x in this rectangle.

(Rectangle with diagonal x, side 3.4 cm, angle 36°)

2 A wheelchair ramp is 90 cm long. One end is placed on a step 14 cm above the horizontal floor.

Calculate the angle of the ramp to the floor at the other end. Give your answer correct to two decimal places.

GO TO
Section 1: Trigonometry in right-angled triangles

STEP 2

3 Write down the exact value of:
  a sin 45°
  b cos 45°
  c tan 45°

(Right-angled triangle with sides 1, 1, $\sqrt{2}$ and angles 45°, 45°)

GO TO
Section 2: Exact values of trigonometric ratios

STEP 3

4 How deep underwater is the seabed if the cable is laid at a 40° angle to the seabed and the cable is 30 m long?

(Diagram of ship with cable 30 m at 40° to seabed)

GO TO
Section 3: Solving problems using trigonometry

GO TO
Chapter review

Section 1: Trigonometry in right-angled triangles

You already know that there are special relationships between the sides of right-angled triangles and that you can use Pythagoras' theorem to find missing sides when two sides are known. You also know that the ratio of corresponding pairs of sides in similar triangles is always the same.

These facts are important for understanding and using trigonometry.

Naming the sides of right-angled triangles

The hypotenuse is the longest side of a right-angled triangle, opposite the right angle.

The other two (shorter) sides are named in relation to the acute angles in the triangle.

In these triangles, one of the acute angles is labelled θ (the Greek letter theta).

The sides can then be labelled **opposite** (that is, opposite angle θ) and **adjacent** (that is, adjacent to angle θ).

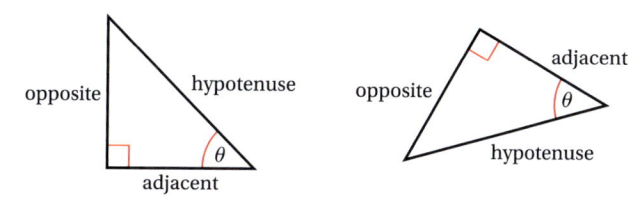

This system of naming the sides is fundamental to working with trigonometry, so make sure you understand how it works for triangles in any orientation before moving on.

WORKED EXAMPLE 1

In the right-angled triangle XYZ which side is:

a the hypotenuse?
b opposite angle Y?
c adjacent to angle Z?
d Which angle is adjacent to side XY?
e Which angle is opposite side XZ?

a YZ — The hypotenuse is the line opposite the right angle.

b XZ — Angle Y is the internal angle at vertex Y.

c XZ — Angle Z is the internal angle at vertex Z.

d Angle Y — The line XY is next to angle Y.

e Angle Y — The line XZ is opposite angle Y.

Find answers at: cambridge.org/ukschools/gcsemaths-studentbookanswers

The ratio of sides in similar triangles

This diagram shows three similar right-angled triangles. The green sides are opposite angle θ and the red sides are adjacent to it. You can see that the ratio of $\frac{\text{opposite}}{\text{adjacent}}$ sides is $\frac{1}{2}$ for all the similar triangles.

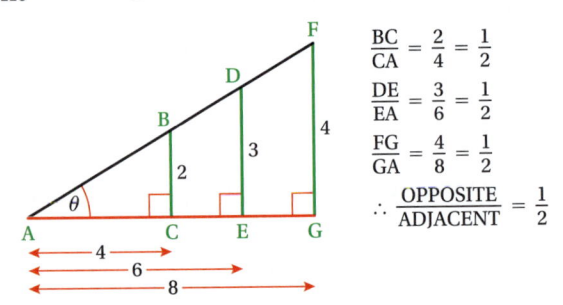

$\frac{BC}{CA} = \frac{2}{4} = \frac{1}{2}$

$\frac{DE}{EA} = \frac{3}{6} = \frac{1}{2}$

$\frac{FG}{GA} = \frac{4}{8} = \frac{1}{2}$

$\therefore \frac{\text{OPPOSITE}}{\text{ADJACENT}} = \frac{1}{2}$

Similar triangles show that for a given angle in a right-angled triangle, the ratio of corresponding sides will always be the same, regardless of the size of the triangle. Every angle therefore has a fixed value for the ratio of any two of its sides.

Depending on which sides you compare, the ratio of sides is given a special name. You will work with three ratios: sine, cosine and tangent.

The trigonometric ratios

In similar triangles, the ratio $\frac{\text{opposite}}{\text{hypotenuse}}$ is the same in each one, and the ratio $\frac{\text{adjacent}}{\text{hypotenuse}}$ is the same in each one, as is the ratio $\frac{\text{opposite}}{\text{adjacent}}$.

These ratios are called the trigonometric ratios (shortened to trig ratios) and they are named as follows:

The **sine** ratio (sin θ) is the ratio of the side opposite the angle to the hypotenuse.

The **cosine** ratio (cos θ) is the ratio of the side adjacent to the angle to the hypotenuse.

The **tangent** ratio (tan θ) is the ratio of the side opposite the angle to the side adjacent to the angle.

$\sin \theta = \frac{a}{c} = \frac{\text{opposite}}{\text{hypotenuse}}$

$\cos \theta = \frac{b}{c} = \frac{\text{adjacent}}{\text{hypotenuse}}$

$\tan \theta = \frac{a}{b} = \frac{\text{opposite}}{\text{adjacent}}$

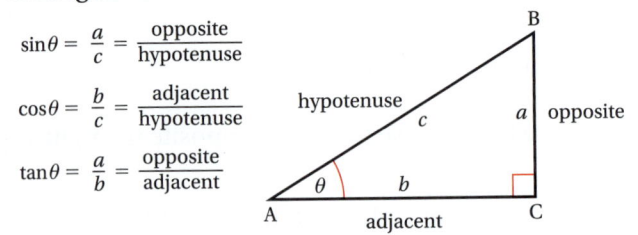

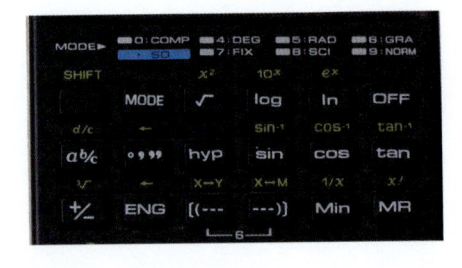

The three ratios have the same value for a particular angle no matter how long the sides are.

For example, sin 30° is $\frac{1}{2}$ or 0.5 for **any** right-angled triangle. This means that the ratio of $\frac{\text{opposite}}{\text{hypotenuse}}$ is $\frac{1}{2}$ if the angle you are working with is 30°.

You can find the ratio for any angle using your calculator. Make sure you know how to find and use the trig function keys.

32 Trigonometry

WORKED EXAMPLE 2

a For triangle ABC, find the ratio of sides used to calculate:
  i sin A. **ii** cos A. **iii** tan A.

b Use your calculator to find the value of each of the following trig ratios. Give your answers to 3 significant figures where necessary.
  i cos 32° **ii** sin 18° **iii** tan 80°

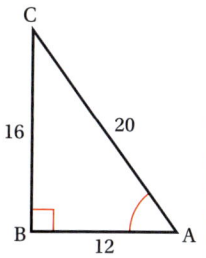

a
  i $\sin A = \dfrac{\text{opposite}}{\text{hypotenuse}} = \dfrac{16}{20} = \dfrac{4}{5}$

  ii $\cos A = \dfrac{\text{adjacent}}{\text{hypotenuse}} = \dfrac{12}{20} = \dfrac{3}{5}$

  iii $\tan A = \dfrac{\text{opposite}}{\text{adjacent}} = \dfrac{16}{12} = \dfrac{4}{3}$

Substitute in the appropriate lengths for each ratio.

b
  i cos 3 2 = 0.848
  ii sin 1 8 = 0.309
  iii tan 8 0 = 5.67

Press the appropriate button then enter the number for each ratio. Check your calculator to see how it works, as some calculators work differently to others.

EXERCISE 32A

1 Identify the sides relative to the angle given.

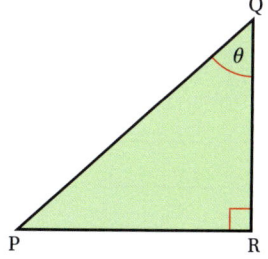

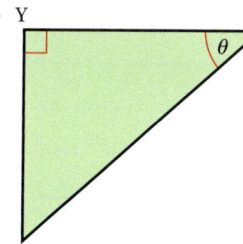

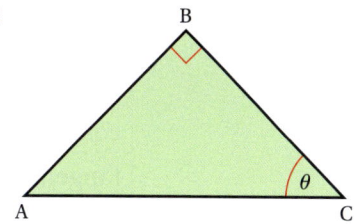

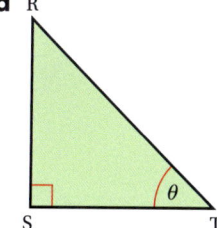

2 For each triangle identify which trig ratio you have the sides for, then write the ratio.

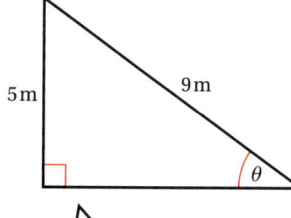

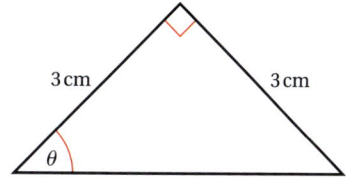

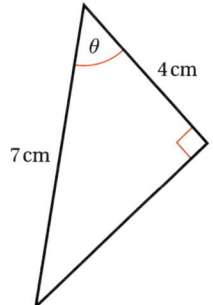

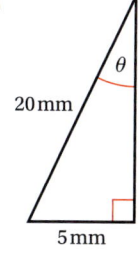

Find answers at: cambridge.org/ukschools/gcsemaths-studentbookanswers

3) Which trigonometry ratio would you use to find the marked angle?

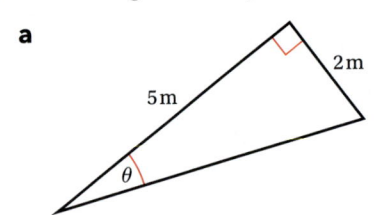

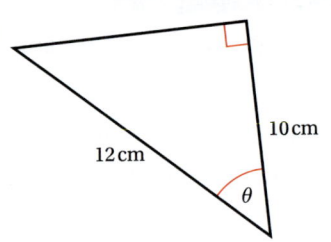

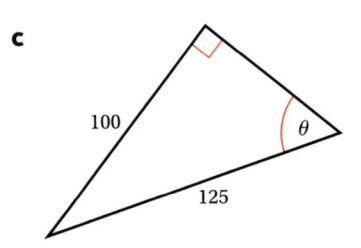

a) [triangle with 5m, 2m, angle θ]

b) [triangle with 12cm, 10cm, angle θ]

c) [triangle with 100, 125, angle θ]

4) Use your calculator to work out the value of each trigonometric ratio.

Trigonometric ratio	Value to 3dp
sine 40°	
cosine 40°	
tangent 45°	
sine 25°	
cosine 60°	
tangent 60°	
sine 30°	
cosine 30°	
tangent 30°	

5) Find the sine, cosine and tangent of the missing angle, giving your answers to 3 dp.

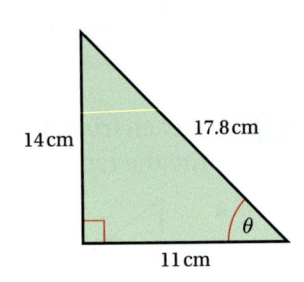

[triangle with 14cm, 17.8cm, 11cm, angle θ]

Tip

If you have two sides of a right-angled triangle you can find the other side using Pythagoras' theorem. If you have one side and at least one of the acute angles, you will need to use the trigonometric ratios.

Solving triangles

Finding unknown sides or angles is called solving the triangle. You can use trigonometric ratios to do this.

Finding unknown sides

If you know an angle (other than the right angle) and one side in a right-angled triangle, you can use the ratios to form **equations** that you solve to find the missing lengths.

You will not be told which ratio to use. You have to pick the right one based on the information that you have about the triangle.

You can remember the ratios using the mnemonic SOH-CAH-TOA and the formula triangles.

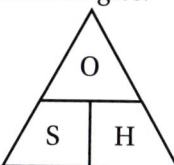

SOH: $\sin = \dfrac{\text{opposite}}{\text{hypotenuse}}$

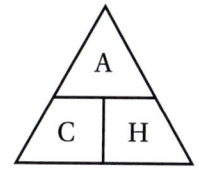

CAH: $\cos = \dfrac{\text{adjacent}}{\text{hypotenuse}}$

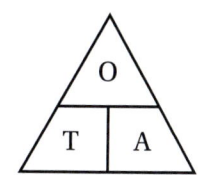

TOA: $\tan = \dfrac{\text{opposite}}{\text{adjacent}}$

> **Tip**
>
> Circle the angle you are working with and mark the sides H, A and O to help you see which values you have and which you need. To remind yourself how to use formula triangles, see Chapter 12.

WORKED EXAMPLE 3

1 In triangle ABC, angle B = 90°, AC = 15 cm and angle C = 35°. Calculate the length of AB correct to one decimal place.

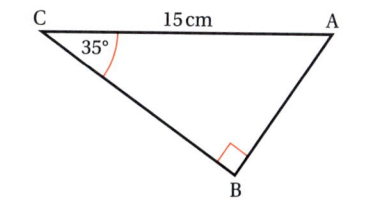

1 Given:

angle C = 35°

AB is opposite C

CA = 15 cm and is the hypotenuse.

$\sin 35° = \dfrac{\text{opposite}}{\text{hypotenuse}}$

Write down the information that you have been given and anything you can work out from the diagram.

AB is opposite the given angle (35°) and you have the length of the hypotenuse, so use the ratio with O and H, which is sin (SOH).

$\sin 35° = \dfrac{AB}{15}$

Substitute in the known values and solve for AB.

$AB = \sin 35° \times 15$

Multiply both sides by 15 to get AB on its own.

[sin] [3] [5] [×] [1] [5] [=]

Use your calculator to find this value.

AB = 8.6 cm (1 dp)

2 In triangle XYZ, angle Z is a right angle and angle X = 71°. Side YZ = 7.9 cm. Calculate the length of XZ correct to one decimal place.

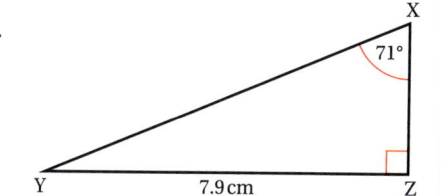

2 Given:

angle X = 71°

YZ = 7.9 cm = opposite side

XZ is the adjacent side

$\tan 71° = \dfrac{\text{opposite}}{\text{adjacent}} = \dfrac{7.9}{XZ}$

Use the ratio with OA which is tan (TOA). Multiply both sides by XZ to get rid of the fraction.

$7.9 = XZ \times \tan 71°$

$\dfrac{7.9}{\tan 71°} = XZ$

Divide by tan 71° to get XZ on its own.

[7] [.] [9] [÷] [tan] [7] [1] [=]

Do the calculation on your calculator.

XZ = 2.7 cm (1 dp)

Find answers at: cambridge.org/ukschools/gcsemaths-studentbookanswers

GCSE Mathematics for OCR (Foundation)

EXERCISE 32B

1 For each triangle, choose the appropriate trigonometric ratio and find the length of the side marked with a variable. Give your answers correct to two decimal places.

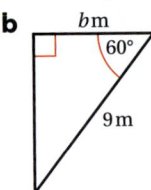

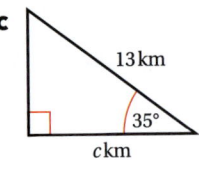

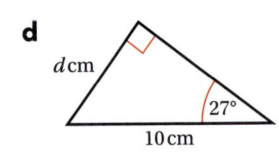

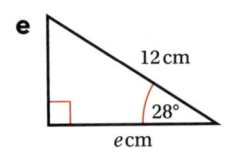

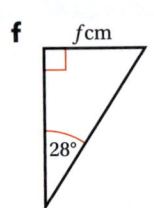

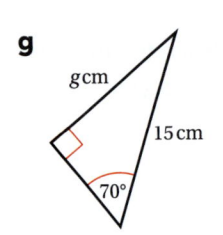

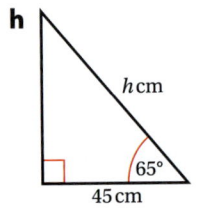

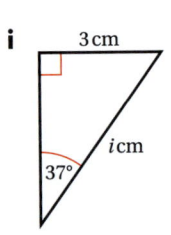

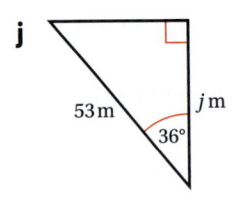

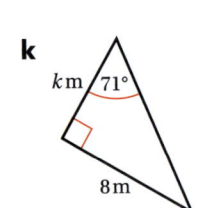

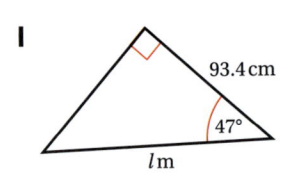

a 2.0 m, 25°, a m

b b m, 60°, 9 m

c 13 km, 35°, c km

d d cm, 27°, 10 cm

e 12 cm, 28°, e cm

f f cm, 28°

g g cm, 15 cm, 70°

h h cm, 65°, 45 cm

i 3 cm, 37°, i cm

j 53 m, j m, 36°

k k m, 71°, 8 m

l 93.4 cm, 47°, l m

2 Find the length of side x using trigonometry.

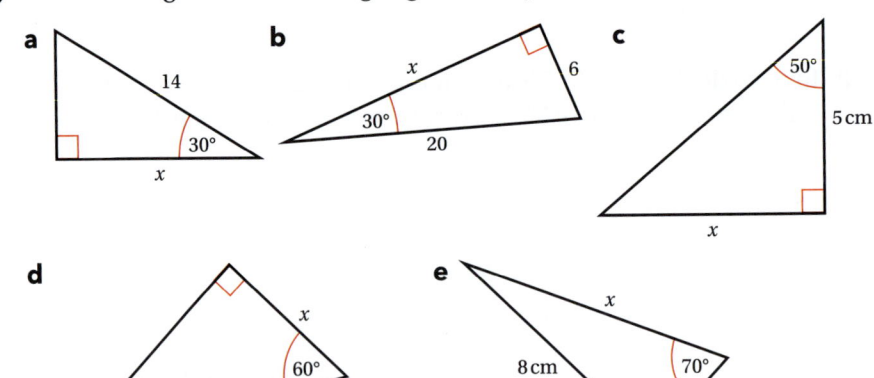

a 14, 30°, x

b x, 6, 30°, 20

c 50°, 5 cm, x

d x, 60°, 10

e x, 8 cm, 70°

Calculator tip

Your calculator can 'work backwards' to find the size of the unknown angle associated with a particular trigonometric ratio. To find the angle if you have the ratio, key in the inverse trigonometric function on your calculator, $\sin^{-1}$, $\cos^{-1}$ or $\tan^{-1}$.

Finding unknown angles

You can use the ratio of sides to find the size of unknown angles. You find the ratio using the side lengths in the same way as before but then you need to work out the **angle** in degrees that is associated with that ratio.

To find the size of unknown angles using the trigonometric ratios you need to use the inverse function of each ratio. On most calculators these are the second functions of the sin, cos and tan buttons. They are usually marked sin⁻¹, cos⁻¹ and tan⁻¹.

WORKED EXAMPLE 4

a Given that tan $x = 5$, what is the size of angle x?

b Find the size of angle x in each triangle to three significant figures.

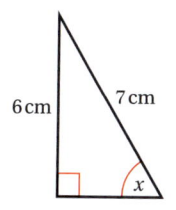

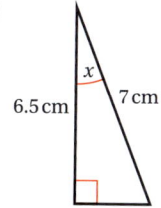

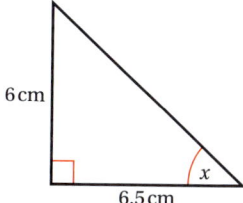

i (triangle with sides 6 cm, 7 cm, angle x at bottom right, right angle at bottom left)

ii (triangle with sides 6.5 cm, 7 cm, angle x at top)

iii (triangle with sides 6 cm, 6.5 cm, angle x at bottom right)

a SHIFT tan 5 = 78.69006753   Using your calculator.

Angle x is 78.7° correct to 1 dp.

b i $\sin x = \dfrac{\text{opposite}}{\text{hypotenuse}} = \dfrac{6}{7} = 0.857$ Write down the relevant information from the diagram. Find the ratio as before.

$\sin^{-1} 0.857 = x = 59.0°$ Use the inverse sin key on your calculator to find the angle in degrees.

ii $\cos x = \dfrac{\text{adjacent}}{\text{hypotenuse}} = \dfrac{6.5}{7} = 0.929$

$\cos^{-1} 0.929 = x = 21.8°$

iii $\tan x = \dfrac{\text{opposite}}{\text{adjacent}} = \dfrac{6}{6.5} = 0.923$

$\tan^{-1} 0.923 = x = 42.7°$

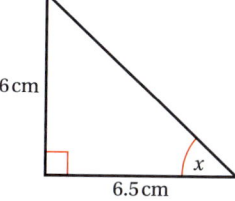

WORK IT OUT 32.1

For a ladder to be safe it must be inclined between 70° and 80° to the ground.

The diagram shows a ladder resting against a wall.

Is the ladder positioned safely?

Which of these calculations gives you the answer that you need?

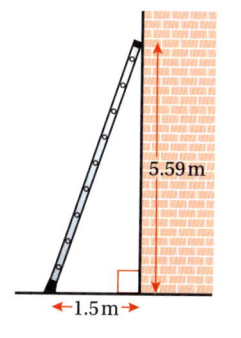

(Diagram: ladder against wall, 5.59 m along wall, 1.5 m along ground, Not to scale)

Option A	Option B	Option C
$\sin x = \dfrac{1.5}{5.59} = 0.268$	$\cos x = \dfrac{1.5}{5.59} = 0.268$	$\tan x = \dfrac{5.59}{1.5} = 3.73$
$\sin^{-1} 0.268 = 15.56°$	$\cos^{-1} 0.268 = 74.43°$	$\tan^{-1} 3.73 = 74.9°$

Find answers at: cambridge.org/ukschools/gcsemaths-studentbookanswers

EXERCISE 32C

1 Use your calculator to work out the value of each angle to the nearest degree.

a $\sin^{-1} 0.017$
b $\cos^{-1} 0.866$
c $\tan^{-1} 1$
d $\sin^{-1} 0.866$
e $\cos^{-1} 0.985$
f $\tan^{-1} 1.732$
g $\sin^{-1} 0.999$
h $\cos^{-1} 0.707$
i $\tan^{-1} 0.268$

2 a Find the sine, cosine and tangent of the following right-angled triangle and find the size of angle θ.

b The answers should all be the same. Why is there a small difference?

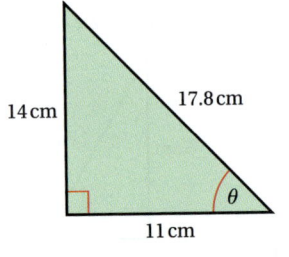

3 Calculate the value of θ for each ratio.

a $\sin \theta = 0.682$
b $\cos \theta = 0.891$
c $\tan \theta = 2.4751$
d $\sin \theta = 0.2588$

4 Find the size of each marked angle. Give your answers correct to 3 significant figures.

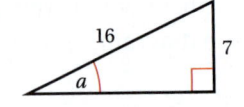

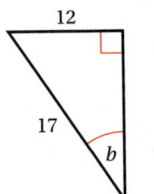

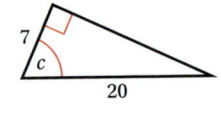

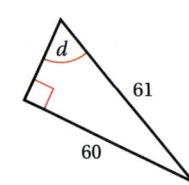

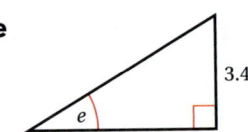

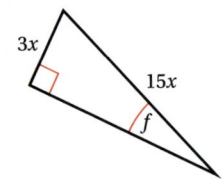

5 PQR is a right-angled triangle.

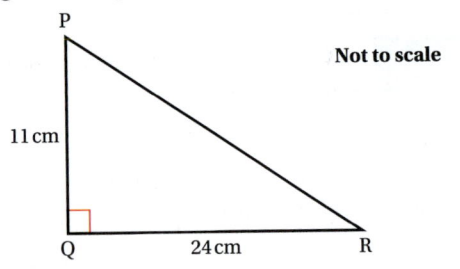

Calculate the size of angle PRQ.

6 What is the size of angle x?

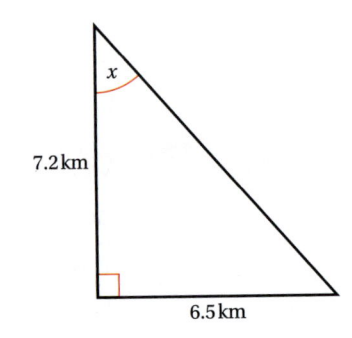

7 For each of these, sketch the triangle and calculate the required value.

  a In triangle ABC, angle B = 90°, BC = 45 units and angle C = 23°.
  Calculate the length of AB.

  b In triangle PQR, angle R = 90°, PQ = 12.2 cm and angle P = 57°.
  Calculate QR.

  c In triangle EFG, angle G = 90°, EG = 8.7 cm and angle E = 49°.
  Calculate the length of FG.

  d In triangle XYZ, angle Y = 90°, XZ = 36 units and angle X is 25°.
  Calculate the lengths of:
  i XY.   **ii** YZ.

8 For each triangle, draw a sketch and then calculate the required values.

  a In triangle ABC, angle C = 90°, BC = 6.7 units and AB = 9.8 units.
  Calculate angle A.

  b In triangle DEF, angle D = 90°, DF = 13 units and EF = 17 units.
  Calculate angle F.

  c In triangle GHI, angle I = 90°, HI = 8.2 cm and GI = 13.7 cm.
  Calculate the sizes of:
  i angle G.   **ii** angle H.

  d In triangle JKL, angle J = 90°, JK = 85 mm and KL = 113 mm.
  Calculate the sizes of:
  i angle K.   **ii** angle L.

  e In triangle MNO, angle N = 90°, NO = 29.8 cm and MN = 20.6 cm.
  Calculate:
  i angle O.   **ii** angle M.   **iii** MO.

  f In triangle PQR, angle Q = 90°, PQ = 57.3 mm and QR = 45.1 mm.
  Calculate:
  i angle P.   **ii** angle R.   **iii** PR.

Section 2: Exact values of trigonometric ratios

When you work out trigonometric ratios on your calculator you often get approximate (or truncated) values because the sides of right-angled triangles are not always perfect squares.

Some values of sin, cos and tan can be calculated exactly.
You need to know the exact values of the sin, cos and tan ratios for 0°, 30°, 60°, 45° and 90° angles, except for tan where there is **no** ratio for 90°.

Angle θ	$\sin \theta$	$\cos \theta$	$\tan \theta$
0°	0	1	0
30°	$\frac{1}{2}$	$\frac{\sqrt{3}}{2}$	$\frac{1}{\sqrt{3}}$
45°	$\frac{1}{\sqrt{2}}$	$\frac{1}{\sqrt{2}}$	1
60°	$\frac{\sqrt{3}}{2}$	$\frac{1}{2}$	$\sqrt{3}$
90°	1	0	tan 90° is undefined

> **Tip**
>
> Think back to the graphs of these functions you saw in Chapter 19. If you zoom in on the axis for the curve between 0 and 90° you see the values of each ratio.

Find answers at: cambridge.org/ukschools/gcsemaths-studentbookanswers

You can find the exact values of sin, cos and tan ratios for 0°, 30°, 60°, 45° and 90° using two special right-angled triangles.

Sine, cosine and tangent ratios for 30° and 60°

Take an equilateral triangle (triangle M with side length 2 units. If this is cut in half, you get triangle N where the angles are 90°, 60° and 30°.

Triangle M   Triangle N

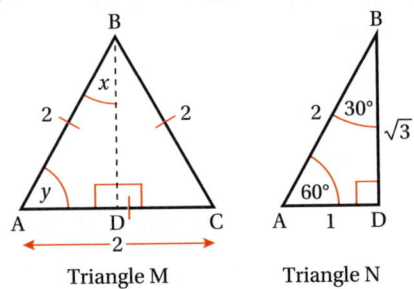

Angle $y = 60°$ (angles of equilateral triangle are equal).

Angle x is bisected by BD, so it is 30°.

BD is the perpendicular bisector of the base.

So, AD is 1 unit long.

Using Pythagoras, you can find the length of BD to be $\sqrt{3}$. You can use this triangle to calculate the value of the following ratios:

$$\sin 30° = \frac{\text{opposite}}{\text{hypotenuse}} = \frac{1}{2} \qquad \sin 60° = \frac{\text{opposite}}{\text{hypotenuse}} = \frac{\sqrt{3}}{2}$$

$$\cos 30° = \frac{\text{adjacent}}{\text{hypotenuse}} = \frac{\sqrt{3}}{2} \qquad \cos 60° = \frac{\text{adjacent}}{\text{hypotenuse}} = \frac{1}{2}$$

$$\tan 30° = \frac{\text{opposite}}{\text{adjacent}} = \frac{1}{\sqrt{3}} \qquad \tan 60° = \frac{\text{opposite}}{\text{adjacent}} = \frac{\sqrt{3}}{1} = \sqrt{3}$$

Sine, cosine and tangent ratios for 45°

The diagram shows a right-angled isosceles triangle with the equal sides 1 unit long.

Using Pythagoras, the hypotenuse is $\sqrt{2}$.

The base angles (x) are each 45°.

$\sin 45° = \text{opposite/hypotenuse} = \dfrac{1}{\sqrt{2}}$

$\cos 45° = \text{adjacent/hypotenuse} = \dfrac{1}{\sqrt{2}}$

$\tan 45° = \text{opposite/adjacent} = 1/1 = 1$

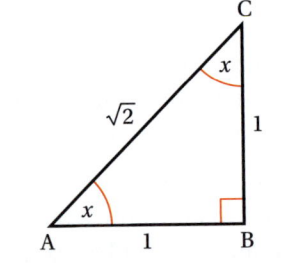

You need to know these exact values of special angles. You can always draw the triangles above to find them if you forget.

Square root form

You should have noticed that some trigonometric values are expressed in square root form, for example, $\sqrt{3}$. Square roots can be rational or irrational numbers.

$\sqrt{4}$ is rational because it can be expressed as a whole number (2).

$\sqrt{5} = 2.23606...$ is irrational as the square root cannot be expressed as a whole number.

It is more accurate to leave an irrational number as it is in a calculation or on a diagram because it gives the exact value rather than a rounded one. When you are asked to give an exact answer and you have an irrational number, you should leave your answer in square root form.

> **WORKED EXAMPLE 5**
>
> Without using your calculator, find the value of x. Leave your answer in exact form.
>
> **a** $x = \dfrac{3}{\tan 45°}$ **b** $x = \sin 30° \times 6$ **c** $x = \tan 60° \times 2$
>
> **a** $x = \dfrac{3}{\tan 45°} = \dfrac{3}{1} = 3$ $\tan 45° = 1$ (you need to learn this).
>
> **b** $x = \sin 30° \times 6 = \dfrac{1}{2} \times 6 = 3$ $\sin 30° = \dfrac{1}{2}$ (you need to learn this).
>
> **c** $x = \tan 60° \times 2 = 2 \times \sqrt{3} = 2\sqrt{3}$ $\tan 60° = \sqrt{3}$ (you need to learn this). Your answer needs to be in exact form so leave the square root sign in place. You know from Chapter 1 that root signs act in the same way as brackets in terms of the order of operations, so you can simplify your answer by removing the multiplication sign.

EXERCISE 32D

1 Copy and complete this table. Use it to memorise the exact values of the trigonometric ratios for the different angles.

Angle θ	$\sin \theta$	$\cos \theta$	$\tan \theta$
0°			
30°			
45°			
60°			
90°			tan 90° is undefined

2 Without using your calculator, identify the connection between $\sin x$ and $\cos (90 - x)$. Think about complementary angles.

> **Tip**
>
> Think about sin 30° and cos 60°; sin 45° and cos 45°; cos 30° and sin 60°.

3 You have an equilateral triangle with side length 7.

Find the perpendicular height of the triangle using each of the trigonometric ratios.

Section 3: Solving problems using trigonometry

The trigonometric ratios can be applied to many different types of measurement problems. If the question does not include a sketch, it is useful to draw one. Make it large and clear and mark what you know on it. This will help you to identify the correct ratio to use to solve the problem.

Find answers at: cambridge.org/ukschools/gcsemaths-studentbookanswers

Angles of elevation and depression

Many trigonometry problems involve lines of sight. (In other words, the straight line from your eyes to an object you are looking at.)

Problems that involve looking **up** to an object can be described in terms of an **angle of elevation**. This is the angle between an observer's line of sight and a horizontal line.

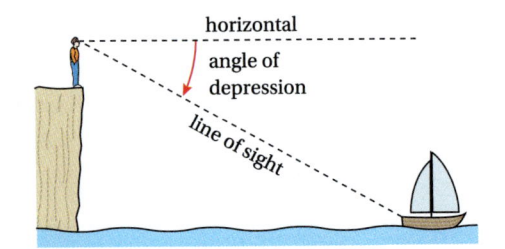

> **Key vocabulary**
>
> **angle of elevation:** when looking up, the angle between the line of sight and the horizontal.
>
> **angle of depression:** when looking down, the angle between the line of sight and the horizontal.

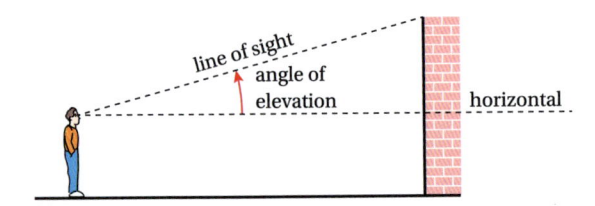

When an observer is looking **down**, the **angle of depression** is the angle between the observer's line of sight and a horizontal line.

WORKED EXAMPLE 6

From the top of a lighthouse 105 m above sea level, the angle of depression of a boat is 5°.

How far is the boat from the shore? Give the answer to the nearest metre.

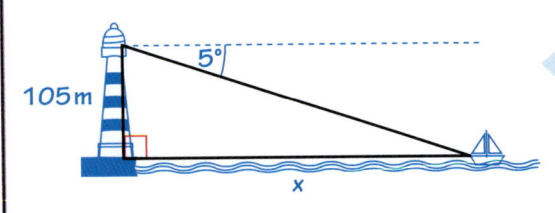

Sketch a diagram of the information you have.

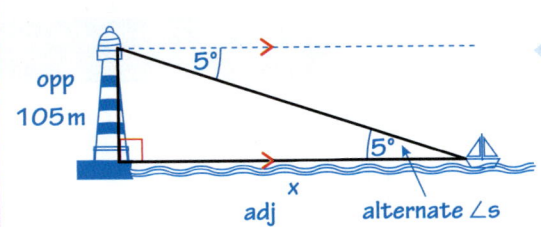

Look at the diagram carefully and mark on any additional information you can: the angle of depression is alternate to the angle at the boat (the sea level is a horizontal line parallel to the horizontal from which the angle of depression is measured). You need to find x. This is the side adjacent to 5°.

The side opposite the angle is 105 m.

You need the ratio with OA, which is tan (TOA).

$$\tan 5° = \frac{105}{x}$$

$$\tan 5° \times x = 105$$

$$x = \frac{105}{\tan 5°} = 1200.155492$$

$x = 1200$ m (to the nearest metre)

32 Trigonometry

Problem-solving framework

A ship is laying cable along the sea bed.

The angle of the cable to the sea bed is 40° and at this angle, the length of cable between the sea bed and the sea level is 40 metres.

The ship is 50 kilometres offshore and travelling north-west.

What is the depth of the sea bed?

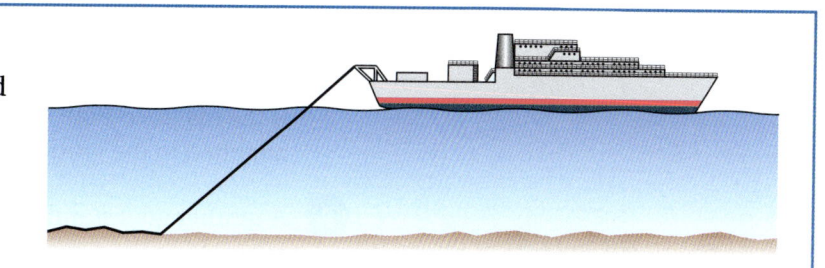

Steps for approaching a problem-solving question	What you would do for this example
Step 1: What have you got to do?	Find the depth of water.
Step 2: Is it helpful to draw a sketch?	You are given an angle and a length and asked to find another length, a sketch of the resulting triangle would be useful. 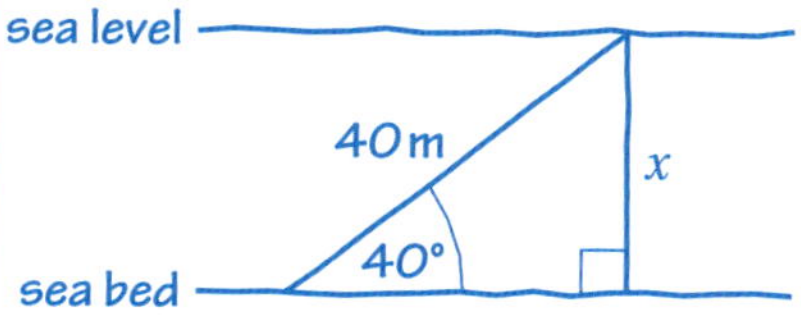
Step 3: What information do you need? What information don't you need?	Angle 40° and length of cable as the hypotenuse is 40 m. That the ship is 50 kilometres offshore and the direction in which it is travelling are irrelevant.
Step 4: What maths can you do?	You have a right-angled triangle, an angle and the length of the hypotenuse. You cannot use Pythagoras as you do not know two lengths, so use trig. Decide which trigonometry function – sin, cos or tan? The required length is opposite the angle, so use sin (SOH). $\sin 40° = \dfrac{x}{40}$ $0.6428 \times 40 = x$ $= 25.71$ m The depth of the sea bed is 25.71 m (2 dp)
Step 5: Have you answered the question? Is your answer correct?	Yes – answer seems reasonable given that the length must be less than 40 m and as sin 30° = 0.5 so half of 40 m would be 20 m.

EXERCISE 32E

1 Measure the marked angles in each diagram in degrees. Say whether it is an angle of depression or an angle of elevation.

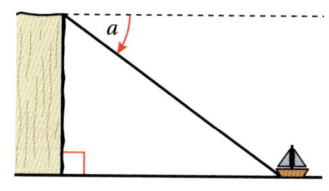

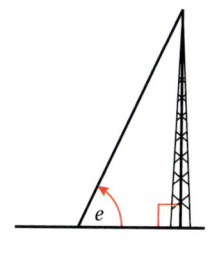

A   B   C   D

Find answers at: cambridge.org/ukschools/gcsemaths-studentbookanswers

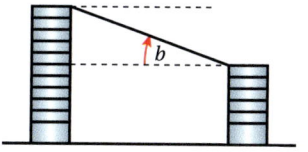

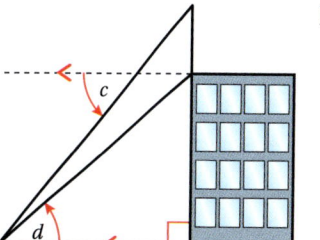

GCSE Mathematics for OCR (Foundation)

2 Look at diagram A on the previous page.
If the boat is 800 m from the base of the cliff, work out the height of the cliff.

3 Look at diagram D.
If the distance from the top of the mast to the point where the cable is attached to the ground is 35 m, how high is the mast?

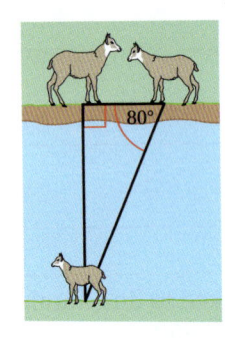

4 A mother goat stands on one side of the river with one of her kids 100 m away along the river bank. The younger of her kids swam across the river and is calling for her. Assuming there is no water current,
  a what distance does the mother goat need to swim straight across the river to reach her baby?
  b What distance is the line of sight from the mother and younger goat to the older kid, once the mother reaches the other side?

5 A slide is 4.2 m long and makes an angle of 63° with the horizontal. Calculate the height of the slide.

6 Carol is in a hot air balloon at point C in the sky.
CG is the vertical height of the hot air balloon above the ground.
David is standing on the ground at point D.
The distance between points D and G is 27 m.
The angle of elevation from David to the hot air balloon is 53°.
Calculate the length of CG.

7 Two boats are sailing out at sea a distance of 25 m apart. The angle of depression from the top of a lighthouse to one boat is 35° and to the other boat is 55°.
How tall is the lighthouse?

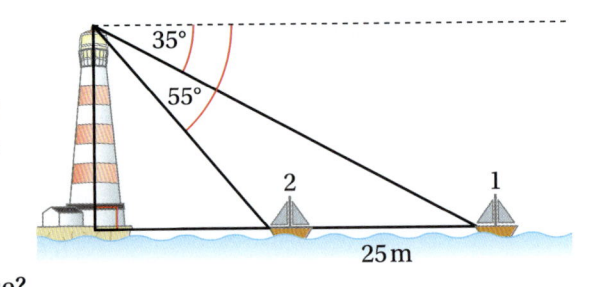

8 Mike is standing 15 m away from a flagpole. The angle of elevation from his line of sight to the top of the flagpole is 60°.
  a How tall is the flagpole?
  b If he moves another 10 m further away from the flagpole, how will the angle of elevation to the top of the flagpole change?

9 Two observers in different positions at A and B are watching a rare bird on a tree at C. The angle of elevation from A to C is 56° and the angle of elevation from B to C is 25°. 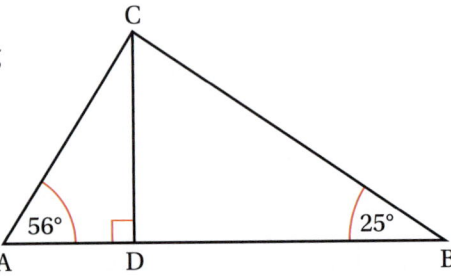
  a If person B is standing 15 m from D (the base of the tree), calculate the height of the bird above the ground (the length of CD).
  b Calculate the distance of person A from D.

10 A person is standing at a point P, 30 m away from a signal tower for a mobile phone operator. The angle of depression from the top of the tower to P is 56°.

Calculate the height of the tower.

11 A tree surgeon uses an instrument to measure that the angle of elevation from her point of view to the top of a tree is 20°. She is standing 10 m away from the tree.

   a If she assumes that the tree is perfectly perpendicular, how would she calculate the height of the tree?

   b To check her calculation, she moves another 10 m away from the tree in a straight line, and measures the angle of elevation again.

   What should the angle measurement be now if her first measurement and calculation were correct?

Checklist of learning and understanding

Trigonometric ratios

- In a right-angled triangle, the longest side is the hypotenuse. For a given angle θ, the other two sides can be labelled opposite (to angle θ) and adjacent (to angle θ).
- The sine, cosine and tangent ratios can be used to find unknown sides and angles in right-angled triangles.
  - $\sin \theta = \dfrac{\text{opposite}}{\text{hypotenuse}}$
  - $\cos \theta = \dfrac{\text{adjacent}}{\text{hypotenuse}}$
  - $\tan \theta = \dfrac{\text{opposite}}{\text{adjacent}}$
- You can find the value of a ratio using the sin, cos and tan buttons on your calculator.
  To find the size of an angle, use the inverse functions for each ratio.

Exact values

- You can find the exact values of sin, cos and tan for special angles. Some exact values contain square roots.

Chapter review

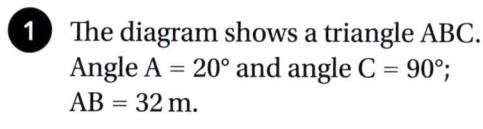

1 The diagram shows a triangle ABC.
Angle A = 20° and angle C = 90°;
AB = 32 m.

Calculate the height BC.

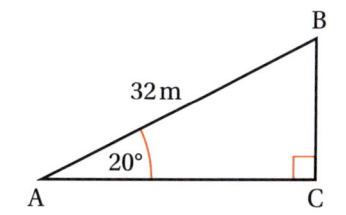

Find answers at: cambridge.org/ukschools/gcsemaths-studentbookanswers

2 A ladder leans against the side of a house. The ladder is 4.5 m in length, and makes an angle of 74° with the ground.

How high up the wall will it reach? (This length is marked x in the diagram.)

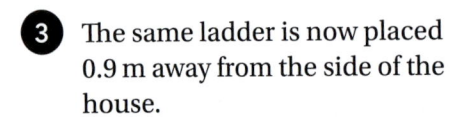

3 The same ladder is now placed 0.9 m away from the side of the house.

What angle does the ladder now make with the ground? (This angle is marked y in the diagram.)

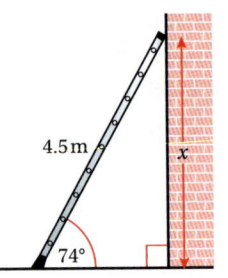

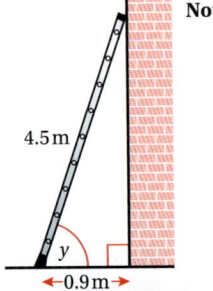

4 The dimensions of the lean on the Leaning Tower of Pisa are shown on the diagram.

From the information given, what is the actual height of the tower?

5 Triangles ABC and PQR are similar. AC = 3.2 cm, AB = 4 cm and PR = 4.8 cm.

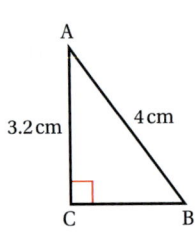

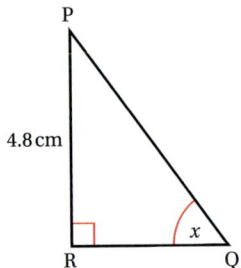

Explain why $\sin x = 0.8$.

33 Discrete growth and decay

In this chapter you will learn how to …

- set up and solve problems involving growth and decay, including simple and compound interest.

For more resources relating to this chapter, visit GCSE Mathematics Online.

Using mathematics: real-life applications

Many real-life situations involve growth (increase) or decay (decrease) as time passes. Population numbers, growth of bacteria, disease infection rates, world temperature patterns and the value of money or possessions may all increase or decrease over time.

"My computer program calculates interest on a daily basis. This means whatever is in the account gains interest, not just the initial investment."
(Investment broker)

Before you start …

Ch 11, 13	You must be able to convert percentages to decimals.	**1** Write each of the following as a decimal. **a** 5% **b** 190% **c** 0.4% **d** 12.5%
Ch 13	You must be able to find a percentage of a quantity using multiplication.	**2** Find, using multiplication only: **a** 68% of £300 **b** 2% of $80 **c** 4.5% of £56 **d** 114% of $650 **e** 99.5% of £1540
Ch 10	You need to be able to increase or decrease a quantity by a given percentage by multiplying by a suitable decimal.	**3** Carry out the following increases and decreases using only multiplication. **a** Increase $44 by 22% **b** Increase £35 by 5.5% **c** Decrease £13 by 44% **d** Decrease $170 by 8%

Find answers at: cambridge.org/ukschools/gcsemaths-studentbookanswers

GCSE Mathematics for OCR (Foundation)

Assess your starting point using the Launchpad

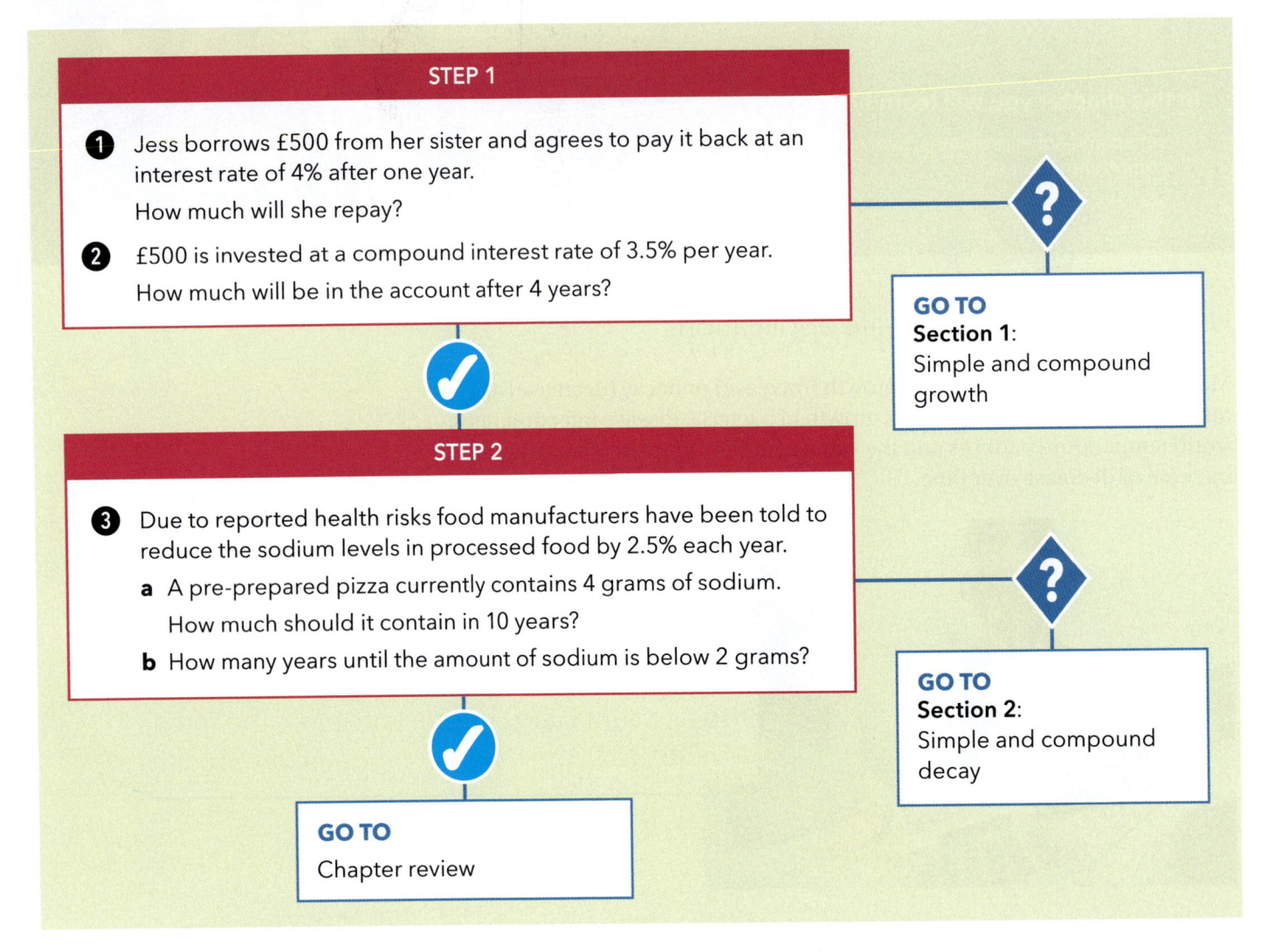

STEP 1

1 Jess borrows £500 from her sister and agrees to pay it back at an interest rate of 4% after one year.
How much will she repay?

2 £500 is invested at a compound interest rate of 3.5% per year.
How much will be in the account after 4 years?

GO TO
Section 1: Simple and compound growth

STEP 2

3 Due to reported health risks food manufacturers have been told to reduce the sodium levels in processed food by 2.5% each year.
  a A pre-prepared pizza currently contains 4 grams of sodium.
  How much should it contain in 10 years?
  b How many years until the amount of sodium is below 2 grams?

GO TO
Section 2: Simple and compound decay

GO TO
Chapter review

Section 1: Simple and compound growth

Simple interest

When you borrow money or buy things on credit you are normally charged interest for the use of the money. When you invest or save money, you are paid interest by the bank or other institution in return for leaving your money with them.

The amount of money you invest or borrow is called the principal.

Simple interest is interest paid on the original principal. The same interest is paid for each time period.

For example:

Suppose you borrow £1000 at an interest rate of 5% per year.

Each year you will be charged 5% × £1000 = £50.

In other words the interest will be £50 for each year of the loan period.

Simple interest (I) can be worked out using a formula:

$$I = PRT$$

Where P is the principal amount,

R is the rate of interest as a percentage,

T is the time period over which the interest is calculated.

33 Discrete growth and decay

Compound interest

When using compound interest, we calculate the interest on the principal amount plus any interest that has been added. So using our previous example, after the first loan period, the bank would work out the interest you owe based on £1050 (principal plus interest), not £1000.

WORKED EXAMPLE 1

Charlotte deposits £500 into a savings account for six years. The bank pays interest on the savings at 5% per year.

Compare the amount each year for 6 years when the interest is calculated using simple interest to the amount when the interest is compounded annually.

Year	Simple interest	Compound interest
1	£500 + 5% = £525	£500 + 5% = £525
2	£525 + (5% of £500) = £550	£525 + 5% = £551.25
3	£575	£578.81
4	£600	£607.75…
5	£625	£638.14…
6	£650	£670.04…

For simple interest, £25 is added every year; the interest stays constant. For compound interest, £25 is added in the first year, £26.25 (5% of £525) is added in the second year … each year the amount of interest earned increases.

Charlotte would get a greater return on her investment if she used an account that offered compound interest.

WORK IT OUT 33.1

The population of Europe is growing at a rate of 0.2% per year. The current population is 739 million. What will the population be in 3 years' time?

Three students attempted the question. In pairs, decide who has got the correct answer. Also decide which you think is the most efficient method to find the answer.

Kayleigh	Tom	Zac
Find 0.2%: 0.2% of 739 000 000 = 0.002 × 739 000 000 = 1 478 000 The same growth for 3 years: 3 × 1 478 000 = 4 434 000 Add it on: 739 000 000 + 4 434 000 = 743 434 000	Year 1: Find 0.2% of 739 000 000 = 0.002 × 739 000 000 = 1 478 000 Add it on: 740 478 000 Year 2: Find 0.2% of 740 478 000 = 0.002 × 740 478 000 = 1 480 956 Add it on: 741 958 956 Year 3: Find 0.2% and add it on 1 483 918 + 741 958 956 = 743 442 874	Increase by 0.2% means there is 100.2%, do this three times in a row. 739 000 000 × 1.002 × 1.002 × 1.002 = 739 000 000 × 1.002^3 = 743 442 874

Find answers at: cambridge.org/ukschools/gcsemaths-studentbookanswers

Working with compound interest and growth rates is very much like working with function machines. Each time an output is produced it goes back to becoming an input and the process is repeated. This keeps going for the allotted period of time. This kind of process is called iterative – it iterates or repeats.

> **Tip**
>
> Always show your working for these questions. Write down what you type into the calculator so you can check it and so that your teacher and the examiner can see how you have calculated your answer.

For example, let's suppose that the population of starlings in a park increases each year at a rate of 10%. To increase a quantity by 10% we multiply by 1.1 (100% + 10% = 110%, or 1.1).

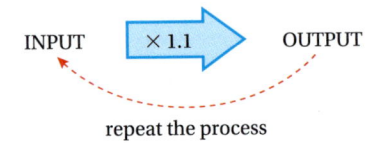

INPUT → × 1.1 → OUTPUT

repeat the process

If the population started with 80 starlings and you wanted to predict how many there would be in five years' time the first input would be 80.

$80 \times 1.1 = 88$

$88 \times 1.1 = 96.8$ (notice that if our model was to stop here we would round sensibly; however, we use the unrounded value to ensure the following year's prediction is more accurate)

$96.8 \times 1.1 = 106.48$

$106.48 \times 1.1 = 117.128$

$117.128 \times 1.1 = 128.8408$, so we would predict that there will be 129 starlings in five years' time.

This could be re-written as

$80 \times 1.1 \times 1.1 \times 1.1 \times 1.1 \times 1.1$ (you can simplify this to 80×1.1^5).

EXERCISE 33A

1. Copy and complete this table for simple interest at the given rate.

Investment	Interest rate	1 year	2 years	6 years	n years
£250	2%				
£1500	4.5%				
	3%	£51.50			

2. £300 is invested for three years with a compound interest rate of 2%.

    How much is in the account after:

    a 1 year?   **b** 3 years?   **c** 8 years?

3. £1000 is invested with a compound interest rate of 3%.

    Plot a graph showing how much money is in the account over the first 10 years of the investment.

33 Discrete growth and decay

4 A colony of bacteria grows by 4% every hour. At first the colony has 100 bacteria.

How many will exist after 24 hours?

5 The population of Ireland is growing at an annual rate of 1.7%. In 2014 the population was 4.6 million.
   a If this growth rate remains constant how many people will be living in Ireland in 2024?
   b How many new inhabitants are there?
   c Use this model to show how many people there were in Ireland in 2012. Comment on the validity of your answers.

6 The Bank of England's target inflation rate is 2%. This tells you how much the cost of living, food, fuel and rent is likely to go up each year. In 2015 a month's rent is given as £450.

Assuming that the Bank targets are correct, how much is this likely to be 20 years later?

7 Gavin is saving for a new bike. The model he wants costs £255. So far he has saved £200. Gavin's dad has offered to pay him 8% interest for every month that Gavin does his homework, cleans his room and loads the dishwasher.

How long is he going to have to wait for the bike? Show working to explain your answer.

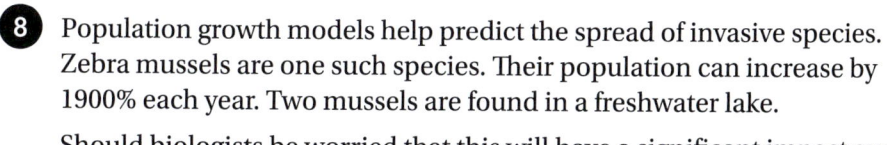

8 Population growth models help predict the spread of invasive species. Zebra mussels are one such species. Their population can increase by 1900% each year. Two mussels are found in a freshwater lake.

Should biologists be worried that this will have a significant impact over the next 10 years? Give details to explain your response.

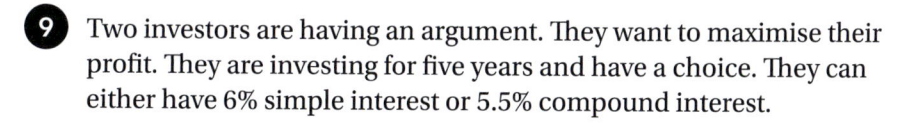

9 Two investors are having an argument. They want to maximise their profit. They are investing for five years and have a choice. They can either have 6% simple interest or 5.5% compound interest.

Which should they choose? Would the answer change if they were investing for four years?

10 £100 000 is invested at a rate of 5% compounded for 10 years.
   a How much more money is earned using compound interest compared to simple interest?
   b What simple interest rate would be needed to achieve the same earnings?

11 House prices are rising. A two-bedroomed house cost £195 000 last year and now costs £216 450.

If the price keeps rising at the same rate how much will this house cost in three years' time?

Find answers at: cambridge.org/ukschools/gcsemaths-studentbookanswers

12 Which of the following investment models gives the highest earnings?

Model 1	Model 2	Model 3
Year 1: 5% interest	Years 1–3	Years 1–3
Year 2: 4% interest	4% compound interest	3.9% simple interest
Year 3: 3% interest		

13 A colony of bacteria grow by 5% every hour.
How long does it take for the colony to double in size?

Section 2: Simple and compound decay

When the value of something goes down we say it has depreciated. For example, a brand new car will show a **depreciation** in value of about 30% in the first year of ownership alone.

> **Key vocabulary**
>
> **depreciation**: the loss in value of an object over a period of time.

WORKED EXAMPLE 2

The value of a new computer depreciates by 30% per year. If it cost £1200 new, what will it be worth in two years' time?

Method 1
Value after 1 year = £1200 − (30% of £1200)
= £1200 − £360
= £840
Value after 2 years = £840 − (30% of £840)
= £840 − £252
= £588

> Each year the value decreases by 30%. Work out the new value after one year by subtracting 30% of the cost when new. To calculate the value after two years, subtract 30% of the value after one year from the value after one year, and so on, working one year at a time.

Method 2:
Value after 1 year = 70% of £1200 = £840
Value after 2 years = 70% of £840 = £588

> Decreasing an amount by 30% is the same as finding 70% of the amount.

When the number of individuals in a population declines over time, it is called decay rather than depreciation.

For example, if the population of squirrels is in decay, it means that each year there are fewer and fewer animals in the population. If the rate of decline is 10%, each year 10% of the squirrels disappear, leaving 90%. So from one year to the next the number of animals is $n \times 0.9$, where n is the total number of squirrels in the previous year.

WORK IT OUT 33.2

For every 1000 m you climb, the atmospheric pressure decreases by 12%. If the atmospheric pressure at sea level is 100 300 pascal (Pa), what would the pressure be for a skydiver at an altitude of 4000 metres?

Three students attempted the question. In pairs, decide who has got the correct answer, and also the most efficient method to find the answer.

Bob	Jenny	Ethan
12% of 100 300 = 0.12 × 100 300 = 12 036 4 × 12 036 = 48 144 100 300 − 48 144 = 52 156 Pa	Decrease by 12% leaves 88% 88% of 100 300 = 0.88 × 100 300 = 88 264 88% of 88 264 = 77 672.32 88% of 77 672.32 = 68 351.6416 88% of 68 351.6416 = 60 149.444608 Pa	Decrease by 12% leaves 88%, do this four times in a row. 100 300 × 0.88 × 0.88 × 0.88 × 0.88 = 100 300 × 0.88^4 = 60 149.444608 Pa = 60 149.4 Pa (1 dp)

Tip

A pascal is the SI unit of pressure, equal to one newton per square metre.

EXERCISE 33B

1 The value of a compact car depreciates each year by 8%. A new compact car costs £11 000. How much will this be worth in:

 a 1 year?   b 3 years?   c 8 years?

2 Copy and complete this table:

Initial cost	Depreciation rate	1 year	2 years	6 years
£400	2%			
£2 500	15%			
£50 000	3.5%			

3 The pesticide DDT is banned in many countries, including the UK, because it builds up in animal tissue over time to dangerous levels. However, DDT in the soil is absorbed by the soil (i.e., it decays) at a rate of 7% a year.

If a farmer used 2 kg of DDT on a field in the year 2000, how much would remain in the field in 2014?

Find answers at: cambridge.org/ukschools/gcsemaths-studentbookanswers

4 The rate at which water flows out of a tank with an opening at the bottom depends on the amount of water left in the tank. For one particular tank the height of the water left will reduce by 15% every five minutes. Which of the following graphs depicts this?

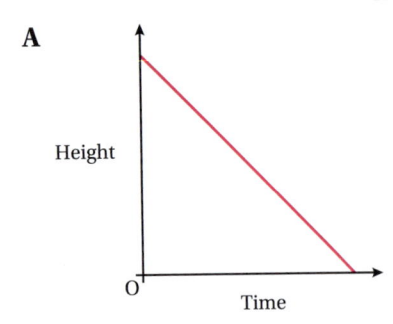

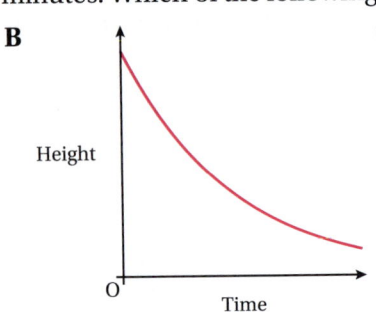

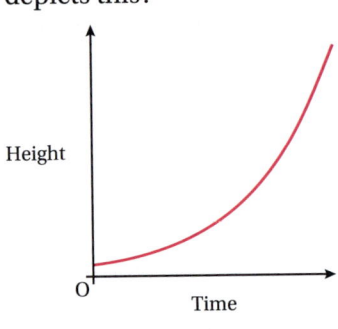

A, **B**, **C** (graphs of Height vs Time)

5 At the start of an experiment there are 8000 bacteria. A chemical is introduced to the population causing a reduction of 1600 in the population in an hour.
   a What percentage decrease in population is this?
   b Assuming the same rate of decrease, how many bacteria would you expect to be alive after eight hours?
   c How long until fewer than 100 bacteria are alive?

6 For every 1000 m higher you climb, the atmospheric pressure decreases by 12%.
   If the sea-level atmospheric pressure is 100 300 pascal (Pa), what would the pressure be if you jumped out of a balloon flying 39 km above sea level?

7 The population of Bulgaria is decreasing at a rate of 0.6% per year. In 2014 the population was 7.4 million people.
   a How many people are expected to be living in Bulgaria in 2020?
   b How many years until the population dips below 7 million?

8 The cost of mobile phones has been falling. Three years ago the latest model cost £400 with no contract; now the latest model costs £342.95.
   If the price keeps falling, how long until the current model costs less than two-thirds of today's price?

Checklist of learning and understanding

Simple and compound growth
- Simple growth, such as simple interest, is a fixed rate of growth, calculated on the original amount.
- The formula $I = PRT$ can be used to calculate simple interest, where P = principal amount, R = the rate of interest as a percentage, and T is the time period over which the interest is calculated.
- Compound growth, such as compound interest, is calculated on the principal for the first period and then compounded by calculating it on the principal plus any interest paid or due for each previous period.
- You can work out compound growth using a multiplier for each period.

Simple and compound decay
- A drop in value of an object over time is called depreciation.
- A decline in a population is called decay.
- Simple and compound decay is found by working out the percentage decrease using repeated subtraction or by working out the percentage remaining.

Chapter review

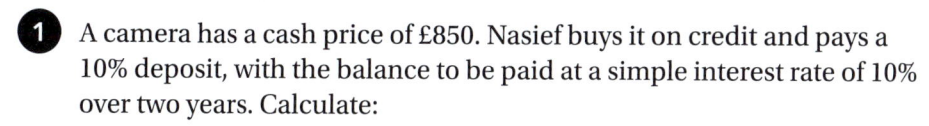

1. A camera has a cash price of £850. Nasief buys it on credit and pays a 10% deposit, with the balance to be paid at a simple interest rate of 10% over two years. Calculate:

   a the amount of his deposit.

   b the balance owing after deducting the deposit.

   c the amount of interest paid in total over two years.

   d the monthly payment amount for 24 equal monthly instalments.

   e the difference between the cash price and what Nasief actually paid in the end.

2. Salma invests her money in an account that pays 6% interest compounded half-yearly.

   If she puts £2300 in the account and leaves it there for two years, how much money will she have at the end of the period?

3. Frances invests £30 000 at 6% per year **compound** interest.

   How much will the investment be worth after 3 years? *(4 marks)*

   © OCR 2013

4. A car valued at £8500 depreciates by 30% in the first year, 20% in the second year and a further 12% in the third year.

   How much is it worth after three years?

5. Each year the education department arranges a quiz. There are 140 students in the competition to start with. During each round, half of the quiz contestants are eliminated (rounded to the nearest whole number).

   How many students will still be participating after round 4?

6. Tamsin collects antiques. Each year the value of her collection increases; it is currently worth £30 000. She is told by an antiquities dealer that her collection will increase in value as follows:

   by 2% after one year

   by 5% after two years

   by 11% after three years.

   What is the value of her collection at the end of each year?

Find answers at: cambridge.org/ukschools/gcsemaths-studentbookanswers

34 Direct and inverse proportion

In this chapter you will learn how to ...
- understand proportion and the equality of ratios.
- solve problems involving direct and inverse proportion, including graphical and algebraic representations.
- understand that x is inversely proportional to y is equivalent to x is proportional to $\frac{1}{y}$.
- interpret equations that describe direct and inverse proportion.

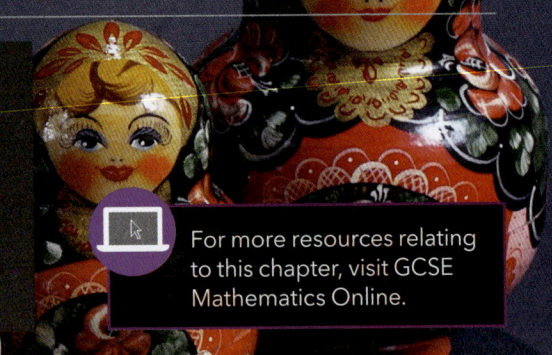

For more resources relating to this chapter, visit GCSE Mathematics Online.

Using mathematics: real-life applications

Proportional reasoning is very common in daily life. You use proportional reasoning when you mix ingredients for a recipe, convert between units of measurement or work out costs per unit. It is an area of maths where you can use many different methods to solve particular problems.

"I test out new dishes on my family. Then I have to scale up the recipes in proportion so that they taste just as good. Sometimes it may be for just a few people at one table in my restaurant, at other times it may be for a whole room of wedding guests." *(Chef and restaurant owner)*

Tip

Review the sections in Chapter 23 on equivalent ratios and fractions to prepare for this chapter.

Before you start ...

Ch 10, 12	You need to know how many minutes there are in fractions of an hour.	**1** How many minutes are there in: **a** half an hour? **c** a third of an hour?	**b** a quarter of an hour? **d** a fifth of an hour?
Ch 10, 12	You need to be able to find what fraction of an hour a given time is.	**2** What fraction of an hour is: **a** 5 minutes? **b** 24 minutes? **c** 54 minutes?	
Ch 8, 14	You should know how to substitute values into formulae.	**3** $g = 3b$ **a** What is the value of g when $b = 7$? **b** What is the value of b when $g = 72$? **c** What is b when $g = 1.2$?	

34 Direct and inverse proportion

Assess your starting point using the Launchpad

STEP 1

1
  a A recipe for blueberry muffins makes 12 muffins. It uses 180 g of blueberries.
  What amount of blueberries is needed to make 30 muffins?
  b A car is travelling at 80 km per hour. How far would it travel in 75 minutes?
  c €1 = $1.40
  How many euros is a t-shirt that costs $24?

GO TO
Section 1: Direct proportion

STEP 2

2 The cost of carpeting a hallway is proportional to the area of the hall. One hallway measuring 15 m² costs £97.50.
  a Find a formula for the cost, c, of carpeting a hallway with area, a.
  b How much would it cost to carpet an area of 32 m²?
  c What area can be carpeted for £328.90?

GO TO
Section 2: Algebraic and graphical representations

STEP 3

3 Ten people have enough food for a six day camping trip.
  a How long would the food last if there were only five people?
  b Two more people join the group unexpectedly. How long would the food last if there were 12 people?

GO TO
Section 3: Inverse proportion

GO TO
Chapter review

Find answers at: cambridge.org/ukschools/gcsemaths-studentbookanswers

Key vocabulary

direct proportion: two values that both increase in the same ratio.

Tip

You learnt about ratio in Chapter 22.

Section 1: Direct proportion

When two quantities vary but remain in the same **ratio** they are said to be in **direct proportion**. A simple example would be the volume and price of petrol. The more petrol a driver puts into the car, the more it costs.

Scaling up recipe ingredients involves direct proportion. If you want to make double the amount of food, you need to use double the amount of ingredients. Other examples are the number of hours someone works and the amount they get paid at an hourly rate, and exchange rates between two currencies.

Decide whether each of these examples represents a directly proportional relationship:

- The time spent riding your bike and the calories you burn.
- The distance you travel and the cost of your rail ticket.
- The amount of water in a kettle and the number of cups of tea you can make.
- The cost of buying woodchips for a primary school play area and the size of the play area.
- The time it takes to walk to school and the number of friends you walk with.

In problems involving variables in direct proportion, you might be given a rate such as price per litre. If not, it can be helpful to find this rate.

Scaling up or down

Consider the following problem.

A car travels 12 miles in 15 minutes.

a At what speed is the car travelling?

b How far would the car go in 75 minutes?

c How long would it take the car to travel 80 miles?

Think how you would find the answers to these questions.

One approach is to assume that distance and time are directly proportional to each other, which allows us to develop a **mathematical model** of the problem.

Key vocabulary

mathematical model: a representation of a real-life problem; assumptions are used to simplify the situation so that it can be solved mathematically.

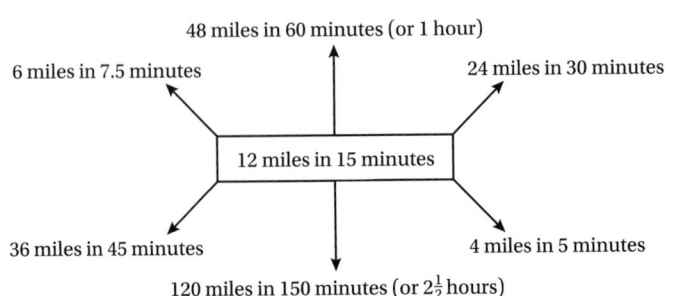

Using the assumption that distance and time are directly proportional to each other, we can write down a range of combinations of time and distance that would represent the same speed and use these to answer the questions. The diagram shows some combinations.

- 48 miles in 60 minutes (or 1 hour)
- 6 miles in 7.5 minutes
- 24 miles in 30 minutes
- 12 miles in 15 minutes
- 36 miles in 45 minutes
- 4 miles in 5 minutes
- 120 miles in 150 minutes (or $2\frac{1}{2}$ hours)

a Having scaled the quantities up it is easy to see that the speed of the car is 48 miles per hour.

b The car would travel 36 miles in 45 minutes and 24 miles in 30 minutes. Hence it would travel 60 miles in 75 minutes.

c The car would travel 4 miles in 5 minutes. Multiply both of these quantities by 20 to find that it would do 80 miles in 100 minutes (or 1 hour and 40 minutes).

These are not the only combinations you could write down or the only ones that you could use to answer the original questions.

Unitary method

Finding the rate for one unit and using this to calculate other values, is called the **unitary method**. In the example above you are told that the car travels 12 miles in 15 minutes. If you calculate how far the car travels in one minute (12 ÷ 15 = 0.8) you find the rate per minute and you can multiply this value as required to find the distance travelled in x minutes.

Similarly, you could calculate how long it takes the car to travel one mile (15 ÷ 12 = 1.25 minutes).

Sometimes it is easier to just scale the values up or down as necessary, and sometimes the new values won't be a neat multiple or factor and the unitary method would be easier to use. Either method works, use whichever one you prefer.

> **Tip**
>
> Very often when working with proportion problems it helps to write down a proportion fact you know and consider what would happen if one side is halved, doubled, tripled, multiplied by 10 and so on. These notes will often then help you to solve the original problem. For example, if you know that six eggs make two cakes then half the number of eggs, three, will make just one cake.

WORKED EXAMPLE 1

While in Florida, Danny bought a T-shirt. It cost $18. He paid on a debit card. When he returned home the charge on Danny's debit card statement was £10.71. He bought a pair of jeans for $32. Assuming the bank uses the same exchange rate, what would this charge appear as on his debit card statement?

$18 = £10.71
$1 = £0.595
32 × 0.595 = £19.04

In this example scaling up and down is too inefficient and it is better to use the unitary method. In other words, start by finding the exchange rate of dollars to pounds. This is very much like an equivalent ratio problem in Chapter 22. Divide both sides by 18. Now use this rate to find the cost in pounds of $32.

This example works out nicely. In reality, quite often exchange rates result in fractions of pence or cents. In these cases exchange desks often round the values down no matter how close you are to the pound above.

EXERCISE 34A

1 A bluefin tuna fish can travel 3 km in just 20 minutes.

List some other distance–time facts about the fish assuming that it always travels at a constant rate.

2 Each day a cat eats 40 grams of dried cat food.

How many grams would it eat in two weeks?

3 Patrick works for four hours and gets paid £22.

What is his rate of pay per hour?

Find answers at: cambridge.org/ukschools/gcsemaths-studentbookanswers

4 Jelly beans cost £1.20 for 100 g.
   a How much would 50 g cost?
   b How much would 300 g cost?
   c How much would 1 kg cost?
   d What weight of jelly beans could you buy with £4.20?

5 On holiday Ben uses his mobile to call home. A 12 minute call costs £4.20.
   a How much would it cost to ring home for 18 minutes?
   b Danny calls home for 20 minutes and it costs him £6.40.
   Whose phone is better value, Ben's or Danny's? Why?

6 Look at this pancake recipe. It serves 8 people.

   100 g plain flour
   2 eggs
   300 ml semi-skimmed milk

   a Copy and complete this table.

Ingredients	8 people	4 people	16 people	12 people	20 people
Plain flour	100 g				
Eggs	2				
Semi-skimmed milk	300 ml				

   b If you have 2 litres of milk, 500 g of plain flour and 9 eggs and make as much pancake mixture as possible, how many will it serve?

7 The fastest train in Europe is the French TGV from Paris to Le Mans. It travels at 320 kilometres per hour. Assuming that the train is going at its full speed:
   a How far does it travel in 2 hours?
   b How far does it travel in 30 minutes?
   c How far does it travel in 15 minutes?
   d How far does it travel in 1 minute?
   e How far does it travel in 10 seconds?
   f The equator is approximately 40,000 km long.
      If it were possible, how long would it take to travel around it in a TGV train?

8 The fastest animal on land is the cheetah. It can reach speeds of up to 120 kilometres per hour but for only a short burst of time.
   How far would it travel at this speed in 15 seconds?

9 £1 = $1.68. Copy and complete this table:

Pounds £	£1	£2	£5	£15				£124.53
Dollars $					$26.88	$71.40	$80.50	

10 Before going to Australia Finley exchanges £175 into Australian dollars. He gets an exchange rate of £1 = AU$1.81.

How many Australian dollars does he get?

11 When returning from her holiday Amber exchanges her $44 back into pounds. The exchange rate is £1 = $1.68.

How many pounds does she receive?

12 Paint is sold in a variety of tins. However, the price per litre remains unchanged.

   a Find the cost of each of these tins of paint.

   i 750 ml   **ii** 1 litre   1.5 litres = £18   **iii** 5 litres   **iv** 25 litres

   b Is this the way items are usually priced?

13 Lucy exchanges £50 for €60.50.

   a What is the exchange rate from pounds to euros?

   b What is the exchange rate from euros to pounds?

Section 2: Algebraic and graphical representations

Direct proportion problems can be represented graphically or generalised through the use of algebra. This allows you to solve problems concerning the same relationship, either by reading information off a graph or by using an algebraic formula.

WORK IT OUT 34.1

Which of these graphs show a pair of variables that are directly proportional to each other?

Explain your choice. How can you tell that the variables in the other graphs are not directly proportional to each other?

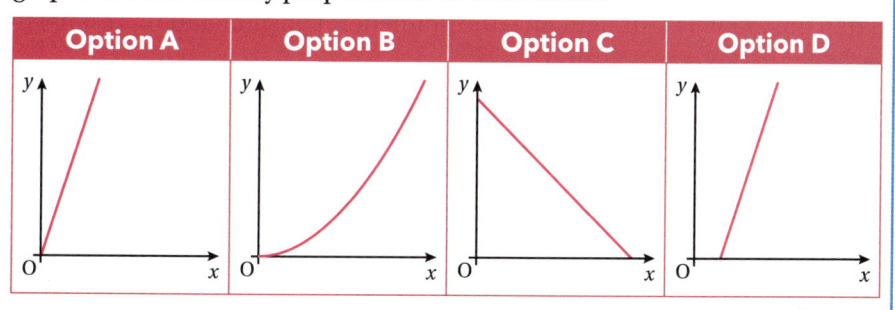

Option A	Option B	Option C	Option D

Find answers at: cambridge.org/ukschools/gcsemaths-studentbookanswers

> **Tip**
> Relate this back to the work you have done on equivalent fractions and ratios.

The graph of a directly proportional relationship has a fixed gradient and goes through the origin. We can express this relationship algebraically.

The mathematical symbol $\propto$ is used to indicate that two values are proportional.

$y \propto x$ means that y is proportional to x

This tells us the following relationship between x and y:

$$\frac{y_1}{y_2} = \frac{x_1}{x_2} \text{ or } \frac{y_1}{x_1} = \frac{y_2}{x_2}$$

If you pay per minute to use your mobile phone the time you speak, t, is proportional to the cost of the call, c. Hence $t \propto c$.

This means that for some fixed value k (often called the constant of proportionality), you can write a formula linking the time and cost:

$c = kt$

> **Tip**
> Be careful with units in questions. In this example the cost is in pence and time in minutes. To use the formula you'd need to make sure all quantities were in pence and minutes and convert any that were not.

If you pay 75p for a 15 minute call, you can calculate the value of k by substituting the known values into the formula.

$c = kt$
$75 = k \times 15$
$5 = k$

So the formula linking the cost in pence, c, and time in minutes, t, is $c = 5t$.

WORK IT OUT 34.2

Which of these formulae represent variables that are directly proportional to each other? Can you explain why (or why not)?

Option A	Option B	Option C	Option D
$y = 3x + 5$	$10w = h$	$\frac{s}{t} = 7$	$d^2 = 4f$

Gradients and ratios

If you plotted a graph to illustrate the car journey described earlier in the chapter where the car travels 12 miles in 15 minutes, the resulting graph would be a straight line showing distance against time. This is called a distance–time graph. The line shows direct proportion because at time 0 the car has travelled 0 miles. You know that these two variables are in direct proportion, and therefore are increasing in the same ratio.

You have seen this kind of relationship before, in the gradient of a straight-line graph:

$$\text{gradient} = \frac{\text{vertical rise}}{\text{horizontal run}} = \frac{\text{difference in } y\text{-values}}{\text{difference in } x\text{-values}}$$

The gradient is a rate of change, it tells you how y changes as x changes. When the graph is a straight line, the gradient is constant and represents two variables in direct proportion.

If you are given a straight-line graph, you can use it to calculate the ratio between two variables by using two points on the line to calculate the gradient. Exchange rates, conversion charts and distance–time graphs are all examples of straight-line graphs that show direct proportion.

> **Tip**
> You will learn more about distance-time graphs in Chapter 37.

In a distance–time graph, time is plotted along the x-axis and distance along the y-axis. The gradient is therefore: $\frac{\text{distance}}{\text{time}}$.

In the car example above, the car travelled 12 miles in 15 minutes. At the start it would have travelled 0 miles in 0 minutes and so you have two points on the graph (0, 0) and (15, 12). You could calculate the speed using the ratio $\frac{\text{distance}}{\text{time}} = \frac{12}{15} = 0.8$ miles/minute.

The gradient of a distance–time graph tells you the speed of a moving object.

EXERCISE 34B

1 When planning a skiing holiday in Switzerland, Ethan compares two resorts. The exchange rate from pounds to Swiss francs is £1 = CHF1.48.

Which resort is a better deal? How many pounds cheaper is it?

	Accommodation	Food	Ski rental	Flights
Bun di Scuol	£340	£65	£300	£69
Flims-Laax-Falera	CHF444	CHF148	CHF164.28	CHF213.12

2 The graph shows how to convert between pounds and Bulgarian lev (ЛВ).

  a What is the exchange rate from pounds to lev?

  b What is the exchange rate from lev to pounds?

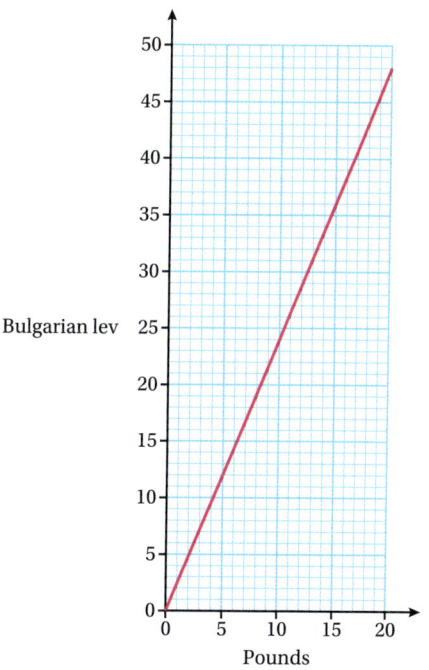

3 During a year abroad Aaron had to change currencies on a regular basis. Use the following exchange information to answer the questions below.

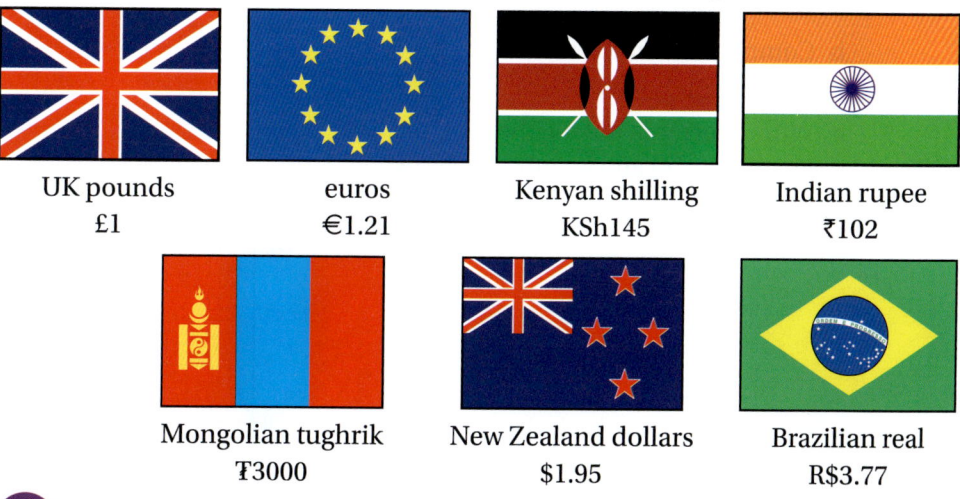

UK pounds £1

euros €1.21

Kenyan shilling KSh145

Indian rupee ₹102

Mongolian tughrik ₮3000

New Zealand dollars $1.95

Brazilian real R$3.77

Find answers at: cambridge.org/ukschools/gcsemaths-studentbookanswers

a Aaron exchanged £350 into euros.
How many euros did he get?

b Aaron had KSh40 600.
How many pounds is this?

c When in Kenya Aaron went on a safari drive. He had booked this before going out at a cost of £185. He paid in Kenya.
How many Kenyan shillings did it cost?

d When he left India Aaron exchanged Indian Rps 5202 into Mongolian tughrik.
How many tughrik did he receive?

e Aaron paid €11 for a hostel in France, KSh1305 in Kenya, Rps500 in India, ₮6500 in Mongolia, $15 in New Zealand and R$20 in Brazil.
Put these prices in order of expense, cheapest first.

4 What information would you need to collect to compare how crowded two school playing fields are? How would you carry out the comparison?

5 This is a time–distance graph for two runners.

a How far had runner A travelled after 30 minutes?

b How long did it take runner B to travel 18 km?

c Which runner is going faster?

d What is the speed of each runner?

e What assumptions have been made when drawing this graph?

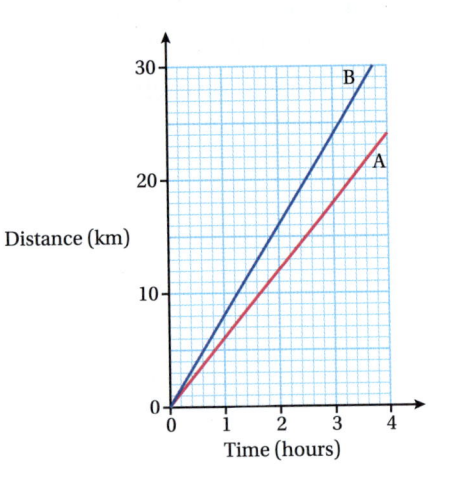

6 The graph shows the cost of telephone cable.

a What is the cost per metre?

b Complete this formula:
cost = _____ × length.

c Write a formula linking the cost, in pounds, (*c*) and length, in metres, of wire (*l*).

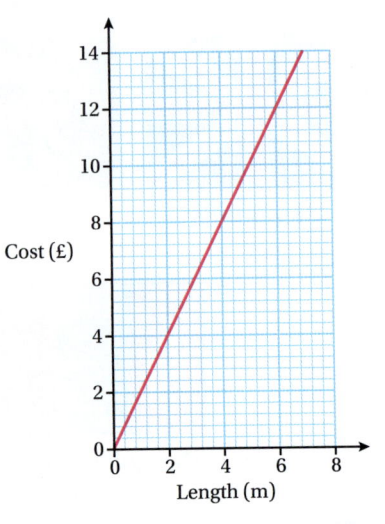

7 The graph shows the number of new cars a factory can make.
The number of cars being produced is directly proportional to the number of days that the factory stays open.

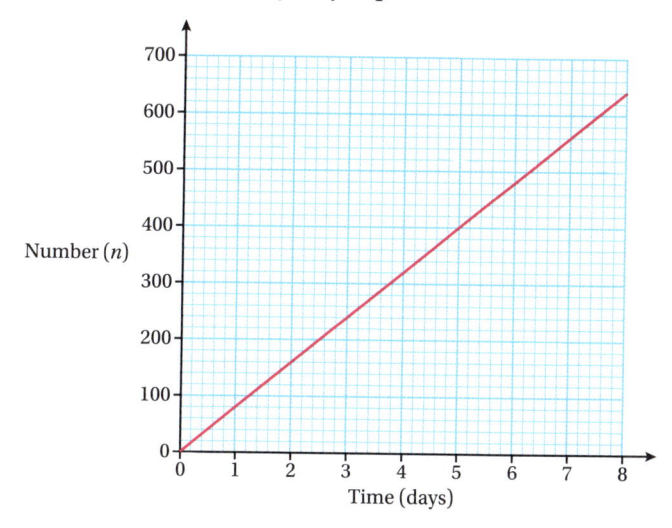

Find a formula for the number of cars (n) being produced in terms of the number of days (d) the factory remains open.

What assumptions have been made?

8 The length of an object's shadow is directly proportional to the object's height. Use this diagram to help explain why this is true.

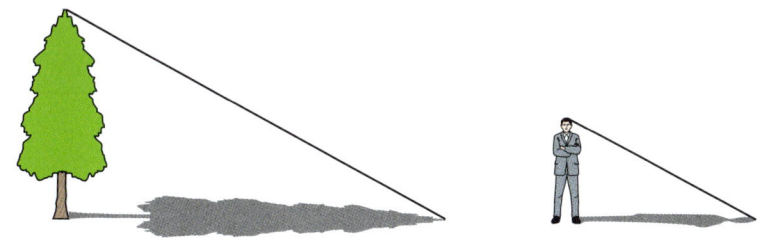

At one specific time in the day a man of height 1.8 metres has a shadow of 1.35 m.

  a Find a formula for the length of an object's shadow (s) in terms of its height (h).

  b The Angel of the North is 20 m tall.
  How long would its shadow be at the same time?

  c The shadow of the tallest upright stone at Stonehenge at this time is 502.5 cm.
  How tall is the stone?

  d Measure your height and use this method to find the height of your school.

9 Two variables p and q are directly proportional.
When $p = 6.5$, q is 52.

  a Find a formula for q in terms of p.

  b Find the value of q when p is 3.8.

  c Find the value of p when q is 14.8.

Find answers at: cambridge.org/ukschools/gcsemaths-studentbookanswers

10 Wheelchair ramps have to be designed with a specific steepness allowing their safe use. One such, well-designed, ramp has a horizontal distance of 4 metres and a height gain of 60 cm.

Find a formula for the horizontal distance (d) in terms of the height gain (h).

Section 3: Inverse proportion

In some instances one quantity decreases as the other one increases. For example, if you increase your speed, the time it takes to travel a fixed distance is reduced. If you add more workers to a job, each working at the same rate, the overall time it takes to complete the job goes down. These types of relationship are inversely proportional.

The graph of a pair of inversely proportional variables never quite touches the x- or y-axis, but comes closer and closer to them.

WORK IT OUT 34.3

A rectangle has a fixed area of 24 cm². Its length, x, and height, y, can vary. Which of the graphs below represents this situation? How did you come to your decision?

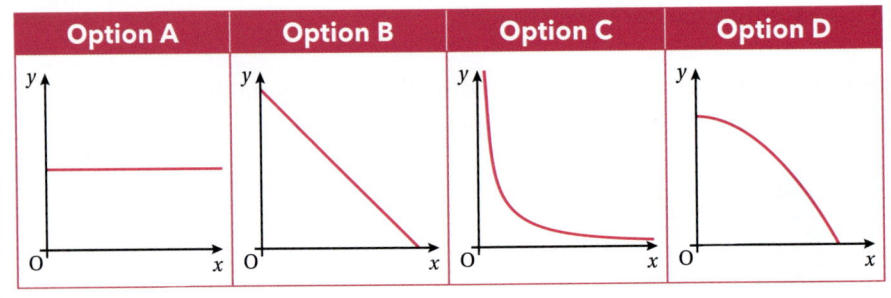

Option A	Option B	Option C	Option D

Key vocabulary

inverse proportion: a relation between two quantities such that one increases at a rate that is equal to the rate at which the other decreases.

In the example of a rectangle with a fixed area (Work it out 34.3), its length and height are in **inverse proportion**. When one of these dimensions increases, the other must decrease for the area to remain the same.

For example, with a length of 2 cm and a height of 12 cm a rectangle has an area of $2 \times 12 = 24$ cm².

If you increase the length by a factor of 3 (2×3) you get a length of 6 cm.

If the length increases to 6, the height has to decrease by a factor of 3 to get 4 cm ($12 \div 3$), in order to maintain the same area.

Length × height = 24 or $xy = 24$ or $y = \dfrac{24}{x}$

Generally, if x is inversely proportional to y:

$$y \propto \dfrac{1}{x}$$

$$y = \dfrac{k}{x}$$

You find k by substituting in one pair of values you know fits the relationship. In the case of a rectangle with area 24 cm², use as an example the length of 2 cm and a height of 12 cm.

$$12 = \dfrac{k}{2} \text{ so } k = 24$$

$$y = \dfrac{24}{x}$$

WORKED EXAMPLE 2

It takes 4 people 3 days to paint the school hall.

- **a** How long would it take 1 person to paint the school hall?
- **b** How long would it take 2 people?
- **c** How long would it take 6 people?
- **d** The job needs to be completed in a day. How many people are needed?
- **e** What assumptions are being made?

a $4 \div 4 = 1$; $3 \times 4 = 12$
12 days

> The number of people is inversely proportional to the number of days as the number of people increases the number of days it takes decreases. If you divide one value by an amount, you have to multiply the other value by the same amount to keep them inversely proportional. It will take 1 person 4 times as long to do the job as 4 people.

b $1 \times 2 = 2$, $12 \div 2 = 6$ (or $4 \div 2 = 2$, $3 \times 2 = 6$)
6 days

> It would take 2 people half the time it takes one person; or twice as long as it takes 4 people.

c $1 \times 6 = 6$, $12 \div 6 = 2$
2 days

> Use the values you calculated for one person to work out the time taken for 6.

d $3 \div 3 = 1$, $4 \times 3 = 12$
12 people

> **Alternatively**, you could have used the values for one person. You can use any of the values calculated as they are all in the same proportion.

e The assumptions are that everybody works at the same rate, and that several people can paint the hall at the same.

EXERCISE 34C

1 While on holiday you budget to buy five souvenirs at $2.40 each.
  - **a** How much money do you intend to spend?
  - **b** How many souvenirs costing $0.80 each could you buy with your budget?
  - **c** If you need eight souvenirs of equal value, how much should you pay for each souvenir to keep within your budget?

2 Speed (s miles per hour) and travel time (t hours) are inversely proportional. The faster you travel the less time a journey takes. For a journey between Cambridge and Manchester this can be represented by $s = \dfrac{180}{t}$.
  - **a** It takes 4 hours to make the journey. What speed is this?
  - **b** How long will it take to do the journey at 60 miles per hour?
  - **c** It takes 2 hours 15 minutes to make the journey. What speed is this?

Find answers at: cambridge.org/ukschools/gcsemaths-studentbookanswers

3. A water tap is running at a constant rate (r litres per minute) filling a pond (in m minutes). The greater the flow of water the less time it takes to fill the pond up. This can be represented as $r = \frac{600}{m}$.

Copy and complete the table and then draw a graph to represent this situation.

m minutes	10	20	30	40	50	60	70	80	90	100
r litres per minute										

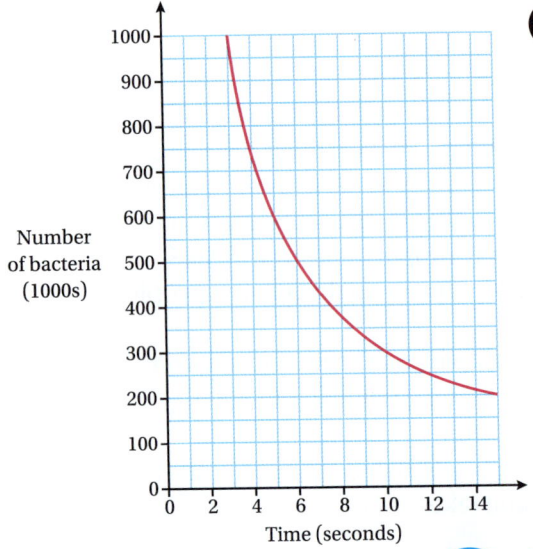

4. A scientist is analysing the efficiency of a new antibacterial agent by exposing a large colony of bacteria to the agent and recording the size of the population over time. The graph shows the relationship between the number of bacteria in the colony and time after first exposure to the agent.

a How many bacteria are there in the colony 10 seconds after exposure?

b How many bacteria were in the colony after 1 second?

c Find a formula for the size of the colony, p, in terms of the number of seconds exposed to the agent, t.

Checklist of learning and understanding

Direct proportion

- If two quantities are directly proportional to each other they increase and decrease at the same rate. For example, if one is tripled so is the other, if one is halved so is the other.
- A formula for a direct proportion relationship between two variables x and y is $y = kx$, where k is the constant of proportionality and can be found by substituting in known values.
- The graph of two directly proportional variables is a straight-line graph of the form $y = mx$, where m is positive.

Inverse proportion

- If two quantities are inversely proportional to each other then as one increases the other decreases. For example, if one is tripled the other is divided by three, if one is halved the other is doubled.
- A formula for an inverse proportion relationship between two variables x and y is $y = \frac{k}{x}$, where k is the constant of proportionality and can be found by substituting in known values.
- The graph of two inversely proportional variables is of the form $y = \frac{m}{x}$, where m is positive. It looks like:

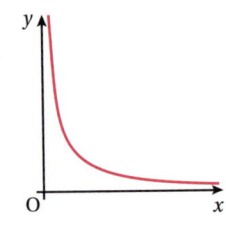

34 Direct and inverse proportion

Chapter review

For additional questions on the topics in this chapter, visit GCSE Mathematics Online.

1 Wine gums cost 90p for 200 grams.
   a How much would 800 grams cost?
   b What mass of wine gums would you get for £2.75?

2 Look at this stir-fry recipe. It serves six people.
   120 g chicken
   300 g vegetables
   15 tbsp of soy sauce

   If you have 300 g of chicken, 500 g of vegetables and 60 tbsp of soy sauce and make the most stir-fry possible, how many will it serve?

3 This is a graph for converting pounds (£) to Danish kroner (DKK).

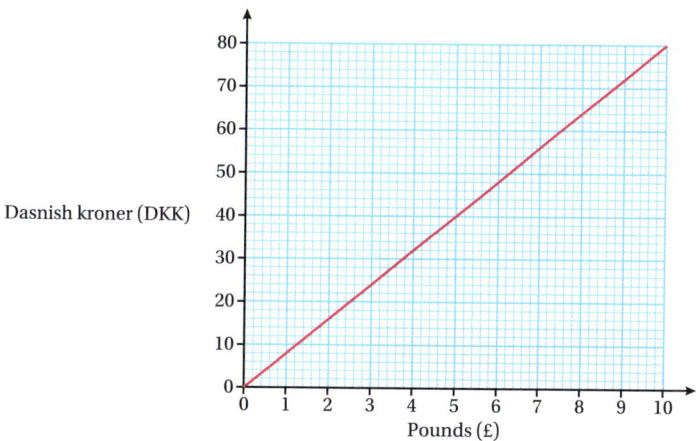

   a Use the graph to convert £6 to Danish kroner (DKK). *(1 mark)*
   b Work out the gradient of the line. *(2 marks)*
   c Convert 152 DKK to pounds. *(2 marks)*
   © OCR 2013

4 The graph shows the cost of buying electrical wire.

   Write a formula for the cost, c, in terms of the number of metres bought, m.

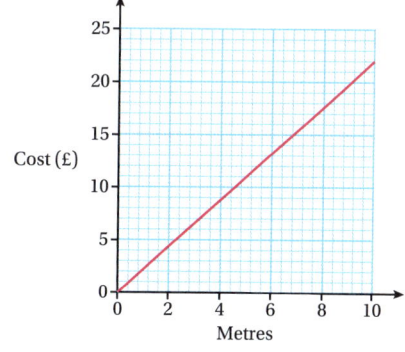

5 It takes three hairdressers an hour to style the hair of models for a fashion show.

   How long would it take nine hairdressers at the same rate?

6 The rate at which water flows into a pond is inversely proportional to the time it takes to fill up. It takes 2 hours for the pond to fill when water flows in at a rate of 50 litres an hour.

   Find a formula for the time in hours, t, in terms of the flow rate of the water, w.

Find answers at: cambridge.org/ukschools/gcsemaths-studentbookanswers

35 Collecting and displaying data

In this chapter you will learn how to ...

- work out properties of populations or distributions from a sample, recognising the limitations of sampling.
- interpret and construct appropriate tables, charts and graphs.
- choose the best form of representation for data and understand the appropriate use of different graphs.

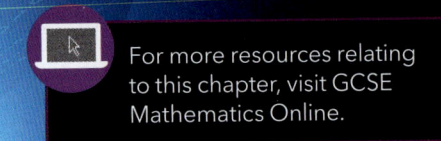

For more resources relating to this chapter, visit GCSE Mathematics Online.

Using mathematics: real-life applications

We live in a very information-rich world. Knowing how to construct accurate graphs and how to interpret the graphs we see is important. Many graphs in print and other media are carefully designed to influence what we think by displaying the data in particular ways.

"When we have data, we need to display it so that our message has the maximum impact."

(Newspaper editor)

Tip

The key to displaying data is to choose the graph or chart that clearly shows what the data tells us without the reader having to work too hard. Getting the scale and labelling right makes a big difference when creating graphs and charts.

Before you start ...

KS3	You need to be able to sort and categorise data.	**1** What would be suitable categories for a set of adult heights ranging from 1.39 m to 1.85 m?
Ch 12, 17	You need to be able to use scales properly.	**2 a** What is each division on this scale: 200 — 300 **b** A scale between 0 and 100 has five divisions. Which numbers should go alongside each division?
Ch 6, 9	You need to be able to measure and draw angles to create pie charts.	**3 a** Measure these angles: **b** Draw an angle of 72° accurately.

35 Collecting and displaying data

Assess your starting point using the Launchpad

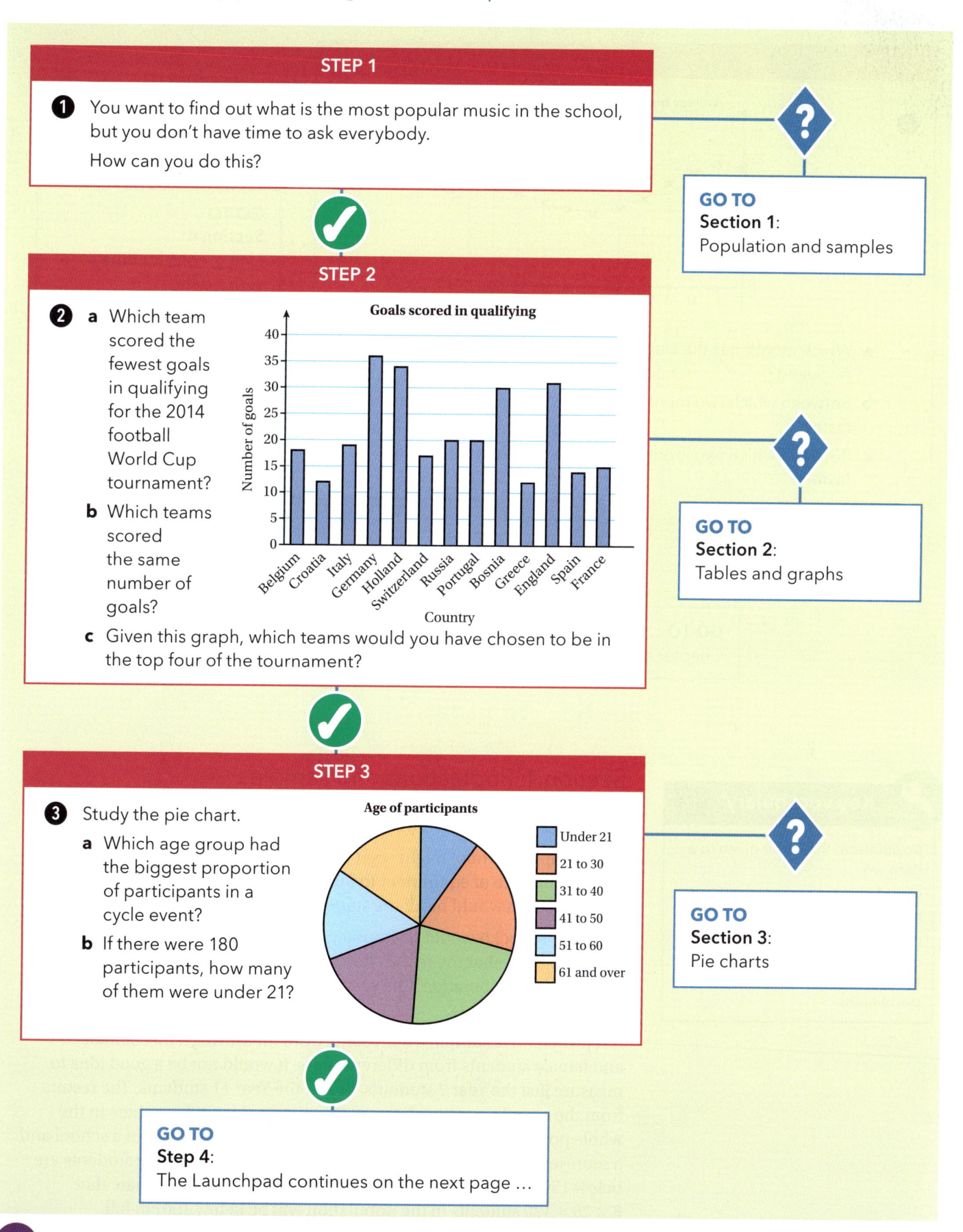

STEP 1

1 You want to find out what is the most popular music in the school, but you don't have time to ask everybody.
How can you do this?

GO TO
Section 1: Population and samples

STEP 2

2 a Which team scored the fewest goals in qualifying for the 2014 football World Cup tournament?

b Which teams scored the same number of goals?

Goals scored in qualifying (bar chart: Belgium, Croatia, Italy, Germany, Holland, Switzerland, Russia, Portugal, Bosnia, Greece, England, Spain, France)

c Given this graph, which teams would you have chosen to be in the top four of the tournament?

GO TO
Section 2: Tables and graphs

STEP 3

3 Study the pie chart.

a Which age group had the biggest proportion of participants in a cycle event?

b If there were 180 participants, how many of them were under 21?

Age of participants
- Under 21
- 21 to 30
- 31 to 40
- 41 to 50
- 51 to 60
- 61 and over

GO TO
Section 3: Pie charts

GO TO
Step 4: The Launchpad continues on the next page …

Find answers at: cambridge.org/ukschools/gcsemaths-studentbookanswers

537

GCSE Mathematics for OCR (Foundation)

Launchpad continued ...

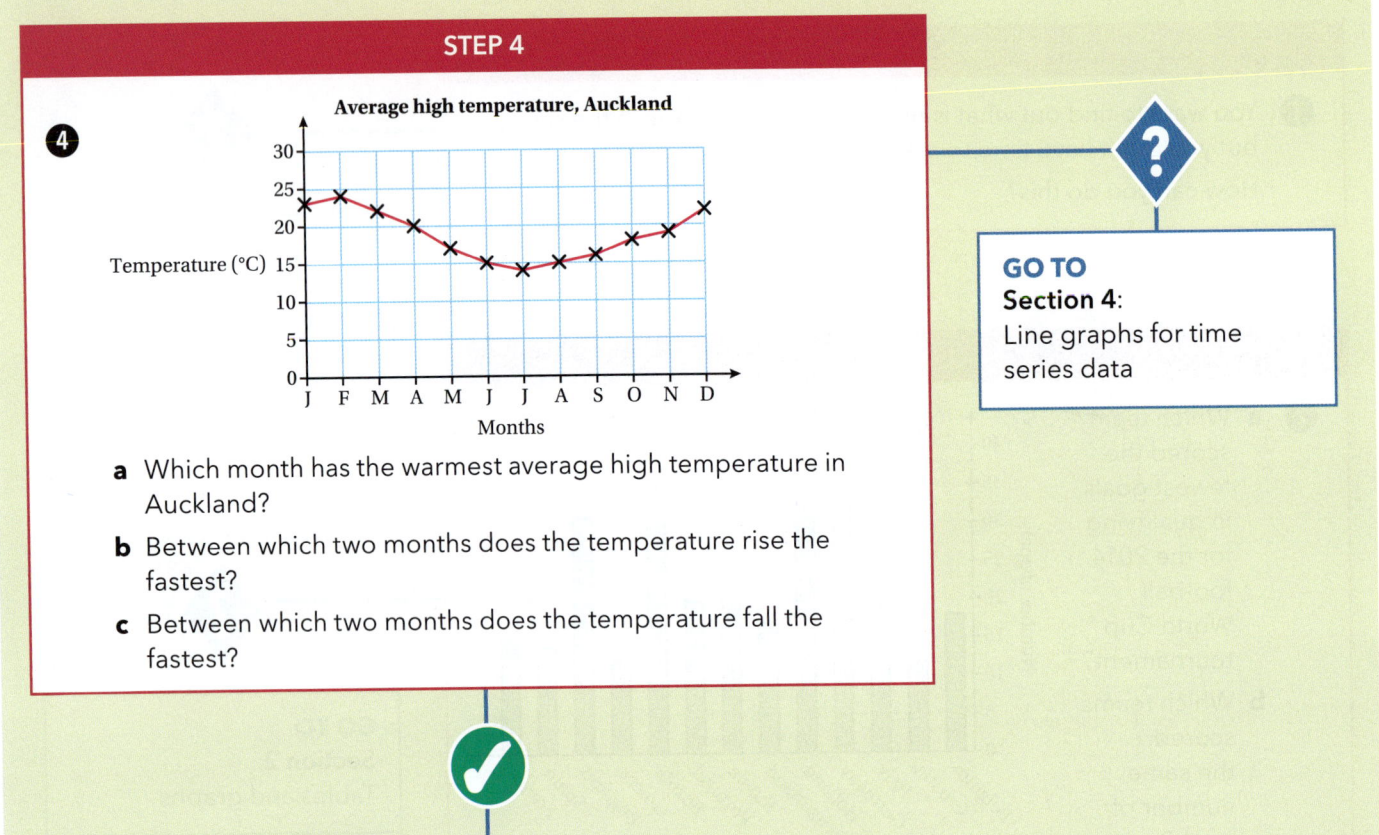

STEP 4

④
Average high temperature, Auckland

[Graph: Temperature (°C) vs Months J F M A M J J A S O N D]

a Which month has the warmest average high temperature in Auckland?
b Between which two months does the temperature rise the fastest?
c Between which two months does the temperature fall the fastest?

GO TO
Section 4: Line graphs for time series data

GO TO
Chapter review

Key vocabulary

population: the name given to a data set.
sample: a small set of data from a population.
representative sample: a smaller quantity of data that represents the characteristics of a larger population.

Section 1: Populations and samples

A statistical **population** is a set of individuals or objects of interest.

For example, a school might want to find the mean height of students to decide what size of equipment to buy for the gymnasium. In this example, the population would be all the students in the school.

In a large school it would be impractical to measure each student's height. It is more likely that the researcher would choose some of the students as a **sample** of the population. The sample needs to be a **representative sample** to provide useful data.

A representative sample would come from measuring a mix of male and female students from different years. It would not be a good idea to measure just the Year 7 students, or just the Year 11 students. The results from the sample can then be used to estimate the total numbers in the whole population. For example, say there are 1000 students in a school and a representative sample of 50 students is chosen. Six of these students are below 150 cm tall. $1000 \div 50 = 20$, so it is reasonable to estimate that $6 \times 20 = 120$ students in the population will be below 150 cm tall.

538

A representative sample can be created by taking a factor that is unrelated to the property being measured, for example creating the sample by using all the students whose first name begins with a letter drawn at random. As the starting letter of your name has no effect on your height, this should give you a representative sample.

Although the sample can't guarantee we will get the heights of the biggest and smallest students, it should make sure that we get a good idea of the spread of the data.

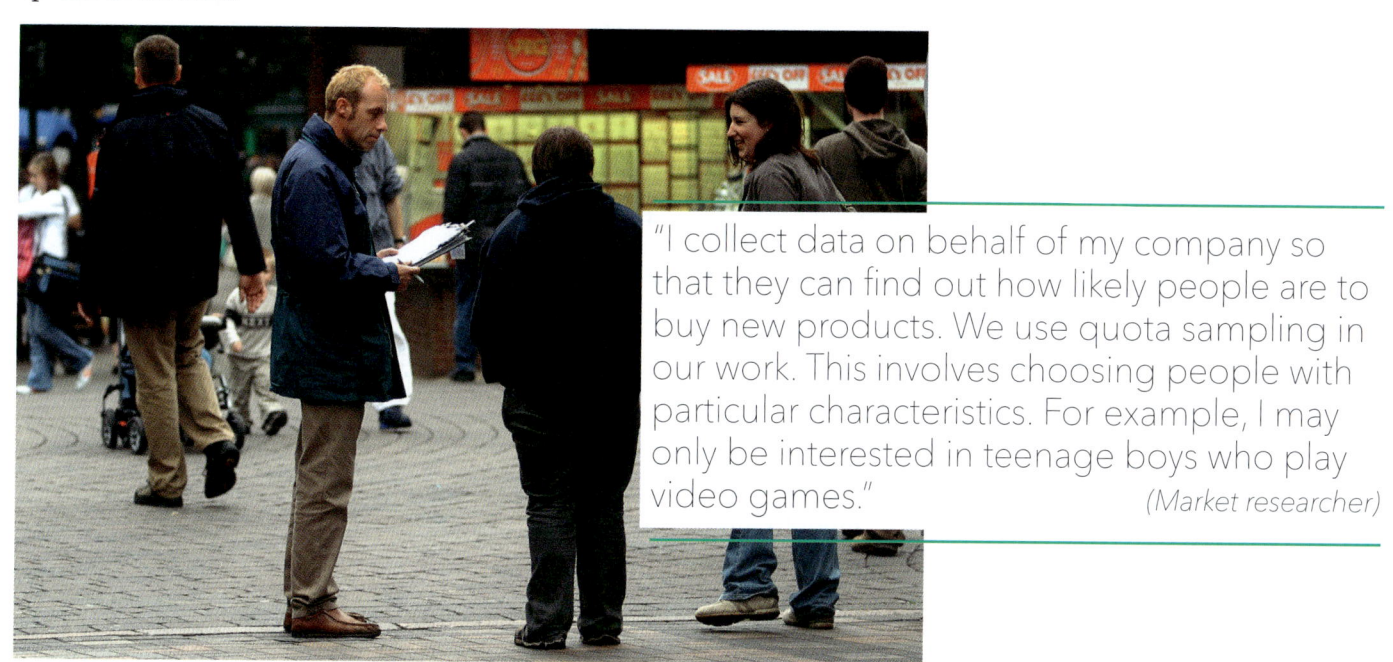

> "I collect data on behalf of my company so that they can find out how likely people are to buy new products. We use quota sampling in our work. This involves choosing people with particular characteristics. For example, I may only be interested in teenage boys who play video games."
>
> *(Market researcher)*

Random sampling

In a random sample, each member of the population is equally likely to be chosen for the sample. For example, if you had a list of all the students in the school you could use a computer program to pick 10% of them at random from the list.

Other methods of random sampling include numbering all the items in the population and then choosing numbers at random using a random number generation application.

In reality, it is often difficult to choose a genuinely random sample. For example, if you are doing a survey for a school project you are mostly likely to use **convenience sampling** because you would probably survey friends and family members, that is, your sample is chosen based on being easier for you to obtain. This method could result in a biased sample.

Care must be taken to avoid **bias** in a sample. This can happen if one section of a population is favoured. For example, choosing telephone numbers at random from a list might appear to be a sensible way to sample a population, but it excludes people who don't have a telephone who therefore won't be represented in the sample.

In statistics, the population may be divided into groups using a particular system. **Stratified sampling** is quite common. This involves dividing the sample into groups (strata) and then choosing a random sample from

Key vocabulary

bias: something that affects the chance of an event occurring in favour of a desired outcome.

Find answers at: cambridge.org/ukschools/gcsemaths-studentbookanswers

each group. The size of the sample chosen from each group should be in proportion to the size of the group within the population. For example, in a school population you could use the year groups as strata. If the Year 9 students make up 30% of the school population, then 30% of the sample should come from that group.

Another method of sampling is **capture/recapture**. This method is used by biologists and ecologists to estimate a population size when counting would be impossible or impractical. A sample of the population is captured and marked then released back into the population. A new sample is then recaptured and the number of previously marked animals noted. The total population size can be estimated by multiplying the number of animals marked in the first sample by the total number of animals caught in the second sample and dividing the result by the number of marked animals caught in the second sample.

WORK IT OUT 35.1

A market researcher has been asked to conduct a survey using a random sample of shoppers at a shopping mall. She suggests four options.

a Which is the only option that would produce a random sample?

b Explain why each of the other three options does not produce a random sample.

Option A	Option B	Option C	Option D
Ask all the women with children.	Ask people between 8 am and 8.30 am.	Stand outside a book shop and ask everyone who comes out.	Stop and ask every 10th person who walks by the researcher.

EXERCISE 35A

1 Which of these methods are likely to give a random sample?

A Selecting all the odd numbered houses in a street.

B Calling people on their home telephones during the day.

C Selecting everybody who is wearing trainers.

D Calling the person whose name is at the top of each page of the phone book.

E Drawing a series of names from a hat.

Give reasons for your answers.

2 A market research company wants to find out how many people are likely to buy a new baby food.

a Suggest a good place to conduct a survey of young parents.

b 35 of the 50 parents asked said they would be interested. How many parents would you expect to be interested in a population of 1000 parents?

3 A gym owner wants to know how many running machines to buy. She asks every member whose surname begins with an 'S' whether they will use a running machine.

   a If 15 of the 28 in her sample say 'yes', what would be a sensible number of machines to buy if there are 300 members overall?

   b Does she really need this many machines?

   c Is there a better way of sampling her members to make sure she gets a realistic number of machines?

4 At the end of 2012 there were 28.7 million cars on the roads of Britain.

   Surjay and his friends conduct a random survey of the cars passing the school and discover that of the 50 cars recorded, 3 had a sun roof, 1 had a faulty exhaust and 4 had chips on the windscreen.

   Use this information to estimate how many cars in Great Britain have:

   a a sun roof.   **b** faulty exhausts.   **c** chips in the windscreen.

5 A school wishes to consult the pupils on a change to the school uniform. They decide to use a stratified sample of 100 students.

   How many students should be chosen from each year group given the school population is as follows?

	Year 7	Year 8	Year 9	Year 10	Year 11
Boys	98	107	184	154	145
Girls	72	121	172	162	168

6 An ecologist is trying to estimate the population of badgers in a certain area.

   She catches 65 badgers and marks them.

   They are then released back into the wild and a further sample caught a week later.

   In the second batch she catches 52 badgers, of which 21 were marked.

   Use this information to estimate the badger population in the area.

Section 2: Tables and graphs

Using tables to organise data

When you have many pieces of data you can use a table to organise them and make them simpler to work with.

A frequency table is a table used to collect or record data that shows the 'frequency' of an event, or how often it happens.

> **Tip**
>
> You worked with frequency tables in Chapters 23 and 24 when you dealt with probability.

For example, the number of goals scored by each of the 20 premiership teams one weekend was as follows:

   5   1   3   0   1   2   4   1   1   2
   0   3   1   0   0   4   0   1   3   0

Find answers at: cambridge.org/ukschools/gcsemaths-studentbookanswers

In a frequency table these results would look like this:

Number of goals scored	Tally	Frequency
0	ⅢⅡ I	6
1	ⅢⅡ I	6
2	II	2
3	III	3
4	II	2
5	I	1

Using bar charts to display data

The data in the frequency table above can be shown on a bar chart.

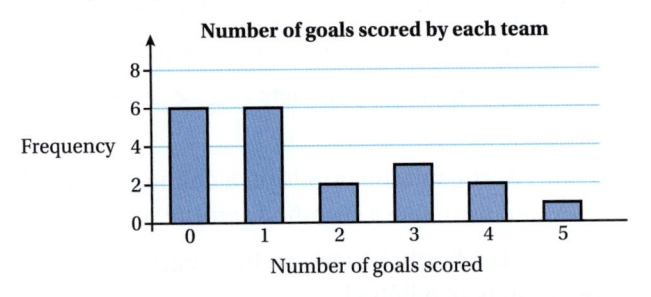

Number of goals scored by each team

The chart has a title, a scale on the left and accurately drawn bars.

Note that there is a gap between each bar and each one is labelled.

Bar charts are used to display **discrete data**. The number of goals scored by each team is discrete data because it can only have certain values.

It must be a whole number; you can't score $\frac{1}{2}$ a goal or 2.34 goals.

Sometimes it is helpful to sort data into categories. Pairs of shoes in a cupboard could be categorised into 'brown shoes', 'black shoes', and so on. Each piece of data can only be in one category. This is known as **categorical data**.

A vertical line graph (or bar line chart) is very similar to a bar chart but the number of data in each category is represented by a line rather than a bar.

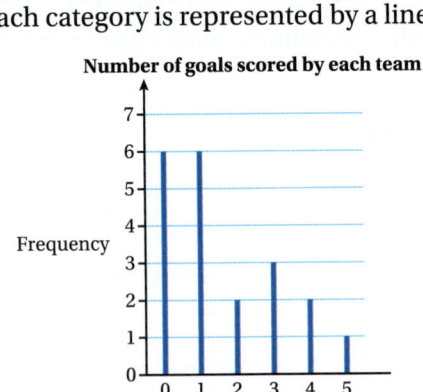

Number of goals scored by each team

This data could also be shown using a pictogram.

In a pictogram for this data a symbol could be used to represent either each goal or a number of goals.

> **Key vocabulary**
>
> **discrete data**: data that can be counted and that only has one possible value; it is counted in integers.
> **categorical data**: data that has been arranged in categories.

In this example each ball represents two goals:

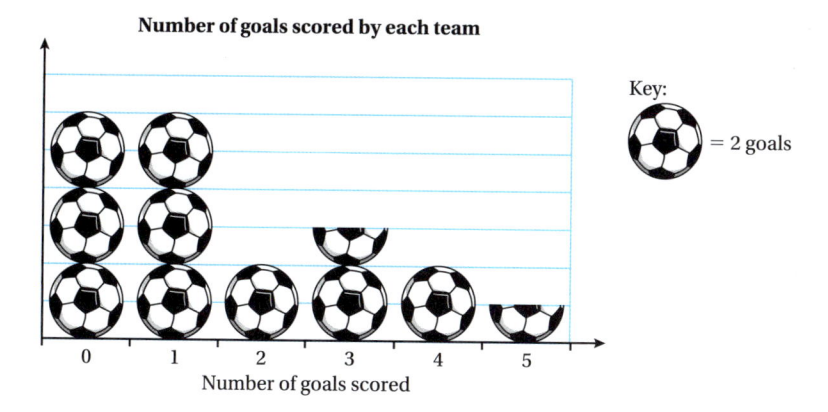

Number of goals scored by each team

Key: ⚽ = 2 goals

Number of goals scored

Note that a pictogram should always have a key to indicate what the symbol represents.

WORK IT OUT 35.2

Ramiz records the number of mistakes he makes in a series of maths tests.

2 3 1 3 4 2 0 3 2 6 1 1 3 2 4 2

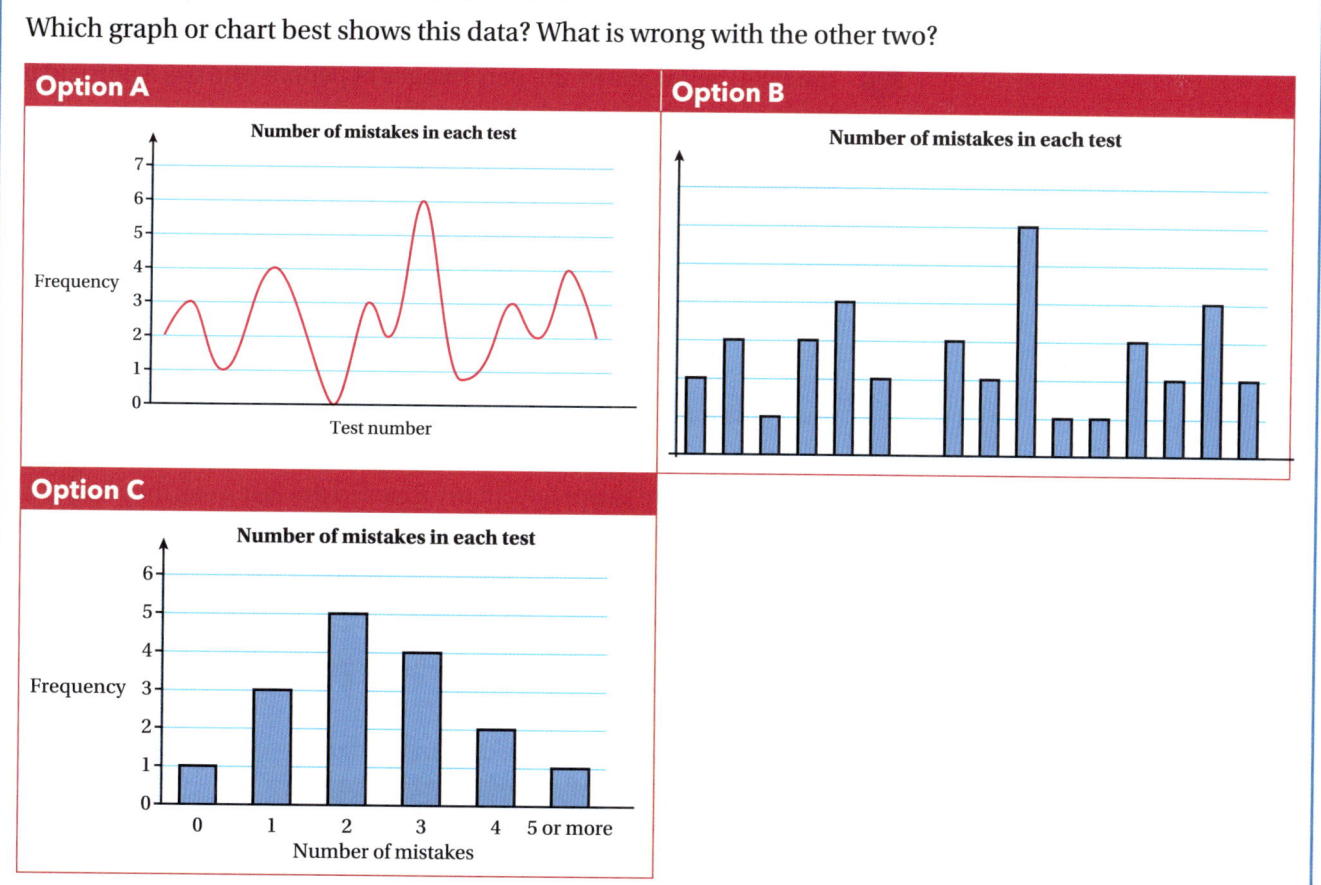

Which graph or chart best shows this data? What is wrong with the other two?

Option A
Number of mistakes in each test

Frequency
Test number

Option B
Number of mistakes in each test

Option C
Number of mistakes in each test

Frequency
Number of mistakes (0, 1, 2, 3, 4, 5 or more)

543

It is not always possible to say that one type of graph is better than another. The type of graph you draw depends very much on what data you have collected.

These guidelines can help you choose an appropriate graph for different kinds of data:

- Use bar chart or vertical line charts for discrete data that can be categorised.
- Use a pie chart or a composite bar chart if you want to compare different parts of the whole or show proportions in the data.
- Use a line graph for numerical data when you want to show trends (changes over time).
- Use scatter diagrams when you want to show relationships between different sets of data (you will deal with these in Chapter 36).

> **Tip**
>
> You might also have heard a composite bar chart called a compound bar chart; they are the same thing.

EXERCISE 35B

1. In an extended family of 30 members, 10 have blond hair, 9 have black hair, 6 have brown hair and 5 have grey hair.

   Draw a vertical line graph to show this information.

2. The table below shows the percentages of people who use a particular mode of transport to work in a factory.

Mode of transport	Percentage
Car	36
Bus	27
Cycle	19
Walk	18

   Show this information in a bar chart.

3. 30 students were asked how many times in the last week they had visited the snack shop. Their responses were:

   1 2 1 2 1 5 1 3 2 1 2 1 3 2 1 2 0 2 3 2 0 2 0 1 2 0 0 3 1 2

   a Draw a frequency table for this data.

   b Present this information on a suitable graph.

4. Construct a bar chart for the data in this table.

Favourite holiday destination	Frequency
UK	9
Spain	15
France	17
USA	12
Greece	8

5 A group of students were asked to choose their favourite snacks. The results are in the table below.

Favourite snack	Number of students
Fruit	6
Crisps	8
Chocolate bar	9
Pizza slice	12
Cookie	7

Draw a pictogram to show these results.

6 The graph below shows the monthly rainfall in Lowestoft over a year.

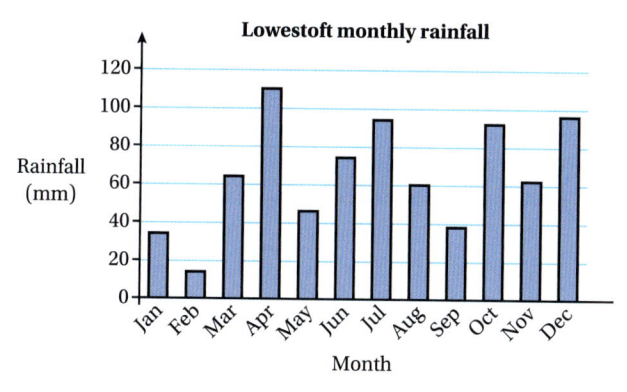

a In which month was the rainfall heaviest?

b Estimate the amount of rain that fell in April.

c Which was the driest month?

d Spring is March, April and May. Estimate how much rain fell in the spring.

e The average annual rainfall for Lowestoft is approximately 575 mm.

Was this a wetter or drier year than average?

7 Jenny is carrying out a survey of what sort of snacks are bought from a shop outside her school.

She writes down the items that people buy:

Chocobar	Apple	NRG drink	Juicebar	crisps	NRG drink	Chocobar	NRG drink	Juicebar
Juicebar	crisps	Cheese puffs	Gum	Cheese puffs	Fruit chews	NRG drink	NRG drink	Chocobar
Chocobar	Juicebar	Chocobar	crisps	Chocobar	Gum	Chocobar	Cheese puffs	crisps
Cheese puffs	crisps	NRG drink	Fruit chews	NRG drink	Cheese puffs	NRG drink	Juicebar	Gum
NRG drink	Chocobar	Apple	NRG drink	Chocobar	Juicebar	crisps	Chocobar	Cheese puffs
Gum	Fruit chews	Gum	crisps	Apple	crisps	Fruit chews	Fruit chews	Fruit chews
Juicebar	crisps	Cheese puffs	Fruit chews	Gum	Cheese puffs	Fruit chews	crisps	Cheese puffs

a How could Jenny have been better organised before she started her survey?

b Use Jenny's data to create a table to show what was bought in the shop.

c Jenny will get extra credit if she can categorise her data.

Adjust your table so that the data is classified in an appropriate way.

Find answers at: cambridge.org/ukschools/gcsemaths-studentbookanswers

GCSE Mathematics for OCR (Foundation)

Tip

You might have heard a multiple bar chart called a comparative bar chart; they are the same thing.

Multiple and composite bar charts

A multiple bar chart is useful when you want to compare data for two or more groups. For example, to compare shoe sizes of male and female students in Year 9 you would show the data for male and female students in matching pairs of bars like this:

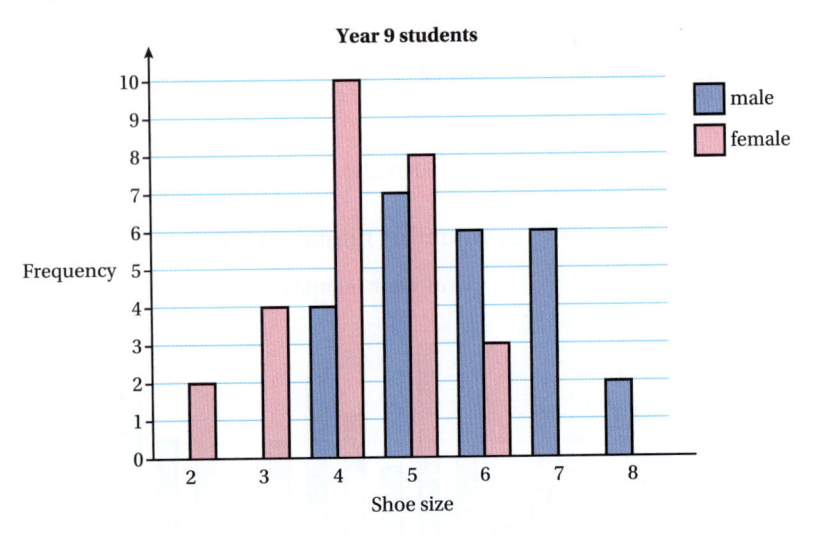

Notice that:

- The graph has a key to show what each colour bar represents.
- The two bars for male and female students who wear each size touch each other, but there is an equal space between each pair of bars.

Composite bar graphs are used to show parts of a whole. The total height of each bar represents a total amount. The height of the bar is divided into parts that show each category's share of the total amount.

To interpret a composite bar chart you need to work out what each bar represents and then do a calculation to find the fraction or percentage of the total that each part represents.

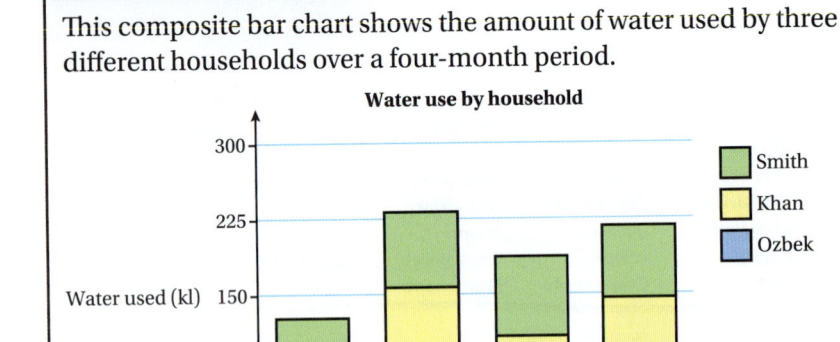

WORKED EXAMPLE 1

This composite bar chart shows the amount of water used by three different households over a four-month period.

Continues on next page …

546

a What does each bar show?

b Which household used the greatest amount of water in month 1?

c Describe the trend in water use for the Ozbek household over this period?

d One household had a leaking pipe in this period. Can you work out from the graph who this was and when it happened?

a The top of each bar shows the total water used by three households in a month. Each coloured segment shows the fraction of the total used by each household.

b The Khan household.

> The yellow section is bigger than the other two.

c In months 1 and 2 they used very little water. In month 3 the amount of water used increased quite dramatically and in month 4 it went up a little more.

d It is most likely the Khan household as they had a large jump in consumption in month 2. However, it could be the Ozbeks as well. If their water pipe started leaking in month 3 and wasn't fixed, it could account for the big increase in their consumption.

EXERCISE 35C

1 Study the bar graph carefully.

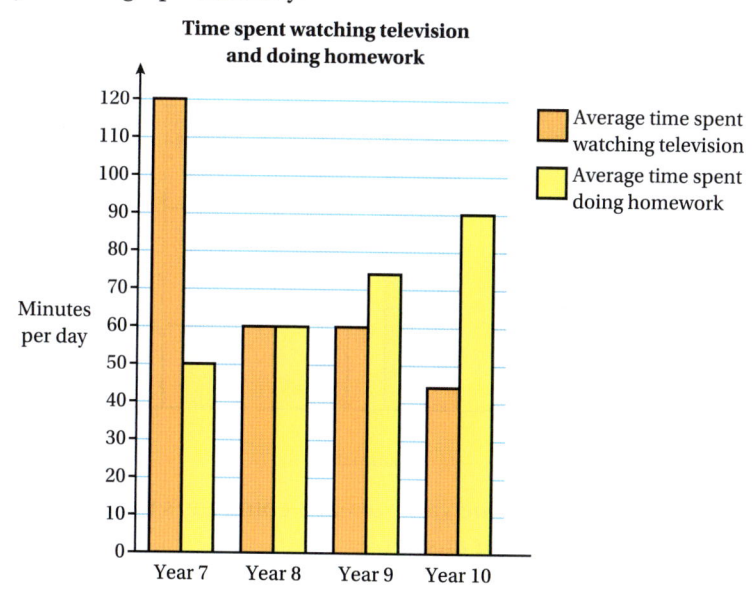

a What two sets of data are shown on this graph?

b Describe the trend in the amount of time spent watching TV as students move into higher years.

c What happens to the amount of time spent on homework as TV watching time decreases?

d How much time do Year 10 students spend on average each day on

　i homework?　　　**ii** watching TV?

GCSE Mathematics for OCR (Foundation)

2 Patrick runs a computer company. He keeps a record of his costs and his income for four large projects in a year.

He drew this graph to compare his costs and his income for each project.

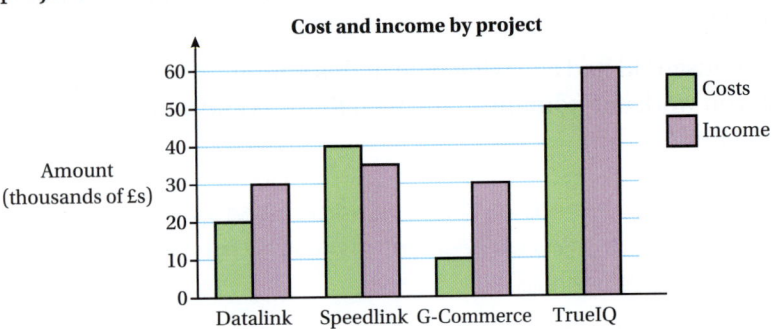

Cost and income by project

a Which project brought in most money?
b Which project brought in least money?
c Which project had the highest costs?
d Which project had the lowest costs?
e Which project gave Patrick the biggest profit?
f On which project did Patrick lose money? How can you tell?
g How much profit did Patrick make altogether?

Tip

Remember that profit = income − cost.

3 Carefully study this composite bar graph showing the proportion of total sales and how they are made for four different companies and answer the questions about it.

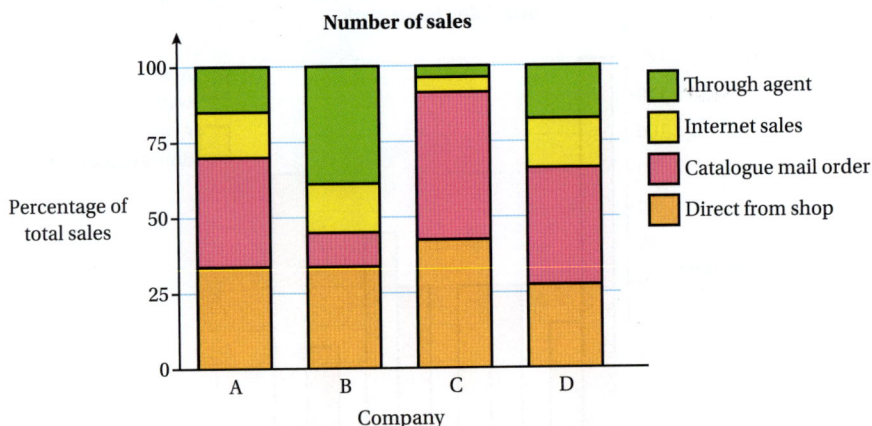

Number of sales

a Can you work out the value of each company's total sales from this graph? Explain your answer.
b Which of the companies does the greatest proportion of sales direct from the shop?
c Which company makes the least of its sales through agents?
d Which company makes almost half of its sales by catalogue mail order?
e What fraction of Company A's sales are done over the Internet?
f Describe the breakdown of sales by type for Company D.

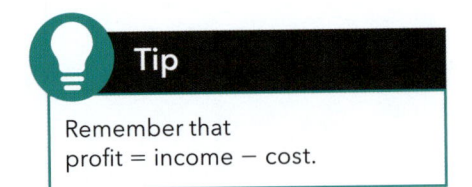

548

4 The chart below was drawn by a medical student writing a paper based on a World Health Organization (WHO) report on malaria.

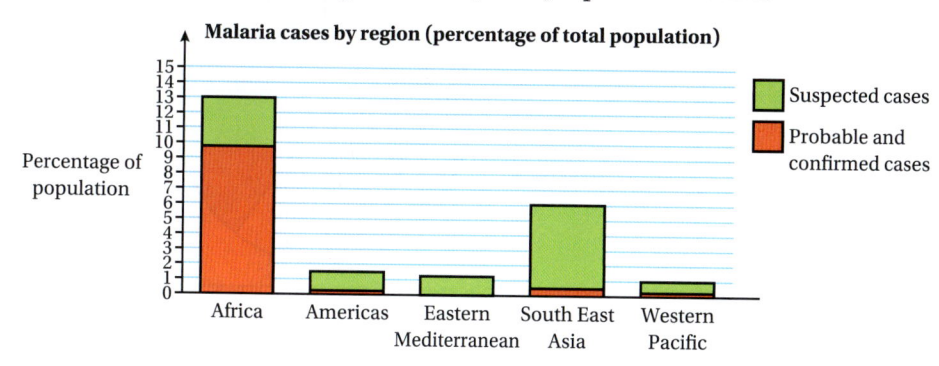

Malaria cases by region (percentage of total population)

Legend: Suspected cases; Probable and confirmed cases

According to the chart:

a What percentage of the population of Africa had or were suspected of having malaria?

b In South East Asia what percentage of the population were suspected of having malaria?

c Were any of the suspected cases in the Eastern Mediterranean confirmed? How can you tell?

d Which region of the world has the biggest problem with malaria?

e The student used a report that was published in 2010. Do you think the student should include the date in their paper? Why? Is the data a good representation of the prevalence of malaria today?

> **Tip**
> You will learn more about misleading data in Chapter 36.

Section 3: Pie charts

A pie chart is useful for displaying data when you are interested in the relative sizes or the proportions of the data.

Pie charts are always circular, so the sum of the angles at the centre must always be 360°.

When drawing pie charts that have data as percentages, each 1% will be represented by 3.6° because 360 ÷ 100 = 3.6.

In this example, data has been collected that shows the area in which students in a class live:

Area	Frequency	Percentage
Reepham	12	40.0%
Whitwell	6	20.0%
Booton	3	10.0%
Cawston	2	6.7%
Salle	7	23.3%

There are 30 students altogether. Each percentage is worked out by dividing the number of students in that area by the total number of students, and multiplying by 100; for example, for Reepham: $\frac{12}{30} \times 100 = 40\%$

Find answers at: cambridge.org/ukschools/gcsemaths-studentbookanswers

The pie chart below shows this data:

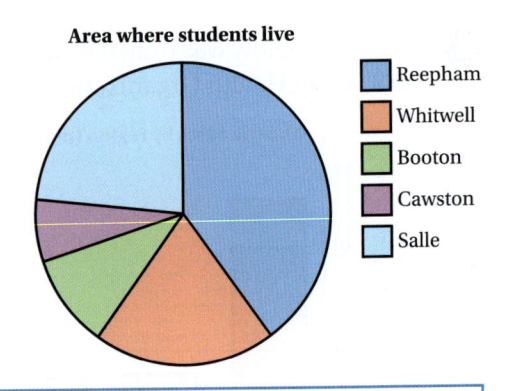

Area where students live
- Reepham
- Whitwell
- Booton
- Cawston
- Salle

WORK IT OUT 35.3

A survey of how many minutes late a sample of 20 trains are gives the following results:

1 0 2 0 3 1 5 4 1 3 6 4 3 5 2 4 3 2 2 4

Which of the pie charts best shows this information? Explain what is wrong with the other two pie charts.

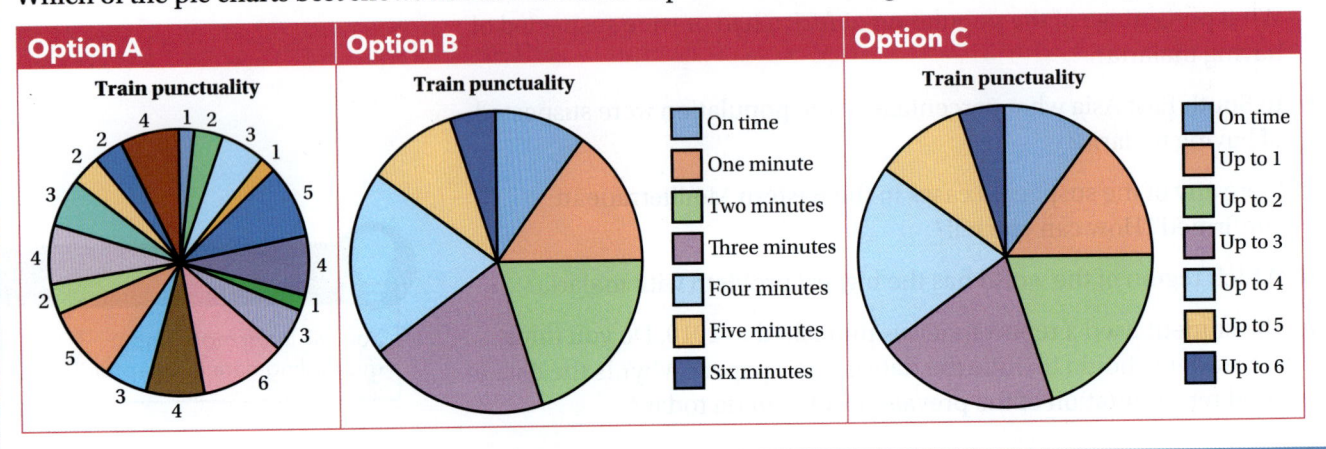

Option A — Train punctuality

Option B — Train punctuality
- On time
- One minute
- Two minutes
- Three minutes
- Four minutes
- Five minutes
- Six minutes

Option C — Train punctuality
- On time
- Up to 1
- Up to 2
- Up to 3
- Up to 4
- Up to 5
- Up to 6

EXERCISE 35D

1 Create a pie chart to represent this data:

Electricity generation	Proportion used
Gas	28%
Other fuels	2.6%
Coal	39%
Nuclear	19%
Renewables	11.4%

2 The pie charts below show the population of two different countries by age.

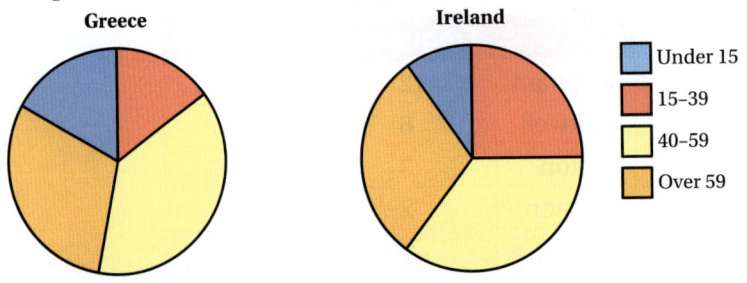

Greece   Ireland

- Under 15
- 15–39
- 40–59
- Over 59

a Write down two differences between Greece and Ireland.
b Which country has the biggest proportion of over 59s?
c There are more under 15s in Ireland than Greece. Is this statement true?

35 Collecting and displaying data

3 This pie chart shows the favourite leisure activity of 72 students.

a Use a protractor to measure the sector for music. Use this measurement to work out how many students prefer music.

b Which is the most popular activity?

c How many students prefer reading?

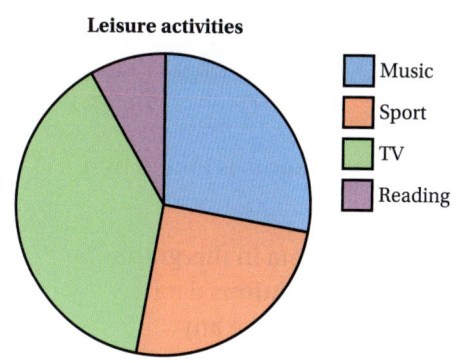

Leisure activities
- Music
- Sport
- TV
- Reading

4 The department of transport maintains data for the different types of vehicles on the road in the UK. Data for vehicles other than cars is shown for 1994 and 2013.

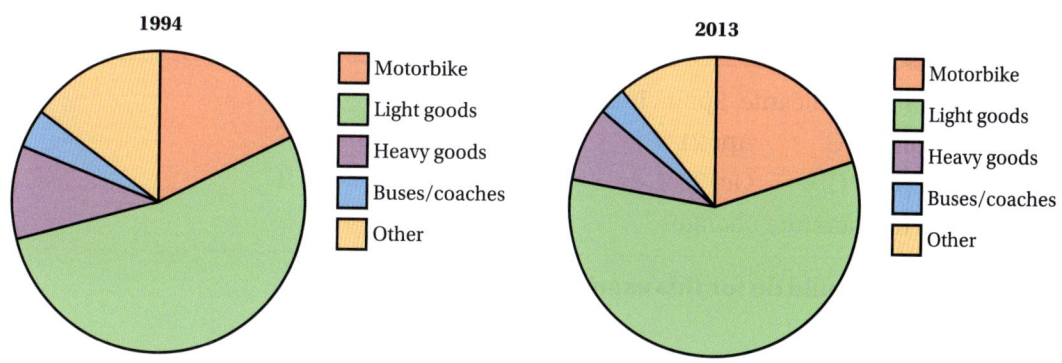

1994 / 2013
- Motorbike
- Light goods
- Heavy goods
- Buses/coaches
- Other

a Give two differences between the proportions for 1994 and 2013.

b If there were 6.075 million vehicles other than cars on the road in 2013, calculate the number of light goods vehicles there were.

c What percentage of vehicles other than cars were motorbikes in 2013?

5 This data shows the destinations of students leaving a sixth form college.

Destination	College A	College B
Higher education	32	46
Further education	45	72
Employment	28	31
Gap year	12	24
Unemployment	15	22

Create two pie charts and use them to argue that one college is more successful than the other.

Section 4: Line graphs for time series data

Some data that you collect changes with time. For example, the average temperature each month for a year, the number of cars passing through a junction each hour or the number of minutes on your mobile phone you have left to use by the end of the month.

Line graphs are useful for showing how data changes over time. When time is one of the variables it is always plotted on the horizontal axis of the graph.

Find answers at: cambridge.org/ukschools/gcsemaths-studentbookanswers

The maximum temperature at a weather station is recorded at noon every day. Data which shows change over time like this is called time series data.

Monday	Tuesday	Wednesday	Thursday	Friday	Saturday	Sunday
15 °C	17 °C	18 °C	21 °C	16 °C	20 °C	14 °C

Each of the points is joined by a straight line.

The type of data in this graph is called **continuous** data because it can take any numerical value (within a range) and can be measured.

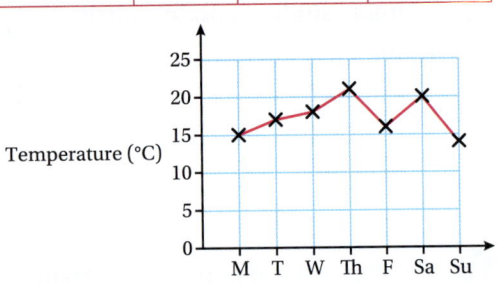

The height of students in your class would also be continuous data.

Problem-solving framework

The average temperature each month in Alicante, Spain, is as follows:

Jan 17 °C   Feb 18 °C   Mar 20 °C   Apr 21 °C   May 24 °C   Jun 28 °C
Jul 30 °C   Aug 31 °C   Sep 29 °C   Oct 25 °C   Nov 20 °C   Dec 18 °C

Display this data to show how the temperature changes.

Steps for approaching a problem-solving question	What you would do for this example
Step 1: If it is useful to have a table, draw one.	<table><tr><td>J</td><td>F</td><td>M</td><td>A</td><td>M</td><td>J</td><td>J</td><td>A</td><td>S</td><td>O</td><td>N</td><td>D</td></tr><tr><td>17°C</td><td>18°C</td><td>20°C</td><td>21°C</td><td>24°C</td><td>28°C</td><td>30°C</td><td>31°C</td><td>29°C</td><td>25°C</td><td>20°C</td><td>18°C</td></tr></table>
Step 2: Identify what you have to do.	You need to choose a suitable means of displaying the data and then draw it.
Step 3: Start working on the problem using what you know.	We know that a time series graph shows changes over time, so it would be a good visual way of showing how the temperature varies. Choose a suitable scale and plot each point on the axes using the table. Join the points to make a line.
Step 4: Check your working and that your answer is reasonable.	Check the shape of the graph. Does it get warmer in the summer and colder in the winter? Is that right for the location? Are there any unexpected sharp increases or decreases?
Step 5: Have you answered the question?	Yes, the graph shows how the temperature changes through the year.

552

35 Collecting and displaying data

EXERCISE 35E

1 a Construct a time-series graph for the average temperature (in °C) in a particular city, which is given in the table below.

Month	Jan	Feb	Mar	Apr	May	Jun	Jul	Aug	Sep	Oct	Nov	Dec
Average Temp (°C)	15.2	16.5	17.2	19.1	19.6	20.1	22.2	24.1	21.3	19.3	17.6	16.6

b Use the time-series line graph to write a brief description of how the average temperature varies in this particular city.

2 The table below gives the annual profit (in £million) of a company over a ten-year period. Construct a time-series graph of the information.

Year	Year 1	Year 2	Year 3	Year 4	Year 5	Year 6	Year 7	Year 8	Year 9	Year 10
Profit (£million)	2.2	1.8	2.3	1.2	0.6	1.1	2.2	3.1	3.7	4.2

3 The table below gives the number of teeth extracted at a dentist's surgery each month for a year.

Month	Jan	Feb	Mar	Apr	May	Jun	Jul	Aug	Sep	Oct	Nov	Dec
Number of teeth	54	47	49	60	41	45	36	11	38	42	32	22

a Represent this information on a time-series graph.

b Briefly describe how the number of teeth extracted each month changed over the year.

c Why might the number of teeth extracted fall during August?

4 The table below gives the position of a particular five-a-side football team in a league of 10 teams at the completion of each week throughout the season.

Round	1	2	3	4	5	6	7	8	9	10	11
Position	2	3	5	7	6	5	6	7	5	5	4

Round	12	13	14	15	16	17	18
Position	5	3	4	3	3	4	3

a Represent this information on a time-series graph.

b Describe the progress of the team throughout the season.

Find answers at: cambridge.org/ukschools/gcsemaths-studentbookanswers

5 The data below shows the value of sales at a service station on a main road over a period of three years. Each quarter represents three months (a quarter) of the year. The quarters are labelled 1 to 12 in the corresponding time-series graph.

Sales quarter	Sales £thousand
Quarter 1	64
Quarter 2	82
Quarter 3	83
Quarter 4	65
Quarter 5	77
Quarter 6	89
Quarter 7	96
Quarter 8	58
Quarter 9	79
Quarter 10	92
Quarter 11	101
Quarter 12	66

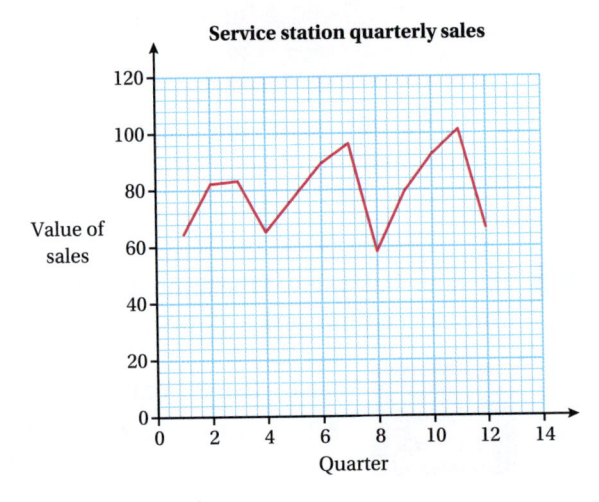

a In which quarter of each year is the value of sales highest?

b In which quarter of each year is the value of sales lowest?

c Compare the sales figures for the first quarter of each year. Are the sales figures improving from one year to the next?

6 The table below gives the numbers of garden sheds sold each quarter during 2012–2014.

Number of sales	Q1	Q2	Q3	Q4
2012	27	32	56	41
2013	33	35	65	45
2014	38	41	72	51

a Represent this information on a time-series graph.

b Describe how the shed sales have altered over the given time period.

c Does it appear that shed sales are seasonal?

7 Study the following graph.

Road traffic by vehicle type (commercial and public service vehicles) in the UK

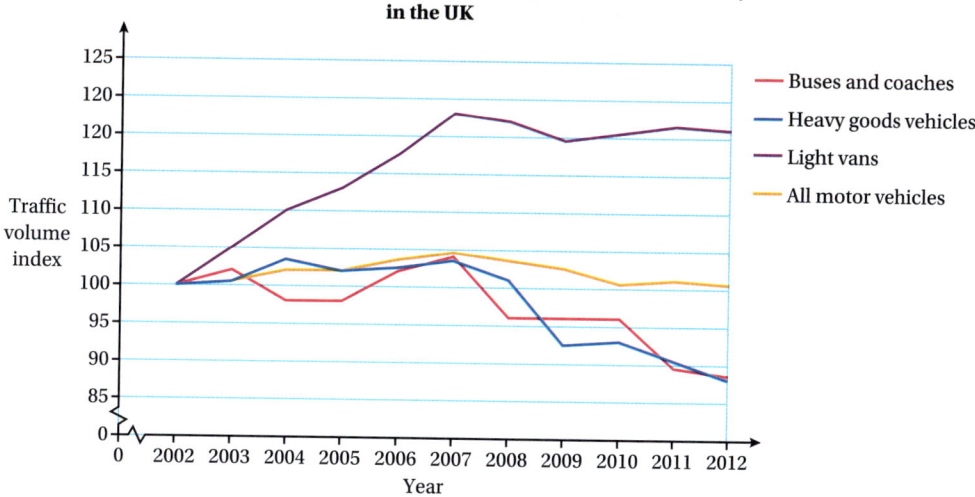

— Buses and coaches
— Heavy goods vehicles
— Light vans
— All motor vehicles

a Describe the trend in numbers of light vans.
b What has happened to the number of all motor vehicles?
c Suggest why the number of heavy goods vehicles might have decreased. Can we answer this by just using the graph?

8 This graph shows how the water level in a pond varies from month to month.

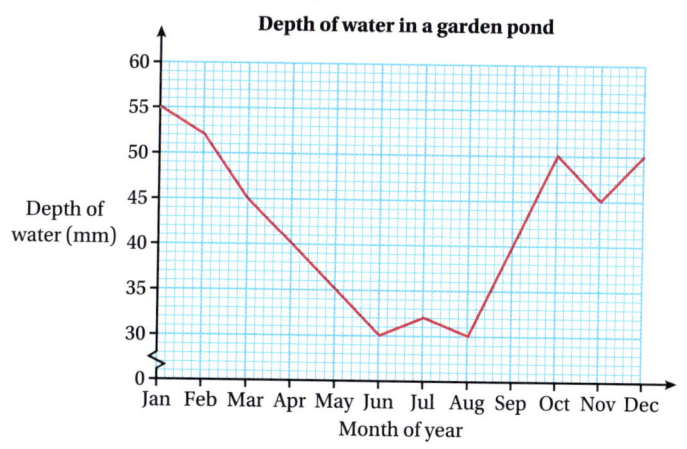

Depth of water in a garden pond

a When is the lowest depth of water?
b What do you think might have happened in July?
c When does the water level drop most rapidly?
d How much water is in the pond in May?
e What is the difference in depth between August and September?

Checklist of learning and understanding

Sampling

- A population is a set of individuals or objects of interest.
- A sample is a small set of data from a population; a **representative sample** is one that represents the characteristics of a larger population.
- In a random sample, each member of the population is equally likely to be chosen for the sample.

Find answers at: cambridge.org/ukschools/gcsemaths-studentbookanswers

Tables and graphs

- A frequency table is a method of organising data by showing how often a result appears in the data.
- Data can be displayed using a number of different graphs.
- All graphs should be clearly labelled and scaled, including a title.
- Vertical line graphs and bar charts are a good way of showing discrete data, where the height of each bar or line determines the frequency.
- Multiple bar charts are a good way of comparing data for two or more groups; a composite bar chart is good for showing the component parts of a data set.
- Pictograms are an interesting visual way of displaying discrete data.
- Pie charts are used to compare categories of the same data set.

Line graphs

- Line graphs for time series data are useful for showing trends and changes over time.
- Time is always along the x-axis.

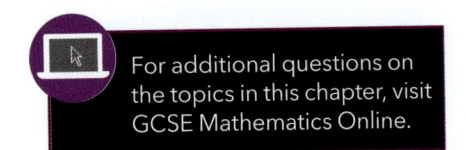

For additional questions on the topics in this chapter, visit GCSE Mathematics Online.

Chapter review

1. Bonita needs to find out how students travel to school, so she decides to take a representative sample.

   a Suggest two ways in which she could do this.

   b Bonita asks a representative sample of 50 students and gets the following results:

Car	15
Walk	17
Bus	6
Taxi	7
Bike	5

   If there are 600 students in the school, what is a sensible estimate of the number of students who walk to school?

2. Kimberley surveys her classmates to find their favourite pizza. The results are shown in the table below:

Cheese and tomato	5
Seafood	8
Meat	2
Roast vegetable	6
Pepperoni	7

   Choose a suitable scale and draw a pictogram to represent this data.

35 Collecting and displaying data

3 Two adults are comparing how much money they spend each month.

Expenditure per month (£)	Josh	Ben
Rent	840	450
Food	250	300
Transport	350	160
Savings	250	40
Entertainment	110	250

  a Draw suitable graphs to enable you to compare the proportions of money they spend.
  b Write two sentences comparing their spending habits.

4 The profits for two companies are given for each quarter of a two-year period below:

	Company profits (£)	
	Company A	Company B
1st quarter 2013	134 820	125 912
2nd quarter 2013	138 429	189 355
3rd quarter 2013	140 721	130 969
4th quarter 2013	131 717	156 548
1st quarter 2014	103 746	219 357
2nd quarter 2014	197 028	151 296
3rd quarter 2014	187 883	249 216
4th quarter 2014	168 414	102 158

Use the data to plot a suitable graph to compare how profits change.
  a Which company is the most successful?
  b Which is the biggest change between quarters?

5 Alec asked 120 people on holiday where they were going to spend the afternoon.
He then drew a pie chart from his results.
His results and the angles he worked out are shown below.
  a Complete the table. *(3 marks)*

Number of people	Activity	Size of angle
42	Swimming pool	
	Beach	138°
5	Lounge	
	Sightseeing	81°

  b Complete the pie chart for Alec. *(2 marks)*

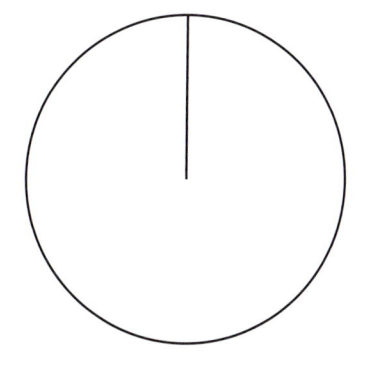

© OCR 2013

Find answers at: cambridge.org/ukschools/gcsemaths-studentbookanswers

36 Analysing data

In this chapter you will learn how to …

- calculate and compare summary statistics for ungrouped and grouped data.
- recognise when data is being misrepresented.
- plot and interpret scatter diagrams and use them to describe correlation and predict results.
- identify outliers and understand how they can indicate errors in data.

For more resources relating to this chapter, visit GCSE Mathematics Online.

Using mathematics: real-life applications

Analysing large sets of data enables financial and insurance companies to make predictions about what might happen in the future. Car insurance premiums are worked out according to typical or 'average' behaviour of large groups of people.

"We group drivers together by age and gender and use statistics to find typical driving behaviour for each group. Young drivers have more accidents, so their insurance costs more."

(Insurance broker)

Tip

Knowing how to calculate averages and measures of spread gives us tools to compare different sets of data. Make sure you know what these are and when to use the different measures.

Before you start …

KS3	You should remember how to find the mean, median, mode and range of a set of data.	① Find the mean, median, mode and range of the following sets of data. Give your answers correct to one decimal place. **a** 2 4 2 7 3 5 4 2 3 1 **b** 40 20 30 60 50 10
Ch 18	You should be able to plot coordinates on a set of axes.	② Write down the coordinates of points A, B and C on the line.
Ch 18	You should be able to recognise whether a gradient is positive or negative.	③ Use the graph above. **a** What is the gradient of the graph? **b** What is the equation of the line?

36 Analysing data

Assess your starting point using the Launchpad

STEP 1

1 Answer the questions about these three sets of data:

A	10	5	9	10	8	12	7
B	3	4	5	6	6	10	12
C	7	10	11	14	18		

   a What is the median of set C?
   b Which data set has a mode of 10?
   c Which set of data has the smallest mean?
   d Which data set does not have a mode?
   e How would the mode, median and mean of set B change if you added the value 14 to the set?

2 The frequency table shows the ages of a group of students visiting the Natural History Museum.

Age (years)	14	15	16	17
Frequency	23	17	13	9

   a What is the modal age?
   b What is the mean age of the students in this group?
   c What is the range of ages in the group?

GO TO
Section 1: Summary statistics

STEP 2

3 This graph appeared in a newspaper article.

Explain how this graph could be misleading.

Massive increase in home price

(Bar chart: Average house price in £, 2012 ≈ 168 000, 2013 ≈ 170 000; y-axis from 167 000 to 171 000)

GO TO
Section 2: Misleading graphs

GO TO
Step 3: The Launchpad continues on the next page …

Find answers at: cambridge.org/ukschools/gcsemaths-studentbookanswers

559

Launchpad continued ...

STEP 3

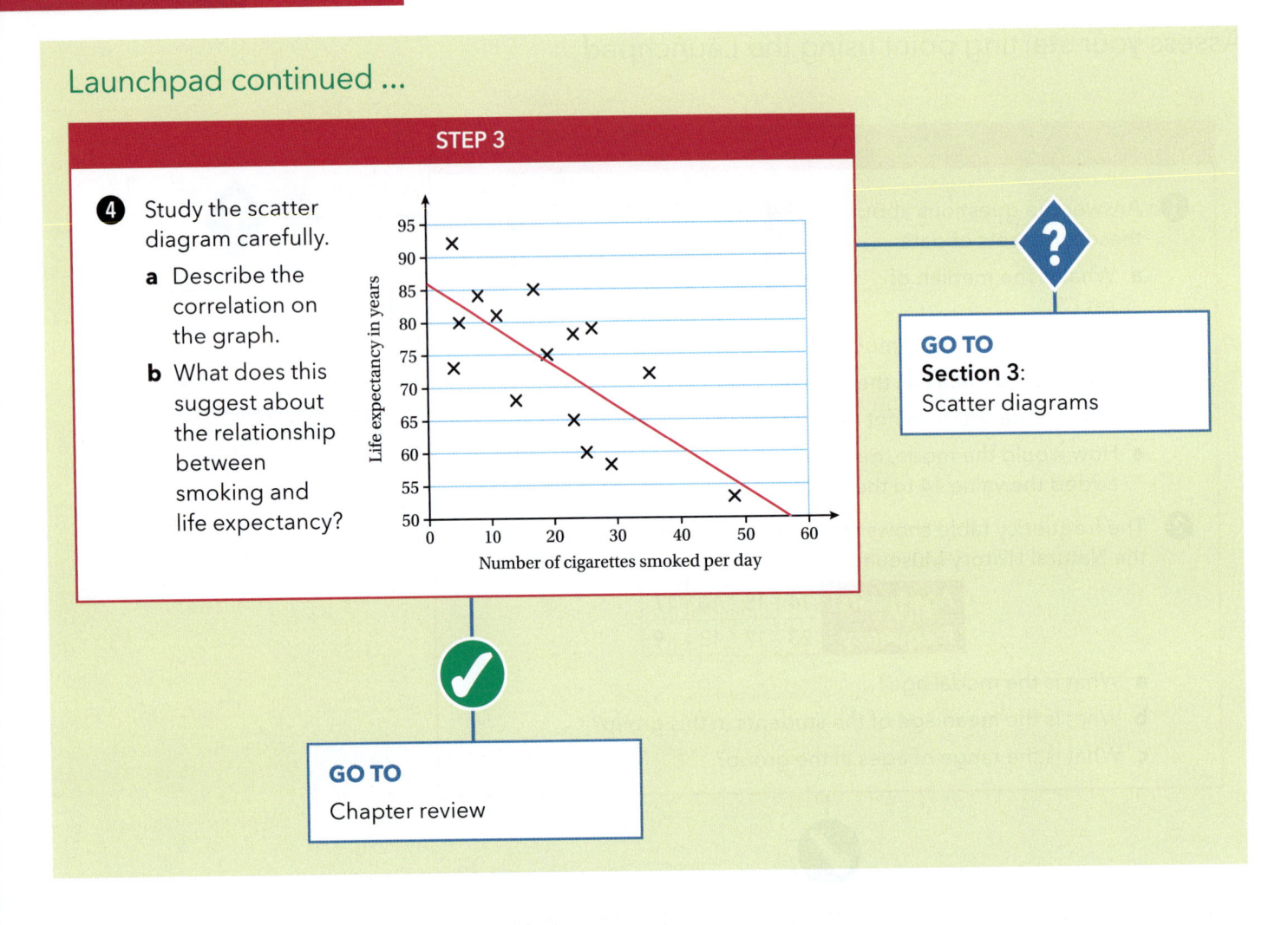

4 Study the scatter diagram carefully.

a Describe the correlation on the graph.

b What does this suggest about the relationship between smoking and life expectancy?

GO TO Section 3: Scatter diagrams

GO TO Chapter review

Section 1: Summary statistics

In statistics you are often asked to give a single value that summarises the data and tells you something about it. You have learnt to use four different values to summarise data:

- the mean – $\dfrac{\text{sum of values}}{\text{number of values}}$
- the mode – the value with the highest frequency
- the median – the middle value when the values are arranged in size order
- the range – the difference between the highest value and the lowest value.

The mean, median and mode are all types of averages, or measures of central tendency.

The range is a measure of spread or dispersion. The range is useful for determining whether the mean is distorted or not.

To describe and compare two sets of data, calculate the averages and range and write sentences to summarise what you notice.

Choosing the correct average

The type of average that you choose depends on the situation and what you want to know.

The mean is the average that is used most often. The mean is useful when you want to know a typical value. If the data is very spread out (it has a big range) then the mean will not be typical.

For example, the boss in a company earns £20 000 per month. Her nine employees earn £2000 each. This gives a mean salary of £3800, which is not typical.

In this situation, the median salary is £2000 and the modal salary is £2000. Both are more representative than the mean.

When the data is not numerical, you have to use the mode as the average.

The mode is most useful when you need to know which item is most common or most popular.

You would use the mode when you wanted to show:
- which clothing size was bought most often
- what shoe size is most common
- what brand of mobile phone is the most popular.

The average you choose can affect how you see the data.

For example, Jeanne asks her friends how many different hobbies they have had in the past year. These are their answers:

1 1 2 1 3 40 1

She works out the mean number of hobbies:

$$\frac{1 + 1 + 2 + 1 + 3 + 40 + 1}{7} = \frac{49}{7} = 7$$

> **Tip**
>
> A very high or a very low value in a set of data is called an **outlier**. If there is an outlier then the mean will not be a typical value.

The mean suggests that Jeanne's friends have had an average of 7 different hobbies each in the past year.

But that is not a very representative average and it does not give the typical number of hobbies. The mean number of hobbies is high because one friend had many more different hobbies than the others.

Jeanne doesn't think the mean is a good average for her set of data, so she finds the median:

1 1 1 1 2 3 40

This gives her an average of 1 hobby. That seems more typical. The mode is also 1 because most people have only had one hobby. The median and the mode are more representative and they are not affected by outliers in the data, so they are better averages in this case.

Find answers at: cambridge.org/ukschools/gcsemaths-studentbookanswers

WORKED EXAMPLE 1

Josh has developed a website and is monitoring how many hits it receives per hour.

In the first two days (48 hours) it receives the following numbers of hits per hour (arranged in numerical order):

100	105	106	106	107	107	108	110	117	118
135	137	145	148	148	148	153	155	157	159
162	171	171	179	183	183	185	185	189	199
201	203	204	209	216	220	223	224	224	227
229	230	231	233	234	235	237	238		

a Find the following summary statistics:
 i the mean, median and mode   **ii** the range.

b Josh is trying to sell advertising on his website. Write a mathematical sentence he could use about the number of hits his site is receiving.

c Josh compares his data to a similar website run by Delia. Delia's data set has the following data values:
 mean = 180 hits
 median = 140 hits
 mode = 135 hits
 range = 200

What can Josh say to compare the two sets?

a i Mean = $\frac{\text{sum of values}}{\text{number of values}} = \frac{8394}{48}$ = 174.88 hits

Median = $\frac{179 + 183}{2}$ = 181 hits.

> Median of the data is halfway between the 24th and the 25th data values.

Mode = 148

> The value 148 is the mode because it occurs three times.

ii The range = 238 − 100 = 138.

b There is a consistent hit rate of over 100 hits per hour with 175 hits per hour on average.

> You need to decide which measure of average you are going to use.

c Although the mean of the hits is a bit higher for Delia's set, the median is much lower for her set than it is for Josh's. This indicates that the mean of Delia's hits is influenced by a few high values, but usually the number of hits is lower. Delia's data shows a wider range, showing that the data is more spread out, and therefore less consistent.

Finding the mean from a frequency table

You can also find the mean when data is set out in a frequency table.

WORKED EXAMPLE 2

Leona is investigating the number of spots a typical ladybird has.
She observes and records the following data.

Number of spots	Frequency
1	4
2	7
3	12
4	14
5	9
6	7

Calculate the mean number of spots.

Number of spots	Frequency	Number of spots × frequency
1	4	4
2	7	14
3	12	36
4	14	56
5	9	45
6	7	42
Total	53	197

Add an extra column to the table and calculate the number of spots in total.

197 ÷ 53 = 3.72

Divide the total number of spots by the number of ladybirds

Analysing grouped data

Data is sometimes grouped together before it is analysed. The groups are known as class intervals. Note that they **do not** overlap.
For example,

Marks scored	Frequency
0–9	6
10–19	6
20–29	4
30–39	5
40–50	9
Total	30

> **Tip**
> You learnt about class intervals in Chapter 35.

When you only have the grouped data in a frequency table, it is not possible to calculate precise values for the mean, median, mode and range because you don't know the individual values.

Find answers at: cambridge.org/ukschools/gcsemaths-studentbookanswers

GCSE Mathematics for OCR (Foundation)

You can identify the modal and median classes from the table.

- The modal class is the class interval that has the most elements, not the individual value that appears the most. In the table above the modal class is 40–50 marks.

- To estimate the median of grouped data, find the class interval in which the middle value occurs. It is only possible to say that the median is within that group. In the table there are 30 values, the middle value is between the 15th and 16th values, so it must fall into the class 20–29 marks.

Estimating the mean of a frequency distribution

To estimate the mean of grouped data, find the midpoint of each class interval. The midpoint is found by adding the lowest and highest possible values for each class interval and dividing by 2. Multiply each midpoint by the frequency for each class interval. Find the total of these products, and divide by the total number of values you have.

WORKED EXAMPLE 3

Ben goes fishing and records the masses of the fish he catches in the table below:

Mass (m) in kg	Frequency	Midpoint	Midpoint × frequency
$2 \leq m < 4$	5		
$4 \leq m < 6$	8		
$6 \leq m < 8$	4		
$8 \leq m < 10$	9		
$10 \leq m < 12$	3		

a Complete the table.
b Find the modal class.
c Estimate the mean, median and range.

a
Mass (m) in kg	Freq	Midpoint	Midpoint × frequency
$2 \leq m < 4$	5	3	15
$4 \leq m < 6$	8	5	40
$6 \leq m < 8$	4	7	28
$8 \leq m < 10$	9	9	81
$10 \leq m < 12$	3	11	33

b The modal class is $8 \leq m < 10$

> The modal class is the class with the highest frequency.

c Total of the midpoint × frequency values is 197.
Estimated mean is 197 ÷ 29 = 6.79 kg

> The total frequency is 29. The mean is only **estimated** because the data is grouped you cannot know its exact value.

The median class is $6 \leq m < 8$ kg.
Range = 12 − 2 = 10 kg.

> There are 29 values, so the middle value is value number 15. This occurs in the interval $6 \leq m < 8$ kg.

564

EXERCISE 36A

1 A large company has kept a record of how many days each employee is absent from work each year.

The results are in the table below:

Days absent (d)	Frequency	Midpoint	Midpoint × frequency
$0 \leq d < 5$	15		
$5 \leq d < 10$	23		
$10 \leq d < 15$	19		
$15 \leq d < 20$	12		
$20 \leq d < 25$	6		
Total			

a Complete the table.
b Use the information to find the modal class.
c Estimate the mean, median and range.

2 For a charity event, several students are throwing rubber darts at a Velcro dart board while blindfolded.

The scores they achieve are given in the table:

a Choose suitable class intervals and group the data.
b Estimate the mean, the median and the range of the scores.
c Is it sensible to estimate the range?
d What is the modal group?

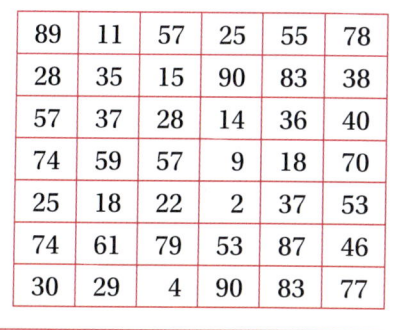

89	11	57	25	55	78
28	35	15	90	83	38
57	37	28	14	36	40
74	59	57	9	18	70
25	18	22	2	37	53
74	61	79	53	87	46
30	29	4	90	83	77

3 A health club has measured its members' heights (in metres) before buying some new gym equipment. The data is given in the table:

a Use group intervals of every 5 cm, starting with the group $1.45 \leq h < 1.50$.
Estimate the mean and the median.
b What is the modal class?
c Use class intervals of every 10 cm, starting with the class $1.40 \leq h < 1.50$.
What difference does this make to your estimates of the mean and median?

1.68	1.68	1.58	1.72	1.58	1.75	1.89
1.84	1.55	1.65	1.66	1.84	1.55	1.81
1.47	1.55	1.58	1.66	1.55	1.61	1.68
1.57	1.57	1.69	1.65	1.75	1.55	1.73
1.64	1.85	1.53	1.65	1.77	1.66	1.75
1.75	1.59	1.88	1.82	1.62	1.69	1.67
1.63	1.66	1.84	1.77	1.52	1.84	1.53

4 30 runners complete a marathon race. Their times are given below (to the nearest minute):

2 hours 45 mins	3 hours 25 mins	3 hours 46 mins	4 hours 15 mins
5 hours 8 mins	4 hours 49 mins	4 hours 18 mins	3 hours 38 mins
3 hours 43 mins	3 hours 5 mins	2 hours 55 mins	4 hours 23 mins
4 hours 25 mins	3 hours 39 mins	3 hours 20 mins	4 hours 1 min
3 hours 33 mins	4 hours 6 mins	5 hours 11 mins	2 hours 51 mins
4 hours 35 mins	3 hours 19 mins	4 hours 47 mins	4 hours 28 mins
5 hours 5 mins	4 hours 19 mins	2 hours 46 mins	3 hours 18 mins
3 hours 53 mins	4 hours 35 mins		

a Group the data into suitable class intervals.
b Find the modal class.
c Estimate the mean, median and range.

Find answers at: cambridge.org/ukschools/gcsemaths-studentbookanswers

5 The mass of fruit from a farm is recorded in the table below.

Mass of fruit in kg	Frequency	Midpoint of class interval	Midpoint × frequency
$200 \leq m < 250$	15		
$250 \leq m < 300$	11		
$300 \leq m < 350$	13		
$350 \leq m < 400$	7		
$400 \leq m < 450$	2		
$450 \leq m < 500$	2		
$500 \leq m < 550$	2		
Total			

a Calculate an estimate of the mean mass of the fruit.

b In which interval does the median lie?

c In which interval does the third quartile lie?

Comparing two or more sets of data

Summary statistics allow us to compare sets of data and make decisions about them. One summary statistic on its own does not give enough information about the whole set. Think about the following:

Set A might have a similar mean value to Set B, but the median is lower than the median of Set B. This shows us that there are a few higher values in the set that have made the mean higher, but that more of the values are low.

One set might have a higher mean than the other, but the range of the data might be much wider, which shows us that many of the values are very different from the mean or median.

EXERCISE 36B

1 The results from two maths tests are given.

A	35	68	55	52	49	63	61	69	35	53
B	47	34	71	41	60	44	57	74	67	64

Describe and compare the results.

2 Two cricketers are having an argument about who has had the better season.

They have both batted 16 times, and the number of runs they have scored in each innings is given below.

Ahmed	27	16	36	27	55	35	51	38	44	17	41	53	7	43	48	49
Bill	2	30	44	11	26	32	13	46	40	44	0	45	15	34	14	24

a Compare and describe their records.

b Who do you think has had the better season?

3 Yusuf has recorded the time it takes to get home on two different buses. Which bus route should he use?

Bus 127	17	17	21	23	19	20	19	18	21	22	19	22	21	20
Bus 362	23	26	20	15	15	20	26	19	18	15	16			

Explain your answer. Does it matter that he has more data about the 127 bus?

4 A factory needs to choose between two machines that are both capable of bottling soft drinks.

Both manufacturers have provided data about how many bottles each machine fills per hour.

Machine A

Bottles (b)	Frequency
$200 \leq b < 250$	36
$250 \leq b < 300$	48
$300 \leq b < 350$	59
$350 \leq b < 400$	61
$400 \leq b < 450$	21

Machine B

Bottles (b)	Frequency
$200 \leq b < 250$	16
$250 \leq b < 300$	58
$300 \leq b < 350$	63
$350 \leq b < 400$	78
$400 \leq b < 450$	15

Use estimates of the mean, median and the range along with the modal group to decide which machine to choose.

5 The following statement in a newspaper seems to be incorrect.

According to latest figures, half the population weighs more than 70 kg. The "average" person weighs 80 kg.

Can you give an example of a sample of 5 people with mean weight of 70 kg and median weight of 80 kg?

6 a According to the Office of National Statistics, the 'average' price of a house in the UK in July 2014 was £272 000.

What would be the best type of average to measure house prices?

Explain why you think so.

b Give an example of when using the mean as a measure of central tendency would be the most useful.

c Give two examples when using the mode as a measure of central tendency is the most useful.

Section 2: Misleading graphs

One of the advantages of using graphs is that they show information at a glance. But graphs can also be misleading because most people don't look at them very closely.

When you look carefully at a graph you might find that it has been drawn in a way that gives a misleading impression. Sometimes this is intentional, sometimes it is not. You need to be able to look at graphs and know if they are misleading or wrong.

Find answers at: cambridge.org/ukschools/gcsemaths-studentbookanswers

When you look at a graph, you have to think about:

- the scale and whether or not it has been exaggerated in any way to give a particular impression.
- whether or not the scale starts at 0; this can affect the information shown and give a misleading impression.
- whether bars or pie diagrams have 3D sections which make some parts look much bigger than others.
- whether the scales are labelled and whether or not the graph has a title.
- whether the source of the data is given.

Here are some examples of misleading graphs.

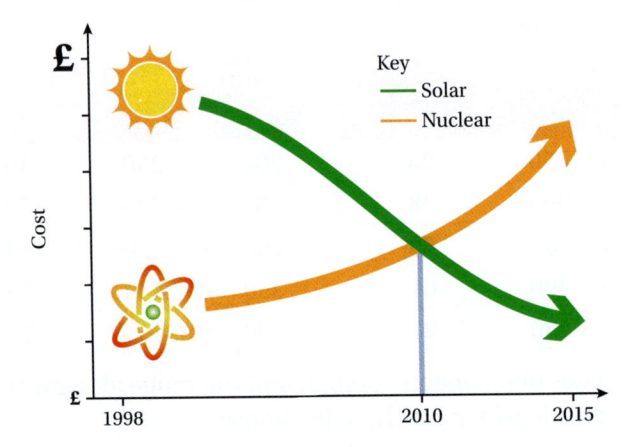

This graph seems to suggest that the price of solar energy is dropping quickly while the cost of nuclear power is increasing.

There are no values on the vertical scale, so it is not possible to decide whether that is really true and no source is given for the information. The scale could be £5 million at the bottom and £10 million at the top, in which case the graph would be very misleading.

You also don't know what costs are being compared. The graph could be comparing the cost of building a nuclear power station (very expensive) and the cost of installing 25 solar panels (much less expensive).

This graph is suggesting that recycling has increased dramatically from 1980.

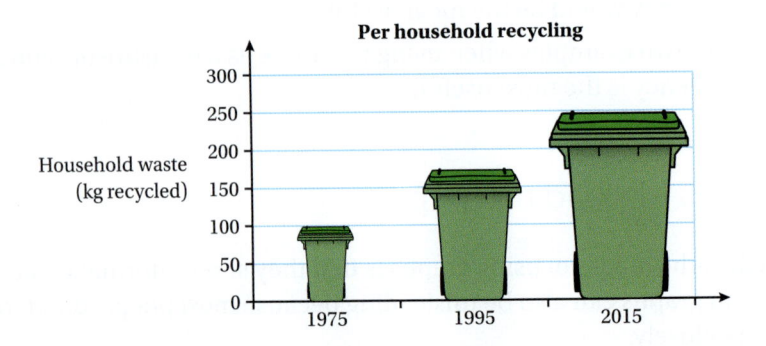

The graph uses proportion to mislead. If you look at the scale, you will see that the amount of recycled material has increased from 100 kg to 250 kg, so 2.5 times more material is recycled. The bin, however, is about six times bigger, so it looks like much more is recycled.

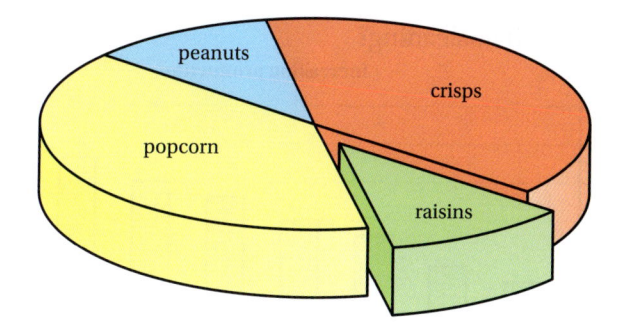

By drawing the pie chart in this orientation and making the sectors 3D, it looks like raisins are just as popular as peanuts and that popcorn is more popular than crisps. The real figures show that only 5% chose raisins and 11% chose peanuts, so the green sector that sticks out represents less than half of the blue sector. The other two sectors each represent 42% but they don't look the same size in this graph.

WORKED EXAMPLE 4

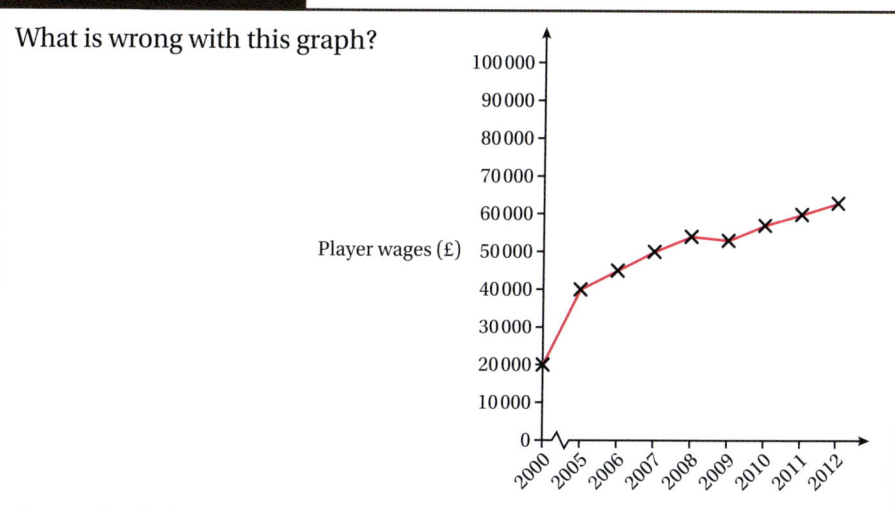

What is wrong with this graph?

The scale of the vertical axis goes as high as £100 000, which makes the increases in wages from year to year appear to be less significant. The small scale makes the slope appear flatter, suggesting the increases aren't very large but actually the scale increases by increments of £10 000.

EXERCISE 36C

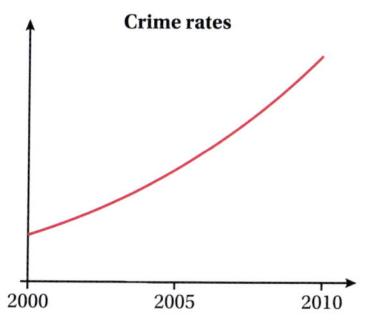

1. Identify the error in this graph.

Find answers at: cambridge.org/ukschools/gcsemaths-studentbookanswers

2. How is this graph misleading?

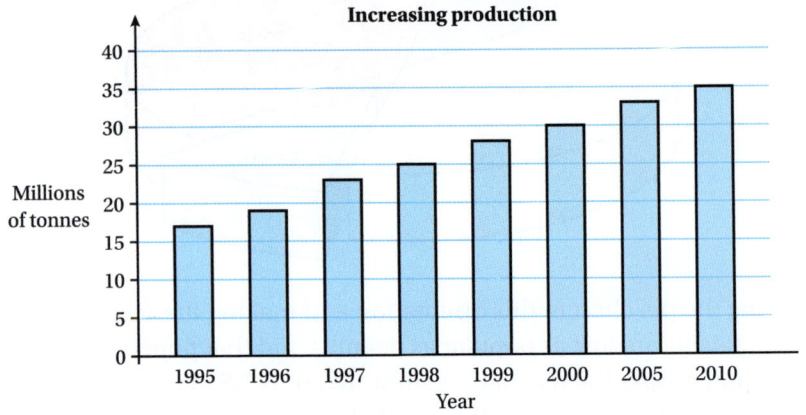

Increasing production

(Bar chart: Millions of tonnes vs Year — 1995: ~17, 1996: ~19, 1997: ~23, 1998: ~25, 1999: ~28, 2000: ~30, 2005: ~33, 2010: ~35)

Why might someone have drawn the graph like this?

3. What is wrong with this graph?

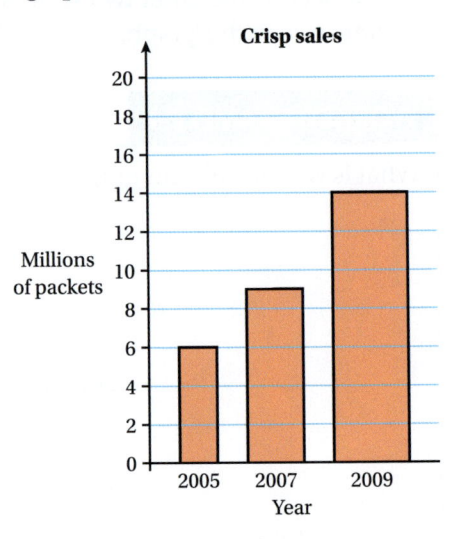

Crisp sales

(Bar chart: Millions of packets vs Year — 2005: 6, 2007: 9, 2009: 14)

4. Look carefully at the graph.

   a What is misleading about this graph?

   b Why do you think it has been drawn this way?

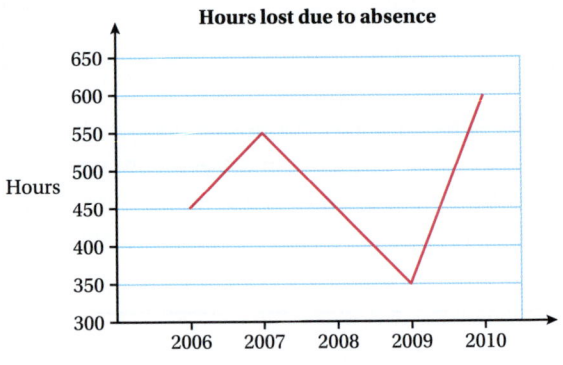

Hours lost due to absence

(Line graph: Hours vs Year — 2006: 450, 2007: 550, 2008: 450, 2009: 350, 2010: 600)

5. The same data has been presented in this 3D graph.

   a Which year has the most days lost, 2006 or 2008?

   b Why is it hard to tell?

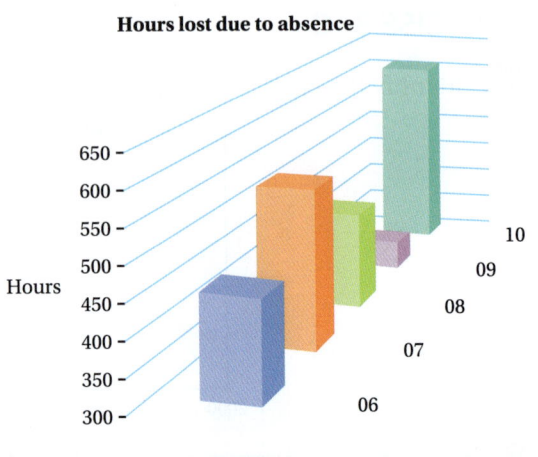

Hours lost due to absence

(3D bar chart showing years 06, 07, 08, 09, 10 with Hours axis from 300 to 650)

6 You are given the following data showing viewing figures for various TV programmes (in millions).

Week beginning	Britain's Got Talent	The Crimson Field	Gogglebox
7 April	10.03	6.89	2.75
14 April	8.45	6.31	3.37
21 April	8.63	6.25	3.48
28 April	8.45	6.01	3.47
5 May	8.58	6.33	3.54

Choose one of the TV programmes and create a graph which shows how well it has performed. You can use any type of graph, but must not change the numbers.

Section 3: Scatter diagrams

A scatter diagram is used to show whether or not there is a relationship between two sets of data collected in pairs. Data that is collected in pairs is called **bivariate data**.

For example, you could record the number of hours different students spend studying and the results they get in a test. This would give two pieces of data for each learner: time spent studying and test results. You can think of these as a pair of number coordinates (x, y).

In bivariate data, both sets of data are numerical, so each pair of data can be plotted as a point using coordinates on a pair of axes.

Once you have plotted the data, you can look for a pattern to see whether there is a relationship or **correlation** between the two variables or not. The diagrams below show the typical patterns of correlation and what they mean.

Key vocabulary

bivariate data: data that is collected in pairs.

Key vocabulary

correlation: a relationship or connection between data items.

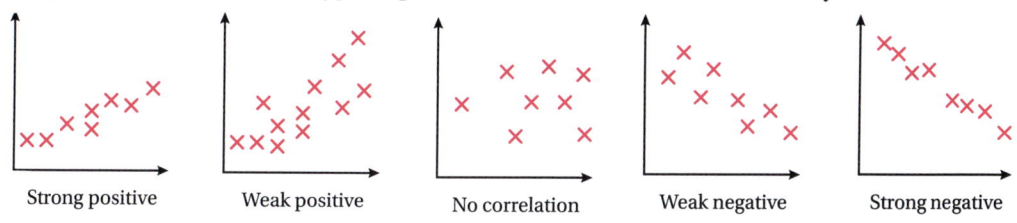

Strong positive | Weak positive | No correlation | Weak negative | Strong negative

WORKED EXAMPLE 5

Nick says people who are good at maths are also good at science.

Use this data to draw a scatter diagram and comment on whether Nick is correct or not.

Maths average (%)	Science average (%)
20	22
32	30
45	39
38	40
60	60
80	70
80	72
90	90
80	25
60	65

Continues on next page …

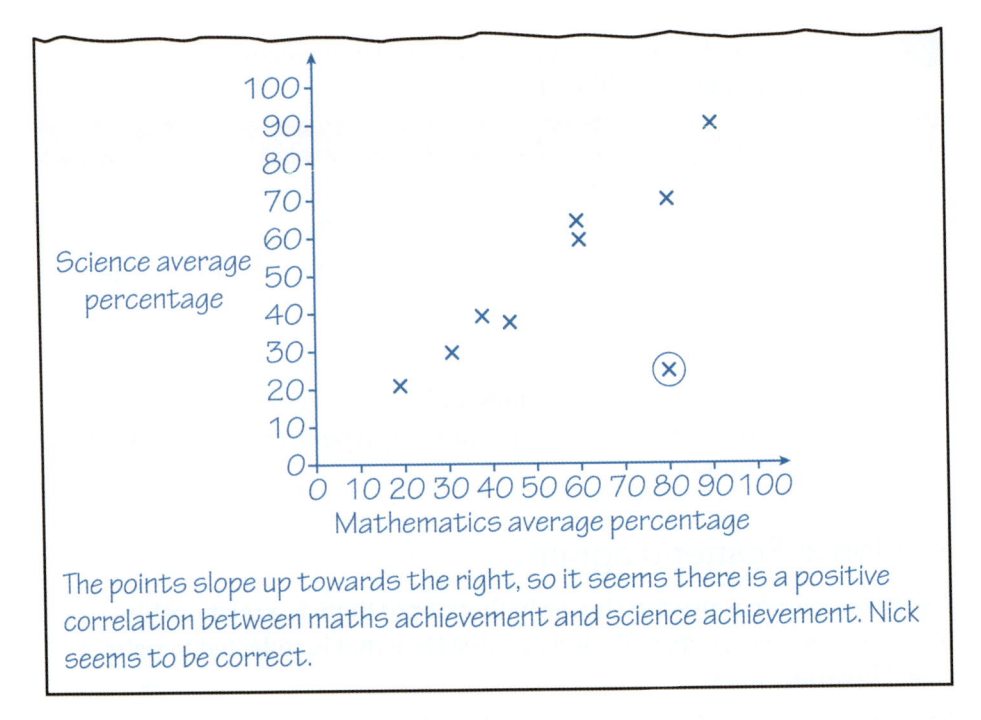

[Scatter diagram: Science average percentage (vertical axis) vs Mathematics average percentage (horizontal axis), both scaled 0 to 100. Points plotted show a positive trend, with one circled outlier at approximately (80, 25).]

The points slope up towards the right, so it seems there is a positive correlation between maths achievement and science achievement. Nick seems to be correct.

Key vocabulary

dependent variable: data that is measured in, and affected by, an experiment.

Look at the graph in the worked example.

Note that maths is on the horizontal axis and science on the vertical axis.

Science is the **dependent variable** in this case. Nick's statement is that science achievement is dependent on whether or not you are good at maths. Maths is the independent variable so it goes on the horizontal axis.

The pattern of points is used to decide whether there is a relationship. In this case, the points are grouped fairly closely and they form a thick line that slopes up to the right, so you can say there is a **positive correlation** between the scores.

If the line that formed sloped down to the left, you would say there is a **negative correlation**.

If the points are scattered such that no discernible line could be drawn, you would say there is **no correlation**.

Key vocabulary

outlier: data value that is much larger or smaller than others in the same data set.

The point that is circled is far away from the others and doesn't seem to fit the pattern. It shows a student with a high mark for maths but a low mark for science. This point is an **outlier** in this set of data.

It is important to note that correlation is **not causation**. This means that although there might be a relationship between two variables, the change in one cannot be said to be the definite reason for the change in the other; one does not necessarily cause the other.

Lines of best fit

A line of best fit is used to show a general trend on a scatter diagram.

This is a line drawn on the graph passing as close to as many points as possible.

This is the line of best fit for the scatter diagram in Worked example 5.

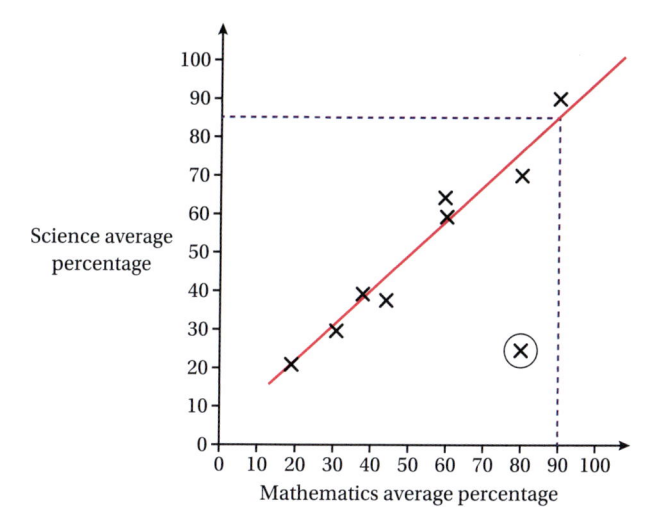

You can use the line of best fit to make predictions based on the collected data.

For example, if you wanted to predict the science results for a student who got 90% for maths, you could find this is 85% using the line. This is shown by the dotted line on the diagram.

EXERCISE 36D

1 Draw a scatter diagram for the following data and draw a line of best fit.

Homework (mins)	10	25	38	65	84	105	135	158
TV viewing (mins)	60	55	50	20	30	15	10	8

What kind of correlation is this?

2 Draw a scatter diagram to show the relationship between car engine size and fuel economy (miles per gallon).

Miles per gallon	64	60	59	58	55	49	47	42
Car engine size (litres)	1.1	1.3	1.4	1.6	1.8	2	2.5	3

3 Mike has an ice cream stall in the local park.

He writes down the number of ice creams he sells and the maximum temperature each day for a week.

Ice creams sold	86	89	45	69	84	25	78
Maximum temperature	25°C	26°C	19°C	23°C	25°C	15°C	21°C

a Draw a scatter diagram to show the correlation between ice cream sales and the temperature.

b Can you suggest any other factors that might affect sales?

4 During a census the number of people living in each house is recorded.

House number	1	3	5	7	9	11	13	15	17	19	21
Number of residents	1	5	1	4	2	5	6	3	5	3	6

a Draw a scatter diagram to show this data.

b What kind of correlation is this?

Find answers at: cambridge.org/ukschools/gcsemaths-studentbookanswers

5 The table below shows the athlete's height and the height jumped by the last 10 men's high jump world record holders.

	Athlete height (m)	Height jumped (m)
Sotomayor	1.95	2.45
Sjoberg	2	2.42
Paklin	1.91	2.41
Povarnitsyn	2.01	2.4
Jianhua	1.93	2.39
Wessig	2	2.36
Mogenburg	2.01	2.35
Wszola	1.9	2.35
Yashchenko	1.93	2.34
Stones	1.96	2.32

a Draw a scatter diagram showing this data.

b Is there a correlation between the height of the jumper and the height he jumped?

Outliers

Outliers are data values that lie outside the normal range for a set of data. In science experiments they might be 'freak' results or the result of inaccurate measurements. It can be difficult to decide when it is reasonable to disregard an outlier, but if it is an obvious error then the value is usually just ignored.

However, if outliers are genuine results and not errors, they can't be ignored just because they spoil a pattern. Outliers will have an impact on calculating the mean and the range of a set of data, but less so when finding the median and the mode.

On a scatter diagram an outlier will be a point that is away from the main scatter of points, or might fit the line of best fit but be at an extreme value.

WORKED EXAMPLE 6

A coach records the 100 m times of her 10 athletes at the start and the end of a week of intense training. Nine of the athletes were faster than their previously recorded times, but one athlete was 2 seconds slower. The team showed a mean improvement of 0.2 seconds.

Can the coach claim to be making a significant impact on her athletes?

Yes, the coach is making an impact on the athletes. Although the mean suggests only a small improvement this is likely to be due to the one negative result. In terms of running times for a 100 m race, 2 seconds is a large value and could have skewed the mean. The athlete with reduced performance is an outlier.

EXERCISE 36E

1 Several students sit a maths test and their scores are given below:

54 50 47 42 54 44 36 37 45 36 55 55 52 85 39

   a What is the mean score in the test?

   b What is the range?

   c What is the median score?

   d What is the median without the outlier?

   e What is the mean without the outlier?

2 Several students sit a maths and an English exam. Their scores are given below.

English	49	42	46	44	53	41	64	14	44	53	55	42
Maths	46	47	43	45	49	48	69	39	33	46	53	44

   a Plot their scores on a scatter diagram.

   b Draw a line of best fit on your scatter diagram.

   c Are any of the points outliers?

3 The time taken to travel by train from Norwich to London in minutes is recorded for 20 journeys:

109	129	98	106	109	156	128	98	99	113
126	99	105	110	126	98	106	114	122	107

On a normal day the journey should take between 95 and 115 minutes, depending on the number of stops at stations.

   a What is the mean journey time?

   b The train company claim that the mean journey time is 111 minutes on a normal day.
Is this right?

Checklist of learning and understanding

Summary statistics

- The mean, median and mode are all measures of central tendency (averages). They can be found precisely for populations that are ungrouped, and estimated for grouped data.
- The range is a measure of spread. It can be found precisely for ungrouped data and estimated for grouped data.

Misleading graphs

- The way that data is presented in graphs can be misleading. Watch out for uneven scales and ways of representing the data to exaggerate changes.

Find answers at: cambridge.org/ukschools/gcsemaths-studentbookanswers

Scatter diagrams and correlation
- Bivariate data is data that is collected in pairs.
- Scatter diagrams can be used to look for correlations in bivariate data. A correlation is a relationship, such as one quantity increasing as another decreases. Bivariate data can have a positive, negative or no correlation.
- Correlation does not mean causation; in other words, identifying a relationship does not necessarily mean that a change in one data set is causing the change in the other.
- Outliers are pieces of data that sit outside the pattern or expected result. They can be ignored if an obvious error, but otherwise should be considered and explained.

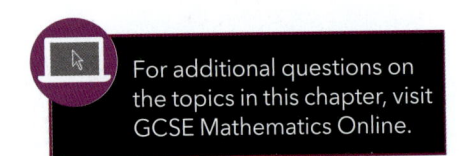

For additional questions on the topics in this chapter, visit GCSE Mathematics Online.

Chapter review

1 Windsurfers need a certain amount of wind to surf, but too much can be dangerous.

A learner would typically surf in a speed of 7 to 18 knots, but an expert would prefer to surf at above 30 knots.

Use the data on wind speed in knots measured at the same time each day for the two lakes below to decide which lake is better for beginners and which for experts. Use measures of central tendency and spread to support your argument.

First lake (knots)	0	21	33	13	20	11	35	3	5	3	31
	28	19	19	21	26	40	40	4	24	21	26
Second lake (knots)	15	11	19	11	10	19	23	25	10	18	10
	16	23	15	15	20	22	10	13	11	18	18

2 Study the two line graphs.

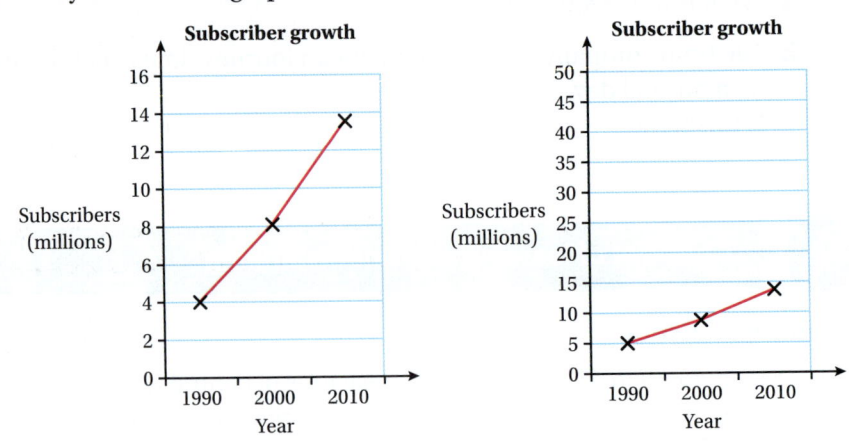

a These two graphs show the same data. Explain why they look different.

b Which graph would you use if you were a mobile phone service provider who wanted to suggest that there had been a huge increase in subscribers over this period? Why?

c Who might find the other graph useful? Why?

36 Analysing data

3 Data for the price of chocolate bars and their mass is given:

Price	45p	80p	£1.50	£3.00	£5.00	£10
Mass	35 g	80 g	175 g	320 g	540 g	1 kg

a Plot the data on a scatter diagram and draw a line of best fit.

b State what type of correlation there is.

4 A group of students did tests in music and French.
Their results were as follows.

Music	34	54	32	46	50	60	26	38	68	77	45	70	62
French	20	61	38	56	51	52	37	44	74	83	89	72	71

a Complete the scatter graph to show these results.
The first eight points have been plotted for you.

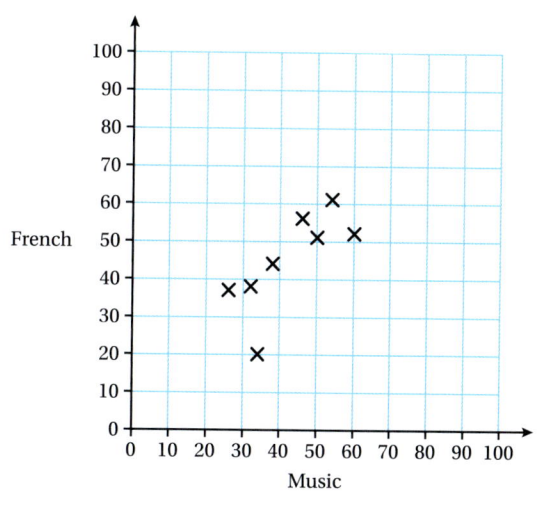

b Draw a line of best fit on your scatter graph. *(1 mark)*

c Describe the correlation shown by the graph. *(1 mark)*

d One of the students in the group, Guillaume, is French and always does much better in French than music.

Draw a ring around the cross that represents Guillaume's results.

(1 mark)

© OCR 2011

37 Interpreting graphs

In this chapter you will learn how to …
- construct and interpret graphs in real-world contexts.
- interpret the gradient of a straight-line graph as a rate of change.

For more resources relating to this chapter, visit GCSE Mathematics Online.

Using mathematics: real-life applications

All sorts of information can be obtained from graphs in real-life contexts. The shape of a graph, its gradient and the area underneath it can tell us about speed, time, acceleration, prices, earnings, break-even points or the values of one currency against another, among other things.

"My car needs to perform at its optimum limits. We generate and analyse diagnostic graphs to calculate the slight changes that would increase power, acceleration and top speed."

(F1 racing driver)

Before you start …

Ch 34	You will need to be able to distinguish between direct and inverse proportion.	**1** Which of these graphs shows an inverse proportion? How do you know this?
Ch 18	You'll need to be able to calculate the gradient of a straight line.	**2** Calculate the gradient of AB.

37 Interpreting graphs

Assess your starting point using the Launchpad

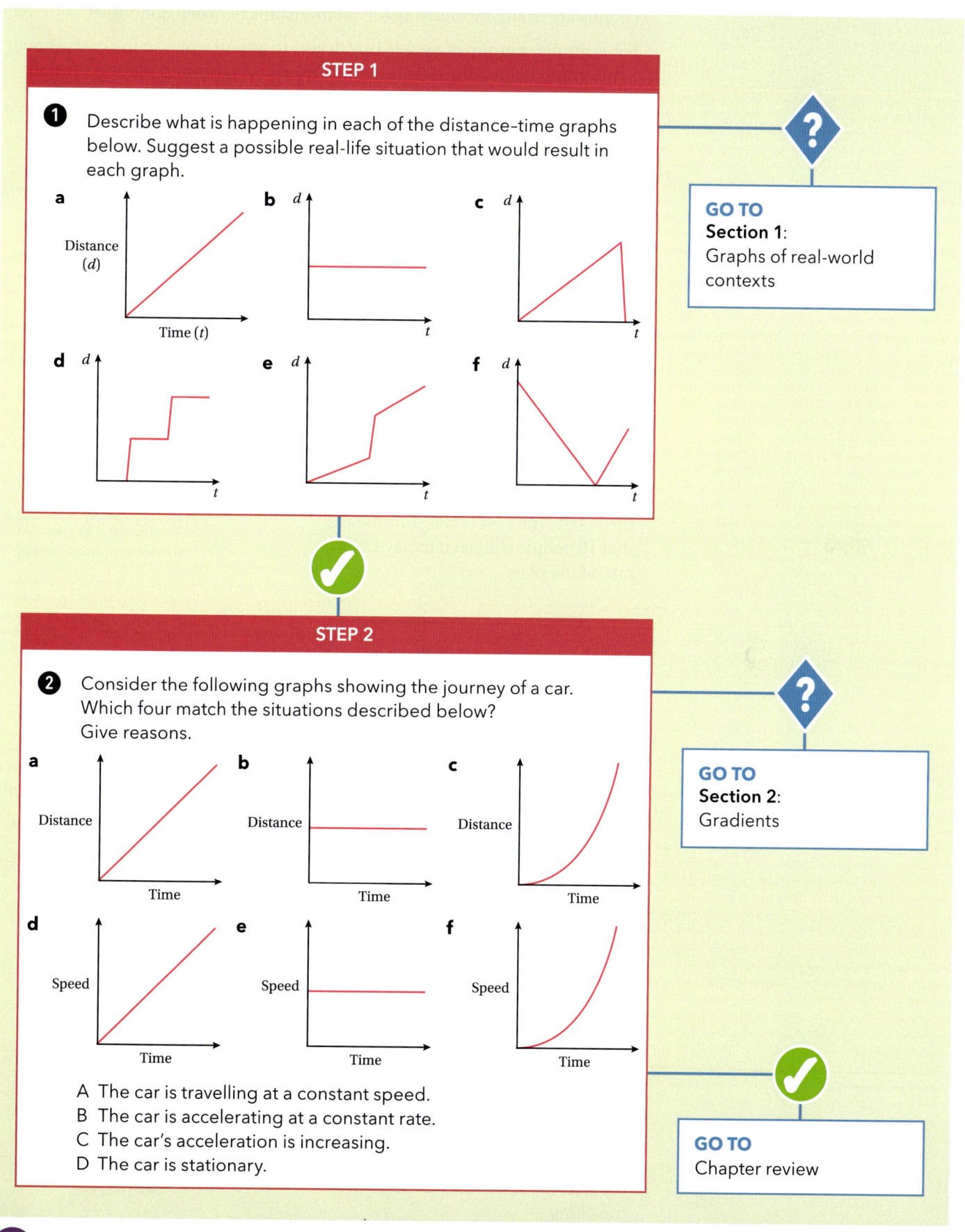

STEP 1

1 Describe what is happening in each of the distance–time graphs below. Suggest a possible real-life situation that would result in each graph.

a, b, c, d, e, f (distance–time graphs)

GO TO
Section 1: Graphs of real-world contexts

STEP 2

2 Consider the following graphs showing the journey of a car. Which four match the situations described below? Give reasons.

a, b, c (Distance vs Time graphs)
d, e, f (Speed vs Time graphs)

A The car is travelling at a constant speed.
B The car is accelerating at a constant rate.
C The car's acceleration is increasing.
D The car is stationary.

GO TO
Section 2: Gradients

GO TO
Chapter review

Find answers at: cambridge.org/ukschools/gcsemaths-studentbookanswers

Section 1: Graphs of real-world contexts

Graphs are useful for showing the relationships between quantities.

For example, a group of people buy tickets to attend a play at the costs shown in the graph below. The tickets include transport costs and seats in the hall.

This graph shows lots of information.

The horizontal axis (or x-axis) shows the number of people attending. The vertical axis (or y-axis) shows the total cost.

The cost depends on the number of people attending. However, there is a cost of £10 regardless of how many people attend – this is a group charge.

There are six marked points on the graph.

This graph is a linear graph, but it does **not** show direct proportion because it does not go through the origin.

Read up from 10 people on the x-axis to the straight line. When you reach the line move across horizontally until you reach the y-axis. The cost is £30. This means that 10 people will need to pay £30 to attend the play.

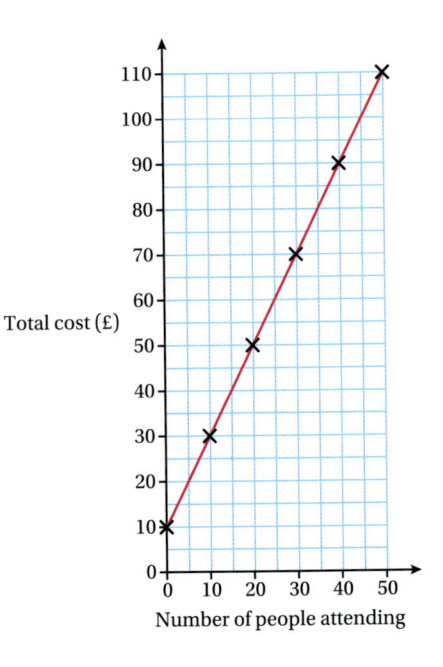

Distance–time graphs

Graphs that show the connection between the distance an object has travelled and the time taken to travel that distance are called distance–time graphs or travel graphs.

Time is normally shown along the horizontal axis and distance on the vertical.

The graphs normally start at the origin because at the beginning no time has passed and no distance has been covered.

Look at the graph. It shows the following:

- a cycle for 4 minutes from home to a bus stop 1 km away
- a 2 minute wait for the bus
- a 7 km journey on the bus that takes 10 minutes.

The line of the graph remains horizontal while the person is not moving (waiting for the bus) because no distance is being travelled at this time. The steeper the line, the faster the person is travelling.

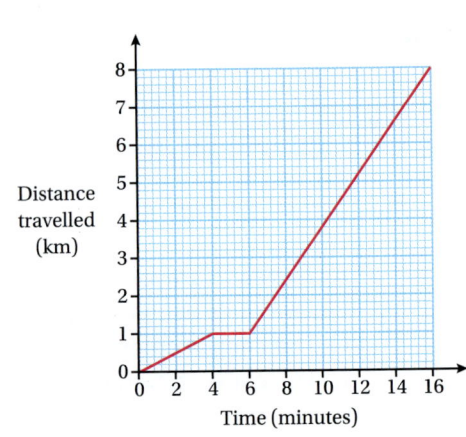

37 Interpreting graphs

WORKED EXAMPLE 1

The graph shows the relationship between the length and width of a hall.

Find the formula for this relationship.

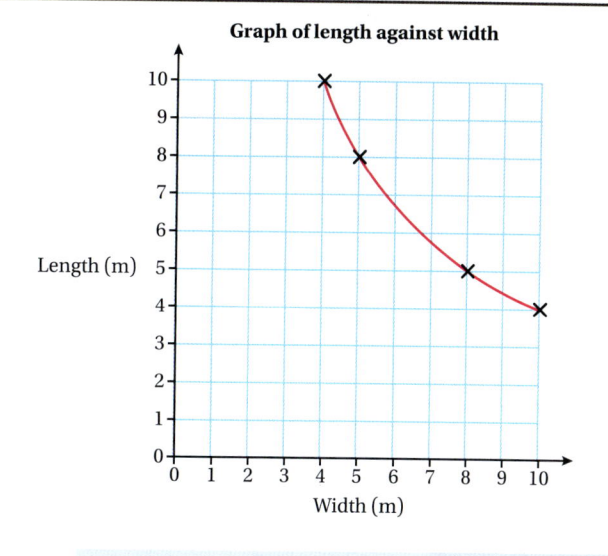

Graph of length against width

(Length (m) on y-axis, Width (m) on x-axis)

(4, 10), (5, 8), (8, 5) and (10, 4) — Write down the coordinates of some points on the line.

$4 \times 10 = 40 \text{ m}^2$

The area of the hall is constant, at = 40 m². — Work out the area of the hall using one of the coordinates, for example when the hall has a length of 10 m and a width of 4 m.

$$\text{length} = \frac{40}{\text{width}}$$

From the shape of the graph, you know that it is showing inverse proportion, so as the length increases the width decreases, therefore your formula will be in the form $y = \frac{k}{x}$. $k = 40$.

Because it shows a real-world context, the graph in Worked example 1 is only valid for that particular range of values.

Graphs are also useful in the real world for reading off values quickly without having to do the whole calculation. They can serve as conversion charts.

> **Tip**
>
> You saw conversion charts in the form of exchange rates in Chapter 34.

WORKED EXAMPLE 2

This graph shows the number of Indian rupees you would get for different numbers of US dollars at an exchange rate of US$1 : Rs 45. This relationship is a direct proportion.

a Use the graph to estimate the dollar value of Rs 250.

b Use the graph to estimate how many rupees you could get for US$9.

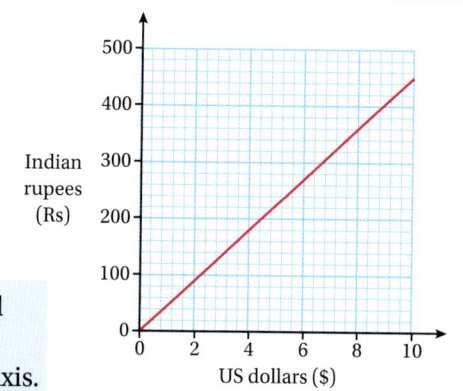

a Rs 250 is worth about $5.50. — Find 250 on the y-axis and read across and down to find the corresponding point on the x-axis.

b You could get about Rs 400 for $9. — Find 9 on the x-axis and read up and across to the find the corresponding point on the y-axis.

Find answers at: cambridge.org/ukschools/gcsemaths-studentbookanswers

581

EXERCISE 37A

1 This graph shows the movement of a taxi during a four-hour period.

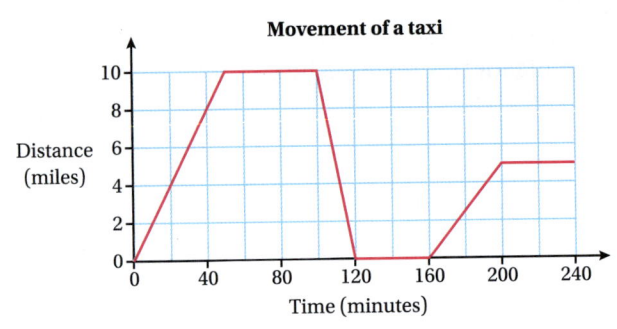

Movement of a taxi

(Distance (miles) vs Time (minutes))

a Clearly and concisely describe the taxi's journey.

b For how many minutes was the taxi waiting for passengers in this period?
How can you tell this?

c What was the total distance travelled?

d Calculate the taxi's average speed during:

  i the first 20 minutes.
  ii the first hour.
  iii from 160 to 210 minutes.
  iv for the full period of the graph.

> **Tip**
>
> You saw in Chapter 14 that
> $$\text{speed} = \frac{\text{distance travelled}}{\text{time taken}}$$

2 This distance–time graph represents Monica's journey from home to a supermarket and back again.

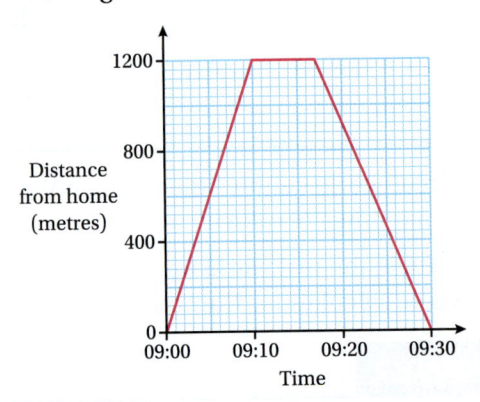

(Distance from home (metres) vs Time)

a How far was Monica from home at 09:06 hours?

b How many minutes did she spend at the supermarket?

c At what times was Monica 800 m from home?

d On which part of the journey did Monica travel faster, going to the supermarket or returning home?

3 A swimming pool is 25 m long. Jasmine swims from one end to the other in 20 seconds.

She rests for 10 seconds and then swims back to the starting point. It takes her 30 seconds to swim the second length.

a Draw a distance–time graph for Jasmine's swim.

b How far was Jasmine from her starting point after 12 seconds?

c How far was Jasmine from her starting point after 54 seconds?

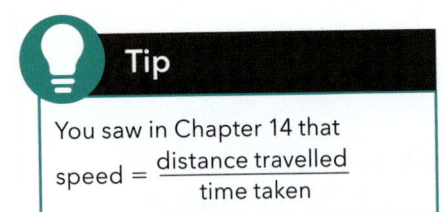

4 A hurricane disaster centre has a certain amount of clean water. The length of time the water will last depends on the number of people who come to the centre.

  a Calculate the missing values in this table.

No. of people	120	150	200	300	400
Days the water will last	40	32			

  b Plot a graph of this relationship.

Section 2: Gradients

Speed in distance–time graphs

The steepness (slope) or gradient of a distance–time graph gives an indication of speed. A straight-line graph indicates a constant speed.

The steeper the graph, the greater the speed.

An upward slope and a downward slope represent movement in opposite directions.

The distance–time graph shown is for a person who walks, cycles and then drives for three equal periods of time.

For each period, speed is given by the formula:

$$\text{speed} = \frac{\text{distance travelled}}{\text{time taken}}.$$

If a line section on a graph is horizontal, the gradient is zero and there is no speed, that is, the object has stopped moving.

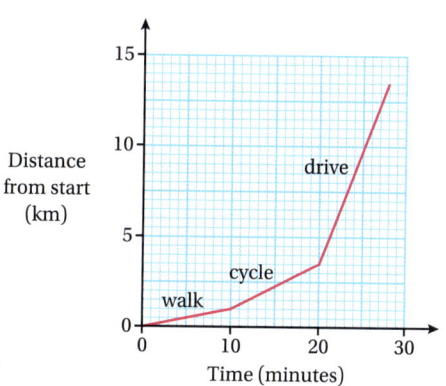

> **Tip**
>
> You learnt about kinematics in Chapter 14. Revise that section if you need to.

Using gradient triangles to interpret changing gradients

Looking at the gradient of a graph along with the axis labels gives a large amount of detail; even when there is no scale given.

This graph shows a car journey.

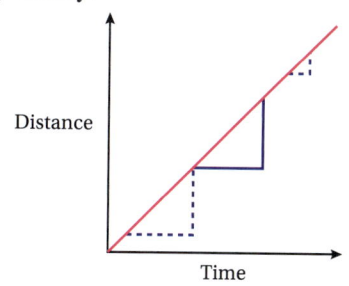

Consider what happens as time moves on. In this case, as time moves on the distance covered increases. So the car is moving.

Now consider the gradient triangles drawn on the graph. It doesn't matter where these triangles are drawn, each is similar to the other, so the sides represent the same gradient $\left(\frac{\text{rise}}{\text{run}}\right)$.

This shows that the car is moving at a constant speed.

Find answers at: cambridge.org/ukschools/gcsemaths-studentbookanswers

In this graph, as time moves on the distance covered increases. So the car is moving.

Now consider the gradient triangles drawn on the graph; each has the same base (unit of time) but a different height.

This time the gradient triangles don't fit the graph as it is not a straight line. Instead, we've laid them against the graph at different places. The hypotenuse of each forms a tangent to the graph.

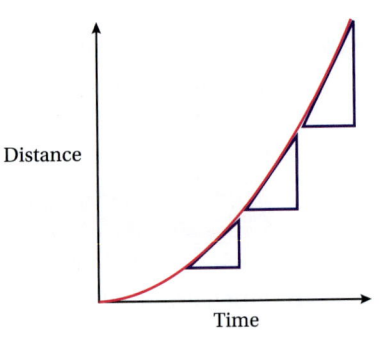

You can see by the slope of each triangle's hypotenuse that the speed is changing along the graph. Moving up the slope, the triangles' hypotenuses are getting steeper – the gradient of the graph is increasing. This shows that the car is speeding up, or **accelerating**.

EXERCISE 37B

1. The following graphs show what is happening to the level of water in a tank.
   Describe what is happening in each case. Justify your answers using gradient triangles.

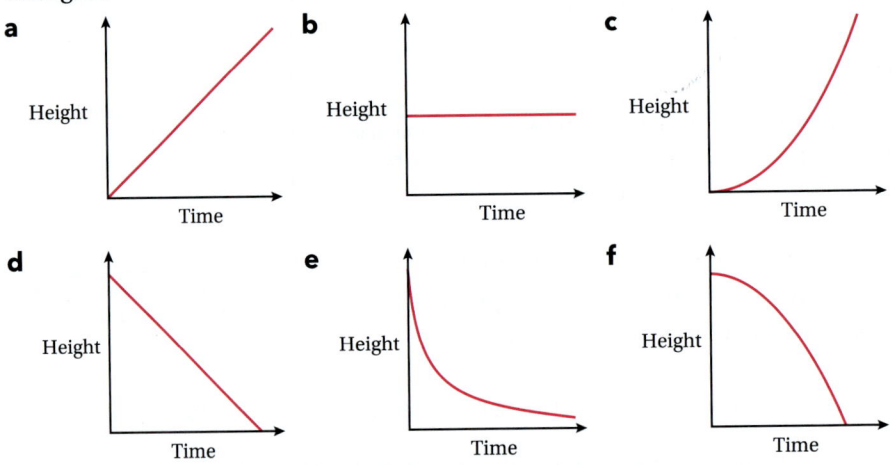

2. The following graphs show what is happening to the price of oil.
   Describe what is happening in each case, justifying your answers using gradient triangles.

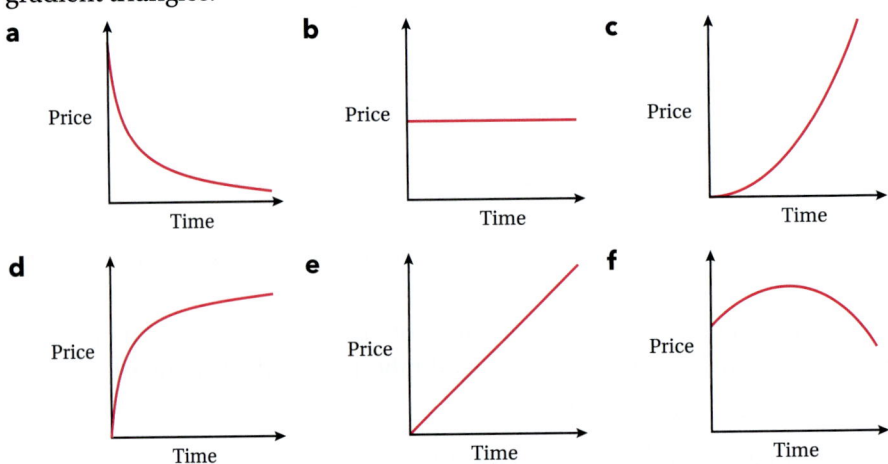

37 Interpreting graphs

3 The following graph is a distance–time graph for a drag-racing car.

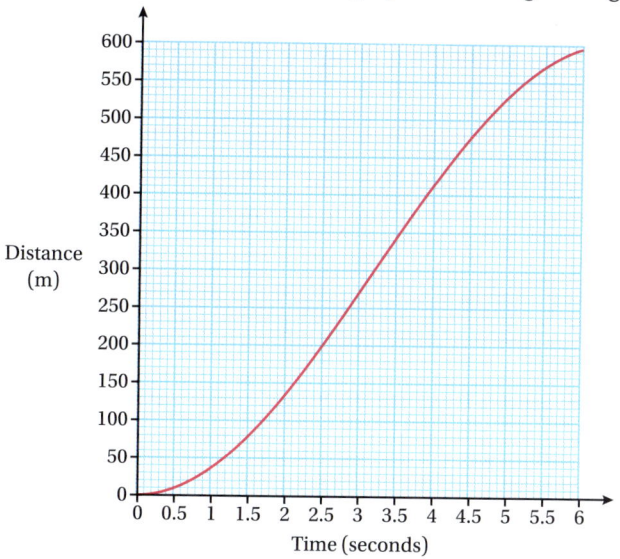

a How far had the car travelled after 2 seconds?
b How long did it take the car to travel 50 metres?
c When was the car going at its fastest speed?
d How fast was the car going after
   i 0.5 seconds?   ii 3.5 seconds?

4 The following graph shows the predicted height of the tide at Milford Haven.

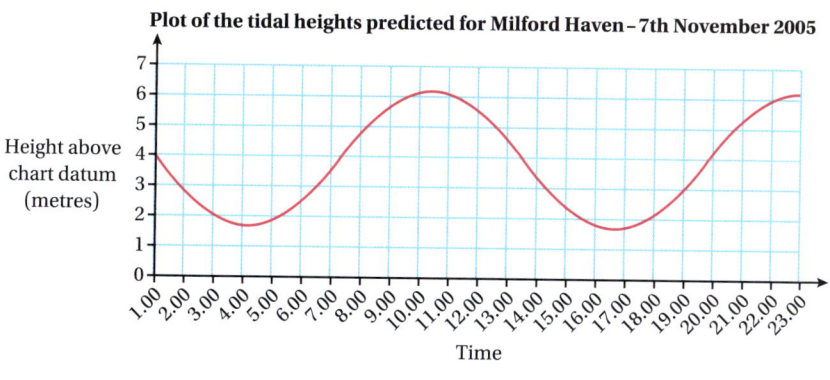

Plot of the tidal heights predicted for Milford Haven – 7th November 2005

a When is the tide coming in at its fastest rate?
b When is the tide fully in?
c How fast is the tide going out at
   i 4pm?   ii 2pm?
d Why would this kind of information be useful?

Checklist of learning and understanding

Graphs of real-world contexts
- Graphs are useful for showing the relationships between quantities.
- Graphs that show the connection between the distance an object has travelled and the time taken are called distance–time graphs.

Find answers at: cambridge.org/ukschools/gcsemaths-studentbookanswers

GCSE Mathematics for OCR (Foundation)

Gradient

- The gradient of a distance–time graph is the speed of the object.
  - If speed is constant the gradient is constant and is represented by a straight line.
  - If the line is horizontal then the object is not moving; the gradient is zero.
- Curved graphs have gradients that change along the graph continually. Gradient triangles can be used to estimate the changes in the gradient.

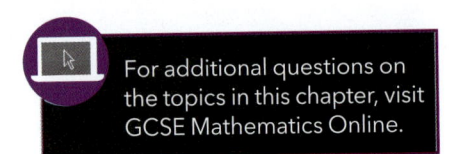

For additional questions on the topics in this chapter, visit GCSE Mathematics Online.

Chapter review

1. The graph shows how the population of a village has changed since 1930.

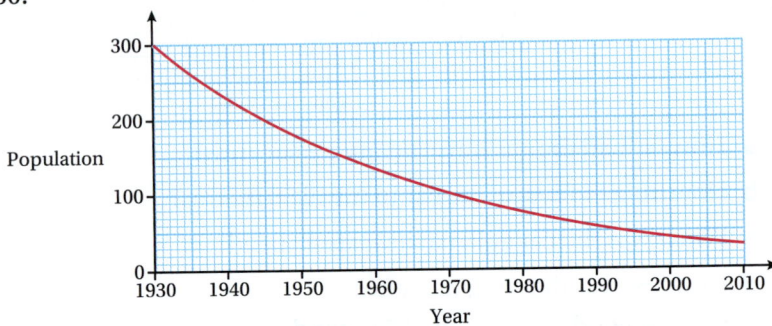

   a Copy the graph using tracing paper and find the gradient of the graph at the point (1950, 170).

   b What does the gradient represent?

2. This graph shows Ben's journey to school.

   a During which part of his journey was Ben travelling fastest?

   b What happened between A and B?

   c Did Ben speed up or slow down at C?

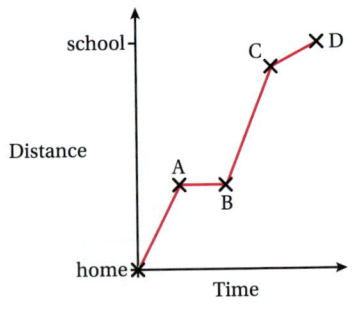

3. The following graph shows the height of water in a cylindrical vase.

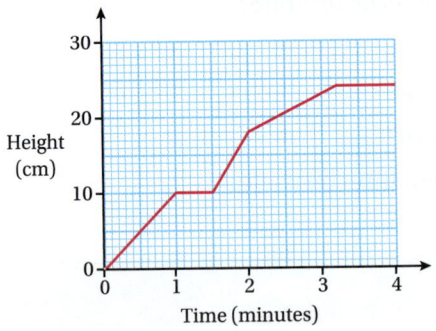

   a The vase was filled to $\frac{3}{4}$ of its capacity. How tall is the vase?

   b Given that the radius of the base was 3 cm, what rate was the water flowing at the beginning?

   c What was the rate between 2 and 3 minutes?

38 Algebraic inequalities

In this chapter you will learn how to ...
- use the correct symbols to express inequalities.
- understand and interpret inequalities.
- solve linear inequalities in one variable and represent the solution set on a number line.

For more resources relating to this chapter, visit GCSE Mathematics Online.

Using mathematics: real-life applications

Inequalities are one way of expressing the ranges of values that have to be met and considered in running a successful business. For example, a business might want wastage to be less than a certain figure, or profit to be greater or equal to a particular amount.

"I work in quality control in food production. One of my jobs is to check that the quality and size of the ingredients we use are within an acceptable range, for example greater than 10 g, but less than 11 g." *(Quality controller)*

Before you start ...

Ch 8	You must be able to solve linear equations.	**1** a If $3x + 2 = 2x + 5$, then $x = $? b If $4(n + 3) = 6(n - 1)$, then $n = $?
Ch 1, 2	You should be confident with ranking numbers in ascending or descending order.	**2** Write this set of numbers in ascending order of size. $\quad -2 \quad 50 \quad -27 \quad \dfrac{1}{3} \quad 1.25 \quad 2\%$
Ch 1, 2	You need to remember the rules for operations with negative integers.	**3** Evaluate the following. a $5 \times (-2)$ b $-5 \times (-2)$ c $12 \div 6$ d $12 \div (-6)$ e $7 - (-1)$

Find answers at: cambridge.org/ukschools/gcsemaths-studentbookanswers

GCSE Mathematics for OCR (Foundation)

Assess your starting point using the Launchpad

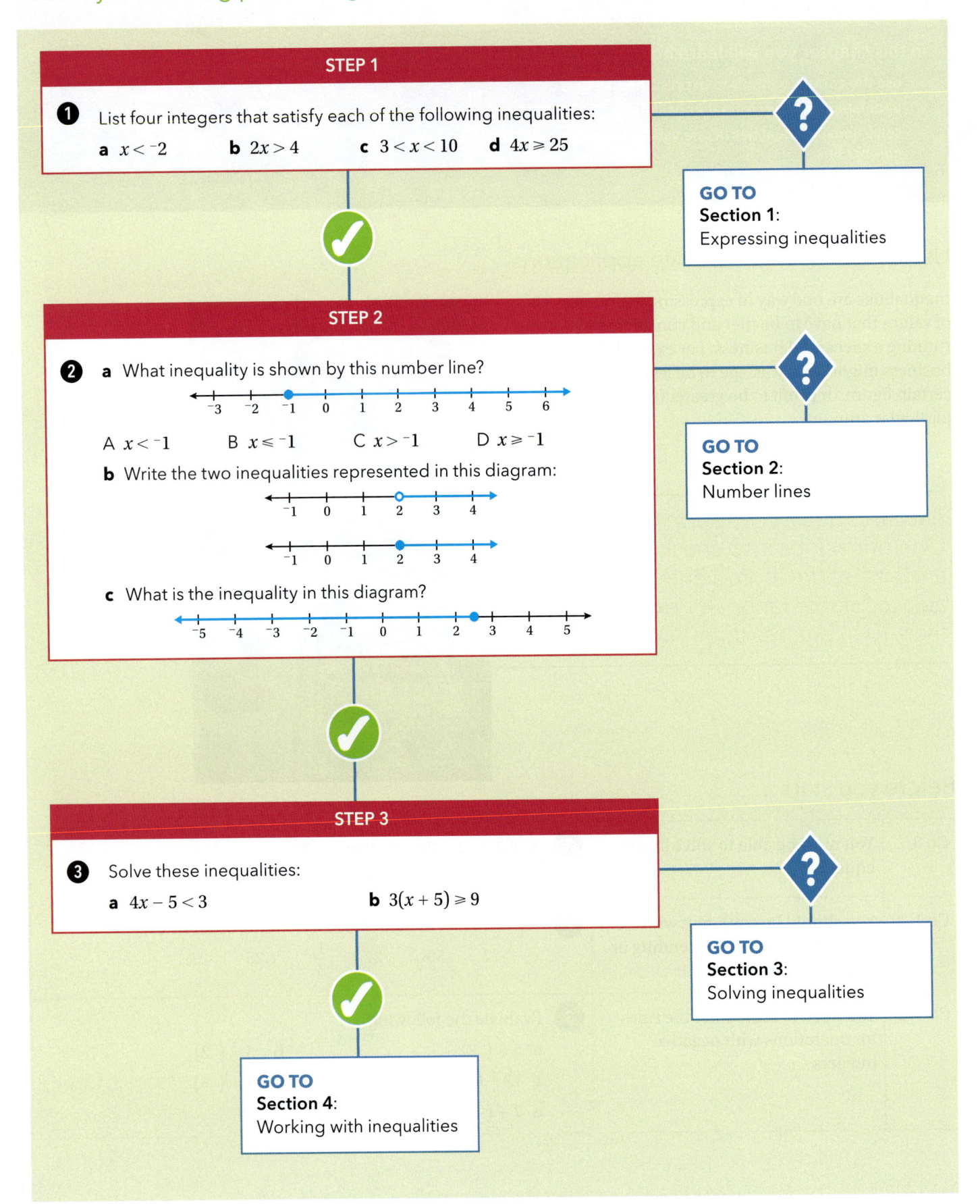

STEP 1

1 List four integers that satisfy each of the following inequalities:

a $x < {}^-2$ b $2x > 4$ c $3 < x < 10$ d $4x \geqslant 25$

GO TO
Section 1: Expressing inequalities

STEP 2

2 a What inequality is shown by this number line?

A $x < {}^-1$ B $x \leqslant {}^-1$ C $x > {}^-1$ D $x \geqslant {}^-1$

b Write the two inequalities represented in this diagram:

c What is the inequality in this diagram?

GO TO
Section 2: Number lines

STEP 3

3 Solve these inequalities:

a $4x - 5 < 3$ b $3(x + 5) \geqslant 9$

GO TO
Section 3: Solving inequalities

GO TO
Section 4: Working with inequalities

588

38 Algebraic inequalities

Section 1: Expressing inequalities

An **inequality** is a mathematical sentence that uses symbols such as $<$, $\leq$, $\neq$, $>$ or $\geq$ in place of an equals sign. The expressions on either side of the symbol are not equal.

The most common inequality symbols are:

- $>$ greater than
- $<$ less than
- $\geq$ greater than or equal to
- $\leq$ less than or equal to

You've already used inequality symbols to give a range of values. For example, $2 < x < 6$ means '2 is *less than* x and x is *less than* 6'. The integer values of x that satisfy this expression are 3, 4 and 5.

Another way to read this statement is to say x lies between 2 and 6.

Inequalities indicate a range of values to be considered. In $a \leq x \leq b$, x is a value that lies between the values of a and b and can be equal to a and b. This statement can also be written in the form $b \geq x \geq a$.

An inequality will have a finite number of integer solutions but an infinite number of real solutions.

Key vocabulary

inequality: a mathematical sentence in which the left side is not equal to the right side.

Applying operations to inequalities

If you apply an operation to both sides of an inequality, then the resulting inequality is true for addition and subtraction. It is also true for multiplication and division of **positive** numbers.

When you multiply or divide both sides of an inequality by a **negative** number, then you need to **reverse** the direction of the inequality symbol in order to make the resulting inequality true.

For example, if you multiply both sides of the inequality $7 > 3$ by $^-2$, then the resulting statement is correctly written as $^-14 < ^-6$.

If $^-x < 3$, this means that $x > ^-3$ (multiplying both sides by $^-1$).

EXERCISE 38A

1 Complete the statements with the correct inequality symbol.

  a If $7 > 3$, then $4 + 7 \,\square\, 4 + 3$
  b If $8 < 13$, then $8 - 5 \,\square\, 13 - 5$
  c If $^-5 < ^-1$, then $^-5 + 3 \,\square\, ^-1 + 3$
  d If $^-4 > ^-11$, then $^-4 - 6 \,\square\, ^-11 - 6$

2 Complete the statements with the correct inequality symbol.

  a If $7 > 3$, then $2 \times 7 \,\square\, 2 \times 3$ **b** If $8 < 13$, then $2 \times 8 \,\square\, 2 \times 13$
  c If $7 > 3$, then $7 \div 2 \,\square\, 3 \div 2$ **d** If $8 < 13$, then $8 \div 2 \,\square\, 13 \div 2$

3 Complete the statements with the correct inequality symbol.

  a If $7 > 3$, then $(^-2) \times 7 \,\square\, (^-2) \times 3$
  b If $8 < 13$, then $(^-2) \times 8 \,\square\, (^-2) \times 13$
  c If $7 > 3$, then $7 \div (^-2) \,\square\, 3 \div (^-2)$
  d If $8 < 13$, then $8 \div (^-2) \,\square\, 13 \div (^-2)$

Find answers at: cambridge.org/ukschools/gcsemaths-studentbookanswers

GCSE Mathematics for OCR (Foundation)

4 List four whole numbers that satisfy the following inequalities.

  a $x > 14$ **b** $x \geqslant 6$ **c** $x \leqslant -2$ **d** $x + 3 \geqslant 7$ **e** $x - 4 \leqslant 5$

5 If $x > 6$ how many values can x take?

6 If $3 < x < 8$, how many integer values can x take? How many values can x take if we include decimal values or fractions?

7 What integer values are given by $6 > x > 2$?

Section 2: Number lines

You can use a **number line** to represent an inequality. When drawing values on a number line the convention is to use an open dot (small circle) if the starting value is not included and a solid dot if the starting point is included.

The expression $x \leqslant 11$ means numbers less than 11 including 11. So a number line representing $x \leqslant 11$ shows values starting from and including 11 with a solid dot at 11.

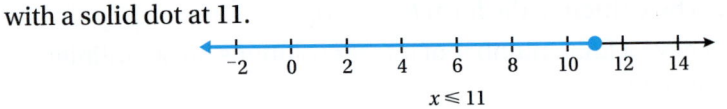

$x \leqslant 11$

The expression $x > 11$ means numbers greater than 11. So a number line representing $x > 11$ starts at 11 but the open dot is taken to mean that 11 is not included.

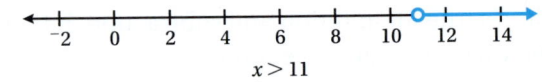

$x > 11$

> **Key vocabulary**
>
> **number line**: line marked with numbers in order, similar to a ruler scale.

EXERCISE 38B

1 Draw number lines to indicate the following inequalities.

  a $x > 4$ **b** $x \geqslant -1$ **c** $x \geqslant -5$
  d $3 \leqslant x \leqslant 10$ **e** $-3 \leqslant x \leqslant 10$ **f** $-10 \leqslant x \leqslant -3$

2 Write the inequalities that are shown in the number line diagrams.

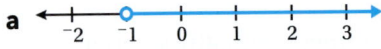

3 Write an inequality to describe each of these diagrams.

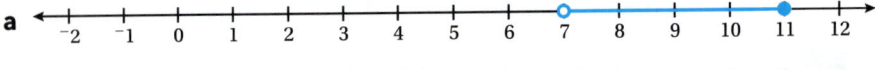

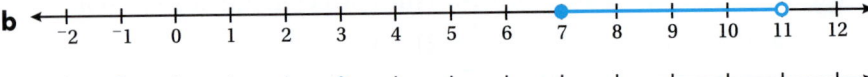

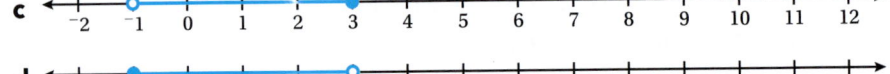

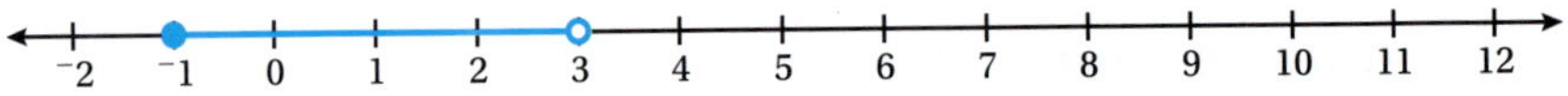

Section 3: Solving inequalities

Solving the linear inequality $4x - 5 < 3$ means finding all of the values for x that satisfy that inequality. You can solve inequalities using the same methods that you used for linear equations.

However, you must apply the rules that you learnt in Section 1:
- If you multiply or divide an inequality by a negative value, the inequality sign must be reversed to make an equivalent inequality.
- If you swap the sides of the inequality you must reverse the signs. For example, if you have $2 < x$ and you want x on the left-hand side, you get $x > 2$. (Think of this as reading the inequality from right to left.)

WORKED EXAMPLE 1

Solve for x. Show your solutions on a number line.

a $4x - 5 < 3$ b $\dfrac{5x - 3}{2} \geq 11$ c $^-5 \leq 3x + 4 \leq 13$

a $4x - 5 < 3$
   $4x < 8$
   $x < 2$

   Add 5 to both sides, then divide both sides by 4.

b $\dfrac{5x - 3}{2} \geq 11$
   $5x - 3 \geq 11 \times 2$
   $5x \geq 22 + 3$
   $5x \geq 25$
   $x \geq 5$

   Multiply both sides by 2 to get rid of the denominator, add 3 to both sides.

c $^-5 \leq 3x + 4 \leq 13$
   $^-5 - 4 \leq 3x \leq 13 - 4$
   $^-9 \leq 3x \leq 9$
   $^-3 \leq x \leq 3$

   Subtract 4 from each expression, then divide all the terms by 3.

EXERCISE 38C

1 Solve these inequalities.

a $x + 3 \geq 7$ b $x - 7 \leq 4$ c $x + 12 > 9$
d $x - 2 < 3$ e $x + 4 \geq {}^-8$ f $x - 10 > {}^-6$
g $x - 5 < {}^-12$ h $2x \geq 6$ i $3x > {}^-15$
j $3(x + 5) \geq 9$ k $2(5x - 2) > 5$ l $2(x - 3) \leq 5$
m $\dfrac{x + 3}{2} \leq \dfrac{3 - x}{2}$ n $^-5x + 3 \geq 78$

2 Solve these inequalities.

a $4x \leq 20$ b $^-10x \geq 130$ c $^-12x > {}^-42$
d $\dfrac{^-x}{2} \leq 5$ e $\dfrac{^-x}{2} > 4$ f $3 - 2x > 5$
g $2 - 5x \leq {}^-8$ h $4(7 - x) < 5$

Find answers at: cambridge.org/ukschools/gcsemaths-studentbookanswers

Tip

Remember, if you multiply or divide both sides of an inequality by a negative number, then you must reverse the inequality sign to make the resulting inequality true.

3 Solve these inequalities.

a $5(x - 2) - 2(3x + 1) > 0$
b $5(2x - 3) < 4(x + 3)$
c $3(x + 4) - 4(x + 2) > 0$
d $2(3x - 7) - 5(2x + 3) \leq 0$

Section 4: Working with inequalities

Often a question that requires inequalities will include 'at least' or 'more than'. Look out for clues in the question.

Problem-solving framework

Suppose you work part-time for £p an hour and you save 25% of what you earn.

Write an inequality that you can use to find the number of hours you will need to work in order to save at least £75 in a week.

Steps for approaching a problem-solving question	What you would do for this example
Step 1: What do you need to do?	'At least' suggests an inequality because you want to know how to get that value and/or more than that value. You need to write an inequality to calculate how many hours you need to work in order to save £75 or more.
Step 2: What maths do you know?	You know how to write simple formulae and expressions to represent real-world contexts (Chapter 14). Let x be the number of hours worked in a week. Given: p is the amount earned per hour in £; savings is 25% of the amount you earn. You need to work out how much you have to earn in a week so that you save £75, so you need to work out what value £75 is 25% of: Let w = how much you earn in a week. $75 = 0.25 \times w$ $w = \dfrac{75}{0.25} = 300$ So, you need to earn £300 in order to save £75. If you earn £p per hour then xp needs to be ≥ 300 in order for the saving to be £75. So, the number of hours you need to work in order to save at least £75 is: $x \geq \dfrac{300}{p}$
Step 3: Have you answered the question? Does your answer seem reasonable?	Yes, you have provided a suitable inequality. Check it seems reasonable using some values. If you worked for £12 per hour then $p = 12$, $300 \div 12 = 25$. If you worked for 25 hours at a rate of £12/hour you would earn $25 \times 12 = £300$. If $p = £20$, $300 \div 20 = 15$. You would need to work 15 hours. The higher the value of p the fewer hours you would need to work. The answer seems reasonable.

WORK IT OUT 38.1

$2x - 5 < 1$

Which is the correct solution? Identify the errors made in the incorrect solutions.

Option A	Option B	Option C
$2x - 5 + 5 < 1 + 5$	$2x - 5 + 5 > 1 + 5$	$2x - 5 - 5 < 1 - 5$
$2x < 6$	$2x > 6$	$2x < {}^-4$
$\dfrac{2x}{2} < \dfrac{6}{2}$	$\dfrac{2x}{2} > \dfrac{6}{2}$	$\dfrac{2x}{2} < {}^-4$
$x < 3$	$x > 3$	$x < {}^-2$

EXERCISE 38D

1 Solve each inequality and draw a number line to show the solution set.

   a $x + 1 > 5$ **b** $2x - 1 < 6$ **c** $\dfrac{x + 1}{2} \geqslant {}^-4$

   d $^-2x + 1 \leqslant 6$ **e** $1 - 5x \geqslant 21$ **f** $3d + 5 \leqslant 5d + 7$

2 If the values for x are whole numbers and satisfy the inequality $0 < x < 10$, copy and complete the Venn diagram with the correct values for x. Label the circles: prime numbers, square numbers, even numbers.

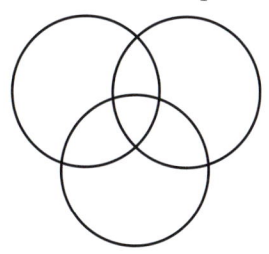

3 To solve the following problems first change the statements given into inequalities and then solve for the variable.

   a When 5 is added to twice p, the result is greater than 17. What values can p take?

   b When 16 is subtracted from half of q, the result is less than 18. What values can q take?

   c The sum of $4d$ and 6 is greater than the sum of $2d$ and 18. What values can d take?

   d A number a is increased by 3 and this amount is then doubled. If the result of this is greater than a, what values can a take?

4 **a** You work part-time for £16 an hour and you save 85% of what you earn each month. The rest you spend on what you like.
How many hours will you need to work in order to buy a video game this month for £45, given that you spent all of last month's spending money?

   b Suppose you work for £p an hour. Write an inequality that expresses the number of hours you will need to work in order to have enough money to buy at least one video game, at £45, a month.

Find answers at: cambridge.org/ukschools/gcsemaths-studentbookanswers

Checklist of learning and understanding

Expressing inequalities

- Inequalities use the symbols $>, <, \geq, \leq, \neq$.
- Inequalities indicate a range of values. In $a \leq x \leq b$, x is a value that lies between the values of a and b and can be equal to a and b. This statement can also be written in the form $b \geq x \geq a$.
- An inequality will have a finite number of integer solutions but an infinite number of real solutions.
- Inequalities can be shown on a number line:
  - A closed dot ● indicates that the starting value is included.
  - An open dot ○ indicates that the starting value is not included.
- If you add or subtract the same number to both sides of an inequality then the new inequality remains true: $a > b$ then $a \pm c > b \pm c$; likewise, if $a < b$ then $a \pm c < b \pm c$.
- If you multiply or divide by the same **positive** number on both sides of an inequality then the new inequality remains true: if $a > b$ and $c > 0$ then $ac > bc$ and $\frac{a}{c} > \frac{b}{c}$.
- If you multiply or divide by the same **negative** number on both sides of an inequality then you need to **reverse** the inequality sign for the new inequality to be true: if $a > b$ and $c < 0$ then $ac < bc$ and $\frac{a}{c} < \frac{b}{c}$.

  For example if $a = 10$, $b = 4$ and $c = {}^-2$:
  $10 > 4$ but ${}^-2 \times 10 < {}^-2 \times 4$, ${}^-20 < {}^-8$ and $\frac{10}{-2} < \frac{4}{-2}$, ${}^-5 < {}^-2$.

Solving inequalities

- Linear inequalities in one unknown can be solved in the same way as equations but the answer includes an inequality symbol and indicates a range of values for the variable.

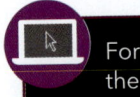

For additional questions on the topics in this chapter, visit GCSE Mathematics Online.

Chapter review

1 Which of the following statements are true?

   a $x + 11 > x - 11$

   b $x \geq 12$ means that a number x is greater than 12.

   c This number line shows the inequality $x \leq {}^-1$:

2 x is a whole number such that ${}^-3 \leq x < 5$ and y is a whole number such that ${}^-4 \leq y \leq 2$.

   Write down the greatest possible value of:

   a $x + y$. **b** $x - y$. **c** xy.

3 I am thinking of an integer. I double it and add 1. The result is less than ${}^-7$. What is the largest integer I can be thinking of?

4 x is an integer.

List all the values of x such that $-1 < 2x \leq 8$.

5 Frozen chickens will be sold by a major chain of supermarkets only if they weigh at least 1.2 kg and not more than 3.4 kg.

   a Represent this range of values on a number line.

   b Write an inequality to represent this range of values in terms of mass (m).

Glossary

A

Adjacent: next to each other; in shapes, sides that intersect each other.

Alternate angles: the angles on parallel lines on opposite sides of a transversal.

Angle of depression: when looking down, the angle between the line of sight and the horizontal.

Angle of elevation: when looking up, the angle between the line of sight and the horizontal.

Arc of a circle: a section of circumference between two points; a minor arc is the shorter distance between two points, the major arc is the larger distance.

Arithmetic sequence: a sequence where the difference between each term is constant.

B

Bias: something that affects the chance of an event occurring in favour of a desired outcome.

Binomial: an expression consisting of two terms.

Binomial product: the product of two binomial expressions; for example, $(x + 2)(x + 3)$.

Bisect: to divide exactly into two halves.

Bivariate data: data that is collected in pairs.

C

Categorical data: data that has been arranged in categories.

Chord: a straight line from one point on the circumference of a circle to another. The diameter is a chord that goes through the centre of the circle.

Circumference: the distance round the outside of a circle.

Coefficient: the number in front of a variable in a mathematical expression. In the term $5x^2$, 5 is the coefficient and x is the variable.

Co-interior angles: the angles within the parallel lines on the same side of the transversal.

Combined events: one event followed by another event producing two or more outcomes.

Common denominator: a number into which all the denominators of a set of fractions divide exactly.

Congruent: identical in shape and size.

Consecutive: following each other in order. For example 1, 2, 3 or 35, 36, 37.

Consecutive terms: terms that follow each other in a sequence.

Constant: in algebra, a constant is a fixed number.

Continuous variable: data that can take any numerical value within a range; it can be measured.

Conversion factor: the number that you multiply or divide by to convert one measure into another smaller or larger unit.

Coordinates: an ordered pair (x, y) identifying a position on a grid.

Correlation: a relationship or connection between data items.

Corresponding angles: angles that are created at the same point of the intersection when a transversal crosses a pair of parallel lines.

Cyclic quadrilateral: any quadrilateral with all four vertices on the circumference of a circle.

D

Decimal place (dp): place value position of a digit to the right of the decimal point.

Degree of accuracy: the number of places to which you round a number, for example to the nearest whole number, 2 decimal places, 3 significant figures.

Dependent events: events in which the outcome is affected by what happened before.

Dependent variable: data that is measured in, and affected by, an experiment.

Depreciation: the loss in value of an object over a period of time.

Diameter: a straight line from one point on the circumference to another, that passes through the centre of the circle; it is twice the length of the radius.

Direct proportion: two values that both increase in the same ratio.

Discrete data: data that can be counted and which only has one possible value; it is counted in integers.

Displacement: a change in position.

E

Elevation: a view of an object from the front, side or back.

Equally likely: having the same probability of happening.

Equidistant: means 'the same distance from'; if all points are equidistant they are the same distance apart.

Equivalent: having the same value; two ratios or fractions are equivalent if one is a multiple of the other because they will cancel to the same simplest term.

Error interval: the difference between the upper and lower bounds.

Estimate: an approximate answer or rough calculation.

Evaluate: to find the value of, that is, to solve.

Event: a set of possible outcomes in an experiment or situation, to which you give a probability.

Exchange rate: the value of one currency used to convert that currency to an equivalent value in another currency.

Expanding: multiplying out an expression to get rid of the brackets.

Expression: a group of numbers and letters linked by operation signs.

Exterior angles: angles produced by extending the sides of a polygon.

F

Factorising: writing a number or expression as a product of its factors.

First difference: the result of subtracting a term from the next term.

Formula: a general rule written as an equation showing the relationship between unknown quantities; the plural is formulae.

Function: an operation between values where each input value gives back only one output value. The square root of 4 can be $^+2$ or $^-2$ so it is not a function.

G

Geometric sequence: a sequence where the ratio between each term is constant.

Gradient: a measure of the steepness of a line.
Gradient = $\frac{\text{change in } y}{\text{change in } x}$.

H

Hyperbola: the curved graph(s) formed by a reciprocal function; the curve of $y = \frac{1}{x}$ gets increasingly close to the x-axis and y-axis but never touches them.

Hypotenuse: the longest side of a right-angled triangle; the side opposite the 90° angle.

I

Image: the new shape (once the object has been transformed).

Included angle: the angle between two lines that meet at a vertex.

Independent events: events that are not affected by what happened before.

Index: a power or exponent indicating how many times a base number is multiplied by itself.

Index notation: writing a number as a base and index, for example 2^3.

Inequality: a mathematical sentence in which the left side is not equal to the right side.

Integers: whole numbers belonging to the set {... $^-3$, $^-2$, $^-1$, 0, 1, 2, 3, ...}; they are sometimes called directed numbers because they have a negative or positive sign.

Interior angles: angles inside a two-dimensional shape at the vertices or corners.

Inverse proportion: a relation between two quantities such that one increases at a rate that is equal to the rate at which the other decreases.

Irrational number: a number that cannot be written in the form of $\frac{a}{b}$ or as a terminating or repeating decimal.

Irregular polygon: a polygon that does not have equal sides and equal angles.

Isometric grid: special drawing paper based on an arrangement of triangles.

L

Line (axis) of symmetry: a line that divides a plane shape into two identical halves, each the reflection of the other.

Linear equation: an equation where the highest power of the unknown is 1, for example $x + 3 = 7$.

Locus (plural **loci**): a set of points that satisfy the same rule.

Lower bound: the smallest value that a number (given to a specified accuracy) can be.

M

Mathematical model: a representation of a real-life problem; assumptions are used to simplify the situation so that it can be solved mathematically.

Midpoint: the centre of a line; the point that divides the line into two equal halves.

Mirror line: a line equidistant from all corresponding points on a shape and its reflection.

Mutually exclusive: events that cannot happen at the same time.

N

Number line: a line marked with numbers in order, similar to a ruler scale.

O

Object: the original shape (before it has been transformed).

Order of rotational symmetry: how many times a shape will fit exactly onto itself when you rotate it through 360°.

Orientation: the position of a shape relative to the grid.

Outcome: a single result of an experiment or situation.

Outlier: data value that is much larger or smaller than others in the same data set.

P

Parabola: the symmetrical curve produced by the graph of a quadratic function.

Parallel vectors: occur when one vector is a multiple of the other.

Perfect square: a binomial product of the form $(a \pm b)^2$.

Perimeter: the distance around the boundaries (sides) of a shape.

Perpendicular bisector: a line perpendicular to another that also cuts it in half.

Plan view: the view of an object from directly above.

Plane shape: a flat, two-dimensional shape.

Plot: draw a graph accurately by marking points on a grid using coordinates.

Polygon: a closed plane shape with three or more straight sides.

Polyhedron: a solid shape with flat faces that are polygons.

Polynomial: an expression made up of many unlike terms with positive powers for the variables.

Population: the name given to a data set.

Position-to-term rule: operations applied to the position number of a term in a sequence in order to generate that term.

Prime factor: a factor that is also a prime number.

Product: the result of multiplying numbers and/or terms together.

Proportion: a comparison of a part, or amount, to the whole; often expressed as a fraction, percentage or ratio.

Pythagorean triple: three non-zero numbers (a, b, c) for which $a^2 + b^2 = c^2$.

Q

Quadratic expression: an expression that can be written in the form $ax^2 + bx + c$, where $a \neq 0$, there are no negative or fractional powers and the highest power is 2.

R

Radius: the distance of any point on the circumference from the centre of the circle.

Random: not predetermined.

Ratio: a comparison of two or more different parts, or amounts, in relation to each other.

Rational number: a number that can be expressed in the form of $\frac{a}{b}$ (or as its equivalent as a terminating or repeating decimal).

Reciprocal: the reciprocal of a number, x, is 1 divided by x, that is, $\frac{1}{x}$. Any number multiplied by its reciprocal is 1. For the fraction $\frac{a}{b}$, the reciprocal is $\frac{b}{a}$.

Reflection: an exact image of a shape about a line of symmetry.

Regular polygon: a polygon with equal sides and equal angles.

Relative frequency: the ratio of the number of times a favourable outcome is recorded to the total number of trials conducted.

Representative sample: a smaller quantity of data that represents the characteristics of a larger population.

Right prism: a prism with sides perpendicular to the end faces (base).

Roots: of an equation are the value(s) that makes the equation true; the root of a function is the value that makes the function equal to zero.

Rotational symmetry: symmetry by turning a shape around a fixed point so that it looks the same from different positions.

Rounding: writing a number with fewer non-zero digits by replacing some digits with zeroes.

S

Sample: a small set of data from a population.

Sample space: a list or diagram that shows all possible outcomes from two or more events.

Scalar: a numerical quantity (it has no direction).

Scale factor: a number that scales a quantity up or down.

Second difference: the difference between each term in the first difference.

Sector: part or slice of a circle that is enclosed by two radii and an arc; the minor sector is the smaller of the two sectors created, the major sector is the larger.

Segment: a chord splits a circle into two segments; the smaller segment is known as the minor segment and the larger is the major segment.

Semicircle: exactly half of a circle; the diameter splits a circle into two semicircles.

Sequence: a number pattern or list of numbers following a particular order.

Set: a collection. The brackets { } are shorthand for 'the set of'. For example, {2, 4, 6, 8} is the set of the numbers 2, 4, 6, 8, which represents the even numbers.

Significant figure: the most significant figure (digit) in a number is the first non-zero digit when reading the number from left to right.

Similar: shapes that have the same shape and proportions but are a different size.

Simultaneous equations: a pair of equations with two unknowns that can be solved at the same time.

Sketch: draw a basic graph showing the direction, gradient and y-intercept; it is not drawn by plotting a table of values.

Solution: all possible roots of an equation.

Subject: the variable which is expressed in terms of other variables; it is the variable on its own on one side of the equals sign. In the formula $s = \frac{d}{t}$, s is the subject.

Substitute: to replace letters in an expression, equation, or formula with numbers.

T

Tangent: a straight line that touches the circumference of a circle at any one point.

Term: a combination of letters and/or numbers. Each number in a sequence is called a term.

Term-to-term rule: operations applied to any number in a sequence to generate the next number in the sequence.

Theorem: a statement that can be demonstrated to be true by accepted mathematical operations.

Transversal: a straight line that crosses a pair of parallel lines.

Truncation: cutting off all digits after a certain point without rounding.

U

Unknown: part of an equation which is represented by a letter.

Upper bound: the largest value that a number (given to a specified accuracy) can be.

V

Variable: a letter representing an unknown number.

Vector: a quantity that has both magnitude and direction.

Vertically opposite angles: angles that are opposite one another at an intersection of two lines. Vertical here means 'of the same vertex or point', not up and down.

X

x-intercept: the point where a line crosses the x-axis when $y = 0$.

Y

y-intercept: the point where a line crosses the y-axis when $x = 0$.

Index

2D shapes *see* plane shapes
'3, 4, 5 rule' 487
3D objects *see* solids
12-hour time system 177-79
24-hour time system 177-79

acceleration 217, 584
accuracy
   degree of 264, 267, 275
   level of 273-74, 276
acute angles 133
acute-angled triangles 60
addition 3, 10, 11
   algebraic expressions 28-29
   decimals 165, 170
   fractions 152, 157
   inequalities 589, 594
   negative numbers 6
   standard form 421, 422
   vectors 428, 431
addition law 392, 393
additive inverse 10
adjacent sides 64, 497, 511
algebraic expressions
   addition 28-29
   brackets in 30-32, 35
   division 29
   evaluation 28
   expansion 30-32
   factorising 33, 36
   multiplication 26, 29
   notation 26, 35
   problem solving with 34, 36
   simplification 28-29, 35
   substitution into 28, 31
   subtraction 28-29
alternate angles 136, 137, 145
angle of depression 508-9
angle of elevation 508
angles
   alternate 136, 137, 145
   around a point 132, 145
   bisecting 80, 83
   co-interior 136, 137, 145
   corresponding 135, 137, 145
   equal 56
   exterior 61, 139, 143-44, 145
   included 452
   interior 61, 139, 141, 145
   measuring and drawing 74-77
   parallel lines and 135-37, 145
   in polygons 141-44, 145
   in quadrilaterals 65
   on straight lines 132-33, 145
   supplementary 136
   in triangles 61, 138-39, 145, 502-3
   types 133
   vertically opposite 133, 145
   vertices of 74
approximation 264, 271, 275
   see also rounding
arcs 54, 234, 240
area
   circles 218, 251, 260
   composite shapes 253-57, 260
   parallelograms 247, 259
   polygons 244-49, 259
   rectangles 90, 100, 110, 244, 259
   sectors 252, 260
   squares 100, 244, 259, 483
   trapezia 248, 259
   triangles 100, 115, 244-46, 259
   units 174-75
arithmetic sequences 39
averages 560-62, 575

bar charts 542, 544, 546-47, 556
bar (line) scales 185
bearings 189-90, 191
BIDMAS 8-9
binary trees *see* frequency trees
binomial products 89, 101
binomials 89, 101, 307
   expansion 101
   multiplication 89-93
bisectors 64, 78
   of angles 80, 83
   perpendicular 78, 82, 86, 435
bivariate data 571, 576
brackets
   in algebraic expressions 30-32, 35
   in equations 107
   order of operations 8-9

calculators
   exponent function 417, 422
   index notation 403
   order of operations 9
   percentages 195, 199
   pi 230, 251
   roots 408
   squares and square roots 483
   standard form 417, 422
   time calculations 177
   trigonometry ratios 498, 499, 502-3, 511
   truncation 270
capture/recapture sampling 540
categorical data 542
centre of enlargement 469-70, 473, 478
centre of rotation 443
certain events 363, 378
chords 54

circles 54, 69
   arcs 54, 234, 240
   area 218, 251, 260
   chords 54
   circumference 54, 218, 230-32, 240
   diameter 54, 230, 232
   radius 54, 230, 251
   sectors 54, 234-35, 240, 252, 260
   segments 54
   tangents to 54
circumference 54, 218, 230-32, 240
class intervals 563
co-interior angles 136, 137, 145
coefficients 94, 284
column vectors 426, 439
combined events 383, 398
   addition law 392, 393
   dependent events 394-95, 398
   independent events 393, 398
   multiplication law 393
   mutually exclusive events 392, 398
   non-mutually exclusive events 392
   representing 383-89, 398
   theoretical probability 390-95, 398
common denominators 149
common difference 42
common factors 15, 96
common multiples 15
comparative bar charts *see* multiple bar charts
compass bearings 189-90
compasses, pairs of 75-77, 86
complements of sets 386, 395
composite bar charts 544, 546-47, 556
composite shapes
   area 253-57, 260
   perimeter 227-28, 236-38
composite solids 344
compound bar charts *see* composite bar charts
compound growth 515-16, 520
compound interest 515, 520
cones
   properties 55, 68, 70, 318, 330
   surface area 341-42
   volume 341, 347
congruent shapes 66, 434
congruent triangles 452-59
consecutive numbers 16
consecutive terms 39
constant of proportionality 528, 534
constants 94, 96, 284
continuous data 552
continuous variables 273, 276

599

convenience sampling 539
conversion factors 173
coordinates 279
correlation 571, 572, 576
corresponding angles 135, 137, 145
cosine ratio 498, 505-7, 511
cube numbers 10, 11, 15, 22, 46
cube roots 10, 11, 15
cubes 66, 67, 68, 317, 335, 409
cubic expressions 307
    graphs of 307-8, 311, 313
cuboids 66, 67, 318, 320
cylinders
    drawing 321
    properties 55, 68, 70, 318, 330, 334
    surface area 338
    volume 338, 347

data
    analysing 558-76
    bivariate 571, 576
    categorical 542
    collecting 538-40
    comparing sets 566
    continuous 552
    discrete 542
    displaying 541-52, 556, 567-69, 575
    grouped 563-64
    misleading graphs 567-69, 575
    time series 544, 551-52, 556
decay 518-19, 521
decimal places 266
    rounding to 266, 269, 275
decimals
    addition 165, 170
    calculations 163-67, 169-70
    comparing 160-61
    conversion to/from fractions 161-62, 169
    converting to/from percentages 195-96, 205
    division 166, 170
    multiplication 166, 170
    rounding to 264
    subtraction 165, 170
degree of accuracy 264, 267, 275
density 183, 191
dependent events 394-95, 398
dependent variables 572
depreciation 518, 521
depression, angle of 508-9
diagrams 56
    see also specific diagrams, e.g. scatter diagrams, Venn diagrams etc.
diameter 54, 230, 232
difference 3, 46
difference of two squares 92-94, 97-98, 101
direct proportion 524, 534
    representation 527-29

scaling up/down 524-25
unitary method 525
discrete data 542
displacement 217, 426
distance-time graphs 528-29, 580, 583-84, 585-86
division 3, 10, 11
    algebraic expressions 29
    decimals 166, 170
    fractions 152-53, 157
    indices 405-6, 410
    inequalities 589, 591, 594
    negative numbers 6
    standard form 419-20, 422
divisors see factors

edges 55
elevation, angle of 508
elevations 326-28, 330
enlargements 434, 467-68, 478
    centre of enlargement 469-70, 473, 478
    properties 473
equally likely outcomes 365
equations 26, 105
    with brackets 107
    graphical solution 121-22, 128
    linear see linear equations
    quadratic see quadratic equations
    roots 111, 128
    simultaneous see simultaneous equations
    solution 111
    unknown on both sides 107-8
equidistant 55
equilateral triangles 53, 60, 139
equivalent 351
equivalent fractions 149-50, 157
error intervals 273, 274, 276
estimates 164, 271, 275
evaluation 28, 211
even numbers 15, 22
events 363
    certain 363, 378
    combined see combined events
    dependant 394-95, 398
    impossible 363, 378
    independent 393, 398
    mutually exclusive 366, 378, 392, 398
exchange rates 179
expansion of expressions 30-32
experimental probability 365, 368-72, 378
expressions 26, 35
    see also algebraic expressions
exterior angles 143
    polygons 143-44, 145
    triangles 61, 139

faces 55
factor trees 17-18

factorisation 33, 101
    algebraic expressions 33, 36
    quadratic expressions 94-96, 112-13
factors 15
    common 15, 96
    highest common 19-20, 22, 33
    prime 17-18, 19-20, 22
favourable outcomes 363, 378, 384
Fibonacci sequences 46, 47, 356
fifty-fifty chance 363
first difference 39, 42
formulae 209
    changing subject 213-14, 220
    kinematics 217
    problem solving with 215-16, 220
    standard 217-18
    substituting values into 211, 220
    writing 209-10, 220
fractional scale factors 471, 478
fractions 149
    addition 152, 157
    conversion to/from decimals 161-62, 169
    converting to/from percentages 195-96, 205
    division 152-53, 157
    equivalent 149-50, 157
    multiplication 151, 157
    properties 149
    of quantities 155-56, 157
    subtraction 152, 157
frequency tables 541-42, 556, 562-63
frequency trees 371-72, 378
functions 44-45, 49, 279
    linear 279, 295, 299-300, 313, 355, 358
    quadratic 302-6, 311, 313
    reciprocal 309-10, 311, 313

geometric sequences 39, 46
golden ratio 355-56
gradient triangles 583-84, 586
gradient-intercept form of equation 284-87, 295
gradients 280
    calculation 280-82, 284-86
    changing 583-84
    distance-time graphs 528-29, 583-84, 586
    parallel lines 289, 295
    straight lines 280-82, 528
graphs 280
    cubic expressions 307-8, 311, 313
    directly proportional relationships 527-29, 534
    displaying data 556, 567-69, 575
    distance-time 528-29, 580, 583-84, 585-86
    horizontal lines 300
    intercept-intercept method 288
    interpretation 580-86

Index

inversely proportional variables 532, 534
linear equations 284–88
   see also straight-line graphs
linear functions 279–80, 295, 299–300, 313, 355
   misleading 567–69, 575
   parallel lines 289–91, 295
   polynomials 308, 313
   quadratic functions 124, 128, 302–6, 311, 313
   reciprocal functions 309–10, 311, 313
   solving equations with 121–22, 128
   straight-line see straight-line graphs
   time series data 544, 551–52, 556
   vertical lines 300
grouped data 563–64
growth
   compound 515–16, 520
   simple 514, 520

highest common factors 19–20, 22, 33
horizontal lines 300
hyperbolas 309
hypotenuse 482, 497
   finding length 482–83, 493

identities 26, 31
images 434, 437, 447
impossible events 363, 378
improper fractions 149
included angles 452
independent events 393, 398
index notation 402, 403, 410
indices 402
   division 405–6, 410
   laws of 405–6, 410
   multiplication 405, 410
   negative 404, 410
   powers of powers 406, 410
   zero 404, 410
inequalities 589
   addition 589, 594
   arithmetic operations and 589, 594
   expressing 589, 594
   multiplication/division by negative number 589, 591, 594
   notation 273, 274, 276
   on number lines 273, 274, 590, 594
   problem solving with 592–93
   solving 591, 594
   subtraction 589, 594
integers 6, 15
   negative 6, 11
   positive 6, 11
   rounding to 264–65
intercept-intercept method 288
interest 514–15, 520

interior angles 141
   polygons 141, 145
   triangles 61, 139, 145
intersections of sets 385, 395
inverse operations 10–11
inverse proportion 532–33, 534
irrational numbers 15, 506–7
irregular polygons 53
isometric drawings 322–25
isometric grids 323
isosceles triangles 60, 61, 139, 485
iterative processes 516

kinematics 217
kites 64

length
   arcs 234, 240
   finding from perimeter 226–27
   hypotenuse 482–83, 493
   prisms 337
   radii 251
   sides of right-angled triangles 98, 482–85, 493
   sides of similar triangles 464–65
   units 7
levels of accuracy 273–74, 276
like terms 28–29, 32, 35
line graphs 544, 551–52, 556
line symmetry 58
line of symmetry 58
line symmetry 70
linear equations 105–6, 128
   gradient-intercept form 284–87, 295
   graphs 284–88
   problem solving with 109–10
   solving 105–6
linear functions 279
   graphs 279–80, 295, 299–300, 313, 355
linear relationships 355, 358
lines of best fit 572–73
loci 81–83, 84–85, 86
lower bounds 273–74
lowest common multiples 19–20, 22

maps 185–86, 191, 355
mathematical models 524
mean 560, 561, 562–64, 575
measurement
   accuracy 273–74, 276
   compound units 180–84, 191
   conversion 173–76, 191
   standard units 173–79, 191
median 560, 561, 563, 575
midpoints 78, 86
mirror lines 434–35, 437, 448
mixed numbers 149
modal class 563, 564
mode 560, 561, 575
money 179

multiple bar charts 546, 556
multiples 15
   lowest common 19–20, 22
multiplication 3, 10, 11
   algebraic expressions 26, 29
   binomials 89–93
   decimals 166, 170
   fractions 151, 157
   indices 405, 410
   inequalities 589, 591, 594
   negative numbers 6, 91
   standard form 419–20, 422
   vectors multiplied by scalar 428–29, 431
multiplication law 393
multiplicative inverse 10
mutually exclusive events 366, 378
   addition law 392, 393
   combined events 392, 398

negative correlation 571, 572
negative indices 404, 410
negative numbers 6, 11
   inequalities and 589, 591, 594
   operations on 6, 91
nets 258, 335
nth term 41–43
number lines 273, 274, 590, 594

objects 434, 437, 447
obtuse angles 133
obtuse-angled triangles 60
odd numbers 15, 22
operations
   inverse 10–11
   order of 8–9, 11
opposite sides 497, 511
order of operations 8–9, 11
order of rotational symmetry 58
orientation 439
outcomes 363, 378
   equally likely 365
   favourable 363, 378, 384
   predicting 368–69, 378
   random 365
   representing 371–72, 378
outliers 561, 572, 574, 576

pairs of compasses 75–77, 86
parabolas 122, 302, 303–4, 311, 313
parallel lines 55–56
   angles and 135–37, 145
   graphs 289–91, 295
parallel vectors 429, 431
parallelograms 63, 64, 247, 259
patterns see sequences
percentages
   calculating 198–99, 206
   comparing 196
   converting to/from 195–96, 205
   expressing quantity as 200–201, 206

601

finding original values 204, 206
percentage change 202-3, 206
probabilities as 364
reverse/inverse 204
perfect squares 91-92, 94, 101
perimeter 224, 240
    composite shapes 227-28, 236-38
    finding lengths from 226-27
    regular polygons 224-25
    sectors 234-35
    see also circumference
perpendicular bisectors 78, 82, 86, 435
perpendicular heights
    cones 341
    parallelograms 247
    trapezia 248
    triangles 245, 346
perpendicular lines 55, 78-79
pi 230, 251
pictograms 542-43, 556
pie charts 544, 549-50, 556
place values 16, 161, 162, 169, 414
plan views 326-28, 330
plane shapes 53
    see also specific shapes, e.g. squares, triangles etc.
plotting 279
polygons 53-54, 69, 141
    angles in 141-44, 145
    area 244-49, 259
    perimeter 224-25
    similar 476
polyhedra 55, 66-68, 70, 317-18
polynomials 307-8, 313
population
    growth and decay 515, 516, 518, 521
    in statistics 538, 555
position-to-term rule 41, 45, 49
positive correlation 571, 572
positive numbers 6, 11
powers 407
    of powers 406, 410
    problem solving with 408
    see also indices
pressure 183-84, 191
prime factors 17-18, 19-20, 22
prime numbers 15, 17, 22
principal 514
prisms
    drawing 320-22
    length 337
    properties 67, 70, 317, 330, 334-35
    surface area 335-37
    triangular 318, 321, 335, 336
    volume 335-37, 347
probability 363, 378
    calculating 365-66
    combined events see combined events
    empirical evidence and 368-69

equally likely outcomes 365
    of event not happening 365-66, 378
    experimental 365, 368-72, 378
    expressing 363-64
    frequency trees 371-72, 378
    mutually exclusive events 366, 378
    as percentage 364
    predicting outcomes 368-69, 378
    problem solving with 373-74
    random outcomes 365
    scale 363, 378
    theoretical 365, 368, 378, 390-95, 398
    tree diagrams 388-89, 393
    two-way tables 371, 378, 383-84
    Venn diagrams 385-87, 395
problem-solving framework 4
product 3, 26
proper fractions 149
proportional reasoning 522
proportions 351, 358
    direct 524-29, 534
    inverse 532-33, 534
protractors 74-75, 86
pyramids
    drawing 322
    properties 67, 70, 318, 330
    surface area 345
    volume 345, 347
Pythagoras' theorem 98, 218, 482-88, 493
    length of hypotenuse 482-83, 493
    length of sides 482-85, 493
    problem solving with 489-90
    proving triangle is right-angled 487-88, 493
Pythagorean triples 487, 493

quadratic equations 111-13, 128
    graphs 124, 128, 302-6, 311, 313
    problem solving with 114-15
    roots 128, 304
quadratic expressions 91
    factorising 94-96, 112-13
quadratic sequences 46, 49
quadrilaterals
    angle sum 65
    problem solving with 65
    properties 54, 63-64, 70
quarter-circles 235, 252
quotient 3

radii 54, 230, 251
random outcomes 365
random sampling 539-40, 555
range 560, 575
ratio scales 185, 186
rational numbers 15
ratios 46, 351, 358, 524
    comparing 355-56, 358
    golden ratio 355-56

sharing 353, 358
    see also trigonometry ratios
reasoning 167-68
reciprocal functions 309-10, 311, 313
reciprocals 10, 153, 404
rectangles 53, 63, 64
    area 90, 100, 110, 244, 259
reflections 58, 434-37, 448
reflex angles 133
regular polygons 53, 224-25
regular polyhedra 68
relative frequency 368, 378
representative samples 538-39, 555
resultant 428
rhombuses 63, 64
right angles 133
right prisms 335
right-angled triangles 60, 61, 485
    length of sides 98, 482-85, 493
    naming sides 497
    proving 487-88, 493
    trigonometry in 497-503
    see also Pythagoras' theorem
roots
    of equations 111, 128
    of numbers 15, 407-8, 410
    problem solving with 408
    of quadratic equations 128, 304
    see also cube roots; square roots
rotational symmetry 58-59, 70
rotations 434, 443-46, 448
rounding 264
    to decimal place 266, 269, 275
    to nearest ... 264-65
    to significant figures 268-69, 275

sample spaces 383, 398
samples 538-39, 555
    random 539-40
    representative 538-39, 555
scalars 428
    vectors multiplied by 428-29, 431
scale 185, 191, 355
scale drawings 185, 188
scale factors 185, 467, 473, 478
    fractional 471, 478
scalene triangles 60, 485
scaling up/down 524-25
scatter diagrams 544, 571-73, 576
scientific notation see standard form
second difference 46
sectors 54, 234, 240
    area 252, 260
    perimeter 234-35
segments 54
semicircles 54, 235, 252
sequences 39, 49
    arithmetic 39
    Fibonacci 46, 47, 356
    generating 44-45, 49
    geometric 39, 46
    nth term 41-43

Index

position-to-term rule 41, 45, 49
    quadratic 46, 49
    special sequences 46, 49
    term-to-term rule 39–40, 49
sets
    set notation 386–87
    Venn diagrams 385–87, 395
shapes
    congruent 66, 434
    plane 53
    similar 434, 476, 478
    see also specific shapes, e.g. squares, triangles etc.
significant figures 268–69, 275, 418
similar shapes 434, 476, 478
similar triangles 463–65, 478
    ratio of sides 498
simple arithmetic progression 46
simple growth 514, 520
simple interest 514, 520
simultaneous equations 115–17, 128
    elimination in 118–19
    graphical solution 122, 128
    problem solving with 119–20
    solving 117–18
    substitution into 117
sine ratio 498, 505–7, 511
sketches 287
    cubic graphs 308
    quadratic graphs 305–6
    straight-line graphs 287–88, 299
slant height 341
solids 55
    2D representations 322–25, 330
    composite solids 344
    drawing 320–25
    elevations 326–28, 330
    plan views 326–28, 330
    properties 66–68, 70, 317–19
    surface area 258, 344, 347
    volume 344, 347
solutions of equations 111
speed 181–82, 191, 217, 582
    from distance-time graph 529, 580, 583–84, 586
spheres
    properties 55, 68, 70, 318, 330
    surface area 342
    volume 342, 347
square numbers 10, 11, 15, 22, 46
square roots 10, 11, 15, 407
    as exact values 99
squares 63, 64, 100, 244, 259
standard form 414–15, 422
    addition 421, 422
    calculators and 417, 422
    conversion to 416
    division 419–20, 422
    multiplication 419–20, 422
    subtraction 421, 422
straight lines 133
    angles on 132–33, 145

    bisecting 78
    parallel 55–56
    perpendicular 55
    vertical and horizontal 300
straight-line graphs 279–80, 311, 313
    features 280–88, 295, 299–300
    finding equations 286
    gradient 280–82, 528
    interpretation 292–93
    linear relationships 355, 358
    sketching 287–88, 299
    x-intercept 280, 283–84, 287
    y-intercept 280, 283–84, 287
stratified sampling 539–40
subjects 209
substitution 211
    checking by 107
    into algebraic expressions 28, 31
    into formulae 211, 220
    simultaneous equations 117
subtraction 3, 10, 11
    algebraic expressions 28–29
    decimals 165, 170
    fractions 152, 157
    inequalities 589, 594
    negative numbers 6
    standard form 421, 422
    vectors 428, 431
sum 3
summary statistics 560–66, 575
supplementary angles 136
surds 99, 511
surface area
    composite solids 344
    cones 341–42
    cylinders 338
    prisms 335–37
    pyramids 345
    solids 258, 344, 347
    spheres 342
symbols 9
symmetry 57–59, 70

tables
    frequency tables 541–42, 556, 562–63
    two-way tables 371, 378, 383–84
tangent ratio 498, 505–7, 511
tangents 54
term-to-term rule 39–40, 49
terms 26, 35, 39
theorems 482
theoretical probability 365, 368, 378
    combined events 390–95, 398
three-dimensional objects *see* solids
tilted squares 483
time
    12-hour and 24-hour systems 177–79
    units 177, 191
time series data 544, 551–52, 556
transformations 434, 447
    enlargements 434, 467–73, 478

    reflections 58, 434–37, 448
    rotation 434, 443–46, 448
    translations 439–42, 448
translations 439–42, 448
transversal 135, 136
trapezia 64, 248, 259
tree diagrams 388–89, 393
triangles 54, 70
    adjacent sides 64, 497, 511
    angles in 61, 138–39, 145, 502–3
    area 100, 115, 244–46, 259
    congruent 452–59
    equilateral 53, 60, 139
    finding unknown angles 502–3
    finding unknown sides 500–501
    isosceles 60, 61, 139, 485
    opposite sides 497, 511
    problem solving with 61–62
    right-angled *see* right-angled triangles
    scalene 60, 485
    similar 463–65, 478, 498
    solving 110, 500–503
    types 60
triangular numbers 46
triangular prisms 318, 321, 335, 336
trigonometry 495
    finding unknown angles 502–3
    finding unknown sides 500–501
    problem solving with 507–9
    ratios *see* trigonometry ratios
    in right-angled triangles 497–503
trigonometry ratios 218, 498–99, 501, 511
    exact values 505–7, 511
    square root form 506–7
truncation 270, 274, 275
two-dimensional shapes *see* plane shapes
two-way tables 371, 378, 383–84

unions of sets 386, 395
unique factorisation theorem 18
unitary method 525
units
    area 174–75
    compound 180–84, 191
    conversion between 173–76
    length 7
    standard units 173–79, 191
    time 177, 191
    volume 175
unknown 105
    on both sides of equation 107–8
upper bounds 273–74

variables 26, 35, 105
    continuous 273, 276
    dependant 572
vectors 217, 426
    addition 428, 431
    column vectors 426, 439

multiplication by scalar 428–29, 431
notation 426, 431
parallel 429, 431
subtraction 428, 431
velocity 217
Venn diagrams 385–87, 395
vertical line charts 542, 544, 556
vertical lines 300
vertically opposite angles 133, 145
vertices
 of angles 74
 of solids 55

viewpoints 322
volume
 composite solids 344
 cones 341, 347
 cubes 409
 cylinders 338, 347
 prisms 335–37, 347
 pyramids 345, 347
 solids 347
 spheres 342, 347
 units 175

x-intercept
 parabolas 303, 304
 straight-line graphs 280, 283–84, 287

y-intercept
 parabolas 303
 straight-line graphs 280, 283–84, 287

zero indices 404, 410